Troes

Mike Halsey, MVP
Series Editor

Apress®

Windows 10 Troubleshooting

Mike Halsey, MVP

Apress®

Windows 10 Troubleshooting

Mike Halsey, MVP
Sheffield, South Yorkshire, UK

ISBN-13 (pbk): 978-1-4842-0926-4   ISBN-13 (electronic): 978-1-4842-0925-7
DOI 10.1007/978-1-4842-0925-7

Library of Congress Control Number: 2016951942

Managing Director: Welmoed Spahr
Lead Editor: Gwenan Spearing
Technical Reviewers: Dustin Harper and Senthil Kumar
Editorial Board: Steve Anglin, Pramila Balan, Laura Berendson, Aaron Black, Louise Corrigan, Jonathan Gennick, Robert Hutchinson, Celestin Suresh John, Nikhil Karkal, James Markham, Susan McDermott, Matthew Moodie, Natalie Pao, Gwenan Spearing
Coordinating Editor: Melissa Maldonado
Copy Editor: Brendan Frost
Compositor: SPi Global
Indexer: SPi Global
Artist: SPi Global

Distributed to the book trade worldwide by Springer Science+Business Media New York, 233 Spring Street, 6th Floor, New York, NY 10013. Phone 1-800-SPRINGER, fax (201) 348-4505, e-mail orders-ny@springer-sbm.com, or visit www.springeronline.com. Apress Media, LLC is a California LLC and the sole member (owner) is Springer Science + Business Media Finance Inc (SSBM Finance Inc). SSBM Finance Inc is a **Delaware** corporation.

For information on translations, please e-mail rights@apress.com, or visit www.apress.com.

Apress and friends of ED books may be purchased in bulk for academic, corporate, or promotional use. eBook versions and licenses are also available for most titles. For more information, reference our Special Bulk Sales–eBook Licensing web page at www.apress.com/bulk-sales.

Any source code or other supplementary materials referenced by the author in this text are available to readers at www.apress.com/9781484209264. For detailed information about how to locate your book's source code, go to www.apress.com/source-code/. Readers can also access source code at SpringerLink in the Supplementary Material section for each chapter.

Printed on acid-free paper

For Lawrence Hall (1942–2014), who taught me everything I know today about how to diagnose, troubleshoot, and repair PCs.

Contents at a Glance

Contents

About the Author

Mike Halsey was first awarded as a Microsoft Most Valuable Professional (MVP) in 2011. He is the author of more than a dozen Windows books, including *Troubleshooting Windows 7: Inside Out*, *Troubleshoot and Optimize Windows 8: Inside Out*, *Beginning Windows 10*, and *The Windows 10 Accessibility Handbook* from Apress. He is also the author of other Windows Troubleshooting books in this series.

Based in Sheffield, UK, where he lives with his rescue Border collies, Evan and Robbie, he gives many talks on Windows subjects from productivity to security, and makes help, how-to, and troubleshooting videos under the banners PCSupport.tv and Windows.do. You can follow him on Facebook and Twitter at @PCSupportTV.

About the Technical Reviewers

Dustin Harper is an IT professional for a large winery company in the United States. He volunteers his time and knowledge among various Microsoft technologies, in person and online. He was first awarded the Microsoft Most Valuable Professional (MVP) award in 2014. He is active on his website (MSTechpages.com), Microsoft Answers, and other tech forums. He also has several industry certifications, including the Microsoft Certified Professional (MCP).

Senthil Kumar leads the Windows app development team at Cleartrip Pvt. Ltd. He previously worked for Trivium eSolutions in Bangalore. His experience spans across various technologies within the Microsoft stack, including Windows Phone, WinForms, ASP.NET, SQL Server, C#, and Entity Framework. He is a Microsoft MVP (Most Valuable Professional) in Windows Platform Development and a Microsoft Certified Technology Specialist (ASP. NET). He is a technical presenter, blogger, mentor, and a Geek. Senthil is actively involved in the local developer communities and is an active member and UG lead for the Bangalore .NET User Group (BDotnet). He is a regular speaker at local user groups and conferences. He has presented at conferences like the Great Indian Developer Summit and Microsoft DevCamps and WebCamps. He blogs at DeveloperPublish.com. You can reach out to Senthil via the Twitter handle @isenthil.

Windows Troubleshooting Series

When something goes wrong with technology, it can seem impossible to diagnose and repair the problem, and harder still to prevent a recurrence. In this series of books, we'll take you inside the workings of your devices and software and teach you how to find and fix the problems using a simple step-by-step approach that helps you understand the cause, the solution, and the tools required.

Series Editor
Mike Halsey, MVP

First awarded as a Microsoft Most Valuable Professional (MVP) in 2011, Mike Halsey is the author of more than a dozen books on Microsoft Windows, and a teacher of many years, Mike Halsey understands the need to convey subjects that can sometimes be complex in clear and nonintimidating ways.

The Windows Troubleshooting Series is, he feels, a great example of how quality help, support, and tutorials can be delivered to individuals of all degrees of technical ability. He hopes you enjoy reading this and many other books in this series, both now and for years to come.

PART 1

■ ■ ■

Getting Started with Windows Troubleshooting

CHAPTER 1

■ ■ ■

Introducing Troubleshooting in Windows 10

If you look back now at the early evolution of PCs and Microsoft Windows, you'd probably wonder how anybody was able to get any work done with them at all. For example, we've had USB devices now for over 20 years, each using the Plug and Play technology that identifies the hardware to the operating system. This technology was later adopted more widely, helping your PC to automatically identify other types of devices and download and install the correct drivers from Windows Update.

Before this technology came about, however, things were very different. Serial and Parallel devices had to be identified and configured manually using setup files, settings tweaks, and scripts. Just getting a serial device to be identified at all could be a challenge that would sometimes occupy a couple of hours.

When it came to the desktop, things weren't that much better. Differences in processor and other technologies from what we use today frequently caused memory leaks, Blue Screens of Death, and crashes. If you were using Windows 95 or 98 there was no easy way to repair the operating system, as even System Restore didn't appear until Windows Me, and that operating system brought its own unique bugs and instabilities that even today cause people to break out in a cold sweat.

With Windows Vista, Microsoft set out to fix all of this. They created a new hardware driver model to reduce, and even eliminate, instabilities and crashes, and completely re-engineered the operating system to make it robust, resilient, and reliable. Even today, a Windows Vista system is pretty good to use, and Windows 7, 8, 8.1, and 10 continued to build on that reliability.

With these operating systems came a whole host of new diagnostic and repair tools and utilities: monitoring apps, image backup utilities, CD and USB recovery media creators, and even a pretty amazing Reset utility that can refresh, reinstall, and update the operating system automatically. It's ironic then that as the reliability of Windows versions has increased, so too has the number of tools provided to troubleshoot and repair problems.

Despite all of this, however, and despite the introduction of non-hardware-serviceable PCs such as Microsoft's Surface range, our PCs are still not consumer electronics devices. They just won't work in the same way as your TV or microwave because of one fundamental difference, the hard drive. Because the operating system and all our drivers and apps have to be installed in a volatile way that permits changes to be made to the files so as to enable updating and new installs and simply to allow us to get stuff done, the risk of damage or corruption will always be present. This is opposed to a consumer electronics device such as a smart TV or refrigerator, which performs a single set of tasks repetitively and in a tightly controlled manner.

© Mike Halsey 2016
M. Halsey, *Windows 10 Troubleshooting*, DOI 10.1007/978-1-4842-0925-7_1

This highlights another irony, that unlike PCs, the consumer electronics devices we use aren't essential to our working lives. They're not what we rely on to "get stuff done." This means when a PC fails to start, or our apps and hardware won't work, it commonly leads to a crisis. For all its troubleshooting and repair utilities, and despite all the work that's been put into making Windows 10 the most reliable and robust edition of the operating system yet, an ecosystem of millions of apps and hardware devices, not to mention the effects of letting end users loose on a volatile file system, means that problems will still occur.

That's where this book comes in. I'll teach you how to become proficient in troubleshooting all aspects of a PC, how to diagnose and repair the most complex of problems, and what the most common and frustrating problems are.

The Three Seashells…

We all learned the "Dem bones" song at preschool, but it's also true that the hip bone isn't just connected to the back bone, but is connected indirectly to every other part of the human body. Everything inside the soft squidgy bag we call our skin is interconnected by muscles, nerves, and tendons. With PCs, things are just as complex. You start with the interconnectedness of all the internal components. These include the motherboard, processor, memory, graphics chip, hard drive, and power supply, but then extend to the BIOS, hardware drivers, software, operating system and screen, printer, and everything else directly connected to the PC.

Beyond this, however, our PCs are still connected to an ecosystem the likes of which are too complicated for the average human brain to comprehend in its entirety. Wi-Fi and Ethernet connections connect our PCs to routers, switches, networked devices, security appliances, telephone exchanges, cellular masts, cloud services, data centers, web sites, biometric scanners, smartphones, tablets, laptops, desktops… the list is pretty endless.

This means that long gone are the days when on a stand-alone PC you'd be diagnosing a problem knowing the cause had to be something local to the machine, such as a driver configuration file, software installation, or hardware component. Now we not only have to take into account all of the PCs and network infrastructure around us, but look to remote servers and even the fabric of the very building the PC occupies, including what is often many hundreds of meters of cabling.

In a way, this actually makes diagnosing problems simpler, though it may not seem like it at first. This brings me to the fundamentals of troubleshooting any problem with a PC, and the three questions where you should always begin.[1]

- What's changed?

- Is anybody else experiencing the problem?

- When did the problem start?

The first of these questions is the most important, as nothing ever goes wrong with a PC without something changing. Perhaps a system, driver, or app update has recently been made, a new app or piece of hardware has been installed, or a fan has failed on the motherboard. Has something been faulty recently? Could an engineer have swapped the component (internal or peripheral) with something that *looks* exactly like, but isn't *really* like, the original? Has there been a power outage, or was the PC moved over the weekend?

Asking what it is that has changed can save valuable time in diagnosing and repairing problems with PCs. To this end, Windows 10 is extremely helpful, keeping records of update and installation operations, even crashes and app failures, all of which could point to a corrupt file or component.

---

[1] I call these questions the three seashells after the now-infamous three seashells encountered in bathrooms by Sylvester Stallone during the cult movie *Demolition Man* (Warner Bros., 1993). They were fundamental to operation of the toilet, but were however completely perplexing to our bemused hero.

Next up is to ask if anybody else is experiencing the same problem. This might include people in your home or workplace, and it immediately helps you diagnose if you're dealing with a problem local to the PC or elsewhere on the network. Outside of this, a quick search on Bing or Google can reveal if anybody else, elsewhere in the world, is being affected by the same problem. Twitter hashtags are a useful resource for this, since if a faulty update or app has been released into the wild, people will begin to complain about it almost immediately, and the feedback you will get online will be instantaneous and give a good indication of both the scale of the problem and any potential fixes that might already exist.

Moving on to when the problem first started is the next step if the answers to questions 1 and 2 haven't already led you to a fix. A PC user might report that a problem has started in the last half hour but might not tell you it's actually a recurrence of a problem that they first saw 2 weeks ago, or that a colleague reported on his own PC the other day.

This is where, as an IT technician, keeping records is a great resource. I dislike paperwork as much as the next person (probably much more in truth), but having a call-logging system in an IT support department that accurately records asset numbers, users, problems, and solutions found can help you see patterns between problems and find solutions more easily.

Some of these links are obvious; when I worked in my first major IT Support job, my colleagues and I were taking calls every day for what felt like a year, for PCs from a major manufacturer (who shall remain nameless) that had bought, what we assumed anyway, to be a large batch of very cheap capacitors which were exploding on motherboards, rendering PCs pretty useless. This made it fairly easy and quick to diagnose a PC where the capacitors were installed, as the end result for the user was fairly consistent, and it was only one particular model of PC affected.

Other links can require more investigation, and throughout this book I'll show you how to undertake those investigations, what to look for, how to find the information you need, and how to repair the problems you find.

The Problems We Encounter

Now that you've been left completely baffled and befuddled by the sheer scope of the causes for problems on our PCs, let's spend some time breaking these down into the main problem areas, examining the possible causes of each one.

Hardware Problems

It's a simplification to think of a hardware problem as a faulty or failed component inside a PC. Sure we do have motherboards, graphics cards, processors, memory chips, and hard drives that fail, but occurrences are very rare. Even the more common failure of a fan or a power supply doesn't come close to explaining what the range and scope of hardware problems on our PCs includes.

Cabling is often a cause of hardware problems on a PC; such problems can often appear to be something else, such as the power supply, network card, or monitor. As a matter of procedure I will always cable-tie and neatly stow cables when installing a new desktop PC, and for a desk where a laptop is to be used, I will use a cable management system to keep them out of the way and tidy. Why do I do this? Well, I'll admit I can be a neat freak and have just a *teeny* amount of OCD (Obsessive Compulsive Disorder), but it's also good practice and can often completely eliminate the risk of cable and other hardware damage.

How many times have you, a friend, a family member, or a colleague tripped on a power, USB, or network cable? This not only risks damaging the cable (by tearing it, stretching it, or damaging one of its plugs) and the socket(s) it's plugged into, but also risks straining a muscle in your leg, hurting a knee if you fall, and even suffering a massive head injury resulting in a concussion and hospitalization... Okay, I might be exaggerating slightly on the last one, but you take my point.

■ **Tip** An essential part of any IT Pro's diagnostic kit is a selection of known good cables. Be they power, video, or USB, it's always helpful to have a suitable cable close at hand that you can guarantee isn't itself faulty.

Hardware problems aren't just isolated to the PC and attached peripherals on which the problem has occurred. Cabling, routers, switches, and other network architecture in a building can be a cause. In these cases, the problem is unlikely to be isolated to a single PC, which aids diagnosis.

Lastly, let's not forget what is by far the most common cause of hardware problems, the driver. I would, in a very unscientific way, suggest that over 99% of hardware problems are caused by incorrect or faulty drivers being installed, or driver files becoming corrupt after installation.

Software and App Problems

If you use an iPad or an Android tablet, then you've only got one port of call to go to for your apps. If you only use Store Apps in Windows 10 then, again, you'll only have one place to go to for them. App stores can present huge advantages for both the developer and the end user. If you use an iOS or Windows 10 device, all apps in the stores are rigorously tested for reliability, stability, and (crucially) malware. Alas, I can't be so confident about Google's app store.

Even so, faulty apps can occasionally make their way through the stores. The autoupdate methods employed by these stores, however, can make it a quick and straightforward job for the developer to distribute a fix. This also helps ensure that all users of the app, which may connect to Internet or other online services and offline and hardware resources, are all the same version, using the same version of the app, and fully up to date with security and stability patches and the latest features.

If you're using Windows 10, though, it's also extremely likely that some, if not most or perhaps even all of the software you use won't come from the Store. These *win32* apps that come as downloads from the Internet, or provided on a CD, DVD, or USB Flash Drive, don't have many of the advantages of Store apps. They might come with an updater, but it's always an updater that can be disabled. They are also not sandboxed from other apps, and the operating system, in the way that Store Apps are. Lastly, the file system containing the component parts of the app is completely exposed, not even requiring a User Account Control (UAC) prompt to gain access, unlike the Store App folders, which are almost completely inaccessible to everybody, including the system administrator.

Networking Problems

How thick are your walls? I ask this because one of the most common networking problems these days is or poor or even nonexistent Wi-Fi connectivity. This might not be so much of an issue in the United States, where walls are commonly made from paper or wood, but in Europe, where buildings can often be hundreds or perhaps even thousands of years old, the walls are slightly thicker and extremely good at blocking radio signals.

Elsewhere, networking presents complex layers of problems that you won't see elsewhere on a PC. Is your network connection problem caused by the network configuration settings on the PC, the driver, the port, the cable, the switch, more cable, the router, yet more cable, the telephone exchange, the cellular mast, a satellite in orbit, or perhaps even a bird that's eaten too much and is stretching an overhead cable when it sits on it or a digger on the building site down the road who has just ripped up the fiber optic cable for the whole neighborhood?

Okay, so I'm likely kidding, as most of the network problems you will encounter will still be local to the PC on which the problem occurs. It's important to bear in mind the connectedness of our PCs with other PCs and systems, though, when diagnosing networking issues.

Startup Problems

There is nothing more annoying, and nothing more common in my own mailbag, than problems caused by a PC that simply refuses to start. A nonbooting PC can be caused by many things from the cabling and power supply (it's also helpful to make sure it's switched on at the mains) to a recent Windows Update or configuration change, power outage, hardware change or upgrade, or perhaps something else entirely.

It's because startup problems are so unpleasant and can seemingly occur at any time that you'll find two chapters in this book teaching you how to repair problems. In Chapter 8 I'll show you how to repair simple and common startup problems, and in Chapter 13 I'll show you what you can do when your copy of Windows appears to be completely dead.

OS Installation and Update Problems

One of the most common problem areas for Windows PCs involves installation and, particularly, updating. When a major update to the operating system is released (what Microsoft used to call a Service Pack) all hell can break loose, and just about everything on a PC can either throw a wobbly (as we say in the UK) or just break completely.

This isn't helped by the SaaS (Software as a Service) approach that Microsoft has taken with Windows 10, enforcing all updates on all users, all of the time, and not giving people the opportunity to opt out. From a security and stability (and a cost-saving) point of view this makes complete sense, having everybody on the same, latest, version in the same way we all are with the Store apps we use. Other problems and headaches can be caused, however, that we'll examine throughout this book.

"Prevention Is Better Than Cure"

If you haven't already guessed by now, the first and most fundamental principle of troubleshooting a Windows 10 PC, or any IT system come to that, is to first set it up in such as way as to try and ensure that problems never occur at all. After all, it's well known that if you are responsible for the IT systems for a major corporation, a medium-sized enterprise, or even a small business and something goes wrong, you'll likely get the "Everything's gone to hell, what am I paying you for!" rant.

Ironically, it's also equally likely that if you create a system in such as way as to ensure that almost nothing ever goes wrong you'll get a variation on the same rant. I for one though know which of the two I'd rather be on the receiving end of; after all, to use another well-known British phrase, "Prevention is better than cure" any day of the week.

To this end, the first three chapters of this book are dedicated to helping you create a PC ecosystem that is, quite literally, bomb-proof (if your office was hit by a major hacking, flood or other natural disaster, or terrorist attack). The next morning (or at most a few mornings after you've finished reading the last chapter of this book[2]) would your business be out of business, or back up and running?

Much of what follows in these first chapters then is based around general principles. These will apply just as equally to your Windows Server system(s) and Internet-facing servers as they will to the PCs on the desks and in the homes and cars of your workers.

Don't think life gets any easier at home. If your college report is due tomorrow and your PC won't start, you're in deep, deep trouble. If your son or daughter can't get online to play a game or chat with their friends, all hell will break loose, and if your partner or significant other can't get online to do whatever the hell it is she does there anyway, then you're actually going to have to spend time *talking* to her instead [shudder!].

---

[2]Should a major catastrophe hit your workplace *before* you have finished reading this book, I wouldn't recommend spending a lot of time sitting at your desk with it in your hands where the boss can see you… they might think you're slacking.

The Security and Maintenance Center

Given that we're now seven pages into this book, it's probably about time to start with some actual tech and features of Windows 10, and the Security and Maintenance Center is where I'd like to start, see Figure 1-1. You can find this in the Control Panel (yes, it's still there, for now anyway). Change the Control Panel view to large or small icons by selecting from the drop-down menu in its top-right corner, and you'll see *Security and Maintenance* listed.

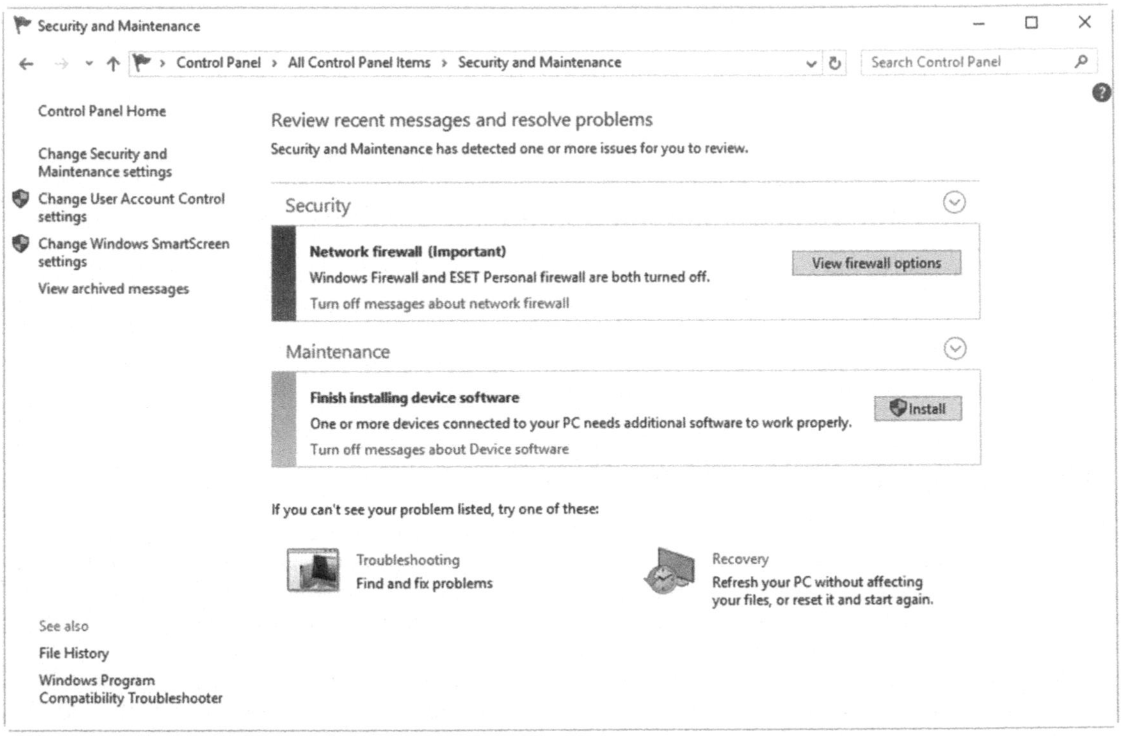

Figure 1-1. *The Security and Maintenance Center*

■ **Tip**   By far the easiest way to access the Control Panel in Windows 10 is to press the Windows key + X on your keyboard (you can also right-click or tap and hold the Windows button on the Taskbar) and to select *Control Panel* from the options menu that appears.

Windows 10 comes with a wide variety of information and status utilities, but the Security and Maintenance Center is certainly the most important for the general operation of a PC. This importance comes about because maintaining good security on a PC is absolutely crucial to the safe and reliable operation of the machine and your copy of Windows 10.

The Security and Maintenance Center is separated into four main areas. The left panel contains quick links to useful links, such as controlling the UAC security subsystem, and the SmartScreen web filtering feature (both of which are crucial to a smooth and malware-free operation for your PC and so shouldn't be deactivated). In the bottom left of the window are quick links to the File History backup and versioning tool, and to the Windows Program Compatibility Troubleshooter.

The first quick link, near the top left of the window, is *Change security and Maintenance settings*, and it is here that you control what messages are displayed.

It's the main section to the right of these links that provides information about the security and maintenance status of the PC. It does this by traffic-lighting two expandable sections. If you don't see any messages highlighted in amber or red, it's because everything is working properly and there are no issues. If you do see one, however, as in Figure 1-1, anything highlighted in amber is an alert that something isn't critical but might require your attention. Anything highlighted in red is a critical alert that needs urgent attention, in this case the PC's firewall has been disabled.

Each of the two expandable sections in the Security and Maintenance panel have small down arrows to their right side. Clicking one of these will expand that section to reveal all of the status information and control links within it. Here you can monitor individual items such as your antivirus status.

Expanding the Maintenance section provides quick links to tools and utilities that can be useful in diagnosing and repairing common problems with a PC, see Figure 1-2.

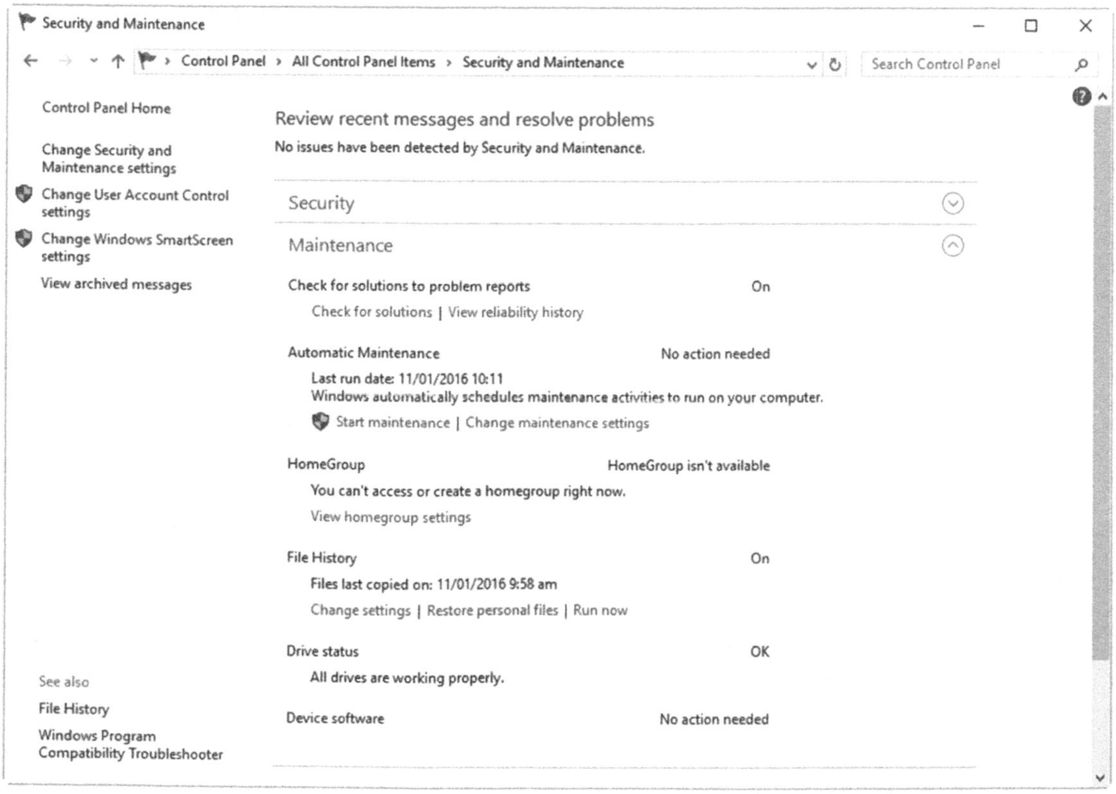

Figure 1-2. *The Maintenance panel contains useful quick links for troubelshooting tools*

Automatically Check for Solutions to Problems

Windows 10 stores information about all events that take place, from routine operations to app crashes, service failures, and driver problems, and it stores all of these in the Event History, which we will look at in detail in Chapter 5. The Security and Maintenance panel, however, contains a quick link to *Check for Solutions [to problems]*. This enables Windows 10 to automatically search online for any automated fixes that Microsoft have made available for common issues and faults. For example, there might be a known problem with a Wi-Fi driver, with a newer version available, or a configuration problem that can be repaired using a Windows Update patch.

Windows Reliability History

Windows' Reliability Monitor, accessed by clicking *View reliability history* in the Maintenance panel, is one of the hidden gems on your PC. It's been around since Windows Vista but is commonly overlooked because it's hidden away, and not highlighted in the Control Panel or Administrative Tools. It displays a horizontal scrolling view with each column in the display a different day when the PC has been in use, see Figure 1-3. If any errors, crashes, or information events have occurred then they will be highlighted by (i) or (x) symbols on the relevant day.

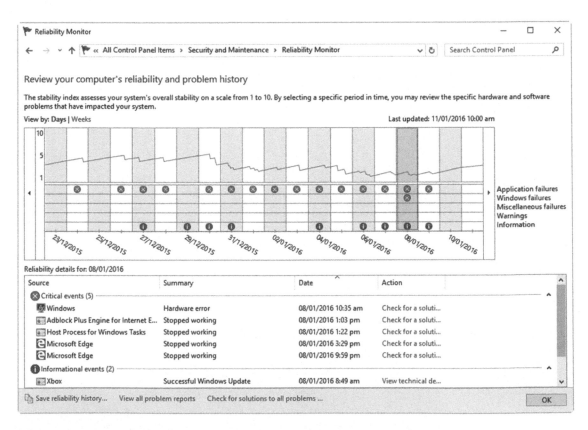

Figure 1-3. *The Reliability Monitor provides information about errors and crashes*

■ **Tip**   If you are supporti/ng a user remotely from a call center, they can open the Reliability Monitor by searching for *reliability* in the Start Menu or Cortana.

Clicking a day will present a list of all the information and error events that occurred, each with a link to its right to either *Check [automatically] for a solution* or to *View technical details* about the problem. The solution checker will launch the same automated process I detailed a little while ago, while the technical details will provide any relevant information about events.

Much more information can be gathered from the Reliability Monitor, however, by double-clicking the event name itself. This will display a wealth of technical information about what happened and what apps, resources, or services were involved, see Figure 1-4.

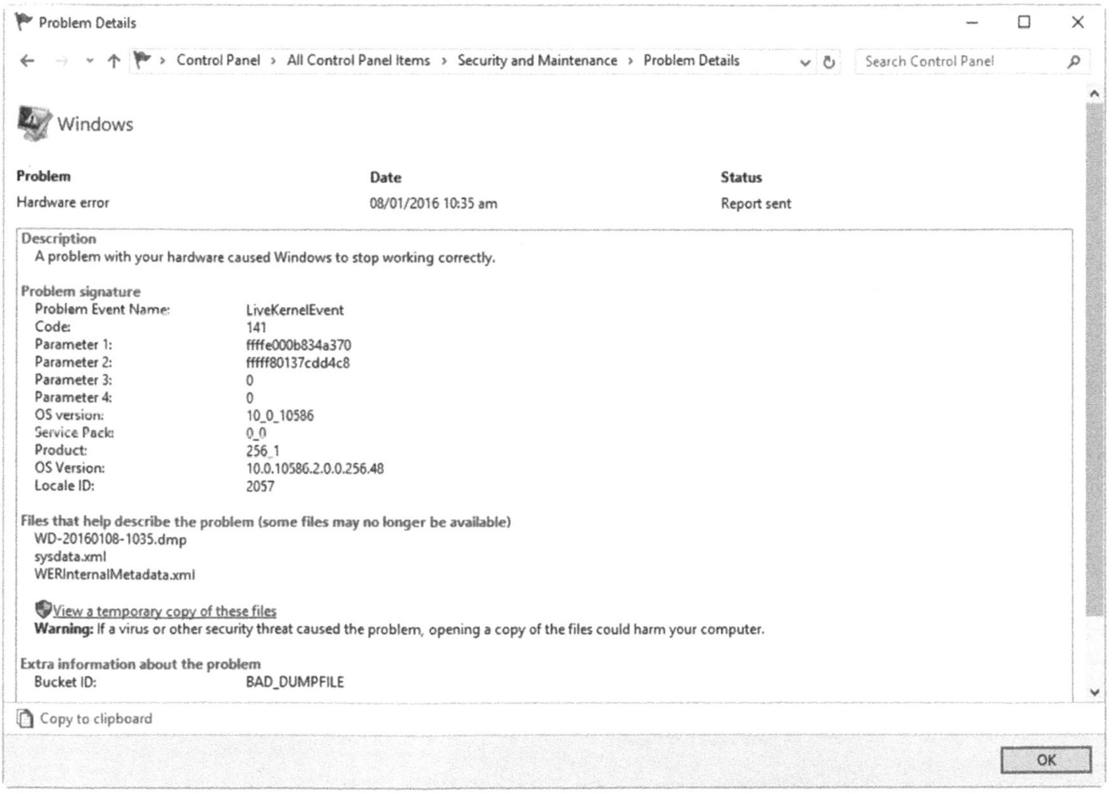

Figure 1-4. Technical details about problems can be found in the Reliability Monitor

The technical information displayed will vary depending on the type of problem Windows has encountered, though it may include the name and folder path of an app or system file or the names of crash (.dmp) reports or .xml files that contain information or other details about the problem. Other useful information that can help diagnosing problems is the inclusion of version numbers for any components involved. You might find, for example, that the driver, system file, or app causing a problem is a different version than those you know are stable and consequently supported. Being able to identify incorrect file versions can help in quickly rectifying some problems.

Below the technical details is a *Copy to clipboard* link. This will allow a user to copy and paste this technical detail into an e-mail if you are remotely supporting a user, or are seeking additional support online or from a colleague.

At the very bottom of the Reliability Monitor window are quick links to *Save [your] reliability history* and *View all problem reports*. These links are less useful for troubleshooting, as they only contain details of problems that Windows has automatically reported to Microsoft in an attempt to find solutions.

Windows Automatic Maintenance

Below the Reliability history in the Security and Maintenance panel are quick links to *Start [automatic] maintenance* and *Change maintenance settings*, see Figure 1-5. This automatic maintenance will perform routine tasks such as running Windows Update, defragmenting any disks that require it, and cleaning up temporary files.

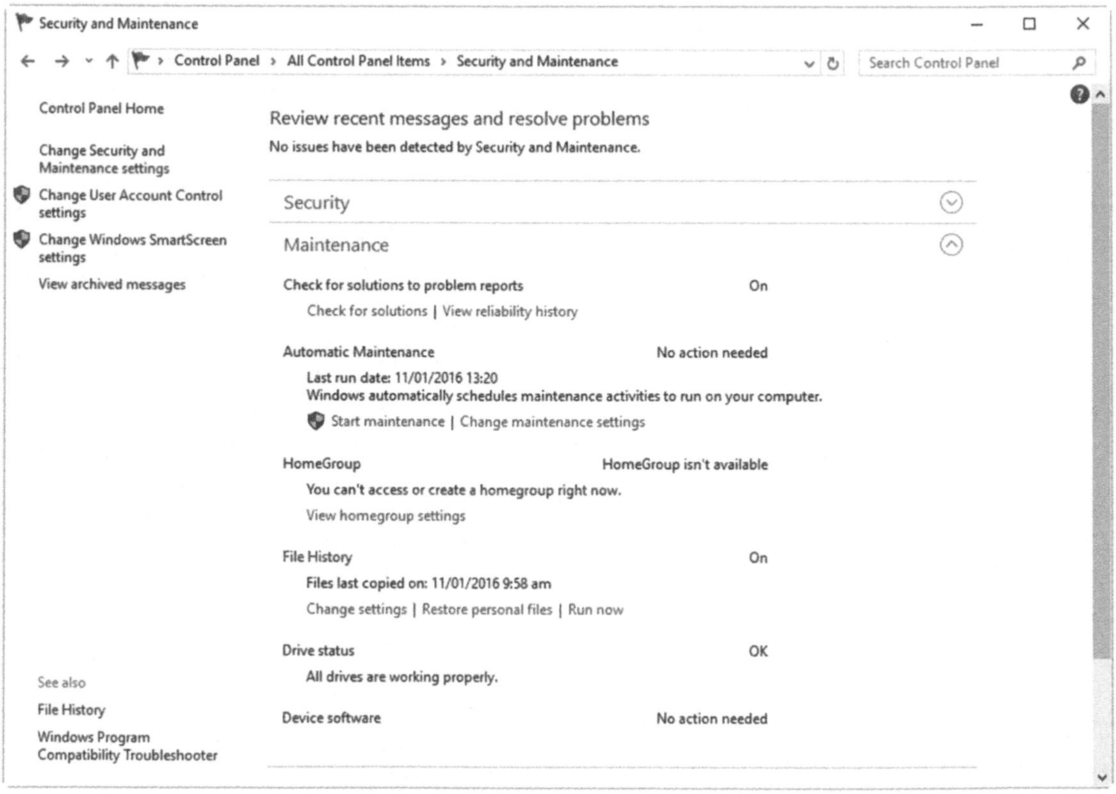

Figure 1-5. *Automatic maintenance can perform routine tasks on a PC*

> ▓ **Note** When files are written to disk, the operating system places the file in the next available free space. On some occasions this free space isn't large enough for the file, and so the file is split into two or more parts. This is especially common if storage space is at a premium, such as can be the case with an ultrabook or tablet. Defragmenting a mechanical hard disk can prevent the disk's read arm from having to access different parts of the disk to access the file, which can slow access times. Solid-state drives (SSD and M.2) do not need defragmenting as they are a random-access storage medium. Defragmenting SSDs can also reduce the life of the drive, as many come with a maximum number of supported write operations during their lifespan. It can be wise to disable defragmentation in the Windows Defragmenter (search for **defrag**) for any SSDs.

Managing Diagnostic Feedback and Privacy

I've mentioned that Windows 10 sends diagnostic information about errors and crashes directly to Microsoft to search for fixes that can be implemented automatically. You may not want information about your PC sent to Microsoft, or a user you are supporting may have changed their privacy settings.

These feedback and diagnostic settings are controlled in the *Settings app* in the *Privacy* section. Click *Feedback & diagnostics* and you'll see an option for **Diagnostic and usage data**, see Figure 1-6. Changing this setting (the options include Basic, Enhanced, and Full) can control how much information is shared with Microsoft. It is not possible to disable feedback completely, but clicking the *Learn more about feedback and diagnostics settings* link takes you to a web page where each of the three settings is explained.

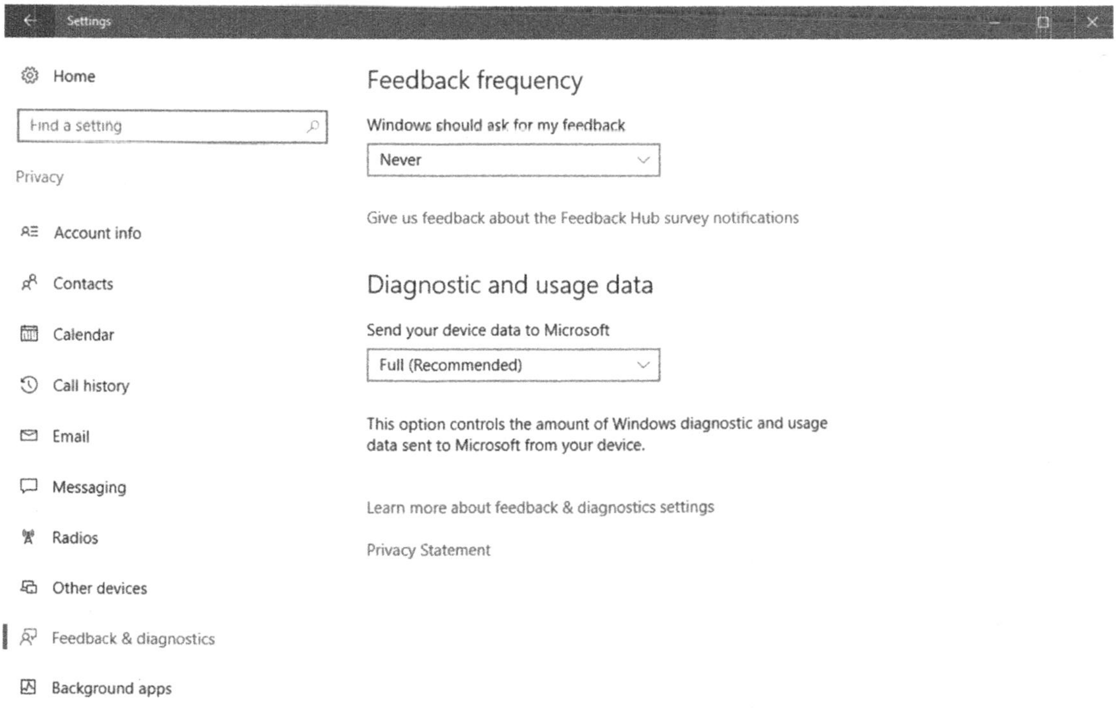

Figure 1-6. You can control what diagnostic information is shared with Microsoft

The Automatic Troubleshooters and Recovery Options

At the bottom of the Security and Maintenance panel are quick links for the Windows Automatic Troubleshooters, which can fix some problems in the OS by resetting components back to their default state, and the Recovery options, which include backup and reset controls for the PC. I will detail these features in depth in Chapter 4 (where I will also cover disk defragmentation and cleanup) and Chapter 2, respectively.

Windows' Security Systems

Windows 10 comes preinstalled on all systems with a variety of security systems, including antivirus protection and a firewall. These systems are crucial to the safe and smooth operation of a PC, and so I want to spend a little time showing you how they can be managed.

Windows Defender Anti-malware

Since Windows 8, Microsoft's operating system has come with inbuilt antivirus software. This is called Windows Defender and isn't to be confused with the Windows Defender anti-spyware package you might have been familiar with from Windows XP, Windows Vista, and Windows 7. In Windows 10 (and with Windows 8), this is a rebadged version of Microsoft's Security Essentials antivirus and anti-malware package.

As packages go it is extremely lightweight, using almost no system resources and not slowing your PC. It's not as effective as some of the dedicated stand-alone packages though and will be disabled if you use one from a third-party such as Eset (which is the package I use), Kaspersky, or Norton.

Windows Defender has two interfaces on a PC. Primarily it is controlled through the Settings app, and you'll find it under *Update & security* listed as *Windows Defender*, see Figure 1-7.

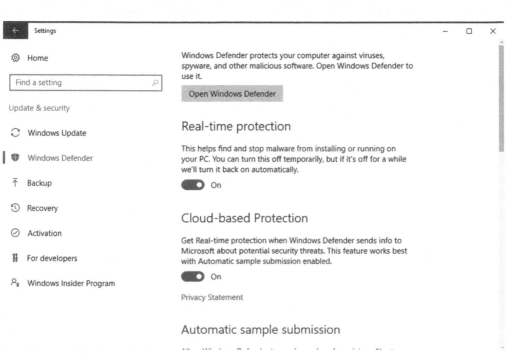

Figure 1-7. *Windows Defender is easily controlled through the Settings app*

Here are basic controls to activate (or deactivate) the anti-malware package, and if you perform troubleshooting on a PC, it's worth having a quick look here to see if Windows Defender is active if no other anti-malware package is installed on the PC, though the System and Maintenance panel will inform you if there is no anti-malware package active at all.

More detailed control (which is a bit of an oxymoron for reasons that will become clear) is available by searching for **Defender** in the Start menu or Cortana to display the full Windows Defender desktop interface, see Figure 1-8.

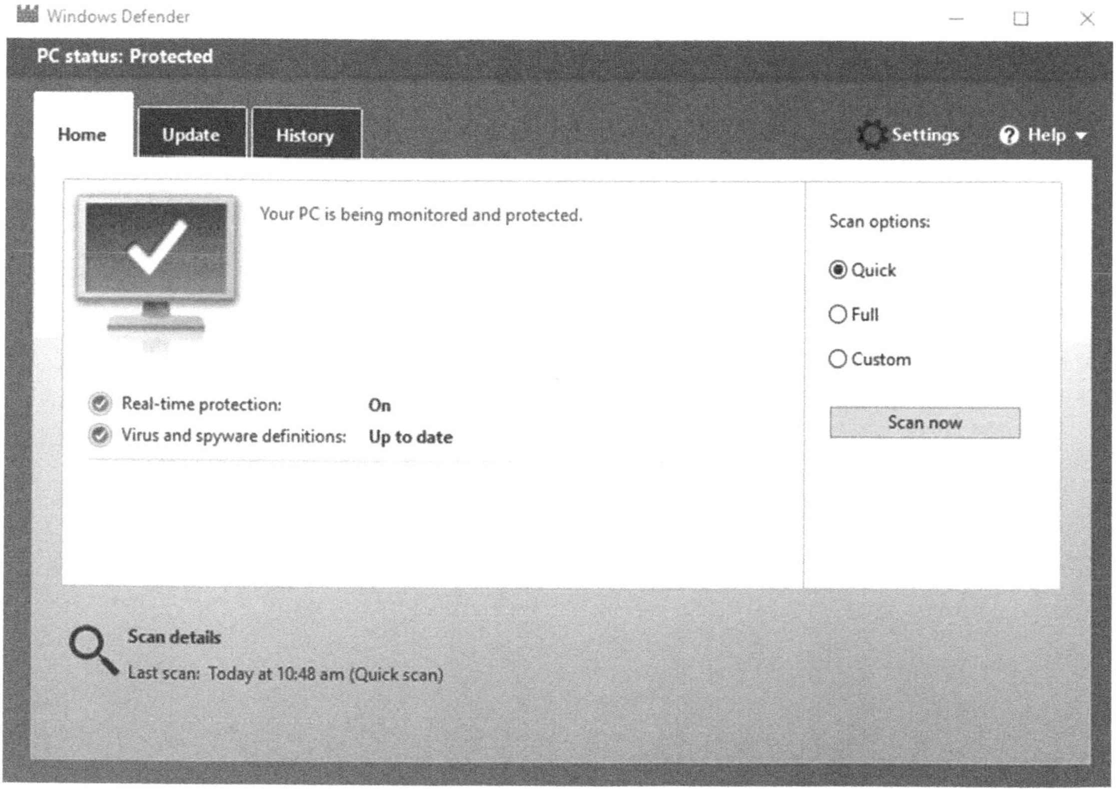

Figure 1-8. The more "traditonal" Windows Defender interface still exists, for now

In time we can expect all of Windows Defender's functions to be subsumed into the Settings app, and this will inevitably come in one of Windows 10's annual updates. If searching for Defender does not reveal this desktop app, then such an update will already have been implemented, and all the settings you need will be in the Settings app.

The desktop Windows Defender app allows you to manually run scans of your PC, including a *Custom [scan]* option which you can use to scan removable media such as USB Flash Drives. Update and History tabs sit across the top of the window from which you can manually update the installed antivirus definitions and view any files that have been quarantined or deleted during scans.

The whole desktop app for Windows Defender is color-coded and will turn amber if it needs an update or red should a virus or other threat be detected. Other than that there's nothing else here, with the Settings button merely throwing you back into the Settings app.

Windows Firewall

When you search in the Start Menu or Cortana for **firewall**, two different options will appear: Windows Firewall with Advanced Security, and Windows Firewall. The former, which I shall detail in full in Chapter 18, allows you to create and modify existing and custom firewall rules. The basic firewall in Windows 10, though, is pretty good and a match for anything commercially available.

Like all the other security features in Windows 10, the firewall, see Figure 1-9, is color-coded so if the firewall has been disabled or if a third-party firewall is being used instead, the panel's sections will be highlighted in red.

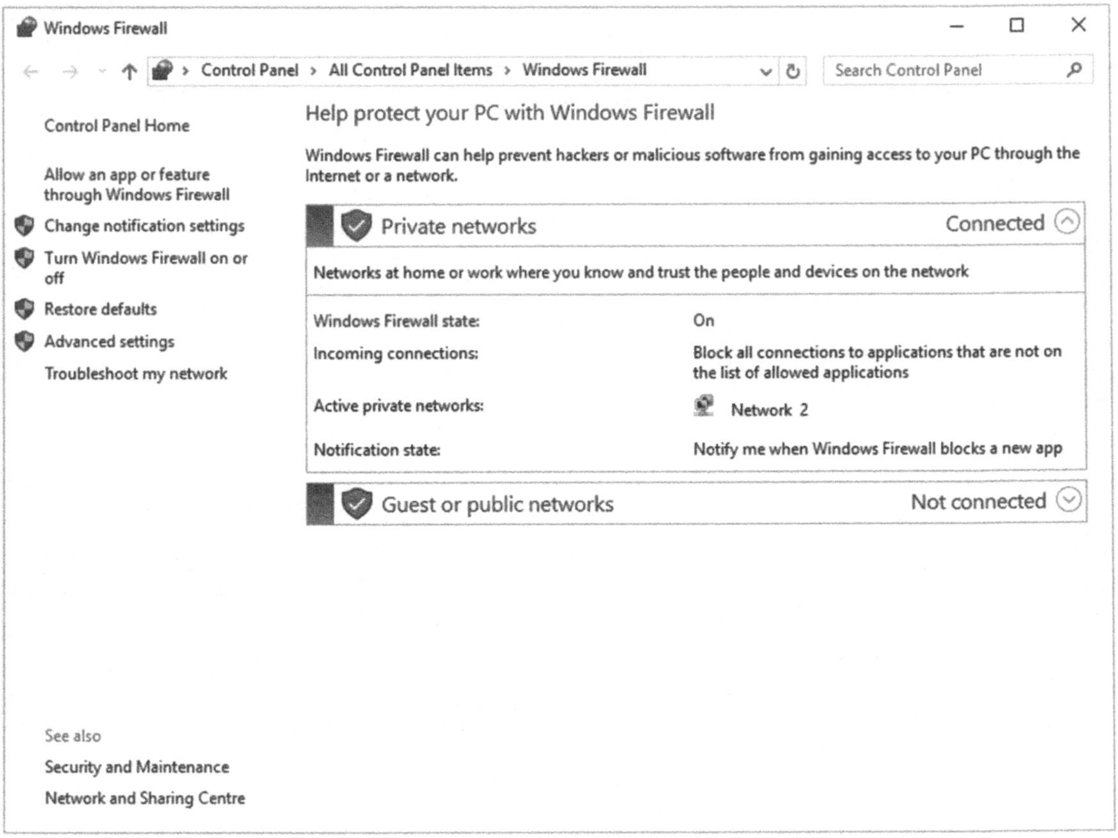

Figure 1-9. *The Windows firewall is basic, but highly effective*

The different network types you can connect to will be listed with the currently connected network expanded to display the network name and details about the firewall settings.

In the left panel are various firewall controls including a link to turn the firewall on or off, useful if it's been disabled by accident or by a user who shouldn't have done so.

In the top left of the window is a link called *Allow and app or feature through Windows Firewall*. This can be used if you find that a third-party service or an installed app or game is being blocked when it shouldn't be. A list of all the installed apps and services on your PC will be displayed, see Figure 1-10.

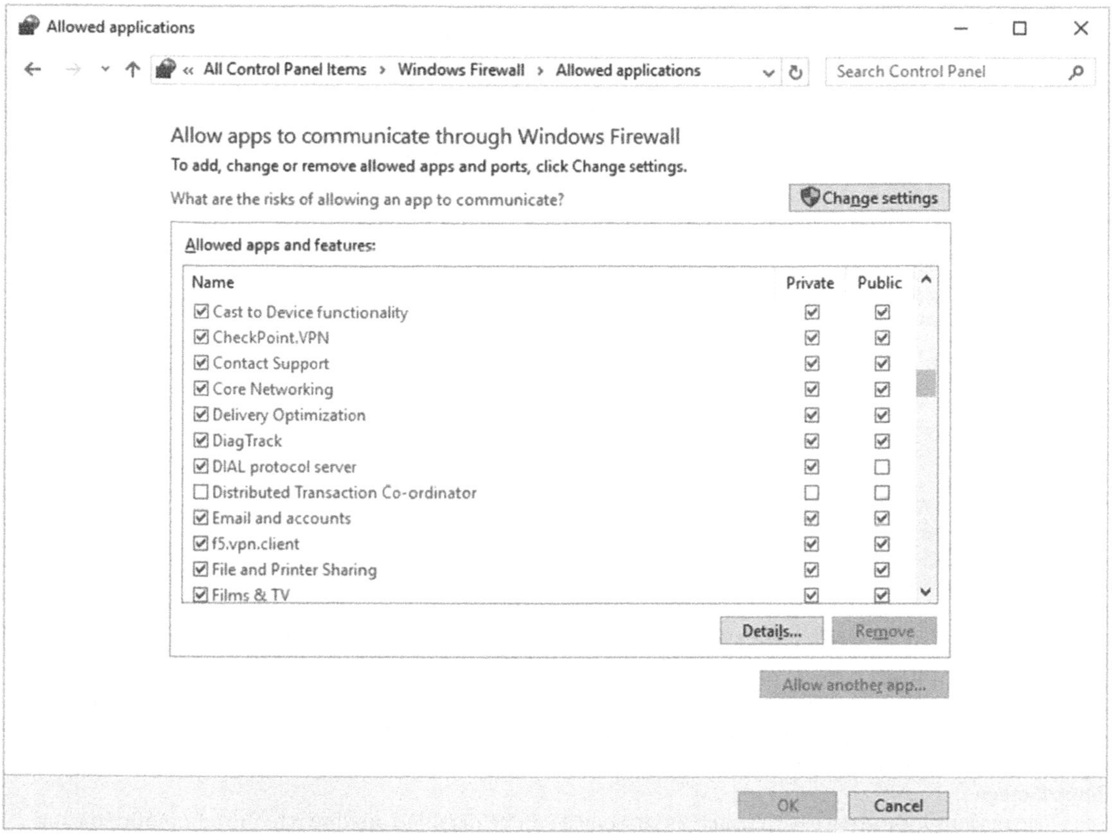

Figure 1-10. *You can manually allow apps and services through the firewall*

To change the settings for a specific app or service, click the *Change settings* button. You will now be able to set access for both Private (home or work) and Public (coffee shop) network types. If the app you want to allow through the firewall doesn't appear in the list, click the *Allow another app* button to display a dialog where you can manually navigate to the app's location on your PC.

Windows SmartScreen

Windows SmartScreen is accessed through a quick link on the left side of the Security and Maintenance panel, and it keeps malware off the PC by checking web links and downloads against lists of known unsafe web sites and files stored by Microsoft and maintained by all the major antivirus and computer security firms.

There are three settings for SmartScreen, see Figure 1-11. The first and default level is to get the approval of an administrator on the PC before running an unrecognized application. The second option does not require administrator approval but will alert the user that the file could be unsafe before he's allowed to run it.

17

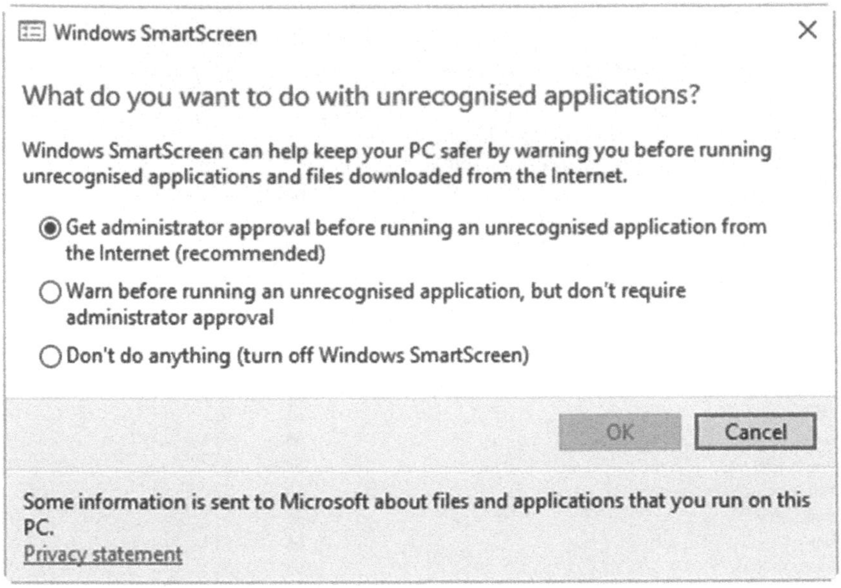

Figure 1-11. *Windows SmartScreen has two levels of protection available*

SmartScreen is an extremely helpful and useful security feature but, alas, it's all too easy for a PC user to deactivate it. If somebody uses the Edge web browser, and opens *Settings*, then *Advanced Settings*, or opens the *Privacy* options in the Settings app, she will see switches which can be used to quickly deactivate SmartScreen.

The reasons for the ease with which SmartScreen can be disabled are down to the automatic sharing of web site links and file download name with Microsoft's security servers, but I personally don't feel these switches provide anywhere near enough information about how important SmartScreen is, and why it should be left activated.

UAC

At the root or Windows 10's security is the UAC feature that was first introduced in Windows Vista, annoying so many people at the time. Back in the days of Vista, you couldn't even so much as change your PC's clock to a different time zone without being warned that this change could harm your computer and were you *really* sure that you wanted to do it.

These days, UAC is a much friendlier affair, and it will alert you only to significant events such as the installation of a new win32 desktop app (Windows Store apps do not trigger an alert as the Store has its own security in place) or if you make changes that could affect anybody else who uses the PC. Changes you make that will affect only your own user account are commonly highlighted with a yellow UAC Shield icon on the *OK* button, to alert you to be cautious.

You can open UAC from a link on the left side of the Security and Maintenance panel, or by searching for **uac** in Cortana or the Start Menu. The main UAC interface has a vertical slider with four settings, see Figure 1-12. These range from *Always notify me*, otherwise known as "annoying mode," through to *Off*, which I certainly do not recommend, as switching UAC off can allow malware to quietly install itself on the PC.

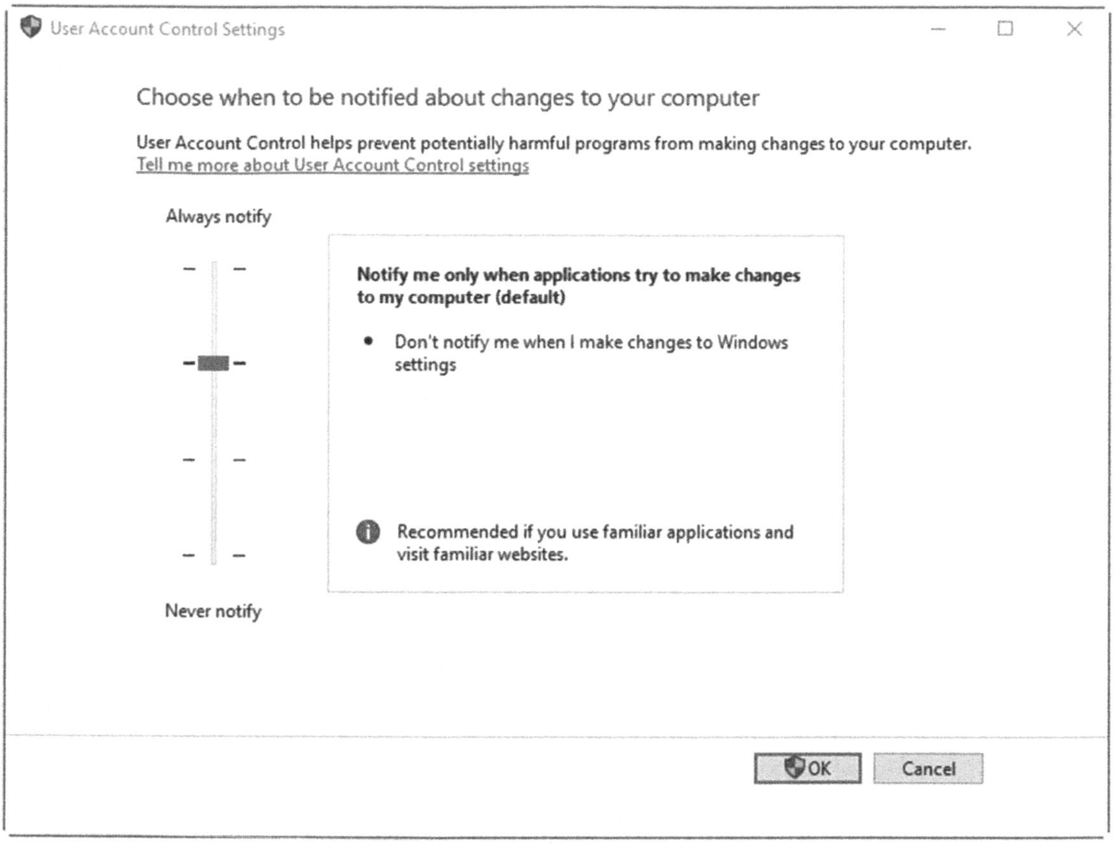

Figure 1-12. *You can control UAC through four different settings*

User Account Management

You might have noticed a common theme running through the section on Windows security in this chapter, that being that users can, and often annoyingly do, deactivate crucial security systems on their PCs because they "find them annoying," "they slow down the PC," which isn't true, or they stop the user "from doing what [they] want," which is very probably a good thing, as if the user wants to do something that's blocked by Windows' security systems, it's very likely they shouldn't be doing it anyway.

When it comes to user accounts, it's important to create them in ways that constrain the user to do only what they ought to be doing, and not necessarily what they *want* to be doing. It might be difficult to prevent a user from spending time on Facebook or eBay, or from playing Minesweeper (though these are fairly innocuous activities that are unlikely to jeopardize the security of the PC), allowing a user access to file-sharing, adult, or gambling web sites (where malware can often hide), or permitting them to install their own apps and utilities on a PC, does present a serious potential security risk, and therefore a serious risk to the stability and operation of the PC and the integrity of its files.

The risks don't end there though! Malware infecting a PC in the business space can quickly spread across the network, affecting other PCs, and even servers and network hardware, and the result can be expensive downtime or even the opening of backdoors into company data that can result in an embarrassing and extremely costly data breach.

Administrators vs. Standard Users

Back in the days of Windows XP, every new user was an Administrator, even the Standard users to a certain extent, because there was no UAC feature to prevent unwanted changes being made to a PC. Administrators can change anything on a PC, anything at all. They can install new software, modify configuration settings, and even delete files in the \Windows operating system folder.

Standard users on the other hand can only make changes that affect their *own* user account, and nobody else's. This can have some downsides in the workplace, especially if a user does need to install the odd extra piece of software (all users can install Store apps), but it's generally accepted that there should be just one Administrator on a PC (usually the person who knows what they're doing) and that everybody else should be a Standard user.

Local Accounts vs. Microsoft Accounts

If you are using PCs in the workplace, you'll most likely have users set up on PCs using Domain or Azure accounts managed by a Windows Server system. Smaller businesses might have users signed into PCs using an Office 365 account, but for everybody else it's the choice between using a Microsoft account to sign into a PC or a local account.

Windows 10 will do everything possible to dissuade you from creating a local account on your PC. Microsoft wants everybody using a Microsoft account because that's what offers the "best experience." I just want to list then the pros and cons using Microsoft and local accounts on a Windows 10 PC (Tables 1-1 and 1-2).

Table 1-1. *The Pros and Cons of Using a Local Account*

Local Account	
Pros	**Cons**
No personal data is shared with Microsoft	Syncing of personalization and Ease of Access settings is not supported
No files are stored in the cloud unless you deliberately set it up	Windows Store cannot be used without Microsoft account sign-in
	OneDrive file sync is not supported without Microsoft account sign-in
	Setup and configuration can take much longer after a reinstall

Table 1-2. *The Pros and Cons of Using a Microsoft Account*

Microsoft Account	
Pros	**Cons**
You get the full Windows 10 experience with all features supported and working	Personal advertising data is shared with Microsoft unless you disable the feature
Profile sync across your Windows 10 devices (PCs, laptops, tablets, smartphones) including personalization and Ease of Access options	Integration is built into Microsoft service you may not wish to use
File backup and sync between PCs are possible using OneDrive	
Setup and configuration is partly handled automatically after a reinstall	

User Identity and Sign-In Management

Windows 10 supports many more ways for a user to sign into a PC than just by using a password, but this isn't always a good thing. These additional sign-in methods include picture passwords, where you draw shapes over a picture, a PIN, such as the one you use for your bank card at an ATM, and Windows Hello, which supports several forms of biometric sign-in from fingerprint readers to iris and facial recognition.

On my desktop PC I have a webcam that is compatible with Windows Hello. This makes it extremely straightforward to sign in to the PC, as all I have to do is sit in front of the PC and have it recognize my face. It's secure, too; in 2015 *The Australian* newspaper tested it with six sets of identical twins and couldn't fool it into signing in the wrong user.

There is a downside to using Windows Hello, though, and this is why I won't use it on a laptop or tablet (i.e., a portable PC). In order to use Windows Hello in any capacity (fingerprint, facial, iris) you must have a PIN set up on the PC. My own Microsoft account password, as tested at howsecureismypassword.net, has 15 characters and 542 octillion possible combinations. A four-digit PIN, however, has only 10,000 possible combinations. Given that the sign-in screen on any Windows 10 PC allows you to switch between the different sign-in methods that are set up on the device, perhaps you can see where I'm going with this one.

You might wonder why I use Windows Hello on my desktop at all, given that a thief could steal the box and hack the PIN. I make sure that all of my PCs are encrypted using Bitlocker, which I'll talk about more in Chapter 18, but my desktop also has the advantage of being securely bolted to a solid wall by use of a land-anchor and a steel cable. Nobody's is getting access to my data without putting some real effort into it.

The sign-in options in Windows 10 are managed in the *Accounts* section of the Settings app, see Figure 1-13. One of the advantages of using this app if you have a Microsoft account is that it allows you to change your Microsoft account password easily, without having to find the security center on the Microsoft web site.

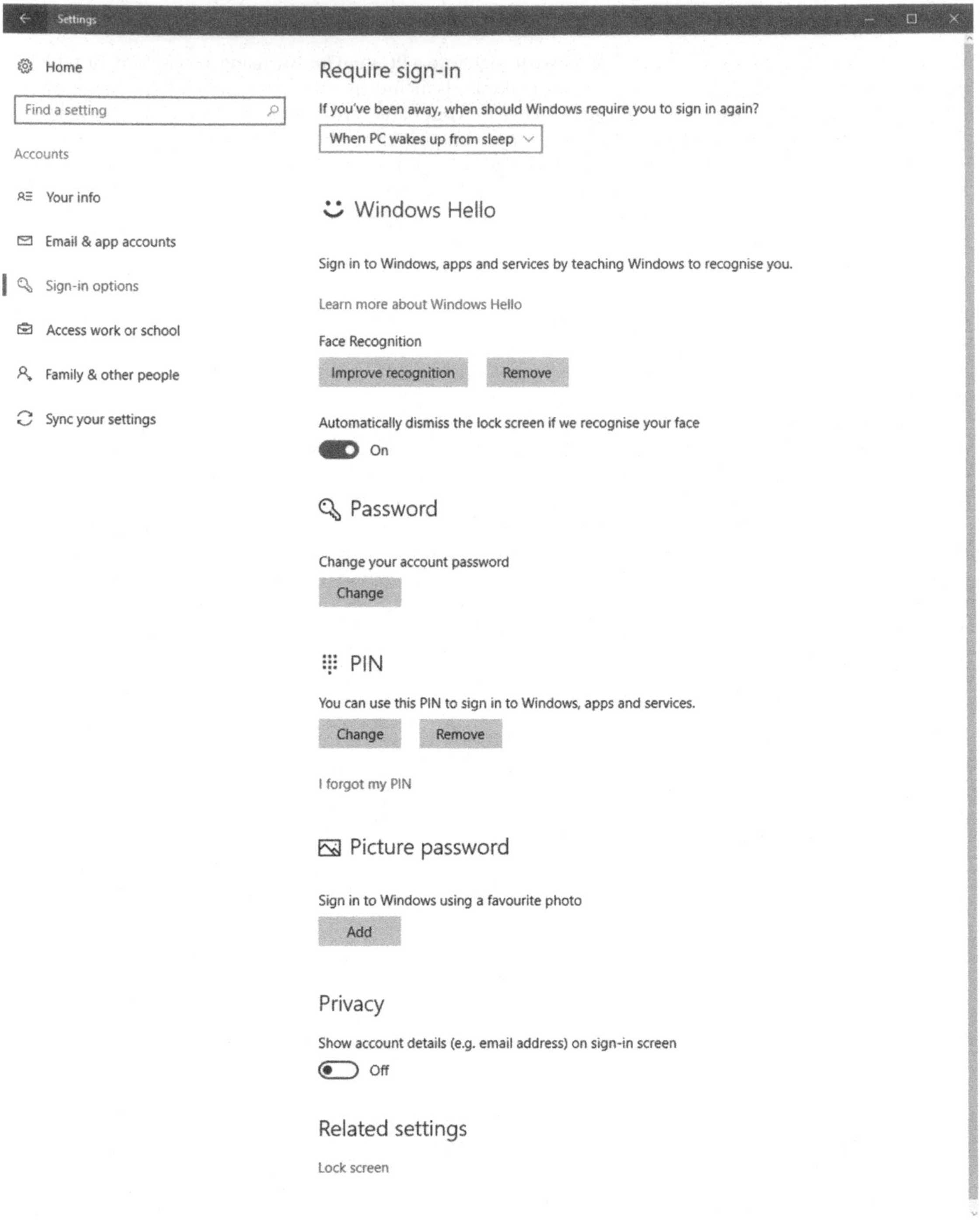

Require sign-in

If you've been away, when should Windows require you to sign in again?

When PC wakes up from sleep ∨

☺ Windows Hello

Sign in to Windows, apps and services by teaching Windows to recognise you.

Learn more about Windows Hello

Face Recognition

Improve recognition   Remove

Automatically dismiss the lock screen if we recognise your face

On

⚷ Password

Change your account password

Change

⠿ PIN

You can use this PIN to sign in to Windows, apps and services.

Change   Remove

I forgot my PIN

🖾 Picture password

Sign in to Windows using a favourite photo

Add

Privacy

Show account details (e.g. email address) on sign-in screen

Off

Related settings

Lock screen

Figure 1-13. You can manage sign-in options in the Settings app

I do stress that if you are using a PC in a business environment, forcing users to create and then enter a long and secure password is by far the best way to ensure the resilience of the PC and your company data. I do have some suggestions for strong password creation however.

How to Create a Superstrong Password: Top Tips!

Here are my top tips for creating superstrong passwords for use on your PC and with websites and Internet services.

- Create passwords that are a minimum of 12 characters in length

- Always use a mixture of numbers, uppercase letters, lowercase letters, and symbols

- Substitute some letters and numbers for other characters. For example you can use a 5 instead of an s or S, an & instead of a or A, () instead of o, O or 0, and / instead of the number 7

- Use a phrase, perhaps a line from a song or poem, instead of a single word to make the password longer

- Append some unique characters representing the service or website the password is for to the beginning or end of the password to make it unique to that service or website. For example, use ebA for eBay, aMa for Amazon, or g()() for Google web services

- Choose a format you will use for each word in your password, for example capitalizing the second letter of each word, and substituting the first vowel with a symbol

An Introduction to Family Safety

While we're on the subject of preventing users from doing things that can adversely affect the security of the PC, it's worth finishing up by talking about children. If you have children then you also have my sympathies, because you'll be all too aware that especially younger children have almost idea of what constitutes a risk, either in the playground or on the Internet.

Windows 10 does include Family Safety features, and when you add a new user to the PC you'll be asked if they are a family member or somebody else. The former option then lets you choose if the person is a child or an adult. Child accounts are automatically hooked into the Family Safety features, which include website filtering, game ratings management, and usage time management for the PC.

For the purposes of maintaining security, it's the website filtering that's the most useful. This can prevent children from accessing adult, file sharing, or gambling websites where malware is often found.

■ **Note**   It's worth mentioning that no Family Safety or Child Protection feature, be they from Microsoft, from a third party, or managed by your Internet Service Provider (ISP) can guarantee to block every attempt by a child to access content that you consider inappropriate. Thus, it is important to maintain good communication with your child on how they can keep themselves safe online, and why it is important for them to do so.

Managing and Deleting User Accounts

As I mentioned earlier, user accounts are managed in Windows 10's Settings app. There's really not much else you can do with them in the Control Panel. If you have a user set up on a PC that's an Administrator when they should really be a Standard user, you can change their account type in *Accounts* and *Family & other people*, see Figure 1-14. Note that you need to be signed in as an Administrator to do this.

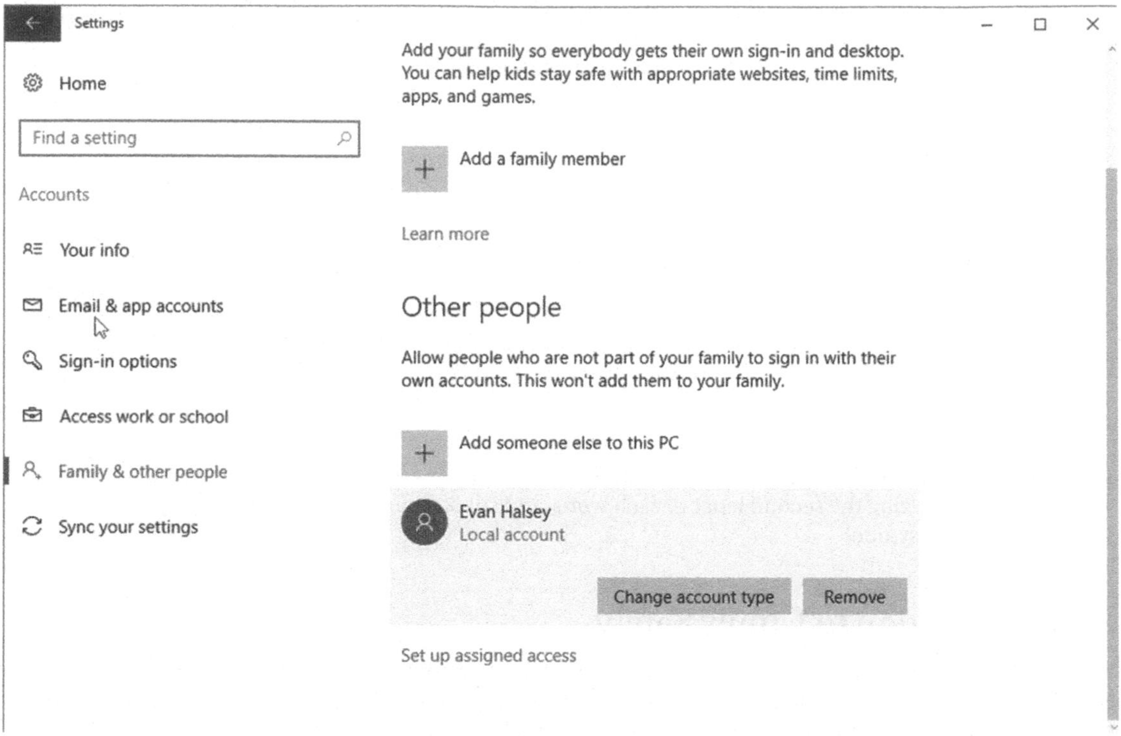

Figure 1-14. *You can change the account type of users in the Settings app*

Sometimes, though, you will want to remove a user from a PC. Clicking in their account name in the Settings app will reveal a *Remove* button. If you performed this action in earlier versions of Windows using the Control Panel tools, you will remember that Windows asked if you wanted the user's files left in a .ZIP folder on your desktop, so that you could save them.

Now, as you can see in Figure 1-15, Windows 10 no longer gives you this option. This might be a pain for removing some users from a PC where you're not certain if their files are all backed up, but it's more secure for the PC overall, as it will not leave any of their files behind that might contain personal information.

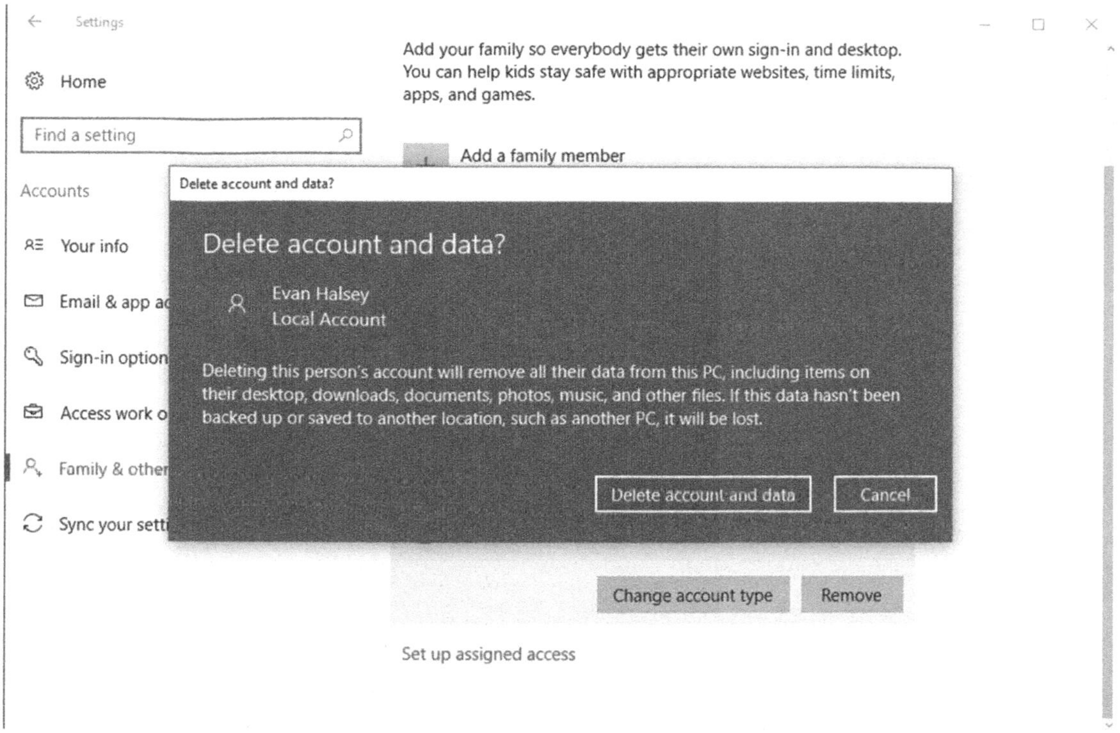

Figure 1-15. *You delete user accounts in the Settings app*

■ **Caution**   Deleting user accounts and their files does NOT securely delete the files and data, which can still be recovered through the use of file recovery apps. To securely wipe currently unused space on your PC you will need a third-party tool such as CCleaner from `piriform.com`. You can also wipe the free space on your PC by opening the Command Prompt (Admin) from the Win + X menu and typing `cipher /w:[directory name or drive letter]`.

Summary

If I had a dollar for every time I told somebody, even whole rooms full of people, how essential it is to the smooth operation of a PC that the basic security and user accounts are properly managed, I'd be writing this book on a beach in the Caribbean rather than in my office in Yorkshire.

What makes things worse is not just that it's extremely straightforward to get the security on a Windows 10 PC right, but that it's also far too simple for nontechnical people to switch off essential functionality.

In the next chapter we'll build on what I've detailed here and look at the tools and utilities available to help make PCs that are resilient and robust, while also being easy to manage and restore should something go horribly.

CHAPTER 2

■ ■ ■

Building a Safe and Secure OS

In the first chapter, as part of introducing troubleshooting in Windows 10 and on different types of PC, I highlighted just how essential it is to maintain good security. Any seasoned IT Pro will confirm this is indeed essential, but no more so than creating a robust installation with a good image backup. I couldn't agree more, so this is the very next item to cover.

It's ironic, however, that so many people spend so much time troubleshooting and diagnosing problems on PCs when the default action of any system administrator seems to be to simply reimage the machine, wiping the current installation completely and reinstalling a fresh image, complete with settings and apps preinstalled. What's not to like about this?

The truth is more complex in that while it *can* be quick and straightforward to simply reimage a PC, it's not always the best option, and in many cases can take considerably longer than tracking down the cause of a problem and repairing it manually.

The reasons for this are many, though they begin with updates for both Windows and your installed apps. Depending on when a system image was made, which could be up to 5 years prior to the current problem appearing on a PC (remember they're only really made when the PC is purchased or a new OS rollout takes place), the sheer volume of updates and new app installs necessary to get the user working again could take a prohibitively long time to install and configure.

There might even be new apps that need to be installed that the company (or the user) began needing after the system image was made, and other configuration changes can slow the process further.

We end in a situation then where what appeared to be just half an hour reimaging the PC and restoring a full backup becomes up to day of sitting in front of the PC installing and updating software, or where a user can't use the machine because it's sitting downloading and configuring apps from the server.

Part of the solution to this lies in Windows 10's clever Reset feature, which I'll detail soon, but first of all I want to show you how to do the most important job you'll ever need to do with ANY Windows PC, laptop, or tablet.

Creating a Recovery Drive

One of the biggest disasters that can hit a PC is the inability for it to boot, or boot reliably, to the desktop. In Windows if you can't get to the desktop, or can't start the PC into its recovery options, then you're faced with having to reinstall the OS, and all your apps and configuration options, from scratch. This, as you can imagine, is a pain!

But! You might say that you have an operating system install DVD for the PC and so you can start the PC from that. But can you? First of all, the PC needs a DVD drive, and unless you have a USB DVD drive handy, a tablet or ultrabook rules that option out immediately.

© Mike Halsey 2016
M. Halsey, *Windows 10 Troubleshooting*, DOI 10.1007/978-1-4842-0925-7_2

■ **Tip**   Creating a Recovery Drive for a PC is the single most useful and essential thing you can ever do to aid troubleshooting and repair of Windows PCs. I urge you to create one for each PC you support, and to recommend to friends, family, and colleagues, they also create a Recovery Drive for each of their Windows 10 PCs.

Then you need a version of the operating system on the DVD that matches the one installed on the PC. There's no point in trying to rescue Windows 10 Pro with an Enterprise DVD, or a 32-bit (x86) installation with 64-bit (x64) media. If you're rescuing a PC then you need the correct media, every time.

I should also mention here that DVDs have a finite shelf life. Sure, an official Windows 10 DVD from Microsoft will last considerably longer than one you burn yourself, but leaving it in a box, on a shelf, perhaps in the sun, will certainly shorten its lifespan. When will you get an official Windows 10 DVD anyway? I will admit that I've not seen a single one yet, because every PC I've encountered has had a free upgrade from Windows 7 or Windows 8.1 (via download) or has used a bootable USB Flash Drive or DVD with an ISO file downloaded from Microsoft's Developer Network subscription service, MSDN, or their volume licensing program. These days, official DVDs are rare.

Fortunately, Microsoft has a tool that helps get around this problem, and it creates a Recovery Drive. This is a USB Flash Drive (8GB is a good size to use) that can optionally include a full backup image of the installed copy of Windows.

■ **Note**   Windows 10 systems installed on BIOS and UEFI firmware create different system partitions and, as such, when you start your PC from a Recovery Drive you need to start in the same way Windows 10 starts. I mention this because many UEFI PCs will permit booting as though it's a BIOS PC, and this may have happened if you installed Windows 10 from DVD or USB Flash. To check, if your Windows 10 installation has only one *System Reserved* startup partition, it's been created in a BIOS boot; if there's more than one, it's UEFI. Check the boot options menu on your PC to make sure you start the PC from Recovery Drive the same way or else it won't be able to repair your copy of Windows.

You can create a Recovery Drive by clicking *Recovery* in the Control Panel. It's not been moved to the Settings app as I write this, but will inevitably be moved at some point, so if it's not in the Control Panel when you look for it, check the *Update & recovery* section of the Settings app instead, as that's where Microsoft will inevitably put it.

With an unused USB Flash Drive plugged into the PC, you can use an "on-the-go" (OTG) cable to plug full-size USB drives into the Micro and Type-C USB ports on tablets; click the *Create a recovery drive* link to open a simple wizard in which you will find a check box to also include a reset (system backup) image for the PC, see Figure 2-1.

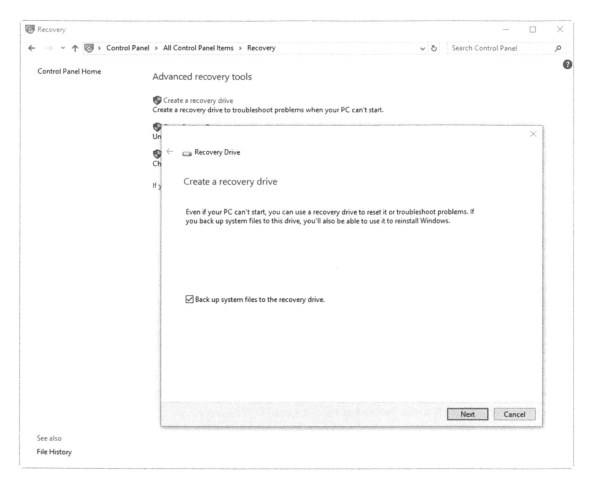

Figure 2-1. *You create a Recovery Drive by selecting Recovery in the Control Panel*

■ **Note** You will need to create a separate Recovery Drive for each PC, and there are several reasons why. First of all, the hardware drivers on PCs will be different, as will the version of Windows 10 you have installed (Home, Pro, Enterprise, etc.), as I mentioned earlier, though you also need different Recovery Drives for 32-bit and 64-bit Windows installations, as one cannot be used to boot into the recovery options for the other. It might seem odd to consider that we even have 32-bit Windows installations these days, but they still exist on low-power, low-cost tablets and convertible laptops.

A Recovery Drive will allow you to start the PC directly into the Recovery options, and I will detail these in full in Chapter 8. Here you can perform actions from a System Restore to a full reimage, as well as gaining access to command-line tools to repair disk and startup problems. You will need to make sure the PC's BIOS or UEFI system is set to permit booting the PC from a USB device in order to use the drive. Some very old PCs that are still in use do not support booting from USB, and for these machines a DVD will still be required.

Backing Up and Restoring Windows 10

At the beginning of this chapter I mentioned that IT Pros will commonly want to reimage a PC when encountering a problem. With Windows 10, however, this raises a question... what system imaging tool do you want to use? This is because there are actually two different ones included with the OS. These tools work in different ways; both have their strengths and weaknesses, and both have specific scenarios in which they are most useful.

Reset

When you install Windows 10 on a PC, it automatically creates its own system backup image called a "Reset" image. This is cleverly maintained because it updates itself on a regular basis with the latest hardware drivers and Windows Updates so that, unlike a static System Image backup, when it's restored it won't need updating with months or years worth of updates and drivers.

But! I hear you say. It's commonly a driver or an update that's the cause of a problem in the first place, so what's the point in this? The Reset feature in Windows 10 stores only those updates and drivers that have been installed on the PC for more than 30 days, the reasoning being that if you've been using them for a month already, there's likely nothing wrong with them as you'd have spotted a problem already.

Even better, the Reset process doesn't wipe your user account(s) or files. A common problem with the System Image backup process is that a user's files need to be stored either on a server or on a separate partition or hard disk to Windows 10 itself, as the process of restoring the backup completely wipes everything currently on the Windows 10 partition, and replaces it with the contents of the backup.

■ **Note**   Windows 8 and 8.1 allowed you to create a custom Reset image, but because of the changes to the operation of the Reset system, this feature has been removed in Windows 10.

A Reset image can be restored from the Settings app, you'll find it in *Update & recovery* in the *Recovery* section, see Figure 2-2. Indeed, it's so straightforward a process that even a nontechnical PC user can do it. You're asked if you want to keep your files and folders, or if you want to wipe the PC (useful if you're selling it or giving it to a friend or family member), and the process is automated from there on.

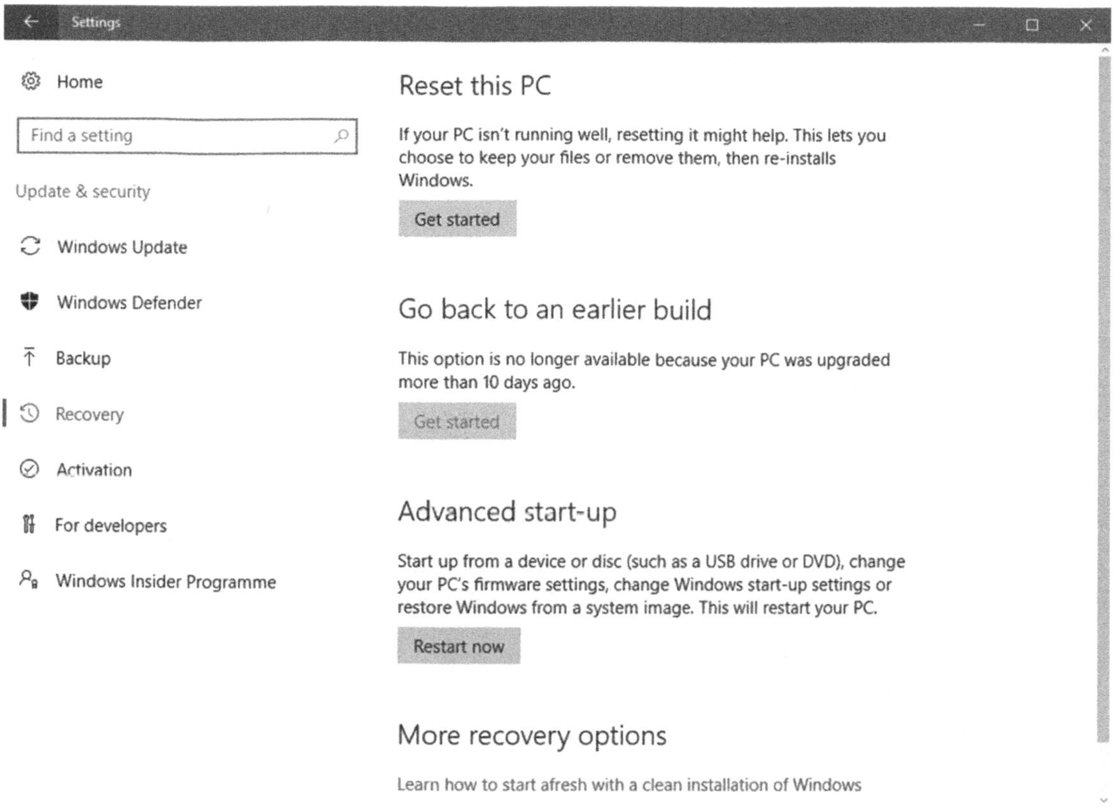

Figure 2-2. You can reset a Windows PC from the Settings app

■ **Note**   Completely wiping a PC using the Reset facility removes all user accounts and files from the PC but *does not* securely erase them. As I mentioned in Chapter 1, **to securely wipe currently unused space on your PC you will need a third-party tool such as CCleaner from** piriform.com**. You can also wipe the free space on your PC by opening the Command Prompt (Admin) from the Windows + X menu and typing** cipher /w:[directory name or drive letter].

On the face of things this sounds like the ideal solution to image backup problems. End users can do it themselves, nondestructively, with all updates and hardware drivers included and with no risk they'll lose any of their files. What's not to like?

As with everything on PCs there is a caveat, and it's an important one. A Reset image won't keep installed win32 desktop apps or any configuration options that can't be easily restored from OneDrive or a domain profile. It doesn't keep Windows Store or Store for Business apps either, though the process of reinstalling these is very straightforward compared to win32 software.

Thus, if the user has the full Microsoft Office suite, Adobe Creative Cloud, or any other non-Store apps on their PC, these will all need to be reinstalled and configured from scratch.

Reset is most useful, therefore, on PCs where win32 desktop apps aren't being used, such as low-power, low-cost tablets on which people are most likely to use only Windows Store apps. However, even here we have a problem, namely, the small amounts of storage allowed by these devices.

■ **Note**   Windows 10 Reset works by using files located in the WinSXS folder to reimage the OS in a way so as to keep it up to date. This means that manual checking and repair of the Reset image in the event of an error or corruption (Reset is intended to be self-managing and robust) isn't possible, as there isn't a single image. While Reset is intended to operate effectively 100% of the time, some IT Pros (myself included) might want to also manually create a System Backup Image… just in case of a disk or partition corruption that would prevent Reset from working.

Restoring a Reset Image on a Nonbootable PC

Reset can be invoked from within the Settings app in Windows 10, as I detailed earlier, and is very easy to operate. However, you might find that your installed copy of Windows 10 isn't bootable, and you cannot launch Reset from the desktop. Alternatively, you might find that the desktop environment is unstable, and crashes such as a Blue Screen of Death (BSOD) occur before you can invoke Reset.

In both cases you can run Reset from the Recovery Options in Windows 10. There are several ways to access this menu.

- From the Settings app, in the *Update & recovery* section, click the *Recovery* tab and then click the *Restart now* button in the *Advanced start-up* section.

- From any power control (the Sleep, Shut-down, and Restart buttons in the Start Menu or at the Sign-in screen) hold down the Shift key while clicking *Restart*.

- Start the PC from the Recovery Drive you created for it, because you *did* create one… didn't you!?

■ **Note**   If your PC is encrypted using Bitlocker (I'll show you how to use this in Chapter 18) you will need your 48-character unlock key. You are prompted to back this up when you encrypt a drive, but if you use a Microsoft account and have chosen to back up the key there (you have to opt in to this at encryption time) you can find your keys stored online at `https://onedrive.live.com/recoverykey`.

When the Recovery options menu loads, you have two further options to choose from depending on whether you want to use the Reset image on the PC's hard drive, or a Reset image you copied to the Recovery Drive automatically when you created it.

To reset a PC from an image on the Recovery Drive, click *Use a device*, see Figure 2-3, and select the USB Flash Drive that's your Recovery Drive.

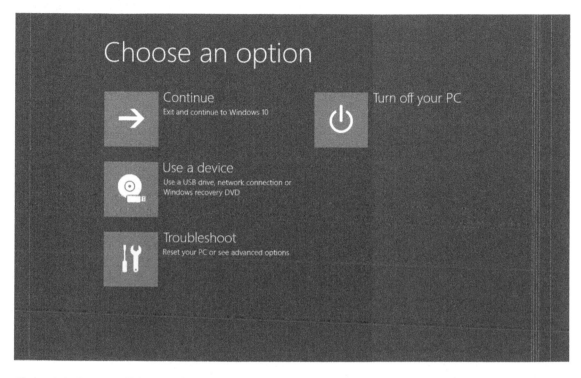

Figure 2-3. *You can click Use a device to reset a PC from an image on a Recovery Drive*

Then, or if you are using the Reset image on the PC itself, click *Troubleshoot* and at the next screen click *Reset this PC*, see Figure 2-4. You will then be guided through the process of restoring Windows 10 using the correct Reset image. Note that you will need to know an Administrator password to complete this process.

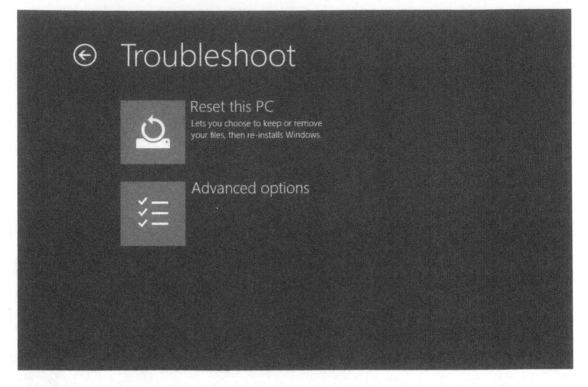

Figure 2-4. *You can reset a PC from the Recovery options*

System Image Backup

If you're a system administrator or an IT Pro, the chances are you'll already be familiar with and have used image backup software such as Symantec Ghost or Acronis TrueImage. Windows has included a System Image Backup feature since Windows Vista, and it offers some compelling benefits over the competition, not the least of which is that backups can be created and restored without the need for any external media (CD, DVD, USB Flash Drive).

Creating a System Image Backup

Oddly, if you search in the Start Menu or Cortana in Windows 10, no combinations of the words **system**, **image**, and **backup** will display a quick link to the System Image Backup utility. There are two ways to access it, and I'll detail both, though I fully expect one of these to be removed in a forthcoming Windows 10 update.

The method I expect to be removed is to click *Backup and Restore (Windows 7)* in the Control Panel, and then to click the *Create a system image* link that appears in the top left of the window. The reason I say that I expect for this to be removed in a forthcoming update is that this is included (as it was in Windows 8) to aid migration of users from Windows 7 who had files backed up using that OS's file backup utility, and in the Windows 8.1 update it vanished. You should not think of this as a long-term feature of Windows 10 and therefore should not use the file backup utility it also provides.

The other (and reliable) method of accessing the System Image Backup utility is to open *File History* in the Control Panel; a *System Image Backup* link will appear in the bottom left of the window. As I write this, clicking the link opens the *Backup and restore (Windows 7)* page, but this as I mentioned is very likely to change, perhaps by the time you read this.

The System Image Backup utility opens as a wizard that offers you three locations for storing your backup, on a local hard disk or partition on the PC (this must be an internal drive; USB-connected drives are **not** supported), on one of more DVDs or on a network location, see Figure 2-5.

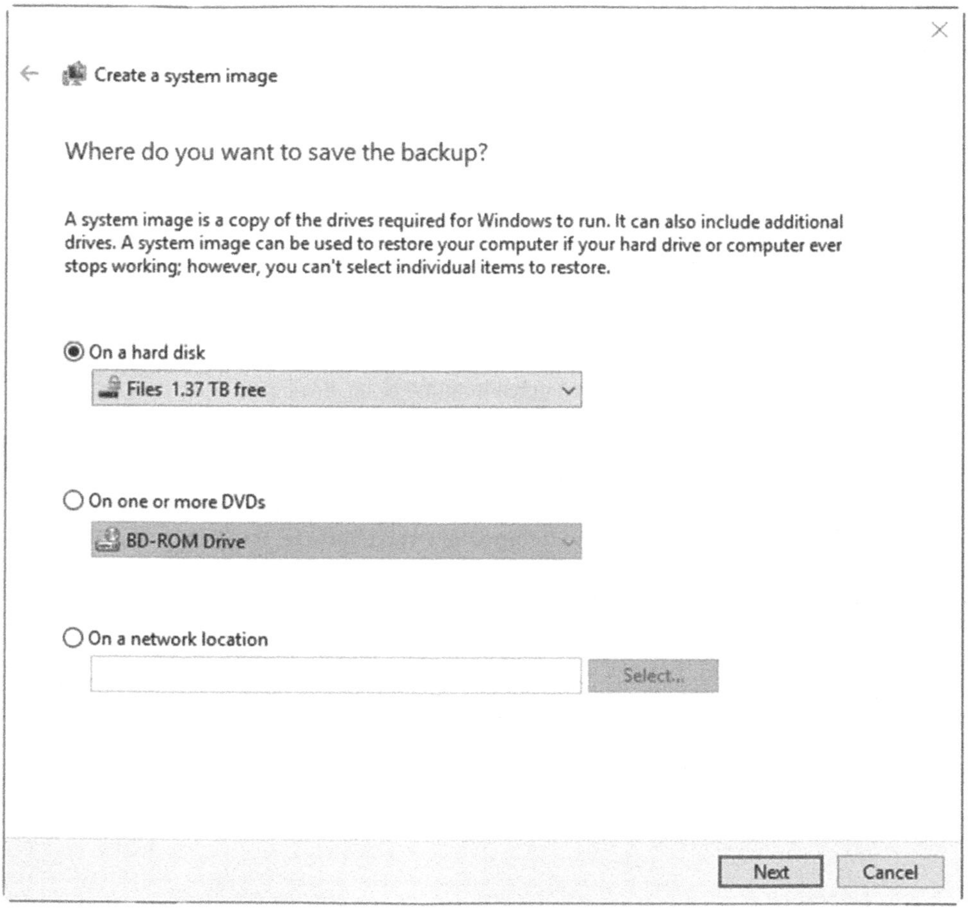

Figure 2-5. *The System Image Backup utility is an easy-to-use wizard*

I want to deal with the issues this can throw up. The first of which is storing your backup on DVDs. Let's set aside for a moment that DVDs tend to have a limited lifespan, and so can't be relied upon for long-term archival storage. A "typical" Windows 10 installation, however, at about 25GB in size would require up to 6 DVDs, and my own installation at around 100GB would require 23 of them. That's a substantial time investment for both creating and restoring the backup, and that's assuming that none of the discs fail in the interim period.

Network storage can also present a problem. You can create your backup on any network location accessible on your PC. This can include server network shares, Network Attached Storage (NAS), and a USB hard disk plugged into your network router, but... **you must never store a System Image backup on a network share you only connect to by Wi-Fi**. The reason for this is that the System Image can be restored only from the Windows 10 Recovery Options, and these have no way to load Wi-Fi drivers, and as such, cannot connect to remote storage by any method other than by a physical network (Ethernet) cable.

There is also the small matter of your files. On some PCs, where files are stored on a server and synced using a roaming user profile, or where all your files are synchronized to a cloud backup service such as Dropbox or Google Drive, and where you don't have many files, you might be content to leave them sitting in your C:\Users folder.

If you use OneDrive however, or if you have more files than can easily and quickly be downloaded from a web service, you should **always** store your files on a separate physical hard disk, or partition on your PC.

The reason for this is that a System Image is a full snapshot of the disk or partition on which Windows 10 is installed, at the time the backup image is taken. When you restore this backup image, that entire disk or partition will be restored exactly as it was at the time the backup was made. If files are stored on this drive or partition in the C:\Users folder (or elsewhere) they will overwritten, and older versions of your files will be restored.

With cloud backup services such as Dropbox or Google Drive this doesn't present too much of a problem, as restoring a backup will require those services to completely resync all of your files downward from cloud storage anyway. OneDrive works differently, however, in that it can simply pick up from where it left off before.

■ **Caution**   While this will sync all of your current files down from the cloud, it will also likely back up all the old versions of files, and files you've long since deleted that are included in your backup, to the cloud again.

There's also the fact that including personal files in a system backup will inflate the size of the backup file, perhaps considerably, and if you need to perform a complete format-and-clean reinstallation of Windows 10, you won't restore them anyway.

I'll show you how to move your Shell User Folders (Documents, Pictures, Music, Video, etc.) and how to create new and manage existing partitions in Chapter 3. Moving your files away from your copy of Windows 10 is a good idea anyway, since if you have a major problem with Windows 10 that requires a clean reinstallation of the OS, you won't lose your files in the process.

When you have chosen your backup location, you will be asked which hard disks or partitions in the PC you wish to include in the backup. Anything you can't exclude because it's essential to the operation of Windows 10 is grayed out, and you're likely to not want to select anything else, see Figure 2-6.

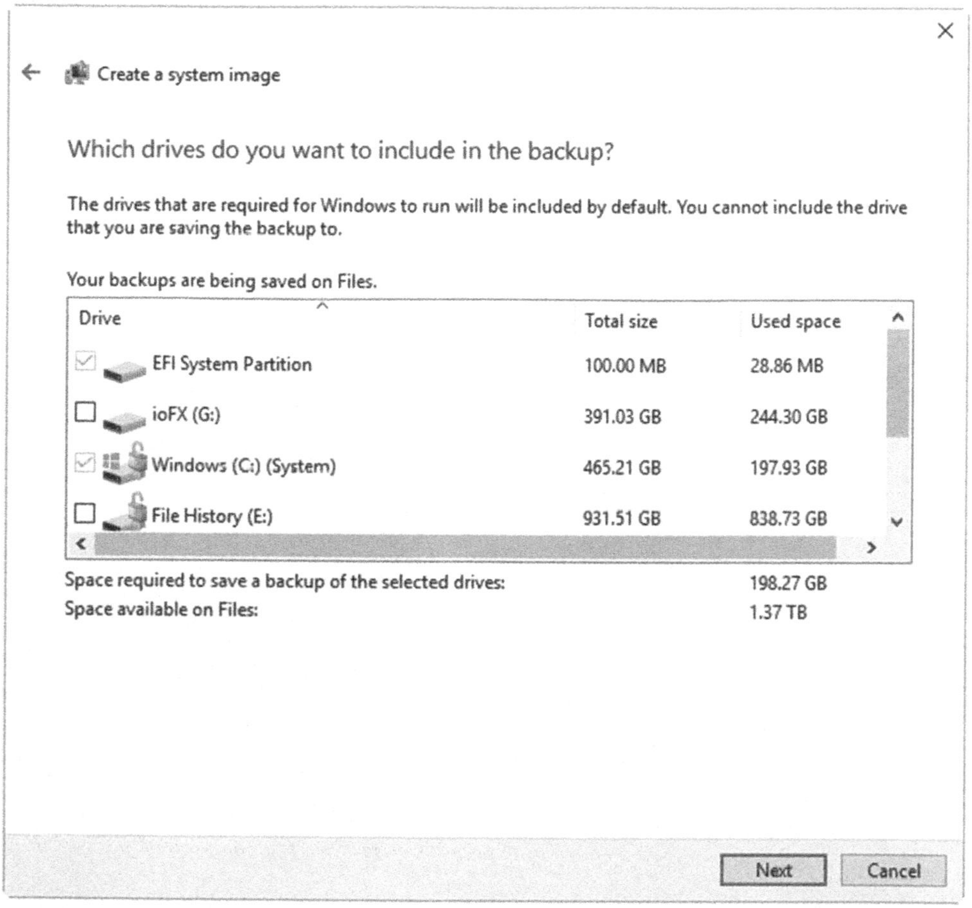

Figure 2-6. *You will be asked what drives or partitions you wish to include in the backup*

I mention this, however, as you may have a small partition on which you store hardware drivers or other setup files for the PC that would be useful to include, or you may have a separate partition on which some win32 apps are installed.

When you click *Next* you will be presented with details of the backup location and partition inclusion options you have selected, and asked to begin creation of the System Image Backup.

Restoring a System Image Backup

As I mentioned a while ago, you restore a System Image Backup from the Windows 10 Recovery Options. There are, just as with performing a Reset, three ways to access these options (Windows 10 starts up far too quickly for the F8 startup menu to be something I can still recommend). You can open the Settings app, click *Update & recovery*, and in the *Recovery* section click the Advanced Startup button. You can also hold down the *Shift* key on your keyboard while clicking Restart from the Start Menu power options or sign-in screen. You can also start your PC from the USB Recovery Drive *that you definitely created!!* You will need to make sure your PC's BIOS or UEFI system is set to permit booting from USB devices, however.

■ **Caution**   Do not encrypt a drive or partition containing a System Image Backup with Bitlocker, as the Recovery Console will be unable to see it and therefore be unable to restore it. This does present some potential security issues, which is another reason to store your files away from your Windows installation and to maintain strong passwords on all user accounts on the PC, as a restored backup will be unencrypted, and you will have to re-encrypt it with Bitlocker afterward.

At the Recovery Options screen, click *Troubleshoot* and then *Advanced Options* as seen back in Figures 2-3 and 2-4. You will then see an option for the *System Image Recovery*, see Figure 2-7.

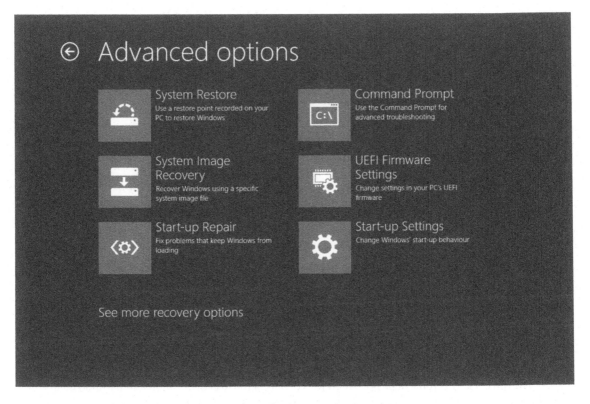

Figure 2-7. *You can restore a System Image from the Recovery Options*

If a system backup image exists on the PC it should be found automatically by the system, if no image is found however, perhaps because you are storing it on a network drive or because the disk containing the backup requires a RAID or other hardware driver, choose the *Select a system image* option, and click *Next*.

If you need to search for a network location, you will be asked for the full address of the network folder containing your System Image Backup in the format \\server\share, see Figure 2-8. Alternatively, you can click *Install a driver* to load a RAID or other hardware disk driver.

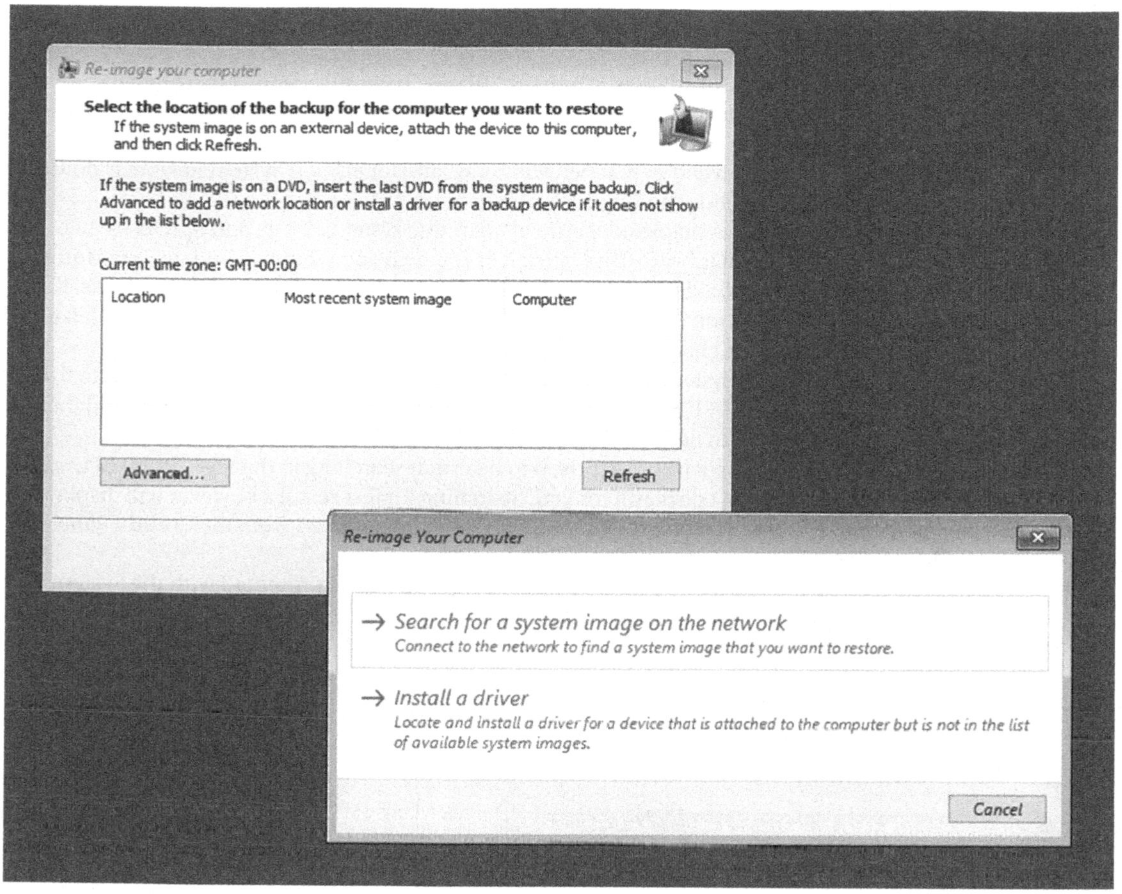

Figure 2-8. *You can search network connections where the PC is connected by an Ethernet cable*

If you do not know this, perhaps because it is managed by your system administrator, you can ask them or, on another PC that also has access to the file share, open its location in File Explorer and then click the icon to the left of the address (breadcrumb) bar to reveal the full network address, see Figure 2-9.

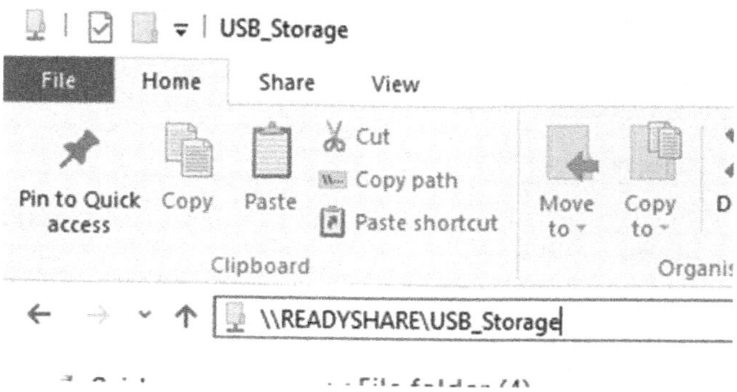

Figure 2-9. *Network addresses can be obtained in File Explorer*

Using Windows System Restore

System Restore has been around since the days of Windows ME, and if like me you're a seasoned (by which I mean, older) IT Pro you'll know that people tended to deactivate it as it was a great place in which viruses could hide, ready to pounce again when a restore was actioned. Fortunately, the advent of User Account Control (UAC) in Windows Vista put an end to that behavior once and for all, and System Restore is now a reliable method to quickly repair a malfunctioning copy of Windows.

What System Restore does is take a snapshot of critical operating system, driver, and app files when a significant change, such as an app or hardware driver install or removal or a Windows Update, is performed. These snapshot files are stored in the hidden System Volume Information folders on your hard disks, if you've ever wondered what they were for. Should a change cause something to become unstable or fail to work, System Restore can roll back the change to undo the damage.

There are several ways to access System Restore. If the PC is completely unbootable, starting into the Recovery Options (perhaps using the USB Recovery Drive you made!!) and clicking *Troubleshoot* and then *Advanced Options* will present a System Restore option, as seen back in Figure 2-7.

From within Windows 10, you might be unsurprised to hear that searching in the Start Menu or Cotana for the words **system** and **restore** won't display it for you. Searching for just **restore** however will display the *Create a Restore Point* option which you can use. Alternatively, opening *Recovery* from the Control Panel will present links to *Open System Restore* and *Configure System Restore*.

If you click *Create a Restore Point* or *Configure System Restore* you will be presented with the System Protection options in the System Properties dialog, see Figure 2-10.

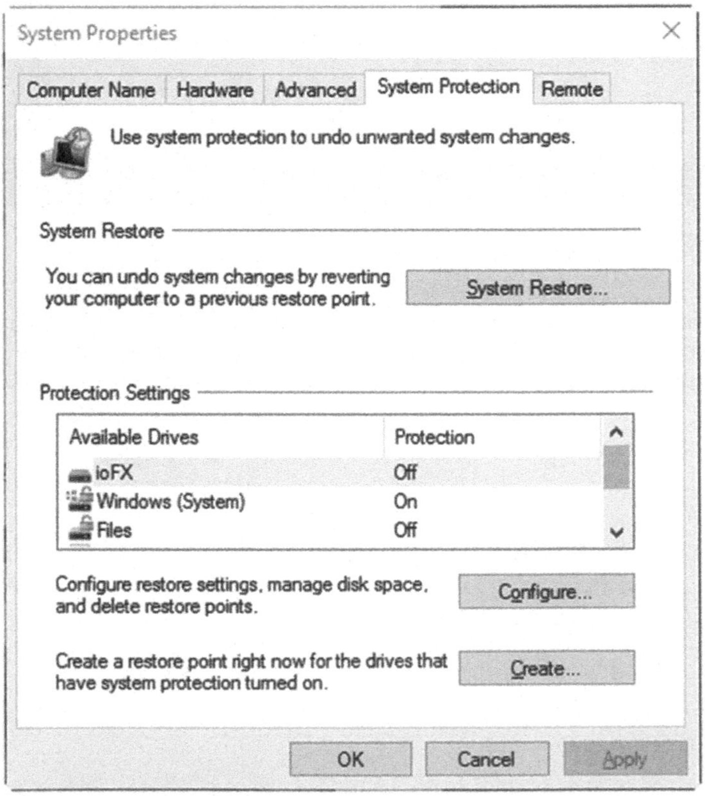

Figure 2-10. *You can create Restore Points manually*

As I mentioned earlier, Restore Points are created automatically when an app or a driver is installed or removed, or when Windows Updates are installed. You can click the *Create* button, however, to manually create a Restore Point if you are making a change that won't trigger the automatic creation of a Restore Point, such as moving the Shell User Folders or editing the Registry.

To restore Windows system files, drivers, and apps back to a previous point in time, click the *System Restore* button or click *Open System Restore* from the recovery panel. This will open a wizard that explains on its first page what System Restore will do.

At the next page, see Figure 2-11, you will be presented with a list of the most recently created Restore Points. In the bottom left of the dialog is a check box to *Show More Restore Points*, should any more exist on the PC.

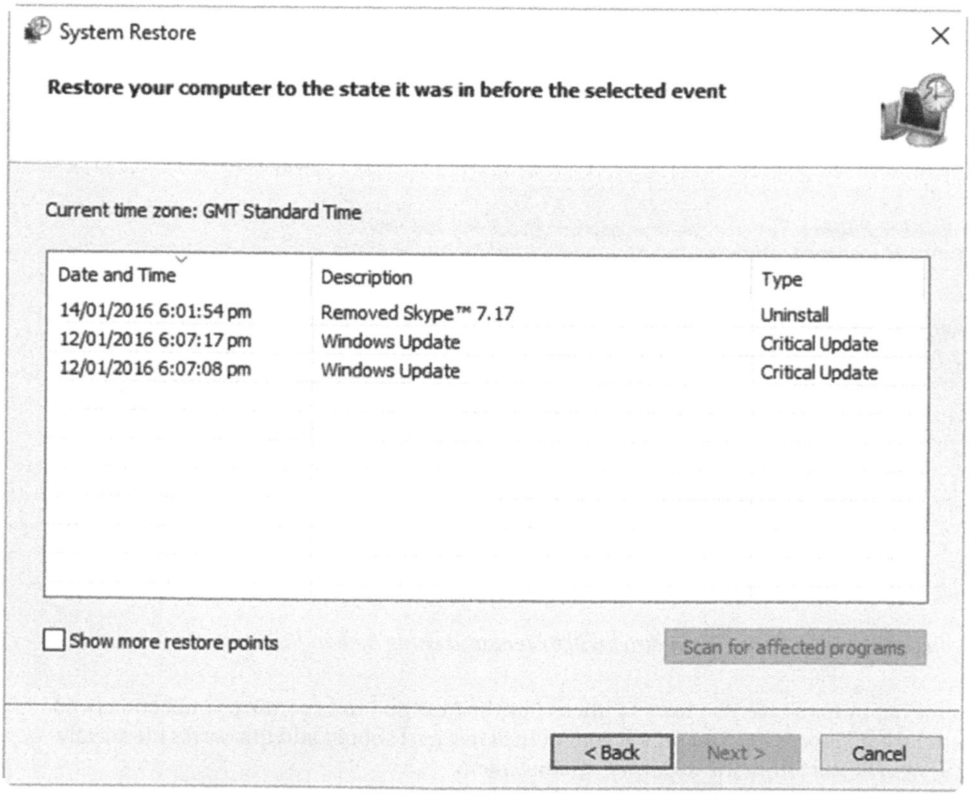

Figure 2-11. Windows 10 stores several Restore Points from which you can choose

Once you have chosen a Restore Point, by clicking it once to highlight it, you can optionally click the *Scan for affected programs* button to see what apps might be rolled back to previous versions or uninstalled, see Figure 2-12, in which you can see that Skype and an update to Google Chrome will be affected.

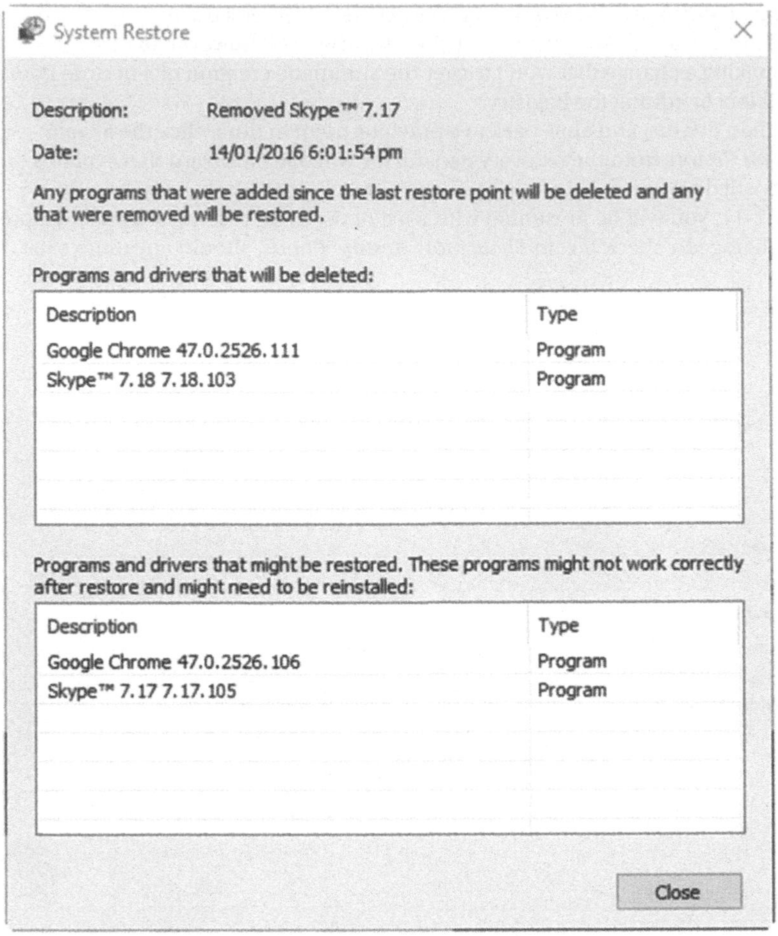

Figure 2-12. *You can see what apps and updates will be removed using System Restore*

When you are happy to restore Windows 10, then click the *Next* button to confirm your actions and begin the System Restore process, during which your PC will restart. I should add this works identically when running System Restore from the Recovery Options menu.

Configuring System Restore

When you install Windows 10, System Restore is configured to run automatically on all the drives on your PC. You might have drives though for files or other purposes that will never be affected by System Restore. Alternatively, you may wish to increase, or reduce, the amount of space System Restore uses on your Windows drive.

You can configure System Restore in the System Properties dialog, accessed by searching for **restore** in the Start Menu or Cortana. Select the disk you want to change the settings for (there may be several in the list) and click the *Configure button.*

As seen in Figure 2-13, you will be able to enable or disable System Protection (another way to describe System Restore that also includes file shadow copies for version control) for that drive, and to change the amount of disk space System Protection uses.

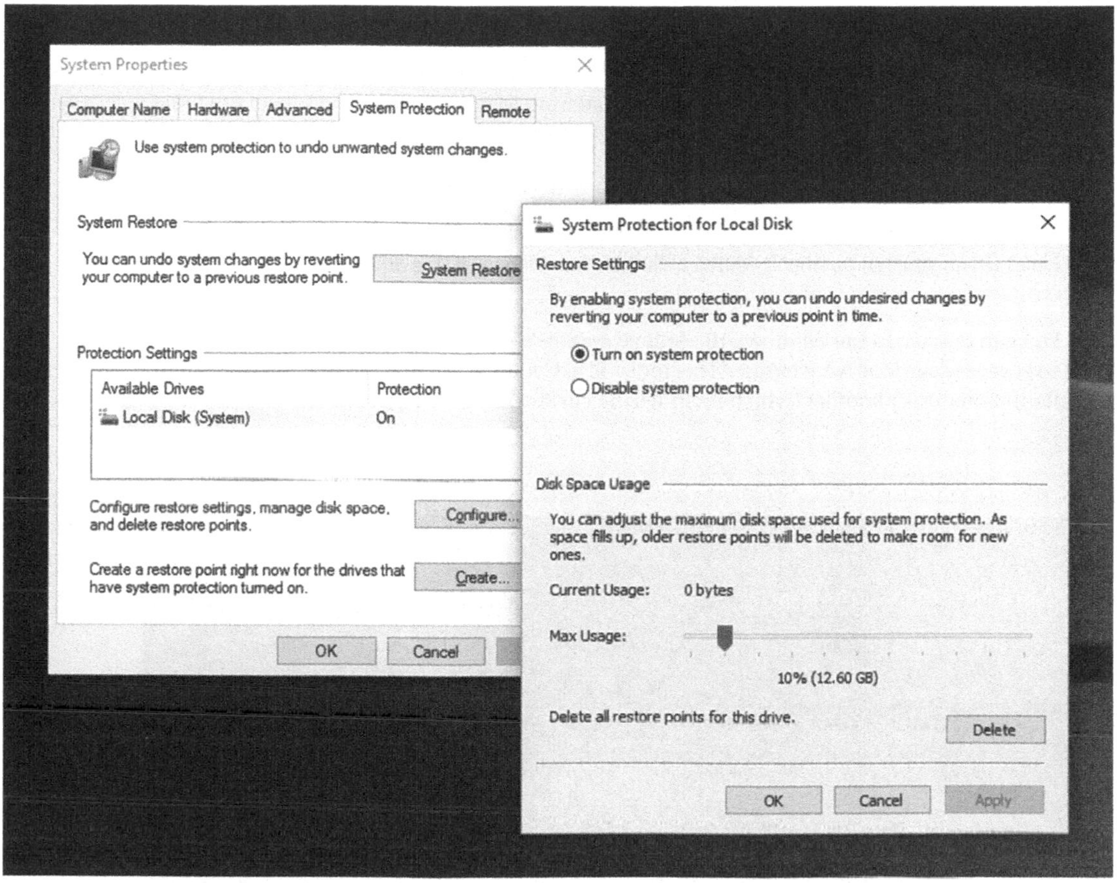

Figure 2-13. You can manage System Restore on each drive or partition in your PC

I should put in a note here about shadow copies of files. These hook into Windows 10's File History feature (if you have it activated) and allow you to roll back to old versions of files should you make a change to a file you didn't wish to make. I'll show you how to use File History shortly. File History does not require the drive on which your files are stored to have System Protection activated, as you can choose where it stores its backups.

Using the Windows 10 Media Creation Tool

Did your PC come with an installation DVD for Windows 10? No, mine didn't either. Installation discs for Windows 10 are now only ever obtained if you specifically purchase a retail copy of the OS in a store. If you purchase a new PC with Windows 10 preinstalled, you won't get a disc, if you took advantage of the free upgrade offer from Windows 7 or Windows 8.1, you won't get a disc either.

If something really goes wrong with Windows 10, however, and you haven't created a USB Recovery Drive (which you did, right!?), Windows 10 needs to be completely reinstalled. If you don't have access to a Windows 10 installer download from the volume licensing program or Microsoft's MSDN web site, or if the A-Team isn't available (though they probably wouldn't be able to help much either if I'm honest), you can create your own installer, either on a DVD or on a USB Flash Drive, at any time.

This can come in handy even if you do have an installation DVD for Windows 10. For one thing, this is because the DVD might contain the wrong version of Windows (Pro when you need Home, for example) but a DVD might also not be much use if you need to reinstall Windows on a tablet or ultrabook that doesn't come with an optical drive. For another, a download from Microsoft will always be of the most recent version of Windows 10, whereas the one on your DVD might require several years of additional patches and updates.

■ **Tip**   If you need to reinstall Windows on a tablet that does not have a full-size USB port compatible with your Flash Drive, you can purchase what's called an "on-the-go" (OTG) adapter cable from good retailers.

You can download the Windows 10 Media Creation Tool free and at any time from www.microsoft.com/software-download/windows10. This tool will ask you if you want to upgrade the current PC or create installation media for another (which includes the current) PC, see Figure 2-14.

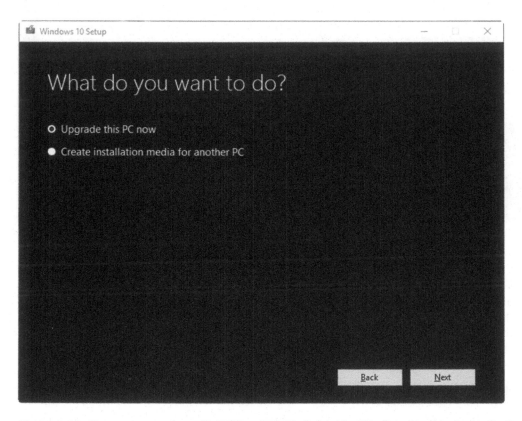

Figure 2-14. You can create a bootable DVD or USB Flash drive for Windows 10 using the Media Creation Tool

You will be asked what language you want Windows 10 to be, what edition of Windows you want (note if it just says Windows 10 it will create media that includes both the Home and Pro versions), and if you want the 32-bit (x86) or 64-bit (x64) version.

■ **Tip**   If you do not know whether you need the 32-bit or 64-bit version of Windows 10, and can still start the PC to the desktop and open *System* from the *Control Panel*, where you will find the current *System type* detailed.

You will then be asked if you want to create a USB Flash Drive (which must be at least 3GB in size, preferably 4GB or slightly more) or download an ISO (disc image) file. Once you have selected an option, you will either be promoted to insert a USB Flash Drive, which will be formatted by the utility, so make sure there's nothing on it you want to keep, or an ISO file will be downloaded.

■ **Note**   If you need to perform a format and clean reinstall of Windows 10, and Windows 10 has previously been installed and activated on the PC, you will not need to enter your product key during the installation process as the OS will recognize the PC and activate automatically when it next goes online. At the product key request page of the installation process, simply click the *skip* button, and continue the installation normally.

If you want to then create a bootable DVD from the ISO file, right-click it in File Explorer and you will see *Burn disc image* appear in the context list of options, see Figure 2-15. You will be prompted to choose the DVD or Blu-ray drive in your PC and to insert a blank disc.

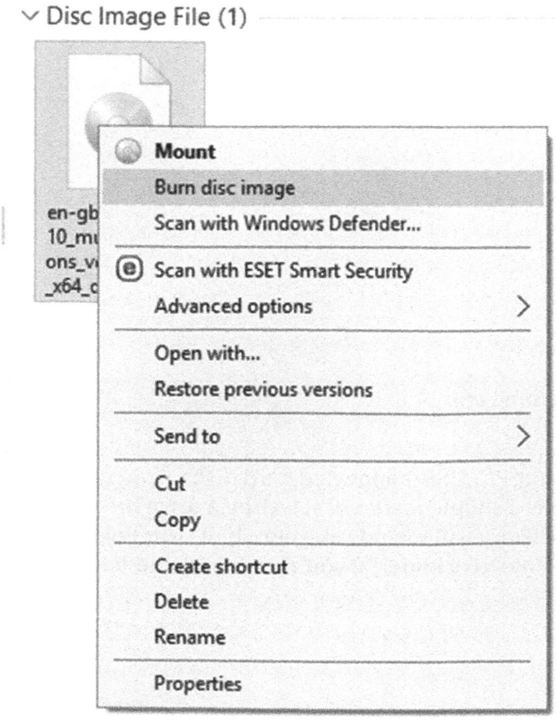

Figure 2-15. You can burn an ISO disc image to a DVD by right-clicking it

Backing Up Your Files with File History

Creating a robust system isn't just about creating a backup image of Windows 10. Your PC would be pretty useless if all your files were lost, so having a reliable file backup routine is essential. Fortunately, Windows 10 comes with an excellent file backup and versioning tool that will be instantly familiar to anyone who's used Time Machine on a Mac.

File History can be found in the Control Panel but is perhaps more easily controlled from the Settings app. Open *Update & recovery* and then *Backup* and you'll be prompted to *add a [backup] drive*, see Figure 2-16.

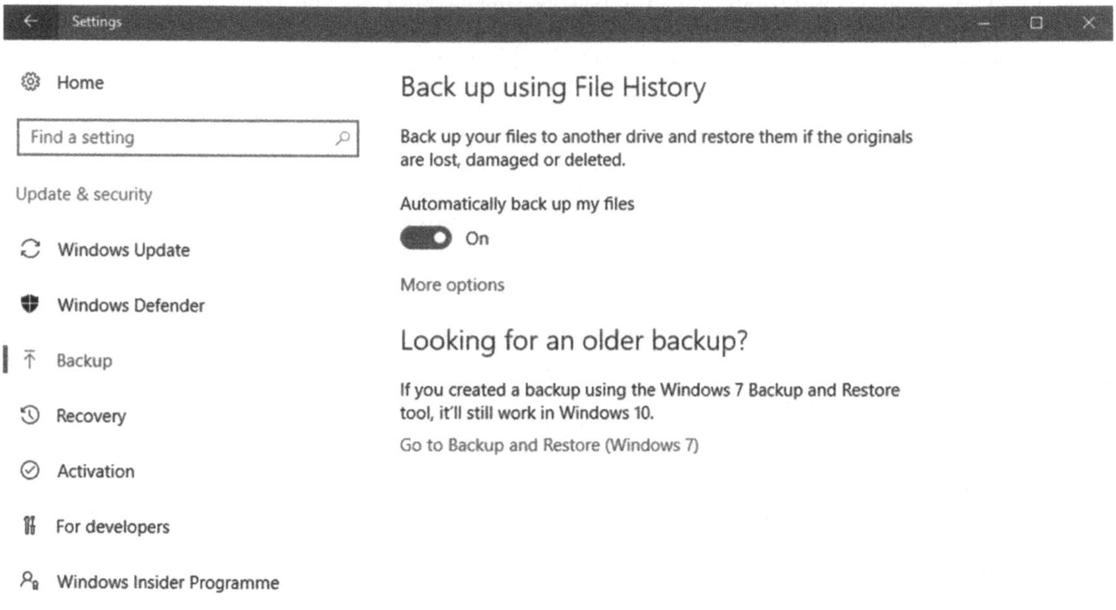

Figure 2-16. *File History is easily controlled from the Settings app*

You can use spare hard disks and partitions in your PC, USB-connected hard disks, or network drives to store your File History backup. Setting it up is a simple matter of selecting a drive on which a **FileHistory** folder will be created. By default, File History will include all your Shell User Folder locations (Documents, Music, Pictures, Video) your OneDrive folder (if you're using it) and anything else in your C:\Users folder.

■ **Tip**   A new version of a file is kept each time a change is made to that file. This includes the file being opened, when its *last accessed* date will be changed. If you have files you open on a regular basis that do not change, such as music or videos, you can prevent your File History drive from filling up with multiple copies of these files by excluding their containing folders from the backup. You should always make sure you *do* keep a backup copy of the files somewhere else, however.

You can manage the settings for File History, though, once it is set up by clicking the *More options* link that will appear in the Backup Settings. This will allow you to control the frequency with which backups are made, how long old versions of files are kept for (this does not include files for which there is only one version), and which folders and included and excluded from the backup, see Figure 2-17.

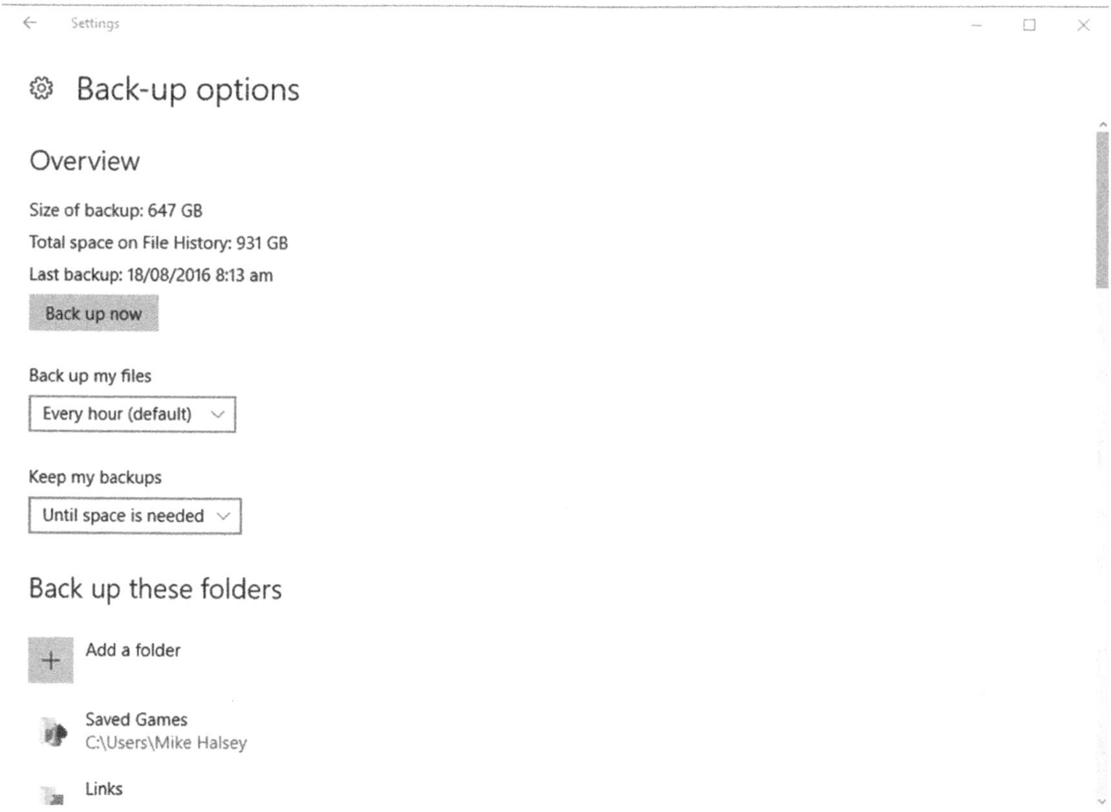

Figure 2-17.   *File History can be managed in the Settings app*

Almost everything you need to do with File History can be done through the Settings app, but the Control Panel offers a couple of additional features, see Figure 2-18.

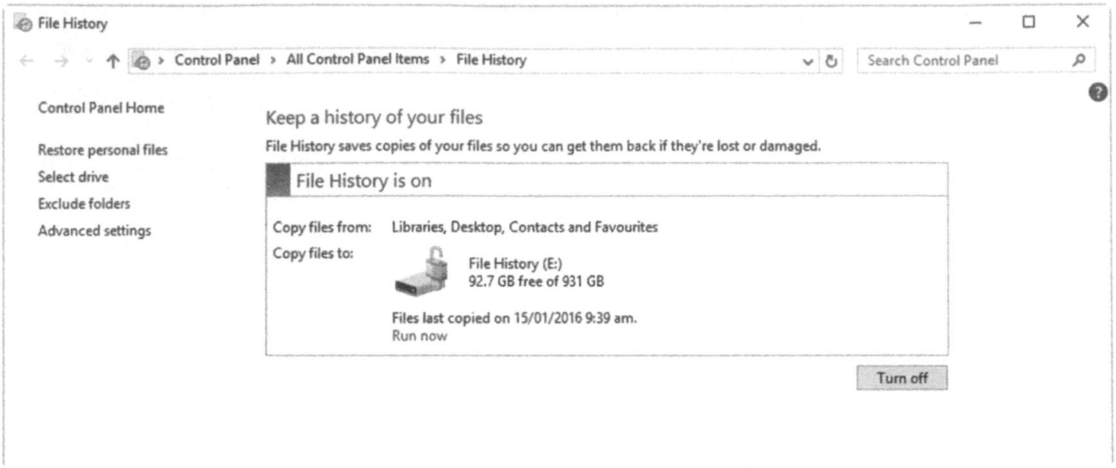

Figure 2-18. *File History in the Control Panel has a few extra options*

Perhaps the most useful of these is seeing how much free space is left on your File History drive. If you find the drive is filling up you can click the *Advanced options* link on the left of the window and then the *Clean up versions* link. Here you can choose to delete all versions of files older than a specific age or, if you're comfortable that you don't need to restore anything, all but the latest one.

Restoring Deleted and Previous Versions of Files

You can restore deleted and older versions of files in File History either by clicking the *Restore personal files* link in the File History, Control Panel applet, or in any File Explorer window by clicking the *History* button in the ribbon, see Figure 2-19.

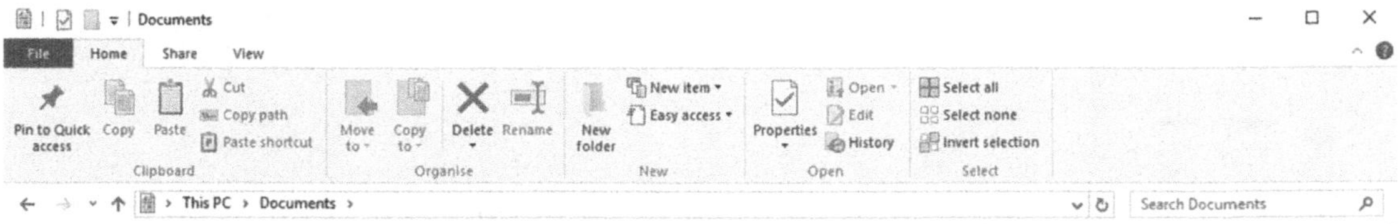

Figure 2-19. *You can restore files directly from File Explorer*

This will open File History at the current drive and folder point, though you can still navigate anywhere within your backup from there. The File History restore window has navigation (back, forward, and up) buttons in its top left and an address bar showing the current folder, see Figure 2-20.

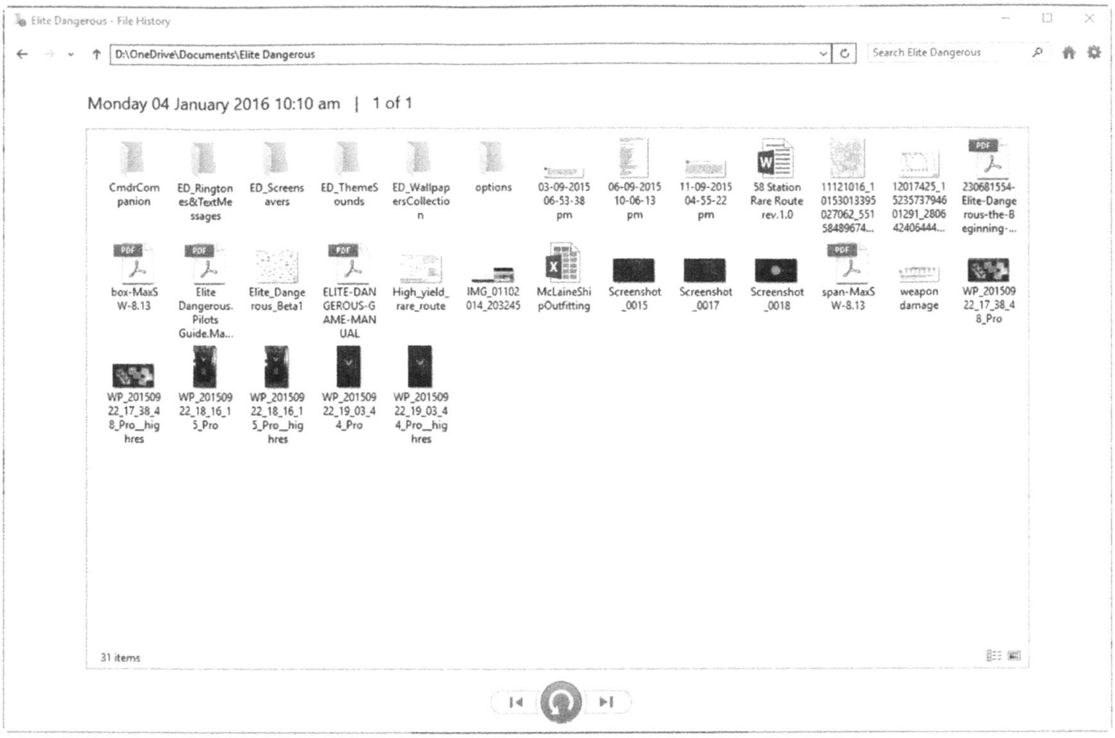

Figure 2-20. *The File History restore panel is easy to navigate and use*

At the bottom of the window are back and forward (by date and time) buttons, with a big green Restore button between them. Once you have navigated to the folder you want to restore deleted or modified file(s) from, use the time buttons to find the correct day and time the backup copy was made, select the file(s) or folder(s) you wish to restore, and hit the big green button. It really is that easy.

■ **Tip** File History does not encrypt your files' backup, so you might want to ensure that Bitlocker or Bitlocker To Go is activated on your File History drive. I will show you how to set these up in Chapter 18.

File History is excellent at picking up where it left off after a Windows reset or reinstall, though you will need to activate the feature again. If you really want to dig into the store location for File History, however, all the files are stored in plain, easily accessible format, just as any other file on a hard disk would be. The only difference is that the date and time the backup was made are appended to the end of the file name.

Setting Up and Managing OneDrive

Microsoft's cloud backup and file sync service, OneDrive, comes baked into Windows 10, and while File History might be a great way to keep backup copies of all your files, it won't help if your home or office catches fire (I know, I'm a cheery person really). Now I'm going to add a caveat to this section, as Microsoft *will* be making significant changes to the OneDrive client in Windows 10 and, knowing my luck, some of those changes will appear right at the moment this book goes to print.

I do know what some of the changes are, however, so I'll give you a heads-up, as they might what you're seeing when you read this. The first is that the OneDrive client, which is a little cloud icon that sits in the system tray to the right of the desktop Taskbar, will support both OneDrive and OneDrive for Business accounts (the latter coming with an Office 365 business or enterprise subscription).

The second is that we will be getting the placeholders feature back. This feature, so popular in Windows 8.1, allowed File Explorer to display all of the files you had, whether stored locally on the PC or in OneDrive in the cloud, and you could make files and folders available offline or online only, by right-clicking them. Once this is implemented we can expect to see "Store [all] files offline" and "Store [all] files online" appear as right-click options on files, folders, and the OneDrive icon in File Explorer.

Fundamentally, however, the setup process for OneDrive shouldn't change very much (he says, hopefully).

To set up OneDrive on your Windows 10 PC, click the cloud icon in the Taskbar system tray, which should appear gray at that point (white when everything is working well) and you will be asked to confirm the location for your OneDrive files store on the PC, see Figure 2-21.

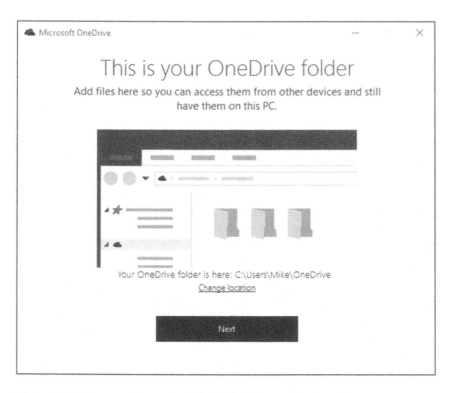

Figure 2-21. *You can change the default OneDrive storage location*

Now, I talked earlier about how you might want to store files on the PC, and this can vary depending on what type of PC you have. If you don't have many files stored in OneDrive (you can purchase more space at any time by visiting onedrive.live.com/options/ManageStorage or by purchasing an Office 365 Personal or Home subscription), or if you are using a PC with limited amounts of storage, such as a tablet or ultrabook, you may not want to store all your files on the PC or have that many to store. In this case, choosing the default storage location C:\User\[YourName]\OneDrive will probably be fine.

If you have a large amount of files stored in OneDrive, however, and want them all stored locally on the PC as well, click the *Change location* link and select where you want the files stored. Remember that if you have or will create a System Image Backup of Windows, as I detailed earlier in this chapter, you should always store your files on a different hard disk or partition to the one on which Windows 10 is installed. I will show you how to do this in Chapter 3.

Next, you will be shown all the files and folders you have stored in OneDrive and asked to select which ones you want downloaded to the PC, see Figure 2-22. You will be alerted, as is the case here, if you have more files than there is space for on the PC. When you have chosen what files and folders you want stored locally on the PC, click Next.

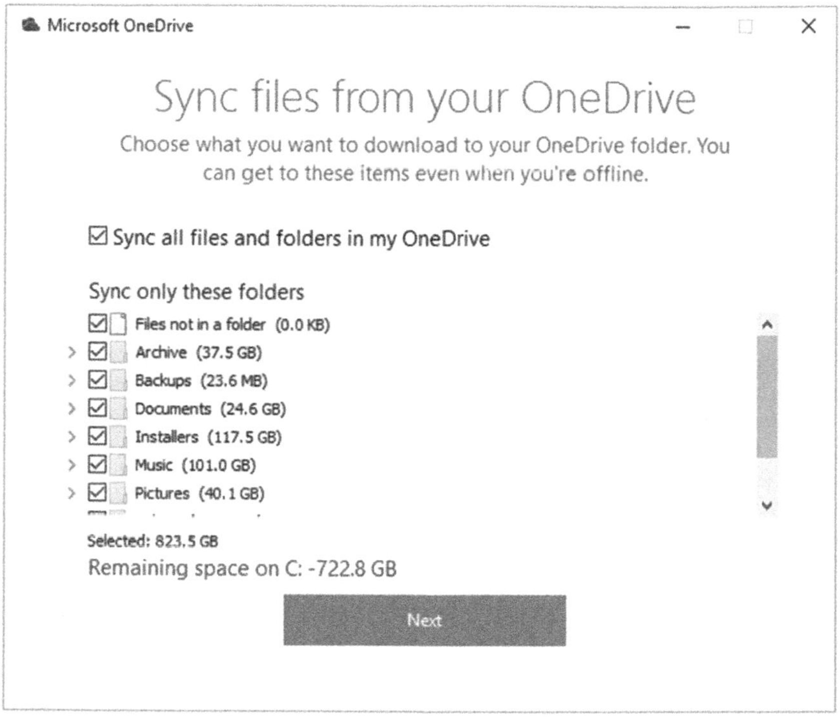

Figure 2-22. *You can choose which folders are synced with OneDrive*

Should you wish to later change which files and folders are stored on the PC, you can right-click the OneDrive icon in the system tray and select *Settings* from the context menu that appears.

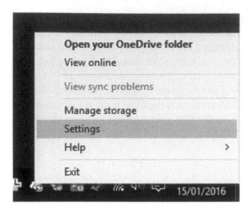

Figure 2-23. *You can change which files and folders are synced locally at any time*

Summary

Back up, back up, back up! Genuinely, the most important part of your PC is its files and apps. Apps can probably be easily replaced, but your files can't. It's crucial therefore to have a robust and, above all, regular backup process in place. Both File History and OneDrive allow you to do this, but other cloud services such as Dropbox, Google Drive, Amazon S3, and LiveDrive are also excellent, and you should shop around to find the best solution to suit your own needs, as some also support offline (local) backups.

With the advice in this chapter followed, you will have created a robust system (and a Recovery Drive!) so that no matter what happens, or what goes wrong (short of your only PC blowing up), you'll be able to quickly get back up and running with your files, your apps, and your copy of Windows 10.

In the next chapter, we'll take this all a step further and look at how Windows 10 can be configured in ways that ensure stability, dependability, and durability. This includes the crucial (I think anyway) ability to move your files and data away from your Windows 10 installation.

CHAPTER 3

■ ■ ■

Configuring Windows 10

While creating a robust backup system, and one that permits the quick and (relatively) straightforward restoration of a fully working copy of Windows 10, is both laudable and necessary (just a reminder that you *did* create that USB Recovery Drive?!), what's likely more important is setting up a PC, Windows 10, and your apps in such a way that they don't break in the first place.

Windows 7 was the first operating system from Microsoft I felt really didn't need to be tinkered with or modified in any way to make it operate well. That's still the case with Windows 10, but knowing what's available, and where to find it, can make creating a robust and resilient system much more straightforward.

The Settings App

The Settings app was first introduced in Windows 8 as PC Settings. The aim at the time was to create a simplified Control Panel containing the settings and options that nontechnical PC users would most likely need. In Windows 10 we've seen Settings expanded significantly, though it's still in its "version 1" form. Over the lifetime of Windows 10 we'll see the full Control Panel and, very likely, the Administrative Tools folded into the Settings interface.

This means that during the lifetime of this book, some Control Panel elements will move into the Settings app (so if I detail a Control Panel applet that you can't find, that'll be why).

You'll probably be familiar with Settings to some extent already; for instance, you probably know that it's opened from the Start Menu, by clicking the *Settings* icon, either in desktop mode or in tablet mode, by first clicking the hamburger icon (so called because its three horizontal lines make it look like one... apparently) and that when you do this, the Settings icon will appear.

The Settings app is divided into nine main categories, see Figure 3-1, and anybody who's used an Apple Mac over the years will immediately feel at home with it.

© Mike Halsey 2016
M. Halsey, *Windows 10 Troubleshooting*, DOI 10.1007/978-1-4842-0925-7_3

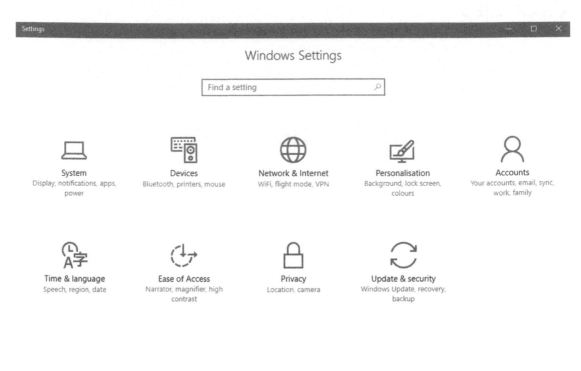

Figure 3-1. *The Settings app consists of nine main settings areas*

The aim with what I will refer to as this version 2 Settings app (the version 1 being that which we saw in Windows 8) is to make it as simple and as straightforward to use for everyday PC users as possible. Thus, the available controls are basic. A good example of this is managing printers. The Settings app will allow you to add and remove printers on your PC, but you need to delve into the *Devices and Printers* panel to access print and management options.

There are also, as you might expect, a great many items which are missing. Some of these are even surprising omissions such as being able to create a USB Recovery Drive for the PC (which you... oh, never mind!) and managing which drives and partitions are protected by System Restore and file versioning. These will inevitably be folded into the Settings app over time.

If you're troubleshooting a PC, there's really not much here currently to work with except for managing Wi-Fi networks, and I'll talk about how you do this in Chapter 9. For setting up and configuring a PC, however, there's more, and I'll detail the most important that are relevant to creating a reliable and resilient PC.

System ➤ Storage

This is where you can select what drive, partition, or external storage medium (such as a Micro SD card) your new documents, music, photos, and video are stored. Crucially, however, it's where you can specify the storage location for Store apps. Changing the storage location here doesn't change the default install location for win32 apps, for which the install location is usually customizable during their installation; it only manages apps that come from the Windows Store or the Windows Store for Business, see Figure 3-2.

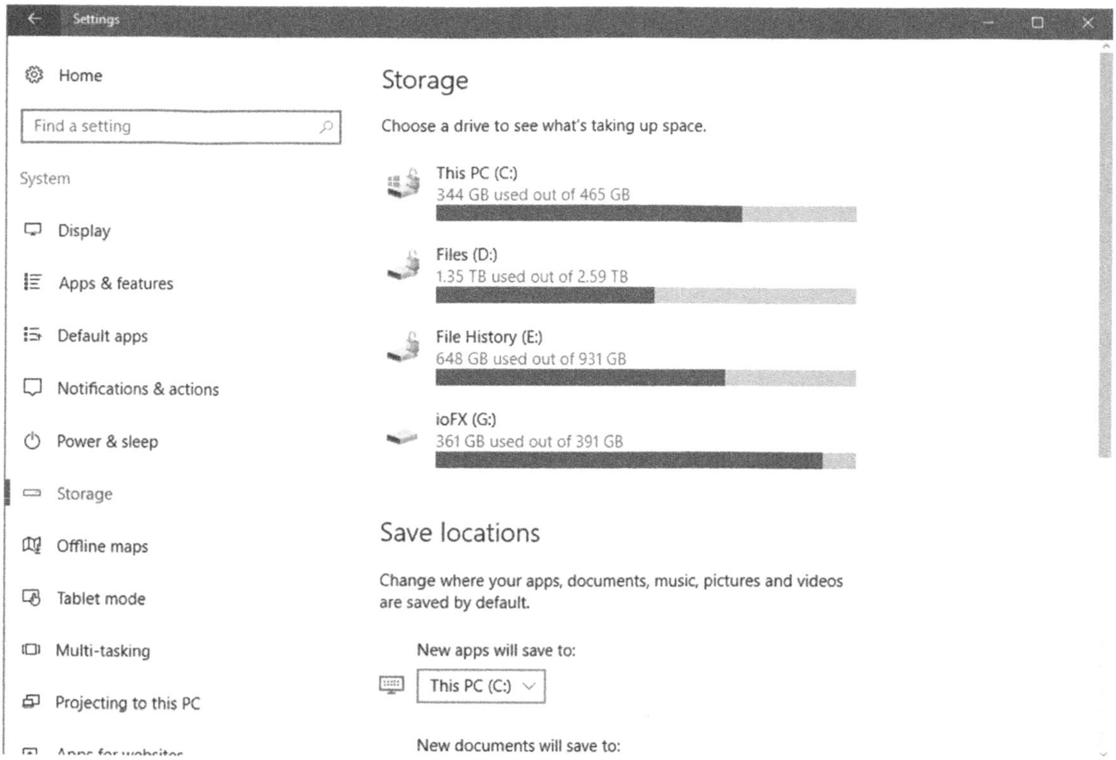

Figure 3-2. *You can manage the Store App install location*

This setting is most useful for people who use tablets (both consumer and pro) in which storage can be at a premium. Some small tablets come with only 16GB of storage, though this can still make them perfectly useful for some tasks in the workplace, and they're certainly useful for people lounging on the couch at home. Even Microsoft's Surface Pro convertible tablets come with a Micro SD card slot for the purposes of storage expansion.

Here comes probably the first top troubleshooting tip to look for, and it's if a user is telling you that they picked up their tablet first thing in the morning to find that, suddenly, none of their apps will work. While it might be tempting to assume they'll need to restart the machine, or it could be a Registry or configuration problem, it's much more likely their 8-year-old child slipped the Micro SD card out of their device so they could use it to store more music on their own smartphone.

System ➤ Default Apps

The Default apps settings, by which I mean which app is started on your PC when you open a specific file type or web link, is one of the few settings that currently reside in both the Settings app *and* the Control Panel (which doesn't offer much more functionality, to be honest). Top tip number two is that if you get a call from a user saying they suddenly can't open their Word documents any more, it's likely because a setting here has been changed, either accidentally by the user, or by another app that's trying to steal the file type for itself.

You can actually do quite a bit to manage your default apps in Settings, see Figure 3-3. The default view will show you which apps are set for the most commonly performed tasks on a PC (e-mail, web browsing, picture and photo viewing, music, and video), and you can click one to change the default app.

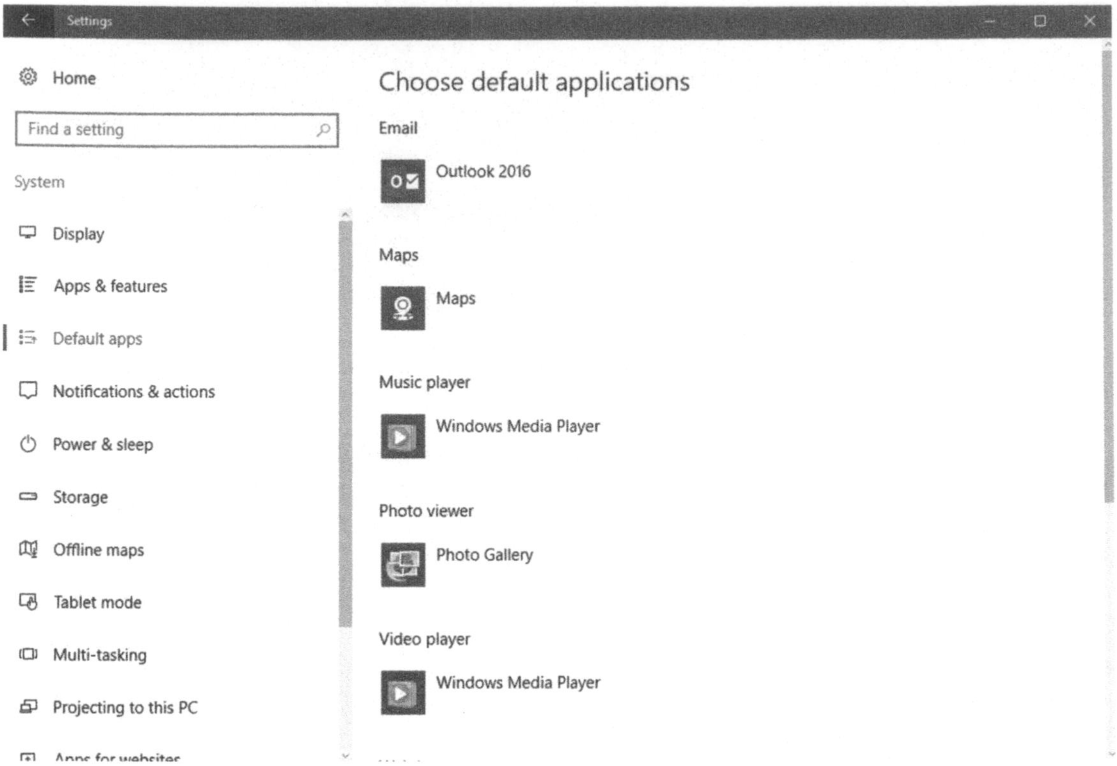

Figure 3-3. *You can manage your default apps in Settings*

Further down the *Default apps* page are several useful quick links.

- *Choose default applications by file type* is useful if your PCs use a custom app that has its own file type. Occasionally, such as after a system configuration change, these file associations can become scrambled. Selecting this option will present a list of all the file types known by Windows 10 on your PC, and you can select the default app for each one.

- *Choose default applications by protocol* is more useful if you have a specific Internet or network link type that is opening with the incorrect app. As an example of this, you might have a convertible laptop with both the Office 365 desktop and Store apps installed, but clicking a link to a PowerPoint file in SharePoint is opening the files in the Store app when the user really wants the win32 app instead.

- *Set default by app* is the one option where you will find yourself back in the Control Panel (for now, anyway). Here you will be presented with a list of all your install apps. You can select one to choose which file associations it has. This is most useful if you want, for example, a music, video, or photos app to open some but not all of the file types associated with it, as you use another app for a specific file type.

System ➤ About

This is where you can point users if you need them to give you information about their PC and their installed copy of Windows 10, see Figure 3-4. You might, for example, want to know what version of Windows 10 they have installed (to maintain app compatibility), what type of OS they have installed (32-bit or 64-bit), or which version of Windows 10 (Home, Pro, Enterprise, etc.) is installed.

Figure 3-4. *You can get information about the PC and Windows 10 from Settings*

Devices ➤ Printers & Scanners / Connected Devices

I'm going to lump these options together, as both have permission options to download drivers and updates for devices over metered (cellular) connections. If you discover that a user is being billed for too much cellular data, you might want to check the settings here to see if these have been accidentally enabled.

Devices ➤ AutoPlay

AutoPlay governs the behavior of Windows when removable media, such as a USB Flash Drive, optical disc, digital camera, or smartphone, are plugged into the PC. A user might know how (and find it helpful) to have the PC perform a specific action, such as opening an app or File Explorer, and might suddenly find that nothing is happening any more.

It's also useful, however, because File History, which I detailed in Chapter 2, can use USB Hard Disks for backup, and if the incorrect setting is selected here (you will find it in the Removable drive drop-down menu) no backups will be made. When you want users to always have an up-to-date backup of their files, this is definitely one to keep an eye on.

Network & Internet

The *Network & Internet* settings really only allow the setting up and removal of connections (Wi-Fi, Ethernet, Virtual Private Network [VPN], dial-up) and you'll still want the full Network and Sharing Center for managing and troubleshooting problems, which I'll talk about in Chapter 9.

This is, though, a useful place for a user to get information about whether network types are set up correctly. If you are remotely supporting a user who can't get access to the work network, you are unlikely to be able to provide Remote Desktop support (we'll cover this in depth in Chapter 12). It could be, however, that the settings for their VPN or proxy server have been deleted (you might be surprised what users feel they don't need on their PCs).

Accounts

Similarly to the Network and Internet settings, the Accounts settings contain things that a user might feel they want to change or tweak, and in doing so they might accidentally delete or corrupt a setting. Changing their account picture is one thing, but users don't like typing long and complicated passwords into their PCs. If you've not locked down password management in Group Policy, then you might find a user creating a very basic PIN or picture password on a laptop that contains sensitive company or customer data.

The settings for Azure Active Directory (Azure AD) and Mobile Device Management (MDM) are also found here however. These are essential for company network access to Office 365, and for a company to be able to remotely support (and check the integrity and security of) a PC or Bring Your Own Device (BYOD) machine.

Lastly, the *Sync your settings* options might be seen by some as an annoyance that ties their PC to Microsoft's OneDrive service, but if you have a PC user with specific accessibility needs, making sure that Settings Sync is active can make the difference between a usable and a completely unusable PC.

Time & Language

If you support people who travel with their laptop or tablet around the world, then they'll need to know how to correctly set the Time and Region settings. At its simplest these settings allow a user to change their current time zone and country (Windows 10 is pretty good at managing everything else).

Occasionally, however, a user might find that a specific app or online service won't work or reports an error. If the user has recently been traveling, these are good settings to check, not just because some online services are location-specific (i.e., only available in certain countries) but because if the clock as set on the PC doesn't match what an app or service expects to see, errors and sign-in failures can sometimes occur.

Update & Security ➤ Windows Update

Windows Updates cannot be disabled or ignored in Windows 10, at all! Microsoft enforces a strict policy that all security and stability updates will be pushed to all Windows 10 PCs, and not even businesses with thousands of devices will be immune. However, there are some caveats with this.

If you use Windows 10 Pro or Enterprise, feature upgrades (not essential security and stability ones, mind) can be deferred for a period of a few months, see Figure 3-5. In Enterprise (and this is managed through a server), these updates, which include new and updates features in the OS, can be deferred for a period of 10 years.

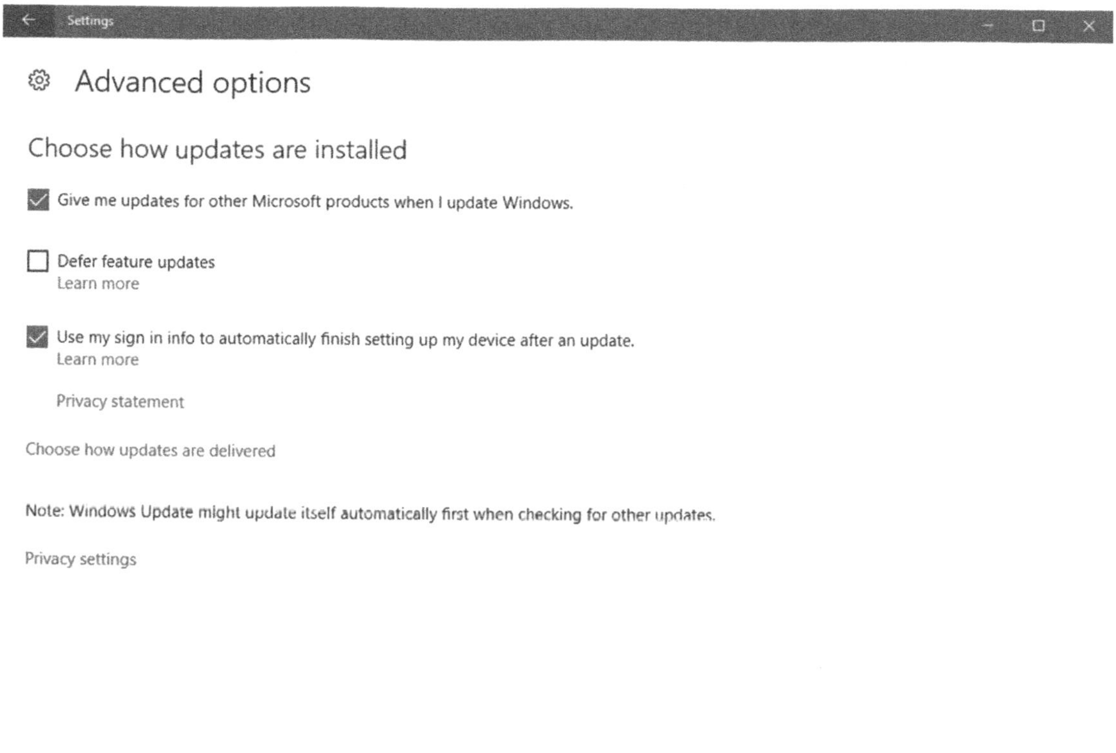

Figure 3-5. *Windows 10 Pro and Enterprise editions permit deferral of upgrade installs*

These deferment branches are called "Current Branch for Business (CBB)", which any PC running Windows 10 Pro or Enterprise can take advantage of, and "Long-Term Servicing Branch (LTSB)."

If there's one thing that users like fiddling with, it's Windows Update. Either they'll hate updates coming down the pipe and try to turn them off, or they'll be bored for a few minutes and think they should check if their PC needs any. Users who are able to check or uncheck the *Defer upgrades* option could find themselves, potentially at any rate, creating security or stability problems that they'll then blame on anything other than their own actions.

If you have users who sign into their PCs using a Microsoft account, such as people who occasionally use their own PC, or who work from home, you might find them signing up to the Windows 10 Insider Preview program. This will download alpha and beta builds of future Windows 10 versions, and these are very commonly known to be unstable and break apps and services.

Update & Security ➤ Windows Defender / Backup

Again, these are settings worth keeping an eye on. Unless you use third-party anti-malware and file backup solutions, you do not want users deactivating these settings. It is perfectly possible for a user to deactivate the Windows Defender package (though Windows 10 will then nag them incessantly to turn it back on again) but it's certainly something of which you should be aware.

Update & Security ➤ Activation

Like the *Settings* ➤ *About* panel, Activation can provide valuable information about whether the currently installed version of Windows 10 is activated and, therefore, fully operational. It might be that after a

59

reinstallation Windows 10 does not activate properly. Here you can check the activation status, manually activate Windows 10 on that PC, or if necessary change the product key to the correct one.

Update & Security ➤ For Developers

PC users always believe they know what is best for security on their PCs, and it's entirely possible that some users might look at the Developer Features options and see that the *Sideload apps* setting is active. "This might allow malware onto my PC," they could think, and change the setting to *Windows Store apps [only]* as a defense. Should you then get a call from a user saying they can't install company apps from your server, this might be why.

Introducing the Control Panel

Throughout this book, we'll be spending a great deal of time looking at the Control Panel. Unlike the Settings app, however, where I wanted to detail all the things "helpful" users might want to change on their own, the Control Panel is slightly more impenetrable for novice PC users.

The Control Panel is easiest opened from the **Windows key + X** administration menu. In its top right is a drop-down *View by:* menu which permits the displaying of a Category view (similar in some ways to the Settings app), large icons, or small icons, see Figure 3-6. It's been on a crash diet since Windows 8.1 and will be slimmed much further in the years to come, but it remains the place to go for serious PC settings.

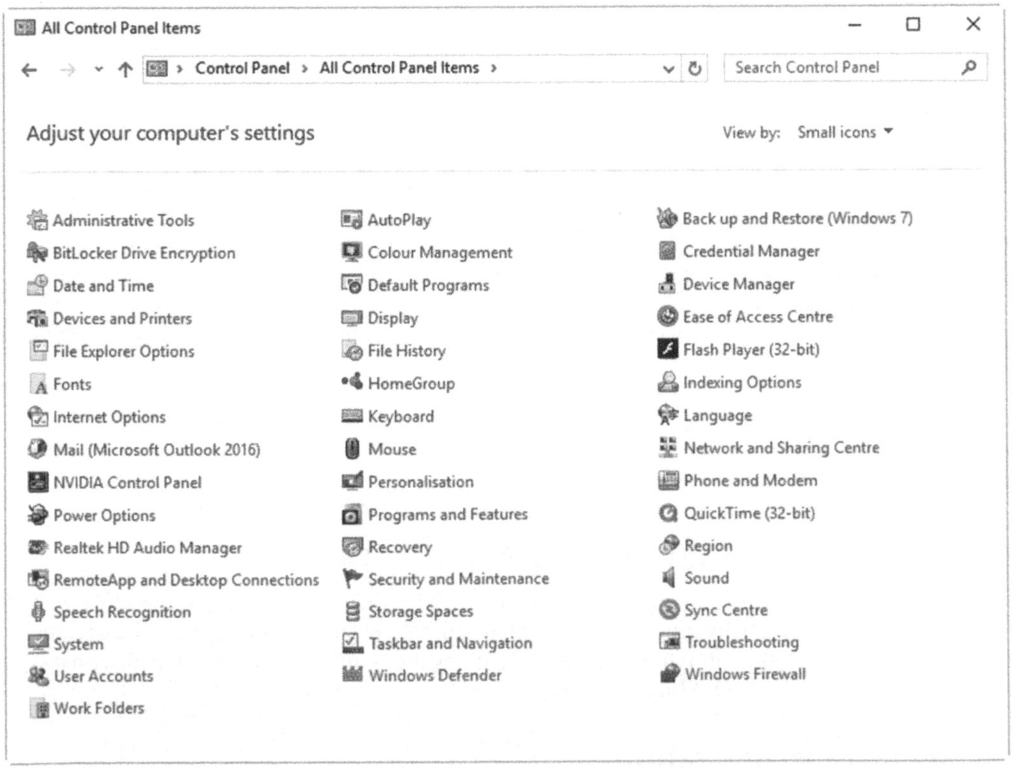

Figure 3-6. *The Control Panel is slimmed from Windows 8.1, but still very useful*

The Control Panel is also home to many subpanels, each of which is significant in its own right. These include the *Devices and Printers* panel, which I'll detail in full in Chapter 7, and the all-important *Administrative Tools*, which contains the advanced management and support utilities for Windows 10 and which I'll cover in depth in various chapters later in this book.

Managing the Virtual Memory, Paging File

While much of the features in Windows 10 can be controlled from the Settings app, there are a couple of settings available in the Control Panel that you might want to change in the Control Panel, the first of which can extend the life of a Solid State Drive (SSD) considerably.

Both of these settings can be found in the *System* section of Control Panel by then clicking the *Advanced System Settings* link in the left of the window. Navigate to the *Advanced* tab in the window that appears, and in the *Performance* section, click the *Settings* button.

At the next pop-up dialog, click the *Advanced tab* and then the *Change* button for virtual memory. You can now change the virtual memory (paging files) settings to a fixed size, that is, where both the initial and maximum sizes are identical, as in Figure 3-7.

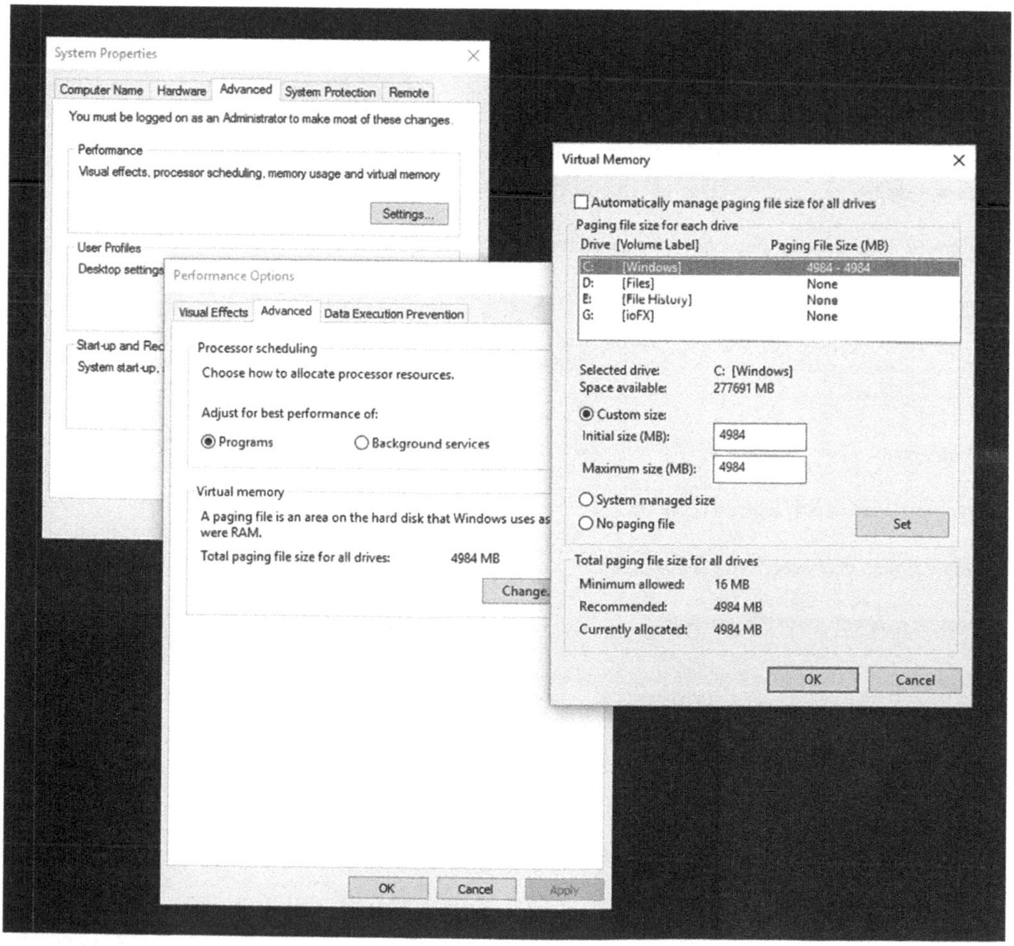

Figure 3-7. *Changing the size of the page file can greatly enhance the life of SSDs*

Windows 10 doesn't really use the paging file as much as previous versions of the OS, as it tends more to keep files in memory than write them to disk. However, the paging file does still exist. This is a temporary store of files that have been swapped out of memory, to speed up the computer and (on older PCs) free up memory space.

By default, the paging file expands and contracts as needed, but all of these file-write operations can slow a disk and even massively shorten the life of an SSD (in fact it can be a good idea to disable the paging file use for SSD systems completely, though this can cause some older software to complain and not work).

Managing Remote Connections to the PC

Additionally, under the *Remote* tab (but also available from the System panel by clicking the *Remote settings* link on the left of the window) are options for allowing or denying remote connections to a PC. If you need to remotely support PCs in the workplace, or are trying to remotely connect to a customer, friend, or family member without success, this is where you should look (or ask them to look, anyway).

You might find that remote connections to the PC aren't permitted, and as such Remote Desktop and using Remote Assistance, both of which I will detail in Chapter 12, won't work. Both of these have their own settings, see Figure 3-8, and you'll need to make sure they are activated if you need them.

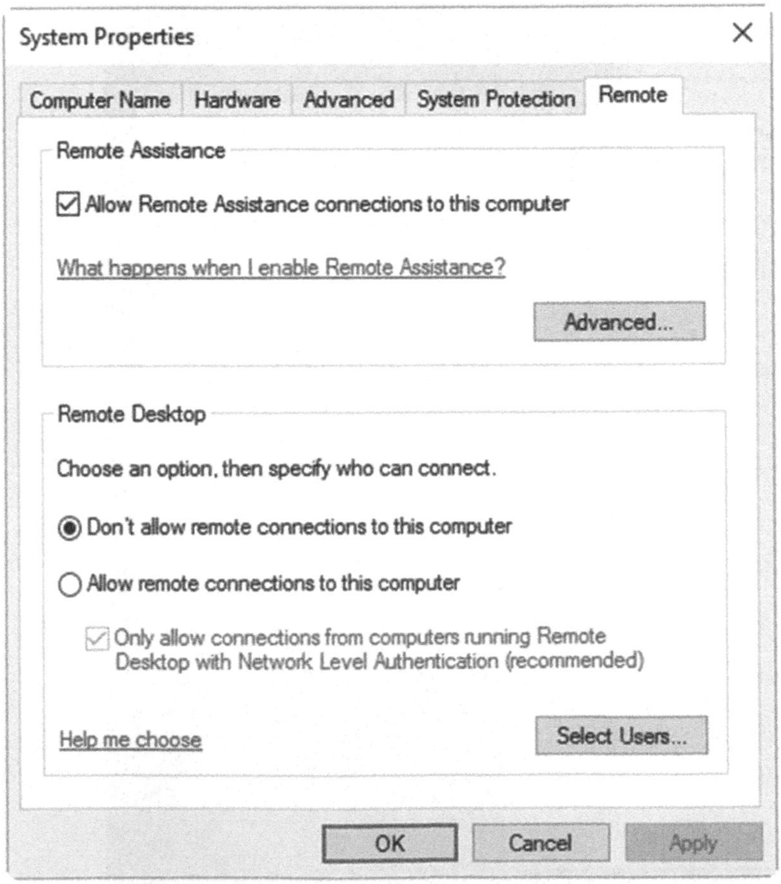

Figure 3-8. *Managing remote connections is essential for PCs requiring remote support*

Moving the Shell User Folders

In Chapter 2, I mentioned that if you create a System Image Backup of Windows 10, regardless of whether you use the utility that comes baked into the OS or a third-party utility from the likes of Symantec of Acronis, it will copy into that backup any files and documents stored in your C:\Users folder. Moreover, when you come to restore this backup (which you will at some point), all the new and updated files and folders in the C:\Users folder will be completely wiped and replaced with the old ones stored in the backup.

If you store all your files in a roaming server profile on a company domain, or if they're all stored in a Service such as Google Drive or Dropbox, that has to sync all of your files back down from their cloud server on a restore, this won't be too much of an issue. For everybody else, however, and let's face it, all these people too, the prospect of losing all your files and documents is a frightening one.

Fortunately, Windows 10 makes it incredibly easy to move your Shell User Folders (Documents, Downloads, Favorites, Pictures, Music, Searches, Videos) away from your Windows installation. Depending on how your PC is set up this may be a process that also requires you to create a new data partition on your hard disk (you'll know this is the case if you only have one disk showing in This PC in File Explorer), but I'll show you how to do that shortly.

To move your Shell User Folders, open File Explorer and click the small arrow to the right of the icon at the beginning of the Address (Breadcrumb) bar. This will drop down a menu from which you should click your name, see Figure 3-9.

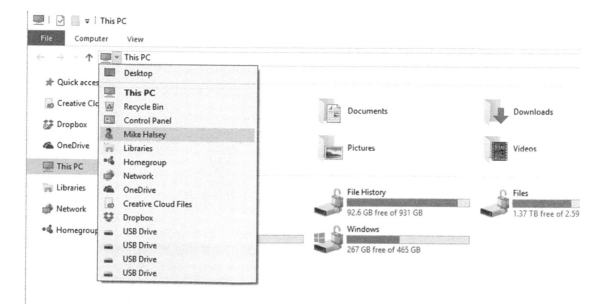

Figure 3-9. *You can access your Shell User folders easily in File Explorer*

When in the Shell User Folder, follow these simple steps...

1. Select all the folders you wish to move. You can select multiple folders by highlighting them all by holding the mouse button and encircling them, clicking the first and holding down the *Shift* key while you click the last, or by holding the *Ctrl* key while you click each one you want to select.

2. Right-click one of the selected folders, and from the context menu that appears, click *Cut*. Alternatively, you can press Ctrl+X.

3. Navigate to the drive or partition and folder where you want to move your user folders.

4. Right-click in a blank space, and from the context menu that appears, click *Paste*. Alternatively, you can press *Ctrl+V*.

It really is as simple as a cut-and-paste operation to move the user folders. You might be asked for confirmation to move some items, but you can cheerfully click "accept" to these questions. When the operation completes, all your user folders will be moved, with the relevant pointers within Windows 10, having been automatically updated for you. It's a good idea to move your user files when you've first signed into the PC, before you've opened any files. This will prevent those files from becoming locked, stopping Windows from being able to move them.

Creating, Managing, and Deleting Partitions

As I mentioned in the last section, moving your Shell User Folders might require you to create a special files partition on your PC. This will be the case if you don't already have a second hard disk or partition available that's large enough for your files.

This is an easy operation to perform, though there are a couple of steps you might want to perform first to free up slightly more space on your drive, namely, running the *Disk cleanup wizard* to clean temporary and other unwanted files, and then defragmenting your hard disk. Note that defragmenting the drive here also applies to SSDs, which you would not normally defragment. This is because you want all the files on the disk as close to the beginning of the disk as possible.

The first operation is to shrink the size of your Windows partition; you can do this in the *Disk Management* console, which is most easily accessed from the **Win + X** administration menu. When the console appears, right-click your Windows drive, and from the menu that appears, select *Shrink*, see Figure 3-10.

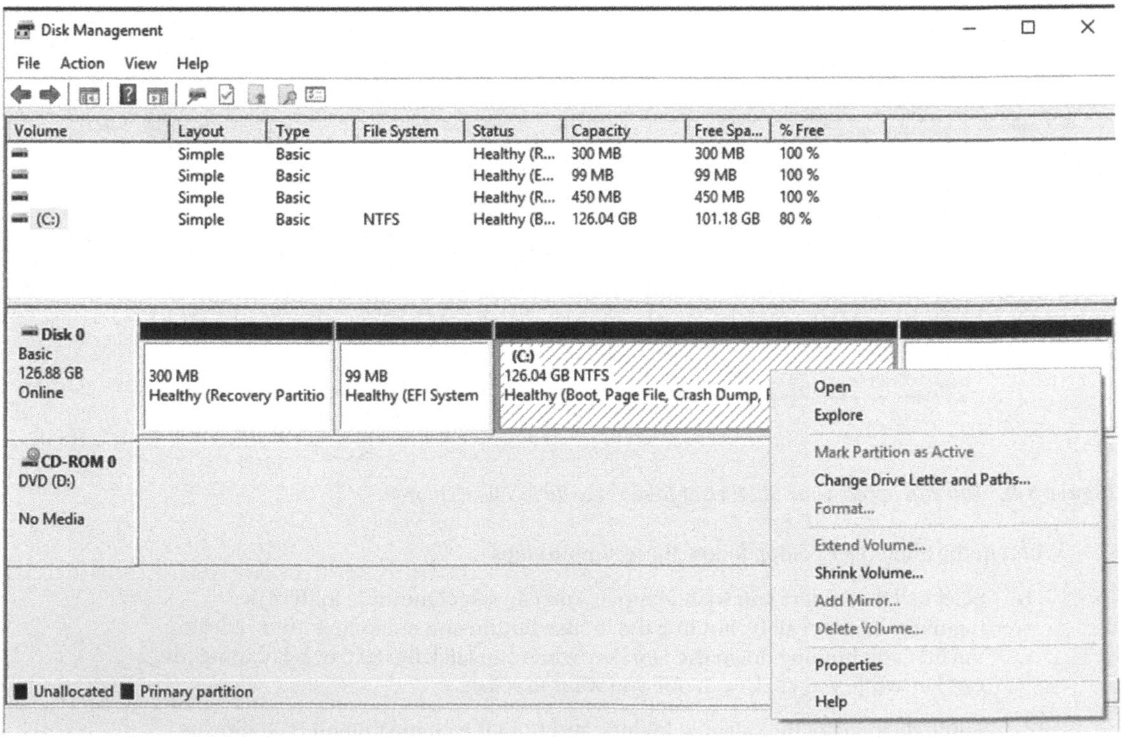

Figure 3-10. *You need to shrink your Windows partition in the Disk Management Console*

You will be asked how much you want to shrink the partition by (if not much is available to you, try cleaning temporary files and defragmenting the disk again), see Figure 3-11.

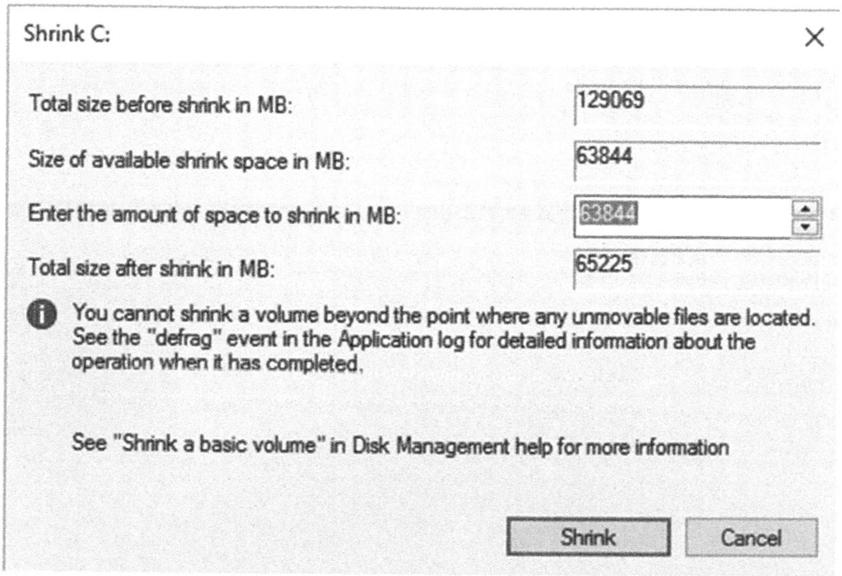

Figure 3-11. *You will be asked how much space you want to shrink the drive by*

When you are deciding how much space to shrink the drive by, think about how much space you will need on your Windows partition. For general usage, 50GB is a good size (meaning the *Total size after shrink in MB* box should read around 51200). A heavy PC user or enthusiast might want 100GB (102400) or 200GB (204800) and a gamer might want up to 300GB (307200) or more.

After the partition has been shrunk, right-click in the *unallocated* space to its right and select *New simple volume* from the options that appear, see Figure 3-12.

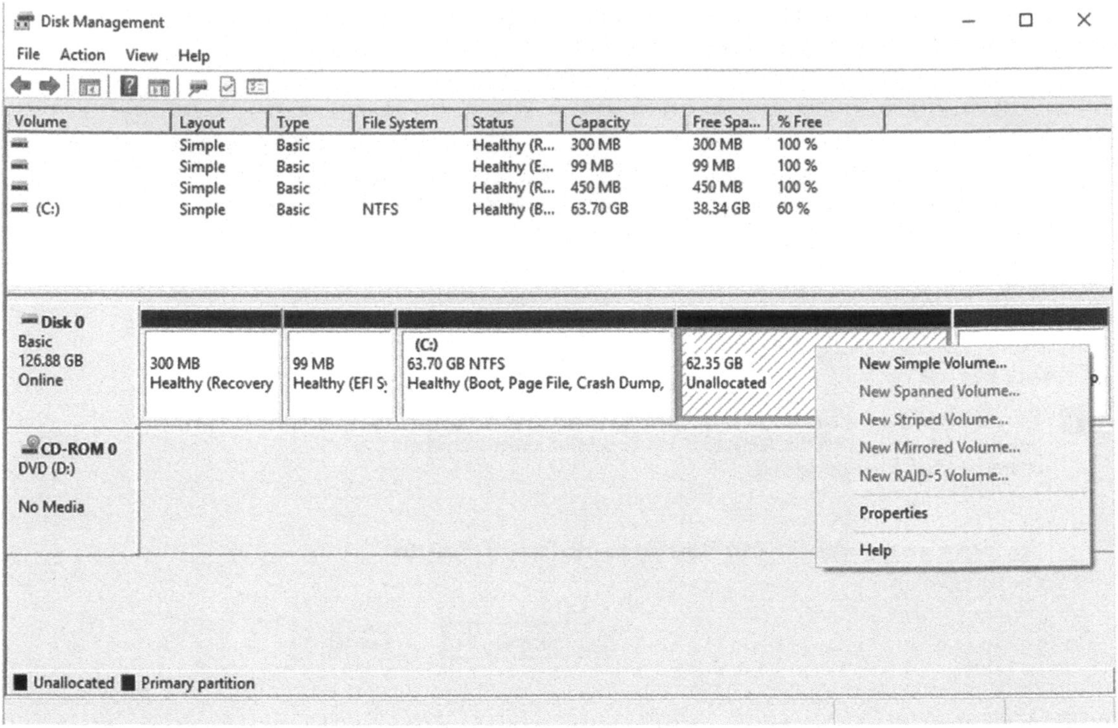

Figure 3-12. *After shrinking a volume you need to create a new one in the free space*

A wizard will appear with the amount of recommended space for the partition, also being the maximum space available for it. Give the drive a drive letter and (optionally) a name and click Finish to complete the partition creation. This will give you a new partition on which you can store your files and documents, see Figure 3-13.

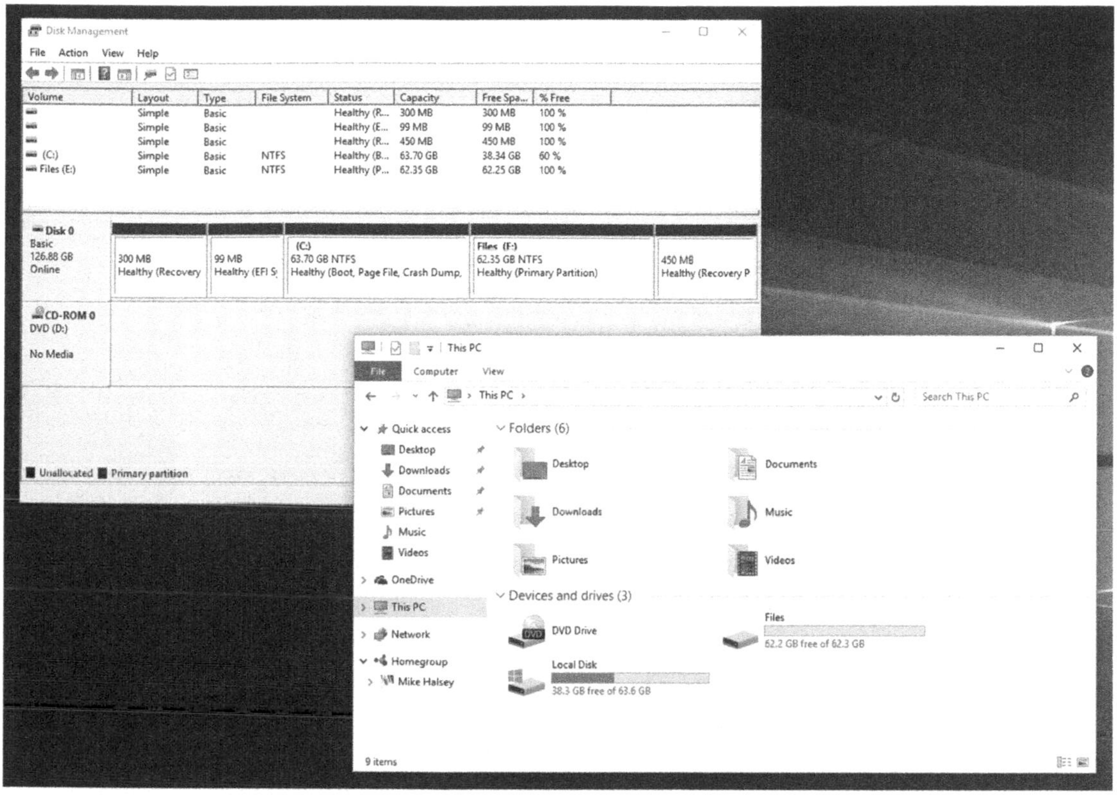

Figure 3-13. *Your newly created partition will appear in File Explorer, ready for use*

Managing Startup Apps

Everybody wants a PC that starts and gets to the desktop quickly, and Windows 10 starts faster than any other version of Windows before it. This process can be slowed significantly by apps that are set to run at Startup. This can include system tray utilities from companies like Adobe, some of which are essential for apps to run, sync utilities for backup and cloud services, updater apps from companies like Apple and Google (that you can run manually when you want to check for updates to apps), and the preinstalled software that comes with your PC when you purchase it, officially known in the trade as "crapware."

Startup apps in Windows 10 are managed through the Task Manager. There are several ways to open this. You can press **Ctrl+Alt+Del** on your keyboard and select Task Manager from the menu that appears, you can right-click in a blank space on the Taskbar and select *Task Manager* from the menu that appears, or you can run *Task Manager* from the **Win+X** administration menu.

When in the Task Manager, click the *Start-up* tab, and here all of the apps that run at startup on your PC will be listed, see Figure 3-14.

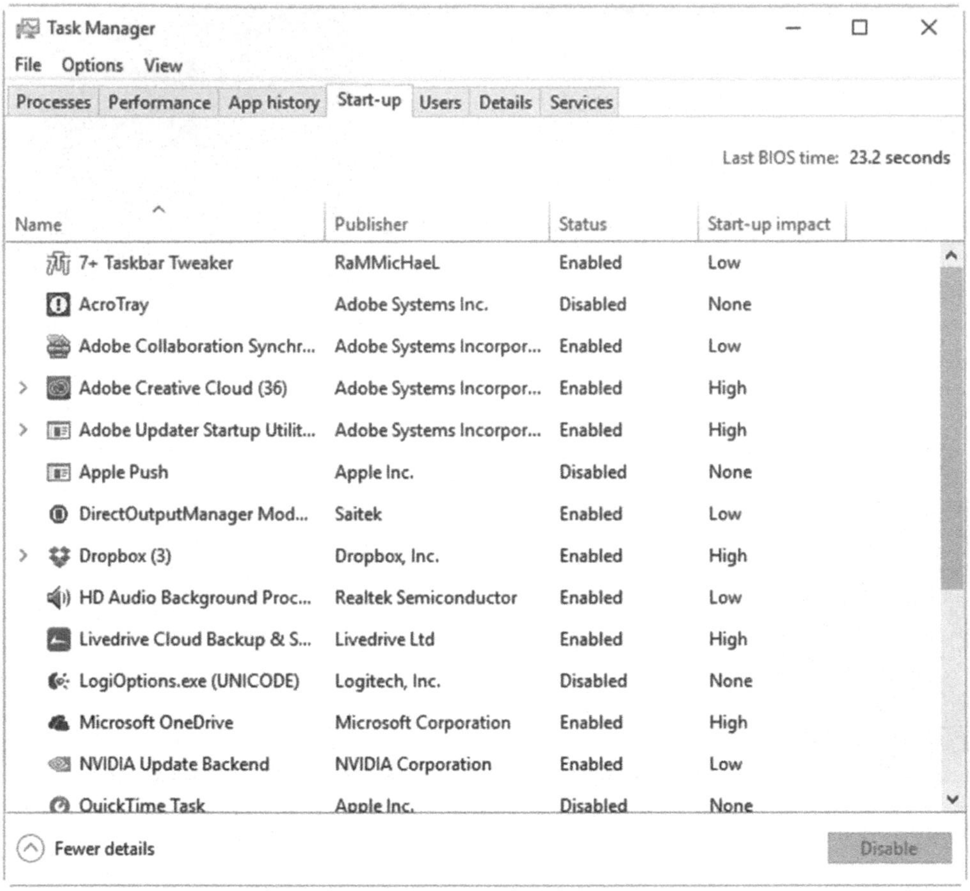

Figure 3-14. *You manage Startup apps in Task Manager*

Each one has a Startup impact assessment rating next to it of Low, Medium, or High. This is the effect that program has on slowing your PC's startup. Choose the apps you want to disable (you can easily re-enable them afterwards as they stay in the list) by selecting one and then clicking the *Disable* button in the bottom right corner of the window.

Summary

In this chapter, I've covered everything you need to know to set up, configure, and back up Windows 10 and your files and documents so as to minimize problems, and so that if something drastic does go wrong, you can recover fairly quickly.

Speed is the most important aspect of supporting PCs, however, as time always costs money, and other problems can still arise such as compatibility with older "legacy" apps, especially custom company apps, managing Internet Explorer when that's required for the workplace Intranet or for compatibility with specific plug-ins, and more besides. In the next chapter, then, we'll look at some of the common problems that you can face on PCs, with a focus on diagnosing and repairing them quickly.

■ ■ ■

CHAPTER 4

Fixing Windows 10 Quickly

While it's always better to prevent problems from occurring in the first instance, when they do occur, fixing them quickly, and even having a user repair a problem on their own remotely, is always preferable to a time-consuming reimage or reinstall.

The holy grail of repairing a Windows PC has always been to fix any problems within 30 minutes or less, and while some straightforward problems might make for easy fixes, others can prove more bothersome. In this chapter I'll show you the common ways to fix problems quickly and simply.

The Disk Cleanup Wizard

The Disk Cleanup Wizard is one of those venerable tools that's been in Windows since the dawn of time. Indeed, like other tools including Paint and Notepad, it almost feels sometime like the OS was built around the need to use them. This tool, however, is much more useful than for just cleaning out temporary files to "free up a bit of space."

You can run the Disk Cleanup Wizard most easily by searching for **disk** or **clean** in the Start Menu or Cortana. If you have more than one disk or partition on your PC, you'll be asked which disk you want to clean (it should default to the drive on which Windows 10 is installed).

The main options present a list of check boxes that include the obvious temporary files and setup files, see Figure 4-1. There's much more to it than this, however. Why clean up temporary files in the first place, though; they don't cause problems, do they? In rare cases they actually can but there's no way to know for sure unless you delete them.

© Mike Halsey 2016
M. Halsey, *Windows 10 Troubleshooting*, DOI 10.1007/978-1-4842-0925-7_4

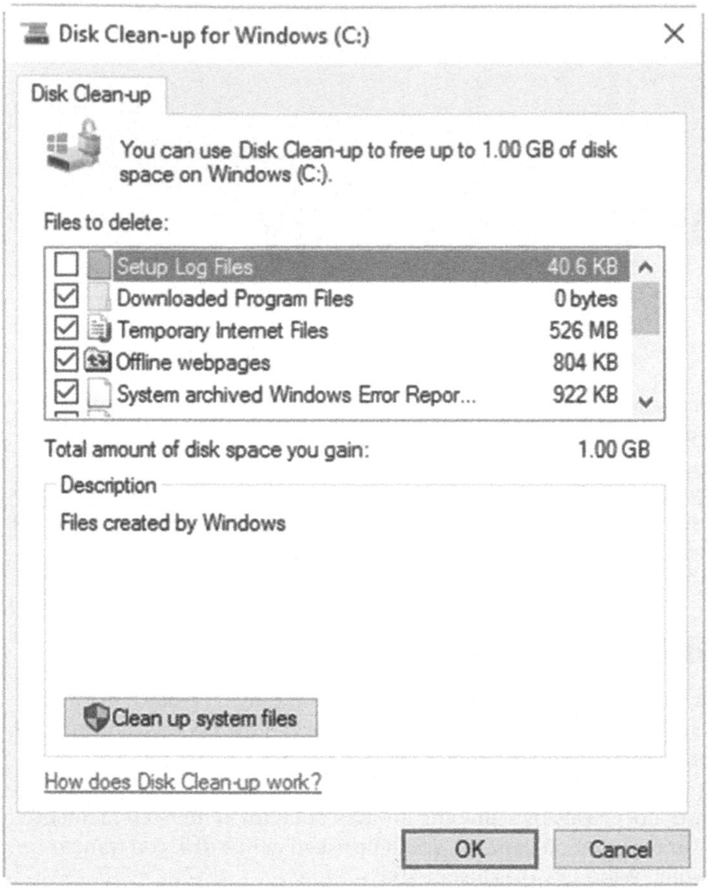

Figure 4-1. *At its simplest, the Disk Cleanup Wizard removes temorary and unwanted files*

Clicking the *Clean up system files* button will reveal additional options. These can include "Windows temporary installation files" which, if you've recently upgraded the PC to Windows 10, can consist of the previous Windows installation. Windows 10 protects these files for 30 days after the upgrade so it can be rolled back if necessary. However, they can occupy many gigabytes of space, and on a tablet or ultrabook with a small SSD, this can fill much of the available storage on the device.

Clicking the *More options* tab presents an option to clean up *System Restore and Shadow Copies*. These reside in the *System Volume Information* folders that are hidden on each hard disk or partition. Should System Restore become corrupt, deleting the restore points can reset it.

■ **Tip**　If you want more power, flexibility, and control than the Disk Cleanup Wizard offers, the market leader in disk maintenance and cleanup is the excellent **CCleaner**, available for free from `piriform.com`.

Managing IE and Edge

If we didn't have web browsers on our PCs, the machines wouldn't, in all honesty, be of that much use to us. Imagine picking up an original IBM PC (with both hands obviously as they were really heavy) or an original Palm handheld (much easier, that one) and finding that neither has an Internet connection. What would you use them for?

Unfortunately, both Internet Explorer 11 (IE11) and Edge are baked into Windows 10, so if they should become corrupt in some way, uninstalling and reinstalling them simply isn't possible. So when your web browser *does* become corrupt (which does happen) what do you do? Is the solution simply to install Google Chrome? Managing IE and Edge is straightforward too, which again is good news.

Cleaning Temporary and Other Files from IE and Edge

While the Disk Cleanup Wizard is a great, easy-to-use tool for deleting temporary files from your PC, your web browser can collect additional files you may want to clean from time to time, for example if the browser is appearing to slow down on startup and use.

To manage temporary and other files in IE, click the Settings icon in the top right of the browser and then click the *Internet options* link from the menu that appears. This will open into the *General* tab of a pop-up dialog. Click the *Delete* button and you will be presented with check boxes for the things you can delete from the browser's cache, see Figure 4-2.

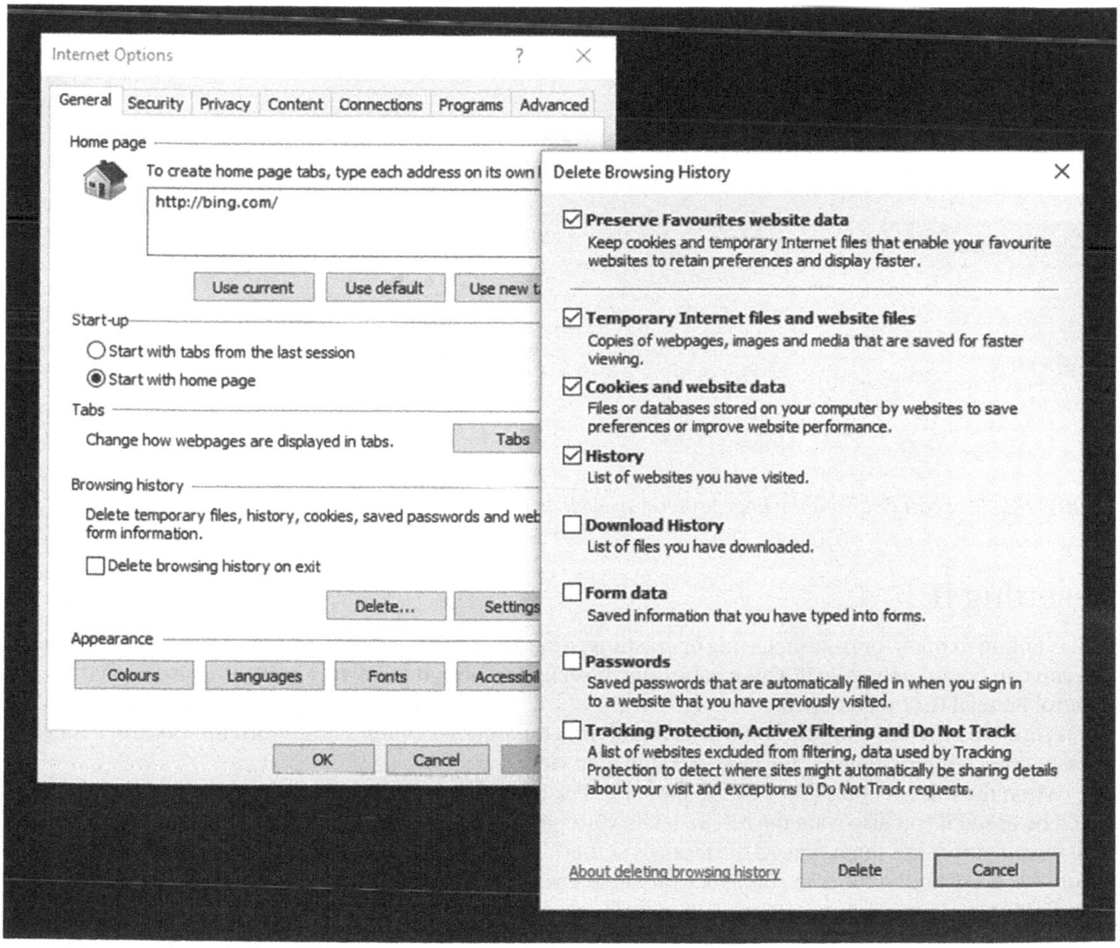

Figure 4-2. You can delete temporary files and much more from IE11

With the Edge Browser, click the menu icon (the three horizontal dots) near the top right of the browser window, then click the *Settings* link. Next, click the *Choose what to clear button* and you will be presented with check boxes for what you can clear from the browser, see Figure 4-3.

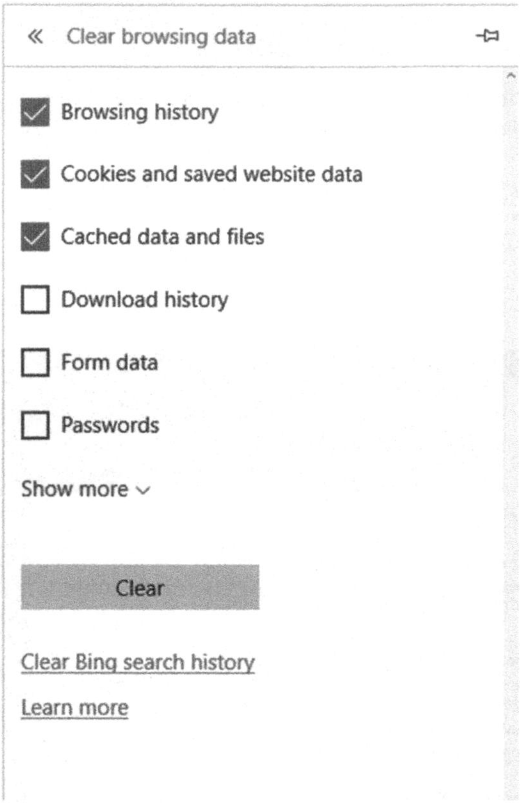

Figure 4-3. *You can clear out the Edge browser as well as IE11*

Resetting IE

If IE is failing to open, or is misbehaving or crashing, it's not possible to uninstall it or install a newer version, but you can completely reset it. This can be done both from within the browser itself, and also from the Control Panel if IE11 won't open.

From the browser, click the Settings icon and then the *Internet Options* link. From the Control Panel click *Internet Options* in either the large or small icon view.

When the Internet Properties dialog appears, click the *Advanced* tab, followed by the *Reset* button. You'll be asked if you also want the rest to delete your personal files (such as temporary files, cookies, and web form data) at the same time as the reset, as something here might be contributing to the corruption, see Figure 4-4. Performing the reset, though, won't delete your Internet Favorites, as they are stored in your Shell User Folder.

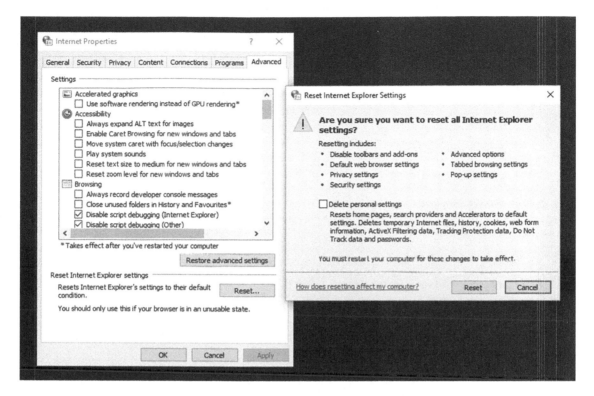

Figure 4-4. *You can completely reset IE11 in Windows 10*

Click *Reset* when you are ready and this will restore IE11 to its "out-of-the-box" state and get the web browser working again.

Resetting the Windows Store and Store Apps

Resetting Edge is a very different proposition as, being a Windows Store app instead of a win32 app, it operates very differently and its core files are never accessible to the end user or other apps. Because Store apps are completely sandboxed from both the OS and each other, corruptions are far less likely.

On occasion, however, you might find that Edge won't open, won't update, or is misbehaving in some other way. You can fix this by resetting the Windows Store and its core app management files.

In the Start Menu or Cortana, search for **wsreset**, and when it appears in the search results, right-click it and run it as an Administrator (this is very important), see Figure 4-5.

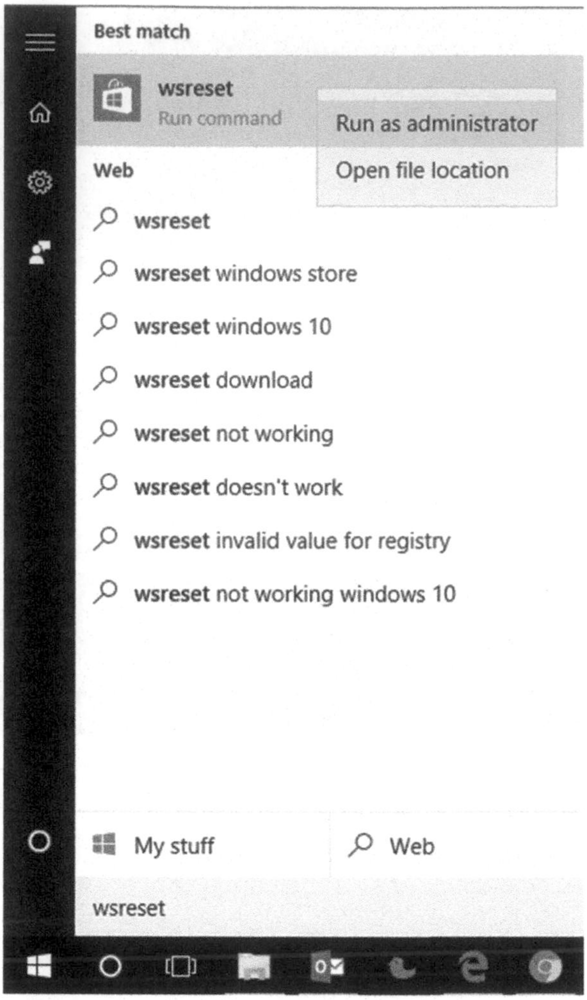

Figure 4-5. *This app resets the cache for the Windows Store and can reset apps*

The WSReset app will report that it's cleared the cache for the Windows Store but also seems to do much more. If you ever find the Windows Store isn't working, or won't download or update apps, this is how to fix it. However, it will also repair problems with installed Store apps themselves. Microsoft has never detailed how this functionality works for security reasons, but it's a useful fix to know about.

When you have run WSReset, you should then open the Windows Store app and check for any updates to Edge (or any other app you might be having difficulty with) before opening the app again, in case of a corruption to the core app files.

Defragmenting Your Hard Disks

Fragmentation occurs because when you save files on your hard disk, Windows 10 will try to save the file in the first accessible space. Should this space not be big enough for the file, it will save some of the file there, and place the rest of the file in the next available space. If that space isn't large enough for the remainder of the file, it will be split again. This isn't a problem for new installations of Windows and your apps, or for copying or downloading your files to a clean hard disk for the first time, but as a hard disk gets used more and more, and files are changed and deleted, the number of large blocks of free space diminishes, and file fragmentation begins to occur.

I mentioned in Chapter 1 that SSDs and M.2 drives don't suffer from this, the reason being that solid-state disks are a random-access memory storage medium, and therefore pulling a file from multiple locations doesn't slow them down. What slows down mechanical hard disks is the movement of the read-arm across the spinning disk platters.

Having fragmented disks on a PC can really slow down the operation of the PC, from Startup to file access, if mechanical disks are used. Windows 10 includes an automatic maintenance system, detailed in Chapter 1, that will automatically defragment drives. What can happen, however, is that defragmentation set to occur when the PC is in use can also slow it down, and if the defragmentation is set to occur when the PC is likely to be switched off, it won't happen at all.

You can change the settings for defragmentation in Windows 10 by searching for **defrag** in the Start Menu or Cortana and clicking *Defragment and Optimize Drives*. The main Defragmenter window lists all of the hard disks and partitions on your PC, along with their fragmentation status, see Figure 4-6.

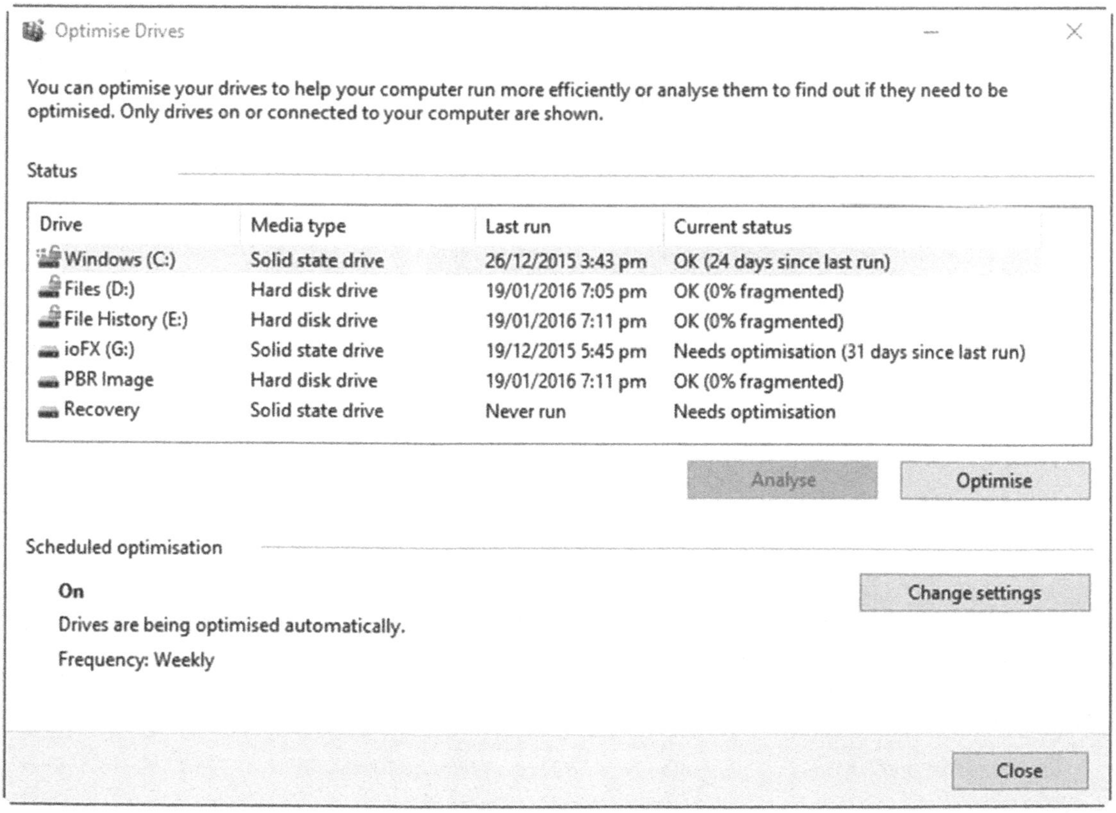

Drive	Media type	Last run	Current status
Windows (C:)	Solid state drive	26/12/2015 3:43 pm	OK (24 days since last run)
Files (D:)	Hard disk drive	19/01/2016 7:05 pm	OK (0% fragmented)
File History (E:)	Hard disk drive	19/01/2016 7:11 pm	OK (0% fragmented)
ioFX (G:)	Solid state drive	19/12/2015 5:45 pm	Needs optimisation (31 days since last run)
PBR Image	Hard disk drive	19/01/2016 7:11 pm	OK (0% fragmented)
Recovery	Solid state drive	Never run	Needs optimisation

Figure 4-6. *Fragmented disks can really slow your PC*

Clicking the *Change settings* button will allow you to choose which drives will be automatically defragmented by Windows 10, and how often this occurs. You can choose to exclude any solid-state drives should Windows 10 have not already excluded them from defragmentation.

■ **Tip**   In Figure 4-6, a solid-state drive (G::) is labeled as "Needs optimization", but it really doesn't. As a random-access memory technology, fragmentation does not slow the drive and can even reduce the life of a drive, as all SSDs and M.2 drives come with a maximum read/write lifespan.

Managing Running Apps and Services with Task Manager

The Task Manager is a fantastic little tool for managing and troubleshooting apps and services, and in Chapter 25 I'll show you how to unlock its full potential. Back in Chapter 3 I showed you how to use it to manage your startup apps, but what about apps and both Windows and third-party services that are already running? How can you troubleshoot and manage those?

You can open Task Manager by right-clicking in a black space on the Taskbar, from the **Ctrl+Alt+Del** menu, or from the **Win+X** menu.

If you have an app that is malfunctioning, won't close, or has hung or crashed, you can manage it from the *Processes* tab in Task Manager. Click the name of the app you want to close and click the *End task* button in the bottom right corner of the Task Manager window, see Figure 4-7.

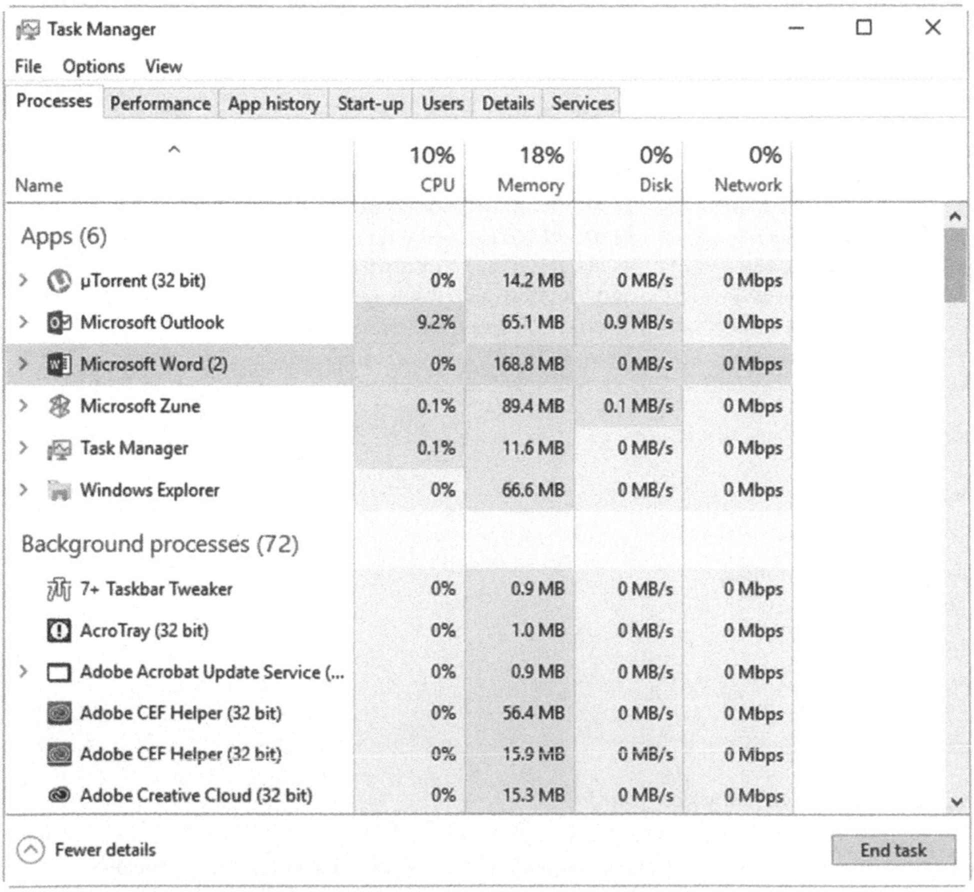

Figure 4-7. *You can manage crashed apps in the Task Manager*

Should you have multiple instances of an app running, and only one has crashed or needs to be forcibly closed, click the ➤ arrow to the left of the app name to expend the list of all running instances of the app. You can then close just the faulty instance.

Sometimes you will have an app that also has dependant apps or services. Think of this as an app consisting of a main app with several sub-apps running at the same time, all for different purposes but all required for the main app to work.

If a sub-app crashes, or if you need to close an app and all of its dependencies for it to work, you can do this from the *Details* tab. Right-click the app, and from the context menu that appears, click *End process tree*, see Figure 4-8.

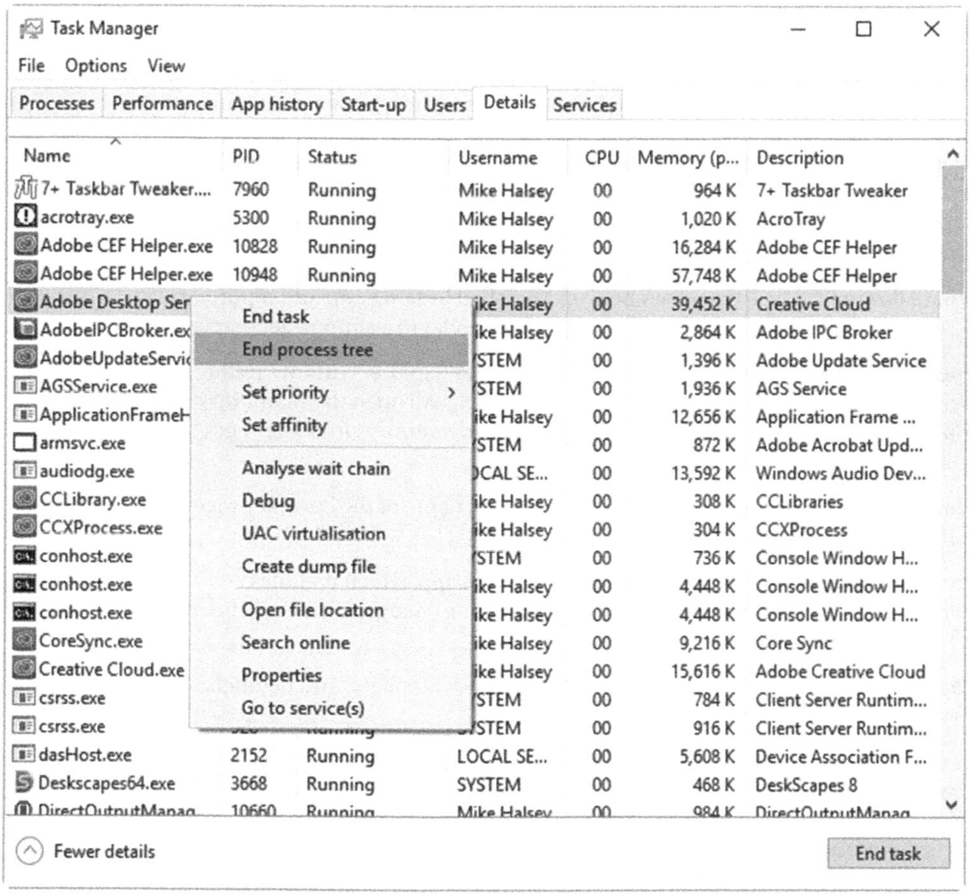

Figure 4-8. *The Details tab allows you to close all the dependancies for an app*

Other app management operations that can be performed by right-clicking an app, service, or process in the Details tab include

- **Set priority**—to change the amount of processor time allocated to the apps from Normal, to Below Normal, Low, Above Normal, High, or Realtime.

- **Set affinity**—to change which processors or processor cores on your PC are assigned to the app (most useful when assigning individual processors to Virtual Machines).

- **Analyze wait chain**—can be used if an app has hung, to identify which resources the app is waiting to use, and is required for the process to continue.

- **Debug**—can be used if you have development software installed on your PC, such as Microsoft Visual Studio, to analyze bugs and crashes in compatible apps and services.

- **User Account Control (UAC) Virtualization**—used when some apps require the user to have full administrative rights, but the user is signed into the PC as a "Standard user" instead. This can be common with poorly written legacy apps. Activating UAC Virtualization enables Windows 10 to virtualize protected areas of the OS, such as the file system and Registry, so that the app can operate normally without hanging or reporting errors.

- **Create dump file**—will create a report on a crashed or hung app and report the location of the file so you may read or copy it, or send it to a support technician.

- **Open file location**—for win32 apps, will open a File Explorer window at the location where the app is installed. For Store apps, it will open the temporary app management folder located in the Windows/SystemApps folder and not the protected app store location.

- **Search online**—will open a browser search for the name of the current process, so that you may research it and discover what it is.

- **Properties**—opens the properties inspector for the app, which includes compatibility settings. Note any compatibility setting changes will only work once the app is restarted.

- **Go to Service(s)**—opens the Services tab in the Task Manager, and highlights any service(s) used by the process.

Services are best described as little applets that are designed to perform a specific task, and that are invoked automatically by Windows 10 or your apps as needed. They can manage your printer queue, security features, cloud syncing, and many more aspects of the OS and apps and are provided by both Microsoft and third-party app developers.

These services aren't built directly into apps because they're most commonly shared between multiple apps. For example, Microsoft provides services for font management, network access and discovery, and Bluetooth connections, which many other apps will want to use. Similarly, some apps systems (Adobe Creative Cloud as an example) will have their own data sharing services.

You manage Services primarily in the Services Administrative panel, which we will look at in Chapter 19. You can stop a hung or crashed service in the Task Manager, however, by right-clicking it and selecting either *Stop* or *Restart* from the context menu that appears, see Figure 4-9.

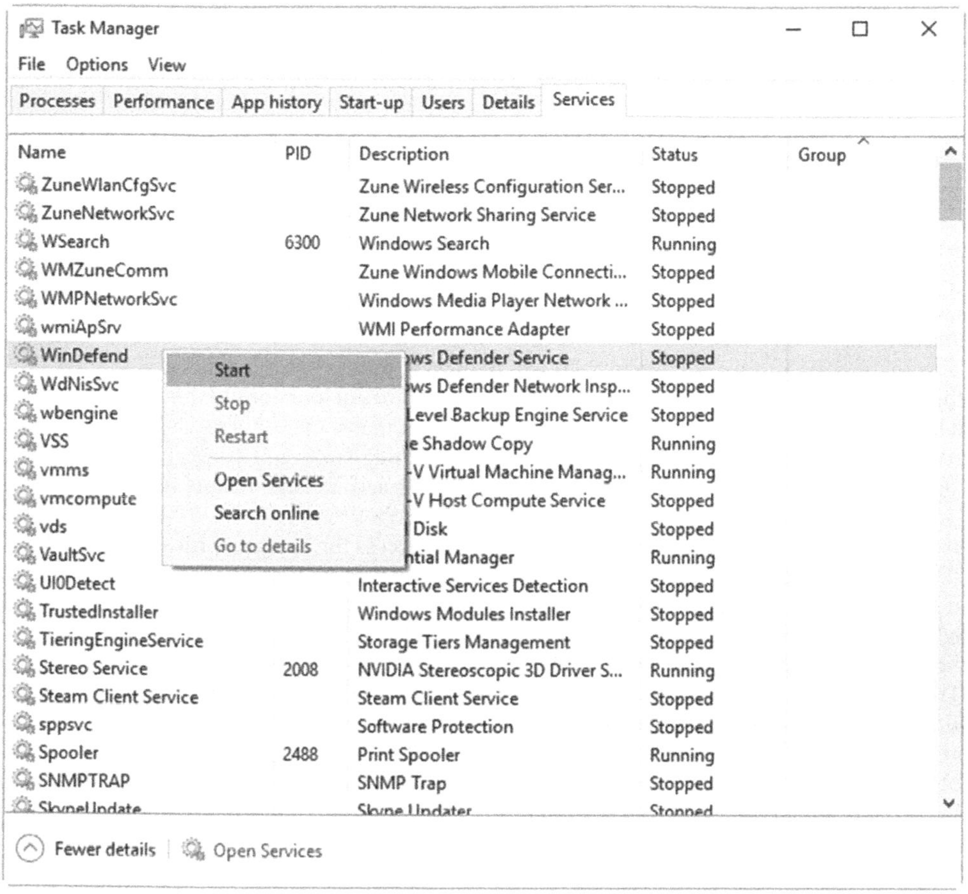

Figure 4-9. *You can start, stop, and reset services in Task Manager*

Services can also be started from the Task Manager if an app or process is reporting that a service it requires isn't running. If you are unsure what a service is, or what it does, you can also search for the service online from this context menu, so as to find out more information about it.

Managing win32 App Compatibility

While we're on the subject of troublesome apps, it's very true that as new versions of Windows have been developed, compatibility with older software has occasionally been broken. In fairness to Microsoft, it does a remarkable job, given all the new hardware, Internet, app, and other protocols that come along on a regular basis, of making sure that older software still has a good chance of working well. As core changes are made to the operating system, however, and as features are removed from Windows, it's inevitable that some app compatibility will break.

A good example of this is an older piece of software I use myself on a regular basis. Microsoft PhotoDraw v2 was released in 2000 and is still popular with a great many people; even though alternatives such as Fireworks or Photoshop can easily outmatch it for power, there's still almost nothing to match it for ease of use.

It's not all good news, however, as while the app works fine almost all of time, I will get an error if I use any of its 3D features; this is because Direct3D, the Windows API it uses, has changed so much over the years that it's now unrecognizable by the software.

"Oh no!" I hear you cry, sarcastically. I know, this is a very minor problem and if it's the worst app compatibility problem I face then I'm a pretty lucky guy. For some people who have software that they just love to use / that was withdrawn and never replaced by an alternative / that nothing else has ever come along to match (delete any of these that aren't applicable to your situation), app compatibility can be a significant headache.

There are several reasons for this. I've already alluded to the first, that as Windows has evolved, its features have changed so much that the APIs and DLLs that perform critical functions in the OS, and that are regularly called by apps, just aren't compatible any more. There's also that some software, especially poorly written software, used workarounds that required the user to have Administrative privileges. I've already detailed one workaround for this with UAC Virtualization a little while ago, but significant headaches can still be caused.

To manage compatibility for a win32 desktop app, you need to access the app properties. Right-click its icon on the Taskbar, and from the context menu that appears, click *Properties*. From the Start Menu, right-click the app and select *More* and then *Open file location* from the context menu. In the window that appears you can then right-click the app and select its *Properties*.

There are several ways to manage app compatibility. Perhaps the easiest of these is to run the Compatibility Troubleshooter, from the button that is under the *Compatibility* tab of the app properties dialog. This will ask you a series of questions about the app, and then set compatibility for you, asking you to run the app and report back if things worked or not.

If you want finer control, there are a couple of things you can do. The Compatibility Mode option, see Figure 4-10, is a drop-down menu that allows you to set compatibility for the app from Windows 8, all the way back to Windows 95. It's notable here, however, that where Service Packs for an OS brought about significant changes to features or performance, such as XP and Vista, additional options are available.

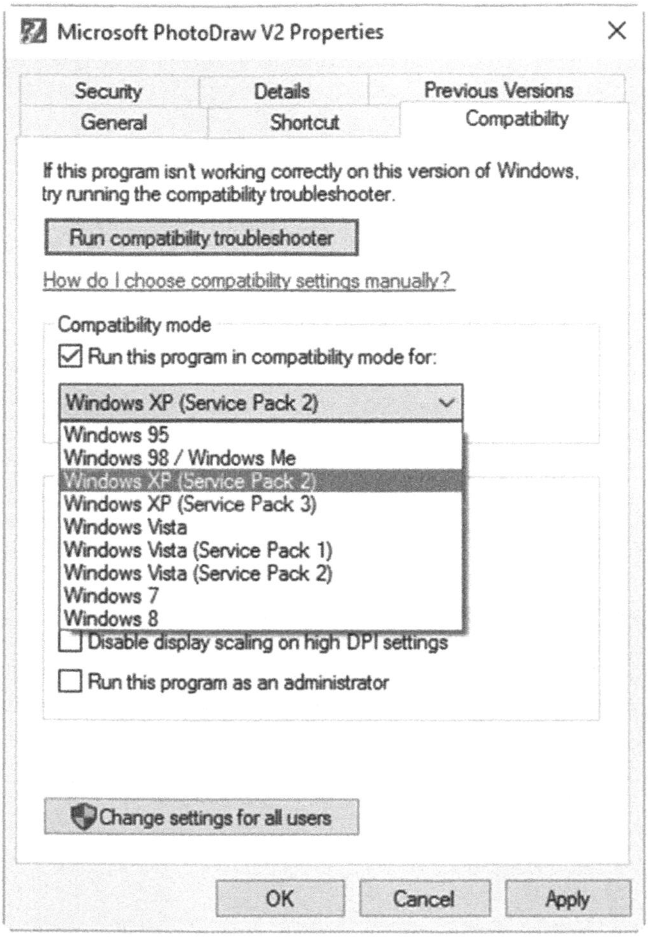

Figure 4-10. *You can set compatibility for apps all the way back to Windows 95*

This might not be enough, however, as you might find that, for example, the app displays incorrectly on high-DPI screens such as UHD/4K monitors or other screens where display scaling is used to make the screen more legible.

■ **Tip**   Some app compatibility can be managed by running a Virtual Machine with an older operating system installed, in which the app ran properly. There are security considerations to make with this approach, however, and I will detail Virtualization in Chapter 20.

Other options are also available, such as forcing the app to run constrained in a 640- by 480-pixel frame, and forcing the program to always run as an Administrator, see Figure 4-11. Bear in mind that this last option is not the same as UAC Virtualization and will require *actual* administrative rights for the use on that PC.

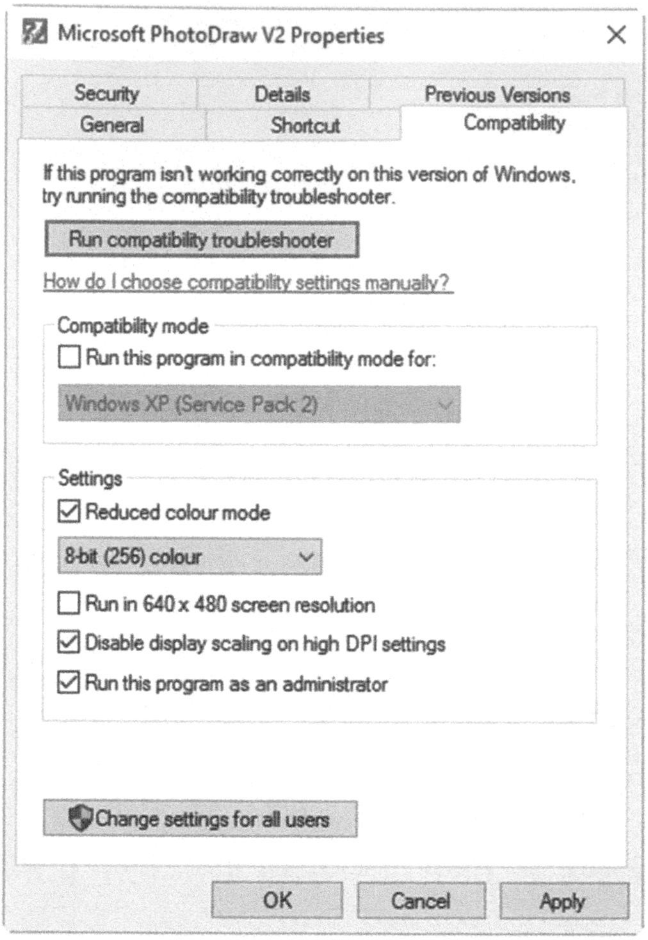

Figure 4-11. *Additional compatibility options are available*

■ **Tip** For large organizations, Microsoft provides two tools to help manage app compatibility: the Application Compatibility Toolkit and Standard User Analyzer. You can download these as part of the Windows 10 Assessment and Deployment Toolkit (ADK) from http://pcs.tv/1P7HwIp, and they're detailed in full in my book *Windows Software Compatibility and Hardware Troubleshooting* (Apress, 2015).

Using the System File Checker

If there were two hidden troubleshooting tools that every systems administrator should know about, and that make me go all "Squeee," one would be the Problem Steps Recorder, which I'll detail in Chapter 12, and the other is the System File Checker. Essentially, the System File Checker scans every file that makes up Windows 10 and compares their integrity details (checksums) against what's stored in its database. If it finds any file that doesn't match, perhaps because it is corrupt or has been altered, then it can replace it with an original.

There are some caveats with this, however. The first is that it will take replacement files from Windows 10 install media, but doesn't work with Windows 10 installations that come on USB Flash Drives. It only works with DVD installation media (so a USB DVD drive will be required for ultrabooks and tablets). The second caveat is that any file it pulls from the DVD must match the version number of the one currently installed on the PC. This means that your DVD must be a Windows install disc that contains the most recent annual update (Service Pack) that's installed on the PC.

This latter issue isn't as much of a problem, however, as it used to be when you had to perform complex operations to merge a Service Pack into a DVD. If you have access to a Volume Licensing or MSDN subscription, you'll be able to download an ISO disc image file that contains the most recently released version of Windows 10. The way Windows Update now works, unless you're in the Enterprise and on the Long-Term Servicing Branch, in which only security and stability updates are installed, this will work fine.

For everybody else, the Windows 10 Media Creator I detailed in Chapter 1 is a great way to get free access to the latest installation ISO file. To burn this file to DVD, right-click it and select the *Burn disc image* option from the menu that appears.

To use the System File Checker, open *Command Prompt (Admin)* from the **Win+X** menu. In the Command Prompt, type `SFC /SCANNOW` and press Enter, see Figure 4-12.

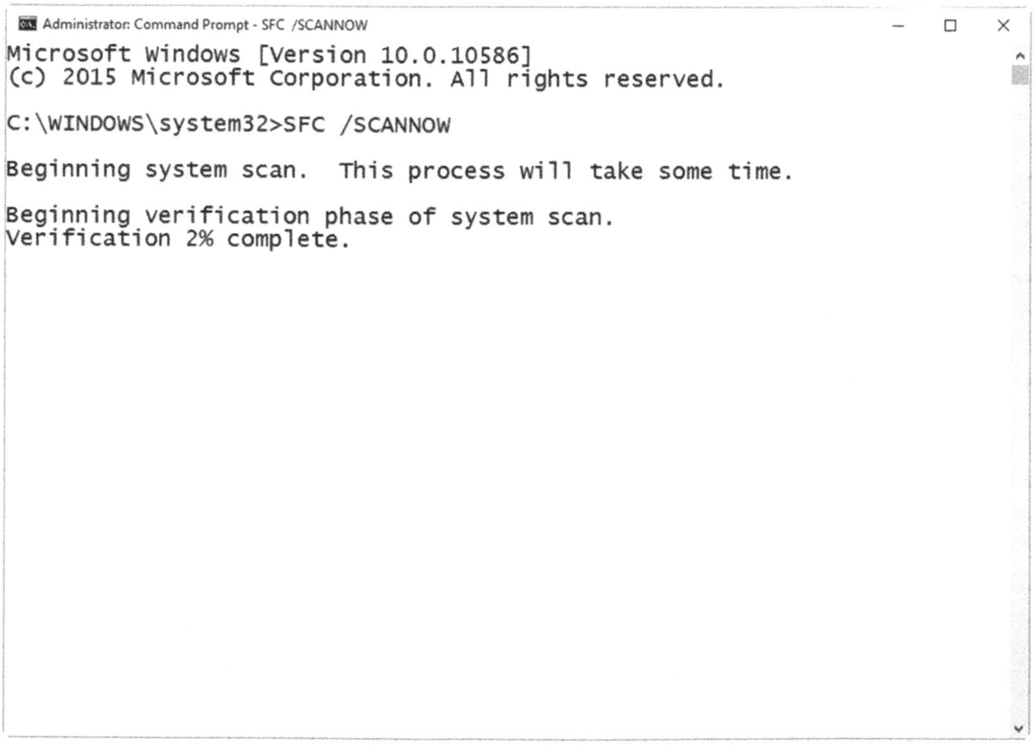

```
Administrator: Command Prompt - SFC /SCANNOW                        —    □    ×
Microsoft Windows [Version 10.0.10586]
(c) 2015 Microsoft Corporation. All rights reserved.

C:\WINDOWS\system32>SFC /SCANNOW

Beginning system scan.  This process will take some time.

Beginning verification phase of system scan.
Verification 2% complete.
```

Figure 4-12. The System File Checker is run from the Command Prompt

If any files are found to have changed or become corrupt, the file will be automatically copied from the DVD (if it's already in your optical drive), or you'll be prompted for the DVD. Other command switches that can be used with the System File Checker are

- **/VERIFYONLY**—Scans the files on the PC but does not attempt autorepair

- **/SCANFILE=C:\Folder\Filename**—Scans a specific file and repairs it if it finds it has changed or is corrupt

- **/VERIFYFILE=C:\Folder\Filename**—As Scanfile, but does not attempt auto repair

- **/OFFBOOTDIR=C:** and **/OFFWINDIR=C:\Windows**—Used with /ScanNow and /ScanFile if the file must be repaired offline (on a restart) because it is a critical system file, or is currently in use

Using the Automated Troubleshooters

Windows' Automated Troubleshooters are something I mentioned briefly in Chapter 1 when talking about the Security and Maintenance Center. Essentially, they are little applets that fix common problems by resetting components to their default state.

As I've already mentioned, you can find the Automated Troubleshooters through the Security and Maintenance panel in the Control Panel, but they also have their own *Troubleshooting* Control Panel applet, see Figure 4-13.

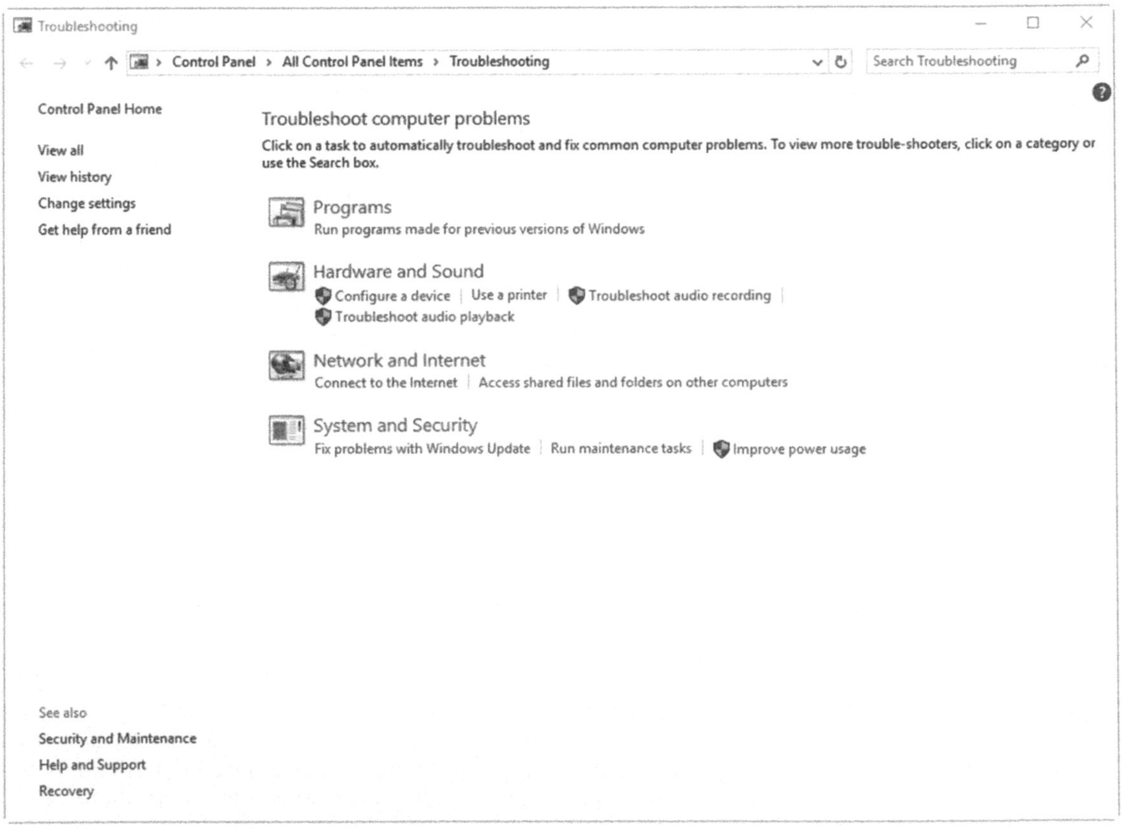

Figure 4-13. The Troubleshooting options from the Control Panel

The Troubleshooters are split into different sections: Programs, Hardware and Sound, Network and Internet, and System and Security. When you run a troubleshooter you will see an *Advanced link*, see Figure 4-14, but this just offers the option to apply or not apply repairs automatically, or in some cases where it might be appropriate, to run the troubleshooter as an Administrator.

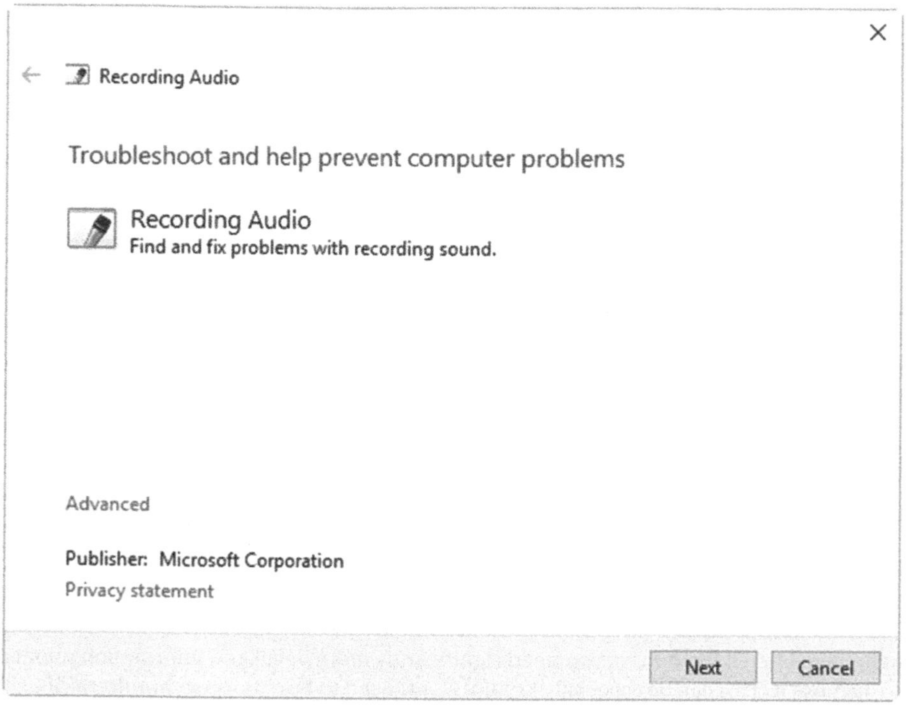

Figure 4-14. *Each troubleshooter is a self-contained wizard*

Each troubleshooter works in its own way. For example, some might ask you questions, while others will get on and try and find any problems they can. As I have already mentioned, the troubleshooters are best for everyday problems, as they work by resetting Windows and other components to their default state. They're not able to diagnose complex problems.

■ **Tip**   You can write your own Automated Troubleshooters for Windows that can be deployed across PCs or a company. These can perform tasks such as resetting printer configurations or VPN connections. All troubleshooters are written in XML and PowerShell, and a guide to creating your own can be found online at `http://pcs.tv/1Wxj4Sd`.

If you find that an Automated Troubleshooter doesn't exist for the problem you want to solve, a look on the Microsoft support web site at `Support.Microsoft.com` can often reveal additional troubleshooters you can download and run, including for Microsoft accounts and the Windows Store.

Microsoft Answers, Service Status Site, and Being a Twit

Something I always encourage people to do before they contact support is to search online for a quick solution to the problem they are facing. By far the best place to go to find these quick solutions is the Microsoft Answers web site, answers.microsoft.com. Here, Microsoft engineers and support staff, technical experts, and many of my fellow MVPs (Hi to Shawn, Rob, Andre, and Barb) will quickly, and with easy-to-understand explanations, answer your technical questions and point you toward solutions.

You might find, for example, that the fix is extremely simple, or that it's not a problem on your PC because lots of other people are experiencing the same issue, or that Microsoft or a third-party company will need to issue a patch or driver update, in which case you'll need to be patient and keep an eye on the problem.

Anything can be searched for online, including error codes (they start with 0x...) and more generic problems. If you are encountering a problem with a Windows Update, new feature, app, or Microsoft service such as OneDrive or Office 365, it can also be a good idea to check both Twitter and the Microsoft service status pages (portal.office.com/servicestatus for Office 365, Outlook.com, and OneDrive.com).

Third-party web sites such as isitdownrightnow.com also exist to help you see the current status of online services, though as I have already mentioned, probably the best by far is Twitter, where a quick search for a name or hashtag will reveal that it takes just a few seconds for the masses to begin complaining when they can't get access to services they need.

Summary

Clearly, some problems within Windows 10 can be fixed quickly and simply. Others can be searched for online for quick fixes and, provided you know where to look, service status pages are available for all Microsoft, and many other, online services.

Sometimes though, quite often if I'm honest, you need significantly more detail and information about a problem in order to diagnose it. This can be especially helpful if you need to hunt through hundreds of online pages to find the one that applies to you, or if you need to send technical data to a support engineer (or if you are the engineer and need to request the information).

In the next chapter, then, we'll look at how you gather this information, what tools exist to help you get access to it, and how you can make sense of what can be some very technical information.

CHAPTER 5

■ ■ ■

Understanding Tasks and Events

It's one thing to have facilities that enable you to fix Windows and PC problems quickly, but this still depends on either you or Windows being able to identify the problem almost at the moment it's seen. If the issue is harder to identify, it doesn't mean you can't still repair the problem in short order, but it really helps if you know what you're looking for.

In Chapter 1 I detailed the Reliability Monitor, an incredibly helpful tool that is a brilliant starting point for diagnosing all types of problems on a PC. These include service and Windows component failures and crashes, app crashes, Windows Update or installation difficulties, hardware driver failures, and more besides.

What happens, though, if you want or need more detailed information about problems? Better still, what if you want to be alerted to the problem when an error or crash occurs? The good news is that Windows 10 includes tools that can do both of these things, and they're fairly easy to use as well.

The Windows Event Viewer

The Windows Event Viewer (sometimes called the Event Log) stores details of everything that happens in the OS, from routine operations to crashes and even Blue Screens of Death (which I now like to call the Blue Unhappy Emoticon of Death).

You can open the Event Viewer by searching for **event** at the Start Menu or in Cortana, or by clicking *Administrative Tools* in the Control panel, and then clicking the *Event Viewer* icon.

Introducing the Microsoft Management Console

This is probably a good time to introduce the Microsoft Management Console (MMC), which is a standard window layout used by the Event Viewer and many other Windows tools and utilities that I'll detail throughout this book, including the Hyper-V virtualization utility.

Figure 5-1 shows the main Event Viewer window). This consists of three vertical panels, each of which I'll cover in more detail. To summarize what you're seeing, however, I'd encourage you to open the Event Viewer on your own PC at this stage and have a look around as you read this: the left panel contains the main categories of views of options available, the right panel contains context-sensitive commands and options, and the central panel contains the main information provided by the particular tool or utility you have opened.

© Mike Halsey 2016
M. Halsey, *Windows 10 Troubleshooting*, DOI 10.1007/978-1-4842-0925-7_5

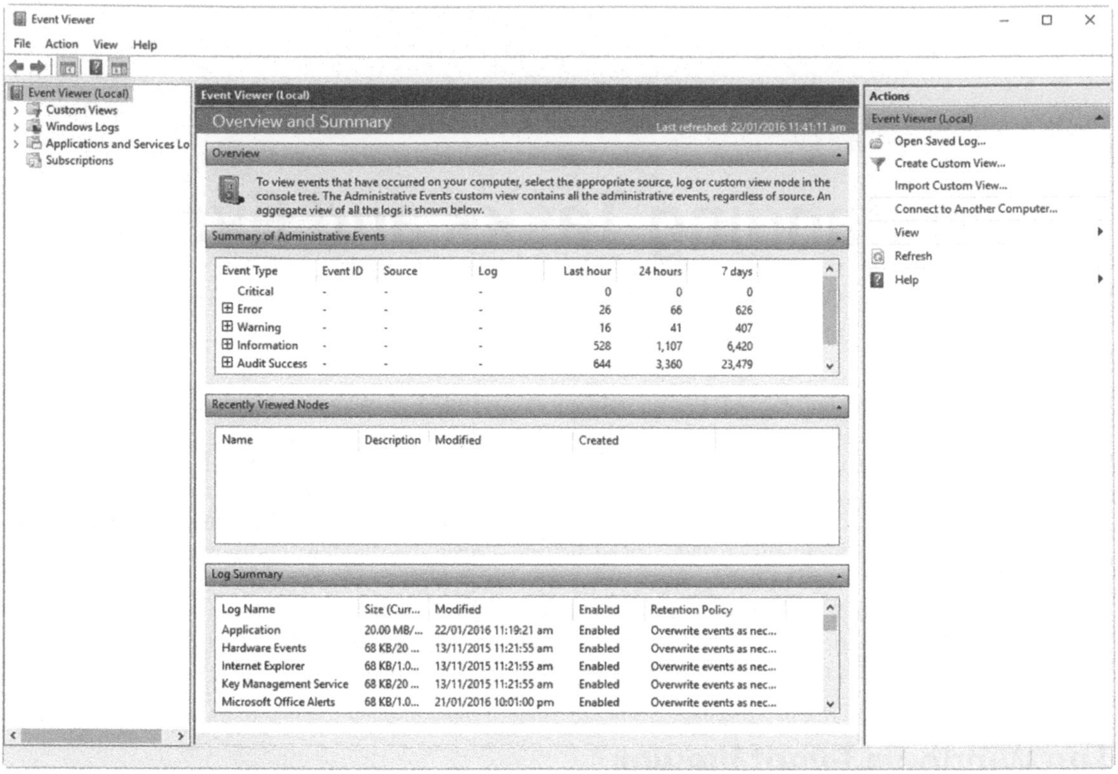

Figure 5-1. *The Event Viewer is split into three vertical panels*

The Category/Views Panel

Obviously, depending on what MMC you have open, the information displayed in the three vertical panels will be different. In the Hyper-V MMC, for example, the left panel will display the available root PCs that can contain Virtual Machines (VM). The Local Security Policy and Group Policy MMCs will display the different groups you can specify policies for. The Advanced Firewall will display options for inbound and outbound security rules, and the Event Viewer, seen in Figure 5-2, displays the different category areas that Windows stores event logs for.

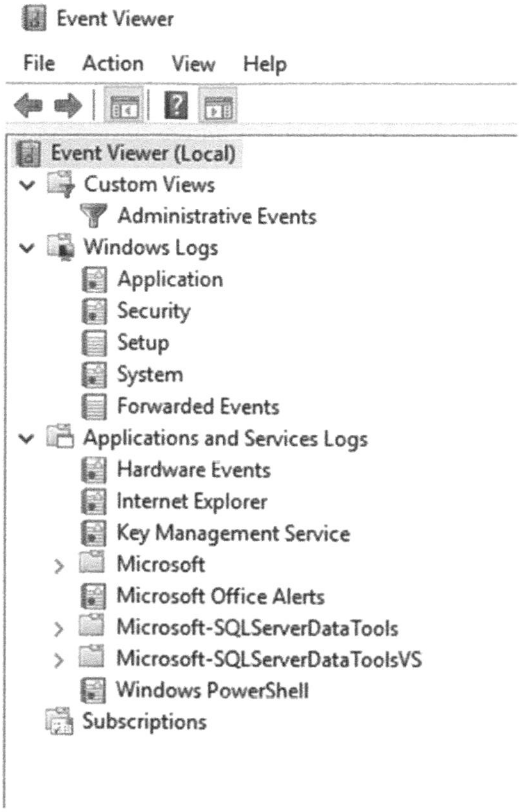

Figure 5-2. *The Category/Views panel is always to the left of the MMC*

In the Event Viewer, the options available in the left side panel allow you to filter the event logs viewed by specific types. These are categorized as follows...

- **Custom Views**—created by your to monitor specific events on a PC

- **Windows logs**—contain Event Log information for Windows events only

- **Applications and Services logs**—contain logs for installed apps and both Windows and third-party services

- **Subscriptions**—allow you to collect logs from multiple remote computers and store them to view locally

The Actions Panel

The Actions panel sits to the right of MMC windows and contains both global and contextual commands and options, see Figure 5-3. These will change depending on which MMC you have open and what you are currently doing in that MMC.

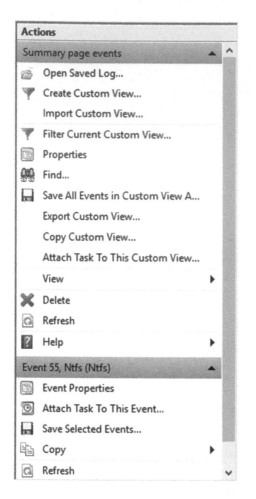

Figure 5-3. *The Actions panel sits to the right of the MMC*

For example, in the Hyper-V MMC, the options will include creating VM and Network Switches. In the Disk Management MMC, they will include disk and partition management tools, and in the Event Viewer they will include ways to interact with, create, save, and view the properties of events and event logs.

The Main Events View

The central panel in the Event Viewer is where the event logs themselves are displayed. When you click the root option in the left panel *Event Viewer (Local)*, you will see the central columns separate into four collapsible panels, see Figure 5-4.

Event Viewer (Local)

Overview and Summary

Last refreshed: 22/01/2016 12:04:43 pm

Overview

To view events that have occurred on your computer, select the appropriate source, log or custom view node in the console tree. The Administrative Events custom view contains all the administrative events, regardless of source. An aggregate view of all the logs is shown below.

Summary of Administrative Events

Event Type	Event ID	Source	Log	Last hour	24 hours	7
Critical	-	-	-	0	0	
⊞ Error	-	-	-	27	63	
⊞ Warning	-	-	-	16	41	
⊞ Information	-		-	537	1,111	

Recently Viewed Nodes

Name	Description	Modified	Created
Applications and Service...	N/A	13/11/2015 11:21:55 am	12/11/2015 3:07:20 pm
Applications and Service...	N/A	13/11/2015 11:21:55 am	12/11/2015 3:07:20 pm
Applications and Service...	N/A	13/11/2015 11:21:55 am	12/11/2015 3:07:20 pm
Applications and Service...	N/A	13/11/2015 11:21:55 am	12/11/2015 3:07:20 pm

Log Summary

Log Name	Size (Curr...	Modified	Enabled	Retention Policy
Application	20.00 MB/...	22/01/2016 11:19:21 am	Enabled	Overwrite event
Hardware Events	68 KB/20 ...	13/11/2015 11:21:55 am	Enabled	Overwrite event
Internet Explorer	68 KB/1.0...	13/11/2015 11:21:55 am	Enabled	Overwrite event
Key Management Service	68 KB/20 ...	13/11/2015 11:21:55 am	Enabled	Overwrite event

Figure 5-4. *The central panel in Event Viewer displays the event logs*

- **Overview**—displays a text description of the view you have open.

- **Summary of Administrative Events**—separates all the event logs stored on the PC into six different categories.

  - **Critical** errors are the ones that result in a sudden PC stop, such as a Blue Screen of Death, a Windows core (kernel) component failure, critical driver stop (such as a critical graphics driver error), or a power problem

  - **Error** messages are generated when a Windows component, app, or service fails

91

- **Warnings** are generated when a Windows component, app, or service generates a message or error that does not cause a stop event to occur

- **Information** is generated whenever a service or component starts, or when an event such as an update, installation, or event in an app is recorded

- **Audit Success** information is generated when a successful routine operation, such as starting up the PC and booting to the Windows desktop, completes

- **Audit Failure** events are generated when a routine operation does not complete or reports an error

- **Recently Viewed Nodes**—quick links to the events you have been viewing most recently.

- **Log Summary**—provides technical information about the currently displayed event or events.

Making Sense of Error Logs

You open event logs by clicking the event categories until you arrive at a list of recorded events, and then click one event to select it. The view will then change to a list of the events for that category in the top center of the window, with details about the currently selected event below it, see Figure 5-5.

Level	Date and Time	Source	Event ID	Task Category
● Error	18/01/2016 8:12:31 pm	Ntfs (Ntfs)	55	None
● Error	18/01/2016 8:12:31 pm	Ntfs (Ntfs)	55	None
● Error	18/01/2016 8:12:30 pm	Ntfs (Ntfs)	55	None
● Error	18/01/2016 8:12:30 pm	Ntfs (Ntfs)	55	None
● Error	18/01/2016 8:12:30 pm	Ntfs (Ntfs)	55	None

Summary page events Number of events: 133

Number of events: 133

Event 55, Ntfs (Ntfs) ✕

General Details

A corruption was discovered in the file system structure on volume I:.

A corruption was found in a file system index structure. The file reference number is 0x5000000000005. The name of the file is "<unable to determine file name>". The corrupted index attribute is ":$I30:$INDEX_ALLOCATION".

Log Name:	System		
Source:	Ntfs (Ntfs)	Logged:	18/01/2016 8:12:31 pm
Event ID:	55	Task Category:	None
Level:	Error	Keywords:	
User:	SYSTEM	Computer:	Workstation
OpCode:	Info		
More Information:	Event Log Online Help		

Figure 5-5. *Opening an error log displays verbose and specific details of the event*

So how do you go about deciphering details of an event in Windows 10? When it comes to diagnosing and troubleshooting problems, there are several useful things you can look for.

- **Frequency of the event**—This can be gathered from checking the event ID (55 in the example given) and matching it to the number of times, and the frequency with which, the event occurs. In this case, a disk file structure error is being repeatedly discovered. Examining the frequency of events might reveal that the error being reported isn't new, but has been occurring for some time.

- **Verbose description of the event**—This is detailed at the top of the *General* information panel. A plain-text description of the event will be given; this can sometimes give you all the information you need on its own. In this case, I have a corrupt file system, on a USB Flash drive.

- **Error code**—These always start 0x; in the preceding example it's 0x5000000000005. Error codes can be incredibly useful when searching the Internet to find solutions to problems.

- **App or Service file name and version numbers**—In Figure 5-6, you will see an error reported when the Skype win32 app has crashed (which was very annoying at the time, as I was preparing for an important webcast with a major firm in the United States). Here we have extremely detailed information, including a 0x error code. Additionally, the Event Log contains details of the exact apps and services, and their file paths, that have crashed. You can also see at the top of the information panel the exact version numbers for those files, in this case *SkypeHost.exe* and *SkyWrap.dll*. Searching for information about file version numbers online can often reveal other people having issues, and perhaps suggestions for more stable installations you can use instead.

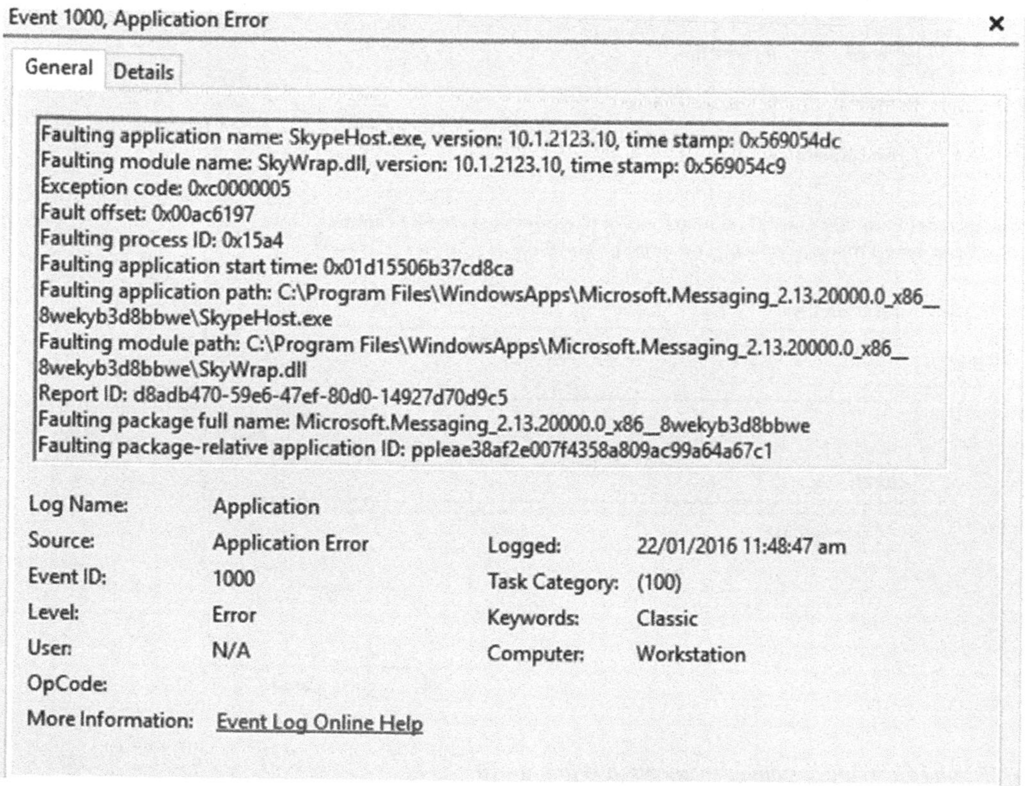

Event 1000, Application Error   ✕

General	Details

Faulting application name: SkypeHost.exe, version: 10.1.2123.10, time stamp: 0x569054dc
Faulting module name: SkyWrap.dll, version: 10.1.2123.10, time stamp: 0x569054c9
Exception code: 0xc0000005
Fault offset: 0x00ac6197
Faulting process ID: 0x15a4
Faulting application start time: 0x01d15506b37cd8ca
Faulting application path: C:\Program Files\WindowsApps\Microsoft.Messaging_2.13.20000.0_x86_
8wekyb3d8bbwe\SkypeHost.exe
Faulting module path: C:\Program Files\WindowsApps\Microsoft.Messaging_2.13.20000.0_x86_
8wekyb3d8bbwe\SkyWrap.dll
Report ID: d8adb470-59e6-47ef-80d0-14927d70d9c5
Faulting package full name: Microsoft.Messaging_2.13.20000.0_x86_8wekyb3d8bbwe
Faulting package-relative application ID: ppleae38af2e007f4358a809ac99a64a67c1

Log Name:	Application		
Source:	Application Error	Logged:	22/01/2016 11:48:47 am
Event ID:	1000	Task Category:	(100)
Level:	Error	Keywords:	Classic
User:	N/A	Computer:	Workstation
OpCode:			
More Information:	Event Log Online Help		

Figure 5-6. *Extremely detailed technical information can be gained from the Event Viewer*

■ **Note**   The *Details* tab in the Event Viewer, when a specific log is displayed, shows the information in a Friendly or XML view that can be copied by right-clicking it (no selection is necessary), and then pasted into an e-mail or other document for a support technician.

Creating Custom Event Views

If you are searching for specific information—perhaps you are asking a user to send you event information from his own PC—you can create a custom view. This will create a subset of the whole Event Log that can be viewed in the Event Viewer under the *Custom Views* section or saved as a file and exported via e-mail or another method to be read on a different PC.

Clicking *Create Custom View* in the Actions panel will allow you to filter the Event Log using a wide variety of methods, see Figure 5-7. You can filter your custom view in the following ways.

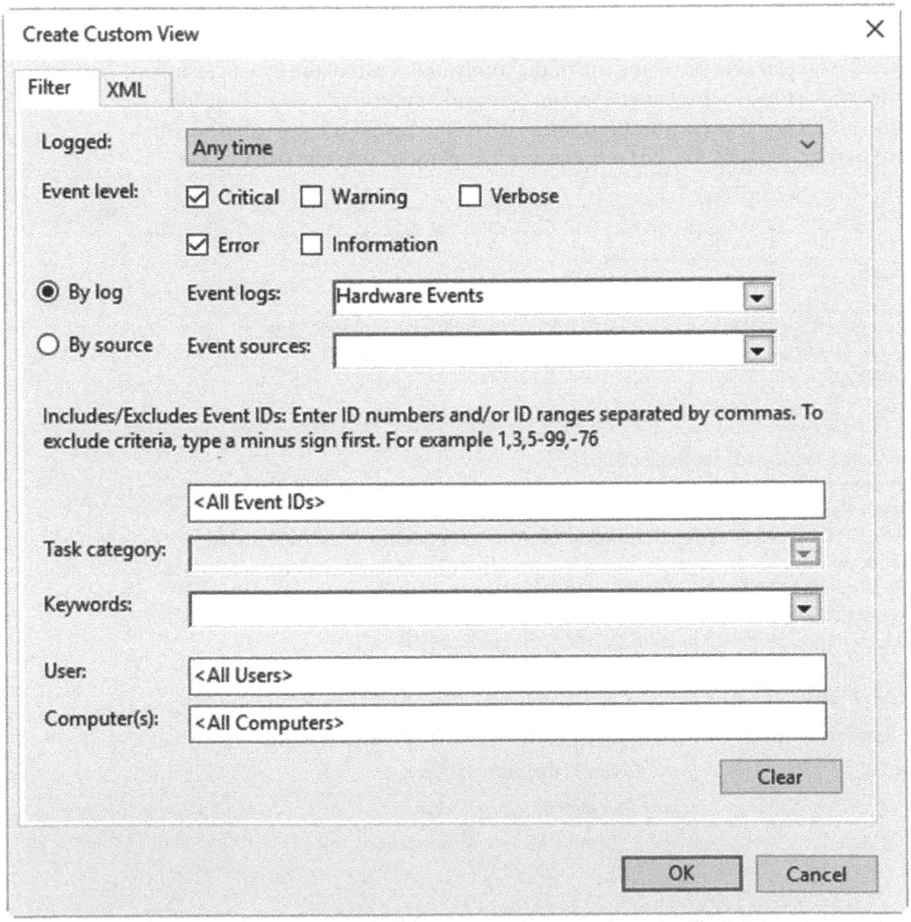

Figure 5-7.   You can create custom event views in Windows 10

- **Logged**—allows you to capture events from any time, the last hour, last 12 hours, last 24 hours, last 7 days, last 30 days, or you can specify a custom date and time range

- **Event level**—lets you specify the error types you want to include from Critical, Error, Warning, Information, or Verbose information

- **By log**—lets you specify the events to keep by their main category, the categories seen in the left panel of the Event Viewer; these include Windows logs, Applications and Services logs, and so on

- **By source**—lists a vast number of Windows services and features from which you can choose; for example, you might want events about the narrator, various Hyper-V services, or specific kernel (core operating system file) errors

- **Event IDs**—you can specify <All event IDs>, the default option, or one or more specific event IDs

- **Task Category**—this is not displayed for all options, but the Task Category is displayed to the right of the event ID in the events list and might be either a number or a text description

- **Keywords**—specific error descriptions you want to select; you can choose from All keywords (the default option), Audit failure, Audit success, Classic, Correlation hint, Response time, SQM, and WDI Diag. When you are viewing the details of an error, the keywords associated with that error will be displayed in the General error details. Selecting keywords can help you find related errors and crashes

- **User**—helps you choose between <all [the] users> on the PC, or a specific user if more than one person uses the PC and only they are experiencing problems

- **Computer**—similar to users, but helps you choose which computer you wish to view events for. This can be used when subscribing to events from remote computers, which I shall cover shortly

---

■ **Tip** When you are viewing a custom view, you can click *Filter Current Custom View* in the Actions panel to narrow the information contained. This can help narrow your searches for problems.

Creating Event Subscriptions

If you are managing multiple PCs on a domain or by using Azure AD, you can subscribe to event logs from multiple computers, and these events will then appear as custom logs in the *subscriptions* section of the Event Viewer.

To have a subscription, both the **Windows Remote Management (winRM)** and **Windows Event Collector (wecsvc)** services must be running on both the machine sending and the machine collecting the logs. In addition to the method detailed in the following, you can also manage these in the Services panel, which I will detail in Chapter 19. You can then set up a subscription by following these instructions...

1. Click *Command Prompt (Admin)* in the **Win + X** menu, and click through the UAC security notification

2. On each source PC, type `winrm quickconfig` and press Enter

3. On the collector PC, type `wecutil qc` and press Enter

4. Open *Computer Management* from the Administrative Tools on each of the source PCs

   a. Select *Local Users and Groups* in the left side panel of the Computer Management Console, then click *Groups* in its drop-down

   b. Right-click in a blank space in the central panel and then click *New Group* from the context menu that appears

   c. To add the collector PC, click *Add*, and then in the dialog that appears, click *Object Types* and select the *Computers* check box

   d. Add the collector PC's name to the local groups information, as you would add a local user account

5. Back in the Event Viewer on the collector PC, click *Subscriptions* in the left panel and then *Create Subscription* in the Actions panel

6. In the wizard dialog that appears, see Figure 5-8, add a subscription name and description, and then select the computers you wish to collect logs from

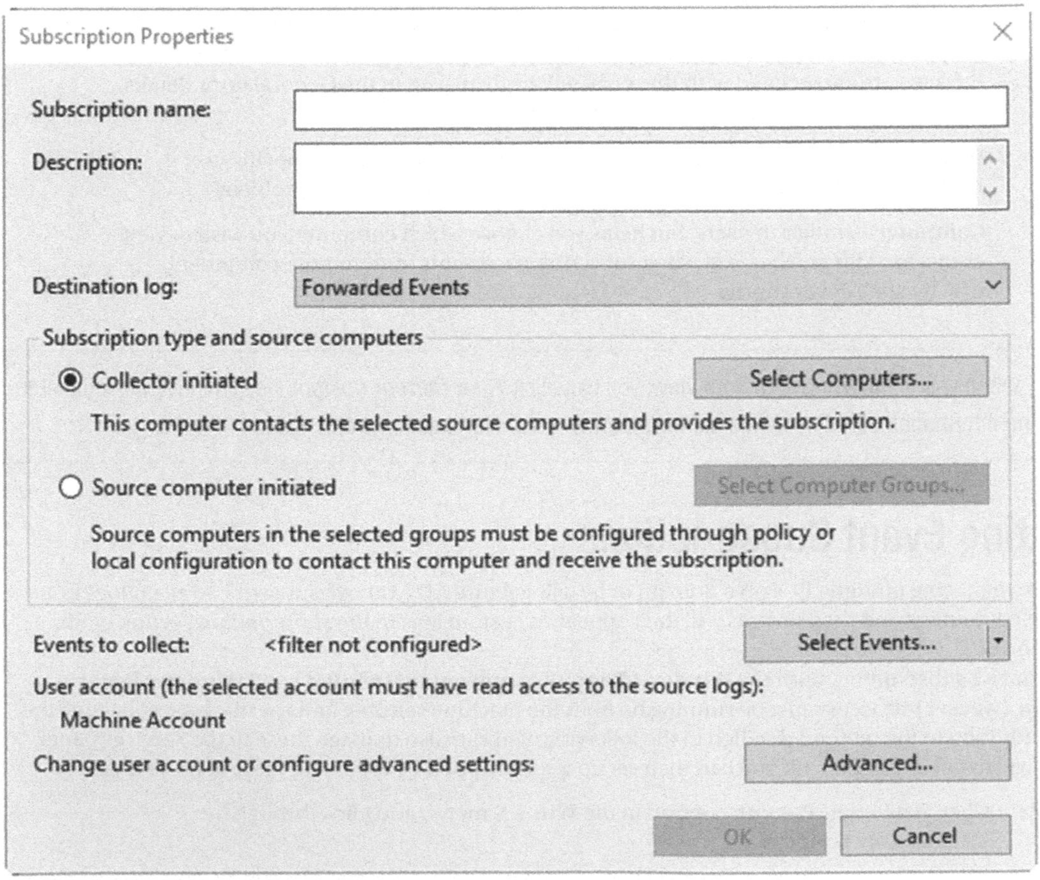

Figure 5-8. *Event subscriptions are created through a wizard interface*

7. Click the *Select Events* button to configure the Event Log collector as detailed in the "Creating Custom Event Views" section of this chapter. Alternatively, you can click the down arrow to the right of this button and import an existing custom view

8. Optionally now, click *Advanced* to specify the user account this subscription is to be for (only required if more than one user account is found on the collector PC), and any bandwidth restrictions you wish to put in place. Note that the `winrm quickcfg` command detailed in step 2 also needs to be run on the collector PC if you want to change the Delivery Optimization (bandwidth) options, and if you are specifying a specific user on the collector PC to use the subscription, that user will need to be added to the accounts on each source PC as well

Attaching a Task to an Event

Sometimes when an event occurs, you want the user on the PC or a support person to be notified. Perhaps even you want a PowerShell script or a repair utility to automatically run to fix the issue. In the Event Viewer, you can do all of these things.

With an individual event selected (you can also attach tasks to custom views to perform an action whenever something new is added), click *Attach Task to this Event* (or Attach Task to this Custom View) in the Actions panel. This will display a wizard dialog.

At the first page of the dialog, check that the event name is correct, or give the task a custom name, and then give the task a verbose description, see Figure 5-9. This can help people identify what the task is for should it no longer be needed.

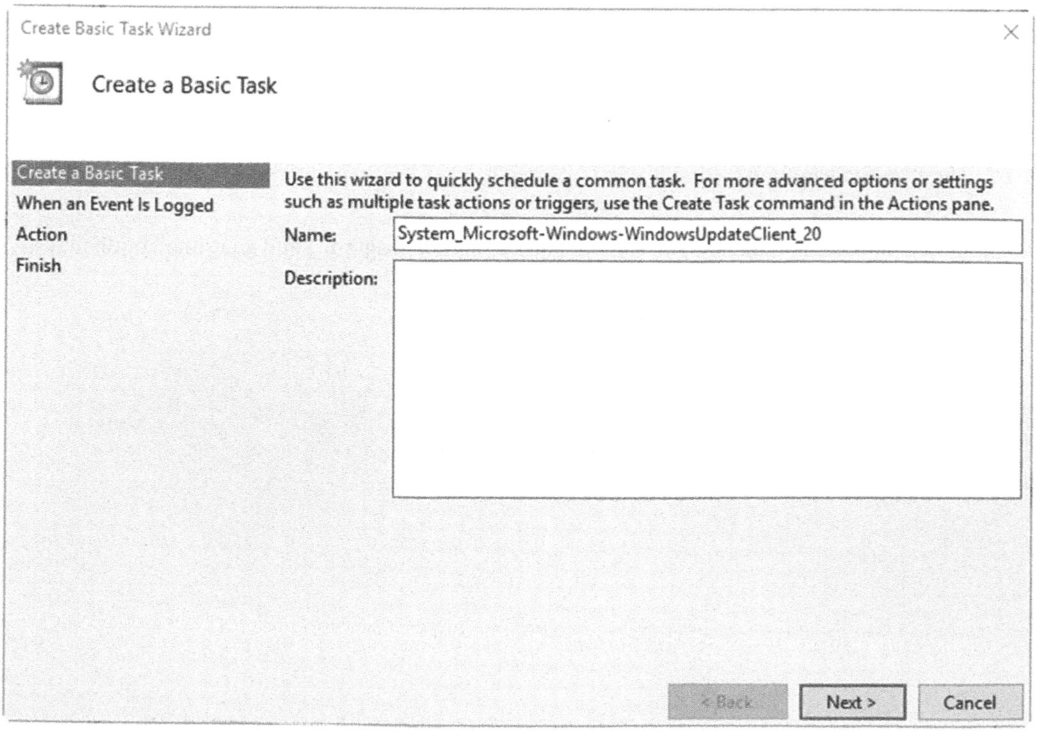

Figure 5-9. You need to give a task a name, and you may also give it a description

Click Next and the next screen is likely going to be grayed out as the event information has already been selected, see Figure 5-10. If the boxes are not grayed out, select the log, source, and event ID information you wish to create the task for.

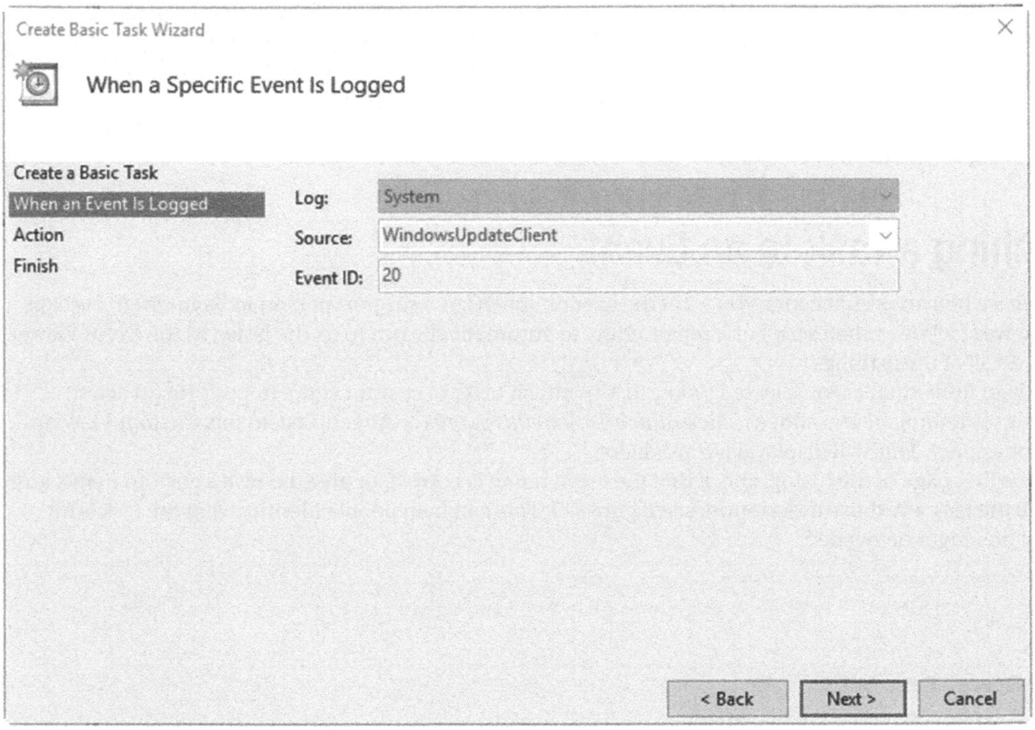

Figure 5-10. *The event information is usually selected for you*

At the next screen, you can choose if you want the task to start a program, send an e-mail, or display a message, see Figure 5-11. We'll look at each of these in turn.

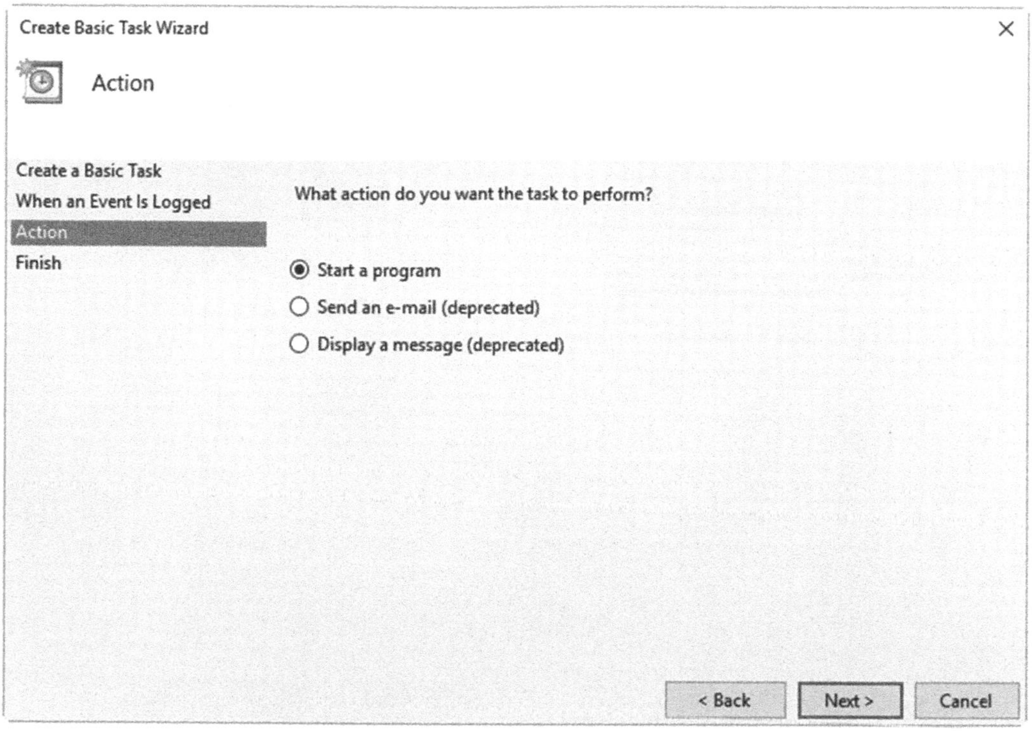

Figure 5-11. At the next screen, you decide what you want the task to do

If you choose to run a program, you can choose an app or a script (command line or PowerShell) to execute when the event occurs. This can include an autorepair script or utility that you have been provided with, or one that you custom-write yourself, see Figure 5-12. You can add command-line arguments if required.

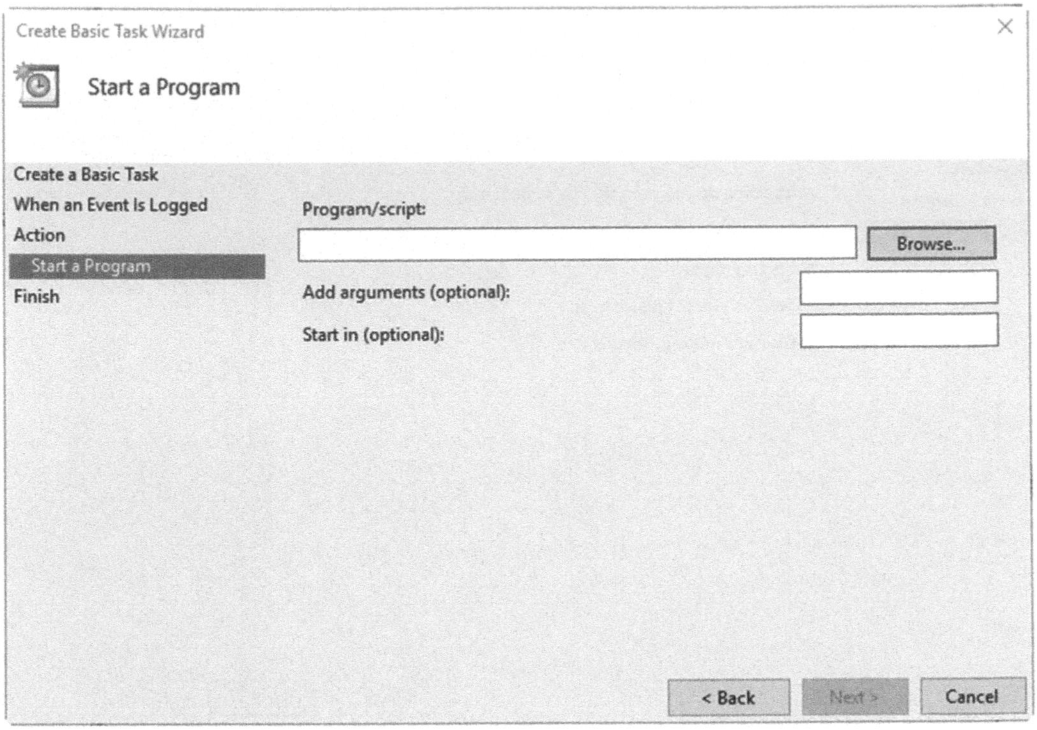

Figure 5-12. *You can choose a program or script to run on the event occurrence*

Sending an e-mail doesn't require an e-mail app to be installed on the PC, see Figure 5-13. You specify the details for the e-mail, which must contain a fixed message, and the SMTP (e-mail out) server. Additionally, you can attach a file to the e-mail, such as an error log. I will detail where these can be found in Chapter 27.

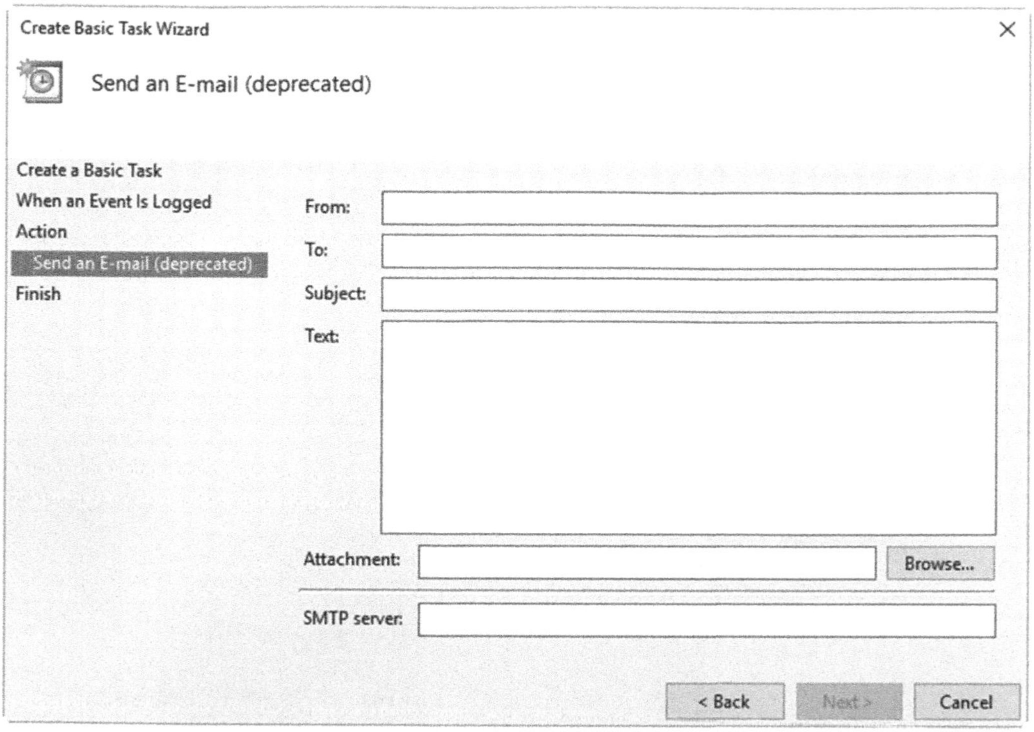

Figure 5-13. Sending an e-mail does not require an e-mail app to be installed on the PC

You can also choose to display a message on the user's screen as a pop-up dialog, see Figure 5-14. This could perhaps ask the user to stop what they're doing and call Support right away, so that up-to-date logs can be collected, but also so that support can be told exactly what it was the user was doing at the time the event occurred.

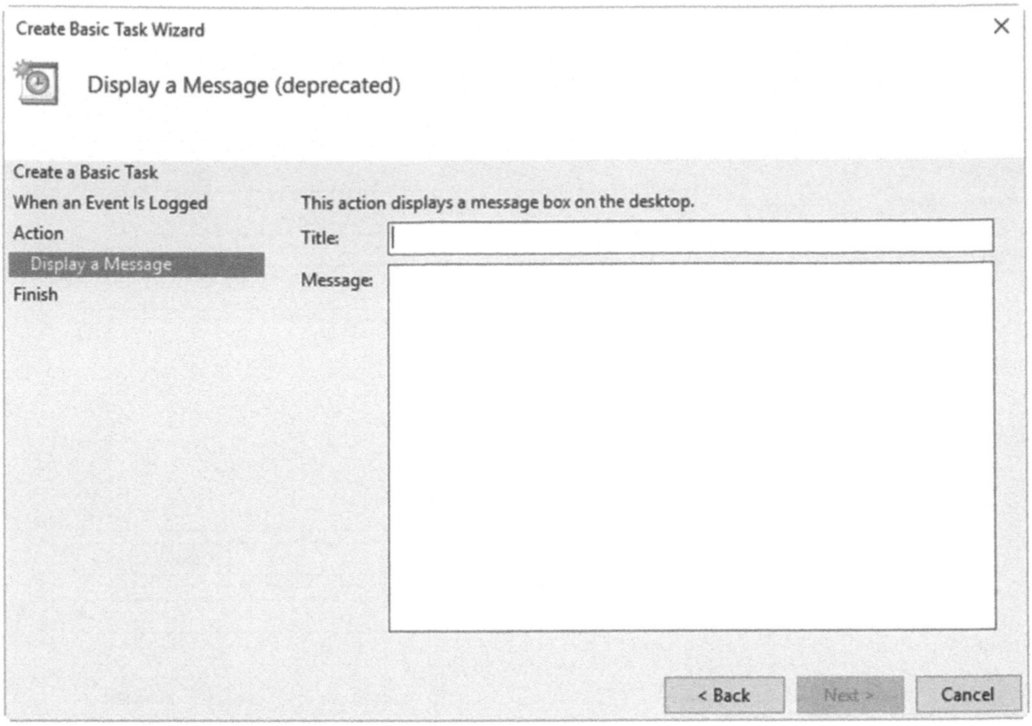

Figure 5-14. A message can be displayed on the user's screen

■ **Note**   Tasks can be managed in the Task Scheduler MMC: search for **task** in the Start Menu or Cortana. Click the *Event Viewer Tasks* section in the left panel, and you can right-click your created event tasks to disable them, export them (for use on other PCs), change their properties, or delete them when they are no longer required.

Saving, Exporting, and Importing Event Information

Sometimes, the information in the Event Viewer will need to be sent to a third-party support person or so that you can digest it properly on the train home. You can save any and all information in the Event Viewer as Event Viewer (.evtx) files. These can then be read in a standard web browser.

In the Event Viewer, select one or more events (you can select all events in a list by clicking the top event, then holding **Shift** when you click the bottom event, or by holding **Ctrl** and clicking all the events you wish to highlight) by right-clicking them and selecting *Save Selected Events* from the drop-down menu that appears, see Figure 5-15. You can also save all events from a custom view by right-clicking the custom view in the left panel.

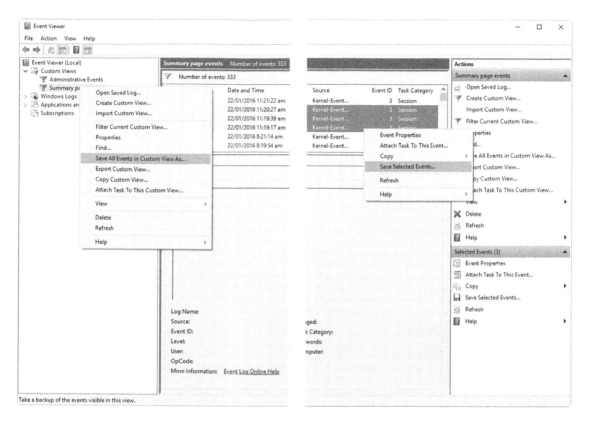

Figure 5-15. *You can save events as XML data in the Event Viewer*

This file can be saved or sent to a support technician and opened by clicking *Open Saved Log* in the Actions panel of the Event Viewer on any Windows PC. It will then appear in the *Saved Logs* section of the Event Viewer, where it can be viewed and reviewed.

Summary

The Event Viewer is a huge repository of useful information, and just about everything you need to know to diagnose and repair problems, crashes, and instabilities can be found within its logs. This is why it justified an entire chapter, all to itself.

When it comes to understanding the inner working of the PC file system, the Event Viewer can be indispensable, though I will detail the Windows file system in full in Chapter 27. In the next chapter, however, we'll look at PC hardware, including all the different technologies you will encounter as an IT Pro.

■ ■ ■

CHAPTER 6

Understanding PC Hardware

The Windows operating system as installed on your PC is extremely complex, literally consisting of tens or even hundreds of thousands of configuration files, shared APIs, drivers, programs, and more besides. The hardware in our PCs isn't any less confusing, and even if you're using a tablet or ultrabook that's not serviceable by the user, because the case is sealed and all components are soldered onto the motherboard, there are still hardware factors you need to know about when troubleshooting problems.

BIOS and UEFI

BIOS (Basic Input, Output System) and UEFI (Unified Extensible Firmware Interface) are the place to start. They exist in ROM (Read-Only Memory) on a chip on the PC's motherboard, and they are referred to as firmware. The firmware is the software layer that exists between the operating system and the PC's hardware; its job is to tell the OS how to communicate with the hardware. Think of it as a hardware driver, as there are similarities, but one that's required by the operating system at the very beginning of startup, so that the OS knows where to find and how to spin up the hard disk and other hardware components, such as the screen, so that it can load its core files and interface.

Firmware shares more in common with the solid-state drives (SSDs) we use in PCs these days than with memory chips, in that it's nonvolatile. This means that like the storage chips on SSDs, but unlike chips on our PCs memory cards, its contents aren't wiped when the electricity supply is switched off.

BIOS was invented in 1975 by a man called Gary Kildall (yup, this was back when one person could invent a technology that we now all take for granted), when it was first used with the CP/M operating system that he also created. IBM created their own BIOS in a deal with Kildall to offer CP/M with their first PCs. The story of how IBM originally contacted Kildall, and the story about how Microsoft's MS-DOS became the dominant PC operating system, which was far more popular with end users than CP/M, has fallen into tech mythology; you can read more about it at http://pcs.tv/1NupOJv.

What I believe to be the far more interesting story is how IBM-compatible machines (and the PC market as we know it) first came about. IBM was unwilling to licence its BIOS to other companies, but the Compaq Computer Corporation really wanted to release IBM-compatible PCs. They couldn't just copy IBM's BIOS, however, as that would have infringed copyright, so instead they set up two teams to manage the task.

The first of these teams reverse-engineered the IBM BIOS), making detailed notes about what it did and how it operated. The second team, working from the notes from the first team, but without having any access to the IBM BIOS themselves, wrote a new BIOS that would perform all the same operations. Because Microsoft had deliberately signed a deal with IBM that allowed them to sell MS-DOS to whoever they wanted, the PC compatibles market was born and no copyright was infringed, at least not according to the law.

IBM did eventually publish the full details of its BIOS, and several other companies including Phoenix Technologies and Award Software created their own compatible versions that are still seen on millions of PCs in use today.

© Mike Halsey 2016
M. Halsey, *Windows 10 Troubleshooting*, DOI 10.1007/978-1-4842-0925-7_6

BIOS served PC makers well for 30 years (even though it was only supposed be used for about 7 years before being replaced). The problem with BIOS is that it wasn't written to support all the technologies that came after it, such as USB. This made it slow to access and identify hardware at the PC's startup, and its operation on a ROM chip with no inbuilt security also made it vulnerable to attack by malware. Some of this malware would corrupt or wipe the BIOS completely, rendering a PC unusable unless complex fixes were implemented and the firmware reflashed.

UEFI was the solution to the woes of the BIOS. It came about from a forum consisting of major technology companies including Microsoft, Apple, Intel, AMD, Dell, and the companies behind the currently-in-use BIOS firmware. The UEFI specification was first written by Intel, and it permitted a more flexible, configurable, scalable, and above all, faster firmware system for PCs; it could also include advanced security to protect both itself and the operating system from malware.

You will typically access the BIOS or UEFI on a PC by pressing Esc, Del, F2, or F12 on your keyboard at PC startup, but tablets will commonly have a button combination to press such as power and volume up. You should check the documentation that came with your device, as the method used will vary depending on the PC you use. The UEFI system can also be accessed from within Windows 10 (and from a USB Recovery Drive). To do this, open the Settings app, then click *Update & security*, then click *Recovery*, and then click the *Restart now* button in the Advanced Startup section. When the boot options menu appears, click *Troubleshoot*, then click *Advanced Options*, and you will see a *UEFI Firmware Settings* button.

BIOS Virus/Malware Attack

As I have already mentioned, one of the biggest issues with BIOS is its complete lack of any type of security. The only security it has, in fact, is User Account Control (UAC) in the host OS blocking malware at the user level. Given that the BIOS is essential in order to get Windows to start on the PC, however, means that it's very vulnerable to attack. There are several different ways to troubleshoot and repair BIOS systems on PCs, and this will depend on what's wrong with the BIOS.

It's actually very rare these days for viruses to attack the firmware on PCs. There are several reasons for this, including that UAC on PCs since Windows Vista is extremely good at defending against viruses. There's also the point that every PC sold since the release of Windows 8.1 has a UEFI firmware system, which was mandated by Microsoft. Malware writers these days simply don't want to take down our computer systems, however. In fact, they need our computers operating so they can either get access to, and steal, our personal data, or use the PC as part of a mesh network to attack companies and governments with Distributed Denial of Service Attacks (DDOS).

That isn't to say that a direct malware attack on a PC's BIOS isn't still possible in some circumstances. Let's say you work for a company or a government department that provides or manages critical infrastructure for a city or perhaps an entire country. This can include phones and cellular networks, Internet access, water, rail, and road, networks, electricity, gas, and even nuclear power. Both governments and a very small number of hacking groups are regularly, perhaps even constantly, trying to disrupt these networks: perhaps to destabilize a country with whom they disagree or to slow down the ambitions of another.

This becomes important when you recognize that critical systems require incredibly robust and stable software and operating systems. By this, I am referring to software and operating systems that have proven themselves reliable over very long periods of time. This means that this infrastructure often runs on very old Windows versions and very old software. Windows XP, which fell out of all support from Microsoft in 2014, is still commonly used by companies, governments, and military forces around the world.

These older operating systems, software, and BIOSes are significantly more vulnerable to attack than a modern PC with Windows 10 and UEFI firmware, despite additional security always being put in place at a network level. The end result is that they present a very tempting target for hackers and government agencies, though it's helpful at least that these PCs don't tend to be restarted very often.

Should a BIOS attack take place, however, or should one be possible on your system, you should make sure you keep a copy of, or a quick link to, the firmware flashing utility or dedicated malware removal tool on the motherboard manufacturer's web site. These can often find themselves removed from the Internet as older hardware falls out of general use (which is why keeping your own copy of the firmware flashing tool is necessary). You will generally run this from a floppy disk (remember those?) at the PC's startup after resetting the BIOS, which I'll talk about in a minute.

Resetting BIOS and UEFI Firmware

While it's not uncommon for BIOS firmware to become corrupt on desktop PCs, it's much less common for UEFI firmware. If you have a small spike in the electricity supply, or if the power is suddenly cut to the PC, the resultant electrical activity can corrupt the firmware as stored on the BIOS chip. Also, if you're updating the BIOS on a PC and the power fails, this too will (fairly obviously) corrupt the BIOS. In this last circumstance you'll also need the reflashing tool you can run from a floppy disk or USB Flash Drive.

Figure 6-1 shows the method by which you can reset the BIOS or UEFI on a desktop PC. There is a battery and what's called a Clear CMOS (Complementary metal-oxide-semiconductor) jumper. You can usually reset the BIOS or UEFI on a PC by moving this jumper, which covers two out of three available pins, to the other end of its base (still covering the center pin), and leaving it for a few seconds before putting it back where it was before. You may also find it helpful to remove the battery.

Figure 6-1. *You can reset a BIOS by removing the battery on the motherboard and resetting the Clear CMOS jumper*

■ **Tip** Some modern desktop PCs come with a button on the back of the machine or on the motherboard that you can press to reset the BIOS or UEFI firmware.

On laptops and tablets, BIOS firmware corruption is rare. This is because, being battery operated and always plugged into grid power by means of a transformer, they are significantly less vulnerable to the electricity spikes that can corrupt a BIOS. However, should a corruption occur you will need to refer to the servicing guide (or an authorized service center) and dismantle the PC's case to find out how the BIOS or UEFI firmware can be reset.

Additionally, if you can load the BIOS or UEFI firmware on the PC, there will be an option to *Restore Defaults* or *Load Optimized Defaults* that you can choose, see Figure 6-2. This will reset the BIOS to its default state.

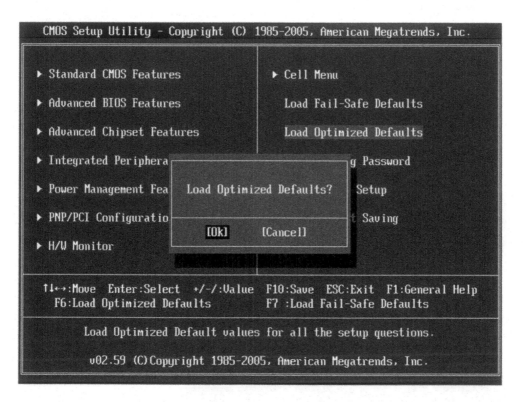

Figure 6-2. *You can Restore Defaults or Load Optimized Defaults from within a BIOS or UEFI*

PCs, BIOS, UEFI, and Overclocking

Overclocking is the process of forcing the hardware in your PC, usually the processor (CPU) and memory, to operate faster than their normal (optimal) speed. PCs are commonly overclocked when they're to be used for speed-intensive tasks such as gaming or video production. Not all PC components support overclocking, and some components can be damaged if forced to work faster than their standard clock speed, which is measured in megahertz (MHz) or gigahertz (GHz).

The overclocking process is managed either in the BIOS or UEFI interface, see Figure 6-3, or through the use of a utility provided by the motherboard manufacturer that then changes settings in the firmware itself.

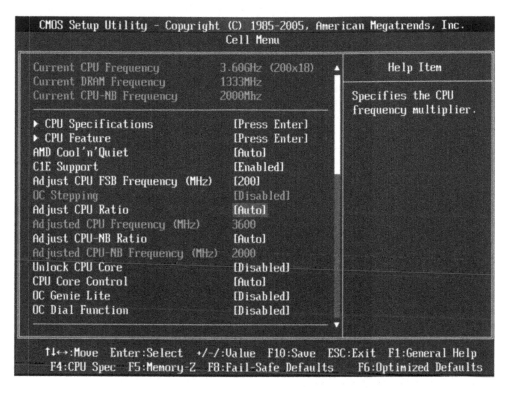

Figure 6-3. *Many PC motherboards support overclocking of components*

Overclocking is a complex process and not for the faint-hearted. It involves manipulating the clock speed (frequency) and power regulation for components that sometimes run on microvolts and have transistors only nanometers (nm) across.

Normally, PCs are very good at recognizing if overclocking is incorrectly configured or can damage the components in a PC. Should this happen, it will likely stop the PC at the firmware screen at startup, report that "Overclocking has failed," and prompt you to reconfigure the firmware with more appropriate settings.

Should a PC be misbehaving, however, and suffering from unexpected crashes, Blue Screens of Death, or overheating, it might be worth checking if overclocking has been enabled on the machine.

Power Supplies

There are two types of power supply for a PC: internal and external. A desktop PC will (unless it's a small-form-factor [SFF] machine) have an internal power supply (PSU). SFF PCs, laptops, and tablets will come with an external "brick" that plugs into grid power when required.

Power supplies fail on PCs more than any other component, and this is especially true of internal PSUs, as they have moving parts in the fans, often sit on the floor, and have vents that allow them to collect dust. Indeed, all electrical equipment will collect dust because of the electromagnetic fields it creates. If you've ever wondered why there always seems to be more dust behind your PC than anywhere else in your home or office, this is why. It's not just dust either, as pet hair will also be attracted by the electromagnetic fields.

There are many PC problems that can be attributed to a faulty power supply. I'd like to detail these each in turn.

- **Failure to Power On**—I want to begin with this, since while it might seem obvious that the power supply in the PC has failed if the PC fails to start, this isn't always the case. If you press the power button on the PC and the lights flicker or turn on for a second before powering off again, then the power supply will be the likely culprit. However, if you press the power button and absolutely nothing happens it could also be the PC's motherboard or the case power button. The power button plugs into the motherboard and sends a signal to the PSU to switch on. If this signal doesn't reach the PSU it can *appear* that is faulty when in fact it isn't. You can test this by jump-starting the PC, which I will detail shortly.

- **Sudden power loss**—This is another problem that may appear to be the power supply when it actually isn't. In some ways this is harder to diagnose, as you can't often jump-start the PC because it needs to be left on for a while before the problem occurs. You can check if other devices in the home or office are experiencing the problem, however, as it could be an electrical wiring fault. Try a different power socket and/or a different power lead before diagnosing the PSU.

- **Blue Screens of Death and other crashes**—If your PC is experiencing sudden and seemingly unrelated Blue Screens of Death or mysterious app crashes, it could be the PSU. Look for a pattern, such as if you're gaming or performing other power-intensive tasks such as rendering video or running a lot of apps simultaneously. A power supply is like an automobile engine, in that over time its power will diminish. A PSU that provided more than enough power for a PC when it was new might not be able to produce enough watts after a few years.

When diagnosing a PSU in a PC, especially if you suspect it's generally down on power, the best method is to unplug some of the power cables from all the components inside the PC that aren't essential. This can include all but the primary hard disk or SSD (M.2 drives plug directly into the motherboard and take their power from that), the optical drive, and any PCIe (PCI Express) or additional graphics cards that may be installed. This can help you determine if the PC will start if less power is being drawn from the PSU. Should this be the case, then it will point to the PSU being old and needing replacement.

Jump-Starting a PC

You'll probably be familiar with the concept of a jump-start. This is when you'll use the battery from one motor engine, usually an automobile, to power the startup of another engine. It works the same way with a PC and this can be a great way to diagnose conclusively whether a power supply has failed, or if it's another component in the PC.

You might have guessed by now that to jump-start a PC you'll need either a spare PC with a similar type of PSU (you can only jump-start desktop PCs with PSU because of this), or you'll need a spare power supply.

It's possible, but fiddly, to jump-start a PC from the power supply in another without first removing the PSU from the other machine's case. The power leads inside a PC aren't very long, however, so it's generally safer and more advisable to perform some minor surgery on the working PC and pop out the PSU.

You don't need to plug every power lead into the faulty PC, just the power leads to the motherboard, which are normally a 24-pin block and a 4-pin block; (optionally) the leads for the primary hard disk or SSD; and, if required, the graphics card. If the PC then springs into life, you'll know that the PSU in the faulty PC is to blame.

The Motherboard

The motherboard in a PC is where it all happens—where the action takes place. In recent years there have been real advances made in motherboard and processor technology that have made them much more reliable and robust. As an example of this, new processors have removed the requirement for motherboards to have a Northbridge chipset.

If you've ever looked at a motherboard, usually a slightly older one now for the reason I detailed, and seen a chip with its own heatsink or fan in the middle of the board, this was the Northbridge. This chip handles all the communications between the processor (CPU), memory, and the installed PCIe expansion cards. As a result, it would have a lot of work to do and get extremely hot. A motherboard with a Northbridge chipset would sometimes fail when this chip would overheat.

So what else can go wrong with motherboards? As the technology involved in manufacturing electronics has evolved, we've moved away from large transistors and resistors, each attached to the motherboard with two short wires (and do you remember valves?). Surface-mount technology means that you can't snap most components on a motherboard, as they're mounted, quite literally, flat to the surface of the board.

There are components that can become gunked with dust (and fine pet hair), break, or fall off. Dealing with this last point first, the most obvious example of this is the connection block on which the wires to the power and reset buttons, and case power and disk activity lights, connect to the board. Some modern PCs come with special blocks that lock these flimsy cables firmly in place. For most PCs, however, it's all too easy for one or more of these wires to become detached from the motherboard, especially if it's moved.

Other components, such as some expansion cards or perhaps a Trusted Platform Module (TPM) encryption card, can also become dislodged when a PC is moved. If this has happens, and a PC is misbehaving, it's a good idea to disconnect the power to the PC and make sure everything is seated properly.

Where there are places that dust and pet hair can collect, such as PCI sockets or in fans, these should be cleaned occasionally, as dust, let's not forget, conducts electricity and collects static. When the components in a PC can often measure in just nanometers, this can make then very vulnerable to even miniscule voltage discharges.

On the subject of fans, bear in mind that these do wear out over time. If a PC is getting old, check the CPU fan especially, as an overheating processor can result in it cracking and becoming useless. Case fans that don't work, or that perhaps have been unplugged because the user thought they were too noisy, can reduce the airflow needed to keep the components in a PC case cool.

The Rear Panel Connectors and Cables

If I had a dollar for every time somebody had plugged something into the wrong socket at the back of a PC, I'd be writing this book from my villa in the South of France. In these days of USB sockets it's easy sometimes to forget that audio often doesn't work because the speakers have been plugged into the wrong audio socket (for reference, it's the green socket you need first), or the monitor has been plugged into the motherboard, when there's a PCI graphics card managing the output instead.

What's often overlooked, however, is good cable management. Some of these cables, VGA and DVI graphics cables for example, are screwed into place. Others, such as USB cables, sit firmly some way inside the rear panel sockets. An accidental kick or sudden bang can damage not just the cable and plug, but the entire back panel and, by definition, the motherboard.

Memory

I was going to say something prophetic about memory, but then the power went out and I forgot it. When diagnosing problems or even potential problems with memory, you can try to remove all but one memory card from the PC and then try different cards in sequence (and in different sockets) to see if a problem exists.

Additionally, Windows 10 includes a specific memory diagnostic utility that can be run by searching for **memory**, funnily enough, in the Start Menu or Cortana. This will prompt you to restart the PC to run its tests, see Figure 6-4. If any memory faults are found, they will be reported upon restarting the PC.

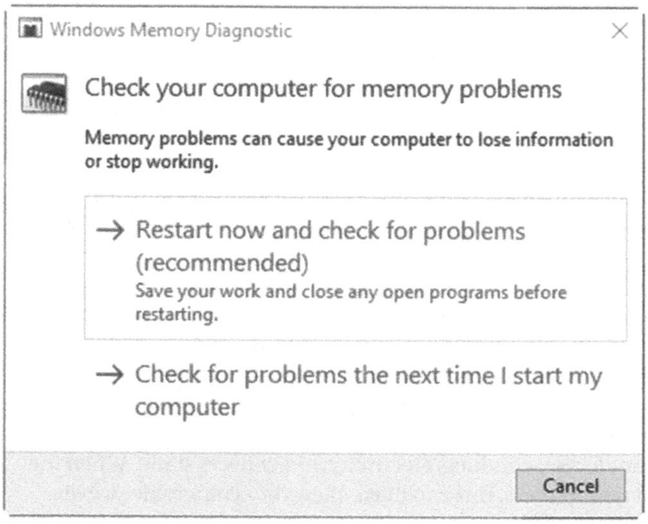

Figure 6-4. *You can test for memory hardware errors from within Windows 10*

Hard Disks, SSDs, M.2, and PCIe Drives

Blimey! Do you also remember a time when you'd plug a regular 3.5-inch hard disk into a PC to use as storage? These days these hard disks are becoming increasingly rare. There have been attempts to release hybrid drives that contain a limited amount of solid-state storage for caching commonly accessed files. These days we're far more likely to be using an SSD or an M.2 drive (which is an SSD on a card that slots directly onto the motherboard).

Some PCs will include a PCIe card that can be used either as storage in addition to the main hard disk or as the boot drive for Windows itself. There is a distinction between the two, as not all of these cards can be used to host the operating system on the PC. They will usually also require additional drivers to operate before Windows 10 can "see" the drive.

There's usually not that much you can do to diagnose hard disk (I'm using the term generically here) faults, but some BIOS and UEFI systems come with monitoring tools, sometimes called SMART monitoring, that will alert you to a disk failure. In Chapter 3, I showed you how to set up and manage disk partitions using the inbuilt Windows 10 Disk Management utility, and in Chapter 11 I'll show you how to manage disk and file permissions.

Expansion Cards

I've mentioned PCIe expansion and graphics cards several times throughout this chapter. They're used for everything from gaming graphics to superfast storage. There's not much that can go wrong with PCIe cards as, unlike previous generations of expansion cards, they don't tend to come loose (not very often anyway) when the PC is moved, and graphics cards often have an additional clip on the socket to hold the card securely in place; moreover, cards that require extra power tend to have those power cables clipped into place.

One of the advantages of troubleshooting PCIe cards is that they can quickly be removed from the PC and placed into another PC to see if the problem recurs. Note that you might need to install drivers on the test PC for the hardware.

Monitors and Cabling

I mentioned cabling earlier in this chapter, but it's really important to get cabling right. You might have a hole in a rear corner of your desk in which you can put cables to keep them tidy, and perhaps a mesh or other type of channel under the back, or just behind the desk in which you can lay cables. These aren't just for aesthetics' sake, they're extremely useful for making sure that your cables are out of the way, that they can't be pinched or snagged easily, and that people won't trip over them.

If you are connecting your PC to a monitor using a VGA or DVI cable, the cable will likely be screwed into the PC at both ends. This means that if somebody trips over the cable, the monitor is likely to come crashing to the floor. Network cables are also prone to this, but if a network cable that's plugged into the back of a PC is caught, the end result will likely be that the cable is stretched and damaged and that the plug might snap.

When it comes to monitors not working, always bear in mind that workers just *love* rearranging their desks. This will mean they'll move their monitor occasionally and unplug and replug the cables at its rear. Should they plug the video cable into the wrong socket at the back of the monitor, they'll not get a picture until they change the input selection on the onscreen display.

■ **Note** Some USB devices, printers, and Wi-Fi dongles especially don't work when unplugged and plugged back in to a different USB port on the PC. I had a bit of an argument a few years ago on my Windows 8 troubleshooting book with a senior member of the Windows Product team at Microsoft about this, in which he said the problem didn't exist because they had no record of it. Believe me, it does exist, but it is easily fixed by unplugging the device and plugging it back into another USB port.

Keyboards and Mice

If there were ever pieces of hardware that could be fixed by simply unplugging and plugging in again, then they are keyboards and mice. It's fairly common, however, with wireless keyboards and mice that come with a USB dongle you plug into the PC, that they won't work when the PC starts. This is because they're not being properly recognized by the PC. Moving them to a different USB port can fix the problem.

■ **Note** I want to talk for a moment about Bluetooth audio. It's a little-known annoyance that Windows 10 PCs can't connect to more than one Bluetooth audio device. So if you have Bluetooth speakers for your laptop, and you also pair Bluetooth headphones with it, an incompatibility will occur and you won't be able to use them.

Summary

This chapter was quite difficult to write, as PC hardware has changed fundamentally in the last few years, and there's now very little that goes wrong with it. From processors that integrate the functions of the Northbridge chipset to USB type-C plugs that will pull free from a PC more easily than older designs, hardware is pretty robust.

Where problems do occur is either with moving parts (such as fans), those that still get extremely hot (like the PSU), driver support in Windows, or limitations within the operating system itself, such as the aforementioned Bluetooth audio limitation.

Safely using hardware is more a case of prevention and cable management than of finding the solutions to problems. Sometimes, though, problems do still occur, and in the next chapter I'll show you how to troubleshoot the most commonly occurring hardware issues.

■ ■ ■

CHAPTER 7

Diagnosing and Repairing Problem Hardware and Peripherals

Getting hardware devices to work with your PC should be a simple matter of plugging the device in, or connecting to it across the network, and getting going. But guess what... it's very often not that simple. At least long gone are the days of parallel and serial devices (well, except for some engineering and other specialist applications) where configuring a device often meant the manual editing of text configuration files, and configuring multiple settings in the Windows Device Manager and on the device itself to get everything to work.

USB (Universal Serial Bus) was designed to eliminate all that, with code embedded into devices that would identify them to the host operating system. Newer peripheral connection technologies such as Thunderbolt (also known as USB Type-C) adopted this system, and devices that connect to your PC over a network or via Bluetooth will also identify themselves, making installation and configuration simple.

In theory, anyway. In practice, it's often not that easy to get devices installed, and when they are installed all that's often needed to get the connection to break is a restart of your PC. In this chapter, we'll look at the common problems associated with installing and troubleshooting hardware, and the steps you can take to fix them.

Getting USB Devices to Work Reliably

USB devices were designed in the mid-1990s to eliminate most of the problems associated with hardware device installation. As I've already mentioned, a USB device identifies itself to the host operating system by means of DEV_ (Device) and VEN_ (Vendor) codes, and I'll talk more about these in Chapter 15. These codes help Microsoft Windows (and all other operating systems) to marry the device with the correct driver, and to configure it appropriately.

There are sometimes problems with USB devices), however. Perhaps the best known of these is that USB drivers sometimes tie a device to a specific port on the PC. This is especially true of printers and Wi-Fi dongles, and means that should the PC be moved, or the device unplugged for some reason, plugging it back into a different USB port suddenly results in the device not working. This can be frustrating for users, and you may get calls from people saying that they cleaned their PC and all of a sudden they can no longer get Internet or network access. Unplugging the USB device and trying different USB ports solves this problem, either by moving the device to the port it was in originally, or by forcing Windows 10 to reload the device drivers if it's plugged into a different USB bus.

© Mike Halsey 2016
M. Halsey, *Windows 10 Troubleshooting*, DOI 10.1007/978-1-4842-0925-7_7

■ **Note** USB game controllers can suffer from mapped-button loss when moved from one USB port to another on a PC.

USB Storage, in the form of Flash Drives, SSDs, and hard disks, are everywhere these days, but who clicks the Safe Eject option hidden in the Windows system tray, see Figure 7-1, when they unplug them?

Figure 7-1. *You can safely eject USB storage devices without causing data corruption*

I will admit to being as guilty of this as most other people. It works fine 99 times out of 100 to just unplug the USB storage device; when you plug it into another PC, or a smart device like a modern television, it just works. It's that 1 time in 100, though, when it doesn't, that can completely corrupt the USB storage drive, rendering everything on it unusable. If you're just transporting files from one PC to another in the office, that can be inconvenient. If, however you're sending someone out of the office with files for a presentation, this can be embarrassing at best, and a major failing at its worst.

By default, Windows 10 sets all USB storage devices to be suitable for "quick removal." You can check this by right-clicking the drive in File Explorer and selecting its *Properties*. In the dialog that appears under the Hardware tab (and making sure the correct device is selected as all your drives will appear in this list), click the *Properties* button; then, at the next dialog, click the *Change Settings* button, and then click the *Policies* tab, which will appear, see Figure 7-2).

■ **Tip** Sometimes a USB Flash Drive or external hard disk will report a corruption error, but will often work fine regardless. A quick *scan and fix* will almost always sort the problem.

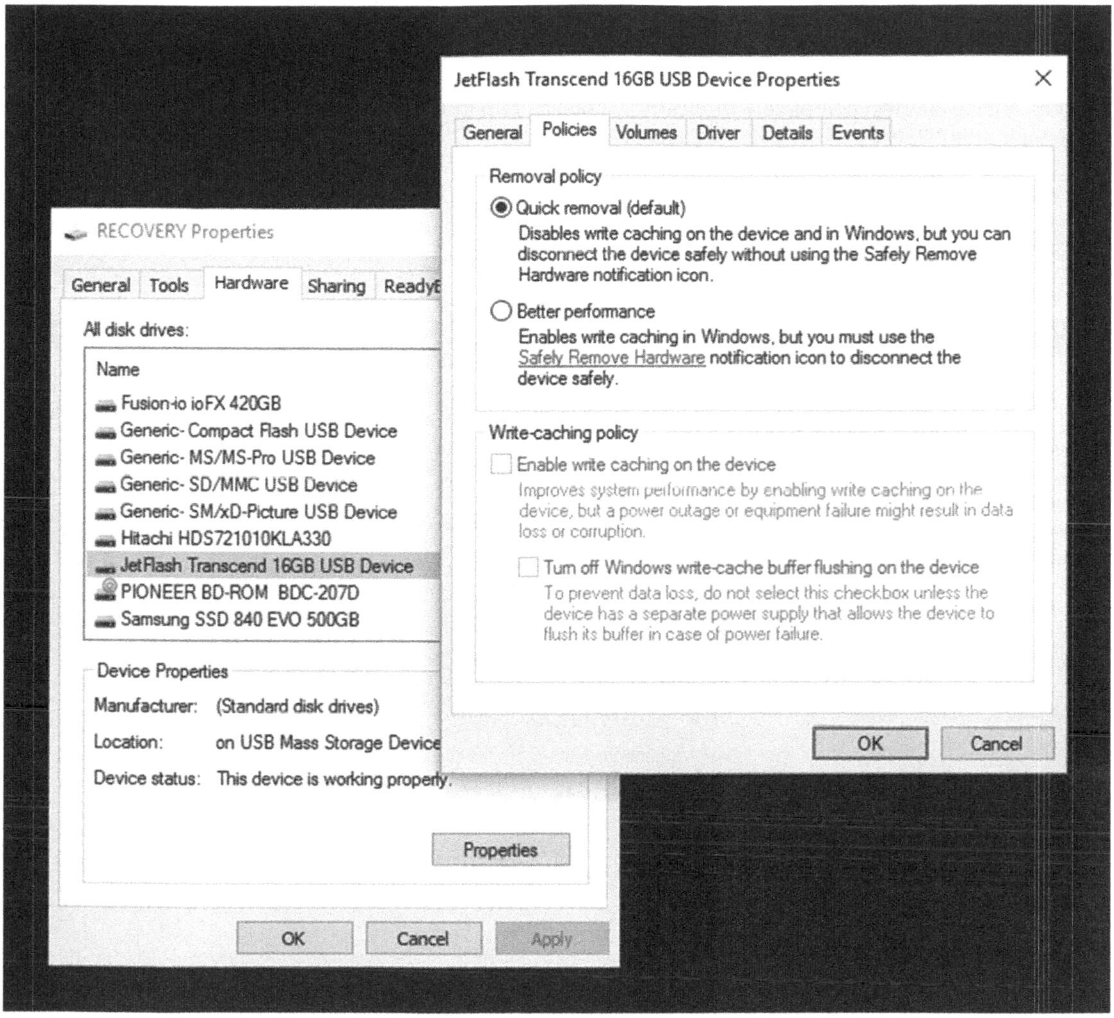

Figure 7-2. *You can check if a drive is configured for quick removal*

■ **Note**   It's worth pointing out that, in a very few cases, and I have experienced this myself, that even setting a drive for quick removal doesn't guarantee the drive will not be corrupted when removed. It's always best practice to tell users to safely eject USB devices before removal as a precaution.

Installing and Managing Bluetooth Devices

Bluetooth was supposed to be the "holy grail" of hardware devices used with PCs and modern computing devices, able to connect completely wirelessly at a range of up to 10 meters. Unfortunately, in more cases than not it's the "Holy cr**!" of device management instead.

Bluetooth devices in Windows 10 are added and removed from the PC primarily through the Settings app, see Figure 7-3. If a Bluetooth device is discovered by your PC, it will appear in the list with a *Pair* button that may also require you to click a pair button on the device, or perform another action, such as typing an authentication code on a Bluetooth keyboard.

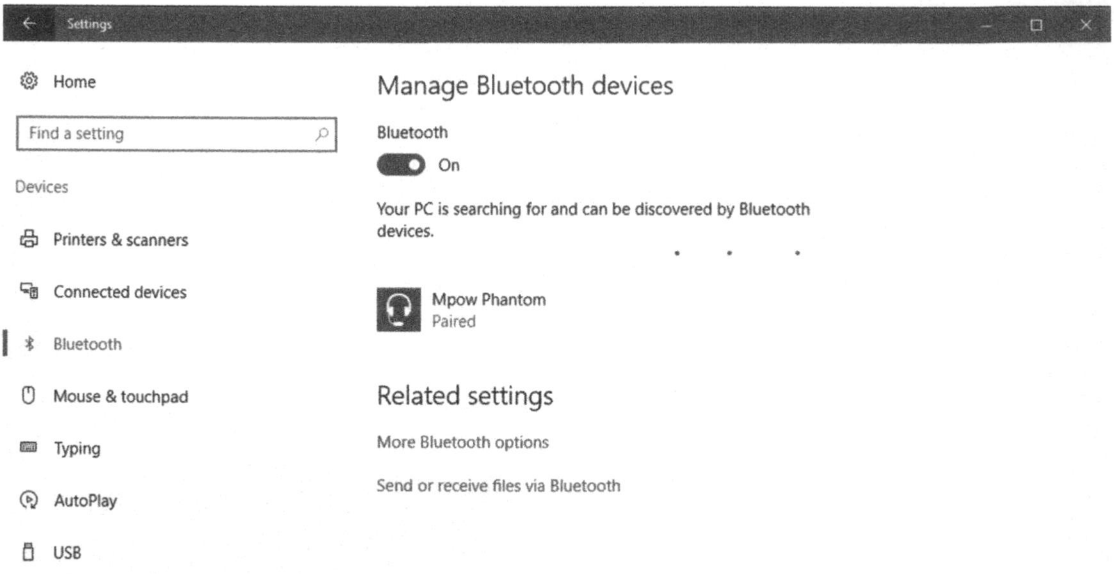

Figure 7-3. *You can add and remove Bluetooth devices in the Settings app*

There are some idiosyncrasies with Bluetooth devices, however. Perhaps the most annoying is that Windows 10 PCs won't connect to more than one Bluetooth audio device. This means if you have both Bluetooth speakers and headphones, you'll need to either choose which one you want to use, or uninstall one before installing the other.

Additionally, some Bluetooth devices don't like being removed (uninstalled) and can sit in the Settings app, trying to uninstall when actually they're not. To get around this, you can also uninstall Bluetooth devices in the *Devices and Printers* panel by right-clicking them, see Figure 7-4.

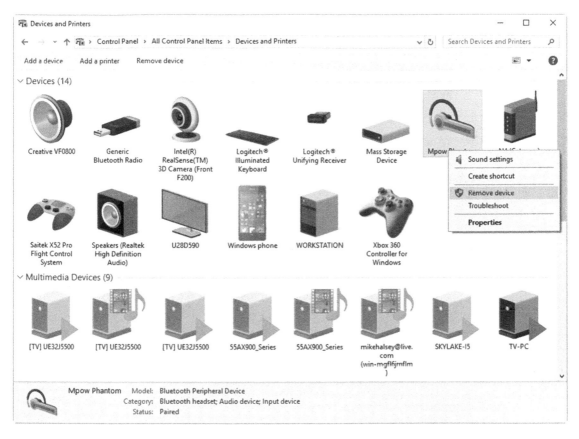

Figure 7-4. *Bluetooth devices can be removed in the Devices and Printers panel*

Sometimes you might find that a PC isn't identifying Bluetooth devices at all. In this circumstance, discoverability for Bluetooth devices might have been disabled. In the Bluetooth section of the Settings app, click *More Bluetooth Options* (note you can also right-click the Bluetooth icon in your system tray and click *Open Settings*). Here are several options which include your PC being discoverable by Bluetooth devices, and whether you are alerted when a Bluetooth device wishes to connect to the PC, see Figure 7-5.

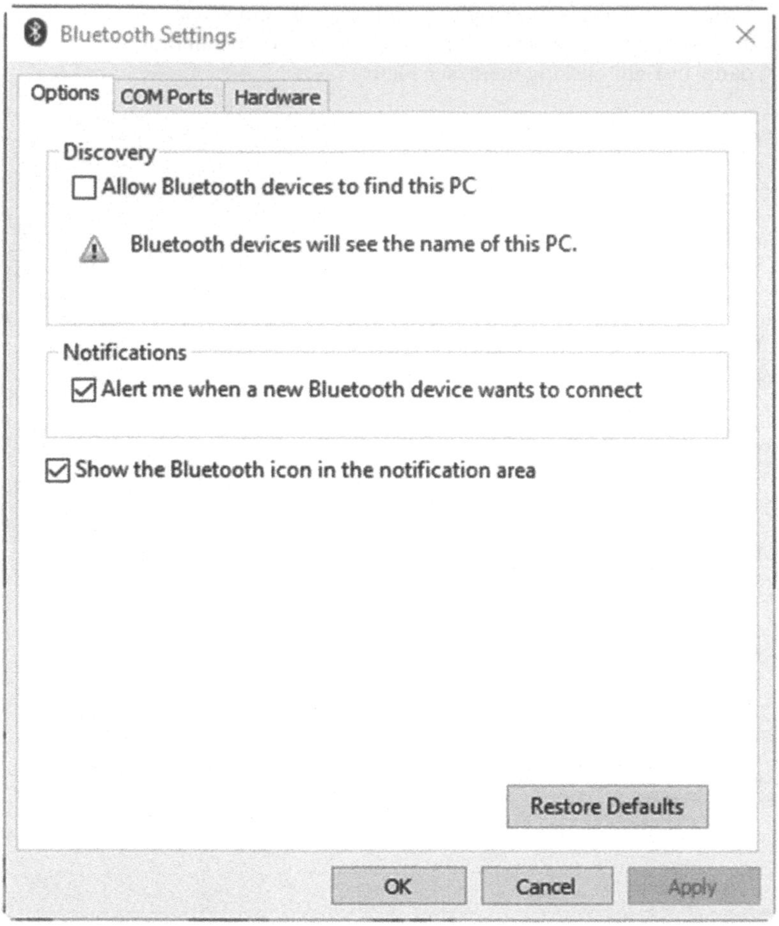

Figure 7-5. *Bluetooth settings that can affect device discoverability are available*

Additionally, the *Hardware* tab in this dialog will provide quick links to your Bluetooth hardware devices, which can be useful if a device is incorrectly installed or configured, or a driver update needs to be applied.

Installing and Configuring Printers

What type of printer do you or your business use? A USB printer? A Wi-Fi printer? A network printer? Perhaps you use a printer that connects via NFC or that uses Wi-Fi Direct to create its own ad hoc wireless network. You might even be using an older Serial or Parallel printer for bespoke applications such as payroll. In short, there are more ways to connect printers to a PC than for any other type of device.

When it comes to configuring printers there are also a plethora of options. You might want to reduce your costs by restricting printing to black ink only, or to enforce duplexing (double-sided) printing. You might want to restrict the hours during which the printer will be available, or enforce security policies on what people can print.

This all means that printers can sometimes be difficult to troubleshoot when something goes wrong, so getting them set up correctly to begin with is the best way to help avoid problems from occurring.

Installing Different Types of Printer

Whatever type of printer you need to install on a PC, you'll do it from the *Devices and Printers* panel, which can be found on a Start Menu or Cortana search, or within the Control Panel. At the top left of this panel are two quick links to *Add a device* (which can include Bluetooth and other devices that aren't automatically detected by Windows), and *Add a printer*. Clicking this second link will start Windows 10 searching for any available printers either attached to your PC, on your local network, or that have set up their own ad hoc network, see Figure 7-6.

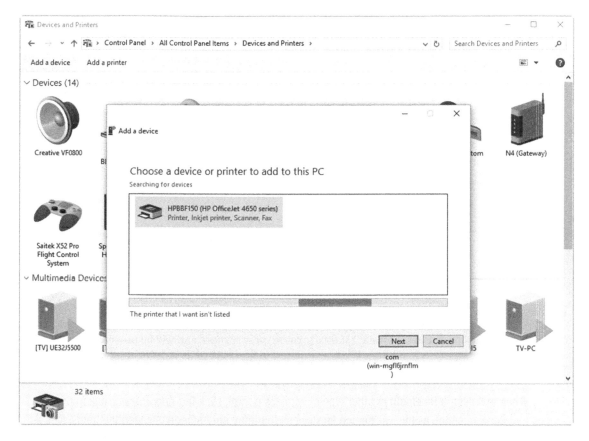

Figure 7-6. *Click Add a printer in the Devices and Printers panel to install new printer*

If your printer isn't discovered however, click the link *The printer I want isn't listed*. This will open a dialog, see Figure 7-7, in which you can install many different type of undiscoverable printer.

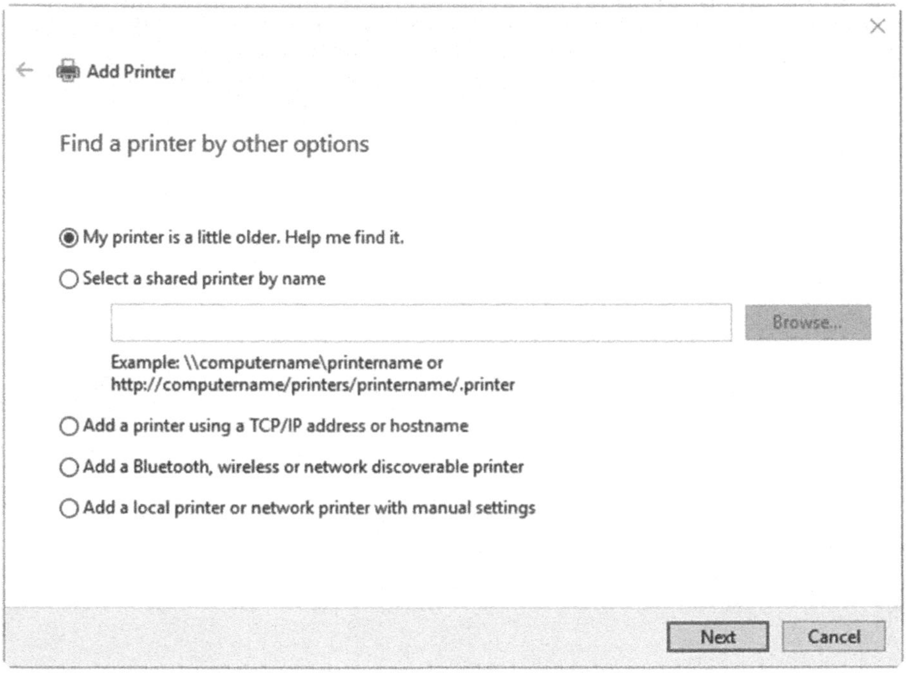

Figure 7-7. *Windows 10 makes it easy to install network and undiscoverable printers*

If you are installing a network printer, there are two ways to do this. The first is to type the network name of the printer; this will come in the format \\computername\printername and will be provided by your IT administrator, or by typing its IP address. I'll show you how to find both of these from another PC shortly.

■ **Tip**   When installing a Bluetooth or other type of wireless printer, click the *Add a device* link in the Devices and Printers panel, as this will search for devices that may not immediately identify themselves as printers, and it is also the utility that the *Add a Bluetooth, wireless or network discoverable printer* option will launch anyway.

If you are installing a Serial or Parallel printer, which cannot be automatically detected by your PC, choose the *Add a local printer or network printer with manual settings* option. This will ask you which port on the PC the printer is attached to, see Figure 7-8. You can also create a new port if you are using software emulation for ports, and have connected the device though a USB adapter.

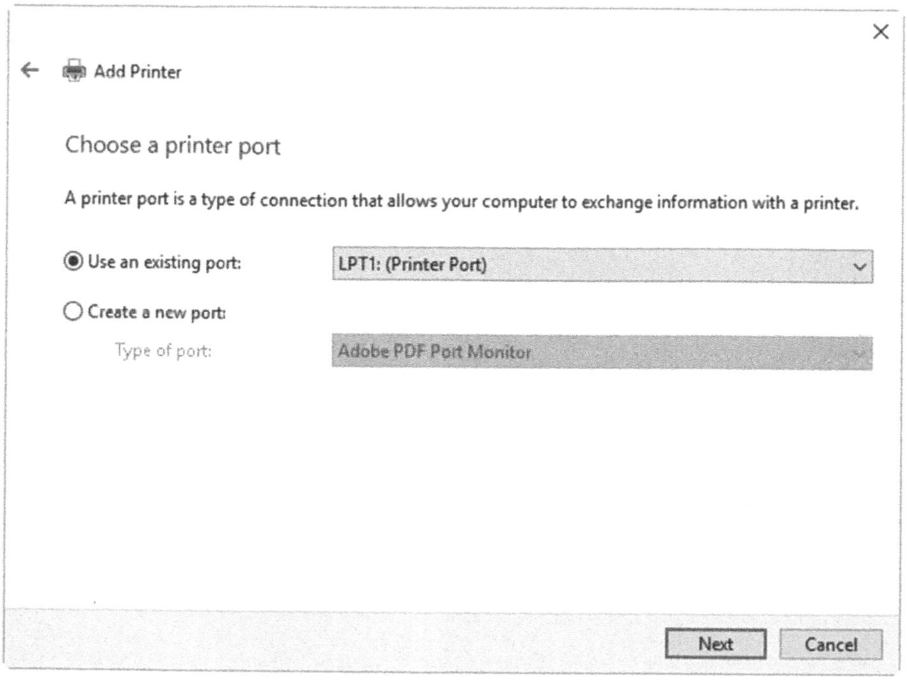

Figure 7-8. *You can manually add Serial and Parallel printers*

If you are unsure what Serial (COM) and Parallel (LPT) ports are available on your PC, open Device Manager from the Win+X menu and expand the *Ports* section, see Figure 7-9. This lists all of the ports installed on the PC with their COM and LPT number assignments.

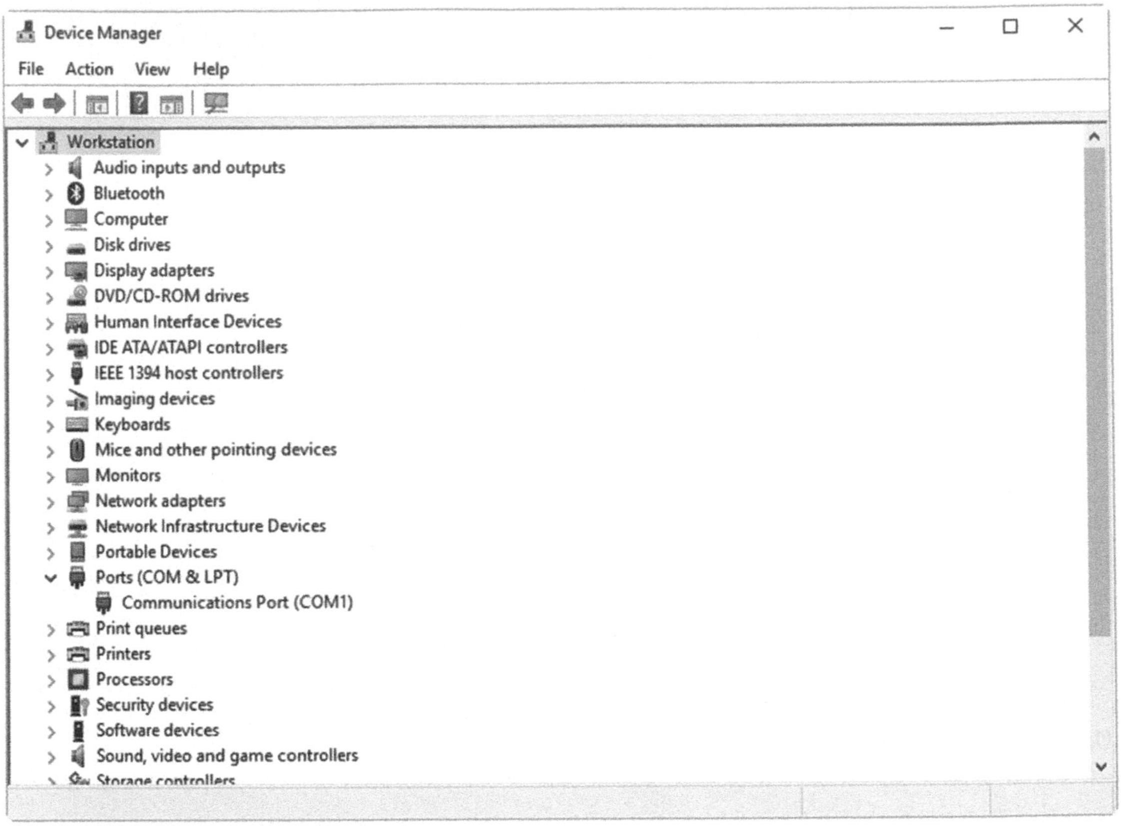

Figure 7-9. *Device Manager lists all the legacy ports installed on a PC*

When you click *Next*, you will be asked to install the driver for the printer. Windows will present a list of all the available drivers (those that ship with Windows or have previously been installed) by manufacturer and model, see Figure 7-10. If you want to install a specific driver from a CD, USB Flash Drive, or floppy disk (remember we're talking about legacy hardware here), click the *Have Disk* button.

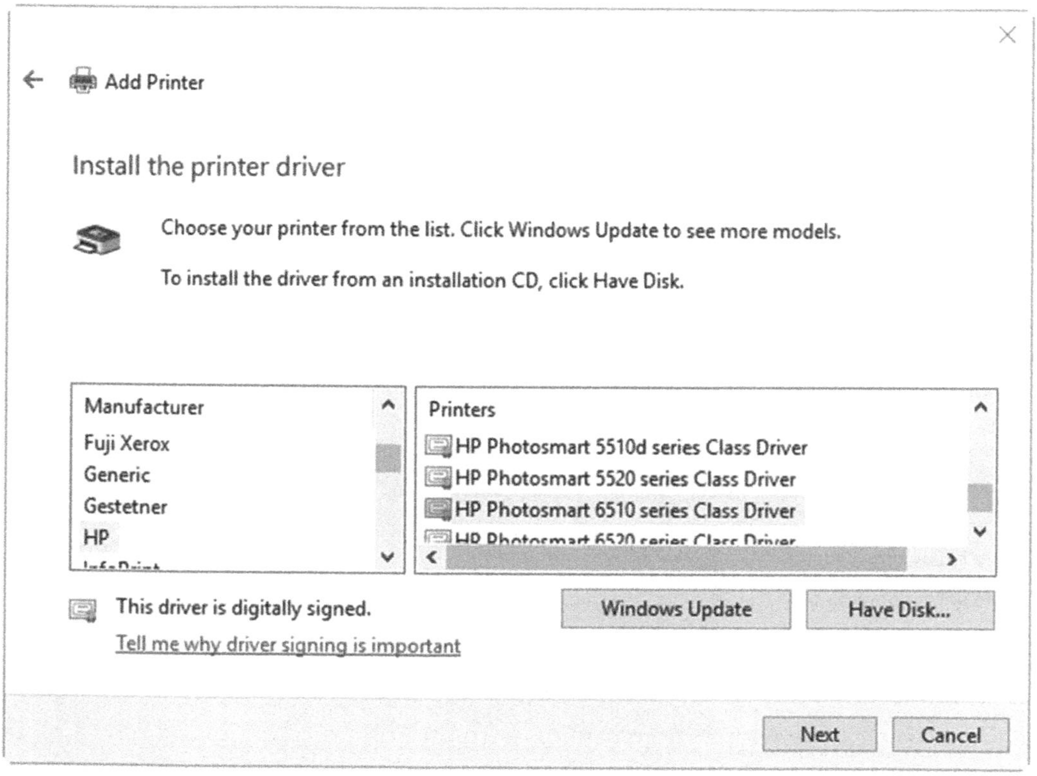

Figure 7-10. You can manually install the driver for a legacy printer

Finding the Name or IP Address of a Printer

I mentioned earlier that if you install a network printer you will need its address and name on the network, or its IP address. Both of these can be obtained from a PC on which the printer is already installed, and looking them up can save a call to IT Support. Let's look at the latter of these first. In the Devices and Printers panel on the PC on which the printer is already installed, right-click the printer and select *Printer Properties* from the menu that appears. In the dialog that opens, click the Ports tab and find your printer in the list, see Figure 7-11.

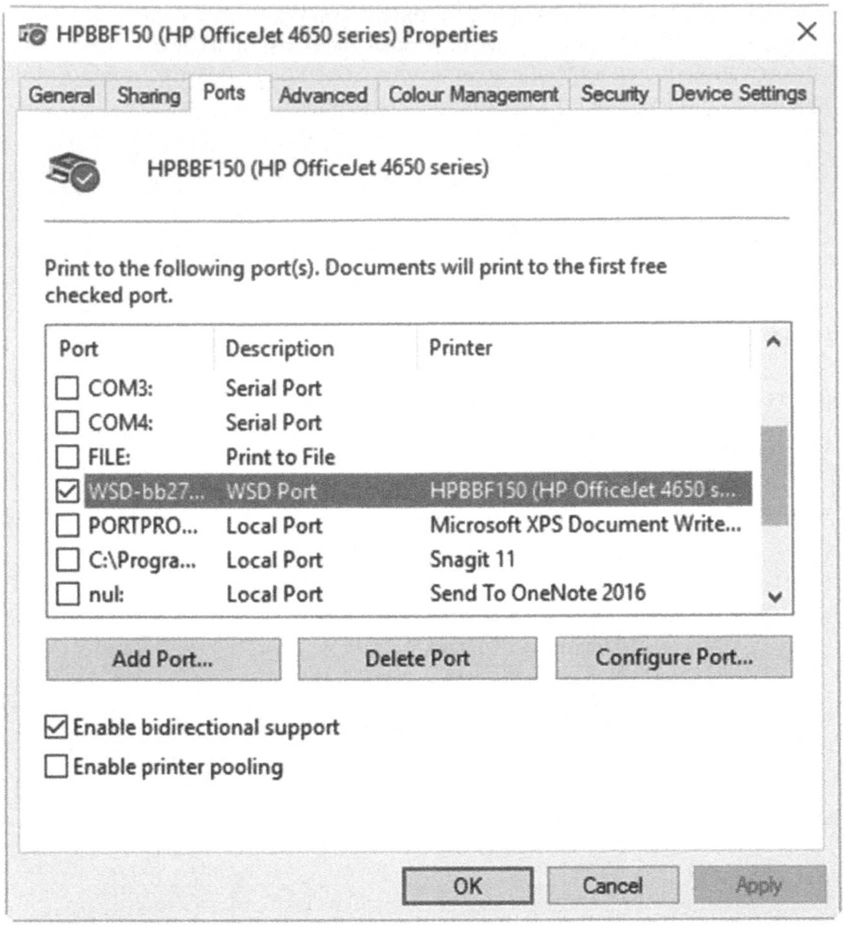

Figure 7-11. *You can often discover the IP address of a printer in its properties dialog*

While this is a good way to reveal the IP addresses of printers in a typical workplace, it doesn't always reveal the information you need. For example, in Figure 7-11 the printer is listed as being on a WSD Port. This stands for *Web Services for Devices*, and these are devices that include Internet functionality, such as being able to print to the printer from anywhere in the world via an app or special e-mail address.

There are a couple of additional ways to get access to a printer's IP address however, though you may not have access to both. The first is to check the IP address in the connected devices page in your home or office router, see Figure 7-12.

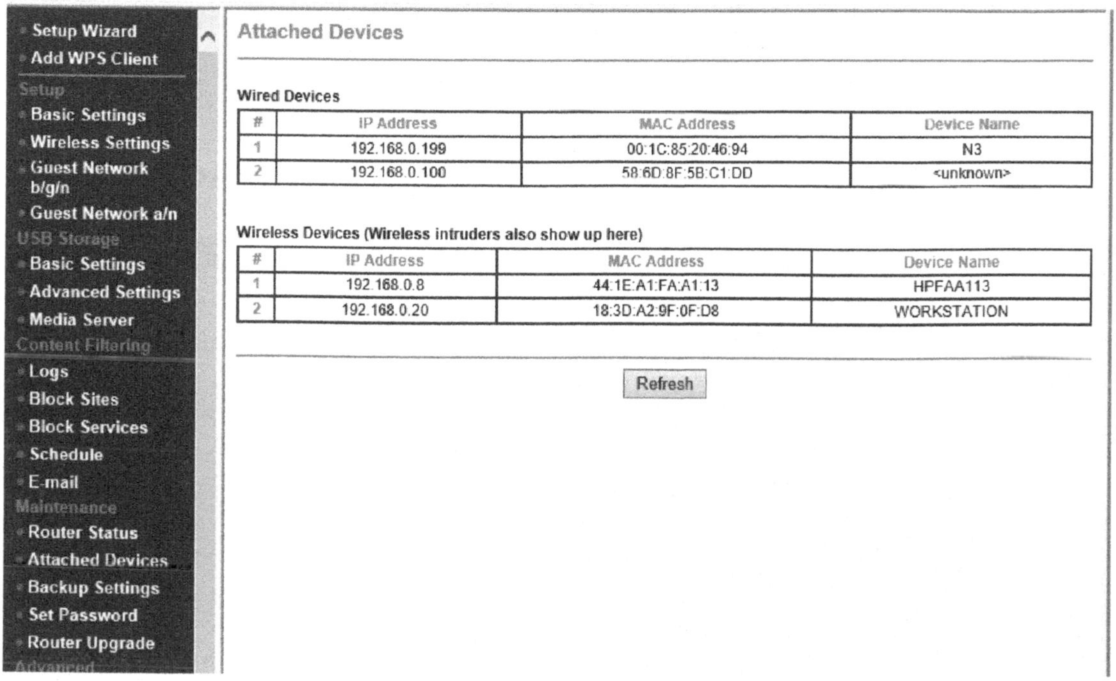

Setup Wizard	**Attached Devices**

Wired Devices

#	IP Address	MAC Address	Device Name
1	192.168.0.199	00:1C:85:20:46:94	N3
2	192.168.0.100	58:6D:8F:5B:C1:DD	<unknown>

Wireless Devices (Wireless intruders also show up here)

#	IP Address	MAC Address	Device Name
1	192.168.0.8	44:1E:A1:FA:A1:13	HPFAA113
2	192.168.0.20	18:3D:A2:9F:0F:D8	WORKSTATION

Refresh

Left navigation menu:
- Setup Wizard
- Add WPS Client
- Setup
- Basic Settings
- Wireless Settings
- Guest Network b/g/n
- Guest Network a/n
- USB Storage
- Basic Settings
- Advanced Settings
- Media Server
- Content Filtering
- Logs
- Block Sites
- Block Services
- Schedule
- E-mail
- Maintenance
- Router Status
- Attached Devices
- Backup Settings
- Set Password
- Router Upgrade
- Advanced

Figure 7-12. *You can check the local IP addresses of devices in your router*

Additionally, and this isn't the case for all printers, click the *Network* link in File Explorer and right-click the network printer. You may see an option such as View device web page, see Figure 7-13, which can open a browser page with status information about the printer itself.

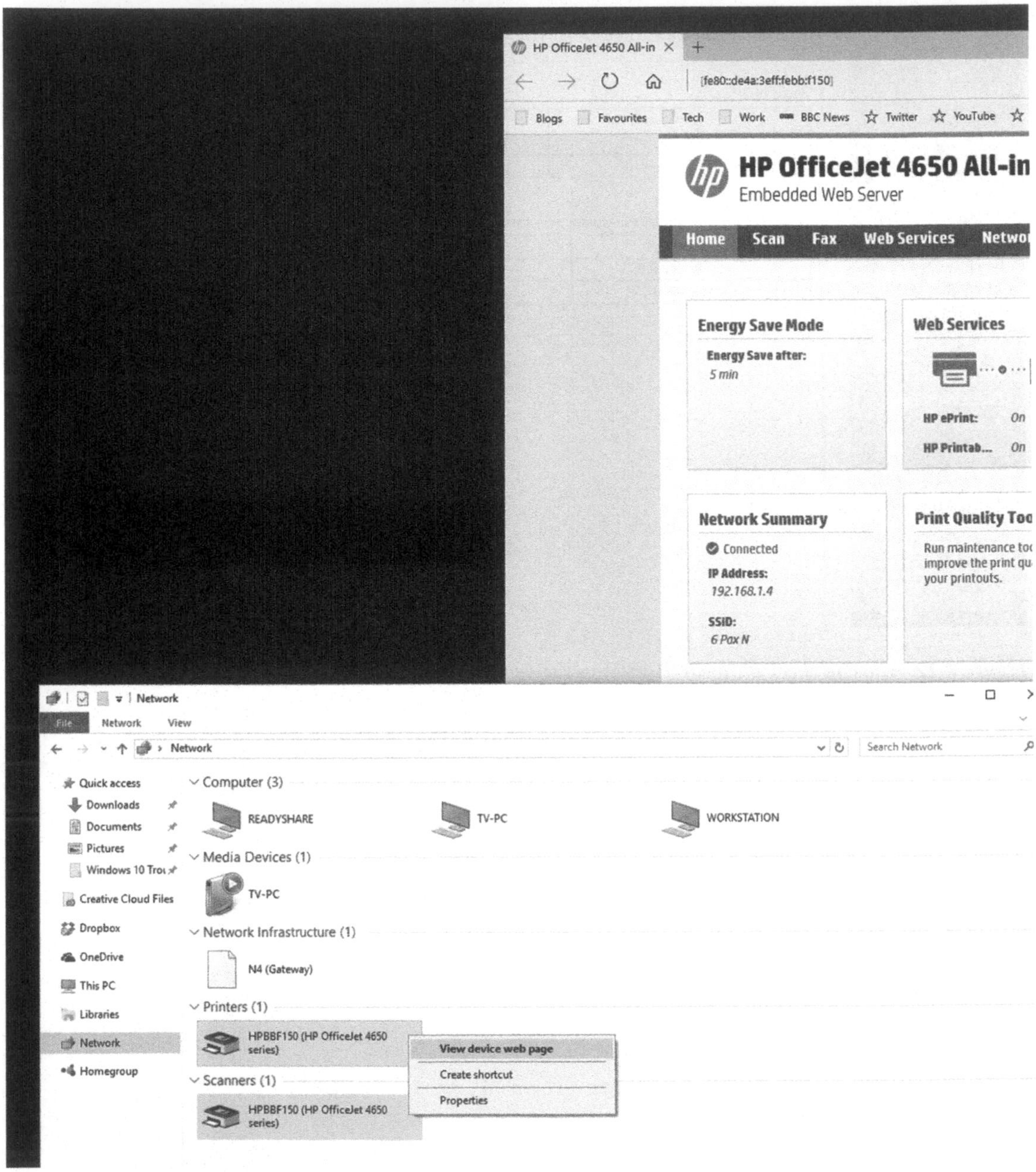

Figure 7-13. *Some printers offer web status pages*

You can also check the *Properties* of the printer with a right-click, which will sometimes reveal its IP address, see Figure 7-14.

Figure 7-14. *Checking the properties of a network printer can sometimes reveal its IP address*

If the printer is shared from a specific PC, there are two places you will need to go to find the information you need, both of which you will need to get from the host PC. The first of these is the computer name. Open *System* from either the Control Panel or the Settings app (you will then need to click *About* in the latter) to reveal the PC name, see Figure 7-15.

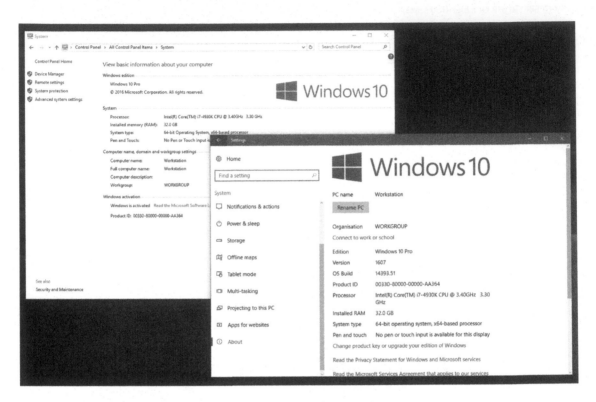

Figure 7-15. *You will need the name of the host PC to install a shared printer*

Next, in the Devices and Printers panel on the host PC, right-click the printer and open the Printer Properties panel. Click the Sharing tab and make a note of the printer name, see Figure 7-16

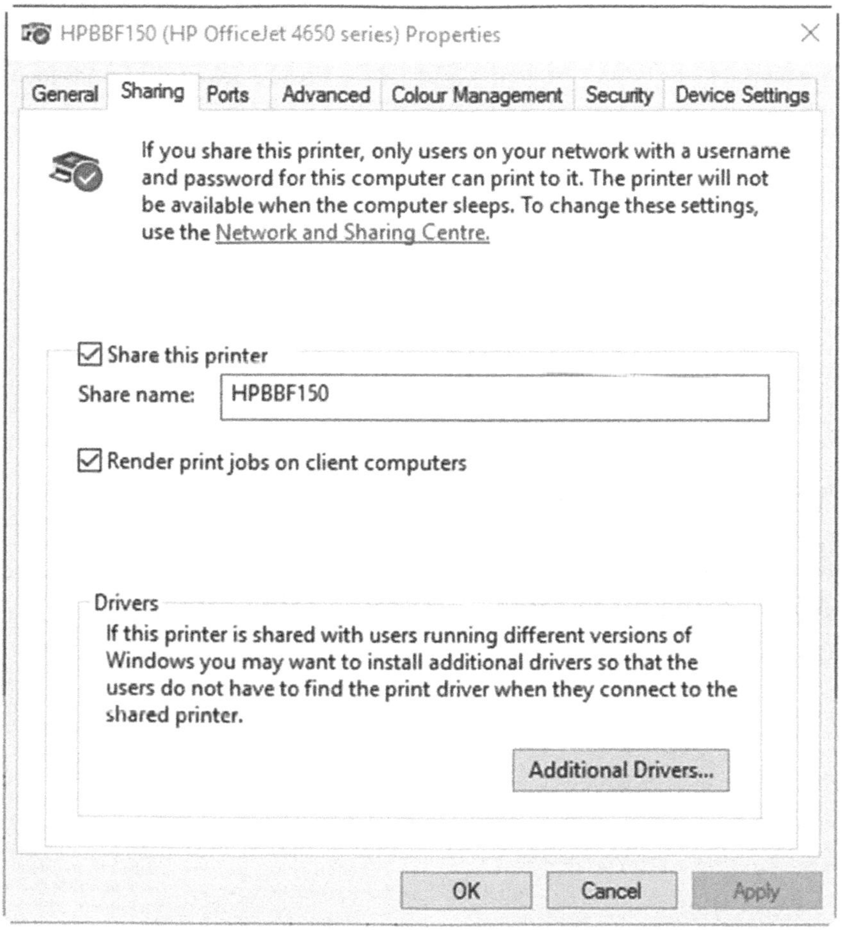

Figure 7-16. You will also need the shared printer name from the host PC

In this example, then, we see that the network address for the printer is \\Workstation\HPBBF150.

■ **Note**　In the Sharing tab of the printer properties on the host PC, you might find it useful to click the Additional Drivers button. The host PC can provide the drivers for the printer automatically to other PCs, but it does not automatically provide both the 32-bit (x86) and 64-bit (x64) drivers. Checking both options can help make sure all Windows 10 devices can easily connect to the printer.

Managing Printing Policies

While not specifically a Windows Troubleshooting issue, you might find that people call you on occasion to complain that they simply can't print the documents they need to. This might be because the printing and security policies set up on the printer are prohibiting their access, so I'd like to spend a short period looking at what these are, and how they are configured.

Policies for printers are managed in the Printer Properties dialog we've already looked at. The Advanced tab contains the first set of policies that can affect users' use of a shared printer, see Figure 7-17.

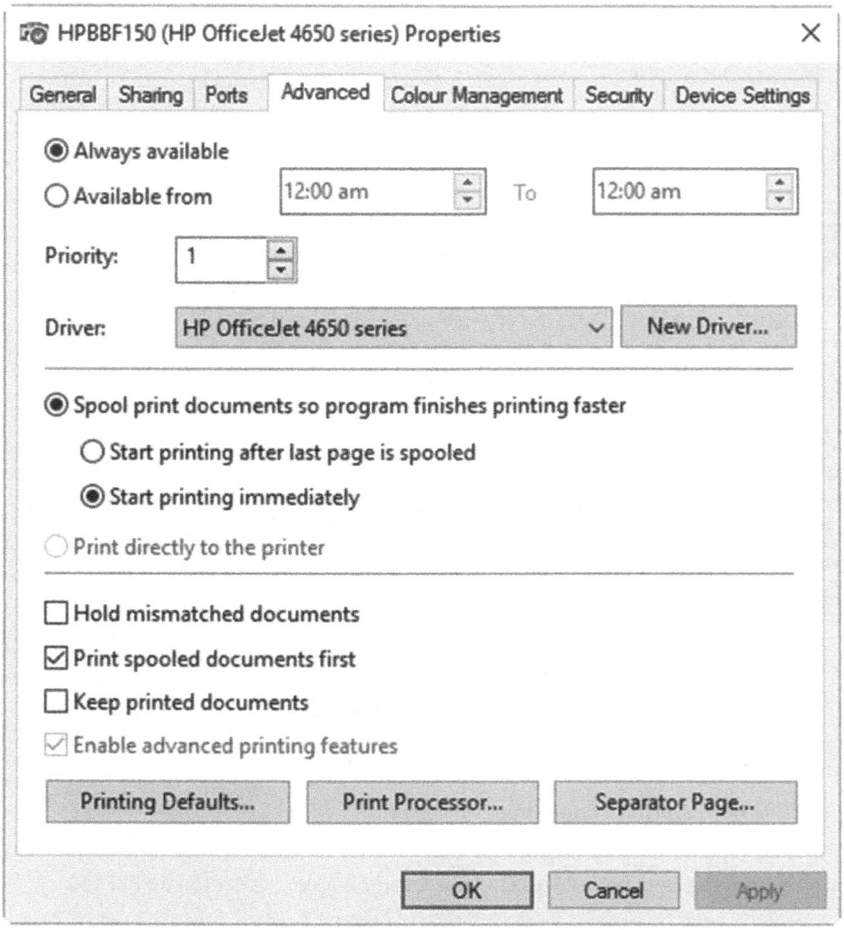

Figure 7-17. *You can set many different policies for a shared printer*

The options available to set for a shared printer (or even the printer connected locally to the PC) include being able to set times of the day when the printer can be used (useful if a teenager at home is fond of printing photos of their favorite pop idol at three in the morning).

At the bottom left of this dialog is a *Printing defaults* button. Click this for control over how and what inks or toner the printer will use when a job is sent to the device. You might want to specify, for example, that all printing should be duplex and only be in black and white, which can save large amounts of money. Should somebody want to print in color, or single-sided, they will then need to manually change the print settings each time they wish to use those different settings.

Should a printer (or the PC) be used for color-sensitive work, such as photo or video editing, clicking the *Color Management* tab will allow you to load and customize individual color profiles for the printer, and for your PC's monitor.

If users are unable to print, this might also be down to them not having access to that specific printer. Access permissions can be managed in the *Security* tab, where you can specify individual or groups of users who can print to, and manage both the print queue and the printer settings itself, see Figure 7-18. This can be useful if you do not want users to be able to change your duplex, black-and-white-only policy back to single-sided and color.

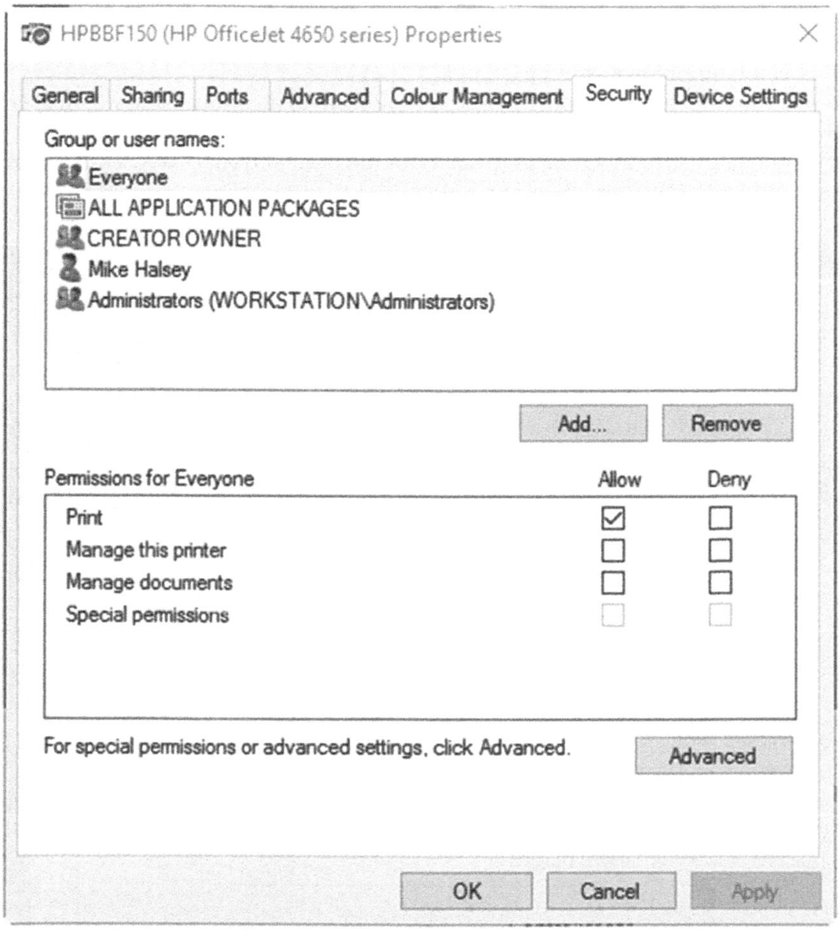

Figure 7-18. You can manage access permissions for individual printers

Have You Tried [Not] Turning It Off and On Again?

So what happens when you can't connect to a printer, or you send a print job and nothing appears at the other end? Normally the response in this scenario is to turn it off and on again. (I can't believe I got all the way to Chapter 7 before saying that!) This isn't always the best approach to take with printers, however, for several reasons.

- Other people might also be using the printer, and you can interfere with their print jobs, which are very likely to be far more important than your own

- Restarting a printer might not clear the print queue, which is managed by each PC connected to the printer

133

So if it's not the best solution to restart the printer if you can't connect to it, or print to it, what do you do? Well, if you're in a home environment let's start by saying you're probably completely fine to turn the printer off and restart it. This can often make the printer spring back into life on a network, though any jobs already sent to it by the PC will be lost. It's not uncommon, especially with Wi-Fi–connected printers?, that you might need to uninstall and reinstall the printer on a PC. This could be for several reasons, such as that the port assignment has become confused or a conflict with another device is confusing the operating system.

Right-clicking the printer in the Devices and Printers panel and clicking *See what's printing* (or double-clicking the printer icon that will appear in the System Tray when a job is sent to the printer) will reveal the printer queue. This is a great way to determine if the user has actually sent the job to the correct printer, which is a **very** common cause of printing failures!

In the print queue window, you will see a complete list of all the jobs sent to the printer, and which user or PC has sent them. Double-clicking a job will open a properties dialog for that job, see Figure 7-19. Here you can manage additional functionality such as setting the priority for the print job (effectively sending it to the top of the queue). You can also see if time restrictions are in effect.

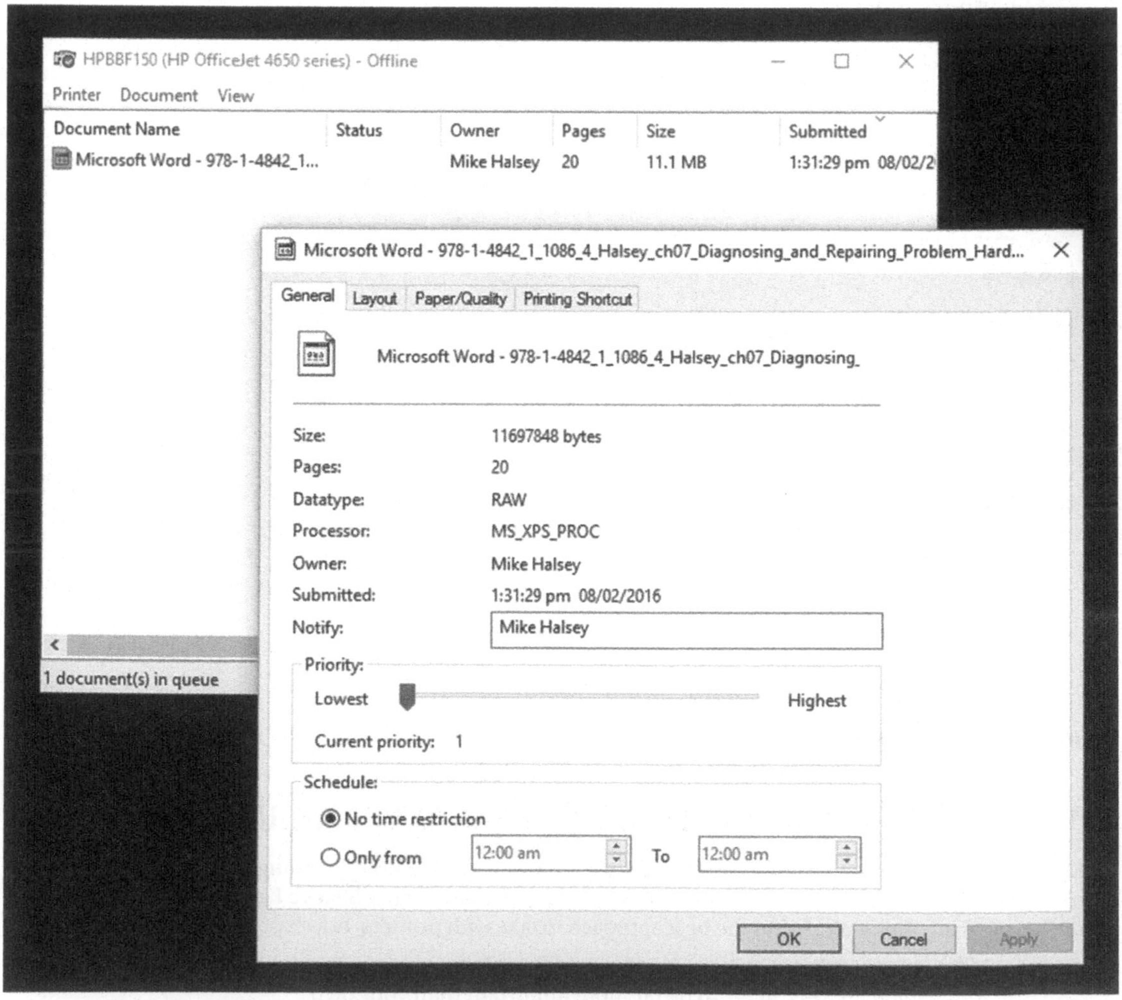

Figure 7-19. You can set print priority and manage other settings from the Print Queue window

If print jobs are snarled up, you can cancel individual jobs by right-clicking them and selecting *Cancel* from the options that appear. Additionally, the Printer menu offers the option to cancel all jobs for the printer simultaneously, see Figure 7-20. It's worth noting, however, that with some badly snarled print queues a restart of both the printer, and the PC that sent the job, might also be necessary?.

■ **Tip** Another way to fix a snarled print queue is to restart the *Print Spooler* service, in the Services panel. I will show you how to do this in Chapter 19.

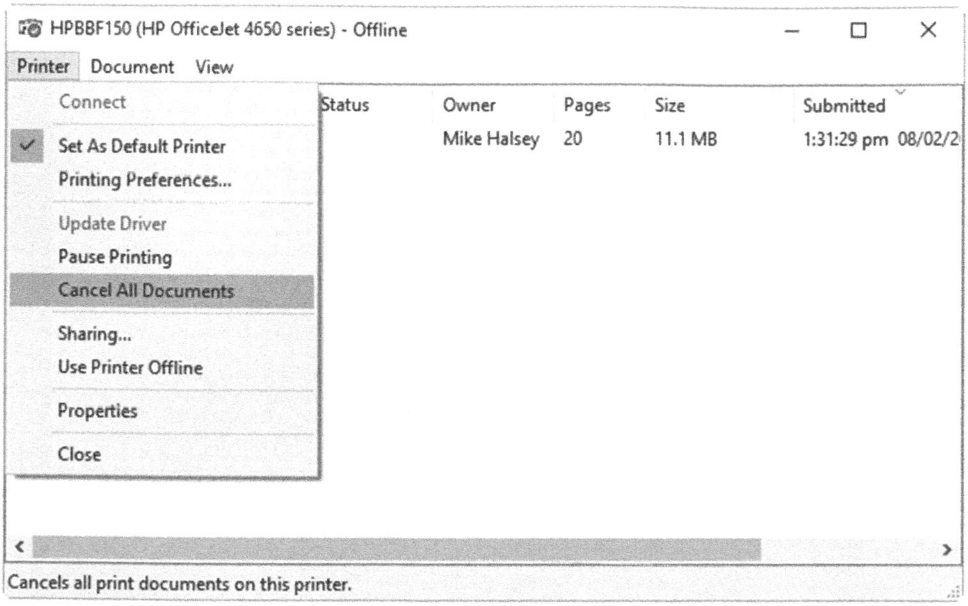

Figure 7-20. *You can completely clear the print queue from the Printer menu*

■ **Tip** Printers contain more moving parts than any other component in an office environment, and as such there's much that can go wrong with rollers and other paper-feed mechanisms. However, should your printing come out blurry or distorted, there will be an option in the printer's own options (you should refer to the printer manual to find exactly where) to clean the print heads or to also realign the heads. Performing these actions can fix some issues with poor-quality output.

Summary

Good management of devices is crucial to making sure that problems don't occur and, as printers are the most used accessory in any home or office environment, good setup and management of a printer can make the difference between a quiet day for a support technician and a very difficult one.

While we're on the subject of having a difficult day, however, nothing can be more bothersome for a user or IT Pro than a PC that fails to start at all, so in the next chapter I'll show you how to fix common startup problems, and use Windows 10's inbuilt tools to get a PC booting to the desktop.

CHAPTER 8

■ ■ ■

Troubleshooting Startup

Nothing is more annoying than a PC that won't boot to the desktop, so knowing how to get a Windows 10 installation working again quickly is a skill every IT technician and professional should know. In Chapter 13, I'll show you how to get inside the Windows 10 boot system and effect manual repairs for the worst scenarios, but as expediency is always the order of the day when it comes to diagnosing and repairing PC problems, I want to start with the things you can do to get Windows booting again quickly.

Have You Tried Turning It Off and On Again?

In order to be able to quickly repair startup problems in Windows 10, it's useful to understand what issues can affect startup, and what the common problems are that occur. There aren't actually too many things that can affect startup, but knowing what's happened can often help quick diagnosis and guide you toward the correct repair method.

- **Improper Shutdown** is by far one of the most common causes of Windows being unable to boot. This can occur either by the user switching the PC off improperly (pressing and holding the power button for four seconds, or switching the PC off by pulling the power cord out of the wall). However, it can also be caused by a power outage, and in some parts of the world these can be quite common. Improper shutdown can corrupt some of the startup files, or perhaps corrupt the startup partition. In this case the more advanced methods detailed in Chapter 13 might be needed if the methods detailed in this chapter don't help.

- **Botched Driver or Update Installation** is another common reason for a PC failing to start. This can include Windows Updates and hardware driver installs and updates. It's worth noting that graphics drivers can be particularly prone to this problem, as they are embedded deep into the OS. These problems can be repaired from the System Rescue Options menu.

- **BIOS or Firmware Update** is something I'll mention even though it's not strictly a Windows startup problem. I detailed how to repair a BIOS or UEFI firmware system in Chapter 6.

■ **Note**   With Microsoft's Surface range of laptops and tablets, many driver updates are named as firmware updates. They're really not; instead, they're motherboard or graphics drivers. This means that if a "firmware update" with a Surface device results in Windows 10 being unable to boot, a System Restore can still often fix the problem.

© Mike Halsey 2016
M. Halsey, *Windows 10 Troubleshooting*, DOI 10.1007/978-1-4842-0925-7_8

- **Hardware Change or Update** can also cause Windows 10 to not start. Perhaps a component has failed (such as the motherboard) and been replaced. With some hardware in the PC (memory, CPU, hard disk) you can swap them out and restart the PC with ease. Motherboards are different, however, and unless you have an identical model, you might be faced with reinstalling Windows 10 from a format due to the way drivers are embedded into the OS. Additionally, adding or changing hard disks in a PC can swap their drive assignments on the motherboard (Drive 0, Drive 1, etc.) and this can result in the PC attempting to load Windows from the wrong drive. Swapping the drive data cables can often fix this problem.

There are ways that can common startup problems can easily be fixed, not the least of which is just turning the device off and on again (yup, that old trick). Additional quick methods exist, however, to help you get up and running quickly.

- **Undoing whatever it is you just did** is usually a good way to get the PC working again, and will normally occur if you have changed the hardware in some way. Perhaps you've installed a new piece, or changed a piece of hardware. Changing things back to the way they were before will often get the PC working again, and give you time to diagnose what caused the problem.

- **Booting with or without the power lead** on a laptop or tablet can solve some startup problems. It might be that a PC is unable to start because it's just not got enough power to get it going. Alternatively, it might be that on a laptop or tablet, a fault with the power brick or the power plug is causing interference that is preventing startup from occurring.

- **Using a minimal boot configuration** can often help too, and can help you diagnose the real cause of the problem. Unplugging all unnecessary cables and devices (network, USB, etc.) and starting the PC without them can sometimes rectify the problem. It's not uncommon for a PC to hang at startup because of a glitch with the network cable or signal. In these cases, unplugging the network cable results in the PC being able to continue booting.

Using Startup Repair

If Windows 10 fails to start correctly two or three times, then the automated Startup Repair system will be invoked. This works by resetting startup components in the OS to their default state, and this can fix some of the easier-to-diagnose and most common startup problems with the OS.

You can run Startup Repair manually from a System Recovery Drive or from Windows 10 installation media by opening the System Recovery menu (Click *Repair your Computer* at the Setup screen if starting from installation media) and then clicking *Troubleshoot* and *Advanced Options*. You will see *Start-up Repair* listed at the next screen, see Figure 8-1.

■ **Note**   If an Administrator password is set on the PC, this will be necessary when performing many tasks within the Recovery Environment.

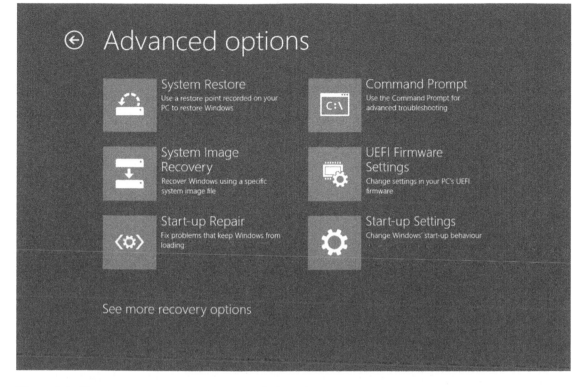

Figure 8-1. *You can run Startup Repair manually from the Recovery Options*

You may be asked for the administrator password and your Bitlocker recovery key if your drive is encrypted. If Startup Repair is able to fix the problem, it'll do so and you'll be asked to restart the PC. If it isn't though, perhaps because it's unable to identify the problem, then you'll be prompted and given the details of the log file it created during the repair process, see Figure 8-2.

Figure 8-2. *You will be shown the location and name of the repair log file if Startup Repair cannot fix the problem*

Clicking *Advanced Options* at this point will return you to the Recovery Options menu, where other repair options are available to you. If you open the log file, you'll be shown details of all the tests performed by Startup Repair, with any errors discovered detailed, see Figure 8-3. You can use this information to help diagnose and get to the root cause of the problem.

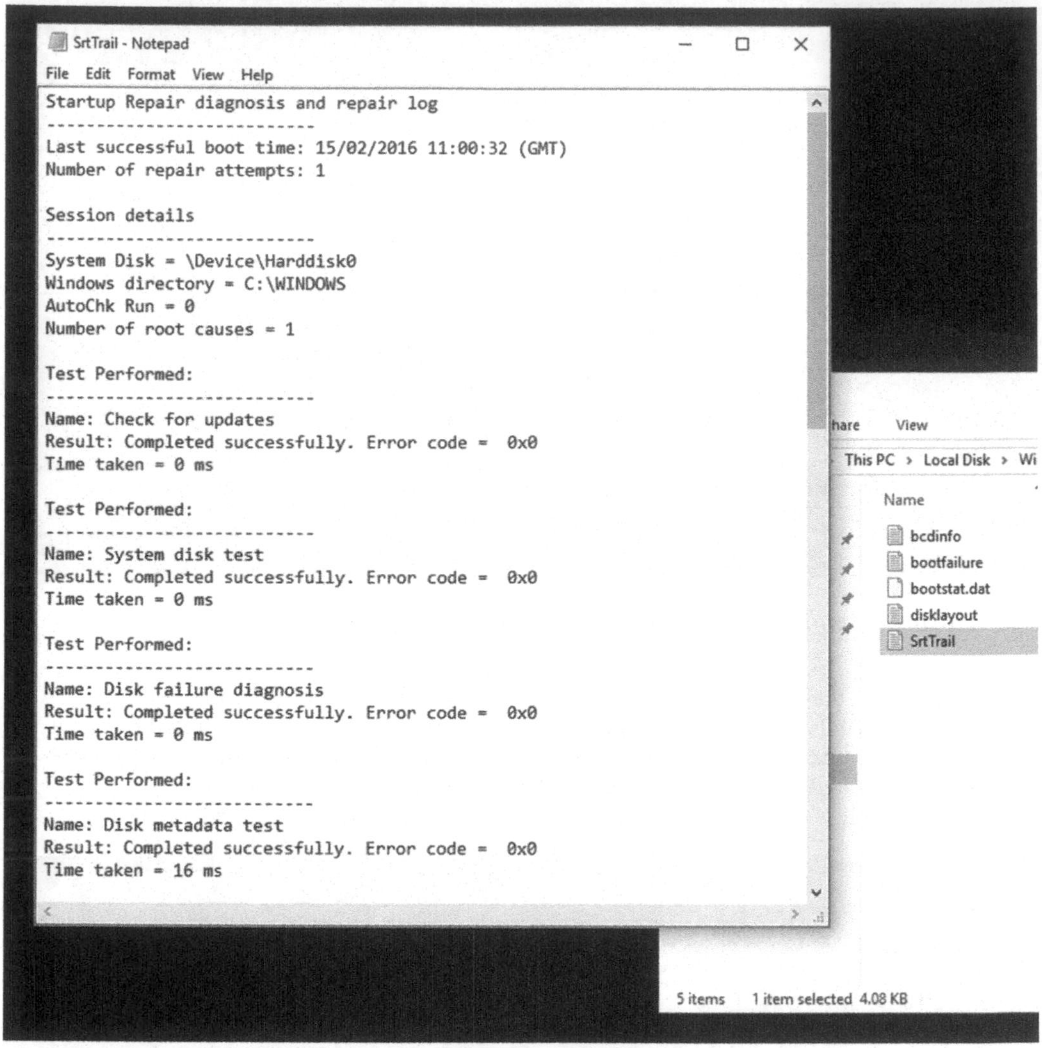

Figure 8-3. *The repair log file contains details of all the tests performed*

To open these log files from the Recovery Options menu, click *Troubleshoot*, then *Advanced Options*, and open the *Command Prompt*. When the Command Prompt is open, type **Notepad** and press Enter to open the text file reader/editor app. In this you can open the log file, see Figure 8-4. Note that you will by default be in a \Windows\System32 folder but you will be on an X: (boot) drive, which is actually a hidden boot partition. You will need to navigate to the drive on which you have Windows installed (usually the C: drive) to see the log files.

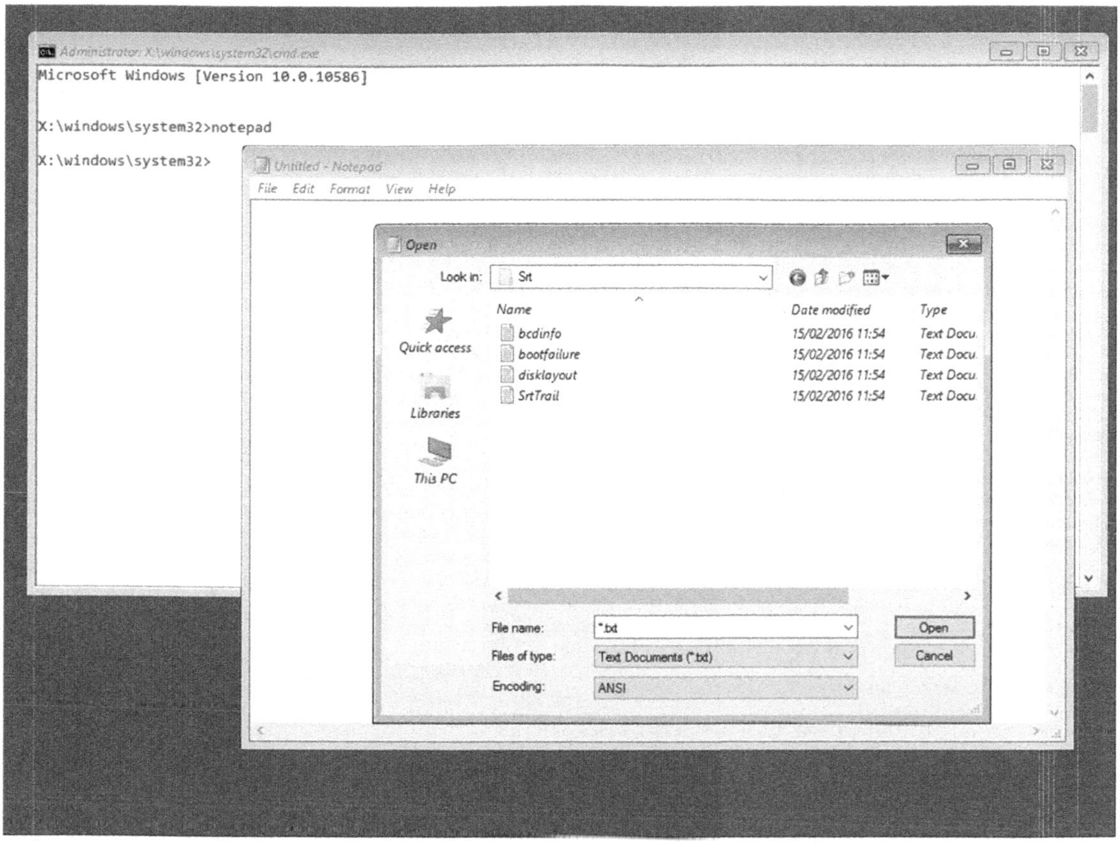

Figure 8-4. *You can open and read log files from the Recovery Environment*

Also in this *Logfiles* folder you will see a **bcdinfo** file. This will provide details of the boot setup for Windows 10 and it can be worth checking, see Figure 8-5.

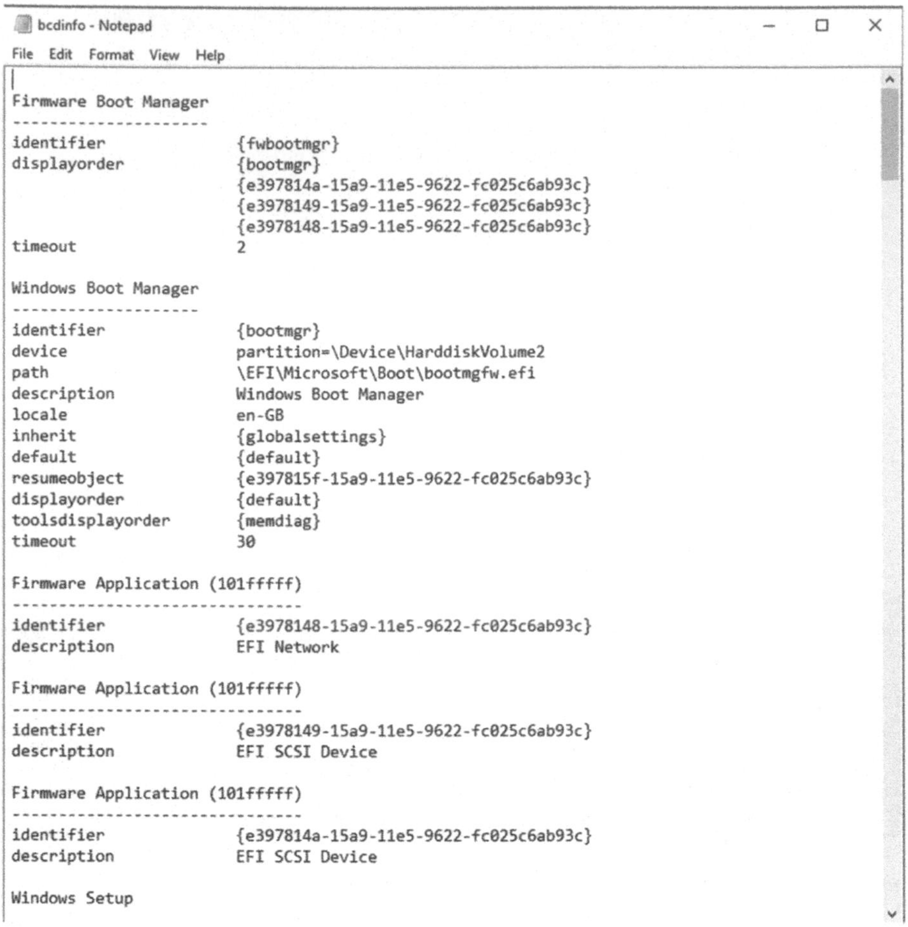


```
Firmware Boot Manager
---------------------
identifier              {fwbootmgr}
displayorder            {bootmgr}
                        {e397814a-15a9-11e5-9622-fc025c6ab93c}
                        {e3978149-15a9-11e5-9622-fc025c6ab93c}
                        {e3978148-15a9-11e5-9622-fc025c6ab93c}
timeout                 2

Windows Boot Manager
--------------------
identifier              {bootmgr}
device                  partition=\Device\HarddiskVolume2
path                    \EFI\Microsoft\Boot\bootmgfw.efi
description             Windows Boot Manager
locale                  en-GB
inherit                 {globalsettings}
default                 {default}
resumeobject            {e397815f-15a9-11e5-9622-fc025c6ab93c}
displayorder            {default}
toolsdisplayorder       {memdiag}
timeout                 30

Firmware Application (101fffff)
-------------------------------
identifier              {e3978148-15a9-11e5-9622-fc025c6ab93c}
description             EFI Network

Firmware Application (101fffff)
-------------------------------
identifier              {e3978149-15a9-11e5-9622-fc025c6ab93c}
description             EFI SCSI Device

Firmware Application (101fffff)
-------------------------------
identifier              {e397814a-15a9-11e5-9622-fc025c6ab93c}
description             EFI SCSI Device

Windows Setup
```

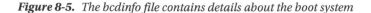

Figure 8-5. *The bcdinfo file contains details about the boot system*

You will see your individual operating systems listed in this file, with Windows 10 listed as *Windows Setup* and *Windows Boot Loader*. Check the driver letter assignments for the OS to see if they are correct. If you need to change these you can use the **BCDEdit** utility, which I will show you how to use in Chapter 13.

The Windows Recovery Options Menu

I've already talked a bit about the Recovery Options menu in this chapter, but I want to show you the other tools available there to help you fix Startup problems in Windows 10 quickly, as there are a few.

As I've already mentioned, there are a few ways to get to this menu, see Figure 8-6. You can start your PC from a USB Recovery Drive, or from Windows 10 installation media (where you'll need to select *Repair your computer* at the installation screen), and Windows 10 will try to load this automatically if it cannot start two or three times.

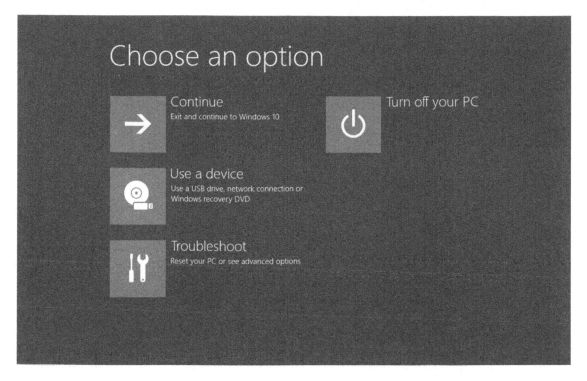

Figure 8-6. The Recovery Options menu in Windows 10 contains many useful tools

It's in the *Troubleshooting* ➤ *Advanced Options* menu that most of the really useful options appear, see Figure 8-7. I want to detail the options that are available here that can help you repair Windows 10 startup quickly.

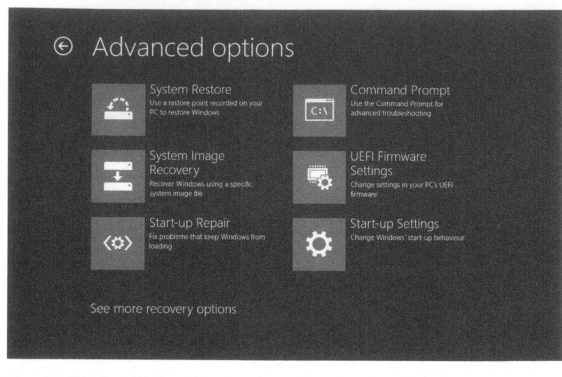

Figure 8-7. *The Advanced Recovery Options are where all the Startup Repair action takes place*

- **System Restore** is most useful if a Windows Update or another installation such as a hardware driver installation has resulted in the PC being unable to start. You can use System Restore to roll the Windows 10 system files back to the point before that installation occurred, whereupon you can install the offending item again, block it, or search for an alternative to install.

- **Command Prompt** is something I'll talk about in more depth shortly.

- **UEFI Firmware Settings** will appear as an option if you are not using the older BIOS firmware system on your motherboard. This is a quick-launch button to open the UEFI settings panel, in which you can check settings such as the disk boot order (which might have become corrupt or altered).

- **Start-up Settings** will open what might be considered a more traditional boot options menu, see Figure 8-8. This includes yet more options.

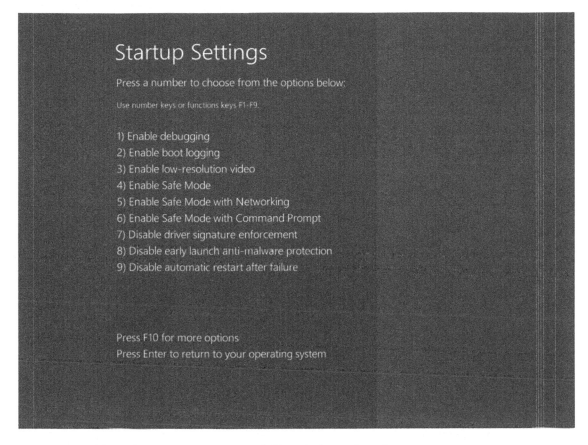

Figure 8-8. *Additional startup settings are available including Safe Mode*

- **Enable Debugging** activates the inbuilt debugger for the Windows kernel (the core OS files). If the PC is connected to another computer running a debugger, this information can be collected by the remote machine for diagnosis. This connection can be made via a null-modem cable, IEEE 1394 (Firewire) cable, or USB. Full details of how to use this feature are available at http://pcs.tv/1XsRKFf.

- **Enable Boot Logging** will start Windows 10 normally, but will create a file called C:\Windows\ntbtlog.txt containing details of all the files and drivers loaded at startup. This file can be accessed using Notepad, either at the desktop or through the Command Prompt, to help you diagnose and repair problems.

- **Enable Low-Resolution Video** will start the PC in an 800- by 600-pixel resolution. It's mostly here for legacy support on older systems, but might prove useful for diagnosing problems with some graphics drivers.

- **Enable Safe Mode / Safe Mode with Networking / Safe Mode with Command Prompt.** I'll detail how to use Safe Mode, which is a reduced-functionality mode, fully in Chapter 19, but it can be a useful environment for uninstalling problematic compoents in Windows 10.

- **Disable Driver Signature Enforcement** will allow unsigned (non-digitally signed) drivers to be loaded at Startup. This can be useful if you are troubleshooting a problem with a driver which has not been submitted to Microsoft's certification process.

- **Disable Early Launch Anti-Malware Protection** can be useful if you suspect it's a problem with your anti-malware software, or an update to that software that's preventing Windows 10 from starting. By default, and for reasons of security, Windows 10 loads your anti-malware software before any other apps. However, if it is causing a problem, start-up can hang at that point unless you select this option to allow the software to start at the same time, and in the same way, as other apps.

- **Disable Automatic Restart After System Failure** can be useful if your PC is displaying a Blue Screen of Death (what I now call the Blue, Unhappy Emoticon of Death) but is restarting automatically before you can read the message. I will detail Blue Screens in more detail in Chapter 11.

Using the Command Prompt to Repair Windows Startup

While it's limited in many ways, and doesn't suport the full range of options available at the desktop, the Command Prompt as run from the Windows Recovery Environment can be a very useful tool for quickly repairing Windows 10 startup problems.

In the Command Prompt here, the following commands are available to you.

- **Attrib** is used to change the permissions (read, write) on files.

- **Bootrec** is a tool I'll detail fully in Chapter 13. It is used to repair the Master Boot Record (MBR) and Boot Configuration Data (BCD) for the PC.

- **Bcdedit** is another tool I will detail in Chapter 13. It is to edit and make changes to the Windows BCD.

- **Cd** is used to change the current directory. You can specify a directory, that is, cd \Windows or go back a folder using cd.

- **Chkdsk** is used to check the hard disk for errors. It is commonly used with the switches /F (fix errors), /R (recovers unreadable information in bad sectors), and /X (forces the colume to dismount if necessary). Additional commands are available and detailed on the /? Switch.

- **Copy** will make a copy of a file in the format Copy C:\Folder1\File.ext C:\Folder2\NewFile.ext.

- **Del** will delete a file.

- **Dir** will list the contents of the current directory or folder.

- **Diskpart** is a tool I'll detail in Chapter 13. It contains powerful disk management and partitioning tools.

- **Icacls** is used to modify file and folder permissions and modify access control lists.

- **Mkdir** is used to create a new folder.

- **More** displays output one screen at a time.

- **Move** can move a file or files from one place to another, and is used with the same syntax as Copy.

- **Ren** is used to rename a file or folder.

- **Rd** can remove an empty folder.

- **Type** displays the contents of a file, such as a log file.

- **Xcopy** is a more advanced version of copy, with more options avaialble.

In addition to these commands, the following apps can be run from the Command Prompt.

- **Notepad**, as I detailed earlier in this chapter, can be used to read log and error files.

- **Regedit** is something I will detail in full in Chapter 19. It is used for making changes to the Windows Registry.

- **Rstrui** is used to start System Restore from the Command Prompt.

Summary

In Chapter 13 I'll detail how you can, if necessary, manually repair the Windows 10 boot system, but the tools and utilities here can help get a nonbooting system working again quickly and in a straightforward manner, and let's be honest, that's what everybody needs when their PC won't start.

Aside from Startup however, there's one other feature of PCs that drives us nuts when it won't work. This is networking. If we can't get access to our network files or (heaven forbid) the Internet, then the world can seem to come crashing down. Needless to say, we'll be covering this in the next chapter.

CHAPTER 9

■ ■ ■

Troubleshooting Networks

Next to being unable to boot a PC to the desktop, by far the most irritating problem anybody can have with PCs is being unable to access networks, especially the Internet. We pretty much live our lives online both at home and at work. If you're wanting to do some shopping or banking, you want to be online. If you need access to the college library system or resources for your dissertation, you need to be online, and if you're collaborating on files with colleagues for an important project, you need network and/or Internet access.

Most network problems, in fairness, are pretty easily fixed, and the good news is that the tools that Microsoft provide as part of Windows can really help in this regard. These tools and utilities haven't changed that much in over a decade now, which makes them both mature and reliable. They're also comprehensive, so let's spend some time looking at what each is, and how they can be used to troubleshoot and repair network and Internet connection problems.

The Network and Sharing Center

The Network and Sharing Center is the main hub for controlling and managing network and Internet connections on the PC, certainly from a troubleshooting standpoint as well as from a management and troubleshooting perspective; the Settings app (which I'll detail later in the chapter) isn't as useful. You can open it either from within the Control Panel, or by right-clicking the network icon in the Taskbar System Tray.

The Network and Sharing Center is standard Windows console fare, with quick links to network utilities in the top left corner, more quick links to related Control Panel items in the bottom left corner, and a panel-style main section containing network connection information, and further links to tools, see Figure 9-1.

© Mike Halsey 2016
M. Halsey, *Windows 10 Troubleshooting*, DOI 10.1007/978-1-4842-0925-7_9

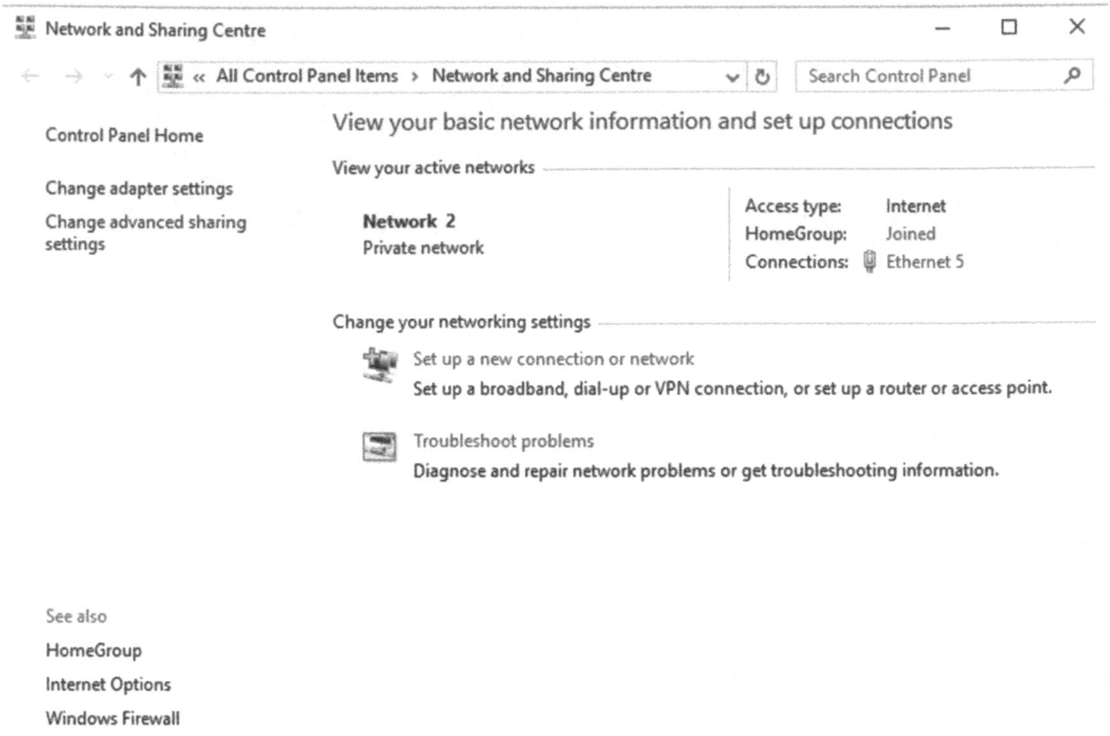

Figure 9-1. *The Network and Sharing Center in Windows 10*

You can get quick information about the current status of a connected network by clicking the *Connections [network name]* link near the top right of the window. This displays details of both the IPv4 and IPv6 connectivity (as you might be connected via one but not the other), the length of time the connection has been active, and the current network speed. Perhaps most useful is the Activity monitor. This will show you in real time the number of data packets being sent and received by the PC, see Figure 9-2.

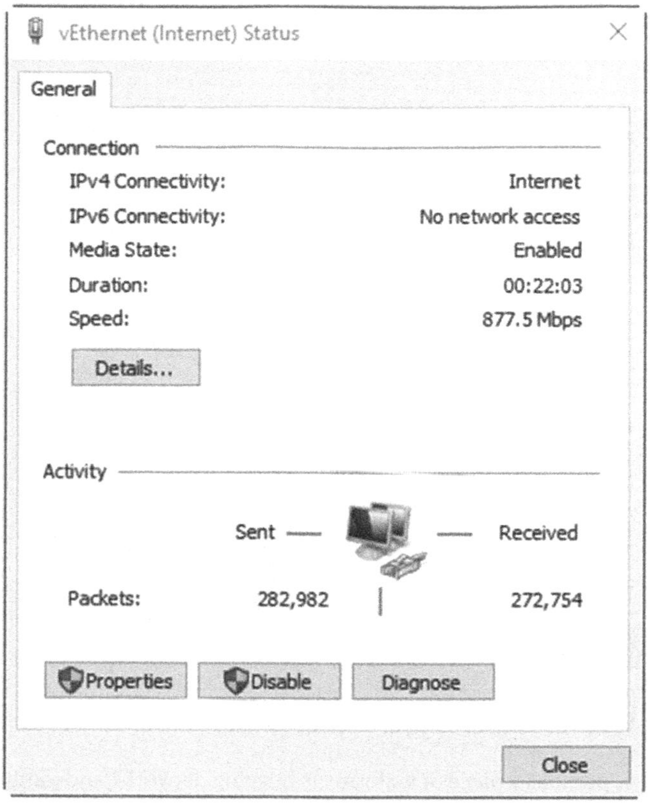

Figure 9-2. You can get quick status information about the current network connection

On a working network connection there should be a fairly constant stream of data passing back and forth, even if you're not doing much with the computer. This data will primarily be handshaking with the router, to maintain the connection, but other apps and services (from Cloud sync and backup apps to Windows Update and time sync) will also be running.

If at any time you want to know exactly what is using your network bandwidth, you can open the Resource Monitor by searching for **resource** at the Start Menu or in Cortana. This will display a full list of all the apps and services that are communicating with a server or the Internet, complete with details on the amount of data they are sending and receiving and, perhaps most usefully, the name or IP address of the local or web server they are communicating with, see Figure 9-3.

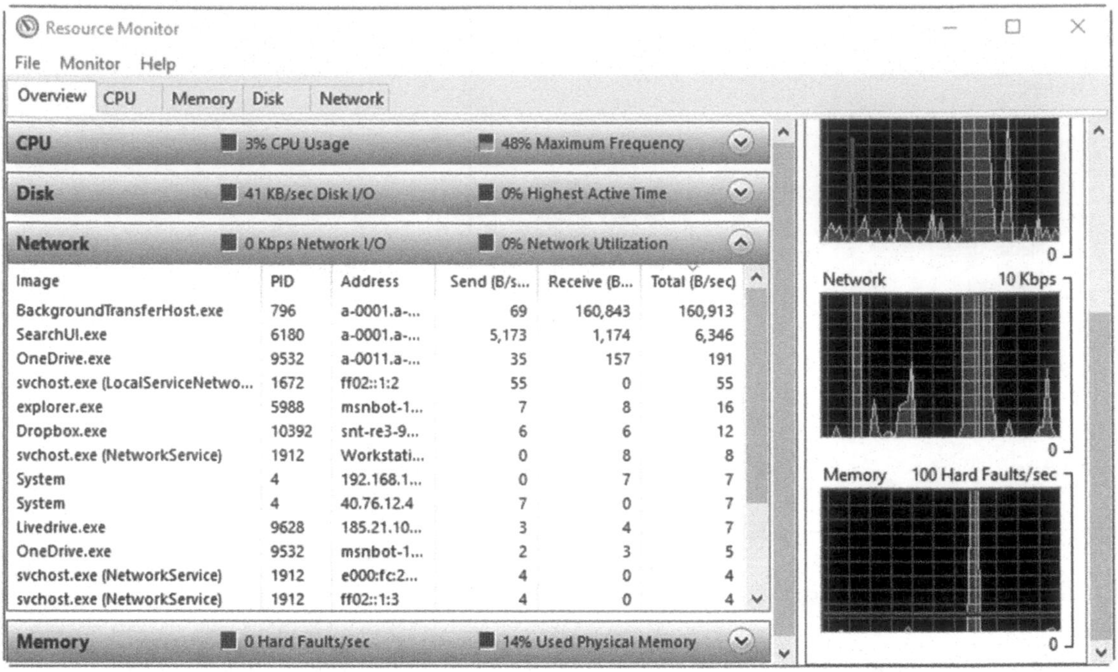

Figure 9-3. *The Resource Monitor can provide details of all network activity*

If you ever suspect that an app or service, or perhaps a piece of malware, is hogging network bandwidth on a PC, the Resource Monitor is definitely the place to check. On a network with multiple PCs, your router may provide a feature whereby you can check the current network usage for each connected PC and device (you should check the documentation that came with your router). You can then use this information to identify the bandwidth-hogging PC, and narrow it down to the specific app or service that's causing the problem.

Configuring Network Connections

Back in the Network Status dialog I showed you in Figure 9-2, there are four buttons which can provide further information about the current network and its status. The first of these is the *Details* button, which will display further information about the current network connection, see Figure 9-4.

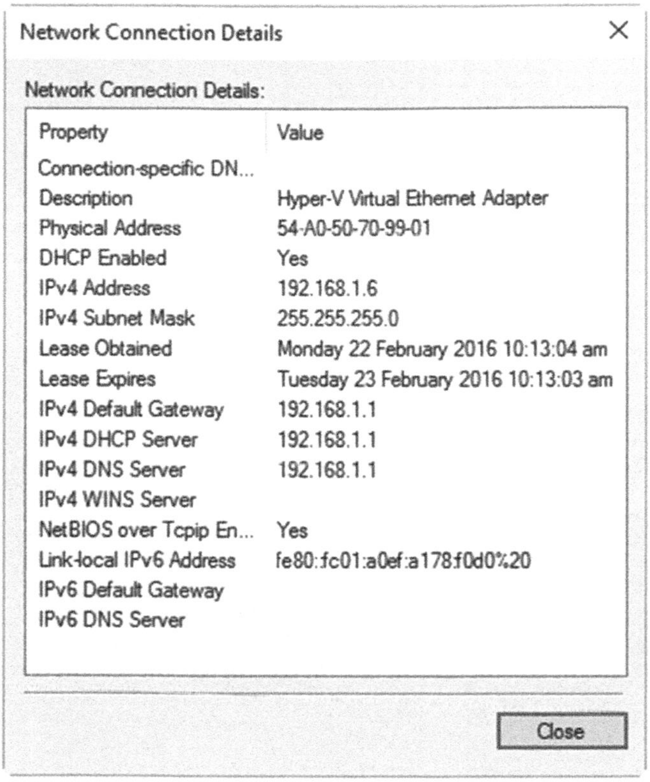

Network Connection Details   ✕

Network Connection Details:

Property	Value
Connection-specific DN...	
Description	Hyper-V Virtual Ethernet Adapter
Physical Address	54-A0-50-70-99-01
DHCP Enabled	Yes
IPv4 Address	192.168.1.6
IPv4 Subnet Mask	255.255.255.0
Lease Obtained	Monday 22 February 2016 10:13:04 am
Lease Expires	Tuesday 23 February 2016 10:13:03 am
IPv4 Default Gateway	192.168.1.1
IPv4 DHCP Server	192.168.1.1
IPv4 DNS Server	192.168.1.1
IPv4 WINS Server	
NetBIOS over Tcpip En...	Yes
Link-local IPv6 Address	fe80:fc01:a0ef:a178:f0d0%20
IPv6 Default Gateway	
IPv6 DNS Server	

Close

Figure 9-4. *You can get advanced information about the current network connection*

This information includes the IP address(es) of the PC on the network and information about the activation status of services such as Dynamic Host Control Protocol (DHCP), which is used to autoassign IP addresses by a router, and which might need to be disabled in some business-specific circumstances.

At the bottom of the Network Status dialog are three buttons. *Disable* is a quick link to disable (and re-enable) the connection. *Diagnose* will launch an automated troubleshooter that can fix some problems by resetting the connection to its default state. The remaining button, *Properties*, will display advanced configuration options for the connection, see Figure 9-5.

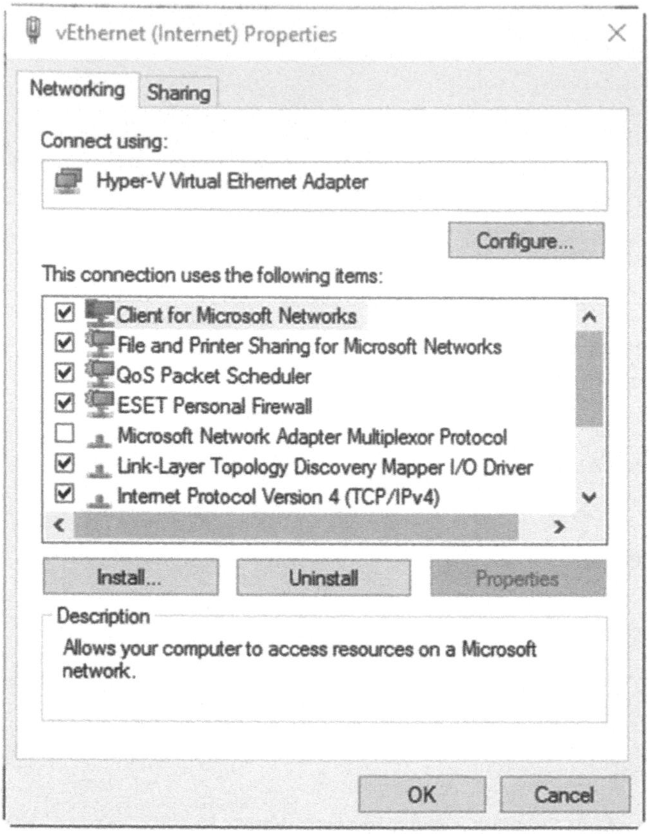

Figure 9-5. *You can manage advanced configuration options for the network connection*

There are two tabs in the Network Properties dialog; I want to deal with the second tab first as it's the more straightforward of the two. The *Sharing* tab contains options that allow the sharing of the computer's network connection with other PCs. Let's say that you have one PC connected to the Internet during a period of Internet down-time, with the only connected PC doing so through the user's cellular phone. This connection can be shared by other PCs but only if all are connected via a wired network. This feature is mostly a legacy hangover from the days when one PC had to be physically plugged into a USB broadband or dial-up modem, though there may still be occasions when it's useful.

Okay, so back to the *Networking* tab, which is by far the more important of the two. Here you will see a list of network services and protocols available to and in use by the network connection. These include, as you saw in Figure 9-5, services such as "Client for Microsoft Networks," which allows the PC to connect to other Windows PCs, and "File and Printer Sharing...," which can also include features and services such as Hyper-V switches.

Perhaps the most useful, certainly from a troubleshooting standpoint, are the IPv4 and IPv6 options. For some, but not all, network services in the list, but certainly for the IPv4 and IPv6 options, you can click the *Properties* button to get access to additional configuration settings.

The IPv4 options, see Figure 9-6, allow you choose if IP (Internet Protocol) and DNS (Domain Name Server) addresses are automatically assigned on handshaking between the PC and the router, or if they should be statically assigned instead. Note that static addresses need to be assigned on both the PC and the router. The Alternate configuration tab allows for laptops and tablets that are used on more than one network. You might, for example, need to assign static IP addresses for PCs at work, but have users switch to router-assigned IP addresses when they take the device out of the workplace.

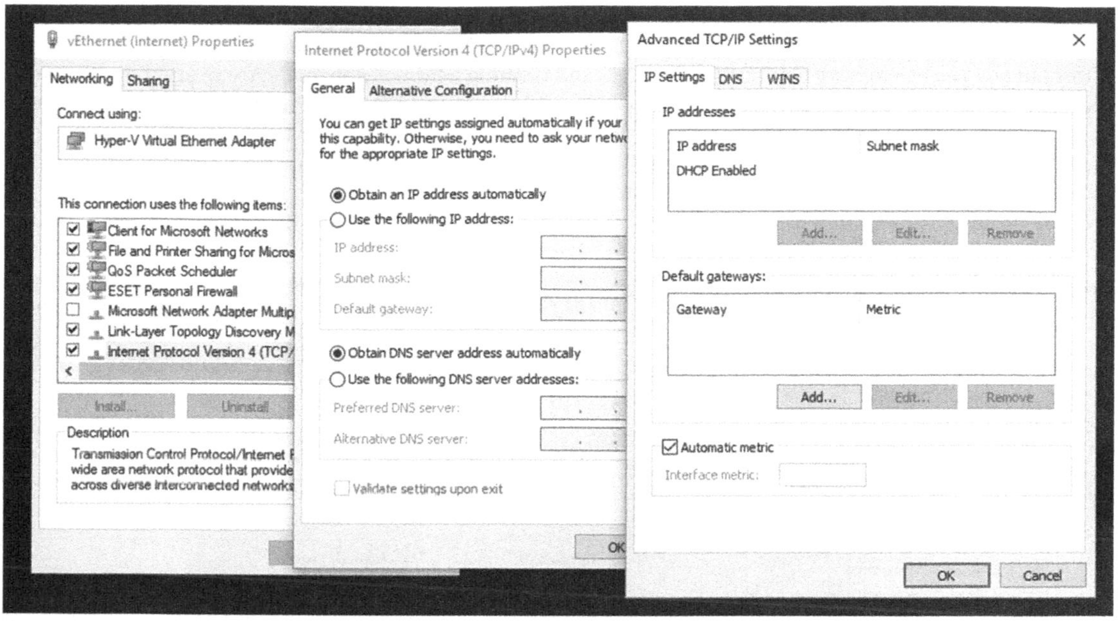

Figure 9-6. *You can manage IPv4 options in Network Settings*

Any additional options that need to be set or checked will be because they are already specified by the network administrator. These can include whether multiple DNS addresses need to be specified for the PC and if the default gateway (normally 192.168.x.x) must be specified.

IPv6 settings can also be configured, although because of the different way that IPv6 operates, not all of the features available for IPv4 connections are available, see Figure 9-7.

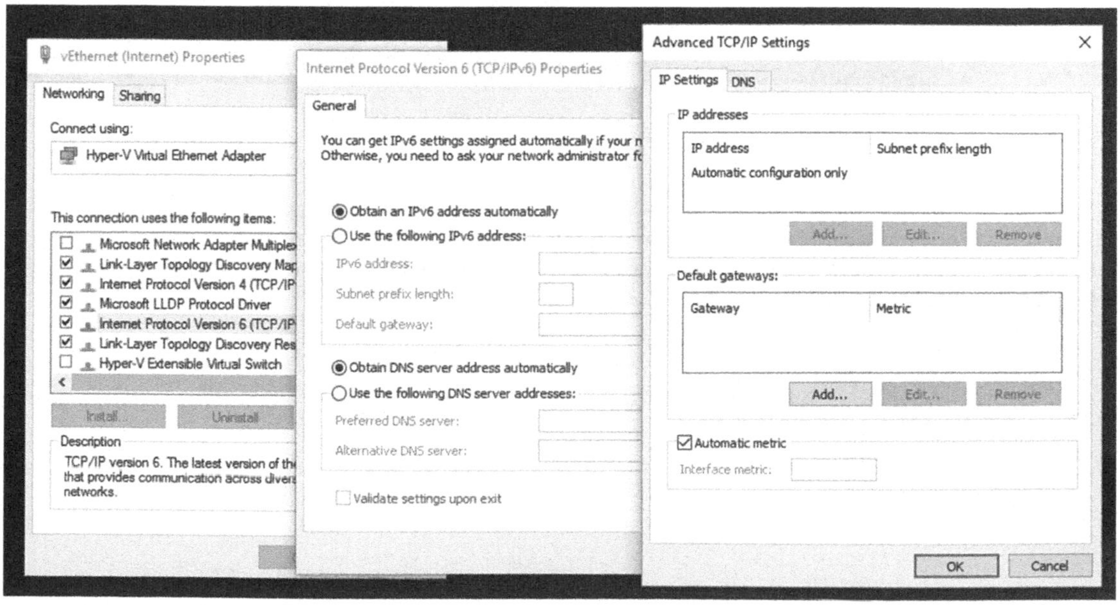

Figure 9-7. *You can configure IPv6 settings in the Network Properties*

You may find that a network Service or Protocol that you require for network access isn't installed. This might be required for high-security implementations or one where custom network hardware is in place. Alternatively, you might have a mission-critical PC still running a Base-T network system, and have to install a specific protocol to permit network connections. To add a missing Service or Protocol, or to install a driver to permit access to another specific PC that requires it, click the *Install* button in the Network Properties dialog. Here you will be prompted for a driver file or disk to install the feature you require, or with a list of available services that Windows 10 can install automatically, but that are disabled by default, perhaps for security reasons, see Figure 9-8.

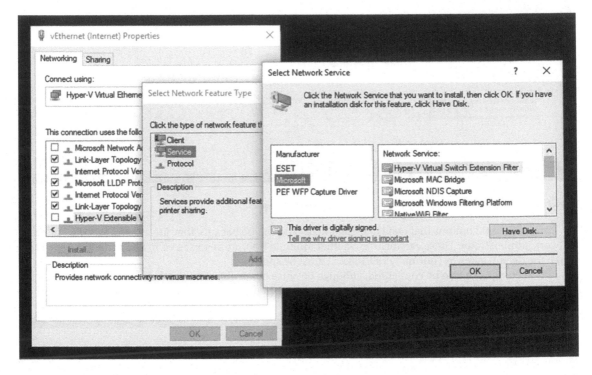

Figure 9-8. *You can install missing network services or protocols*

Lastly, the Network Properties dialog contains the *Configure* button. Clicking this will display the driver options for the network device, and I'll talk you through driver install and maintenance in full in Chapter 15. However, the Advanced tab in the driver properties will allow you to set and change properties for specific hardware driver properties, see Figure 9-9.

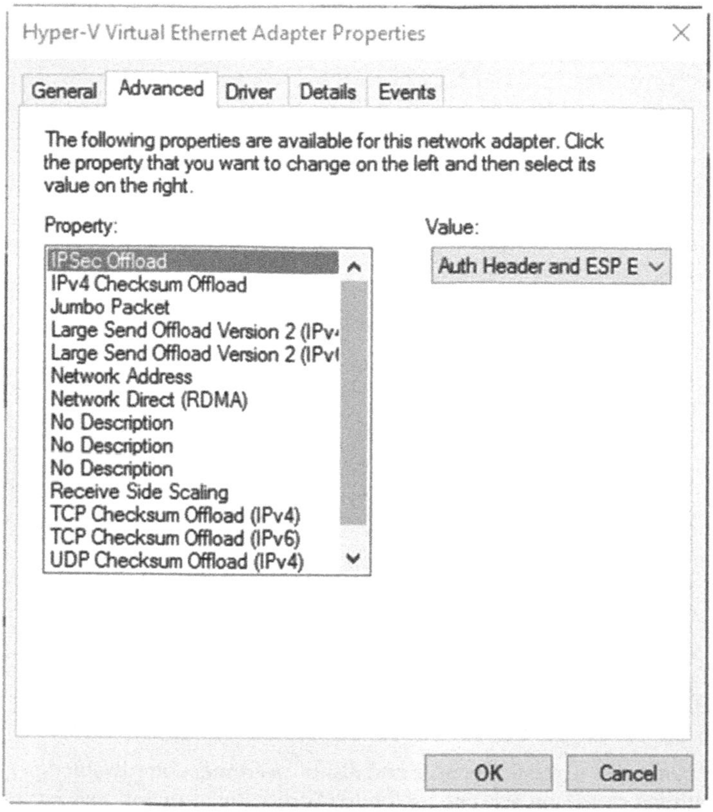

Figure 9-9. *The Configure options permit settings of specific settings for the network driver*

These settings will vary depending on what type of Network connection you have installed, but can include checksum and authentication settings, both of which are used by Windows 10 to determine if data is being sent and received correctly, and without errors.

Managing Network Adapters

In the top left of the Network and Sharing Center is a *Change adapter settings* link. Clicking this will display a list of all the network adapters currently installed on the PC, see Figure 9-10. Double-clicking any of the displayed adapters will open its properties dialog, as detailed earlier, but additional functions are available on a right-click.

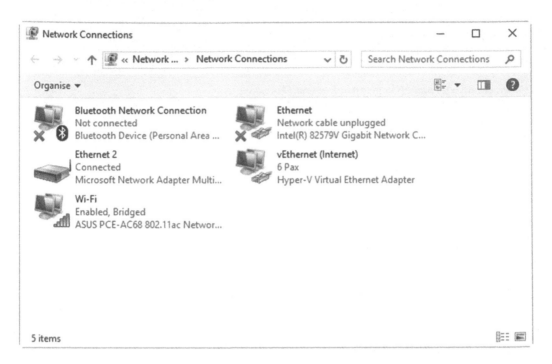

Figure 9-10. You can view details of all the network adapters installed on the PC

These additional functions include being able to quickly enable and disable a connection (disabled connections are shown in Figure 9-10 with red cross icon overlaid on them). Additionally, an option exists to *Bridge* several connections. Bridging allows you to bring multiple connections together as though they were a single connection.

In the example given, you can see that the Wi-Fi connection, which is enabled and connected to a network, is bridged with the Hyper-V network adapter. This enables installed Virtual Machines (VM) to get access to the local network and the Internet. Should a VM in this example be unable to obtain a network connection, I would check this bridge to see if it was active.

You might also use a bridge if, for example, you use two Ethernet adapters on the PC simultaneously to maximize both the speed and the stability of your network connection, perhaps for a bandwidth-intensive activity such as gaming.

Managing Network Connections in the Settings App

Many network management and connection options have been moved to the Settings app in Windows 10. Indeed, we can expect more options to be moved here in the future, perhaps even by the time you read this, as the Control Panel has been gradually reduced in functionality and eventually will be removed from the OS completely.

The Settings app, as I detailed at the beginning of this book, is designed primarily to permit nontechnical PC users to be able to perform the tasks they require, and the *Network & Internet* settings are no different. They allow users to perform actions such as connect to Wi-Fi networks, VPNs (Virtual Private Networks), see Figure 9-11, and to set proxy settings for a network if required.

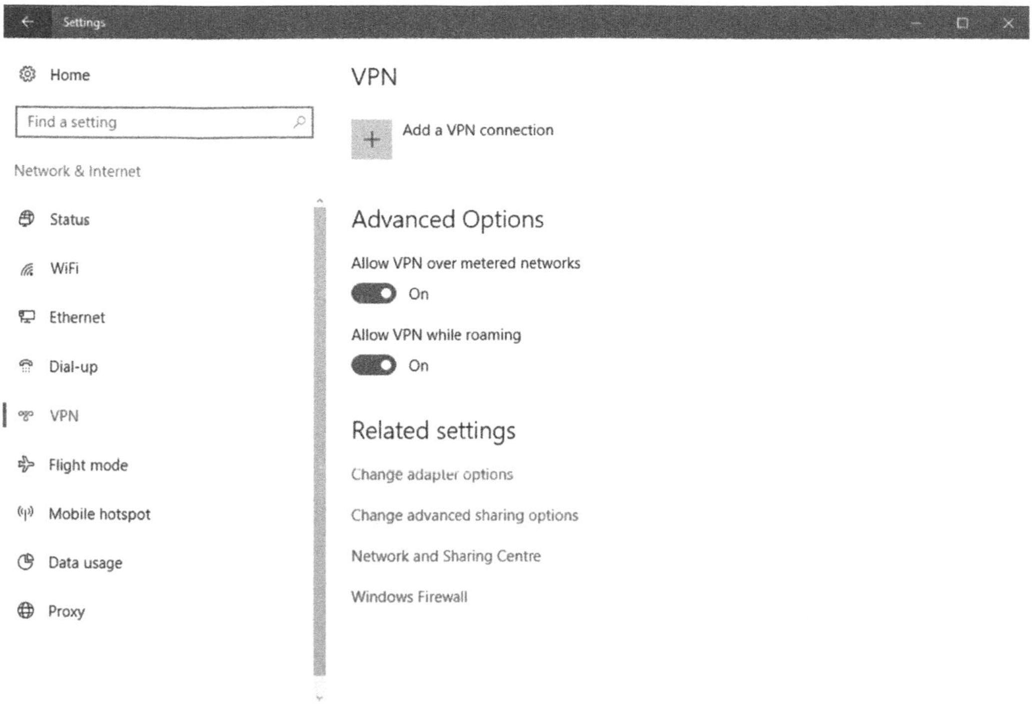

Figure 9-11. *The Settings app is your main hub for creating network connections*

Where links appear below options in the Settings app, these will almost always open Control Panel applets, as detailed earlier in this chapter. Two notable exceptions however are the *Advanced options* and *Manage WiFi Settings* links in the Wi-Fi section (which will not appear if Wi-Fi is not available on your PC).

The first of these will allow you to set the currently connected Wi-Fi network as a metered connection. This can be useful if you have a limited data plan on a PC that does not support unlimited data usage. Setting a Wi-Fi connection as metered will restrict the data used by features as Live Tiles, but can also crucially affect Windows Update, and its ability to search for and download updates and patches to the PC.

The *Manage WiFi Settings* link is significantly more useful, however. It's common that settings for some Wi-Fi connections become corrupt, and suddenly the user is unable to connect to the network. The *Manage known networks* section of this panel allows you to force Windows 10 to forget its settings for any Wi-Fi network. This can be achieved by clicking the network, whereupon a Forget button will appear, see Figure 9-12.

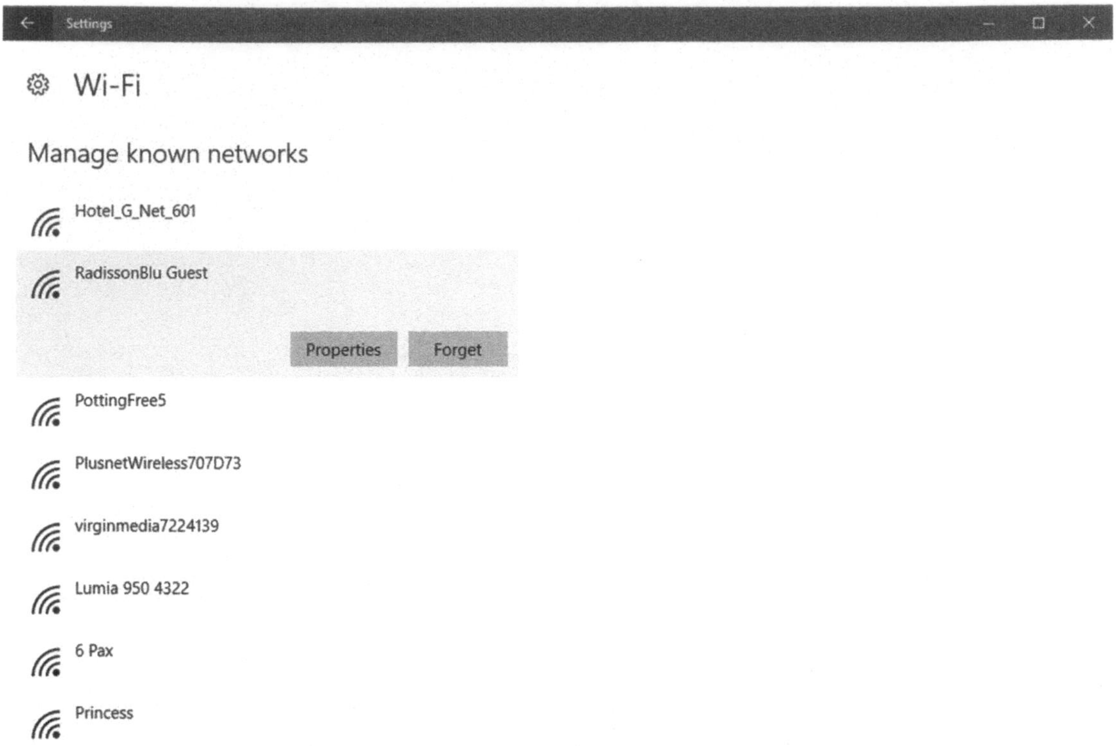

Figure 9-12. You can force Windows 10 to forget individual Wi-Fi networks

---

■ **Tip** You can disable Wi-Fi Sense using the Windows Registry by navigating to `HKLM\SOFTWARE\Microsoft\DataCollection\Default\WifiAutoConnectConfig` and creating a new DWORD called `AutoConnectEnabled` that has a value of `0` (zero).

While Wi-Fi connections can be managed within the Settings app, there's not much available for management of other network types. There's no management available for Ethernet connections at all, as they're just sort of on or unplugged. VPN settings just allow you to add or remove a connection and change the roaming settings for the connection, and the Dial-up connections panel merely throws you into the classic Control Panel.

One exception is the proxy settings, which contain advanced controls should you need to use a proxy server on your PC (perhaps because you work in a security-conscious industry), see Figure 9-13. You can set up proxy servers automatically, through detection by Windows, or manually. Should there be a problem with a connection, it's worth having a look here to see if the proxy server settings have been disabled or have become corrupt.

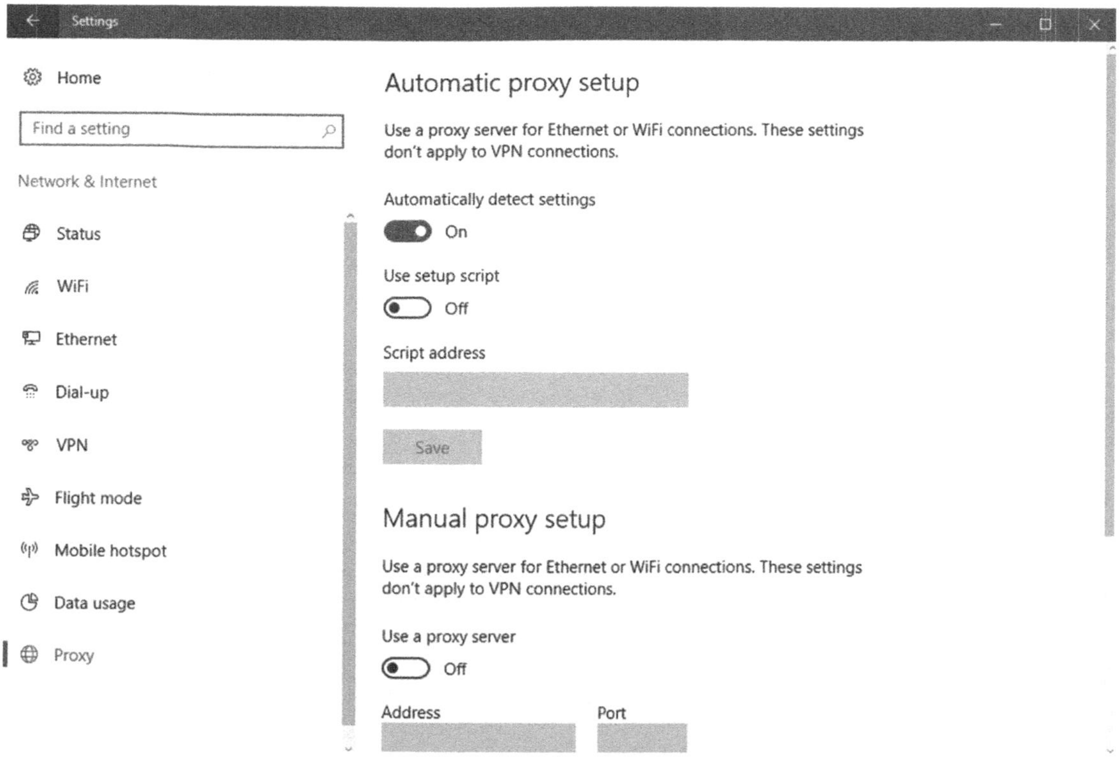

Figure 9-13. You can configure all proxy server settings in the Settings app

Setting Up and Managing Your Router

This may seem like an obvious thing to say to an IT Pro, but it really is crucial to configure a router correctly and make sure that it has a secure access password. The number of times I have encountered routers, even in the business space, where the username and password are both set to "admin" is alarming.

■ **Caution**   The default username and password for almost any router are available to find online, via a quick search for the manual, or the manufacturer's default settings. You should always change the username and password on all routers you own.

The first challenge, however, can be finding the IP address of your router, as different router manufacturers use different default IP addresses, and the router IP address range can be changed by an administrator after installation anyway. As an example, Linksys routers tend to use the default IP address 192.168.1.1. D-Link and Netgear routers however commonly use 192.168.0.1 (by far the most common address), and some Belkin routers use 192.168.2.1.

You can find the IP address of your router by opening *Command Prompt* from the Win+X administration menu and typing the command ipconfig, see Figure 9-14.

```
Command Prompt                                                                    —  □  ×
Microsoft Windows [Version 10.0.10586]
(c) 2015 Microsoft Corporation. All rights reserved.

C:\Users\Mike Halsey>ipconfig

Windows IP Configuration


Ethernet adapter Ethernet:

   Media State . . . . . . . . . . : Media disconnected
   Connection-specific DNS Suffix  . :

Wireless LAN adapter Local Area Connection* 3:

   Media State . . . . . . . . . . : Media disconnected
   Connection-specific DNS Suffix  . :

Ethernet adapter vEthernet (Internet):

   Connection-specific DNS Suffix  . :
   Link-local IPv6 Address . . . . . : fe80::fc01:a0ef:a178:f0d0%20
   IPv4 Address. . . . . . . . . . : 192.168.1.6
   Subnet Mask . . . . . . . . . . : 255.255.255.0
   Default Gateway . . . . . . . . : 192.168.1.1

Ethernet adapter Bluetooth Network Connection:

   Media State . . . . . . . . . . : Media disconnected
   Connection-specific DNS Suffix  . :
```

Figure 9-14. *You can find the IP address of your router from the IP Config command*

In the ipconfig results, look for the "Default Gateway" for your network connection. This is the router through which traffic is directed. This will be the address of your router on the network.

■ **Note**   For most scenarios, looking for the Default Gateway in the ipconfig results will reveal the address of the router; however in some enterprise scenarios, it may instead reveal the address of a security, or web filtering appliance.

Of course, and you'll laugh that I've mentioned this as the second way to find the IP address of the router. You can always go and have a look at the label on the underside of the router, which will more than likely have its default IP address written on it.

When you are signed into the router, please, please, please make sure that the very first thing you do is change its access password to something secure. Once this is done you will find that different manufacturers use different router interface software, and this can even vary across different routers in their own range. Figure 9-15 shows the router interface in my own Netgear router.

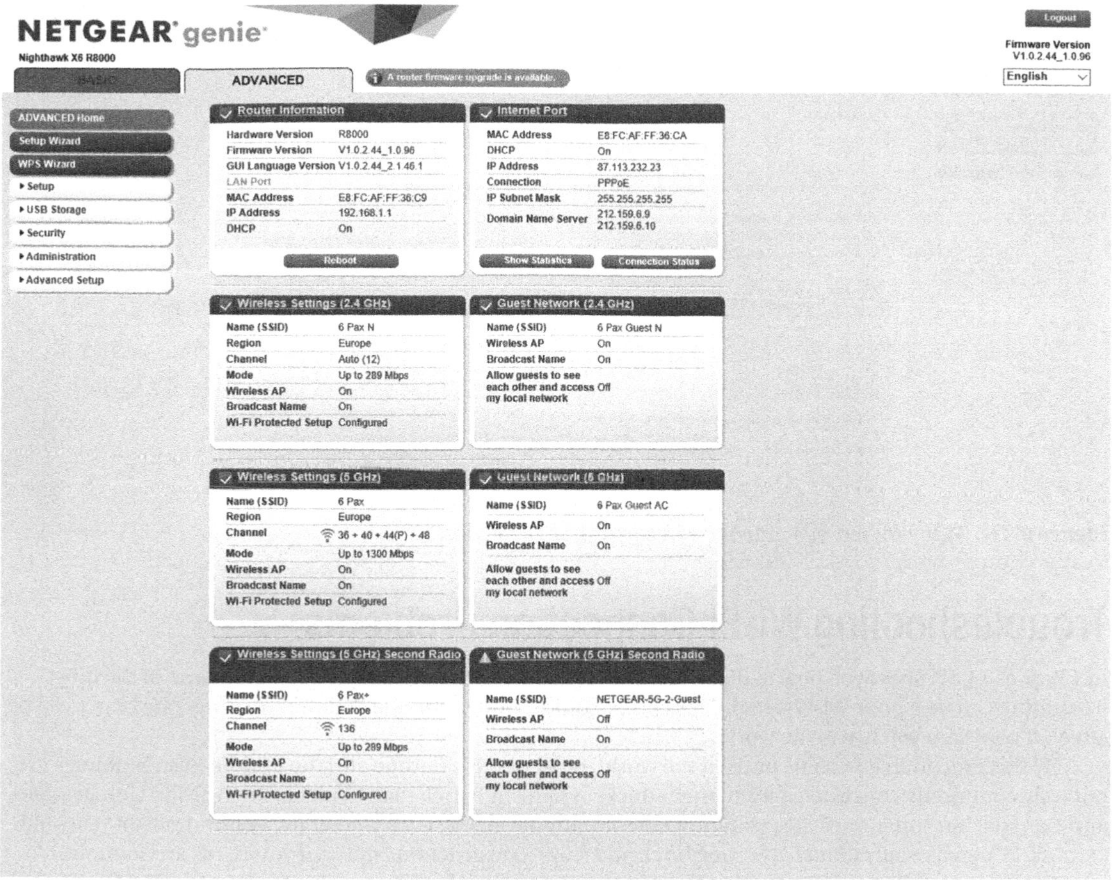

Figure 9-15. *Different manufacturers use different router interfaces, and even different interfaces across their products*

The more advanced the router, the more advanced the features it will provide. These can include web filtering, parental controls, and using USB attached printers and storage with the router. Guest Wi-Fi networks can be extremely useful, especially if you share documents across your network from a USB drive or a Network Attached Storage (NAS) drive. A guest network can provide Internet access for visitors to your home or workplace, without them also having access to devices and storage on the network.

If the router you are using is a free model that was provided by your ISP, it's unlikely to support these advanced features. Routers that you purchase separately, however, do often support advanced functionality such as access control and web site blocking and scheduling, see Figure 9-16.

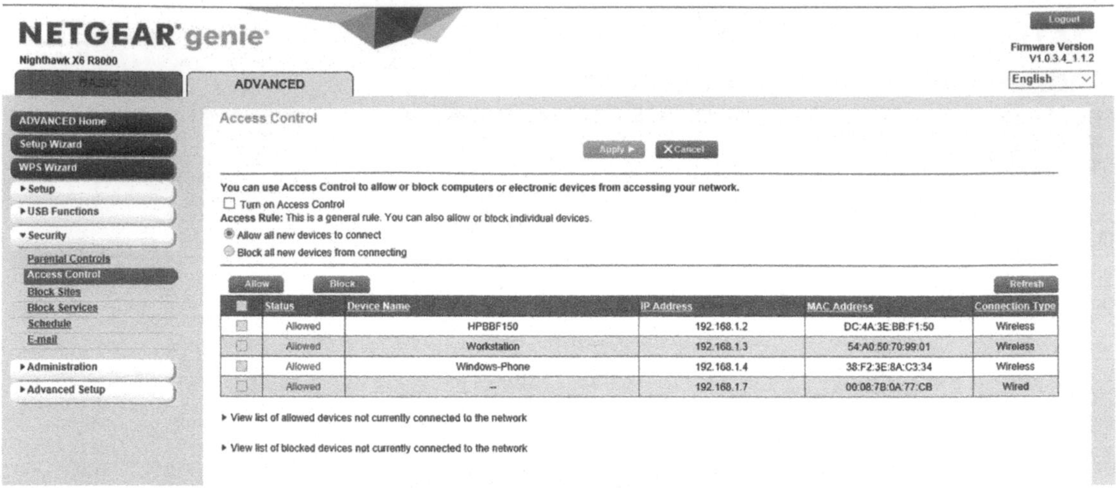

Figure 9-16. *Many routers offer advanced security and other controls*

Troubleshooting Wi-Fi Connection Problems

In Chapter 14, I'll show you how to diagnose and repair complex network problems, but one of the most frustrating can be a poor Wi-Fi signal. This can be caused by a multitude of different things, and can even be affected by where you live in the world.

By this I mean that in some parts of the world, most notably Europe and the Middle East, buildings are not only commonly constructed from much thicker stone and brick than in places such as the United States and Canada, but sometimes these buildings are hundreds, maybe even a great many hundreds of years old.

Wi-Fi signals really don't like strong brick and stone construction, and so if you're (as an example) traveling from the United States to the UK on business and then find that you're getting an awful Wi-Fi signal, it could be the building you're sitting in that's causing it.

Good placement of your Internet router is crucial therefore to maintain a good all-around Wi-Fi signal. Where this isn't possible, Access Point or Wi-Fi repeater hardware can be installed to boost the Wi-Fi signal into parts of a building where it's weak. Additionally, if you have an old Internet router collecting dust, you may be able to reconfigure it as a Wireless Access Point. The settings for this, if your router supports it, will be found in its advanced settings, see Figure 9-17.

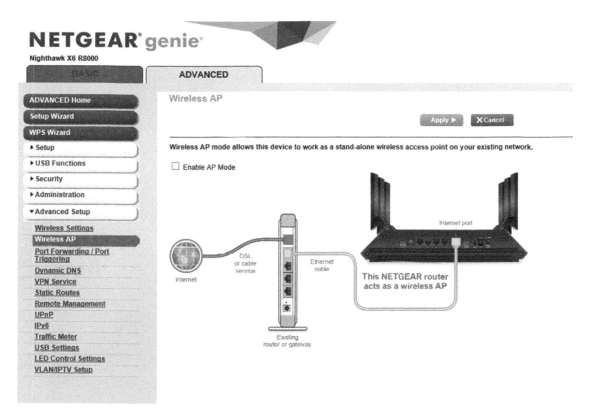

Figure 9-17. Older routers can often be reconfigured as an access point

Other factors can affect Wi-Fi signals, however. These include radio and other signals broadcast from devices such as older televisions and microwave ovens, so keeping these devices away from the PCs in your home of office can assist with maintaining a good Wi-Fi connection.

Lastly, you can also get interference on Ethernet network cabling used for PCs and other systems such as Voice-Over-IP (VoIP) telephony systems. Common network (and other types of) cable are built using a method known as UTP, which stands for unshielded twisted pair. UTP cables are susceptible to interference caused by radio and other signals. Shielded cabling is available, though slightly more expensive, and you might want to consider purchasing shielded cabling when installing network systems in your home or workplace.

Summary

Despite all the network diagnosis and troubleshooting methods covered in this chapter, we've really only scratched the surface of the subject. As we progress to more advanced subjects in this book, we'll cover these things in much more detail in Chapter 14.

In the next chapter, however, we'll deal with that other essential component for Internet access, the web browser. Both the Edge browser and Internet Explorer have advanced configuration and troubleshooting options and features available, but neither can be uninstalled and reinstalled from the OS, so I'll show you how to troubleshoot them.

CHAPTER 10

■ ■ ■

Troubleshoot and Manage Internet Explorer and Edge

If the most important aspect of using our PCs is getting network and Internet access, the second most important is the web browser, of which Windows 10 has two. There are fundamental differences between these browsers as well. Edge is Microsoft's latest web browser and rather than being a "traditional" Windows program, it's really a Store app. This means that the browser can be updated on a regular basis without needing to be part of a major Windows service pack or update.

Internet Explorer (IE) still exists too, primarily to help businesses maintain compatibility with essential plug-ins and older intranet sites. It's hidden by default, but searching for it in the Start Menu or Cortana will display it, after which it will appear automatically in the all apps view in the Start Menu.

Managing IE11

I want to begin with IE, as the type of person most likely to be reading this will be using Windows 10 in a business or enterprise environment. Unlike previous versions of Windows, where as the years progressed so did the version number for the available copy of IE, the version that ships with Windows 10, IE11, will be the very last version of the browser. There will be no updates in the future except for security patches. It's also extremely unlikely (I'd say it's never going to happen) that newly ratified and released Internet browsing standards will be included in IE. IE in Windows 10 is merely there to maintain compatibility with *older* sites, and for anything going forward, Microsoft wants you to use Edge.

There is a caveat with this, however! If your PCs are on the Long-Term Servicing Branch (LTSB) of Windows Update, you will only get security and stability updates and no feature updates for up to 10 years (i.e., the expected lifetime of the PC or system on which Windows 10 is installed). This is to help systems for which stability is paramount to operate without issue. You will commonly find that embedded systems, such as ATMs, POS terminals, and automated business systems, will use LTSB. Nobody uses the desktop interfaces on these systems, at least not very often, and as such installing new interface and feature updates could adversely affect their operation.

Sadly, these updates also include Store apps, which include the Edge browser. If there's no way to guarantee that a future interface or operation update to Windows 10 won't adversely affect the operation of a critical system, there's also no way to guarantee that an app update won't either. As a result, Store apps are excluded from systems on LTSB and can't be installed.

This leaves only IE11 on these systems as an available browser. It will still get security and stability updates as I've said, but it won't get support for new web browsing standards. This is unlikely to affect systems on LTSB, as they're most commonly not used for web browsing. Any Internet activity they have will be through custom apps (such as the interface software for your ATM).

© Mike Halsey 2016
M. Halsey, *Windows 10 Troubleshooting*, DOI 10.1007/978-1-4842-0925-7_10

Why do I mention this? Well, it's important to note that if you're reading this in 2020 or later and wondering why Facebook (if it still exists by then) isn't working on your LTSB PC, this will probably be why, and there will be very little you can do about it, short of installing another web browser such as Google Chrome.

Disabling IE

Edge is a very different beast from IE by virtue of being a Windows Store app. This means that, as with all other Store apps, it runs in its own protected bubble of memory and its core files are hidden away with such tight security that even an Administrator can't access them. As a result, Edge is (as I write this) the most secure web browser available for any OS. As other browsers are recompiled as Store apps, they too will be able to take advantage of this advanced security, but it certainly makes Edge pretty much unhackable.

If security is important to you or your business, you might want to minimize the risk of attack for your systems. You can do this by disabling any part of the OS that's potentially vulnerable. This includes IE, which, as a desktop Win32 app, has its core files visible and vulnerable to anybody with administrative rights.

You can disable IE11 from the *Programs and Features* panel, most easily accessible from the Win+X administration menu. On the left of this panel is a *Turn Windows features on or off* link that, when clicked, will display a list of all the Windows 10 features that can be disabled, or that haven't yet been enabled, see Figure 10-1.

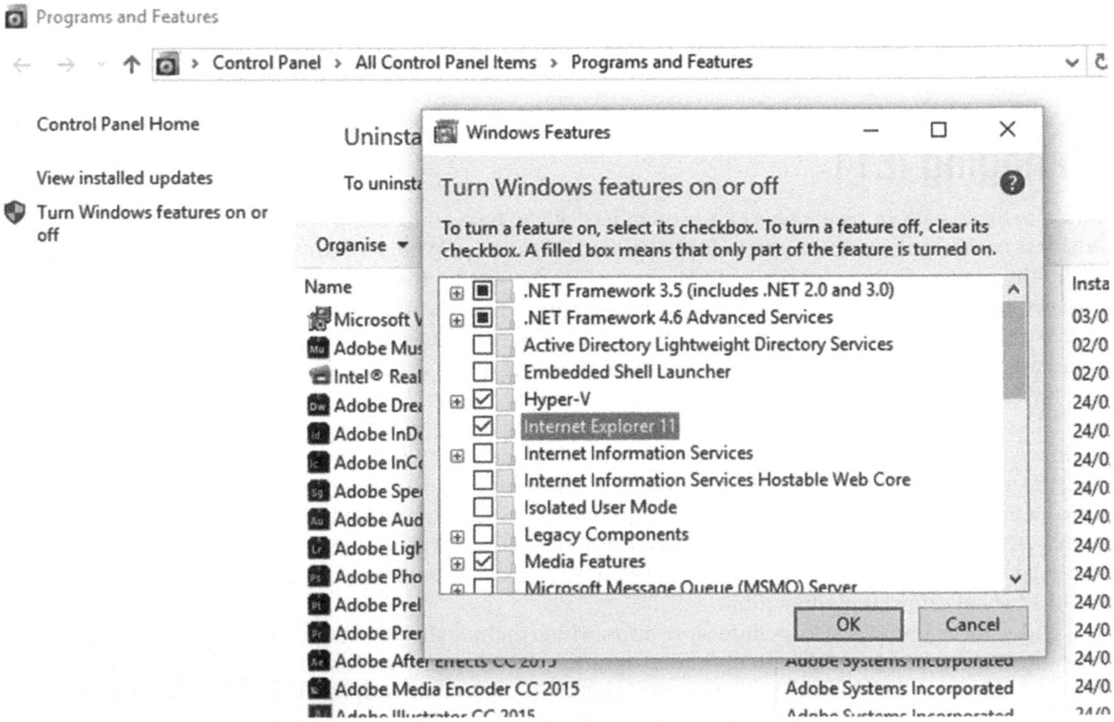

Figure 10-1. *You can disable IE from the Programs and Features panel*

It's worth bearing in mind that much of the underpinnings of IE also forms the basis of other Windows utilities, many of which you can't disable or be without, such as File Explorer. Should a hacking or virus attack modify or delete some core files for IE, it's possible that other UI elements could also be affected. However, disabling IE prevents any users on the PC from being able to access it, and if users can't access it on the PC, it makes it significantly harder for malware to attack it as well.

Managing Temporary Files in IE

The primary way for malware to attack your PC through a web browser is to get you or the browser to download files containing malicious code. These can sit in the temporary files store for your web browser, waiting to be run again, as the temporary files store helps make sure the web pages you visit often load quickly.

The security-conscious among you can manage these temporary files in IE11 through the Internet Options panel. This is available either in the Control Panel or through the Settings icon in the top right corner of the browser.

I'll show you through all the options available in Internet Options in Chapter 17, but under the General tab you will see a *Browsing history* section. Here there is a quick check box option to always *Delete [the] browsing history on exit*, which will delete most temporary files from the PC. Click the Settings button, however, and more options will become available, see Figure 10-2.

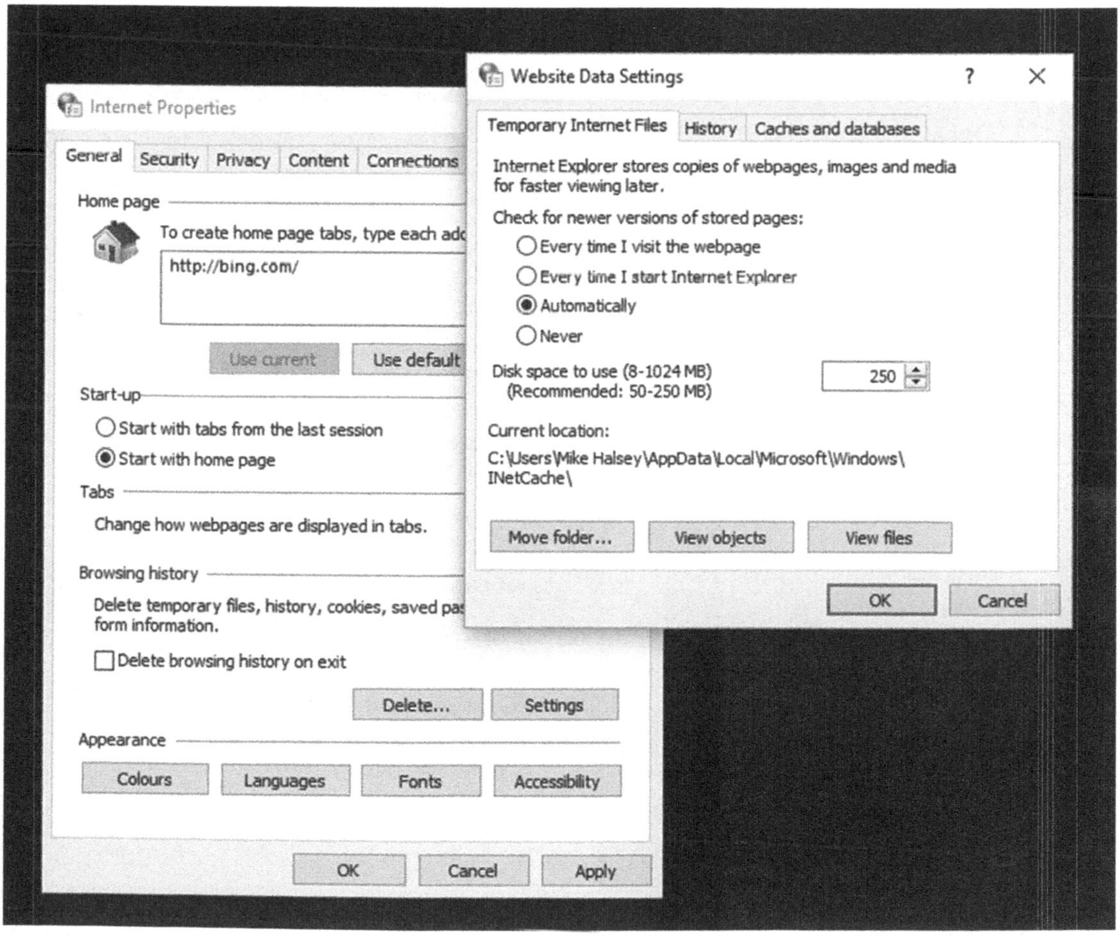

Figure 10-2. *You can manage the default options for managing temporary files in IE11*

Under the *Temporary Internet Files* tab, you can control how often the temporary files are refreshed. The default setting is for IE to manage the setting automatically and refresh the temporary files only if it detects that a web or intranet page has changed. You can, however, force IE to check every time the browser is started, every time a page is visited, or never.

You can also control the amount of space allocated on the PC for temporary files. Unfortunately, this doesn't allow you to eliminate the files altogether, with a minimum required disk space of 8MB, but it can help minimize the space in which malware can reside.

At the bottom of the panel are buttons to move the temporary files store, perhaps to a protected area on the PC, such as a different partition; to *View objects* in the store (these are downloaded programs); and to *View [all the] files* in the temporary file store. Opening this will help you manually delete the files should you wish.

The *Caches and databases* tab will also allow you to determine what if any web sites and intranet sites can store database caches on your PC. You can disable these completely; however, you might find that your intranet requires this feature to be active.

Back in the main Internet Options panel, clicking the *Delete* button will allow you to delete temporary and other files from IE manually. These include form data from web sites and intranets, your downloaded files history, and stored passwords, see Figure 10-3.

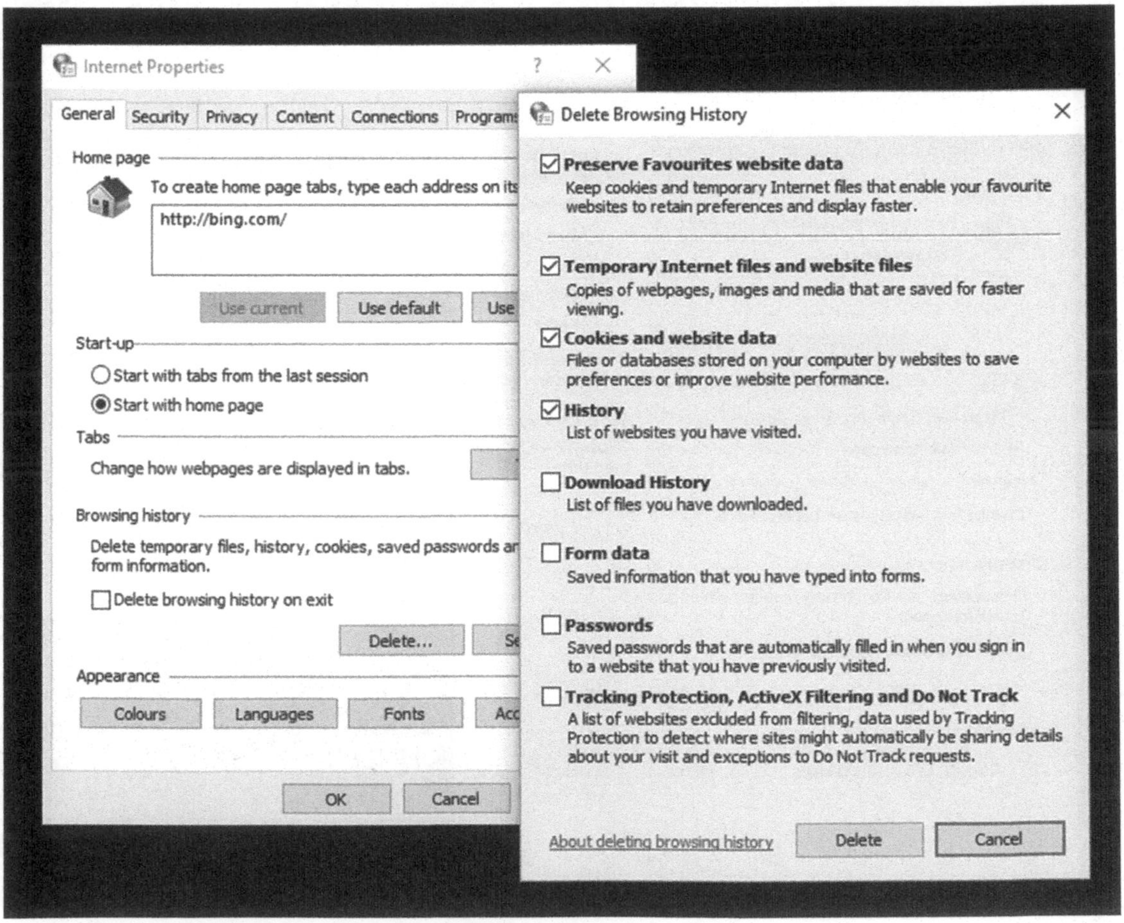

Figure 10-3. You can delete temporary and other files from IE11 manually

Resetting IE11

Something both IE and Edge have in common is that, because they're integral parts of the Windows OS, neither can be uninstalled or reinstalled. This can present a problem should their core files become corrupt. While corruption is far less likely with Edge because of the protected way its core files are stored, with IE, this can be a pain.

With previous versions of Windows you could install a newer version of the browser to fix the problem, or you could manually download the installer for the browser if it was an update of the version that originally shipped with Windows and perform a reinstall.

There is no stand-alone installer, however, that's compatible with Windows 10. Even extracting the installer's core files using software such as WinRar won't help you (this is a great trick for installing software and drivers that I'll detail in full in Chapter 15).

However, all is not lost! IE can be completely reset, effectively reinstalling it and at least setting it back to the point it was at when Windows 10 was first installed on the PC. This doesn't affect any patches and updates that have been installed afterward from Windows Update, but it's a good way to get the browser working again.

You can reset IE11 from the Internet Options panel, which if IE11 isn't working is best accessed from the Control Panel. On the *Advanced* tab you will see a *Reset* button. Clicking this will inform you what the reset process will do, and give you the added option of completely clearing out the browser at the same time, just in case it's personal or temporary files that are causing or contributing to the problem, see Figure 10-4.

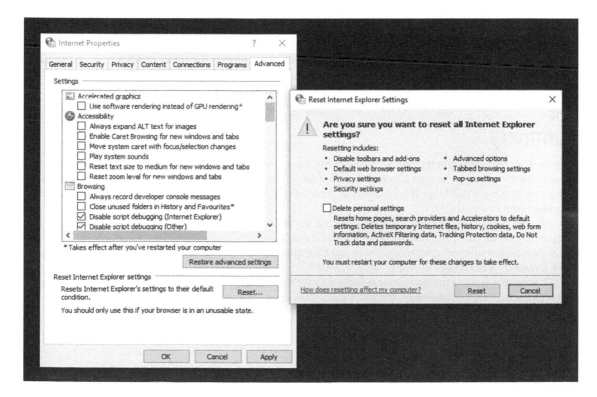

Figure 10-4. *You can reset IE11*

Resetting IE11, and even *Deleting [the] personal settings,* doesn't delete your Internet Favorites, which are stored elsewhere in your Users folder, but it can be a great way of getting a faulty or malfunctioning installation of IE11 working again.

Managing Edge

Microsoft's Edge browser is, as I've already mentioned, considerably more secure than IE11 by virtue of being a Store app, and therefore taking advantage of the sandboxed nature of these apps. There's really not that much to manage in Edge as a result. You can *Clear [its] browsing data* from the settings menu (the three horizontal dots near the top right of the window), and that's about it.

■ **Caution**   It might be tempting to look for the Edge temporary files store and delete the contents of it manually, or for the core Edge files so you can reset the browser. Many web results on these subjects will point to the C:\Users\[Username]\AppData\Local\Packages\Microsoft.MicrosoftEdge_8wekyb3d8bbwe folder, but whatever you do, **DO NOT delete the contents of this folder**. Doing so will break Edge completely in such a way that you'll need to perform a System Restore or perhaps even a reinstall to get the browser working again.

Should you find that Edge isn't working, or is misbehaving, resetting the Windows Store can sometimes help. To do this, search for **wsreset**, and run the wsreset.exe tool as an Administrator. Resetting the Windows Store can often trigger an update download for installed apps, and get them operational once more.

There are ways to uninstall Edge, usually through a script or third-party package. I don't recommend using these as the browser cannot be reinstalled from the Windows Store, it simply doesn't appear there. Uninstalling Edge in this way will probably require a reinstall of Windows 10 to get it operational again.

Summary

Edge and IE really highlight the differences between store and Win32 apps. With IE11 you can pretty much manage the browser and its core files in a variety of ways, but this also means that malware can get access to the core files too. With Edge, the system is far more robust, with access to the app's files hidden even from Administrators.

This isn't to say that damage can't be done, and instructions I found commonly floating around the Internet can render the Edge browser completely unusable and unable to start. The lesson here is to follow any instructions with care, and to make sure you have an image backup of your Windows 10 installation you can fall back on if need be.

I'll show you how to manage compatibility with web sites and intranet sites, and how to manage privacy and security in IE11, in Chapter 17, but we're going to throw ourselves directly into troubleshooting in the next chapter by looking at how we fix the most common Windows 10 annoyances.

PART 2

Becoming a Proficient Troubleshooter

CHAPTER 11

■ ■ ■

Dealing with Common Windows Annoyances

PCs can be annoying, frustrating, irritating things to use when something isn't working as it should. From files that won't open, to disks you can't access, sound that won't play, irritating activation messages two years after you'd activated Windows, Windows Updates that won't install, slow and hanging startup and shutdown, to encryption lockouts, faulty touchscreens, nonfunctioning USB devices, not having a picture on your monitor and Blue Screens of Death (BSOD) with perpetual restarts. Things that might in essence be "straightforward" problems can cause enormous headaches and loss of productivity.

In this chapter, I'll deal with all of these issues and more, and show you how to quickly repair every single one of them. When you fix a PC that has a problem like these, people will look at you wondering how the hell you did it, and how you did it so quickly.

Incorrect File Associations

Few things are more annoying than files that won't open. Whether you're at work, at home or studying, you want the files you have to always open correctly and in the right app. Windows 10 to its credit is fairly good with its notifications; if it doesn't recognize a file type, it will display a helpful dialog with a list of installed apps on your PC from which you can choose.

Where it all falls down, of course, is that because the OS can't recognize the file type, it has absolutely no idea what types of app it should display, and as it can only display a few apps in the dialog, it will commonly get things wrong.

It's a straightforward process to repair file associations, however, and there are two ways to manage it, the first of which is very straightforward for nontechnical PC users. This method is in the Settings app. Navigate to *System* and *Default apps* and you will see default app options for e-mail, maps, music, photos, video, and web browsing, see Figure 11-1. This covers the basics for typical home PC users and will most likely be useful when they have installed a new music or photos app or a new web browser, but it's not opening when they click a file or link.

© Mike Halsey 2016

M. Halsey, *Windows 10 Troubleshooting*, DOI 10.1007/978-1-4842-0925-7_11

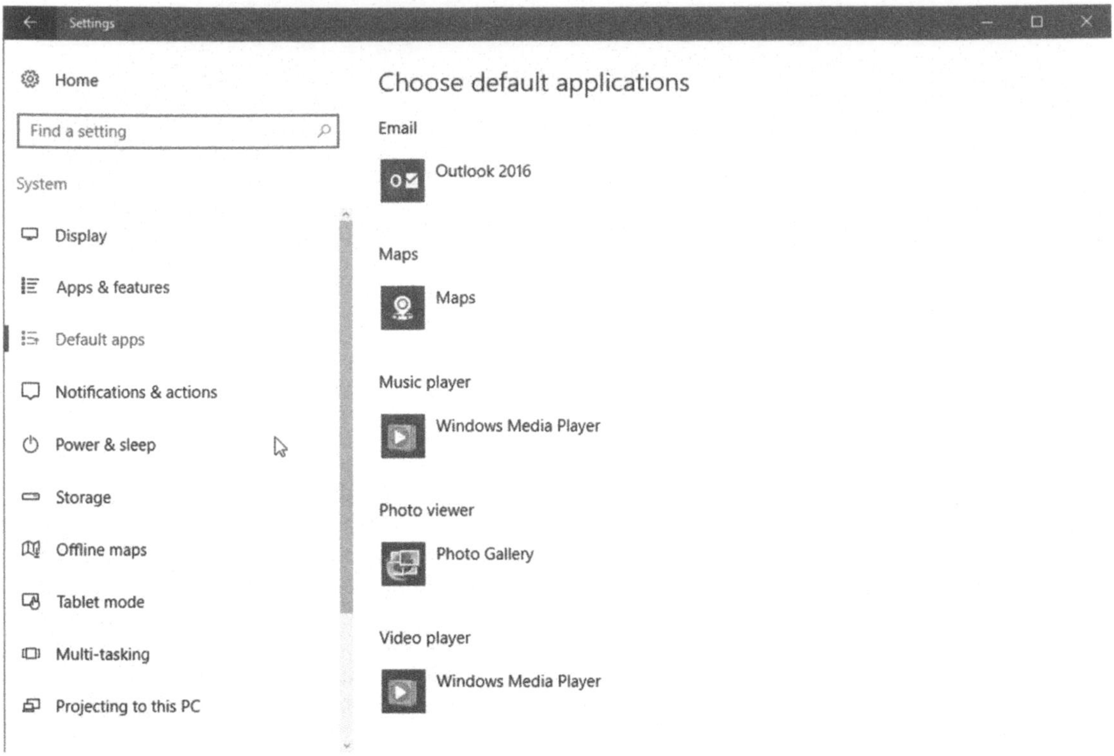

Figure 11-1. *You can set a few app associations in the Settings app*

There are some additional options to help users, however, for other file types. At the bottom of the list are three links. The first of these, *Choose default applications by file type*, which is the option to choose if you have, for example, an Office app that won't open a file, or a file that's opening in the wrong app. To set the file association correctly, you will need to know the file extension of the file you are trying to open. These file extentions are listed on the left side of the window, with their default app association, if one is set, to their right, see Figure 11-2.

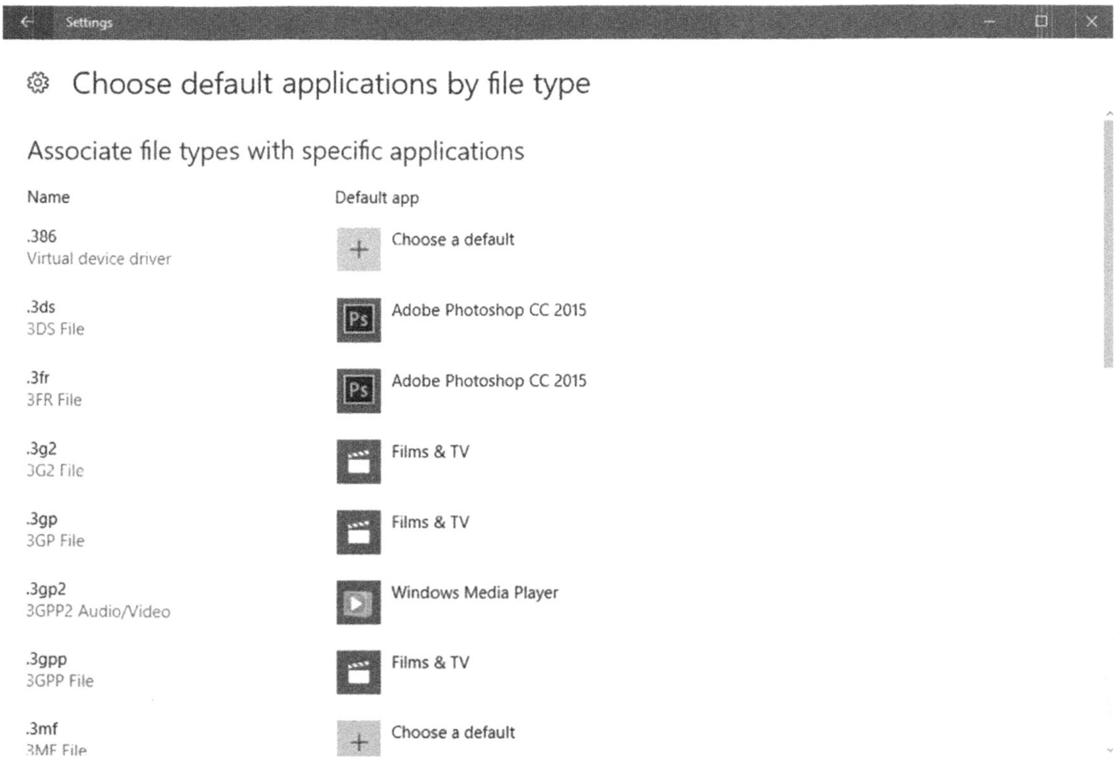

Figure 11-2. *You can set file associations by file type*

Where this method falls down is that clicking the *Choose a default [app]* button will ask you to "Look for an app in the store." This will work for some users and even some businesses, as some win32 desktop apps will be available in the Windows Store. For everybody else, however, you will need to resort to the Control Panel, and I will detail this shortly.

■ **Tip** You can display the extensions for all files in File Explorer from the *View* tab on the Ribbon, by checking the *File name extensions* option.

The second of the three links at the main Default apps page is *Choose default apps by protocol*. A protocol is a nonfile element such as a web link (URL), map, DVD burning command, or create e-mail link. You can see a list of protocols in the left of the window, with their default app association to their right, see Figure 11-3.

Figure 11-3. *You can set app associations by protocol*

The last link at the Default apps page is *Set defaults by app*, and this is where we're thrown into the Control Panel. This will display a list of all the installed Store apps and win32 desktop apps on your PC. You can click one to check its file defaults (as one app might open many different file or protocol types) and set all the defaults for the app, or choose which file types or protocols to associate with that app, see Figure 11-4.

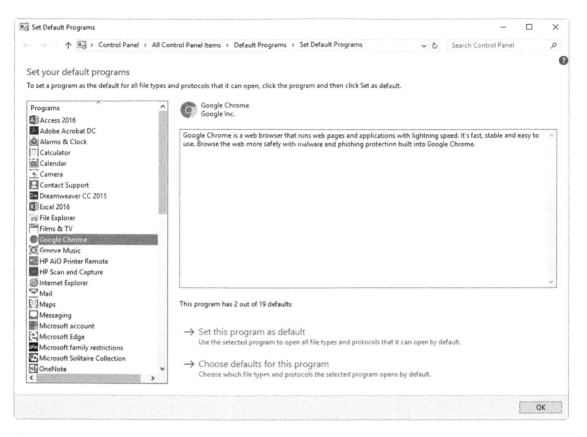

Figure 11-4. *You can get finer control of app associations in the Control Panel*

In the breadcrumb bar at the top of the Set Default Programs window, click the *Default Programs* link to be taken to the main Control Panel options for app defaults. Here you can click the *Associate a file type or protocol with a program* link, and this is where you can assign non-Store apps to open files, see Figure 11-5.

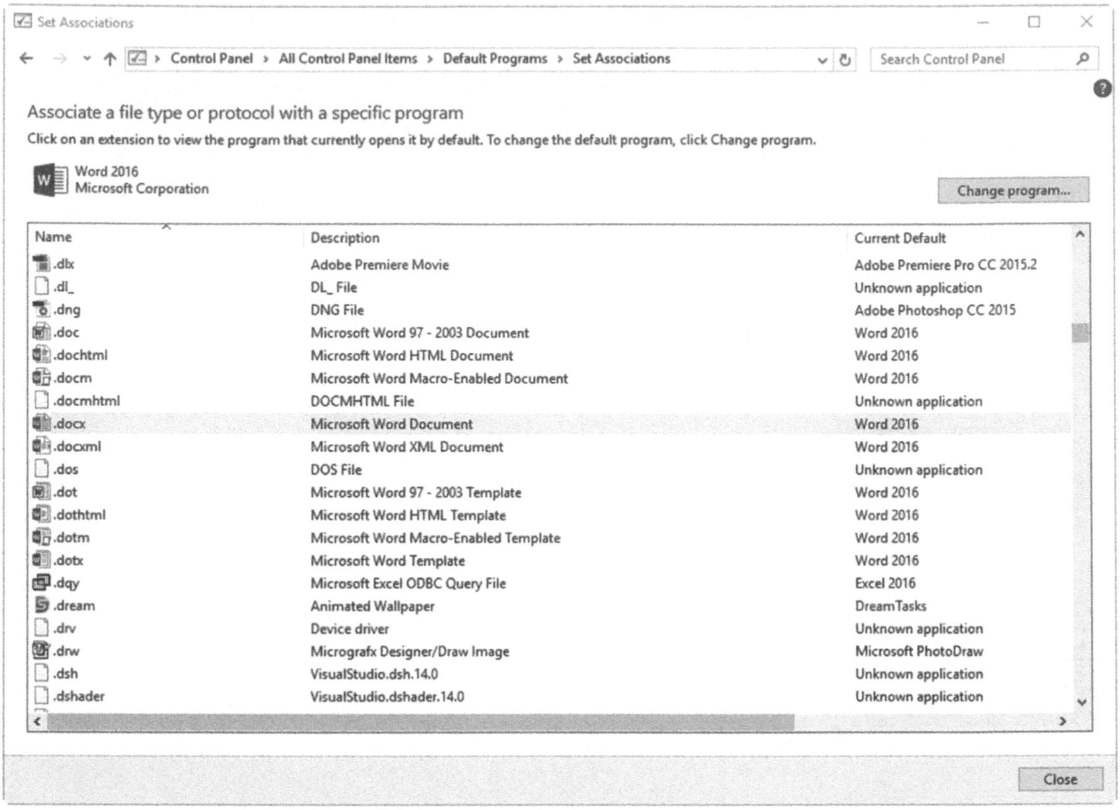

Figure 11-5. *You can set non-Store app associations in the Control Panel*

This is where you will want to point a user if they are reporting that they can't set the file association correctly on their PC.

Setting Disk and File Permissions

Sometimes, however, users simply won't have access to disks, file(s), or folder(s) that they really need, and should be able to get access to. This can occur for several reasons, the most common of which is a reinstallation of Windows. In this scenario a new user account will be set up, but the files required by the user might still be residing in the C:\Users\OldUserName\ folder. When you try to open this folder to move the files to the new user file store, you will get an access error, because the folder is locked and you don't have permission to access it.

To fix this issue, you need to first be signed into the PC as an Administrator. Right-click the file, folder, or disk, and select *Properties* from the context menu that appears; this will open a Properties dialog for the item where you need to navigate to the *Security* tab, see Figure 11-6.

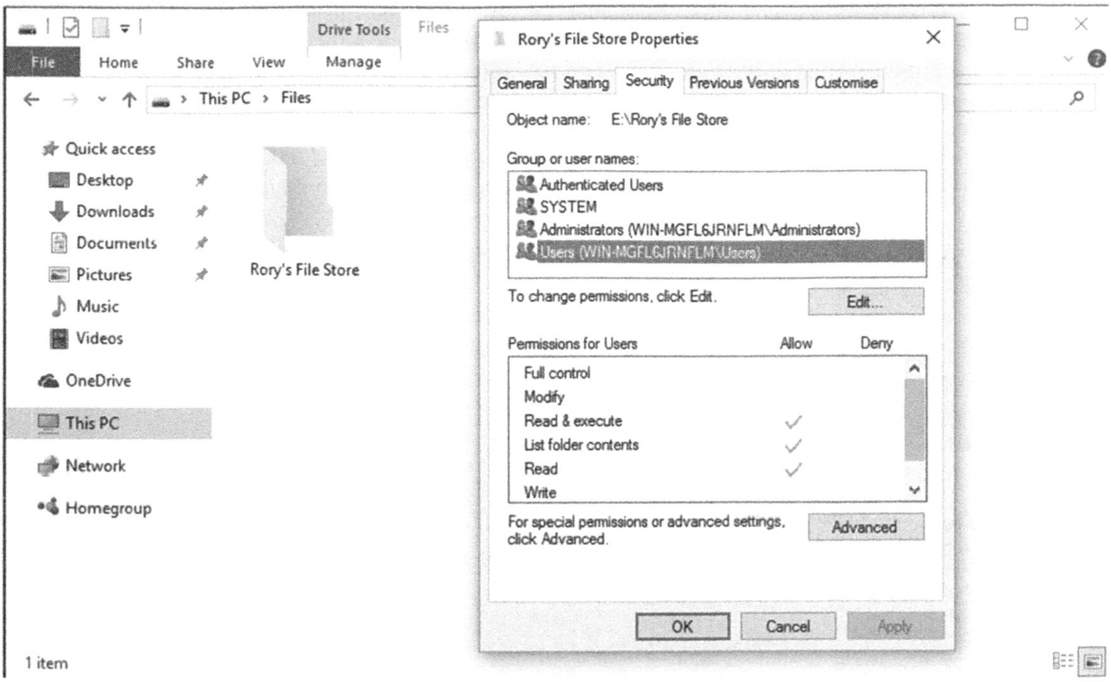

Figure 11-6. *You manage disk and file permissions from within File Explorer*

Here you can see the user groups, and individual users if specified, who are set up on the PC. Clicking one will display their permissions. To change permissions for a user or user group, click the *Edit* button. This will turn each of the available options into a check box. Additionally, it offers *Add* and *Remove* buttons. These are used for adding or removing users from the permissions list, see Figure 11-7.

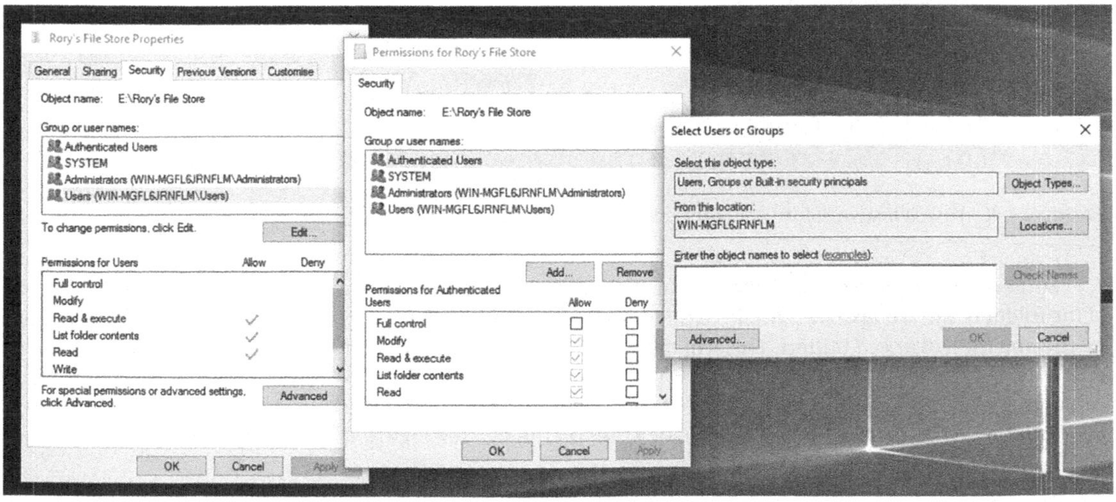

Figure 11-7. *You can add or remove users from the permissions list*

You might want to add a user if the files or folders you are setting permissions for don't reside on the PC, but sit on a network-attached storage drive or on another PC or server to which you have access. Type the name of the user in the format *Computername\Username* and click the *Check Names* button.

If you are unsure of the computer name or the user name, you can click the *Advanced* button, which will allow you to search for users. The dialog that appears will allow you to search different computers on your network, by clicking the *Locations* button, and for user of the PC with the *Find Now* button, see Figure 11-8. You can then double-click a user (or use Ctrl to select multiple users) to select them.

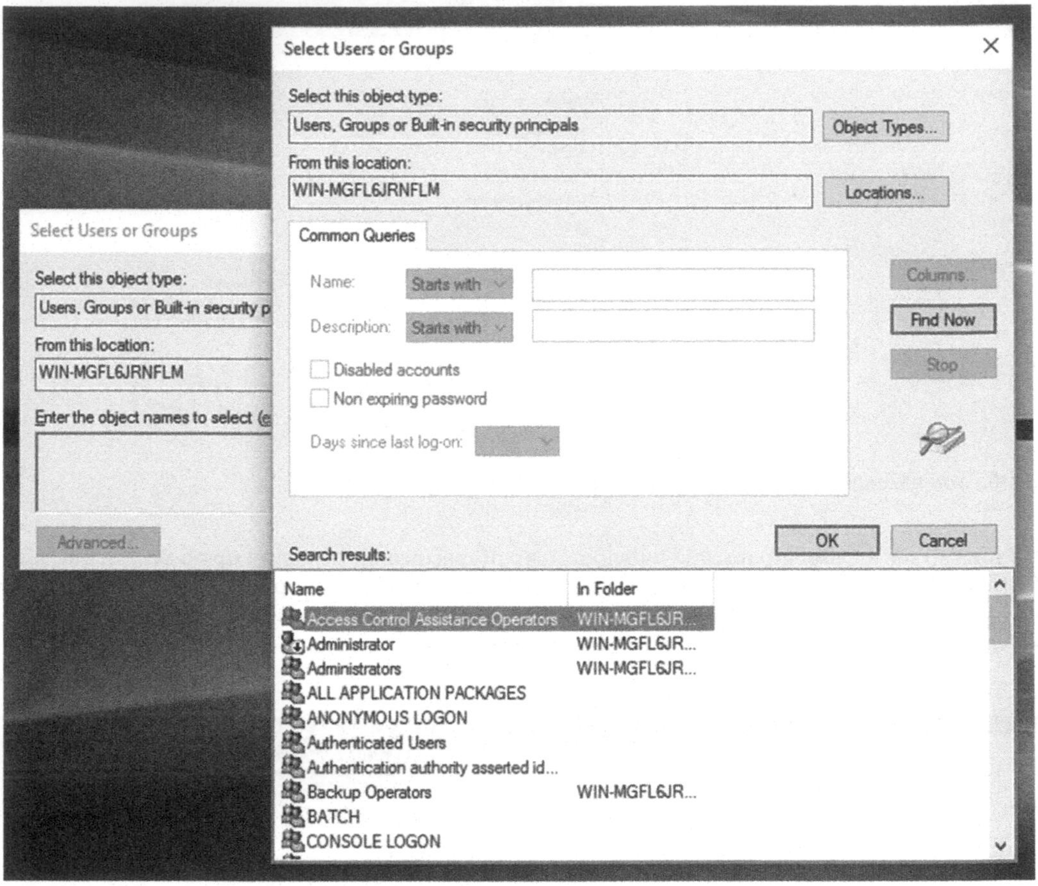

Figure 11-8. *You can search for users on the PC or network*

Sometimes, however, especially as is the case with old user folders, you will want to change the "Owner" of the folder or files to take ownership of them. You can do this from the file, disk, or folder Properties dialog by clicking the *Advanced* button. This will display an advanced permissions dialog, and there are a few different things you can do here. To change permissions, however, click the *Change* button near the top center of the window, next to the current "Owner" name. This will display a user dialog, the same as the one I've just detailed, in which you can search for a user on the PC, see Figure 11-9.

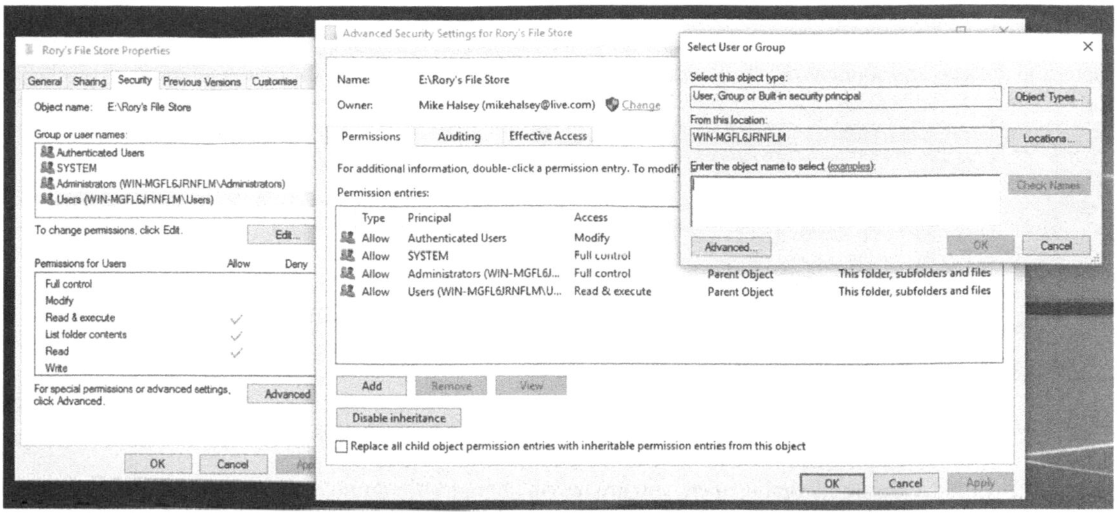

Figure 11-9. *Taking ownership allows you to change the "owner" of files or folders*

Something else that can prove useful if you're having difficulty accessing files or folders is to enable or disable permission "inheritance," using the button and check box near the bottom left of the window. Inheritance is where you have a tree of nested folders and want to either set the permissions for them to be all the same, or disable this feature so that folder permissions are assigned individually.

In short, inheritance is where a folder and its contents will "inherit" their security permissions from the folder above them. This follows all the folders back to the root drive. If you find that, for example, you're creating folders or files that have incorrect permissions, then inheritance is probably not configured. Open the properties for the root folder and enable inheritance for the tree.

Managing Audio Devices

We've all encountered this. You plug some headphones into your PC, connect a Bluetooth speaker, or try to make a call over Skype, and the sound on the PC either doesn't play at all or plays through the wrong device. Now that we commonly use our PCs with hardware such as Bluetooth speakers and gaming headsets, it should be straightforward for people to switch between audio devices, or you would expect Windows 10 to do this automatically.

Alas, when you click the audio icon in the system tray, at the far end of the Taskbar, you're presented in Windows 10 only with a volume slider but no way to change the displayed audio device, see Figure 11-10.

Figure 11-10. *The volume control in Windows 10 doesn't let you switch audio devices easily*

In order to change the audio device, you must right-click the audio icon (you can also open Sound from the Control Panel) and select one of the available options, see Figure 11-11. In truth, the options for playback devices, recording devices, and sounds will all take you to the same dialog, so it doesn't really matter which one you click.

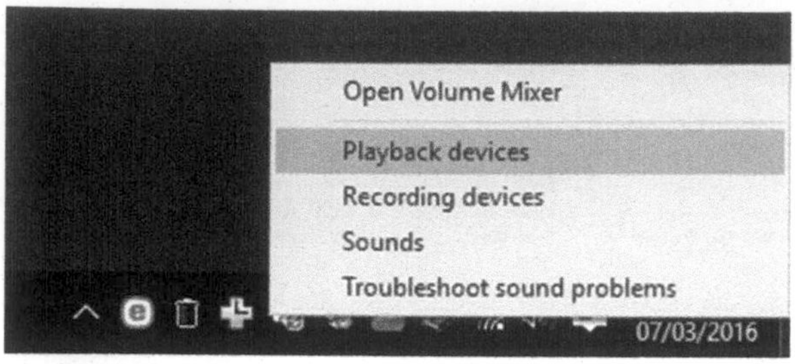

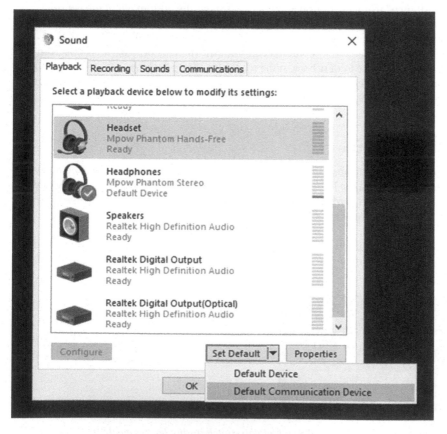

Figure 11-11. You need to right-click the audio icon to change the sound device

Once you have the audio dialog open, you are free to change your audio device to the correct one. It's worth noting, especially with regards to communications headsets, that two "Set default" options are available. Figure 11-12 shows that you can set an audio device either as the default, or as the default for communications. If you merely set a headphone/microsoft set as the default device you will find yourself changing audio devices very often, and not just when you want to make a Skype call.

Figure 11-12. You can set a device as the default device or the default communications device

Troubleshooting Windows Activation

It's not uncommon for a PC to start with a black desktop and a message saying that either your copy of Windows isn't activated, or worse, that it's not a genuine copy of Windows. This is a rare, though annoying circumstance. It occurs because the file containing the registration and activation status of the PC couldn't be found, or wasn't loaded at the PC's startup due to a glitch.

The good news is that this is extremely easy to fix, as all you need to do is restart the PC. Sometimes you may need to fully shut it down and restart it, but a general restart will almost always fix the problem. I say almost always because I have seen only a tiny handful of incidents where the message has persisted. If you are certain that your copy of Windows 10 is genuine (i.e., that you upgraded from Windows 7 or Windows 8.1 when the free offer was on in 2015/16, or because the copy of Windows 10 came with a new PC or you bought a retail copy), then you may need to reset or reinstall Windows.

Information about Windows licensing and activation can be found online at **http://windows. microsoft.com/windows/genuine** and it's not unheard of for independent PC makers (such as those on your Main Street) to sell PCs with pirated copies of Windows.

Troubleshooting and Resetting Windows Update

Sometimes, though fortunately not very often, Windows Update become corrupt and will flatly refuse to either download or install updates. This is more than an annoyance as it will prevent essential security and stability updates from being installed on your PC. It happens when one or more of the downloaded updates are corrupt and unreadable.

Should this happen, you will need to reset Windows Update. You should restart your PC at this point (as if the Windows Update process is running, it will prevent you from deleting some files), and in File Explorer, navigate to C:\Windows\SoftwareDistribution, see Figure 11-13. You should then delete **all** the contents of this folder and Windows Update will be reset.

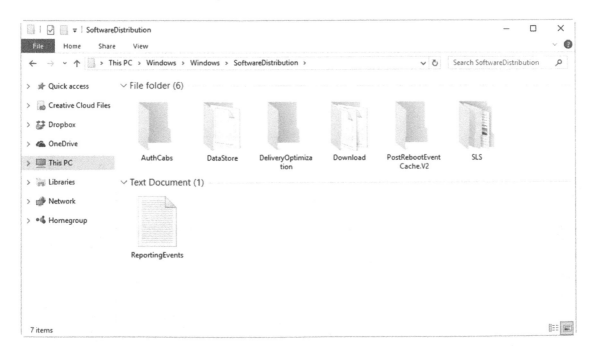

Figure 11-13. *You can delete the contents of the SoftwareDistribution folder to reset Windows Update*

Troubleshooting Power Loss During an Update Installation

Windows 10 is incredibly resilient during the installation of updates, and despite the operating system asking you not to turn off your PC when updates are being installed, doing so is unlikely to harm it. In fact the Windows Update system is **so** resilient that I have tried repeatedly in the past to break the OS by forcing the power off during major update installations, only to fail to break the OS on every occasion. Every time I tried, the installation just restarted when I switched the PC back on.

My best efforts to break my own PC notwithstanding (see the lengths I go to for you all?) it's not beyond the realms of possibility that something could break on a PC at some point in the future. It's easy to rectify, however, so long as you have created a USB Recovery Drive (remember those?). If you start the PC from the Recovery Drive you can run System Restore and roll the OS back to a point before the update installation took place; see Chapter 8 for details on how to do this. This will fix your copy of Windows.

Managing and Resetting Windows Search

In the same way that downloaded Windows Update files can become corrupt, so too can the database used by Windows 10's and Cortana's search engine. Resetting this database (called the Search Index) is a very simple and straightforward operation. Open the Control Panel and then click *Indexing Options* (I won't recommend searching for Indexing options on this occasion). When the Indexing Options dialog appears, click the *Advanced* button, and in the dialog that appears, under the *Index Settings* tab you will see a Troubleshooting section with a Rebuild button, see Figure 11-14. Click this to delete the current index and rebuild it from scratch.

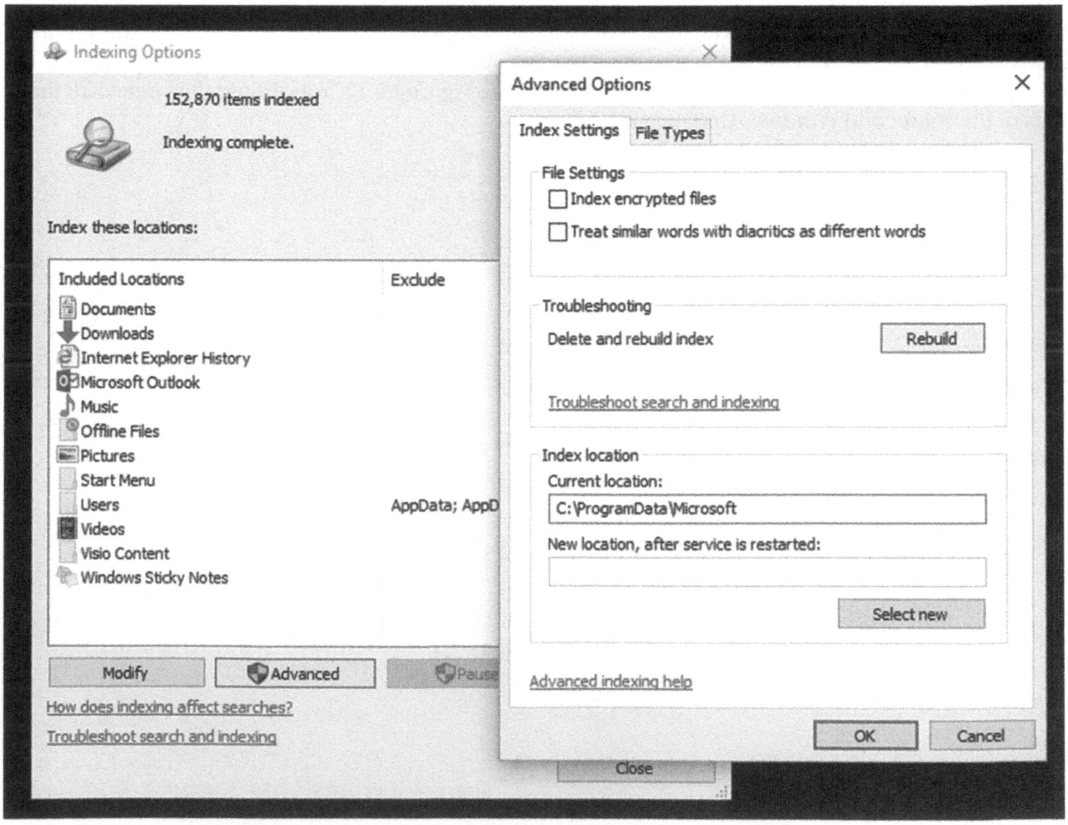

Figure 11-14. *You can ask for Windows to search to delete its database*

Troubleshooting Slow Startup

It wasn't too long ago that we'd switch our computers on in the morning, and then go and make a cup of coffee while the boot sequence ran. After 5 minutes we'd be confident that when we returned to the PC we'd be faced with the sign-in screen. Nowadays a modern PC will start up in seconds, even from cold, which is great news for PC users, but bad news for coffee sellers.

This is especially useful when returning to your PC after a break or from lunch, when you (or more honestly, your boss) wants you working again as quickly as possible. But what happens when you have a normally speedy PC that's suffering from slow startup?

Troubleshooting slow startup is fairly straightforward in Windows 10, as it's almost always going to be your apps that are slowing things down. I say "almost always" because if you have a PC with a mechanical hard disk, it may need defragmenting. A fragmented disk won't slow the PC much, but you will probably notice the difference.

To manage your startup apps, open the Task Manager. You can do this from the *Win+X* menu, from the *Ctrl+Alt+Del* menu, or by right-clicking a black space on the Taskbar. Once the Task Manager is open, click the *Start-up* tab, where you will see all your startup apps listed, see Figure 11-15.

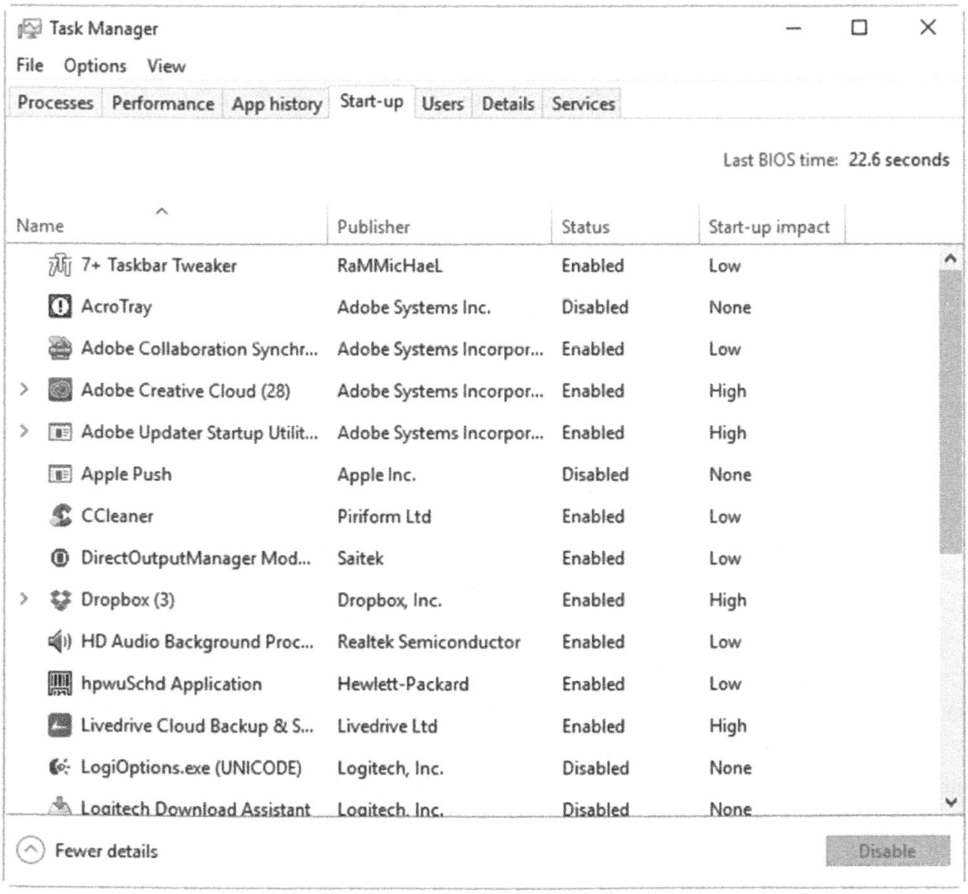

Figure 11-15. *You can manage startup apps in Task Manager*

Next to each is a *Start-up impact* rating. This will appear after the first few startups since an app was installed (obviously, it's impossible for Windows 10 to measure the Startup impact on an app that's only just been installed). The ratings show Low, Medium, or High, with the apps rated high being the ones that will slow your PC's startup the most.

In Figure 11-15 we can see that Adobe Creative Cloud, Adobe Updater, Dropbox, and LiveDrive Cloud Backup are all rated high (which is very annoying as I need all of them!). You can click any startup app and the *Disable* button will become clickable, so you can stop that app from running at startup.

Windows 10 Hangs on Startup

Occasionally you might find that your PC doesn't start at all, and you're left with either a spinning loading icon or just a black screen. There can be several reasons for this…

- Network connections can cause a stalled startup. If your PC is connected to the network via an Ethernet cable, unplug this temporarily and see if startup continues. Should this be the case, it's likely your network driver will need to be updated to prevent this from happening each time you switch on the PC.

- Sometimes a PC will hang at the BIOS/UEFI screen with an error. This will be most commonly because the BIOS/UEFI system is being reset each time the PC starts (which likely means you will need to put a new battery on the motherboard), or because the BIOS/UEFI settings are either corrupt or unstable. You can fix the latter by entering the BIOS/UEFI interface and selecting the "Load optimized defaults" option, or by resetting the BIOS using the motherboard jumper I detailed in Chapter 6.

- If you get the message "No operating system found" it's likely that there is a hard disk inconsistency, either in the BIOS/UEFI or with the disk itself. In the BIOS/UEFI interface, the default boot order might have been changed (perhaps because of a BIOS/UEFI reset) and the PC is trying to load the operating system from another disk, perhaps a network boot or removable drive, where no operating system exists. Alternatively, have the drives in the PC been changed recently? If you have performed maintenance or cleaning on the PC, is the hard disk on which Windows 10 is installed plugged into the same motherboard SATA socket it was before? These are assigned Drive 0, Drive 1, and so on by BIOS and Windows, and the OS boot loader will expect to find its files on the same drive it was installed on.

- Lastly (and this one is almost comical, though you may be surprised how often it occurs), if you have recently installed Windows 10 but keep seeing the setup screen when you start the PC, this is because you need to unplug or remove the USB Flash Drive or DVD containing the Windows installer, and then restart the PC.

■ **Note** Windows 10 never truly shuts down completely, as it always hibernates some part of memory to disk to aid in a quick startup. Sometimes this will become corrupt, causing startup problems. To rectify this, during startup, press and hold the PC's power button for 4 seconds to force shutdown. When you next start the PC, it will start completely fresh.

Windows 10 Shuts Down Slowly

Just as annoying as a slow startup is when the PC won't shut down, or shuts down extremely slowly. Normally when you shut down the PC, if any apps are still running, you will be presented with a list of the apps and asked if you want to force them to shut down, or if you want to wait for Windows 10 to shut them down itself.

Sometimes, if you're like me, you'll hit the force shutdown button and walk away. On other occasions though you might just get up and walk, and then come back some time later to discover the PC is STILL trying to shut down the apps.

There are some changes you can make to the Registry, however, to speed up the shutdown of your PC. You can access the Registry Editor by searching for **regedit** at the Start Menu or in Cortana.

■ **Caution**   Always be careful making changes to the Windows Registry. Make a backup of the Registry from its *File* menu so the Registry can be restored should a change cause Windows to become unstable. This can be achieved from the Recovery Panel if necessary, see Chapter 8 for details of how to run the Registry Editor in the Recovery Panel. If you have encrypted your hard disks using Bitlocker, you should copy the Registry backup file to a nonencrypted drive.

There are two options you can change in the Registry to affect Windows Shutdown...

- HKEY_LOCAL_MACHINE ➤ SYSTEM ➤ CurrentControlSet ➤ WaitToKillServiceTimeout is set by default at 5000 miliseconds (5 seconds). This setting determines how long the OS waits for Windows and third-party services to close before notifying the user the service is not closing. You may wish to increase this number to 50000 if services require longer to quit.

- HKEY_CURRENT_USER ➤ Control Panel ➤ Desktop ➤ WaitToKillAppTimeout will need to be created as it doesn't exist by default in Windows 10, see Figure 11-16. This key determined how long the system waits for user processes to end before notifying the user. The time is stated in miliseconds (20000 being 20 seconds). You can force shutdown by changing the value to **1**, though be aware that forcibly closing any apps with open files may result in loss of data.

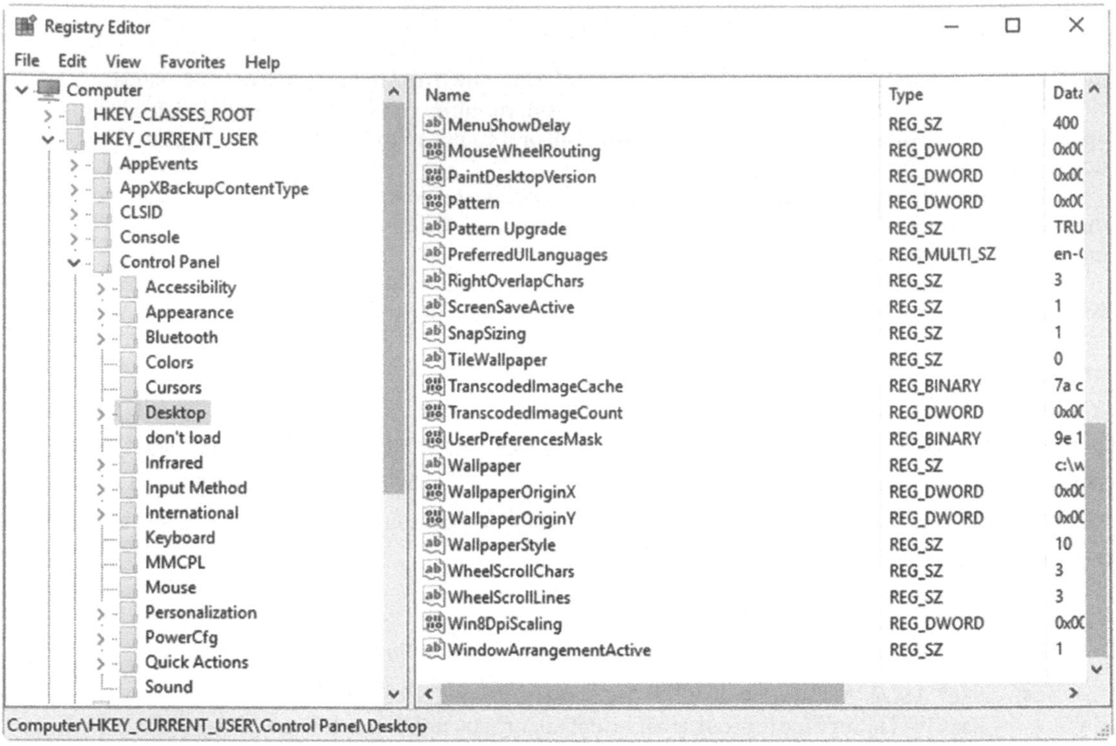

Figure 11-16. *WaitToKillAppTimeout doesn't exist in Windows 10 and needs to be created*

Windows Fails to Sleep/Resume from Sleep

I mentioned a little while back that Windows 10 doesn't really shut down, instead going into a deep hibernation so as to help it restart quickly. By far the quickest, and now extremely common and popular, way to shut down a Windows PC is to put it to sleep. Whether you simply close the lib on your laptop, press the sleep button on your tablet, or activate sleep from the Start menu on a desktop, sleep keeps the current memory active so the PC can start to the desktop within a second or two.

Sometimes this doesn't work however, and you need to troubleshoot the Sleep feature in Windows. There are different sleep states available for PCs, laptops, and tablets and you can check which ones are supported on your hardware by opening a Command Prompt window and typing `powercfg/availablesleepstates`, see Figure 11-17.

```
Command Prompt

Microsoft Windows [Version 10.0.10586]
(c) 2015 Microsoft Corporation. All rights reserved.

C:\Users\Mike Halsey>powercfg /availablesleepstates
The following sleep states are available on this system:
    Standby (S3)
    Hibernate
    Fast Startup

The following sleep states are not available on this system:
    Standby (S1)
        The system firmware does not support this standby state.

    Standby (S2)
        The system firmware does not support this standby state.

    Standby (S0 Low Power Idle)
        The system firmware does not support this standby state.

    Hybrid Sleep
        The hypervisor does not support this standby state.
```

Figure 11-17. *You can use the PowerCFG command to check sleep state compatibility*

In this example we can see the S0, S1, S2, S3, and Hybrid Sleep states and so on, and that only S3 is supported on this PC. But what are these different states and which should you choose for your PC?

- **S0** is a low-power idle state where power is used at a normal rate, but where unused devices, such as the hard disk, can be powered down as necessary.

- **S1** is the first Sleep state for PCs. Power consumption is less than with the S0 state, but greater than the other states. In this state, both the process and commuinications bus clocks are stopped. This is the first state the system goes into when you put it to sleep.

- **S2** is similar to S1 but in this state the processor does not receive power and is reset on startup. This causes the system cache to be lost and causes more of a "reset" to the system than with S1. S2 is engaged after a period of sleep in S1.

- **S3** is very similar to S2; however in this state only power to the system memory is maintained. S3 is engaged after a period of sleep in S2.

- **S4** is the lowest-power sleep state and all devices are powered off. Memory is moved to a Hibernation file on the disk and reloaded on startup. S4 is engaged after a period of sleep in S3.

- **S5** is a shutdown state for the PC. S5 is engaged after a period of sleep in S4, when the power gets low.

- **Hybrid Sleep** is designed for desktop PCs, and is a combination of Sleep and Hibernate: any open documents and files are held both in memory and on the hard disk, so that work can continue even after a power failure.

- **Connected Standby** provides and instant-on sleep state. This power state requires compatible hardware support and suspends the state of the OS, while maintaining it with a tiny power draw.

If you find that a device isn't waking, or is misbehaving when you put the PC to sleep, you can use the **powercfg /devicequery** command to determine what hardware devices in your PC support each sleep state. The command is used in the format **powercfg /devicequery s1_supported** and so on through to **S4_supported**. Each will provide a list of the installed hardware that's okay at that level of sleep.

You can also troubleshoot Sleep and power management on a PC using the **powercfg** command with the switches **/batteryreport**, **/sleepstudy**, and **/energy**, see Figure 11-18. These commands save reports to your hard disk as HTML files that can be opened in a web browser.

```
Administrator: Command Prompt
Microsoft Windows [Version 10.0.14271]
(c) 2016 Microsoft Corporation. All rights reserved.

C:\WINDOWS\system32>powercfg /sleepstudy
Sleep Study report saved to C:\WINDOWS\system32\sleepstudy-report.html.

C:\WINDOWS\system32>powercfg /batteryreport
Battery life report saved to C:\WINDOWS\system32\battery-report.html.

C:\WINDOWS\system32>powercfg /energy
Enabling tracing for 60 seconds...
Observing system behavior...
Analyzing trace data...
Analysis complete.

Energy efficiency problems were found.

2 Errors
13 Warnings
19 Informational

See C:\WINDOWS\system32\energy-report.html for more details.
```

Figure 11-18. *You can troubleshoot power, battery, and sleep issues*

The Battery Report will apply only to laptops and tablets and will provide detailed metrics on power usage and battery capacity over the last few days. The Power Efficiency Diagnostics Report, however, can help you ascertain if the power management options set in Windows are optimal for your device.

In Figure 11-19, you can see a typical Power Efficiency Diagnostics Report. There are warnings here that the power settings for this particular PC, a Surface Pro 3, are not set correctly. The descriptions are all in plain language so you can determine what changes, if any, you can make to improve power management on the PC.

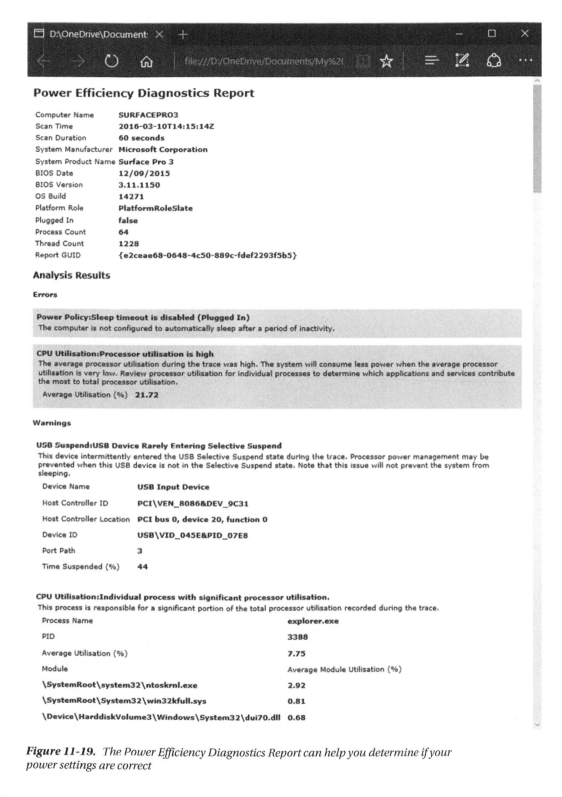

Figure 11-19. *The Power Efficiency Diagnostics Report can help you determine if your power settings are correct*

The Sleep Study provides extremely detailed graphics and metrics to show power consumption for the PC when it is in a sleep state or Connected Standby, see Figure 11-20. The information includes what components in the PC were still drawing power, and how long they were active for during sleep. This includes the "Top Five Offenders" for power usage.

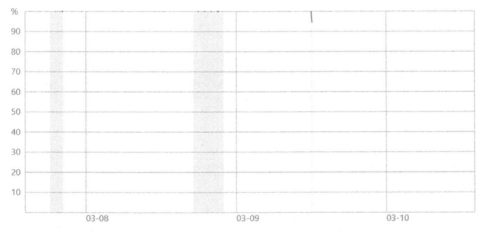

Figure 11-20. The Sleep State report is extremely detailed and useful

Windows 10 is able to wake periodically during sleep to check for updates, perform maintenance, and update Live Tiles in the Start Menu. At the bottom of the Sleep Study are details of all the apps and services that have been active during these wake states, see Figure 11-21. You can use this information to determine if something is waking the PC too often, or using too much power at those times.

Srum Data

Data obtained from the SRUM database.

Energy Estimation

APP ID	TOTAL (mJ)	CPU (mJ)	DISPLAY (mJ)	DISK (mJ)	MBB (mJ)	NETWORK (mJ)	SOC (mJ)	OTHER (mJ)
\Device\HarddiskVolume3\Windows\System32\svchost.exe [mikeh]	258268	2639	0	254932	0	697	0	0
System [SYSTEM]	31736	2553	0	23040	0	6143	0	0
\Device\HarddiskVolume3\Windows\System32\svchost.exe [utcsvc] [SYSTEM]	14878	1269	0	6081	0	7528	0	0
\Device\HarddiskVolume3\Windows\System32\svchost.exe [netsvcs] [SYSTEM]	3262	496	0	2002	0	764	0	0
\Device\HarddiskVolume3\Program Files\ESET\ESET Smart Security\ekrn.exe [SYSTEM]	2516	295	0	44	0	2177	0	0
\Device\HarddiskVolume3\Windows\System32\svchost.exe [LocalServiceNetworkRestricted] [LOCAL SERVICE]	1545	480	0	1061	0	4	0	0
\Device\HarddiskVolume3\Windows\System32\svchost.exe [NetworkService] [NETWORK SERVICE]	1322	775	0	0	0	547	0	0
\Device\HarddiskVolume3\Windows\System32\svchost.exe [LocalSystemNetworkRestricted] [SYSTEM]	1077	168	0	909	0	0	0	0
Memory Compression [SYSTEM]	1015	23	0	992	0	0	0	0
System Interrupts [SYSTEM]	935	621	0	0	0	0	314	0
\Device\HarddiskVolume3\Windows\explorer.exe [mikeh]	326	78	0	144	0	104	0	0
\Device\HarddiskVolume3\Windows\System32\lsass.exe [SYSTEM]	325	325	0	0	0	0	0	0
\Device\HarddiskVolume3\Windows\System32\LogonUI.exe [SYSTEM]	294	4	0	290	0	0	0	0
\Device\HarddiskVolume3\Windows\System32\svchost.exe [RPCSS] [NETWORK SERVICE]	273	273	0	0	0	0	0	0

Figure 11-21. *The Sleep Study also details apps and services using power during wake states*

Armed with all the information the powercfg commands and reports have given you, you can then modify the standard sleep settings for the PC to ensure Sleep operates properly on the PC. In the *Power Options* in Control Panel, click *Choose what the power button does* and then click *Change settings that are currently unavailable.*

Now you will be presented with a list of the available and supported sleep states for your PC, see Figure 11-22. Each, including Fast Start-up, can be disabled should it be causing a problem on the PC. Fast Start-up is the feature I mentioned earlier where some parts of memory are saved to disk as a hibernation file. If you wish for your PC to clean start each time you switch it on, you can disable this feature.

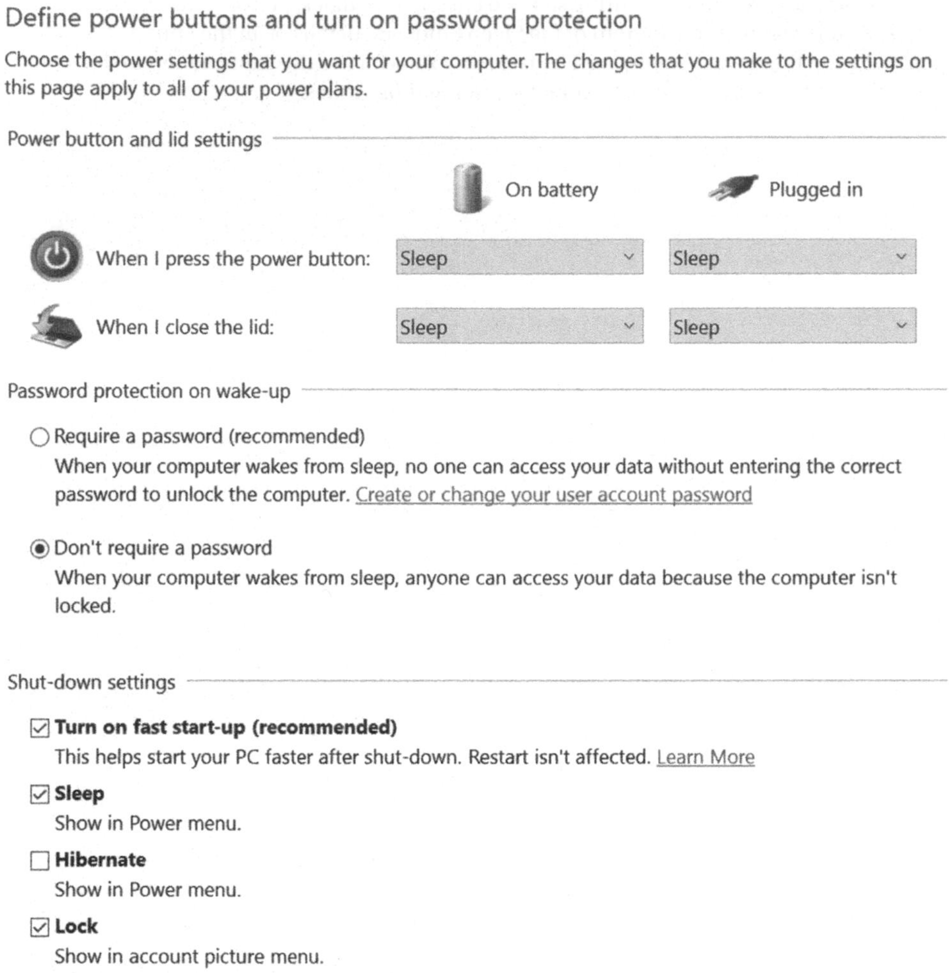

Define power buttons and turn on password protection

Choose the power settings that you want for your computer. The changes that you make to the settings on this page apply to all of your power plans.

Power button and lid settings

	On battery	Plugged in
When I press the power button:	Sleep	Sleep
When I close the lid:	Sleep	Sleep

Password protection on wake-up

○ Require a password (recommended)
When your computer wakes from sleep, no one can access your data without entering the correct password to unlock the computer. Create or change your user account password

⦿ Don't require a password
When your computer wakes from sleep, anyone can access your data because the computer isn't locked.

Shut-down settings

☑ **Turn on fast start-up (recommended)**
This helps start your PC faster after shut-down. Restart isn't affected. Learn More

☑ **Sleep**
Show in Power menu.

☐ **Hibernate**
Show in Power menu.

☑ **Lock**
Show in account picture menu.

Figure 11-22. *You can disable sleep states that are causing problems on your PC*

Gaining Access After Bitlocker Lockout

Sometimes, perhaps after a disk corruption (even a small one can cause this), you can find yourself locked out of the PC until you can enter your 48-character unlock key, see Figure 11-23. It's also worth noting that on some PCs such as Microsoft Surface Pro and Surface Book lines, Bitlocker is enabled automatically if you sign into the device with a Microsoft account.

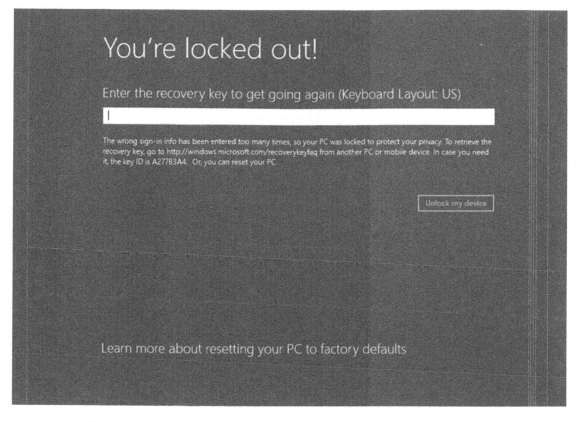

Figure 11-23. You find yourself locked out of your PC by Bitlocker

I strongly recommend that when you encrypt a drive with Bitlocker, you tell Bitlocker to save a copy of the unlock key to your Microsoft account, as then you can save the bookmark *https://onedrive.live.com/ recoverykey* to your smartphone or another device. From this web site you will able to see your Bitlocker recovery keys, so you can enter them on your PC.

Troubleshooting Touch Screen Problems

If a touch screen isn't working on your device, then it will certainly be the driver that's either missing or corrupt. On a tablet device, this can be extremely annoying but there are a couple of things you can do in advance, just to make sure you're okay should this happen.

Having a Bluetooth keyboard and mouse that you can use with the tablet is a very good idea. However you may not want to purchase these, as you might have a USB wired keyboard and mouse that you can use instead. Tablets don't tend to come with full-size USB ports, however, usually shipping with either Micro-USB or USB Type-C ports. If this is the case, it can be extremely wise, especially should you need to reinstall Windows, to purchase a USB On-The-Go (USB OTG) cable. This is a USB extender cable that will plug into your Micro-USB or USB Type-C port, and it has one or more standard USB ports at its other end. I will show you how to troubleshoot hardware drivers in Chapter 15.

USB Type-C and Thunderbolt Problems

Similiarly as with touch screens, any problem you encounter with USB Type-C and Thunderbolt devices not working is likely to be a hardware driver problem. Check in the Device Manager to see if there are any "unidentified" or "uninstalled" devices. I will show you how to manage device drivers in Chapter 15.

No Picture on Desktop PC Monitor or TV

Sometimes, especially after cleaning, moving, or updating a desktop PC, you might suddenly find that you have no picture on your monitor. However, this can also extend to Media Center PCs that you have plugged into a TV via HDMI or DisplayPort.

Regarding standard PC monitors on business PCs, the most common cause is that whoever has been cleaning or moving a PC has plugged the monitor into the wrong video socket, perhaps the one on the motherboard back panel when a graphics card is installed. The cause also could have been a BIOS update, however. On older PCs, a BIOS reset can set the default video output to the motherboard when your monitor is plugged into a PCIe graphics card. To rectify this, you will need to plug your monitor into the motherboard graphics output (you might need a cable adapter for this and it's useful to have one in your toolkit) and change the BIOS setting back.

Situations where TVs and even some monitors have no picture after a PC resumes from sleep are actually very common, and you should check for an updated graphics driver. It's caused by the HDMI or DisplayPort system going into a low-power state during sleep and not waking properly. Unplugging the video cable from the TV and plugging it back in will refresh the connection.

Disappearing and Conflicting Drives

You might already have enocuntered this already as it's not that uncommon. You plug a USB Flash Drive into your PC and it doesn't appear in File Manager. Alternatively, you have a backup set to run periodically to an external hard disk, but one day the drive suddenly disappears from Windows, even though it's plugged in and switched on.

This is caused either when a drive is plugged into the computer and not correctly identified by the OS, or when Windows tries to assign a driver letter that's already in use by another drive. In both cases the new drive will be present, but won't have a drive letter (C:, etc.) so you can't see it in File Explorer.

To fix this, open *Disk Management* from the Win+X menu and look for the disk in the window that appears (it's usually somewhere near the bottom). Right-click the drive and select Change drive letter and paths from the menu that appears. A dialog will appear that will let you add or change the drive letter, see Figure 11-24, after which the drive will appear in File Explorer.

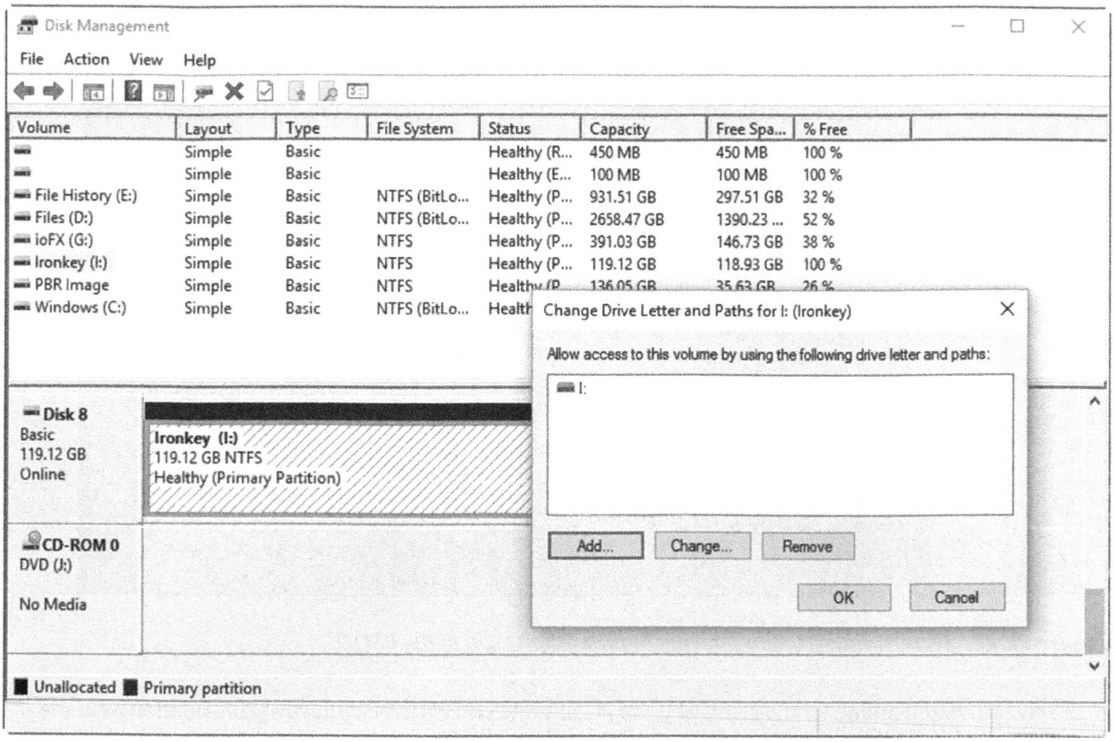

Figure 11-24. *You can assign and reassign driver letters for drivers that require it*

Understanding the BSOD

Microsoft watchers and IT Pros may still refer to Windows 10's critical stop screen as the BSOD, but I prefer these days to call it the "Blue Unhappy Emoticon of Death" because of the change it underwent in Windows 8. This change, if I'm honest, wasn't an improvement as the legacy BSOD provided far more information for the user than the new one does. But, you have to live with what life gives you!

While the legacy BSOD gave you useful information such as the name of the file or driver that had caused the crash, Windows 10's BSOD only gives you an error description. You can find this in the bottom right of the BSOD, see Figure 11-25, where the error is HAL_INITIALIZATION_FAILED.

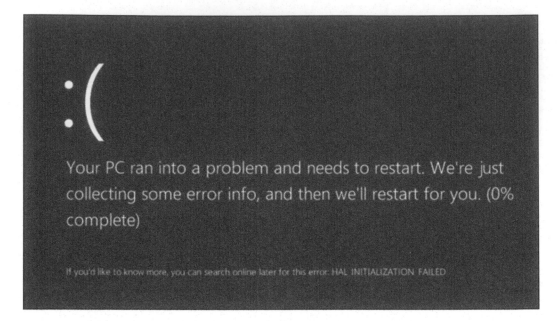

Figure 11-25. *The error description appears in the bottom right of the BSOD*

You can search online for the error, or if the PC has told you it's been collecting information as in the example in Figure 11-25, you will be able to find this in a .dmp memory dump file. Windows Stores these in the \Windows folder as MEMORY.DMP. If you can't find a file when you get back to the desktop, open *System* from the Control Panel, then click *Advanced System Settings* and in the dialog that appears click the *Advanced* tab and the *Settings* button in the Start-up and Recovery section. Additionally, Blue Screens in Windows 10 include a QR code which, if you can open a scanning app on your phone or tablet quickly enough, you can scan to take you directly to a Microsoft support page, related to that error. I say quickly enough, because the blue screen will only remain visible for around 30 seconds before your PC restarts.

In the dialog that appears, you will see options to control Blue Screens, including the dump file name and location, and if the PC should automatically restart after a Blue Screen, see Figure 11-26. You can disable the automatic restart here if you want time to read the error name on the BSOD, but automatic restart (sometimes known as the perpetual restart, as it happens over and over) can also be disabled from the Windows recovery options, as I detailed in Chapter 8.

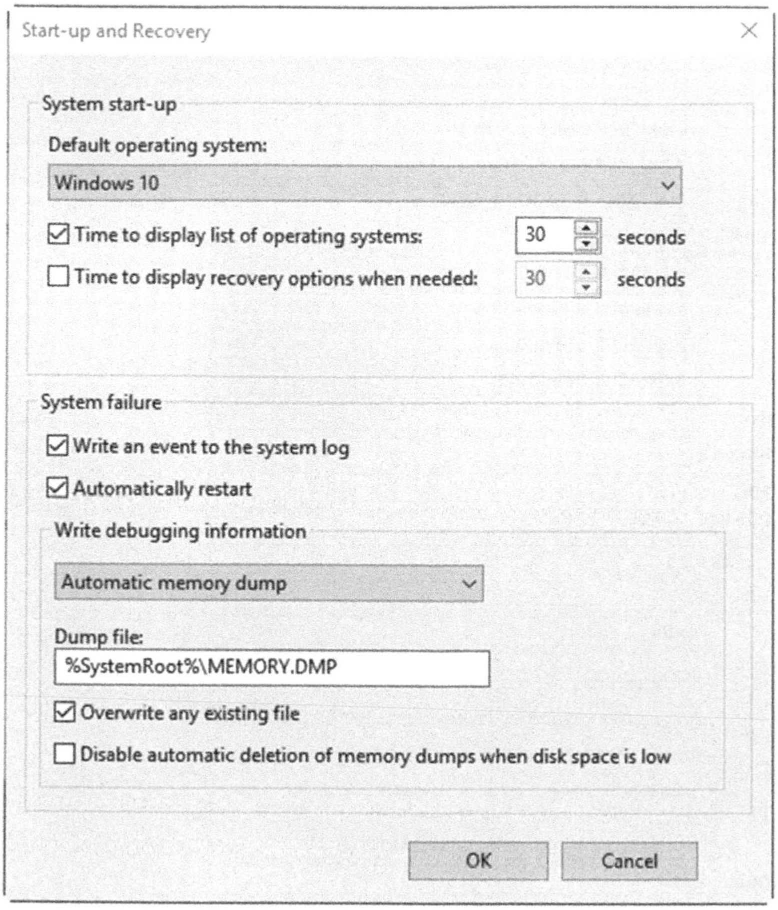

Figure 11-26. *You can find the default location for the BSOD error log in the System options*

The question now is, how do you open and read a .dmp memory dump file? There's no way to easily read this in Windows 10, and you'll need compatible software such as Microsoft Visual Studio to open and read its contents. For this, I recommend a free utility called BlueScreenView, available from www.nirsoft. net/utils/blue_screen_view.html, which will help you find and read BSOD files on your PC.

Reading the MEMORY.DMP file can reveal further information about the cause of the crash. In Figure 11-27 you can see a dump file opened using BlueScreenView, which also details the error code, **0x000000ef** in this case. Searching for error codes online can often reveal much more helpful information than just searching for the error name, see Figure 11-27.

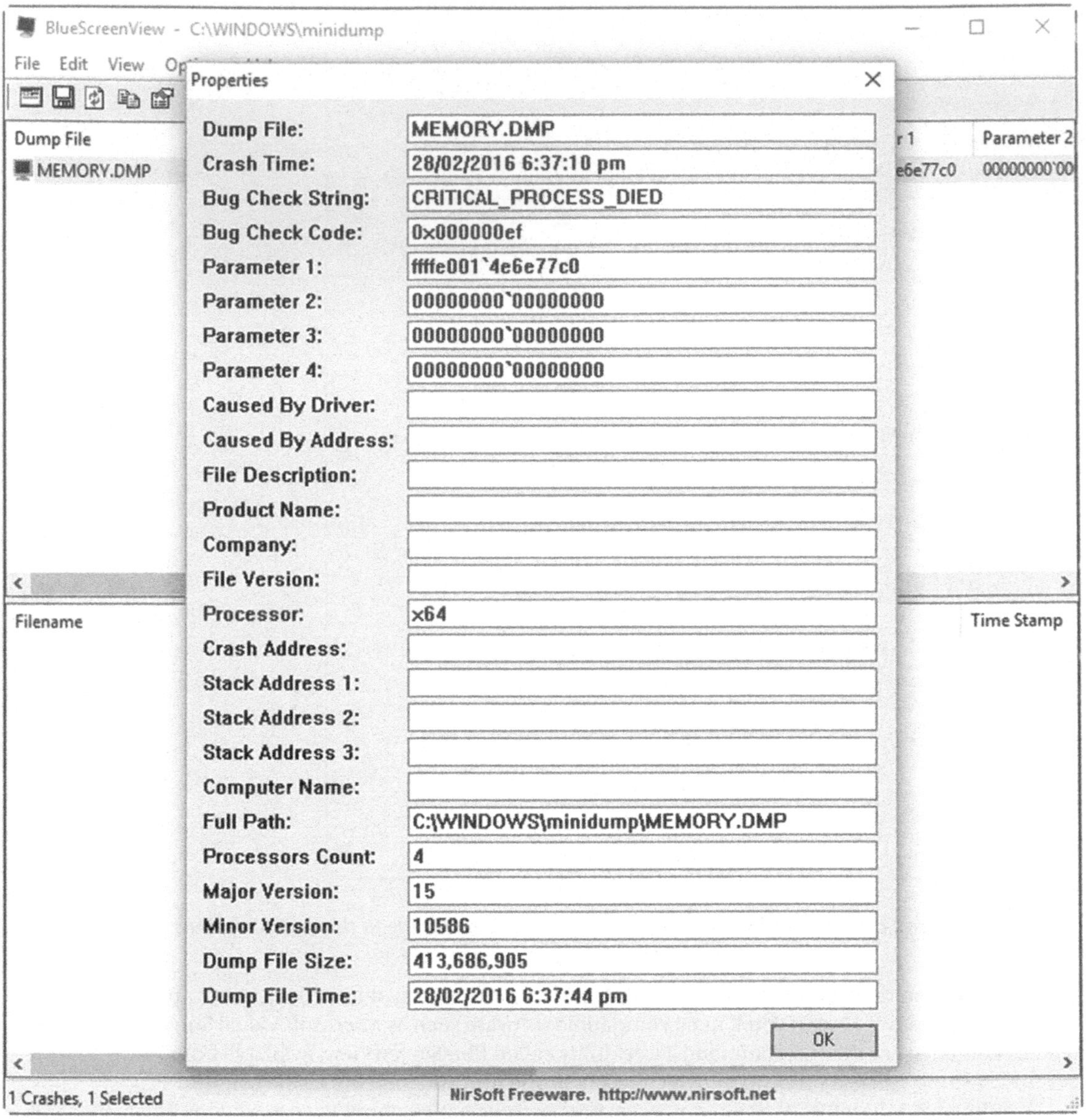

Figure 11-27. MEMORY.DMP files contain more information about crashes

Summary

Windows 10 is not a perfect operating system. Since its release it has included bugs and idiosyncrasies the same as any other OS. While some of these are admittedly Microsoft's fault, it's astonishing to me sometimes how stable, secure, and robust the operating system is, given the almost infinite combinations of software and hardware available for PCs.

While problems such as those listed in this chapter are straightforward to fix, sometimes you're just nowhere near the PC you need to support. In the next chapter, then, we'll examine all the remote support options for PCs, including some little gems of tools you may never have heard of.

CHAPTER 12

■ ■ ■

Remote Help

One of the biggest challenges in either providing or receiving IT Support is that of distance. Long gone are the days when 90% or more of all PCs sold were hulking-great desktops. Now, desktops are still prevalent in offices where workers are static, and for PC gamers at home, but for everybody else the move to laptops and tablets is well established.

One of the challenges with mobile PCs, however, is that you can pretty much guarantee they'll be away from the home or office when they need support. Something will go wrong on the train, or in the airport lounge, or at a remote or a customer's office, or when the user is on their vacation (though in the last instance they'll likely have the sense to enjoy whatever they went there for and leave the PC until they return home). On top of this is the possibility that you will be required to provide urgent support when you're away or out and about.

Partly, this "Murphy's Law" guarantee of problem occurrence is down to the fact that when we're on the move we don't have access to the quick fixes you get when back at base. There's often no good Internet connection for downloading a driver, or a copy of a backup installer on a network share. When it comes to something occurring such as a Bitlocker encryption lockout, which I mentioned in the previous chapter, you can't quickly refer to another PC and find the code you need.

The rest of the problem lies in how people like to work and use their PCs in the 21st century. We enjoy being able to type up notes for a meeting while sit on the train, just an hour before it starts. We like being able to sling our PC into a bag and work on a dissertation in the sunshine of a pub garden.

But if you need to support these people, how can you do so? Well, there are two options, the first of which is with tools the user can use themselves, which is extremely helpful in a place where there is little, no, or patchy Internet coverage. The other tools are remote access and control utilities to help you use the remote PC as if it were sat in front of you on your desk... almost.

The Problem Steps Recorder

One of Windows' best hidden gems is the Problem Steps Recorder, launched by searching for **psr** at the Start Menu or in Cortana, where *Steps Recorder* (Desktop app) will appear as a search result. This is a screen recording and annotation tool that was initially included with the Windows 7 beta builds, to help testers record bugs and problems with the OS. It was so incredibly popular, however, that Microsoft agreed to keep it in the final build, and it remains in Windows to this day.

© Mike Halsey 2016
M. Halsey, *Windows 10 Troubleshooting*, DOI 10.1007/978-1-4842-0925-7_12

The Problem Steps Recorder opens as a toolbar with just four controls, see Figure 12-1. This makes it suitable for use by end users who might have no or only limited technical knowledge.

Figure 12-1. *The Problem Steps Recorder toolbar*

When you want to record a problem on a PC, just click the *Record* button, which will then change to a *Pause* button. This can be useful if you want to omit certain steps from the recording, perhaps because they're not relevant, or perhaps because recording them will contravene a company security or privacy policy. Additionally, an *Add Comment* button, see Figure 12-2, will pause the current recording and present a text box in which a comment can be typed.

Figure 12-2. *Pause and Comment buttons appear when you are recording your screen*

When the recording is finished, click the *Stop Record* button and the toolbar will change to a full window containing the output from your recording session. At the top of this is a save button, see Figure 12-3, that will prompt you to save the recording as a ZIP file, which can then be sent to yourself or another support person for examination.

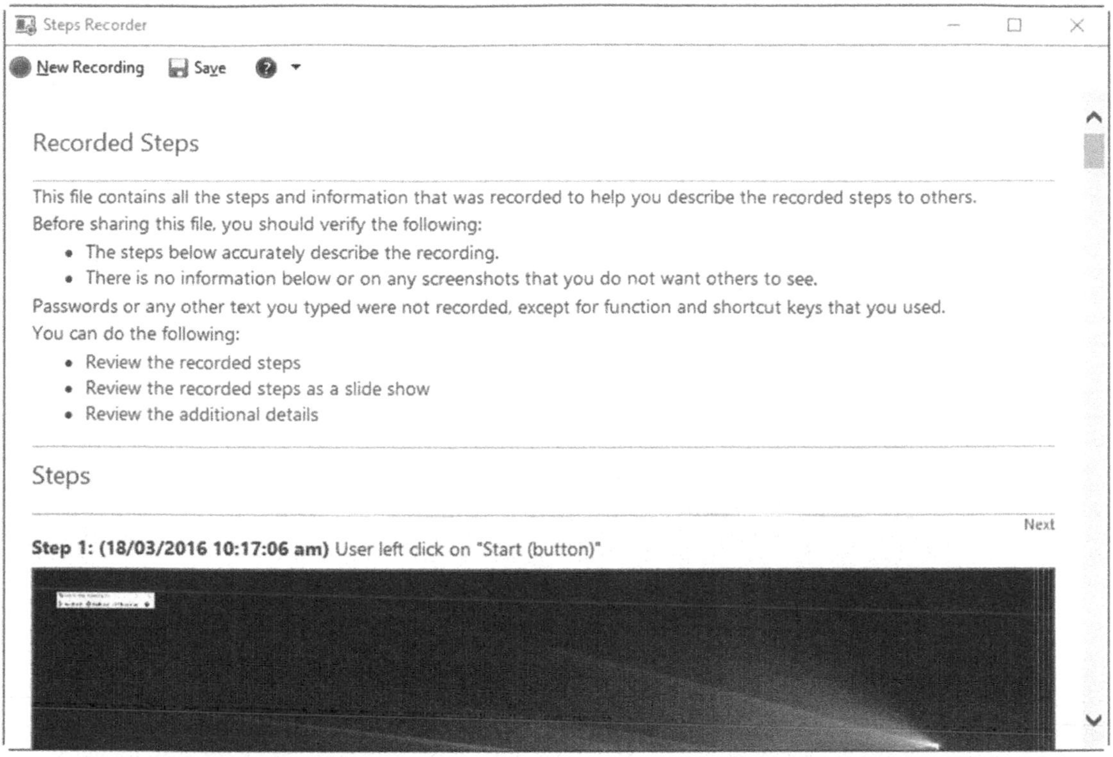

Figure 12-3. *When you stop recording you have an option to save the output file*

This ZIP file contains an HTML document that will open in a web browser and be formatted as you see in Figure 12-3. It's split into different sections. The first section shows a series of annotated screenshots, with the item onscreen that the user has clicked, or that is in focus, highlighted with a green border, see Figure 12-4. This helps you follow the "narrative" of what's going on, and check what's being clicked, activated, and so on. Above each screenshot is a plain text description of what has happened.

■ **Tip** The screenshots can appear very small, especially if the screen being recorded is of a very high resolution, such as the 4K screen seen in Figure 12-4. You can enlarge each screenshot by clicking it.

Previous Next

Step 2: (18/03/2016 10:17:09 am) User left click on "All apps with new apps available (button)" in "Start"

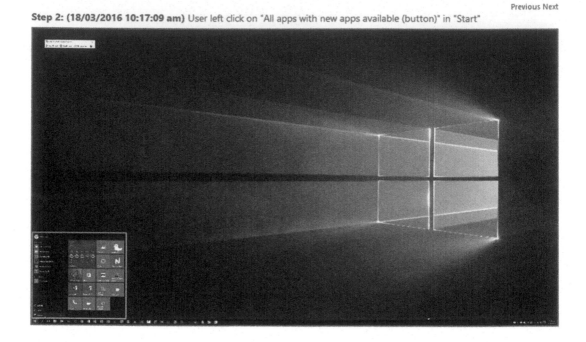

Figure 12-4. Each screenshot is annotated to show what the user is doing

Where the user has written a comment the screenshot will be grayed, and the comment will appear in double quotes above it, see Figure 12-5.

Previous

Step 12: (18/03/2016 10:17:56 am) User Comment: "What's this Direct 3D thing and how do I get it?"

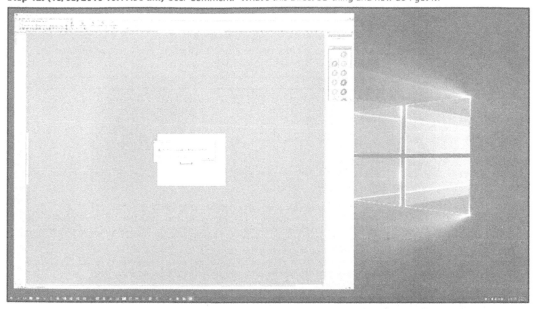

Figure 12-5. *Screenshots hwhere a comment have been typed are grayed out*

At the bottom of the document are technical details, see Figure 12-6. These include the text descriptions from each screenshot, with details of apps, services, or other OS features used, complete with version numbers (which can be incredibly useful when diagnosing problems). The current version number of their copy of Windows 10 is also included, so you can check if an update might be available to help solve the problem.

Additional Details

The following section contains the additional details that were recorded.

These details help accurately identify the programs and UI you used in this recording.

This section may contain text that is internal to programs that may only be understood by very advanced users or programmers.

Please review these details to ensure that they do not contain any information that you would not like others to see.

```
Recording Session: 18/03/2016 10:17:04 am - 10:17:56 am

Recorded Steps: 12, Missed Steps: 0, Other Errors: 0

Operating System: 10586.162.amd64fre.th2_release_sec.160223-1728 10.0.0.0.2.48

Step 1: User left click on "Start (button)"
Program: Windows Explorer, 10.0.10586.0 (th2_release.151029-1700), Microsoft Corporation, EXE
UI Elements: Start, Start, Shell_TrayWnd

Step 2: User left click on "All apps with new apps available (button)" in "Start"
Program: Windows Shell Experience Host, 10.0.10586.122 (th2_release_inmarket.160222-1549), Mi
UI Elements: All apps with new apps available, Button, Start, Windows.UI.Core.CoreWindow

Step 3: User mouse drag start on "All Apps (list)" in "Start"
Program: Windows Shell Experience Host, 10.0.10586.122 (th2_release_inmarket.160222-1549), Mi
UI Elements: All Apps, ListView, SemanticZoom, Start, Windows.UI.Core.CoreWindow

Step 4: User mouse drag end on "Microsoft Silverlight 3 SDK folder, Collapsed (list item)" in
Program: Windows Shell Experience Host, 10.0.10586.122 (th2_release_inmarket.160222-1549), Mi
UI Elements: Microsoft Silverlight 3 SDK folder, Collapsed, ListViewItem, M, ListViewHeaderIt

Step 5: User left click on "Microsoft PhotoDraw V2, Jumplist present (list item)" in "Start"
Program: Windows Shell Experience Host, 10.0.10586.122 (th2_release_inmarket.160222-1549), Mi
UI Elements: Microsoft PhotoDraw V2, Jumplist present, ListViewItem, M, ListViewHeaderItem, A

Step 6: User left click on "Rectangle (button)" in "Microsoft PhotoDraw - [Picture1]"
Program: Microsoft PhotoDraw, 2.0.0.0915, Microsoft Corporation, PHOTODRW.EXE, PHOTODRW.EXE
UI Elements: Rectangle, Standard, MsoCommandBar, MsoDockTop, MsoCommandBarDock, Microsoft Pho

Step 7: User mouse drag start on "PhotoDraw Workspace  (pane)" in "Microsoft PhotoDraw - [Pic
Program: Microsoft PhotoDraw, 2.0.0.0915, Microsoft Corporation, PHOTODRW.EXE, PHOTODRW.EXE
UI Elements: PhotoDraw Workspace , DecoView, Picture1, PhotoDrawChildFrm, Placeholder window
```

Figure 12-6. *Technical details can be found at the bottom of the document*

Recording an App with Game DVR

While the Problem Steps Recorder is an incredibly useful tool that provides an output file that can easily be e-mailed to a support person, sometimes annotated screenshots don't provide all the information you need. This is when one of Windows 10's gaming features can prove useful (and I'll bet you didn't see that one coming).

■ **Note** Game DVR (also known as the Game Bar) feature is available in both the Home and Pro editions of Windows 10, but may be disabled in Windows 10 Enterprise.

Game DVR is opened by pressing the *Windows key + G,* and the user will probably have to confirm that the currently running app is a game. It opens as a toolbar similar to the Problem Steps Recorder, see Figure 12-7. However, Game DVR is locked to a single app and won't record anything outside of that app, so the user should be using an offending app before she launches Game DVR, and this also means it's no good for general recording of the desktop as it can't be launched from a blank desktop.

Figure 12-7. *Game DVR can record video*

At the right of Game DVR is a settings icon that includes General, Shortcuts, and Audio options. The Shortcuts options offer an at-a-glance view of the keyboard commands you use to control recordings with Game DVR, see Figure 12-8.

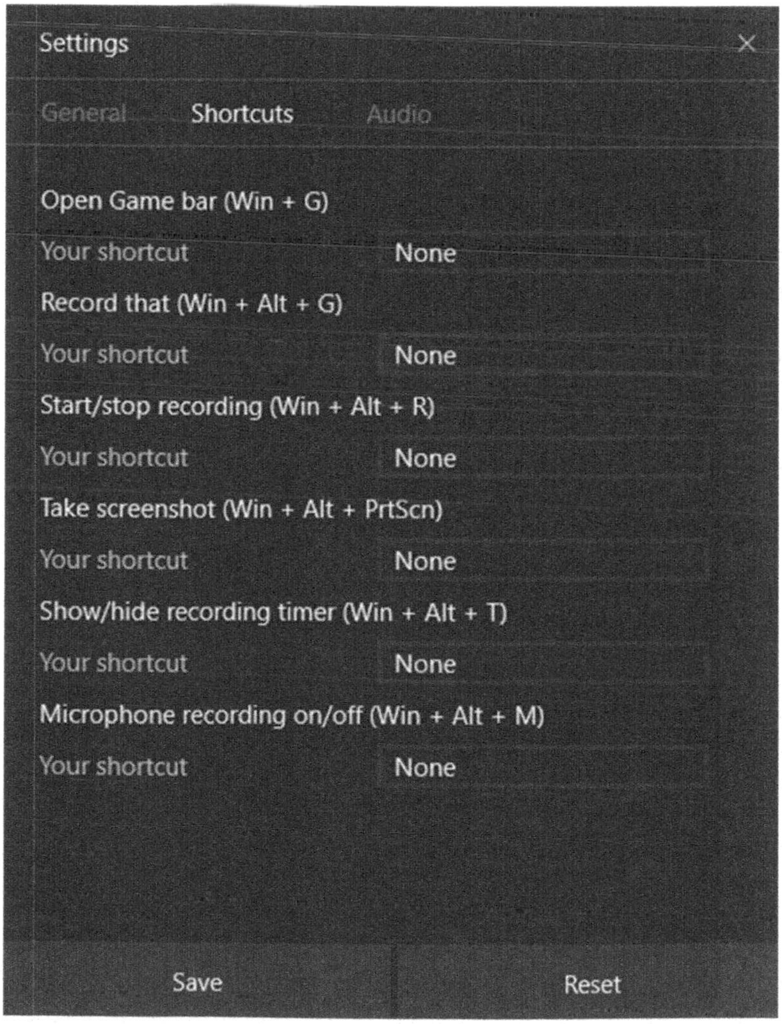

Settings   ×

General   **Shortcuts**   Audio

Open Game bar (Win + G)

Your shortcut   None

Record that (Win + Alt + G)

Your shortcut   None

Start/stop recording (Win + Alt + R)

Your shortcut   None

Take screenshot (Win + Alt + PrtScn)

Your shortcut   None

Show/hide recording timer (Win + Alt + T)

Your shortcut   None

Microphone recording on/off (Win + Alt + M)

Your shortcut   None

Save   Reset

Figure 12-8. *Game DVR settings include details of its control shortcut keys*

When you are recording an app with Game DVR, it will be minimized to the top right of the app window, see Figure 12-9, to indicate that recording is taking place. You can stop a recording by using the *Win + Alt + R* key combination, or by opening the Game Bar again by pressing *Win + G*.

Figure 12-9. *Game DVR signifies it's recording in the top right corner of the app*

When you stop a recording, it will be automaticaly saved as an MP4 video to the *User folders* ➤ *Videos* ➤ *Captures* folder.

Quick Assist

If you sign into your PC using a Microsoft Account, and if both yourself and the person to whom you are providing support are using Windows 10, then a feature called *Quick Assist* can make the task of providing remote support extremely easy, both for yourself and the recipient. You will find Quick Assist in the Start Menu, and you should tell the person to whom you will be providing support to look for it too.

When you Start Quick Assist you will be asked if you want to *Get assistance*, or *Give assistance*, see Figure 12-10. Clicking *Give assistance* will prompt you to sign in with your Microsoft Account, as this support app uses a Microsoft peer-to-peer system to connect the two PCs.

Figure 12-10. *You can give assistance to people who are also running Windows 10*

When you have verified your account, you will be given a six-digit security code that must be typed into the PC where assistance is required, see figure 12-11. The code expires in ten minutes, and you are given quick links to copy the code to your clipboard, so it can be pasted into an instant message or email, or sent directly via email (you will need an installed and configured mail app for this to work). The *Provide instructions* link will tell you where to point the user receiving support, so they can also open Quick Assist.

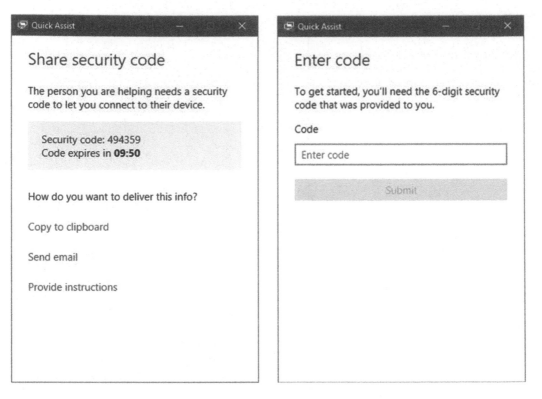

Figure 12-11. A security code must be typed into the Quick Assist app on the PC receiving support

Once the code has been entered, the user receiving support will be told that you will be taking control of their PC, and for their permission for this to happen, see Figure 12-12.

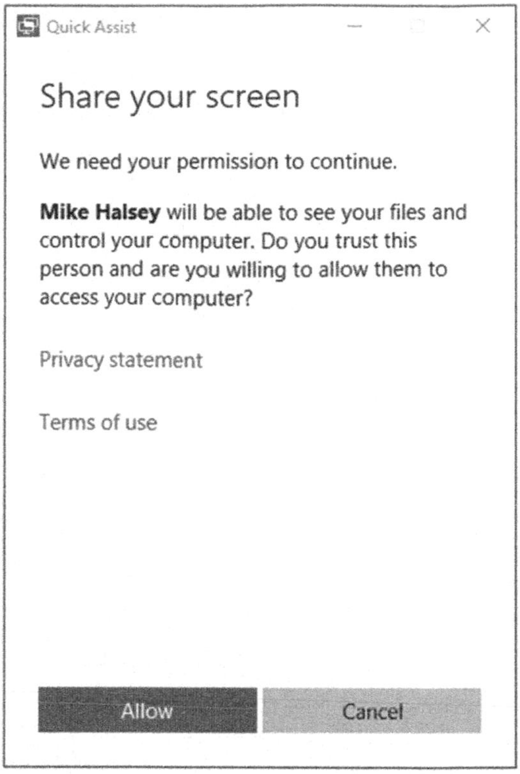

Figure 12-12. *The person receiving support will be asked to confirm you can control their PC*

Once permission has been granted, the main support window will appear, in which you will see the desktop of the remote PC, see Figure 12-13. The controls for the app at this point are very easy to use and intuitive. You can annotate on the screen, perhaps to show the remote user something of which they should be aware. This works because the rmeote user can see what is happening on their screen at all times.

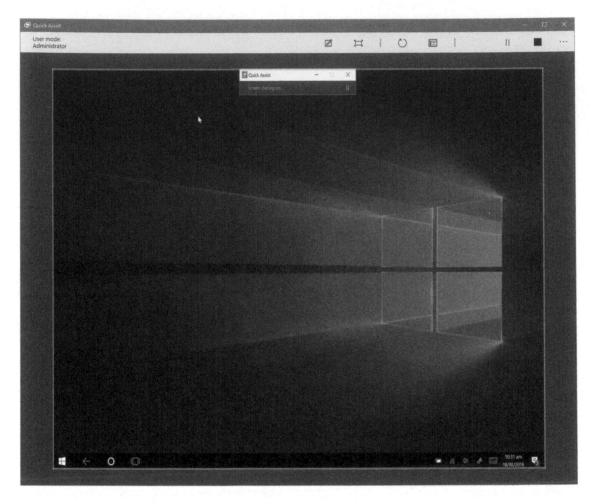

Figure 12-13. *The Quick Assist window is easy to navigate and has simple controls*

Perhaps the most useful feature of the Quick Assist app however is the ability to restart the remote PC. This is a function of Remote Desktop when used in business environments, but the Windows alternative app, Remote Assistance, which I will detail shortly, doesn't offer this functionality. When you have finished providing support to the remote PC, click the *End* button in the top right corner of the window.

Windows Remote Assistance

If you're in a scenario where you can get remote access to a PC but are not using a MIcrosoft Account, there are two ways to achieve this. In a business environment you're best using Remote Desktop, which I'll detail later in this chapter. However, you might be supporting a home user or a small business that doesn't have its own dedicated IT engineer.

There are plenty of third-party remote support packages availble, some of which are free to use. TeamViewer, available from `www.teamviewer.com,` is one of the most popular as it's very straightforward for a nontechnical person to use on their PC, but it's also nonintrusive on their system and offers significant functionality for a support technician.

You don't need third-party software, however, to provide remote support to people, as Windows has for many years included its own Remote Assistance feature called, perhaps unsurprisingly, Windows Remote Assistance. You can find it in the Control Panel, but first it is important to establish that Remote Assistance requests are enabled on the PC that requires support.

To achieve this, search for **Remote Assistance** in the Start Menu or Cortana and click *Allow Remote Assistance Invitations to be sent from this computer*. This will open a dialog, see Figure 12-14, where a check box is visible in which you can approve, or deny, permission for Remote Assist on the PC.

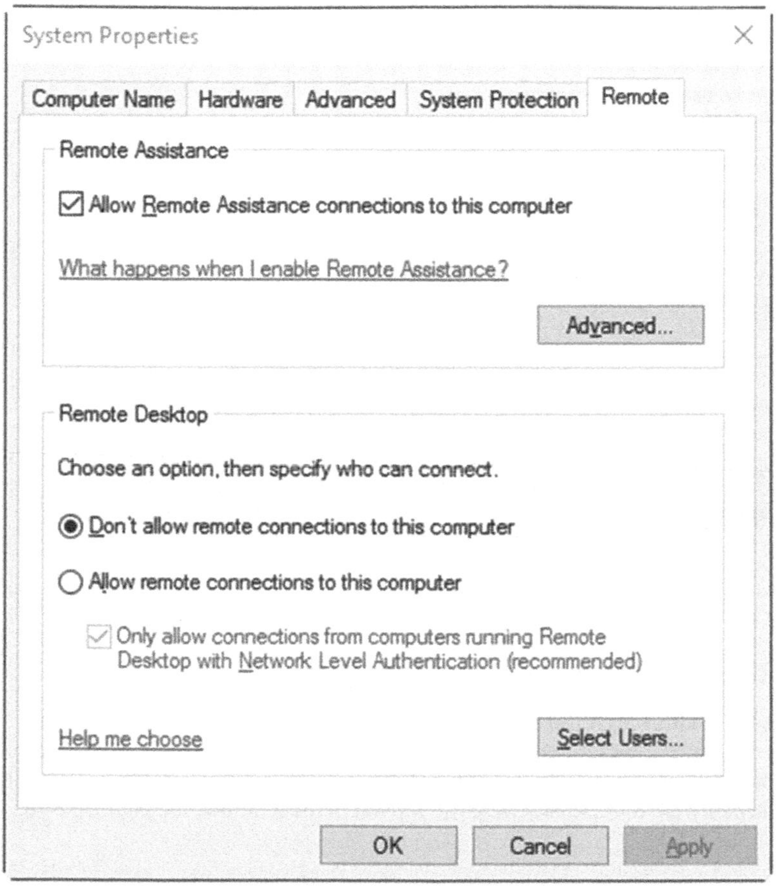

Figure 12-14. *Remote Assistance needs to be activated on the PC requiring support*

You will want the user to make sure the Remote Assistance option is checked. Clicking the *Advanced* button provides additional options you may want the user to check, including whether the PC can be controlled remotely, and how long Remote Assistance invitations remain active, see Figure 12-15.

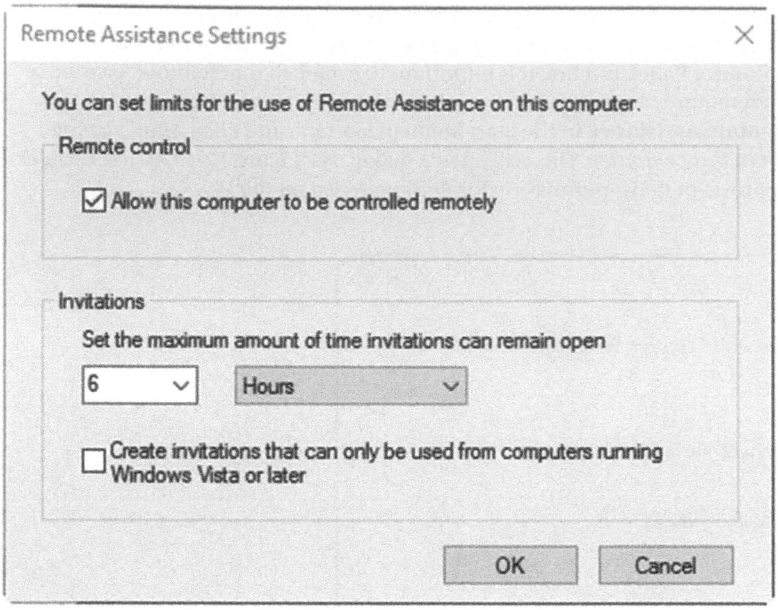

Figure 12-15. *Advanced options are available for Remote Assistance*

■ **Note**   You'll notice this is also the dialog in which Remote Desktop is activated on the PC. We'll be coming back to this later in the chapter.

Sending and Responding to a Remote Assistance Request

Ironically, at this point, the process of talking a user through instigating a Remote Assistance request isn't as straightforward as searching in the Start Menu for Remote Assistance. They'll need to search instead for **Troubleshooting** and open *Troubleshooting (Control Panel)*. When the Troubleshooting panel opens, you'll need to ask the user to click the *Get help from a friend* link near the top left of the window, see Figure 12-16.

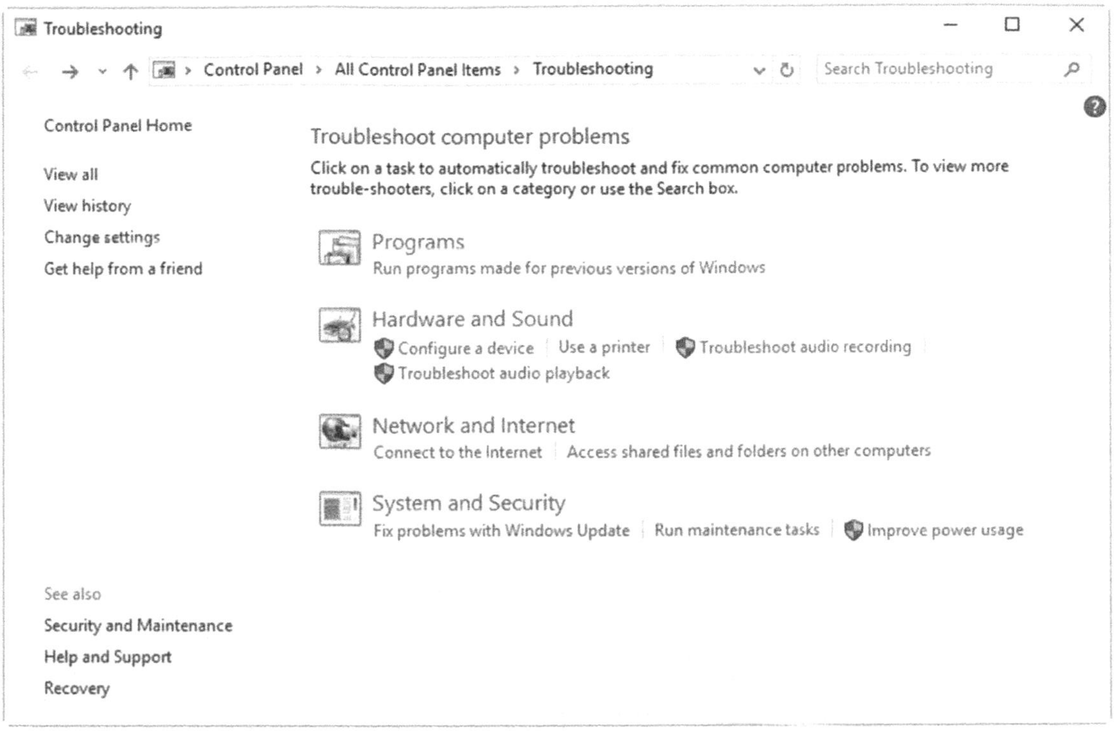

Figure 12-16. *Remote Assistance requests are instigated from the Control Panel*

At the next panel, the user will see an option to "Invite someone to help [them]," see Figure 12-17. Below this, you'll see an *Offer Remote Assistance to help someone* link, but don't think that you can use this to instigate a Remote Assistance session, as it's quite badly worded and only applicable to connections made over a corporate network, where prior configuration has already been implemented on all PCs.

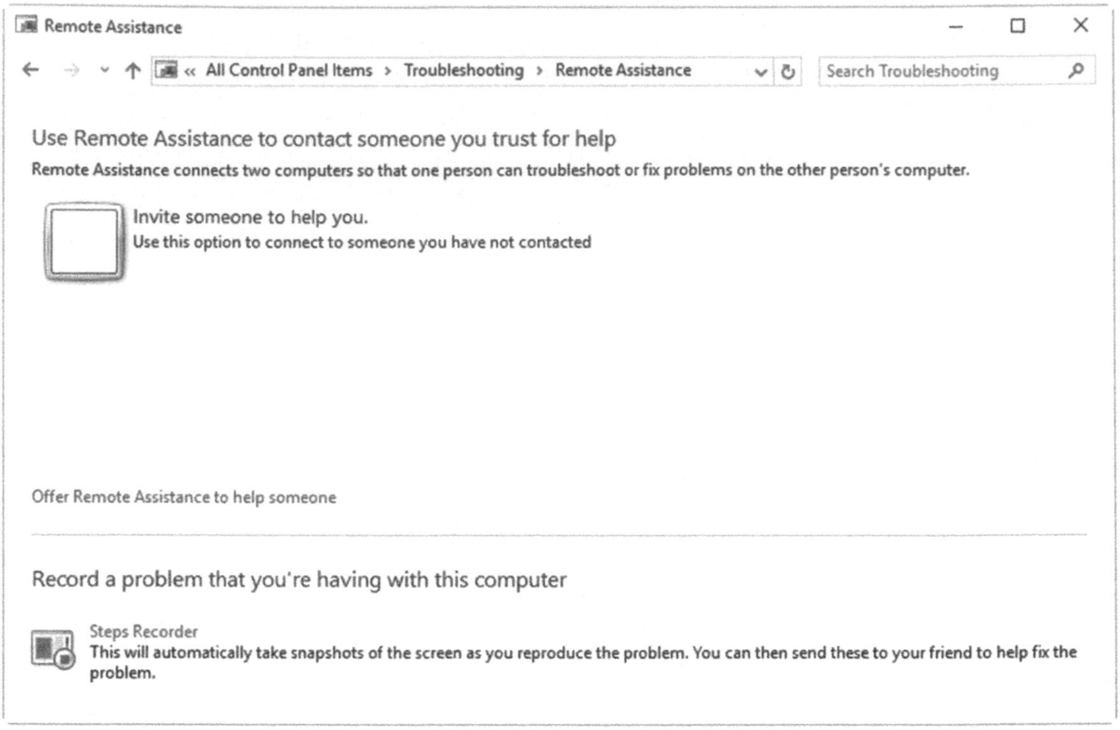

Figure 12-17. Remote Assistance must be initiated from the PC requiring help

When the user requiring help clicks the *Invite someone to help you* button, they will be presented with three options for how to send the request: *Send the invitation as a file, Use email to send an invitation,* and *Use Easy Connect,* see Figure 12-18.

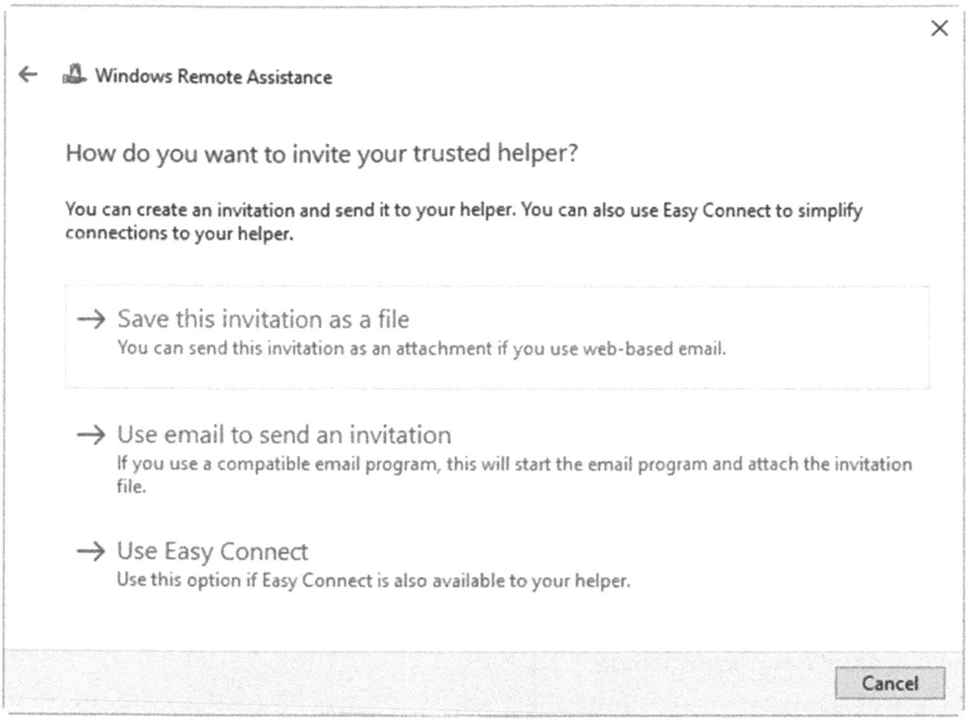

Figure 12-18. *Remote Assistance requests can be sent in three ways*

- **Send this invitation as a file** will save a file to a location of your choice on the PC (the desktop by default). This file can then be attached to an e-mail, and it is best if the user is using either webmail or an e-mail Windows Store app. The reason for this is because the...

- **Use email to send an invitation** option is only available if you are using a Win32 desktop app, such as Outlook as shipped with the full desktop edition of Microsoft Office. It is grayed out for Windows Store apps.

- **Use Easy Connect** is a Microsoft system that uses a Peer-to-Peer network for securely transmitting a Remote Assistance invitation. Easy Connect might be grayed out and unavailable on the PC for several reasons, one of which being that Windows 10 doesn't feel the available Internet bandwidth is good enough to maintain a connection, but it can also be because the Internet router doesn't support Easy Connect.

■ **Note**   In order for a router to support Easy Connect, it must support Peer Name Resolution Protocol (PNRP). You may also need to open access to port 3389 on the router. Details of PNRP compatibility and advanced configuration will be available in your router's documentation. Not all routers will support Easy Connect, and it's likely that cheap, ISP-supplied routers will be light on features.

When an invitation is sent, a dialog displaying an access password is displayed onscreen, see Figure 12-19. This password will be required in addition to the invitation file to provide access to the PC.

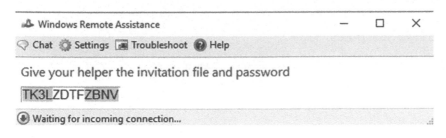

Figure 12-19. *A password is provided for added security*

On the PC providing support, a password dialog will appear when the invitation file is opened, see Figure 12-20. You will probably need to be on the phone to the user at this point so they can tell you the password, but also because you still have to request control of the PC.

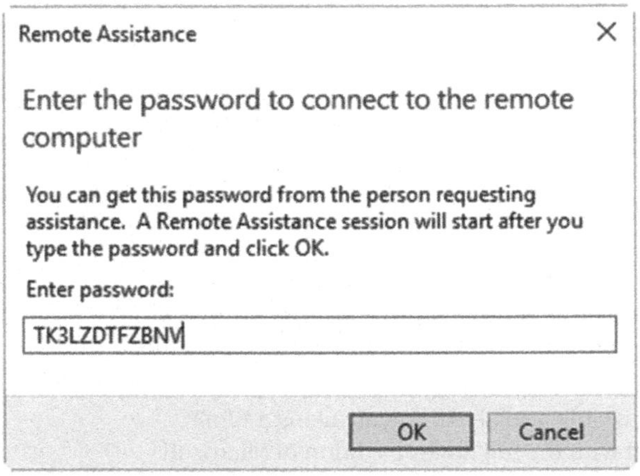

Figure 12-20. *The password needs to be entered on the PC requesting access*

If you are using Easy Connect to provide Remote Assistance, in the *Troubleshooting* ➤ *Get help from a friend* panel, click the *Offer Remote Assistance to help someone* link, and then click the *Use Easy Connect* option. This will open the password dialog.

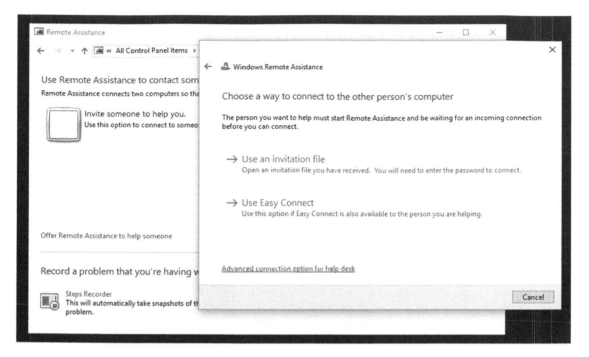

Figure 12-21. *If you using Easy Connect you should connect via the Control Panel*

On the screen of the PC requiring help, a dialog will appear asking for permission to initiate the Remote Assistance session, see Figure 12-22. The user on that PC will have to click *Yes* on this dialog before the session can begin.

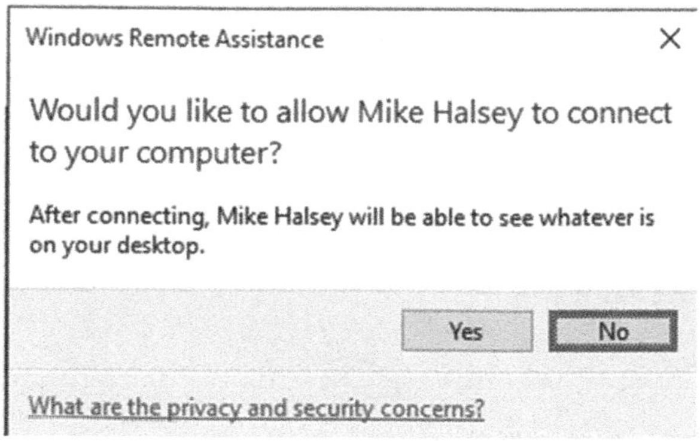

Figure 12-22. *Permission needs to be granted for the Remote Assistance session to begin*

There is one more thing that needs to be done before you can really provide remote support. In the top left of the Remote Assistance window, you will see a *Request control* button, see Figure 12-23.

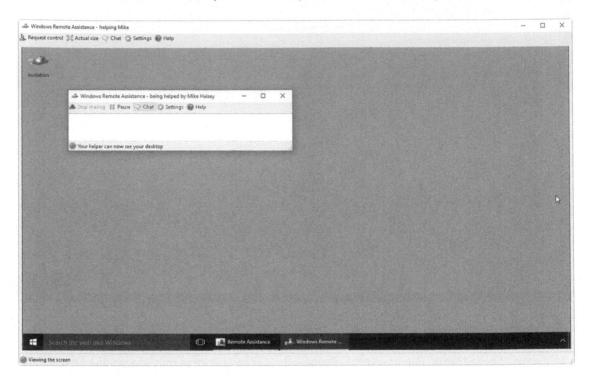

Figure 12-23. *You have to request control of the user's PC*

When you click this, a dialog will appear on the remote PC that only the user of that PC can interact with. This dialog asks for permission for you to share control of their PC, see Figure 12-24.

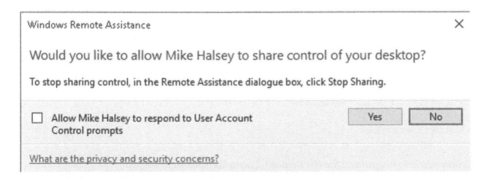

Figure 12-24. *Permission needs to be given for remote control*

It's important to note here that before you ask the user to click *Yes* and give you remote control of their PC, you will probably want them to check the box to *Allow [you] to respond to User Account Control prompts*. If they don't check this dialog, then only they will be able to respond to any UAC prompts that appear during your remote session.

The Remote Assistance dialog on the host PC now changes to present the user on that PC several options, some of which are also available to the person providing support, see Figure 12-25.

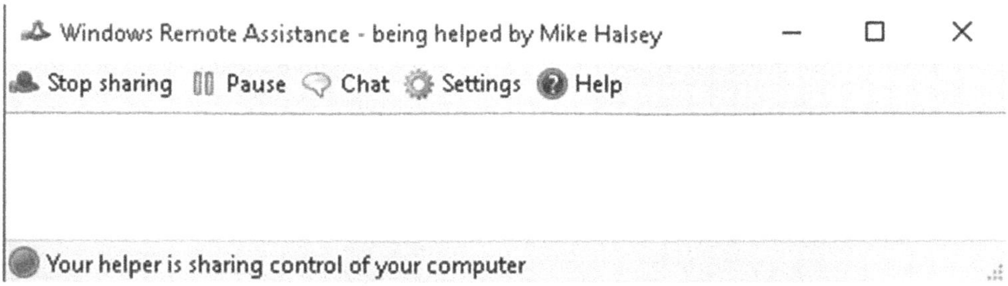

Figure 12-25. *The user of the host PC has various options available*

These include opening a chat window, so you can keep the user informed of what you're doing without needing to keep them on the phone. Settings are also available in which you can change the quality of the connection, see Figure 12-26, and these offer an option for the user receiving support to terminate the connection by just pressing the Esc key on their keyboard should they wish.

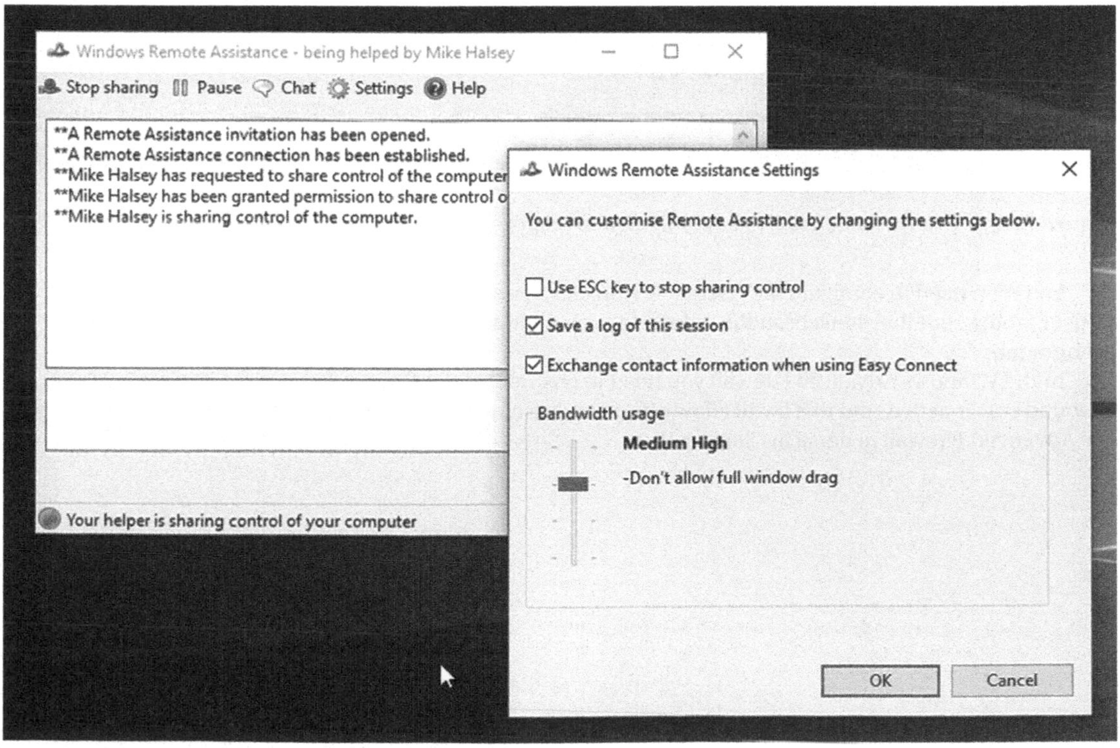

Figure 12-26. *Settings are available for Remote Assistance, as is a chat window*

Sending Unsolicited Remote Assistance Offers

I mentioned earlier in this chapter that you can use Remote Assistance in a company environment without a Remote Assistance invitation needing to be sent. This requires configuration in Group Policy, which you can open by searching for **gpedit** in the Start Menu or Cortana.

This type of Remote Assistance request is called an unsolicited request and, as you can imagine for reasons of security, it's disabled in Windows 10 by default. In the Group Policy Editor navigate to *Computer Configuration* ➤ *Administrative Templates* ➤ *System* ➤ *Remote Assistance* and double-click the *Configure Offer Remote Assistance* policy. You will need to enable this policy on each machine that you want to receive unsolicited Remote Assistance requests, see Figure 12-27. Available options include being able to automatically control the PC, or just view it.

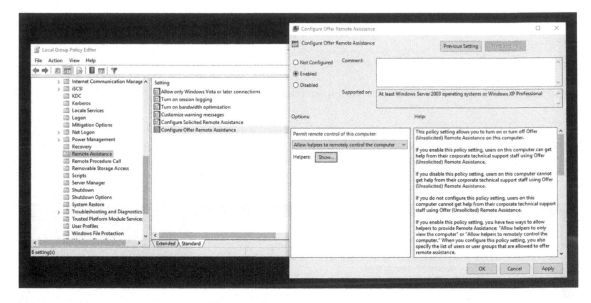

Figure 12-27. *Group Policy needs to be configured to allow unsolicited Remote Assistance*

You then need to configure the "Helpers" who can access the PC. This can be either individual users or user groups, but they must be in the following format: domain_name\username or domain_name\ groupname.

In the Windows Advanced Firewall you need to ensure that the *Remote Assistance (RA Server TCP-In)* inbound rule is active, and that it will allow offers for assistance, see Figure 12-28. I will show you how to use the Advanced Firewall in detail in Chapter 18.

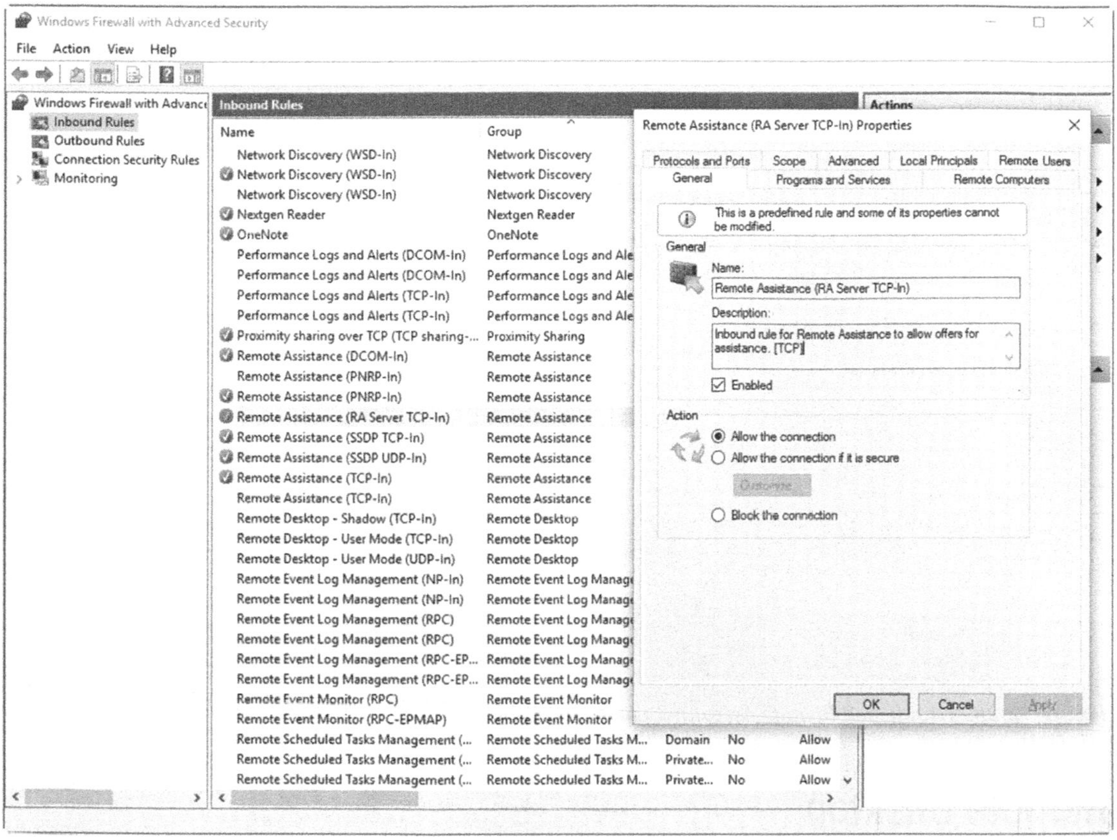

Figure 12-28. *The Windows Firewall also needs to be configured to allow connections*

With these configured, an unsolicited Remote Assistance session can then be instigated from the *Troubleshooting* Control Panel, by clicking *Get Help from a Friend* ➤ *Offer Remote Assistance to help someone*, and then clicking the *Advanced connection options for help desk* link, and entering the name or IP address of the computer to which you want to connect, see Figure 12-29.

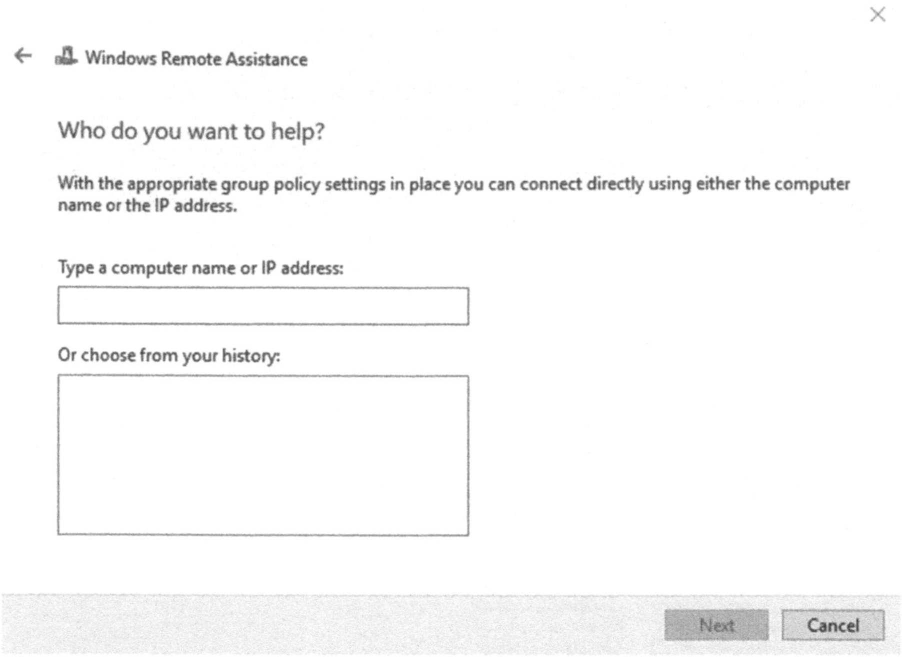

Figure 12-29. *Unsolicited Remote Assistance can be instigated by computer name or IP address*

Remote Desktop

An alternative to Remote Assistance is the Windows Remote Desktop feature, and this is much more common in the workplace. Again, it needs to be activated on each PC. Search in the Start Menu or Cortana for **allow remote**, and open *Allow Remote Access to your Computer* when it appears in the search results.

This is the same dialog we saw when we were making sure Remote Assistance connections can be made with the PC, but you'll see that further down the dialog are options for Remote Desktop, see Figure 12-30.

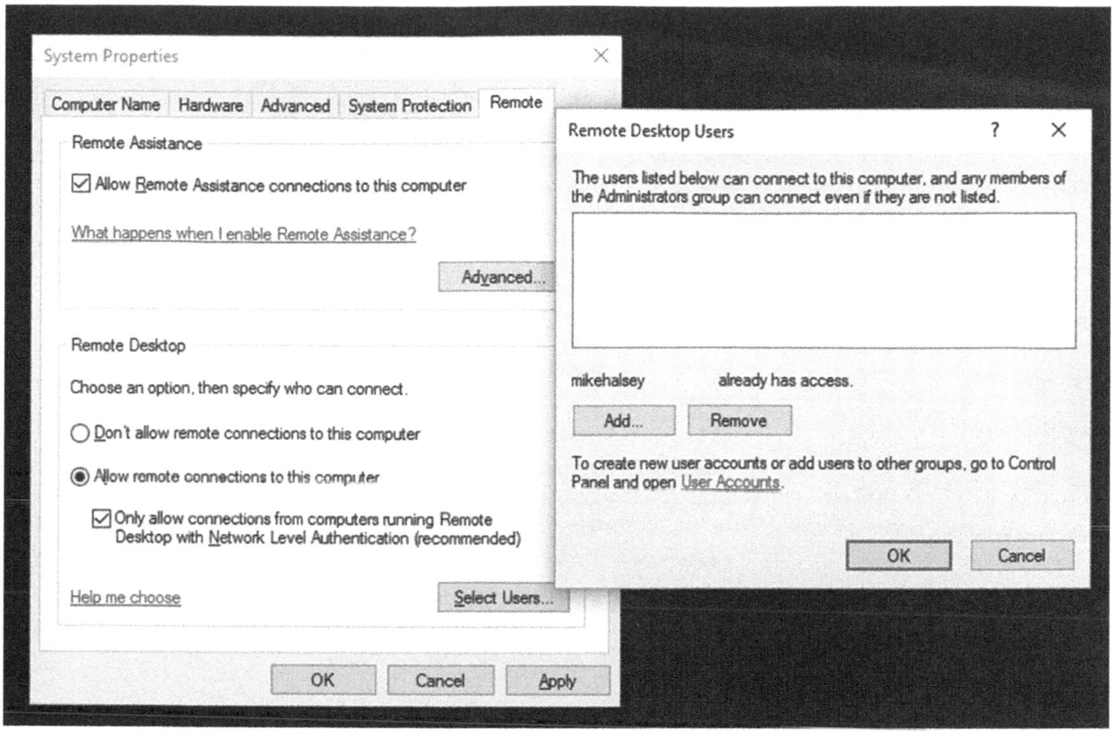

Figure 12-30. *You need to enable Remote Desktop on each PC*

Remote Desktop is disabled by default, so you need to *Allow remote conections to [the] computer* and then click the *Select users* button. Here you can configure which users or user groups can access the PC. These should be in the format, domain_name\username or domain_name\groupname, but clicking the *Add* button will allow you to search for users and groups in the Domain directory.

To initiate a Remote Desktop session, you will need the computer's name. This can be gained either from the System section of the Control Panel, or from the System section in the Settings app, see Figure 12-31.

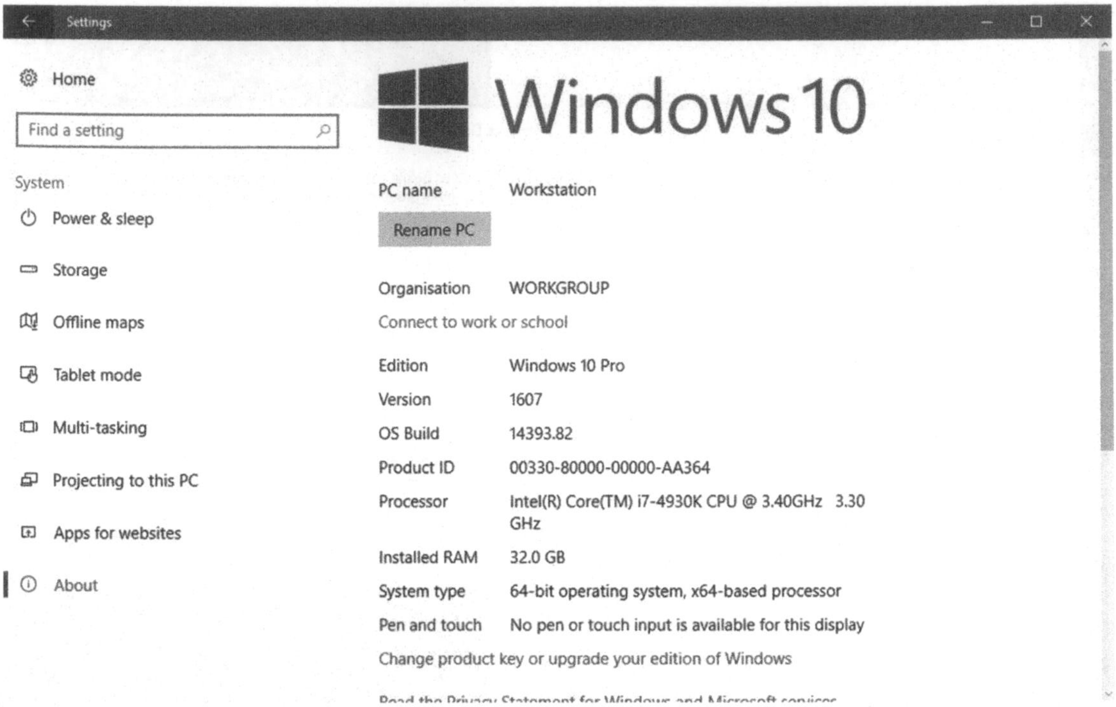

Figure 12-31. You can get the computer name from the Settings app

On the PC you wish to use to access the remote computer, search for **Remote Desktop** in the start Menu or Cortana, and click *Remote Desktop Connection* when it appears in the search results. This will display a dialog in which you enter the name (with domain pointing if necessary) for the computer to which you wish to connect, see Figure 12-32.

Figure 12-32. At its simplest, Remote Desktop just asks you for the name of the PC to connect to

You will be presented with a security dialog and asked to confirm that you do intend to connect to the remote computer, see Figure 12-33. There is a *Don't ask me again for connections to this computer checkbox*, and if you click the *Show details* button in the bottom left corner of the dialog, you can choose if you want to share the drives, clipboard, printers, and other supported Plug and Play devices on your PC with the remote PC.

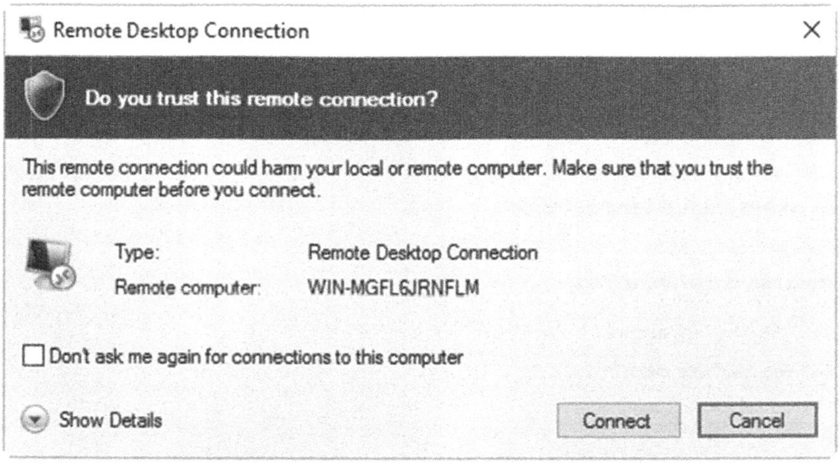

Figure 12-33. *You will be presented with a security dialog before the connection is made*

You will be asked to sign into the remote PC with credentials that have previously been configured as authorized, and you will then be presented with a security certificate for the remote PC that you can review, or click another *Don't ask me again for connections to this computer* check box, see Figure 12-34.

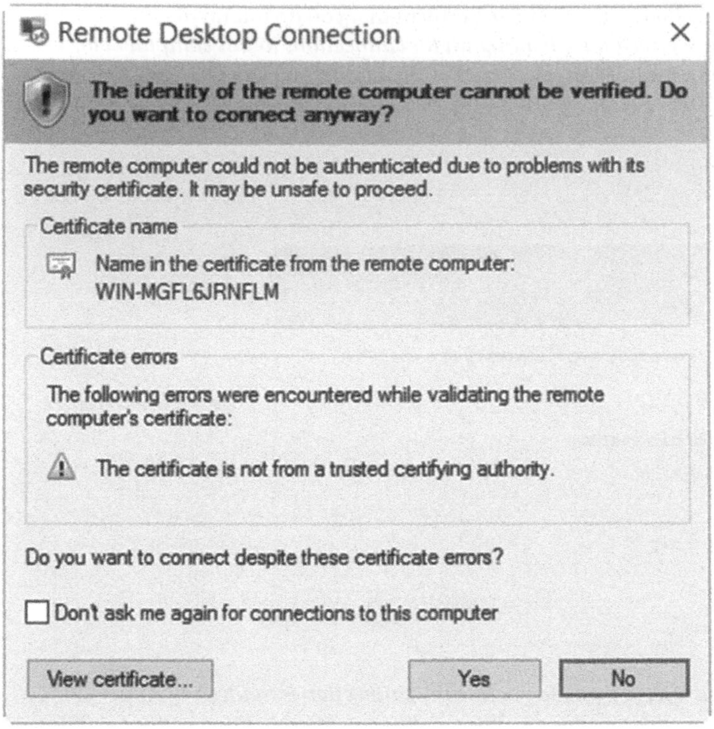

Remote Desktop Connection   ✕

⚠ **The identity of the remote computer cannot be verified. Do you want to connect anyway?**

The remote computer could not be authenticated due to problems with its security certificate. It may be unsafe to proceed.

Certificate name

🔲 Name in the certificate from the remote computer:
WIN-MGFL6JRNFLM

Certificate errors

The following errors were encountered while validating the remote computer's certificate:

⚠ The certificate is not from a trusted certifying authority.

Do you want to connect despite these certificate errors?

☐ Don't ask me again for connections to this computer

| View certificate... | | Yes | No |

Figure 12-34. You are presented with a second security certificate when you sign into the remote PC

When you are using Remote Desktop, any other users will be signed out of the PC, so they won't be able to see what you're doing. Remote Desktop will also run full-screen with a toolbar accessible at the top center of your screen, see Figure 12-35. This toolbar may be hidden, but moving your mouse to the top center of your screen will make it appear, and you can click the *pin* icon to lock it in place so that it is always visible.

Figure 12-35. Full-screen Remote Desktop is controlled by a bar at the top center of your screen

Should you wish to run your Remote Desktop connection with different settings, such as at a different screen resolution, you can click the *Show options* button at the main Remote Desktop Connection dialog. This will expand the dialog to offer options such as display, bandwidth, and advanced settings, see Figure 12-36.

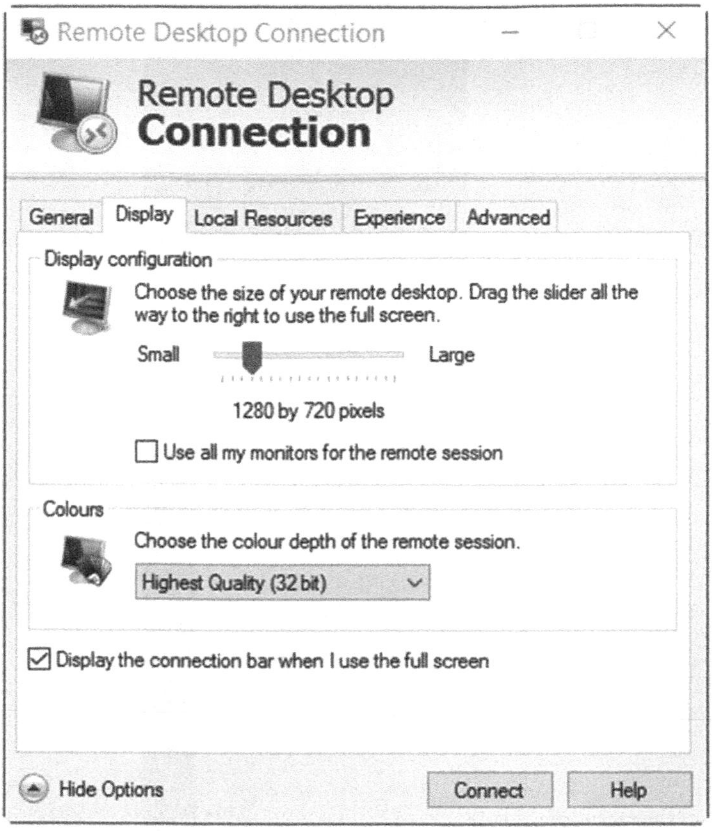

Figure 12-36. Additional options are available for Remote Desktop

You may want to choose, for example, what hard disks are available to the remote PC. This can be useful for transferring files or hardware drivers. You can achieve this by clicking the *Local Resources* tab and then clicking the *More* button in the *Local devices and resources* section. This will open another dialog, in which you can select what hard disks on your PC will be accessible to the remote PC, see Figure 12-37.

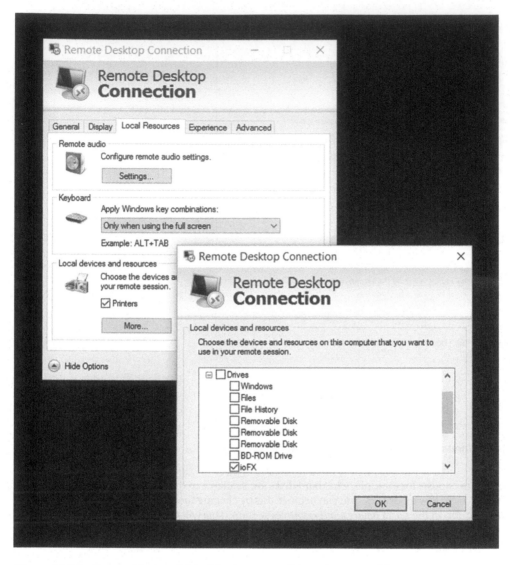

Figure 12-37. *You can choose which drives are accessible to the remote PC*

Summary

Certainly, there are plenty of options available to you for supporting users and troubleshooting PCs remotely, and Remote Desktop is extremely popular in larger businesses. Tools such as the Problem Steps Recorder are easy enough for nontechnical people to use, and that can provide an extremely valuable support option when remote access isn't possible, perhaps because the user is on a metered broadband connection.

Back in Chapter 8, however, I dealt with a far more prickly issue, and one that cannot be easily supported remotely, if at all: Windows 10 PCs that simply won't start up. I showed you how to use the automated troubleshooting and repair options, but in the next chapter I'll show you how to get inside the guts of the Windows Startup system and effect repairs manually.

■ ■ ■

CHAPTER 13

Repairing Windows Startup Problems

In Chapter 8, I showed you how you can use the tools and utilities available in Windows 10 to troubleshoot startup problems. But what happens if Windows cannot be easily or automatically repaired? If you can't get your copy of Windows 10 to boot to the desktop then you can't get any work done at all.

The normal response to a nonbootable copy of Windows is either to reimage the PC, which will inevitably result in huge numbers of Windows updates and app updates needing to be installed... perhaps before you can begin work. Alternatively, you might be faced with completely reinstalling Windows and ALL of your apps and updates, which can take you out of business for up to two full days.

The good news, however, is that you don't necessarily have to do either of these things, as you can effect manual repairs of the Windows boot system, and even rebuild it completely. Over the years, I've had more mail in my mailbox about this than any other subject, so I would expect this chapter to be the most thumbed of this whole book.

Manually Repairing Windows Startup

If Windows 10 won't start, there are different ways to repair the startup files. You can completely rebuild the boot system by creating new boot partitions, should these have become corrupt, and I'll show you how to do this later in this chapter, and I'll also talk you through the different boot partitions in detail. Microsoft does include a facility, however, that will rebuild the boot files on their existing "hidden" partition, and this is a good first step to try to get your PC working normally again.

To do this, you will need either the USB Recovery Drive I prompted you to create back in Chapter 1, and which I'm sure you have sitting somewhere nice and safe by now, or Windows 10 installation media such as a DVD or USB Flash Drive.

■ **Note**   If you do not have a USB Recovery Drive or installation media, you can download a Windows 10 ISO file, which you can burn to DVD, or create USB installation media at www.microsoft.com/software-download/windows10 by installing the Windows 10 Media Creation Tool on another PC.

© Mike Halsey 2016

M. Halsey, *Windows 10 Troubleshooting*, DOI 10.1007/978-1-4842-0925-7_13

If you start the nonbooting PC using Windows 10 installation media, at the *Install* screen, click the *Repair your computer* link in the bottom left corner of the install window. At the Recovery options screen, click *Troubleshoot*, then click *Advanced options*, and then click *Command Prompt*, see Figure 13-1.

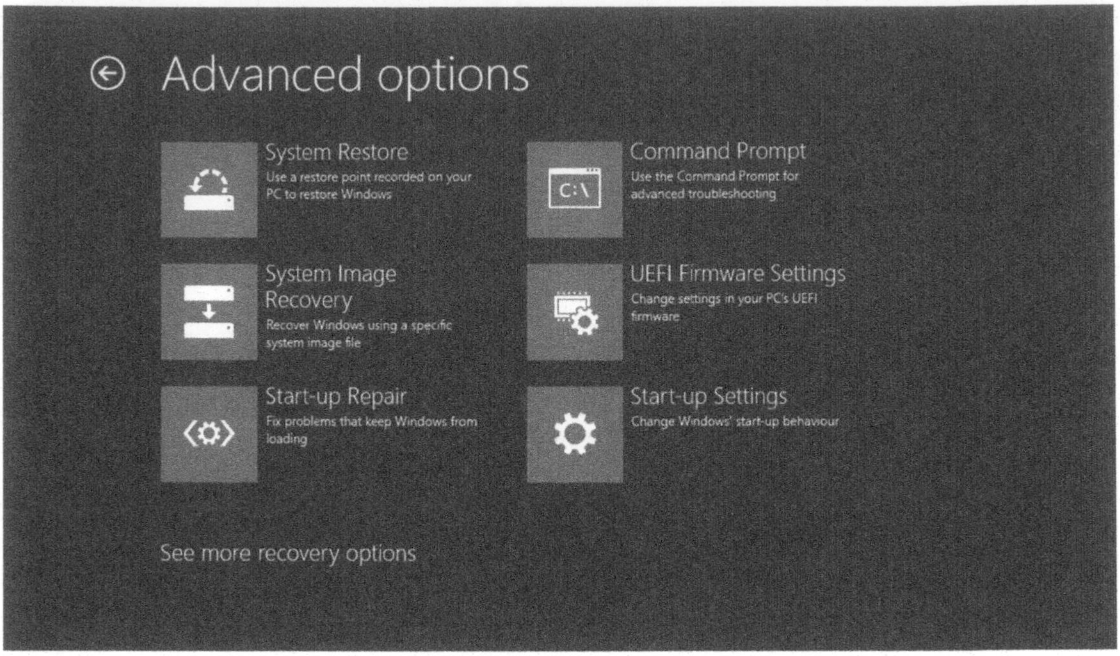

Figure 13-1. *You repair Windows startup from the Command Prompt*

Repairing BIOS Startup Files

When the Command Prompt window is open the commands you type will be different if you have Windows 10 installed with BIOS or UEFI compatibility. If your copy of Windows 10 is installed with a BIOS system (in which you will have one *System Reserved* partition) type these commands.

1. **BcdEdit /export C:\BCD_Backup**, to create a backup of the current boot files (just in case) where C:\ represents the drive on which you want the backup stored. These can later be reimported in necessary with the **/import** switch.

2. **C:**, moves you to the boot drive as seen by the Command Prompt from a Recovery Drive or installation media.

3. **Cd boot**, navigates to the Windows boot folder.

4. **Attrib bcd -r -h -s**, changes permissions on the boot file so you can rebuild it.

5. **Ren C:\Boot\bcd C:\Boot\bcd.old**, renames the boot file so you can create a new one, but keeps it as a backup.

6. **Bootrec /RebuildBCD**, rebuilds the boot files.

■ **Tip** How can you tell if you have a BIOS or UEFI installation of Windows 10? If you can get to the desktop (such as when the PC working fine), open *Disk Management* from the Win+X menu. BIOS installations will have a System Reserved partition before the Windows installation on your hard disk. UEFI installations will have separate Recovery and EFI partitions listed. If you cannot access the desktop, first try the BIOS repair method. If the **Bootrec /RebuildBCD** command reports "Total identified Windows installations: 0", you will have a UEFI installation.

Repairing UEFI Startup Files

As I have mentioned, the process for repairing UEFI startup files is different than those for BIOS installations and so requires a different process for repair. At the Command Prompt, type the following commands…

1. **Diskpart**, to enter the Windows Disk partitioning and management tool.

2. **List disk**, to check the hard disks installed on your PC. Choose the correct hard disk (there may only be one) and note its number.

3. **Select disk=0**, where the number you type matches the disk on which Windows 10 is installed.

4. **List volume**, to see the partitions on the disk listed. You are looking for either a FAT32 formatted partition of around 99MB in size, see Figure 13-2, or a volume labeled BOOT: note its number.

```
Administrator: X:\windows\system32\cmd.exe - diskpart

Microsoft Windows [Version 10.0.10240]


X:\windows\system32>diskpart

Microsoft DiskPart version 10.0.10240

Copyright (C) 1999-2013 Microsoft Corporation.
On computer: MININT-43AQVHN

DISKPART> select disk=0

Disk 0 is now the selected disk.

DISKPART> list volume

  Volume ###  Ltr  Label        Fs     Type        Size     Status     Info
  ----------  ---  -----------  -----  ----------  -------  ---------  --------
  Volume 0     D                       DVD-ROM       0 B    No Media
  Volume 1     C                NTFS   Partition   126 GB   Healthy
  Volume 2          Recovery    NTFS   Partition   300 MB   Healthy    Hidden
  Volume 3                      FAT32  Partition    99 MB   Healthy    Hidden
  Volume 4     E                NTFS   Partition   450 MB   Healthy    Hidden

DISKPART>
```

Figure 13-2. *You want a FAT32 formatted volume of around 99MB or a volume labeled BOOT*

5. **Select volume=3**, where the number represents the number of the correct boot volume.

6. **Assign letter=f:**, to assign a drive letter to the selected volume.

7. **Exit**, to exit the Disk Partitioning tool.

8. **F:**, to select the boot partition, where the letter you type matches the drive letter you assigned the volume.

9. **Cd \EFI\Microsoft\Boot**, to access the boot folder (Note: this could also be \Boot\ or \ESD\Windows\EFI\Microsoft\Boot\ depending on your system).

10. **Ren BCD BCD.old**, to rename the boot file so you can create a new one.

11. **Bootrec /RebuildBCD**, to rebuild the boot files (see the following note about the *BCDBoot* command, if this does not fix the problem).

12. When prompted to *Add [the discovered] Windows installation to the boot list*, type **Y**.

Additional Repair Commands for BIOS and UEFI

There are a few additional commands that you may want or need to run at this point to repair startup.

- **Bootrec /FixMBR**, creates a new Master Boot Record for the disk, and should be used if the MBR file is corrupt.

- **Bootrec /FixBoot**, writes a new boot sector to the disk, and should be used if the disk boot sector is corrupt.

- **Bootrec /ScanOS**, can be used if your Windows 10 installation is not found. This command searches for operating system installations and reports what it finds.

- **BcdBoot C:\Windows /s F: /f ALL**, used if the Bootrec /RebuildBCD command does not repair your boot files. This command creates completely new boot files by coping the necessary files from your Windows installation (which should be on C: at this point, but you can check in *Diskpart* by viewing the disks and volumes as I detailed earlier). The /s switch designates the boot drive and the letter you gave it, in this case F:, and the /f switch specifies the firmware type to create a boot system for. This can be BIOS, UEFI, or ALL.

Recreating or Moving the Boot Partition

Sometimes you need to completely rebuild the Windows boot partition from the ground up, and you might be surprised when this might be required. Let's take the example of when you install Windows 10 on your PC. In Figure 13-3, we can see the Windows installer asking where we want to put the OS, but there's only one physical disk, this being labeled as Disk 0.

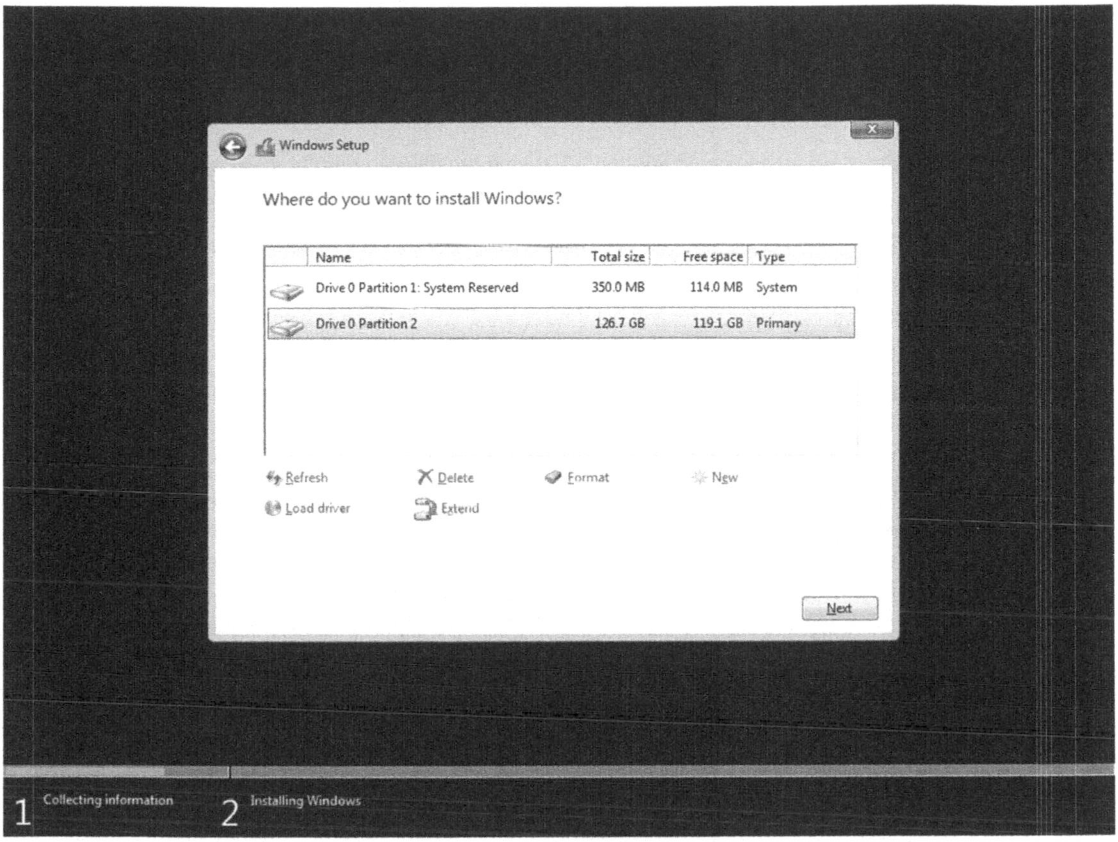

Figure 13-3. *Occasionally, the Windows installer puts the boot files on the wrong disk*

You might have more than one physical hard disk in your PC, however: Disk 1, Disk 2, and so on. Occasionally when you install Windows, the boot partitions will end up on the wrong physical disk. This is most likely because you want to install Windows 10 on a specific disk, but that disk isn't marked as Disk 0 by the BIOS or UEFI system on the motherboard.

Generally speaking, this isn't annoying, as if you just install Windows 10 and leave it, you won't even notice this has happened. If you want to create a System Image Backup of the installed OS though, one of two things will happen.

1. You will try to back up your Windows installation using the Windows 10 Image Backup utility, to be told that there is no available hard disk or partition on your PC on which the backup can be stored. This is because each partition is occupied by either Windows 10, or the boot files, and both need to be included in the backup.

2. Your backup will include the entire contents of the second disk because, unless that disk was completely blank, with no partitions at the time Windows 10 was installed, the boot files will be placed on the first partition on the disk. If this disk contains your files and folders, these will be included in the backup, rendering the backup useless. This is because when you come to restore the backup, you will also restore the contents of your files disk, as they were at the time the backup was made. This will completely wipe any files created or modified since.

There might be other circumstances too in which the boot system in Windows 10 becomes, to use a technical term, completely buggered. In most circumstances, however, it can still be rescued by following these instructions.

■ **Caution**   Rebuilding the boot system in Windows 10 using the following method will render some parts of the recovery system, the Reset backup image, and the USB Recovery Drive creator tool completely useless. You will need to ensure you already have a System Image Backup and a USB Recovery Drive to repair Windows should anything untoward happen to it in the future.

Step 1a: Create a New Boot Partition (Command Prompt)

The first step involves creating a new partition on which the boot system can reside. You can do this from the Disk Management Console on the desktop, but I will show you how to action this from the Command Prompt when you start the PC from a USB Recovery Drive or Windows 10 installation media, as it's most likely that you're doing this because you can't start the PC. I will include side-instructions though on how to achieve this from the desktop. At the *Command Prompt (Admin)* (accessed using the method I described in the "Manually Repairing Windows Startup" section), type the following commands.

1. **Diskpart,** to enter the Disk Partitioning and Management tool.

2. **List Disk,** and make a note of the disk on which Windows 10 is installed.

3. **Select Disk=0,** where the number is the number of the disk on which Windows 10 resides.

4. **List Volume,** to list all the volumes and partitions on the disk.

5. **Select Volume=4**, where the number represents the final (or largest partition on the disk). I say largest, because sometimes a UEFI install can place hidden partitions at the end of the disk.

6. **Shrink desired=500**, to shrink the partition by 500MB. This will craete blank space at the end of the partition.

7. **Create Partition Primary Size=500**, to create a new partition in the available space.

8. **List Volume**, to check the number for the newly created partition; it will be listed as having a RAW filesystem.

9. **Select Volume=5**, where the number represents the number of the new partition.

10. **Format FS=NTFS LABEL="Boot" Quick**, to format the disk.

11. **Assign Letter=f,** to assign a drive letter to the partition temporarily. This should be a letter that is not currently showing as being in use in *List Volume* for any installed disk.

12. **Exit**, to leave the Diskpart tool.

Step 1b: Create a New Boot Partition (Disk Management Console)

If you can get to the desktop, perhaps because the boot folders were placed on the wrong disk during the installation of Windows 10, follow these instructions.

1. Press *Windows key + X* to open the Administration menu.

2. Click *Disk Management* to open the Disk Management Console. You can also open this by searching for diskmgmt.msc in the Start Menu or Cortana.

3. Right-click the last or largest partition on the disk on which Windows 10 is installed (I say largest because sometimes, as in the example in Figure 13-4, the Windows installer places boot partitions at the end of the disk, not giving us space to create a new partition).

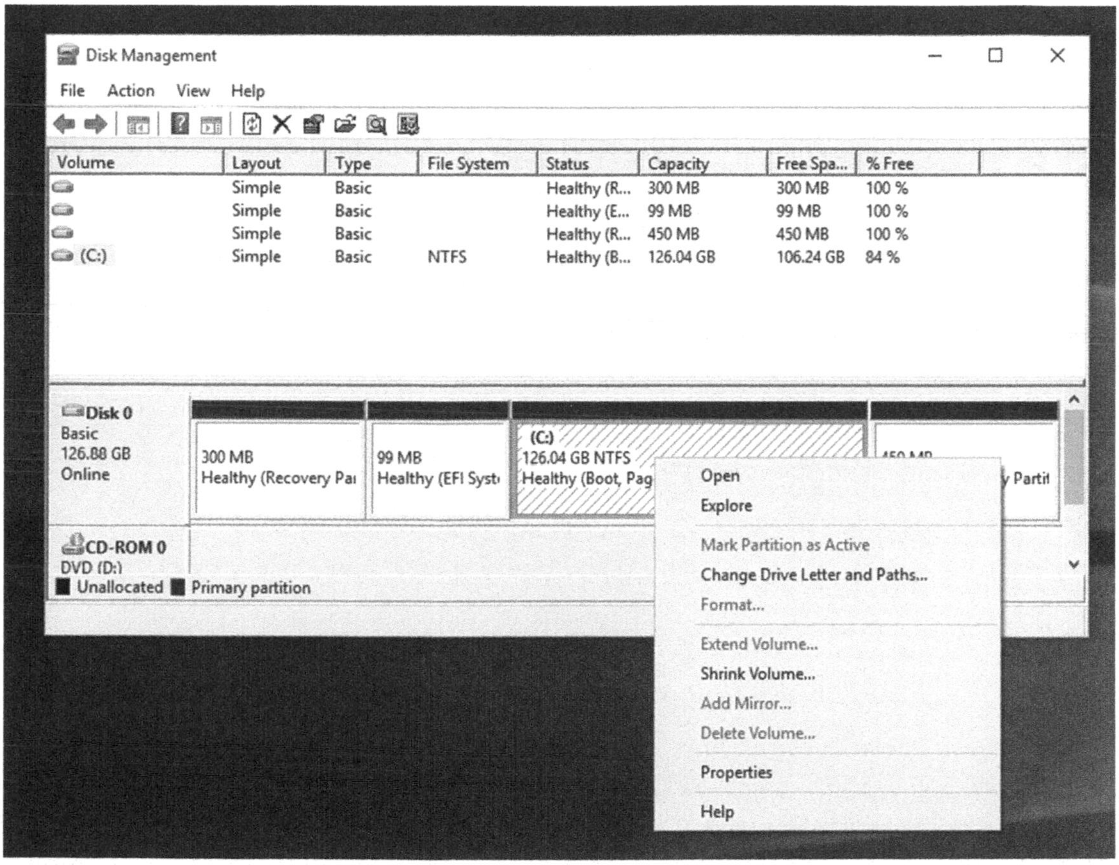

Figure 13-4. *You need to right-click the last or largest partition*

4. Click *Shrink Volume* in the menu that appears.

5. In the dialog that appears, set the *Enter the amount of space to shrink in MB* figure to 500, see Figure 13-5, and click *Shrink*.

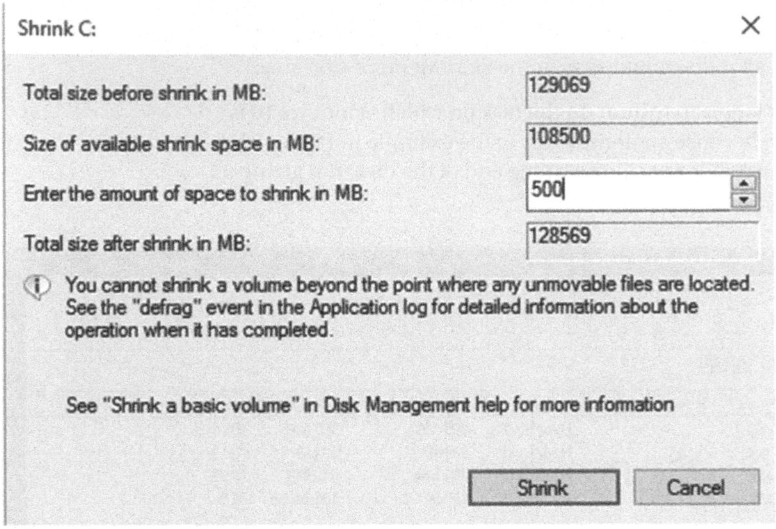

Shrink C: ✕

Total size before shrink in MB:	129069
Size of available shrink space in MB:	108500
Enter the amount of space to shrink in MB:	500
Total size after shrink in MB:	128569

ⓘ You cannot shrink a volume beyond the point where any unmovable files are located. See the "defrag" event in the Application log for detailed information about the operation when it has completed.

See "Shrink a basic volume" in Disk Management help for more information

                                           Shrink   Cancel

Figure 13-5. *You need to shrink the partition by 500MB*

6. In the blank partition space that is created, right-click and select *Create Simple Volume* from the menu that appears, see Figure 13-6.

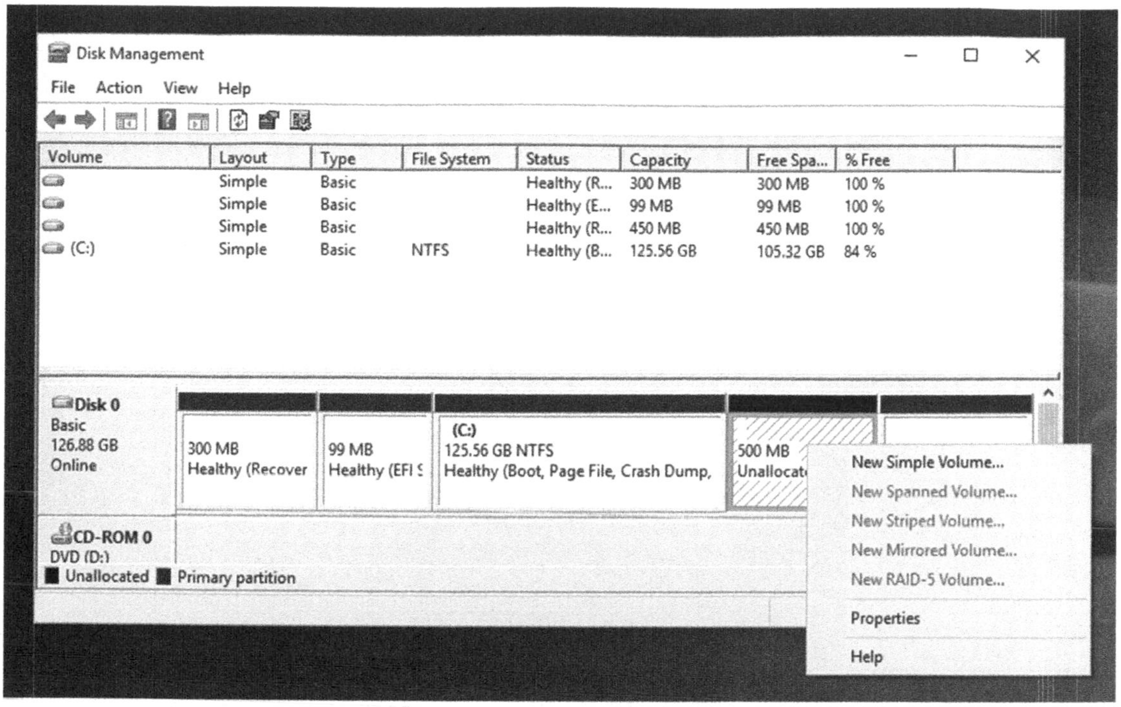

Figure 13-6. *You need to create a new partition in the available space*

7.   In the dialog that appears, click through the options, assinging the maximum available amount of space, making sure it was a drive letter assigned (see Figure 13-7), and that it is formatted as NTFS with the volume name "Boot".

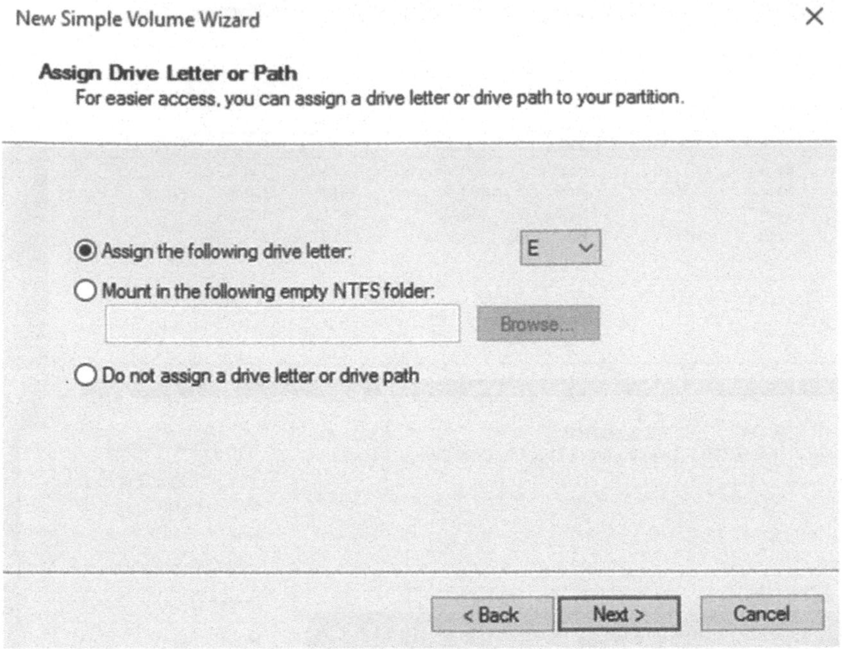

New Simple Volume Wizard   ✕

Assign Drive Letter or Path
For easier access, you can assign a drive letter or drive path to your partition.

◉ Assign the following drive letter: [E ⌄]

○ Mount in the following empty NTFS folder:

[   ] [Browse...]

○ Do not assign a drive letter or drive path

[< Back] [Next >] [Cancel]

Figure 13-7.   *The new partition should have a drive letter assigned*

Step 2: Create the New Boot Files

Once your new boot partition has been created, either from the desktop or the Command Prompt, you need to move the boot files across to it. To do this you must be at the Command Prompt. This can be done either from the Recovery environment or form the Desktop. Should you be doing this from the desktop, run the Command Prompt as an *Administrator*; the option for this is in the Win+X menu. Next, type the following commands.

1. **BcdBoot C:\Windows /s E: /f ALL**, used if the Bootrec /RebuildBCD command does not repair your boot files. This command creates completely new boot files by coping the necessary files from your Windows installation (which should be on C: at this point, but you can check in *Diskpart* by viewing the disks and volumes as I detailed earlier). The /s switch designates the boot drive and the letter you gave it, in this case E:, and the /f switch specifies the firmware type to create a boot system for. This can be BIOS, UEFI, or ALL. If you are not sure what partitions Windows 10 installed on, and which one you have created for your new boot system, use the *List Disk* and *List Volume* commands I detailed earlier.

2. **DiskPart**, to enter the Disk Partitoning tool.

3. **List Disk,** and make a note of the disk on which Windows 10 is installed.

4. **Select Disk=0,** where the number is the number of the disk on which your new boot partition resides.

5. **List Volume,** to list all the volumes and partitions on the disk.

6. **Select Volume=5**, where the number represents the partition you created for your new boot system.

7. **Active**, to mark the partiton as active.

8. **Remove Letter=E**, to remove the drive letter from the partition.

Your new boot system has now been created. When you restart the PC, your old boot partitions will no longer be used. **Bear in mind the caution earlier, however, that performing this task will completely break some parts of the recovery environment, the Reset backup image, and the USB Recovery Drive creator utility.** If these are important to you, perhaps a better alternative is to physically unplug all but the hard disk on which you want Windows 10 installed and perform a clean install, wiping out all your existing partitions on the Windows drive first. I will show you how to do this in Chapter 30.

Setting Up and Managing Dual/Multiboot Systems

Dual and multiboot PCs are still commonplace both in the home and in businesses. There are many reasons why someone might want to configure their PC to boot from two different operating systems. This might be to maintain compatibility with older software that runs fine in an earlier version of Windows, but not in Windows 10. In the IT support space, it might be to have a reference machine you can refer to (though a VM might be a better choice in this example). Some people like to have a dual-boot system to separate their work and home lives, or to have a dedicated OS for gaming.

Whatever the reason to set up a dual-boot system, it's not without its complications, especially with Windows 10. If you already have Windows 10 installed on your PC, and then want to also install an earlier version of Windows, then you can pretty much forget it, as the advances Microsoft has implemented with the boot-loader will render your entire system unbootable should you try. If you want a different version of Windows, or Linux, installed on your PC, though, you should install them in this order...

1. Linux / Windows XP

2. Windows Vista

3. Windows 7

4. Windows 8.1

5. Windows 10

■ **Caution**   I want to mention end-of-support dates for Windows operating systems, as all support for Windows XP ended in 2014. This means that there are no longer any security or stability updates for the OS and any vulnerabilities that still exist will never be patched. Windows XP therefore is a significant security risk unless it's completely sandboxed in a VM, and I'll show you how to do this in Chapter 20. Similarly, the end-of-support dates for other Windows versions are/were (depending on when you're reading this) Vista in April 2017, Windows 7 in January 2020, and Windows 8.1 in January 2023.

Secure Boot

Secure Boot, sometimes called Trusted Boot, is an Intel-designed system that's built into the UEFI firmware systems of modern motherboards. It's designed to prevent the execution of any code at the PC's startup that's not digitally signed and known to the system, such as rootkits and malware.

Microsoft mandated that all new PCs that were sold with Windows 8.1 or Windows 10 must come with Secure Boot available and enabled. This can cause a problem for people who want to dual-boot with older or non-Windows operating systems, as only Windows 8.1 and Windows 10 support it. As such, Windows 7, Windows Vista, Windows XP, and any Linux distribution (at the time of writing this anyway) will simply fail to install on a system where Secure Boot is enabled.

When you are purchasing a new PC, or on an existing PC where you wish to install an older or non-Windows OS, you should check the UEFI firmware settings to see if Secure Boot can be disabled, as it often can. Not all UEFI systems support disabling of Secure Boot, however, especially on cheaper PCs.

Bitlocker and Dual-Boot Systems

Microsoft's full disk encryption feature, Bitlocker, notoriously hates dual and multiboot systems. If you use Bitlocker to encrypt your Windows drive or partition and/or any other partitions, every time you start your PC to Windows you will be asked to enter your 48-character Bitlocker unlock key.

This can be bothersome, so the best solution if you wish to dual-boot your PC is simply not to use Bitlocker on your PC. There are other encryption methods you can use for your files though, such as the Encrypting File System (EFS), and I'll show you how to use this in Chapter 18.

Managing Boot Systems with BCDEdit

Sometimes you need to manually edit the boot menu system in Windows 10. This might be because you have multiple copies of Windows 10 installed in a dual-boot system, and they're all showing up in the startup menu with the same name. It also might be because you have a Linux installation that is configured incorrectly in the boot menu.

You can edit the boot menu both from the desktop or from a USB Recovery Drive or Windows 10 installation media by using the (Boot Configuration Data) BCDEdit command. This works in the Command Prompt. If you are opening the Command Prompt from the desktop, start it from the *Win+X* menu and click *Command Prompt (Admin)*. If you are using the Command Prompt from boot media, start it in the way I described at the very beginning of this chapter.

When you type the command **BCDEdit** into a Command Prompt window, you will be presented with a list of all the operating systems currently installed on the PC that are listed in the Windows 10 boot system, see Figure 13-8.

```
Administrator: Command Prompt                                    —     □     ✕

Windows Boot Manager
--------------------
identifier              {bootmgr}
device                  partition=\Device\HarddiskVolume2
path                    \EFI\Microsoft\Boot\bootmgfw.efi
description             Windows Boot Manager
locale                  en-GB
inherit                 {globalsettings}
flightsigning           Yes
default                 {current}
resumeobject            {e397815a-15a9-11e5-9622-fc025c6ab93c}
displayorder            {current}
toolsdisplayorder       {memdiag}
timeout                 30

Windows Boot Loader
-------------------
identifier              {current}
device                  partition=C:
path                    \WINDOWS\system32\winload.efi
description             Windows 10
locale                  en-GB
inherit                 {bootloadersettings}
recoverysequence        {e397815c-15a9-11e5-9622-fc025c6ab93c}
recoveryenabled         Yes
isolatedcontext         Yes
flightsigning           Yes
allowedinmemorysettings 0x15000075
osdevice                partition=C:
systemroot              \WINDOWS
resumeobject            {e397815a-15a9-11e5-9622-fc025c6ab93c}
nx                      OptIn
bootmenupolicy          Standard
```

Figure 13-8. BCDEdit is run from the Command Prompt as an Administrator

The important object for each to note is its *{identifier}*; this might be a text string, but it could also be a hexadecimal code as in the {e397815a-15a9-11e5-9622-fc025c6ab93c} format seen in Figure 13-8. There are many switches you can use with BCDEdit to edit, create, and delete entries from the Windows 10 boot menu. Of these, by far the most useful for troubleshooting are

- **bcdedit [/store filename] /bootdebug [id] { ON | OFF }** is used to enable or disable the begugger for the specified boot entry. The debug log is stored in the file specified in the command. This might be used in the format *bcdedit /store C:\BootDebugLog / bootdebug {current} ON*

- **bcdedit [/store filename] /bootsequence id [...] [/addfirst | /addlast | /remove]** specifies the boot sequence for a one-time boot. This might be used in the format *bcdedit /bootsequence { e397815a-15a9-11e5-9622-fc025c6ab93c } {current} {ntldr}*

- **bcdedit [/store filename] /copy id /d description** creates a copy of the specified boot entry. This might be used in the format bcdedit /copy { e397815a-15a9-11e5-9622-fc025c6ab93c } /d "Copy of Windows 10"

- **bcdedit [/store filename] /create [id] /d description [/application apptype | / inherit [apptype] | /inherit DEVICE | /device]** creates a new boot entry with the specified ID. The supported application types are *BOOTSECTOR, OSLOADER,* and *RESUME,* and the supported Inherit sypes are *BOOTMGR, BOOTSECTOR, FWBOOTMGR, MEMDIAG, NTLDR, ORLOADER,* and *RESUME.* This might be used in the format *bcdedit /create {ntldr} /d "Compatibility OS"*

- **bcdedit [/store filename] /debug [id] { ON | OFF }** enables or disables the kernel debugger for the specified boot entry. This might be used in the format *bcdedit / debug ON*

- **bcdedit [/store filename] /default id** sets the default boot entry for the PC. This might be used in the format *bcdedit /default { e397815a-15a9-11e5-9622-fc025c6ab93c }*

- **bcdedit [/store filename] /delete id [/f] [/cleanup | /nocleanup]** deletes the specified boot entry and optionally cleans it from the display order. This might be used in the format *bcdedit /delete {cbd971bf-b7b8-4885-951a-fa03044f5d71} /cleanup*

- **bcdedit [/store filename] /deletevalue [id] datatype** deletes an element or value from a boot entry. This might be used in the format *bcdedit /deletevalue {bootmgr} bootsequence*

- **bcdedit [/store filename] /displayorder id [...] [/addfirst | /addlast | /remove]** sets the boot manager's display order. This might be used in the format *bcdedit / displayorder { e397815a-15a9-11e5-9622-fc025c6ab93c } /addlast*

- **bcdedit [/store filename] /enum [type | id] [/v]** lists all the boot entries in the specified BCD store. This can be used with the enum types ACTIVE, ALL, BOOTAPP, BOOTMGR, FIRMWARE, INERIT, OSLOADER, and RESUME. It may be used in the format *bcdedit /enum OSLOADER*

- **bcdedit /export filename** creates a backup copy of the BCD store to the specified file. It might be used in the format *bcdedit /export "C:\BCD Backup"*

- **bcdedit /import [/clean] filename** imports the contents of an exported BCD backup. It might be used in the same format as the export command. The /clean switch is used only on UEFI systems, and it forces the firmware to delete all its existing NVRAM boot entries that are used with Secure Boot.

- **bcdedit [/store filename] /set [id] datatype value [/addfirst | /addlast | /remove]** creates or modifies an element in a boot entry. It might be used in the format *bcdedit /set { e397815a-15a9-11e5-9622-fc025c6ab93c } path \windows\system32\winload.exe*

- **bcdedit /sysstore partition** specifies the partition used for the BCD store. This switch is used only on UEFI systems, and might be used in the format *bcdedit /sysstore C:*

- **bcdedit [/store filename] /timeout** timeout specifies how long the boot loader should wait at the OS loader menu before selecting the default entry. It might be used in the format *bcdedit /timeout 30*, where the number is a representation of seconds.

BCDEdit Identifiers

I've already detailed that the OS identifiers used in the Boot Configuration Data store come in the format {xxxxxxxx-xxxx-xxxx-xxxx-xxxxxxxxxxxx}, but there are others available, such as {current} and {ntldr}, which I've used in the preceding examples. The full list of available identifiers is shown in Table 13-1.

Table 13-1. *Identifiers Used by the BCDEdit Command*

Identifier	Description
{badmemory}	The global RAM defect list
{bootloadersettings}	Global settings to be inherited by all boot loader entries
{bootmgr}	The Windows Boot Manager
{current}	The currently running operating system
{dbgsettings}	The global debugger settings
{default}	An identifier for the default boot entry
{emssettings}	The global EMS settings
{fwbootmgr}	The firmware boot manager boot entry; stored in NVRAM on UEFI systems
{globalsettings}	Global settings that should be inherited by all boot entries
{memdiag}	The memory diagnostic utility
{ntldr}	The Windows legacy loader, NTLDR; used for versions of Windows released prior to Windows Vista
{ramdiskoptions}	Additional options required for RAM disks
{resumeloadersettings}	Global settings that should be inherited by all Windows resume-from-hibernation entries

BCDEdit Data Formats

Additionally, each BCDEdit command is used with data fields such as ID. These are shown in Table 13-2.

Table 13-2. *BCDEdit Data Formats*

Data Format	Description
boolean	A Boolean value that can be set to TRUE or FALSE. You can also use the values TRUE or FALSE, as well as 1 and 0, and YES and NO.
device	A device data type that can be one of BOOT, PARTITION=drive, FILE=[parent]path, or RAMDISK=[parent]path,optionsid
enum	The data type that takes a value from a list.
id	The identifier for a boot entry, known as its GUID.
integer	A 64-bit integer, 32-bit variables are not supported.
list	A boot entry identifier list that contains one or more boot entry identifiers separated by spaces. This list type does not use quotation marks.
string	A string variable. It should be surrounded by quotation marks ("") if it contains spaces.

An excellent and full reference document for the BCDEdit command is available to download from the Microsoft web site **http://pcs.tv/1MBUbPu**.

Examples of BCDEdit Use

This all seems fairly confusing, so I want to detail some real-world examples of how you might use the BCDEdit command with your Windows 10 PC.

- To change the default operating system, the one that appears first in the OS choices list and that will load automatically if no option is selected there, use the command **BCDEdit /default {id}.**

- If an operating system has the incorrect disk or partition associated with it, this can be rectified with the command **BCDEdit /set {id} device partition=X:,** where X: represents the disk or partition on which the operating system is installed. You must then also use the command **BCDEdit /set {id} osdevice partition=X:.**

- To manually add a legacy operating system that isn't appearing in the list, use these commands with the new custom ID {legacy}.

  a. **BCDEdit /create {legacy} /d "Legacy OS Name"**

  b. **BCDEdit /set {legacy} device partition=D:** or the letter of the partition where the legacy OS is installed

  c. **BCDEdit /set {legacy} path /ntldr**

  d. **BCDEdit /displayorder {legacy} /addlast**

- If you are adding a Linux installation to the boot menu, follow these instructions.

  Boot into Linux and launch a Terminal session with root privileges.

  Find which partition Linux is installed on with the command **fdisk -l** (lowercase "L"). The Linux installation will be on a partition labeled as /dev/sda1 or /dev/hda1.

  Install a GRUB (Grand Unified Boot Loader) boot manager on that partition with the command **grub-install /dev/sda1.**

  Copy the Linux boot sector with the command **dd if=/dev/sda1 of /tmp/linux.bin bs=512 count=1.**

  Copy the file linux.bin to a USB Flash Drive as a backup.

  Install Windows 10 on your PC.

  Press *Win+X* to open the Administration menu and run *Command Prompt (Admin).*

  Type **diskpart** to enter the disk management utility.

  Type **select disk=0,** which is more than likely where your boot partition is located.

  Type **list volume** and look for the active or System partition, see Figure 13-9.

```
■ Administrator: Command Prompt - diskpart                                         —   □   ×

C:\WINDOWS\system32>diskpart

Microsoft DiskPart version 10.0.10586

Copyright (C) 1999-2013 Microsoft Corporation.
On computer: WORKSTATION

DISKPART> select disk=0

Disk 0 is now the selected disk.

DISKPART> list volume

  Volume ###  Ltr  Label        Fs     Type        Size     Status     Info
  ----------  ---  -----------  -----  ----------  -------  ---------  --------
  Volume 0    J                        DVD-ROM         0 B  No Media
  Volume 1    G    ioFX         NTFS   Partition    391 GB  Healthy
  Volume 2    C    Windows      NTFS   Partition    465 GB  Healthy    Boot
  Volume 3         Recovery     NTFS   Partition    450 MB  Healthy    Hidden
  Volume 4                      FAT32  Partition    100 MB  Healthy    System
  Volume 5    D    Files        NTFS   Partition   2658 GB  Healthy
  Volume 6         PBR Image    NTFS   Partition    136 GB  Healthy
  Volume 7    E    File Histor  NTFS   Partition    931 GB  Healthy
  Volume 8    F                        Removable       0 B  No Media
  Volume 9    H                        Removable       0 B  No Media
  Volume 10   L                        Removable       0 B  No Media
  Volume 11   M                        Removable       0 B  No Media

DISKPART>
```

Figure 13-9. *You are looking for the System partition on your disk*

You need to temporarily assign a drive letter to the System partition. Type **assign letter=n** and use the next available drive letter.

Copy your *linux.bin* backup file from your USB Flash Drive to the root (active) partition.

Type **remove letter=n** to remove the drive letter.

Create a GRUB entry with the command **BCDEdit /create /d "GRUB" /application BOOTSECTOR**. This will return a unique ID: make a note of it. For the remainder of this example, I will call it {linuxid}.

Type **BCDEdit /set {linuxid} device boot**

Type **BCDEdit /set {linuxid} PATH /linux.bin**

Type **BCDEdit /displayorder {linuxid} /addlast**

Effecting Repairs on the Boot Partition Structures

If the main boot partition becomes corrupt in Windows, you can, as I detailed earlier, create a new one and get your copy of Windows 10 working again. This will, however, break some crucial functionality such as some parts of the Recovery Environment, the Reset backup image, and the ability to create a USB Recovery Drive. But what happens if you want to preserve these, or if you are suffering from a general disk corruption?

Normally in these circumstances you'd run a command such as the venerable CHKDSK, or a third-party disk utility. CHKDSK can be run from a Recovery Drive but isn't very comprehensive. If you can't get Windows 10 to start, however, this becomes very difficult. You could start the PC from a Windows To Go (WTG) drive, but these are designed to hide the underlying PC drives for security reasons. There are ways around this by giving yourself access in the Disk Management Console, but Windows 10 doesn't really come with useful disk partition management tools, and certainly doesn't come with repair tools. You would need these to already be installed on the WTG drive.

In these circumstances I recommend starting the PC from a Linux CD or DVD. It's noninvasive in that it can be run entirely from the removable disk, without needing to be installed, and many distributions (known as distros) come with useful disk and partiton management tools.

I mentioned early in this chapter that BIOS and UEFI installations of Windows have different boot partition structures. BIOS systems use a single *System Reserved* partiton, see Figure 13-10. This contains all the files needed to boot the operating system. This partition is comonly 100MB in size.

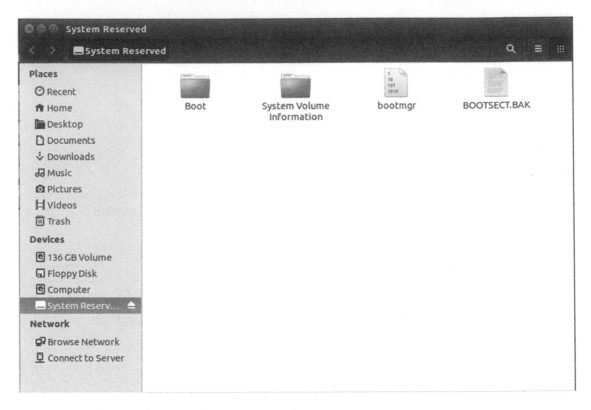

Figure 13-10. *BIOS PCs have a single System Reserved partition*

UEFI systems have a three-partition structure. The first of these is a 100MB *EFI System* partition, a 300MB *Recovery* partition that contains a copy of the WinRE Windows Recovery Environment file, and a third small, hidden partition that's used for storing the security tools used for features such as Bitlocker.

■ **Note**   Some UEFI installations of 32-bit Windows 10 versions have only a System Reserved partition. This will be because they are installed on a PC with a 32-bit processor and older motherboard that does not support all the features of the UEFI specification.

It's the *EFI System* partition, see Figure 13-11, that contains all the boot files for Windows 10. With both the *System Reserved* and *EFI System* partitions, you can, if you're extremely paranoid and have a tin foil hat, make backup copies of all the files in these partitions. It's not normally necessary, however.

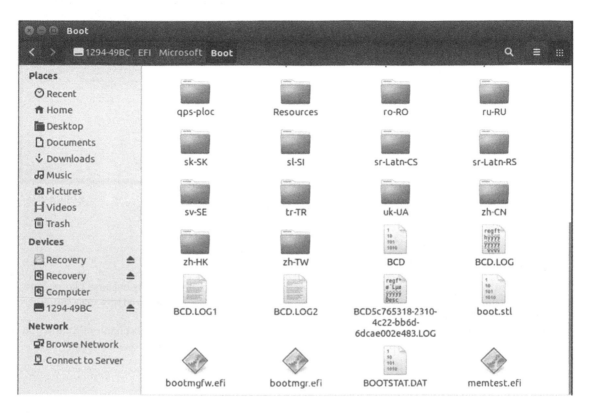

Figure 13-11. *UEFI systems have a three-partition structure, different from BIOS systems*

There are many Linux distros. I'm using Ubuntu here (www.ubuntu.com), but you could use another such as Linux Mint (www.linuxmint.com) or Red Hat (www.redhat.com); many come with disk and partition management tools such as GParted, seen in Figure 13-12. These can report on partitions and check them for errors, repairing those they find if possible. This can be a useful way to repair errors in the partition structure of your PC's hard disk.

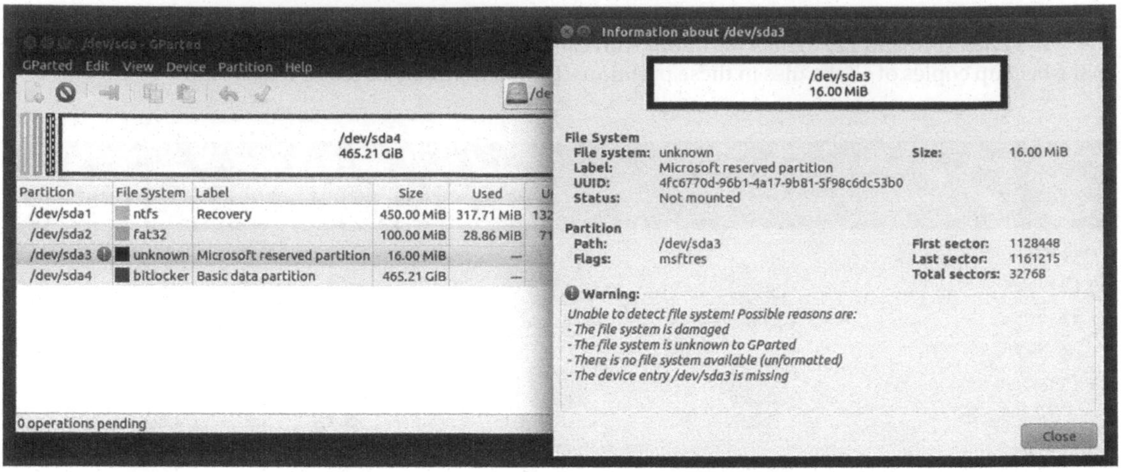

Figure 13-12. *You can get partiton information and even repair partitions from Linux*

Summary

I really wanted to go all out to make this chapter as comprehensive as possible, simply because I know from the size of my mailbag how many people have problems with Windows startup, and just how easy it can really be to avoid a reinstall.

Startup isn't the only thing that can drive PC users "nutzoid," however. In the next chapter I'll show you how to effect advanced repairs on your networking systems to maintain stable connections to your home devices, business servers, and the all-important Internet.

CHAPTER 14

■ ■ ■

Networks and Internet Connections

What use is a computer that doesn't have Internet access? It's odd to think that life wasn't always this way, though I do remember how frustrating it was that my early computers—be they a Sinclair ZX81, ZX Spectrum and QL, Psion Series 3, 3a, and 5 handhelds, or an Olivetti 8086-based PC—couldn't get access to the wider world. All this, of course, was before the World Wide Web (or even DARPANET as it was originally) was invented. Now, it's impossible to think of a device that's not online, from tablets and watches to the refrigerator in your kitchen.

You'll be pleased to learn that this chapter is not a master class in how to connect your fridge to the Internet. What it is, though, is everything you need to know to troubleshoot and repair network connections to your company network and the wider world. Let's face facts: *nothing* is more annoying on PCs than not having an Internet connection, and we've reached the point with society that it can also be a significant barrier to productivity as well with so many company services, such as Office 365, requiring online access.

Checking the Status of a Network Connection

Troubleshooting any problem on a PC, especially one involving networking, is always a methodical process of elimination. Why do I say this? Well, a network problem isn't the same thing as a software compatibility issue as there are always external factors to consider as well. Let's take just one example to focus on, the humble Ethernet cable.

How many times have you, or someone else you know, pulled, tripped over, or damaged a network cable? For our laptops and tablets that now come equipped with fast Wi-Fi, they might be a thing of the past, but in a business environment they are still de rigueur. If an Internet or network connection fails on a PC that's connected via Ethernet, my initial reaction is always to check the cabling first, to ensure that everything is plugged in securely, and that the cable hasn't been pulled or snagged.

After that, it's a case of checking the Ethernet socket and/or the router or switch the cable is plugged into, to see if there's any problem or damage there. Third is to check any other PCs in the vicinity, connected via Ethernet or Wi-Fi (and smartphones count in this as well, though with their cellular connection it can sometimes be harder to tell for certain) if the problem is isolated to the single PC, or exists elsewhere on the network.

These three checks will quickly tell you if you need to go digging around in the PC's networking settings at all, and it's amazing how many times a network problem will be caused by an ISP (Internet Service Provider) issue or outage and people don't associate it with that. In a way it's the old story of the person calling IT Support to report their computer won't switch on, and when asked to check the power cable says they can't see it because the power is out in the building, and it's all dark.

There's a quick and easy way to check the status of a network or Internet connection, and you can find it in the Network and Sharing Center (available by right-clicking the Network icon in the System Tray, or through the Control Panel). At the top center of the window you'll see details of your "active networks," see Figure 14-1. To the right of each, and it's very likely there's only one listed, is a *Connections* link.

© Mike Halsey 2016

M. Halsey, *Windows 10 Troubleshooting*, DOI 10.1007/978-1-4842-0925-7_14

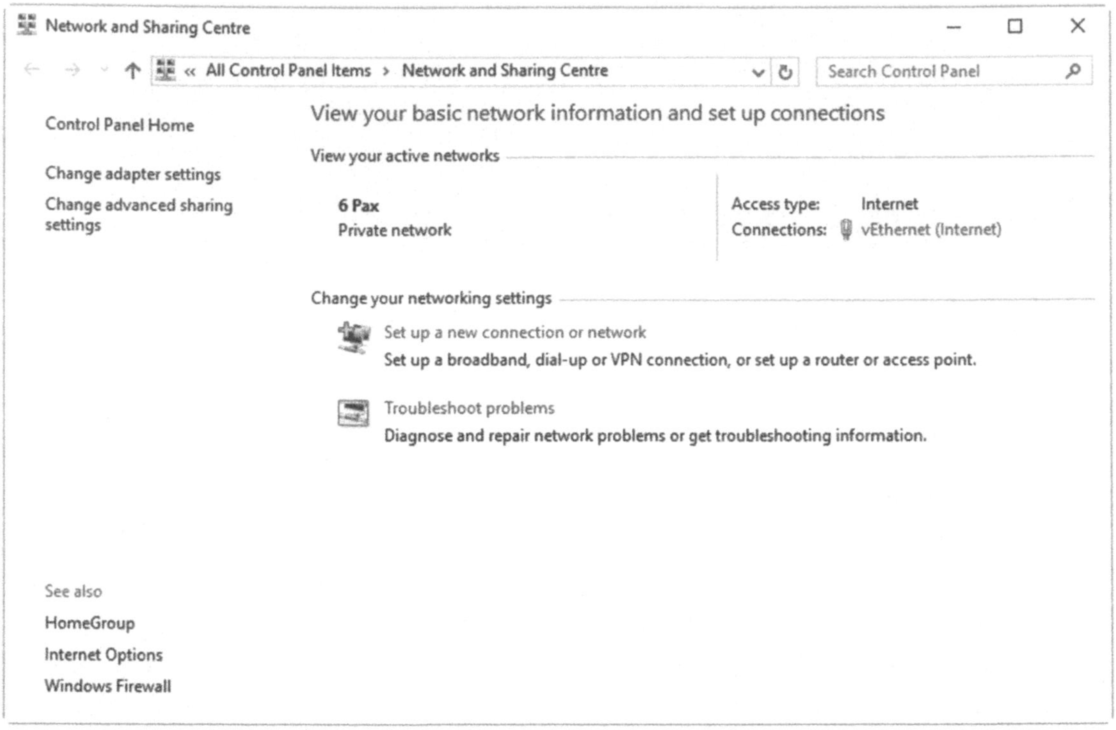

Figure 14-1. *You can check your network connection status in the Network and Sharing Center*

Clicking this connections link will display a status dialog for the network connection, see Figure 14-2. In the bottom half of this dialog is an Activity panel which will show you, in real time, the inbound and outbound packets of data. For a live connection there will be an almost constant stream of small data packets, as the PC performs routine handshaking with the network. If there is no data passing through the network connection, or if the Sent and Received values register as zero, the network connection is definitely down.

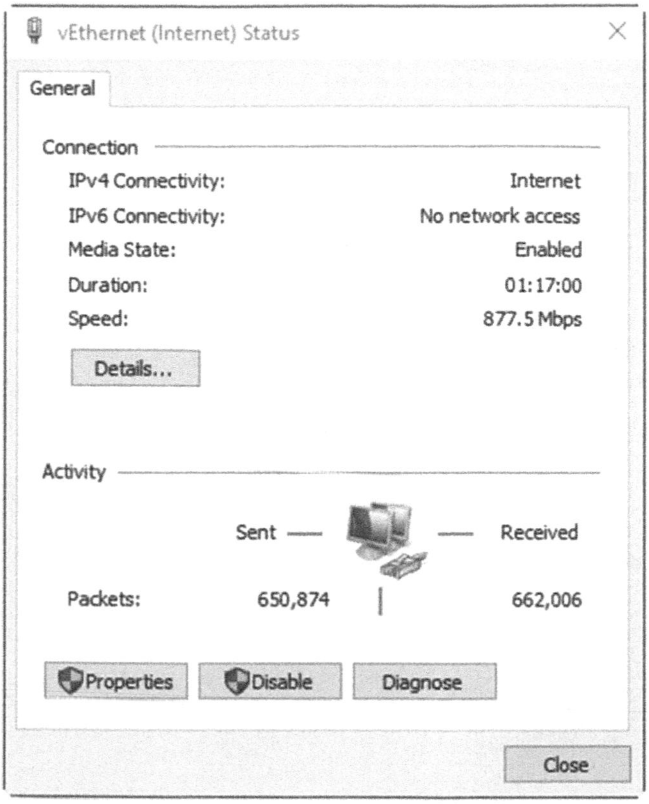

Figure 14-2. *The network status dialog will display real-time traffic information*

As with any detective work, troubleshooting and diagnosing problems with network connections requires some sleuthing. There is a huge amount of information available to you when it comes to networking, however.

From the Network Connection Status dialog, as detailed in Figure 14-2, click the *Details* button for data about your current connection. The dialog that will appear lists a great many useful details, including the name of the network adapter in use, your physical (MAC) address, your IPv4, and if applicable, IPv6 address and details such as the default gateway, which is the address on your network of the router, see Figure 14-3. It may be that some of these details are incorrectly configured, and later in this chapter I'll show you how to fix them.

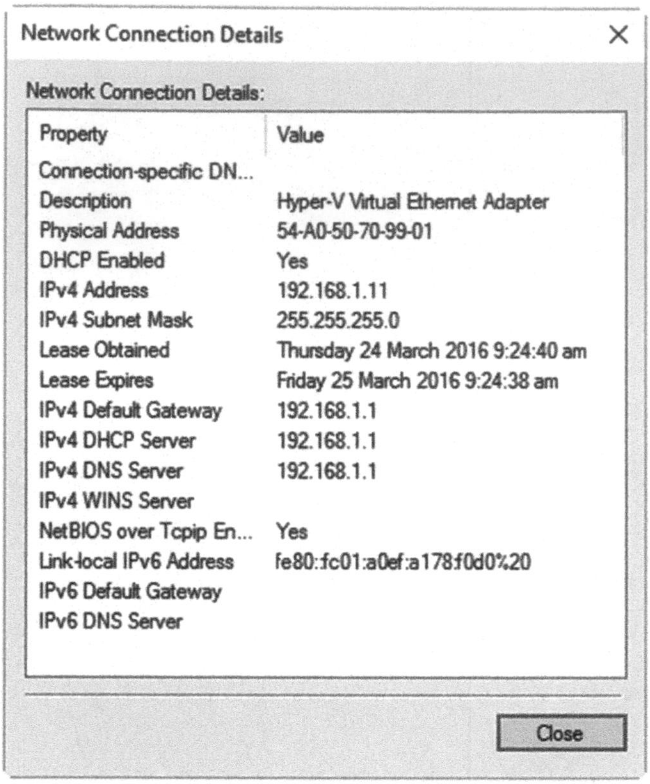

Figure 14-3. *You can get detailed information about the connection, including your IP address*

Back in the Network Connections Status dialog, click the *Properties* button to see which Windows and third-party services are available and enabled for the connection, see Figure 14-4. If you are having difficulty connecting to network shares or other PCs on the network, for example, you might find that the File and Printer Sharing service is not checked and thus not enabled for this connection.

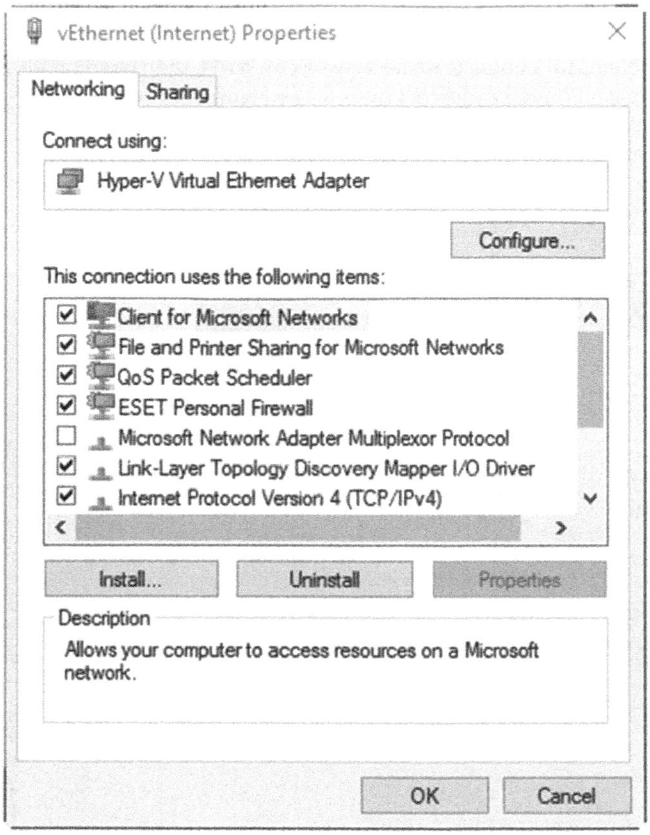

Figure 14-4. *You can check if appropriate Windows services are available for the connection*

You might also find that either the IPv4 or IPv6 connection isn't enabled. This could be because the PC, let's say it's a laptop or tablet, has been configured to work in a specific way on a secure company network, but when you connect to a network at home, as you're using the same network adapter, the settings you need are now incorrect.

■ **Tip**   You can quickly fix some network problems at the Network Connection Status dialog by clicking the Diagnose button. This will run the automatic network troubleshooter, which will reset components to their default state, but one of the most popular methods for quickly repairing network connections, especially if there's a configuration problem, is to manually reset the TCP/IP networking stack in Windows. To do this, from the *Win+X* menu, open *Command Prompt (Admin)* and type the command `netsh int ip reset`.

Displaying Information About Wi-Fi Networks

If the PC you are troubleshooting network problems for connects to the network by Wi-Fi, then opening the Network Connection Status panel will also reveal a *Wireless Properties* button, see Figure 14-5. Clicking this will reveal details such as the SSID name of the network (it's entirely possible the user is connected to the wrong network!) and if you click the security tab, you'll be able to see the security and encryption types that Windows 10 is using to connect to the network. You can check these against another working PC, or in the router settings, to ensure they are correct, as incorrect settings will cause a connection attempt to fail.

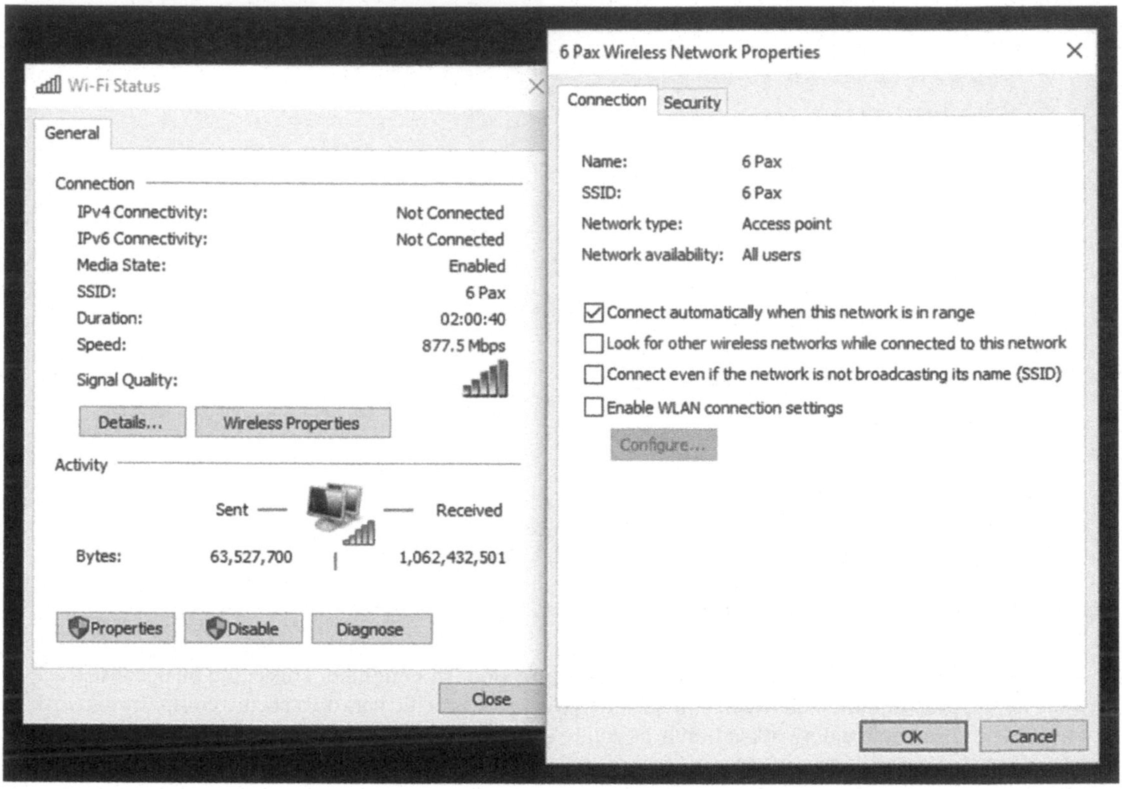

Figure 14-5. *Checking the details of a Wi-Fi connection additionally presents a Wireless Properties button*

You can also discover the password for a Wi-Fi network in the Wireless Network Properties panel, under the *Security* tab, by checking the *Show characters* box for the Network Security Key. This will display the Wi-Fi password for the network to which you are currently connected.

Sometimes you want more advanced information about a wireless network, including perhaps even the password used to access a network to which you're not currently connected. The good news is that both are easily achievable. Simply open a *Command Prompt (Admin)* window and type the command netsh wlan show profiles name="network name" key=clear. Full details for the Wi-Fi network connection will then be displayed, including in the Key *Content field*, the password used to access that network, see Figure 14-6.

```
Administrator: Command Prompt                                                    -    □    ×
Microsoft Windows [Version 10.0.10586]
(c) 2015 Microsoft Corporation. All rights reserved.

C:\WINDOWS\system32>netsh wlan show profiles name="6 Pax" key=clear

Profile 6 Pax on interface Wi-Fi:
=======================================================================

Applied: All User Profile

Profile information
-------------------
    Version                : 1
    Type                   : Wireless LAN
    Name                   : 6 Pax
    Control options        :
        Connection mode    : Connect automatically
        Network broadcast  : Connect only if this network is broadcasting
        AutoSwitch         : Do not switch to other networks
        MAC Randomization  : Disabled

Connectivity settings
---------------------
    Number of SSIDs        : 1
    SSID name              : "6 Pax"
    Network type           : Infrastructure
    Radio type             : [ Any Radio Type ]
    Vendor extension        : Not present

Security settings
-----------------
    Authentication         : WPA2-Personal
    Cipher                 : CCMP
    Security key           : Present
    Key Content            : NetworkPasswordDisplayedHere

Cost settings
-------------
    Cost                   : Unrestricted
    Congested              : No
    Approaching Data Limit : No
    Over Data Limit        : No
    Roaming                : No
    Cost Source            : Default

C:\WINDOWS\system32>
```

Figure 14-6. *You can discover a Wi-Fi network password with a simple command*

Additionally, using the netsh wlan show profiles command on its own will display a list of all the Wi-Fi network connection details stored on the PC, see Figure 14-7. You can use this to check if required network settings are in place, or if a network connection that should not be present is still there after a connection.

```
Administrator: Command Prompt                                                    -    □    ×
(c) 2015 Microsoft Corporation. All rights reserved.

C:\WINDOWS\system32>netsh wlan show profiles

Profiles on interface Wi-Fi:

Group policy profiles (read only)
---------------------------------
    <None>

User profiles
-------------
    All User Profile     : PlusnetWireless707D73
    All User Profile     : virginmedia7224139
    All User Profile     : Lumia 950 4322
    All User Profile     : 6 Pax
    All User Profile     : Princess
    All User Profile     : mvp2015
    All User Profile     : 6 Pax
    All User Profile     : AIR-2602I
    All User Profile     : 6 Pax+
    All User Profile     : EE-BrightBox-htndfh
    All User Profile     : NOKIA 909_0845
    All User Profile     : ZyXEL_A39C
    All User Profile     : NOKIA 909_9800
    All User Profile     : MMU-Visitor
    All User Profile     : BTHub3-2CSW

C:\WINDOWS\system32>
```

Figure 14-7. *You can display details of all the Wireless network details stored on the PC*

Sometimes the settings for a Wi-Fi connection become corrupt, and you need to delete the profile and set it up again from scratch. This can be achieved within the Settings app, but can also be done from a *Command Prompt (Admin)* window with the command `netsh wlan delete profile name "network name"`.

Diagnosing Network Connection Problems

The Network and Sharing Center isn't the only place where you can find detailed information about the status of your network connection. The Task Manager, Resource Monitor, Performance Monitor, and Event Viewer can all provide detailed disgnostic and real-time data about the status of a network connection. I'll show you how to use these tools in depth in Chapter 25, except for the Event Viewer, which I detailed in Chapter 5.

I do want to focus a little more on the Event Viewer in this chapter, however, and show you how to get specific network status reports from it. Then I'll show you how to get network-specific data from the Performance Monitor and Resource Monitor.

Getting Network Diagnostic Reports from the Event Viewer

If you *Create [a] Custom View* in the Event Viewer, you can choose from a veriety of different networking logs of services from which to get reports, see Figure 14-8. These can include everything from "information", which will report, for example, when a successful connection is made or when there is a connection failure, to "warnings", "errors", and "critical [stops]".

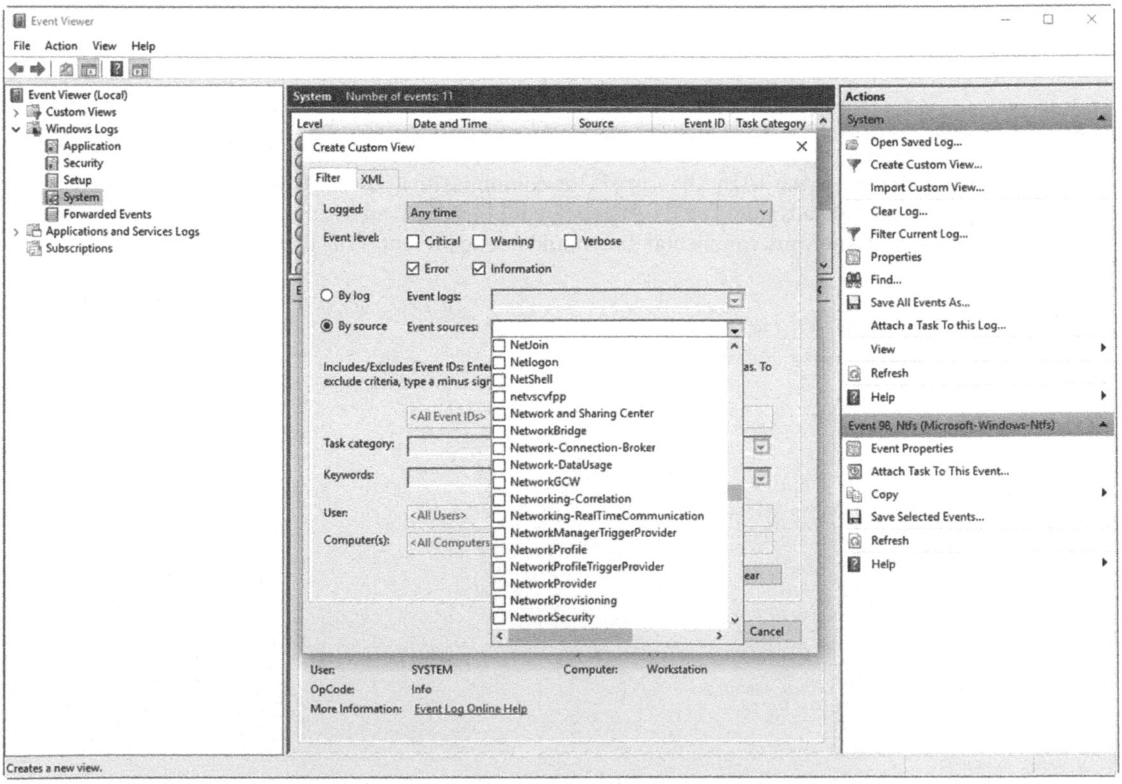

Figure 14-8. *You can receive reports of network errors in the Event Viewer*

Unless you are an experienced System Administrator, however, who *really* knows exactly what to seek for your specific problem, you can get connection reports from the Network-Connection-Broker, NetworkBridge (if you have used bridged connections), Network and Sharing Center, and more. To make things simpler, however, you can select reports "by log" and select "System [logs]" with the event ID **6100**; these will automatically include all the Network Diagnostics events filtered by the Event Level(s) you choose.

See the Status of Your Connection with the Performance Monitor

The Task Manager's Performance tab, which I'll detail more in Chapter 25, allows you to view your current overall network traffic. This can be broken down further, however, with the Performance Monitor, which I'll detail in full in Chapter 25. You can open the Performance Monitor from the Administrative Tools in the Control Panel, or by searching for it in the Start Menu or Cortana.

Clicking the green + icon at the top of the Performance Monitor window allows you to add counters that will be displayed in the main Performance Monitor view as a live bar graph. These include the number of bytes sent and received by the PC, including many other networking metrics, see Figure 14-9.

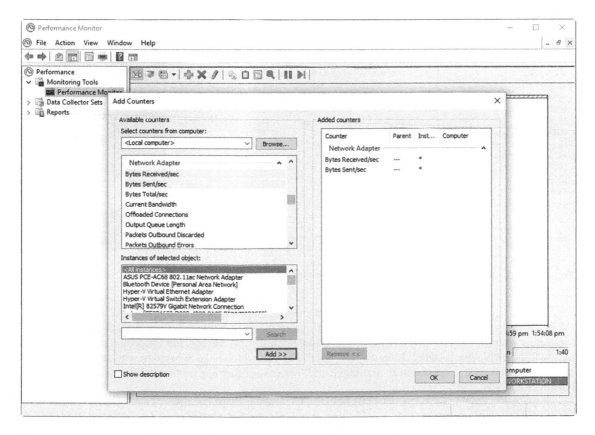

Figure 14-9. *You can get live network metrics from the Performance Monitor*

See What's Using Your Bandwidth with the Resource Monitor

Perhaps, though, you have a situation where you have a working and seemingly stable network connection, but nothing you try and do on that connection is working properly. Maybe activities are failing or timing out. In this circumstance, you need to know exactly what's using all your network bandwidth and why.

This is where the Resource Monitor comes in, which again I'll show you how to use in detail in Chapter 25. In short, however, it is split into four horizontal, colapsible panels. The Network panel, which is the one we're interested in here, shows you exactly what apps, services, and processes are using bandwidth, and exactly how much bandwidth they're using at any given time, see Figure 14-10.

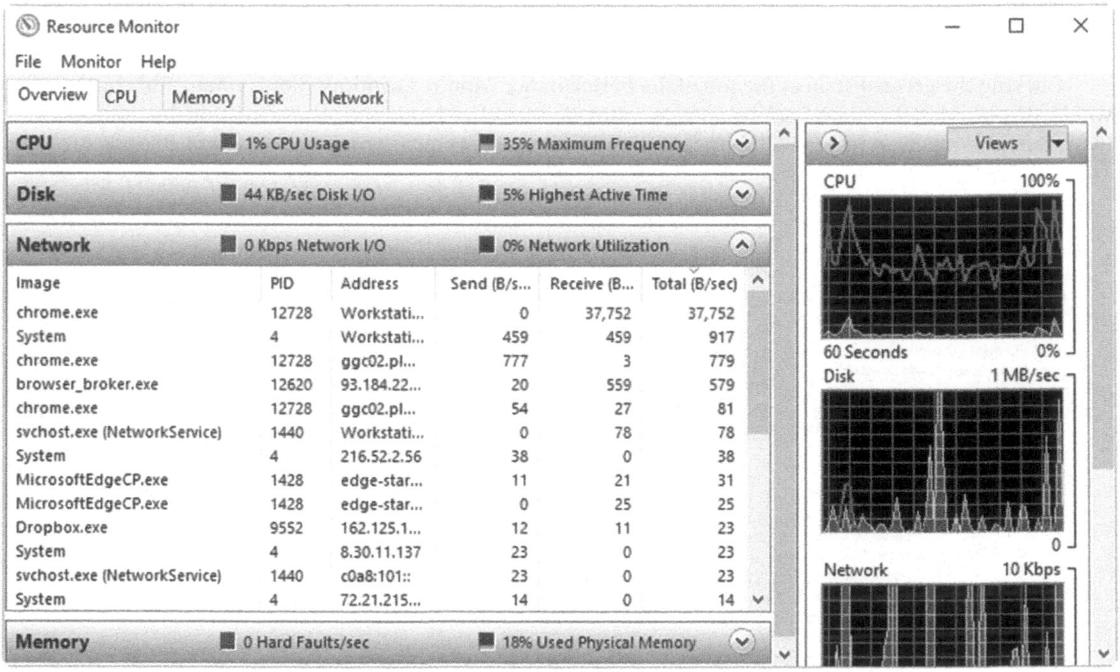

Figure 14-10. *The Resource Monitor can tell you what's using your bandwidth*

You may find that you have a runaway process, maybe an app updater, a poorly coded app, or perhaps even malware on the PC, that is consuming large amounts of network bandwidth, and maybe even swamping your Internet connection. In the preceding example, you can see that Chrome is using the most bandwidth (it's playing relaxing chillout music from YouTube, which I like to listen to while writing these books, should you be interested in such things), and we can see other apps such as Edge and Dropbox using bandwidth as well.

If there was anything here we didn't recognizes, however, perhaps because it's a malware process; we can search for the name of the process online. You do this in Task Manager, under either the Process or Details tab, by right-clicking the process and selecting *Search online* from the menu that appears, see Figure 14-11.

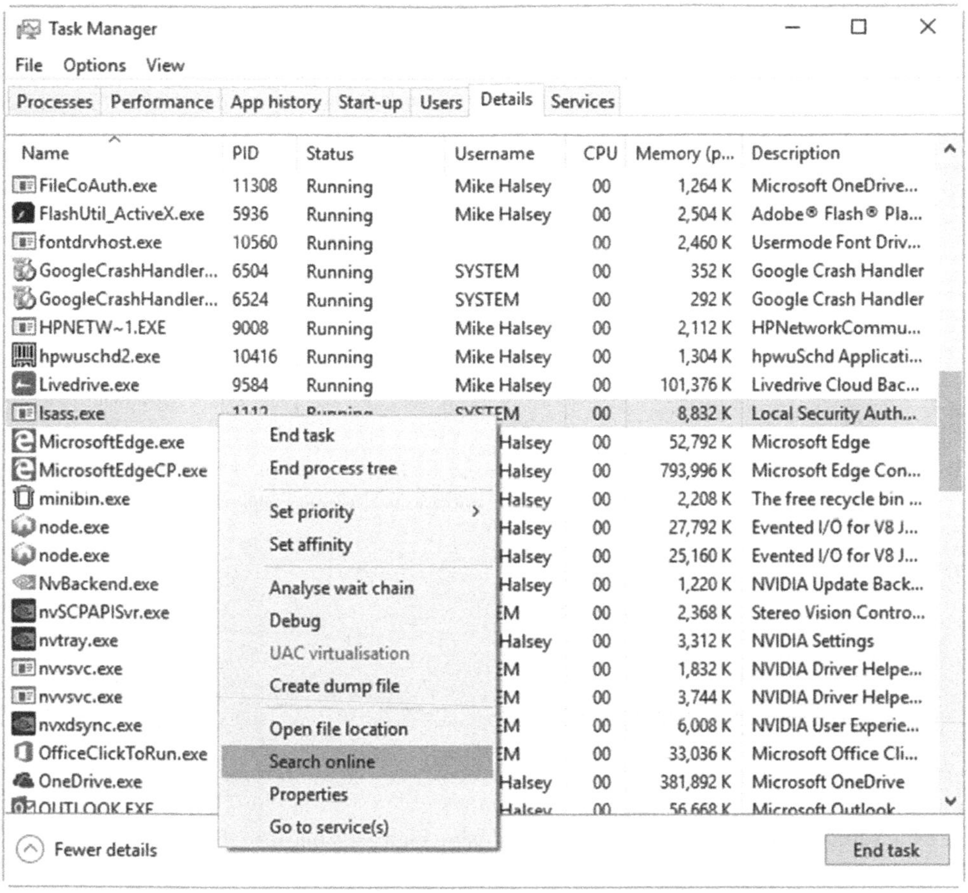

Figure 14-11. *Task Manager lets you search for process details online*

Troubleshooting in the Network and Sharing Center

The Network and Sharing Center, accessed by right-clicking the network icon in the System Tray, or from the Control Panel, isn't just a place for Windows to display infomation about your current network status, as it also contains useful configuration options you might need when troubleshooting a problem. In the top left of the Network and Sharing Center window are two links, *Change Adapter Settings* and *Change Advanced Sharing Settings*. We'll look at the second one of these first.

Occasionally, the sharing settings for a PC might be changed (perhaps by the user accidentally). These settings, however, don't just affect file and folder sharing, but they also affect discovery for other PCs, and network hardware, and for the discoverability of that PC by other hardware and systems on the network.

If you click the *Network* link in File Explorer, Windows 10 is extremely good at prompting you that Network Discovery is switched off, if it's unable to see any other PCs on the local network. Obviously, however, you won't get this message from other PCs that can't see the one on which Network Discovery is deactivated.

The Advanced Sharing Settings panel is split into three main collapsible sections: Private, Guest or Public, and All Networks, see Figure 14-12. Additionally, in a corporate environment you may see an additional option here for your Business Network.

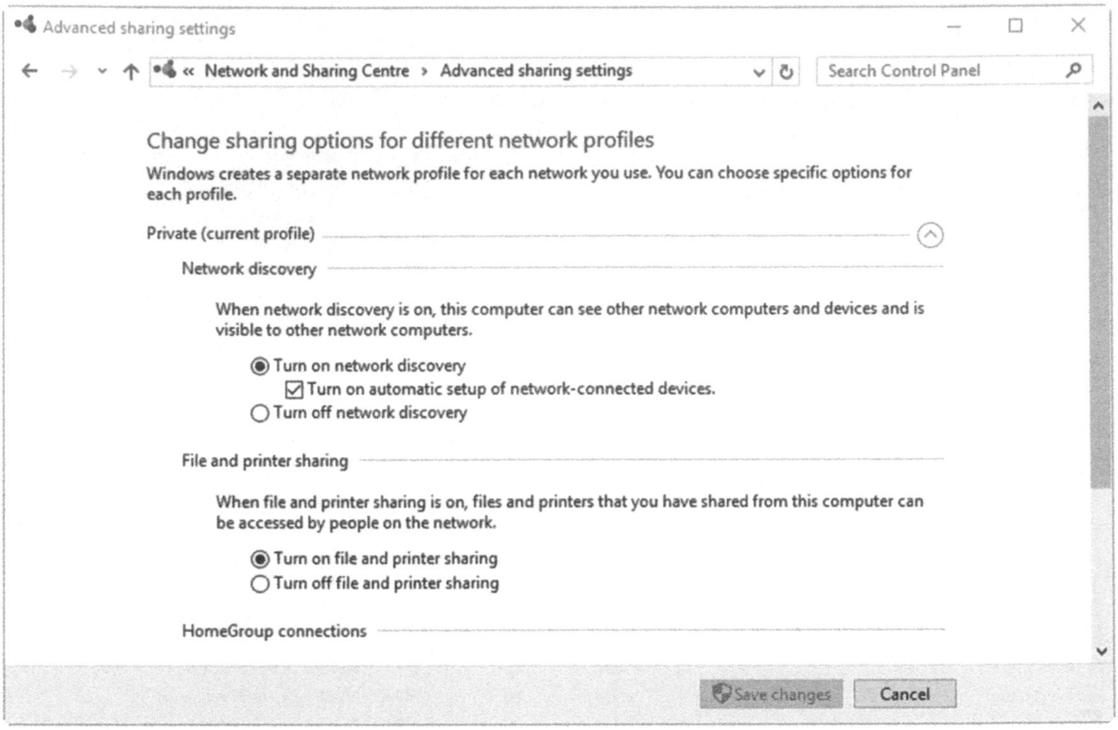

Figure 14-12. *The Advanced Sharing Settings control discoverability as well as sharing*

This is where the settings can occasionally become confusing for a user, because they might say, for example, that they can see all the network storage and devices on their laptop in the office, but not at the remote site they needed to visit. This would be because the worker has connected to the network at the remote site by assigning it a different network type. By this I mean that when you connect to a network in Windows 10, a dialog will appear near the top right of your screen asking if you want to be able to see other PCs on the network, and have them see you. This is exactly the sort of information dialog that people don't read, and where they'll just click one button or another. Consequently, it's all too easy to set the network as Public (can't see the network) when you had intended for it to be marked Private (can see PCs).

I'll show you how to change the network type shortly, but in the Advanced Sharing Settings panel, you can change the individual settings for Network Driver and File and Printer Sharing, for each individual network type by checking the appropriate options. Additionally, the Public network type includes file sharing encryption options. If file sharing is not working correctly on a PC, it may be that this encryption is either disabled (it's enabled by default), or that the setting is configured incorrectly for the security policies on the PC or on the network.

Changing a Network Type Between Private and Public

There are three ways to change a Wi-Fi network connection between Public and Private, and you might want to do this because, as has happened to me in a local pub, the landlord didn't want to give away the Wi-Fi password so typed it into my PC and then hit the *Yes* button when asked "Did [I] want to see other PCs..." before I could stop him. Clearly, this was a Public network, and I didn't want my laptop being seen by any other PCs that were also connected.

The simplest way, from a user perspective, is to go to the Settings app, open the *Network & Internet* section, and under the WiFi section, click the Manage WiFi settings link. This will display a list of all the Wi-Fi networks that are known to the PC. You can click any one and tell the PC to *Forget* the network settings, see Figure 14-13.

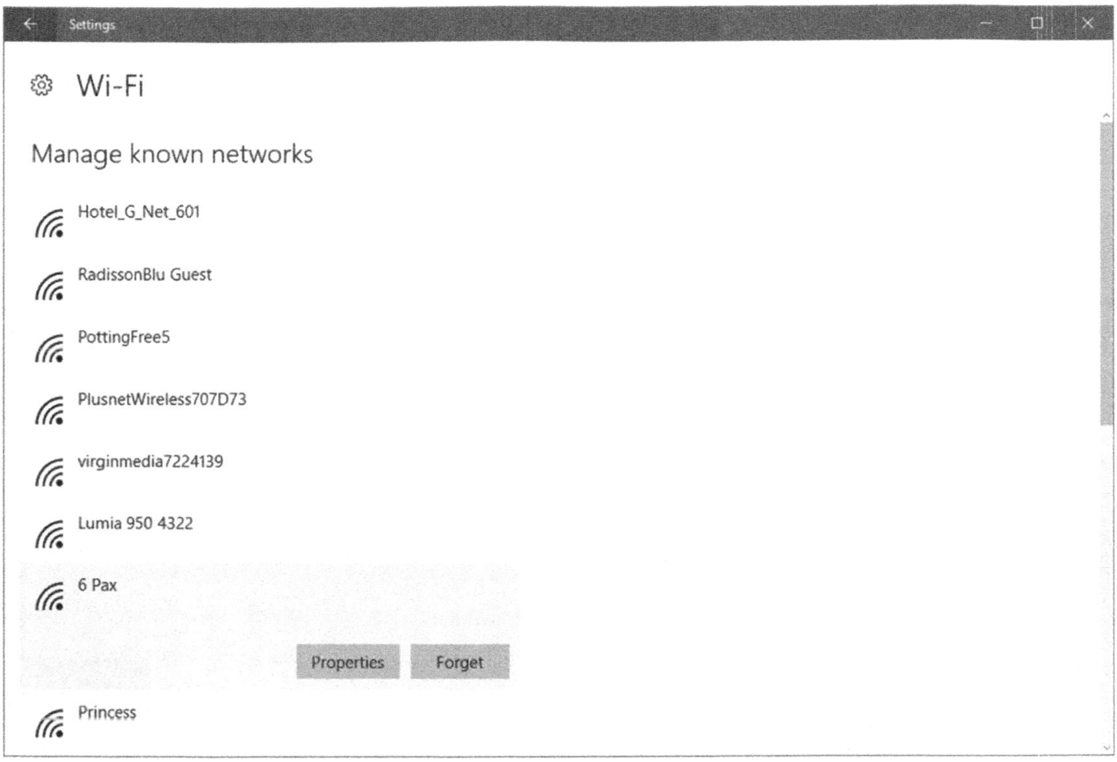

Figure 14-13. *You can tell Windows 10 to forget Wi-Fi networks*

The user will then need to reconnect to the network, for which they will need to know the password. I detailed a couple of methods to retrieve the password earlier in this chapter, should the user not already know what it is. When they reconnect they will be asked if they "...want to see other PCs..." and devices on the network, to which they should click *Yes*, to make it a Private network, or *No*, to make it a Public network.

The other methods of changing the network type require Group Policy and the Registry Editor, and so you might want to perform this change yourself, onsite or via remote access. Both changes will require a restart to take effect, so Remote Access is a good option.

To change the network type using the Group Policy Editor, open Group Policy by searching for **gpedit** in the Start Menu or Cortana and navigate to *Computer Configuration* ➤ *Windows Settings* ➤ *Security Settings* ➤ *Network List Manager Profiles*. This will display the name of the current Wi-Fi network, which you can double-click to open its properties. In the Properties dialog, click the *Network Location* tab, and then you can forcibly change the location type to either Public or Private, see Figure 14-14.

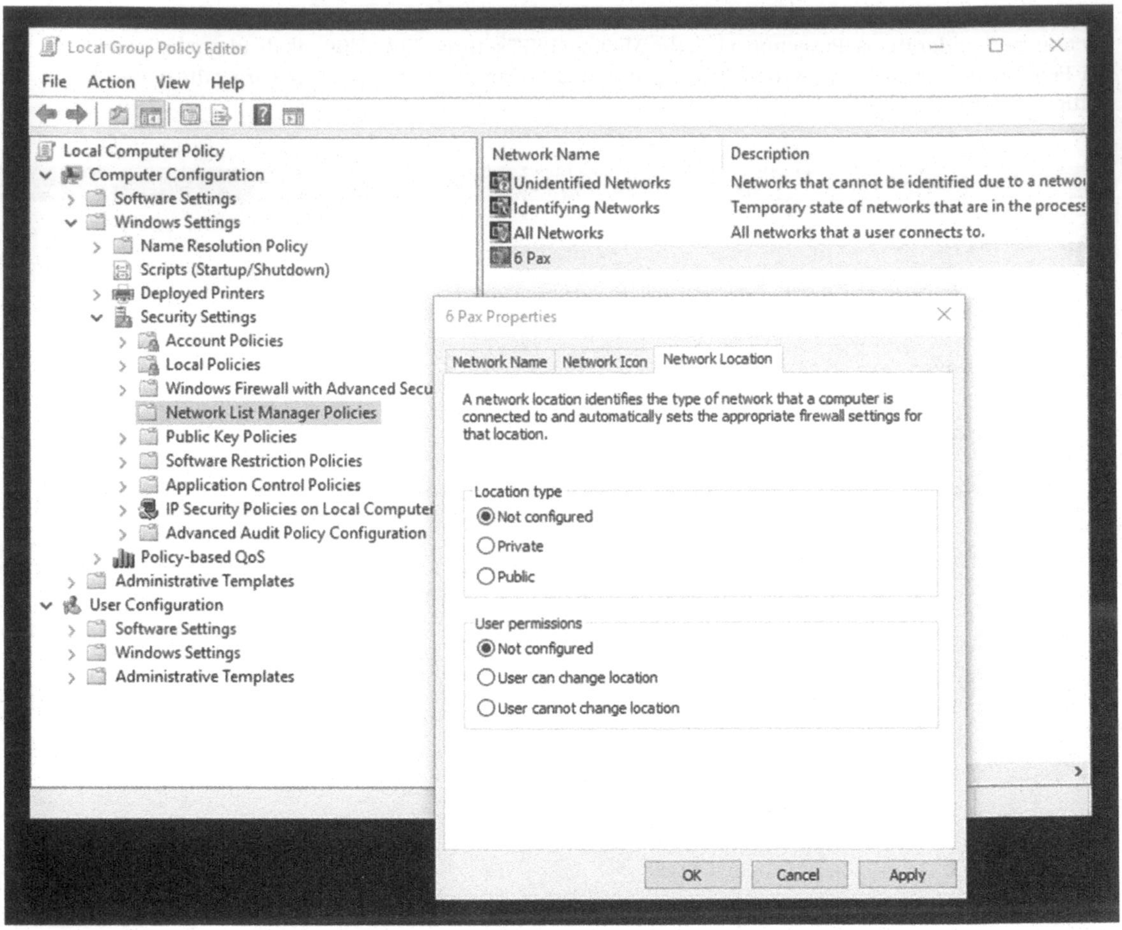

Figure 14-14. *You can change the network type in Group Policy*

If the PC is not running the Pro or Enterprise edition of Windows 10, you won't have access to the Group Policy Editor. The network type can still be changed though in the Registry Editor. I'll show you how to use the Registry Editor in full in Chapter 26, but you should always create a backup copy of the Registry before making any changes.

To open the Registry Editor, search for **regedit** at the Start Menu or Cortana, and when the Registry Editor window opens, click the *File* menu and the *Export* option. This will export a full backup copy of the Registry that can later be restored using the *Import* option if need be. To change the network type, in the left panel of the Registry Editor, navigate to *HKEY_LOCAL_MACHINE* ➤ *Software* ➤ *Microsoft* ➤ *WindowsNT* ➤ *CurrentVersion* ➤ *NetworkList* ➤ *Profiles* and look for the profile that has the *ProfileName* tag with the correct Network SSID, see Figure 14-15.

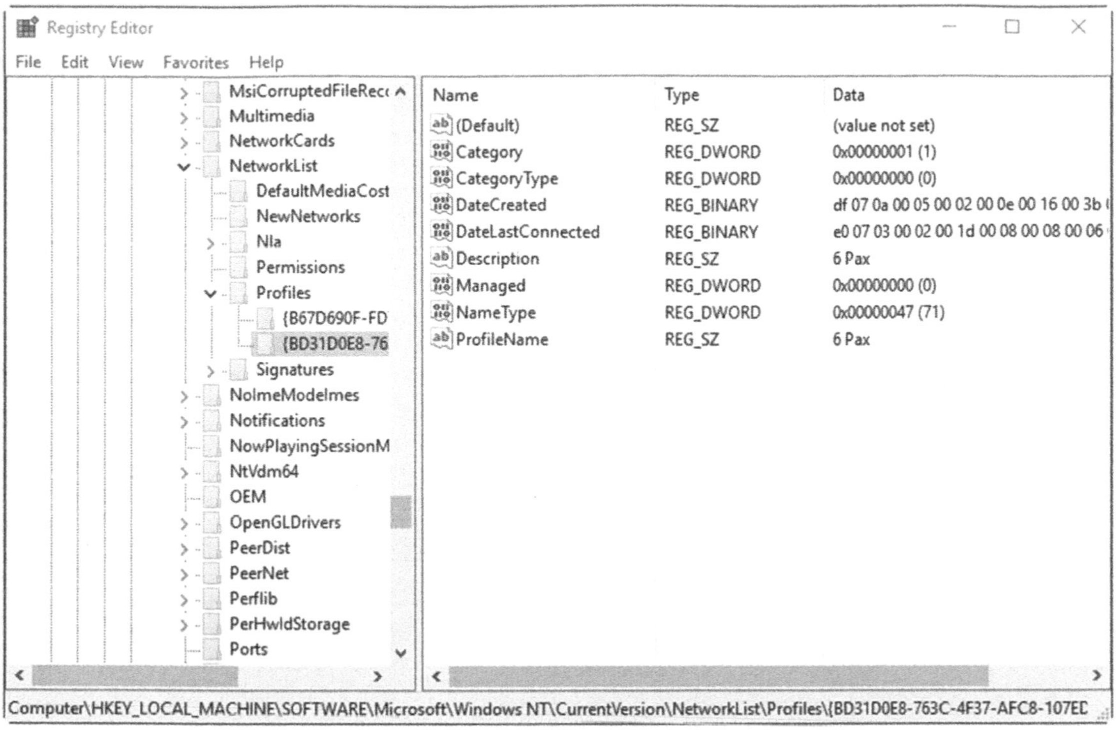

Figure 14-15. *You can change the network type in the Registry Editor*

To change the network type, double-click the *Category* value and change its value to **0** (zero) for a Public network, or **1** for a Private network. You will then, for both the Group Policy and Registry change, need to restart the PC for the change to become effective.

Setting Advanced Network Configuration Options

Sometimes you need to change advanced network configuration options on the PC, perhaps because the IPv4, IPv6, or Default Gateway settings are incorrect. In the Network and Sharing Center, click the *Change Adapter Settings* link (this is also available by clicking *Network Connections* in the Win+X menu), and double-click the network adapter you need to make changes to. In the dialog that appears, click the Properties button to open another dialog in which you can view, manage, and change the network properties for the adapter, see Figure 14-16.

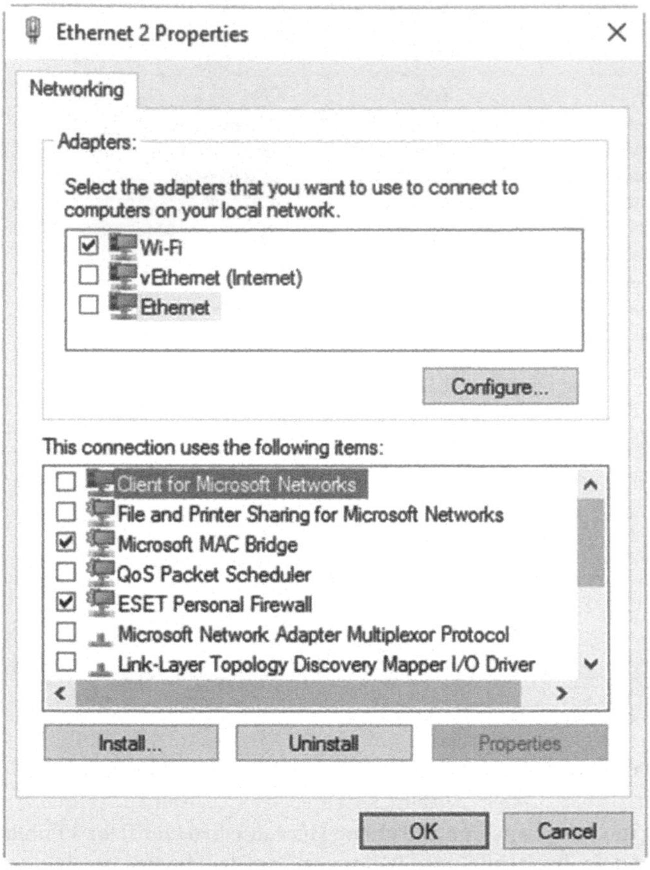

Figure 14-16. *The Network Adapter Properties dialog is where you configure network settings*

In the *This connection uses the following items* panel, you will see a list of the Microsoft and third-party network services used by the adapter. Some will be checked and some won't. You might find that *Client for Microsoft Networks*, which is required for access to Domains and other Microsoft network systems, and *File and Printer Sharing*, are not enabled. Should this be the case, as in Figure 14-16, it's not always necessary to enable them as, in this case, the PC uses Hyper-V with the virtual machines able to connect to the local network and the Internet. This Ethernet 2 connection is a virtual adapter, created by Hyper-V and bridged with the PC's main Wi-Fi adapter.

When it comes to configuring network options, however, it's the *Internet Protocol Version 4 (TCP/IPv4)* and *Internet Protocol Version 6 (TCP/IPv6)* options we'll want to configure, as these determine how the PC connects to the workwork.

If you highlight the IPv4 service and click its *Properties* button, you will be able to configure its IP address and DNS (Domain Name Server) options, see Figure 14-17. By default, these are assigned automatically when the PC handshakes with the router. On your network, however, you might require each PC to have a static IP address, or to connect to the Internet that has a nonstandard DNS address.

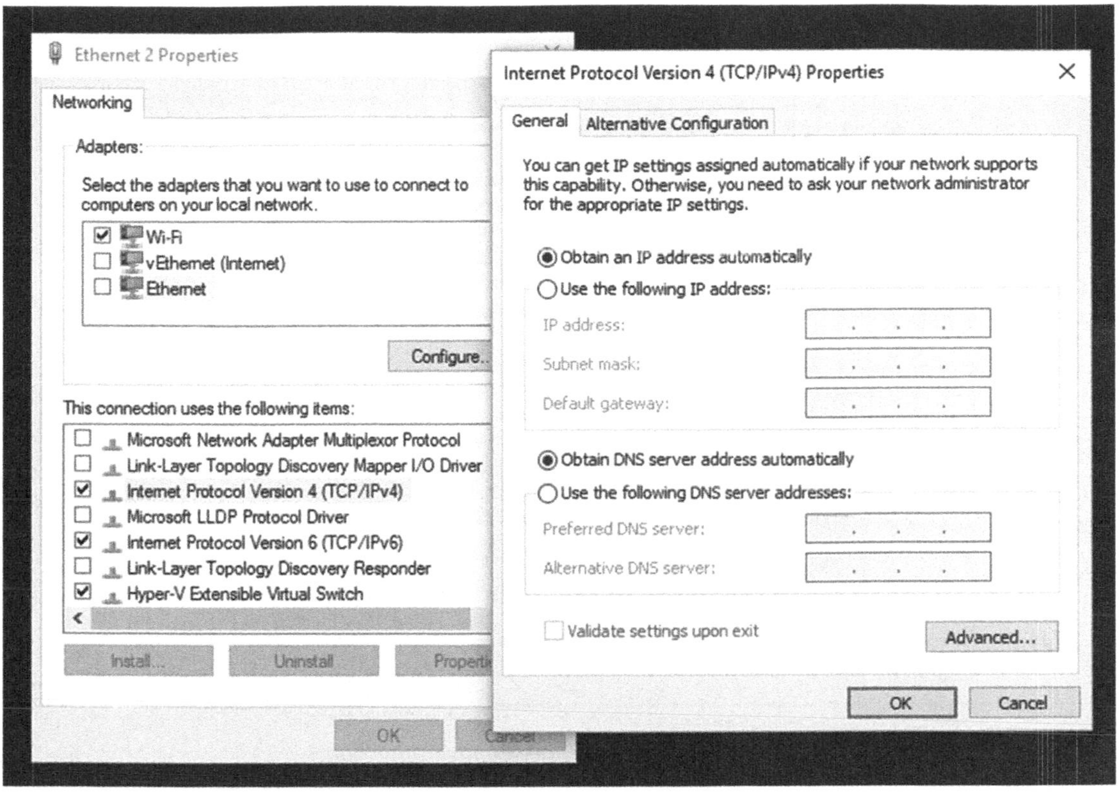

Figure 14-17. *You can set IP and DNS addresses for the IPv4 connection*

The Alternative Configuration tab also allows you to set separate IP and DNS settings for when the PC is connected to other networks, such as for a laptop or tablet that's used in multiple locations such as the office and the user's home.

Clicking the *Advanced* button also allows you set additional options, such as multiple DNS addresses (if different DNS settings are used for different routers in business locations), or if a different Default Gateway (also related to the router configuration) needs to be set for the PC to be able to access the network, and its files and resources.

The IPv6 properties allow you to set very similar options except that there is no Alternative Configuration option, see Figure 14-18, and the Advanced options do not support the WINS (Windows Internet Name Service) protocol.

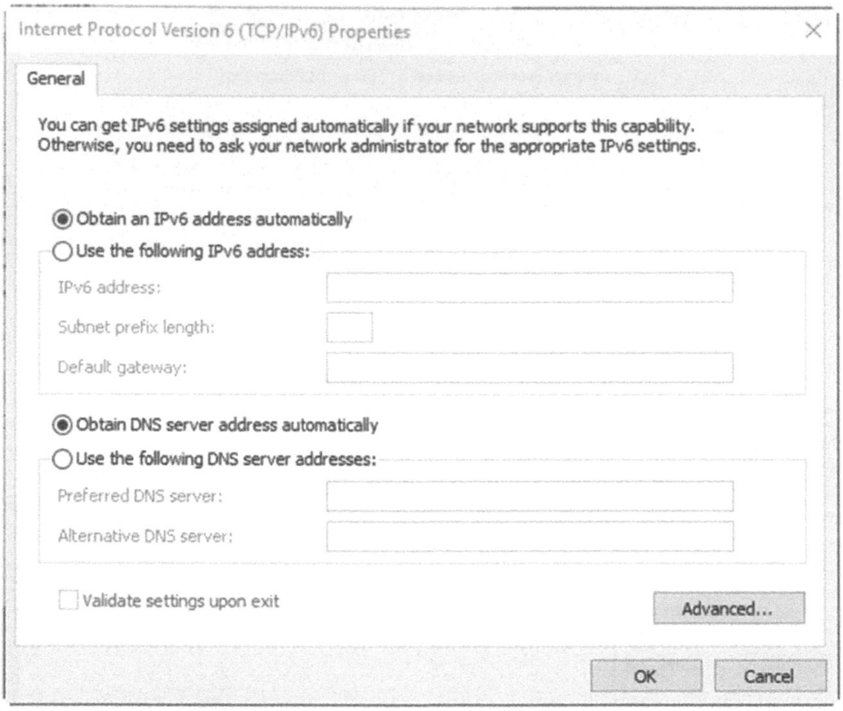

Figure 14-18. *The IPv6 settings do not offer an Alternative Configuration panel*

■ **Note**   You might be wondering what the difference is between a DNS address and the Default Gateway when connecting to your network. In short, the Default Gateway is the network address of the main router (usually 192.168.0.1), though this may be set to a nonstandard address for reasons of security or network stability. A DNS address is used by your ISP to enable a connection to the Internet. Again, for reasons of security, or sometimes because an ISP has a "walled-garden" approach to Internet connections, this might be a nonstandard setting you will need to configure manually.

Summary

It's possible to get a huge amount of detailed information about the status of a network connection in Windows 10. Usually, connections manage themselves as router and switch hardware manufacturers, and ISPs are sensible enough to set their systems to configure connections automatically when they handshake with a new PC. Occasions where this doesn't happen might include secure environments, such as research or government offices, or corporations where there are multiple networks configured to handle extremely large numbers of PCs and network-connected devices.

As configurable as the network options are, there's one thing I have deliberately missed in this chapter, and that's how you can directly manipulate the settings for network driver hardware. Hardware driver configurations can appear an impenetrable business at times, with driver management a tricky task in some circumstances. In the next chapter, we'll look at how we can install, remove, and manage drivers, including how to maniupulate individual properties of the driver to affect its behavior.

■ ■ ■

CHAPTER 15

Managing Device Drivers and PC Resources

Startup, networking, drivers—where will the problems end on our PCs? It can indeed safely be said that one of the biggest headaches when it comes to getting PCs working reliably is hardware drivers. A large part of the problem is that Microsoft simply doesn't control drivers. Sure they have a certification program, and with Windows 10 every device driver must be digitally signed by Microsoft to ensure it's compatible with the OS and won't crash, but life is unfortunately more complex than that.

There's very little, other than warning dialogs, to prevent an administrator on a PC from installing an unsigned device driver, and indeed there are occasions when you may have to do exactly that, such as for older hardware or for bespoke hardware where the manufacturer simply finds the certification process uneconomical. There's also no way to know how the driver will interact with other drivers and apps on the PC, given the limitless scope of the PC ecosystem.

It's not all bad news though as managing device drivers isn't as impenetrable as many people believe, and Microsoft has done a good job of managing compatibility with device drivers. In this chapter, we'll examine every aspect of driver management and look at how you can troubleshoot any driver problem.

Deciphering the Device Manager

The Device Manager is where all hardware, software, and virtualized devices on your PC are managed. It's often accessed from within the Control Panel, but it's most easily accessed from the *Windows key + X* Administration menu.

When you open the Device Manager, you'll be presented with all the devices on your PC grouped by their main category type, see Figure 15-1. This means that all graphics cards, all disks, and all optical drives will be helpfully grouped together. It also means though that any unknown devices will also be grouped together.

© Mike Halsey 2016
M. Halsey, *Windows 10 Troubleshooting*, DOI 10.1007/978-1-4842-0925-7_15

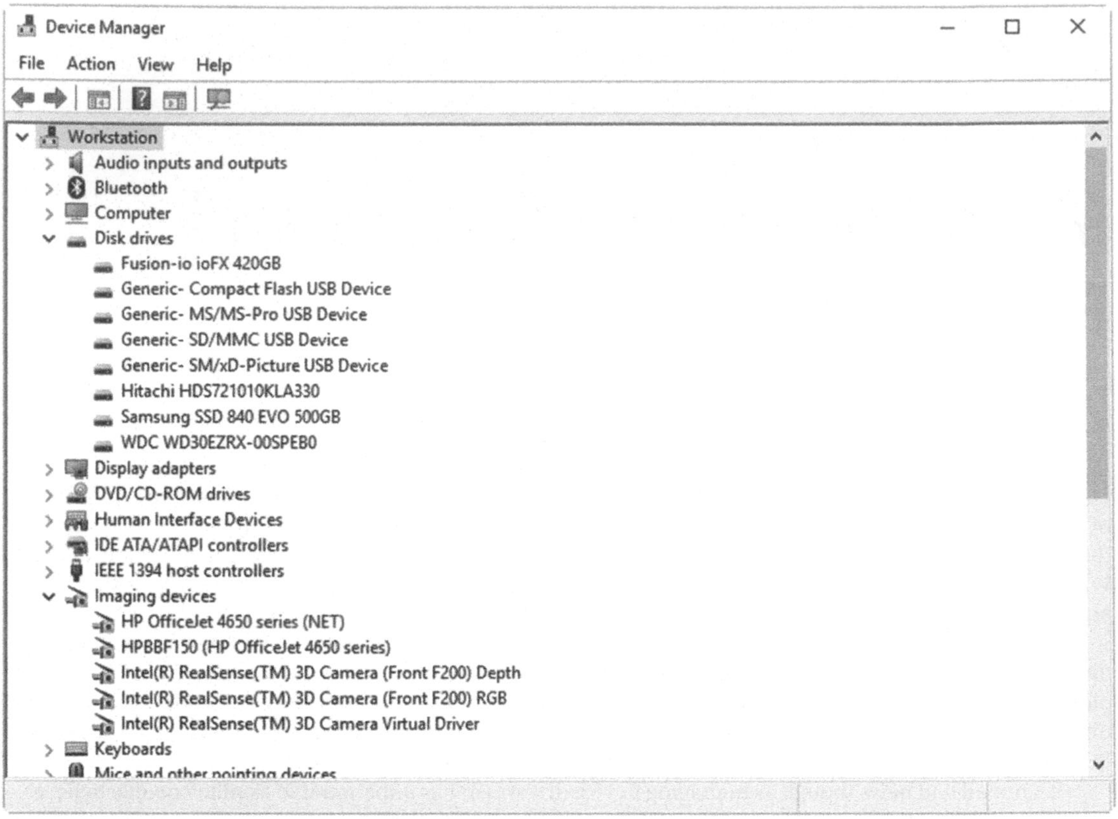

Figure 15-1. *The Device Manager's default view groups device by type*

The *View* menu at the top of the Device Manager window allows you to change the Device Manager so that it displays all your devices in different ways, see Figure 15-2.

- **Devices by Type** is the default view. It groups devices by their main device type category.

- **Devices by Connection** will group devices by how they are attached to the PC, with each device being listed under the device to which it is connected. This view can be useful for troubleshooting nested devices, such as USB devices that are connected to a hub.

- **Resources by Type** displays all allocated resources on the PC, grouped by the type of device that is using the resources. These include Direct Memory Access (DMA) channels, Input/Output ports (I/O Ports), Interrupt Requests (IRQs), and Memory Addresses.

- **Rescources by Connection** displays all the allocated resources by their connection type.

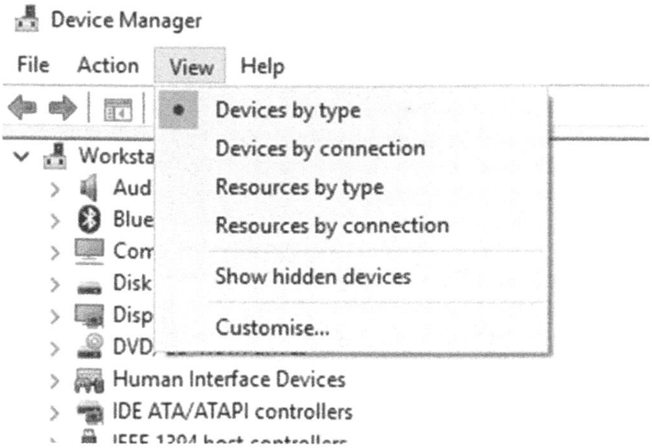

Figure 15-2. Different views are available in the Device Manager

Additionally, in the *View* menu is a *Show Hidden Devices* option. By default the Device Manager shows connected Universal Plug and Play (UPnP) devices. Activating the Show Hidden Devices option will also display non-UPnP devices, such as legacy devices, and also UPnP devices that are installed but not currently connected to the PC.

■ **Tip**   Not all hidden devices are displayed in the Device Manager when the Show Hidden Devices option is activated. There is a category called *Nonpresent Devices*, which you should never have to view because they have been physically removed from the PC, but their Registry entries remain. This view is mostly used during driver development; however, should an error report a problem with a file or Registry entry that you cannot trace to a specific installed driver, you can view nonpresent devices by opening a *Command Prompt (Admin)* window and typing the command SET DEVMGR_SHOW_NONPRESENT_DEVICES=1. These devices will then appear grayed out in the Device Manager when the Show Hidden Devices option is selected.

Identifying and Installing Unknown Devices

When you install a device driver, you will be prompted by Windows 10 to look for the driver automatically, which will search the Driver Store, which comes as part of Windows 10, and will also search Windows Update for a driver if you have an Internet connection. Alternatively, you can install the driver manually by pointing the Device Manager at the specific installer file for the hardware.

Very often, however, the hardware is listed as being an *Unknown device*, see Figure 15-3. Sometimes, after a few Windows Update installs, these devices sort themselves out and are automatically installed. On other occasions, however, you can be left scratching your head, and wondering what the device could be.

Figure 15-3. *Unknown devices appear grouped in an Other Devices category*

If Windows 10 cannot identify a driver, it's still possible to easily discover what it is as long as it's a Plug and Play device. Right-clicking the device and choosing *Properties* from the menu that appears will display detailed properties for that hardware. The *Details* tab in this dialog contains a drop-down options menu. Selecting *Hardware IDs* in this menu will display *VEN_* (Vendor) and *DEV_* (Device) codes that will be (almost always) unique to that device, see Figure 15-4. You can search for these VEN_ and DEV_ codes online to discover what the device is, so as to obtain the correct driver. In the example here it's an Nvidia GeForce GTX 980 graphics card with the codes VEN_10DE and DEV_13C0.

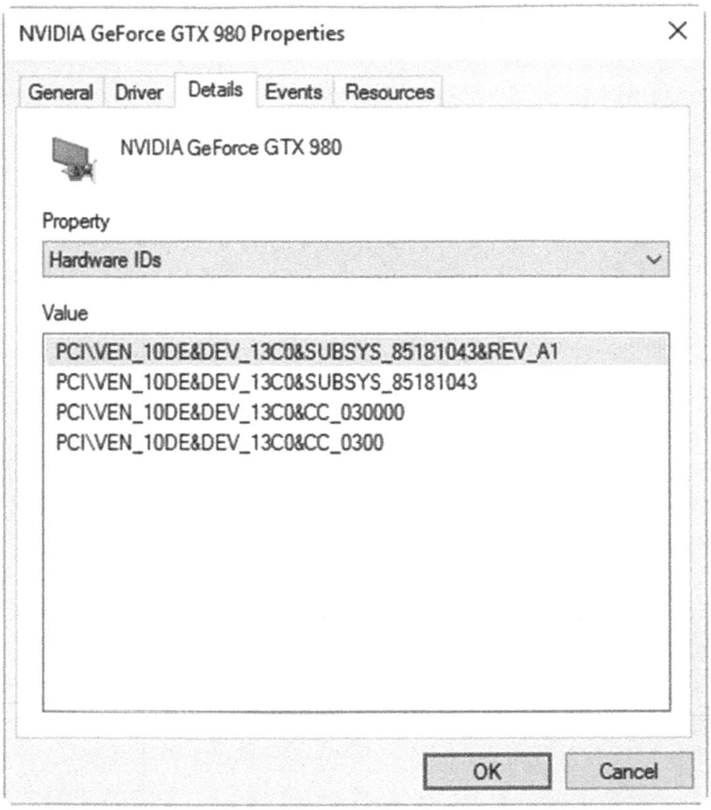

NVIDIA GeForce GTX 980 Properties   ✕

General   Driver   Details   Events   Resources

NVIDIA GeForce GTX 980

Property

Hardware IDs   ⌄

Value

PCI\VEN_10DE&DEV_13C0&SUBSYS_85181043&REV_A1
PCI\VEN_10DE&DEV_13C0&SUBSYS_85181043
PCI\VEN_10DE&DEV_13C0&CC_030000
PCI\VEN_10DE&DEV_13C0&CC_0300

OK   Cancel

Figure 15-4.   *You can identify unknown devices by their VEN_ and DEV_ codes*

Sometimes, you will be installing a legacy driver for a device that's displaying as Unknown, or something that you're certain will have a driver already shipped with Windows 10, or that has been installed previously on your PC. If you don't have access to the driver install media, you can search the Windows 10 Driver Store for the correct driver to install.

1.   Right-click the device and select *Update Driver Software* from the menu that appears.

2.   At the wizard that opens, click *Browse my computer for driver software*, see Figure 15-5.

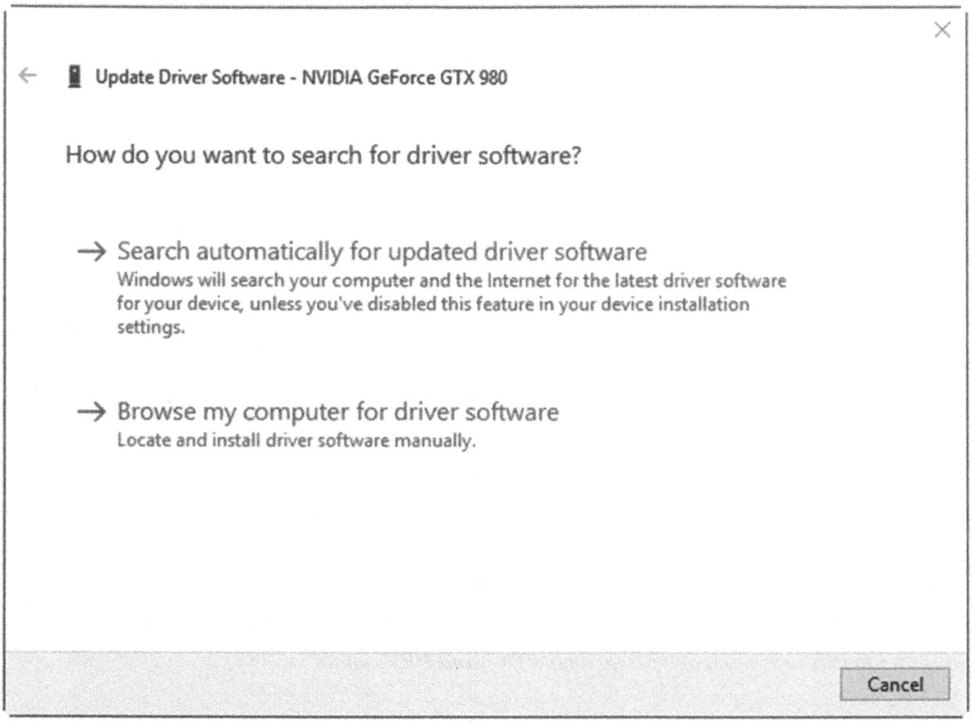

×

← ▌ Update Driver Software - NVIDIA GeForce GTX 980

How do you want to search for driver software?

→ Search automatically for updated driver software
   Windows will search your computer and the Internet for the latest driver software
   for your device, unless you've disabled this feature in your device installation
   settings.

→ Browse my computer for driver software
   Locate and install driver software manually.

Cancel

Figure 15-5. Choose Browse my computer for driver software to install the driver manually

3. At the next panel, instead of clicking the Browser button to search for the driver install file, click Let me pick from a list of devices on my computer, see Figure 15-6.

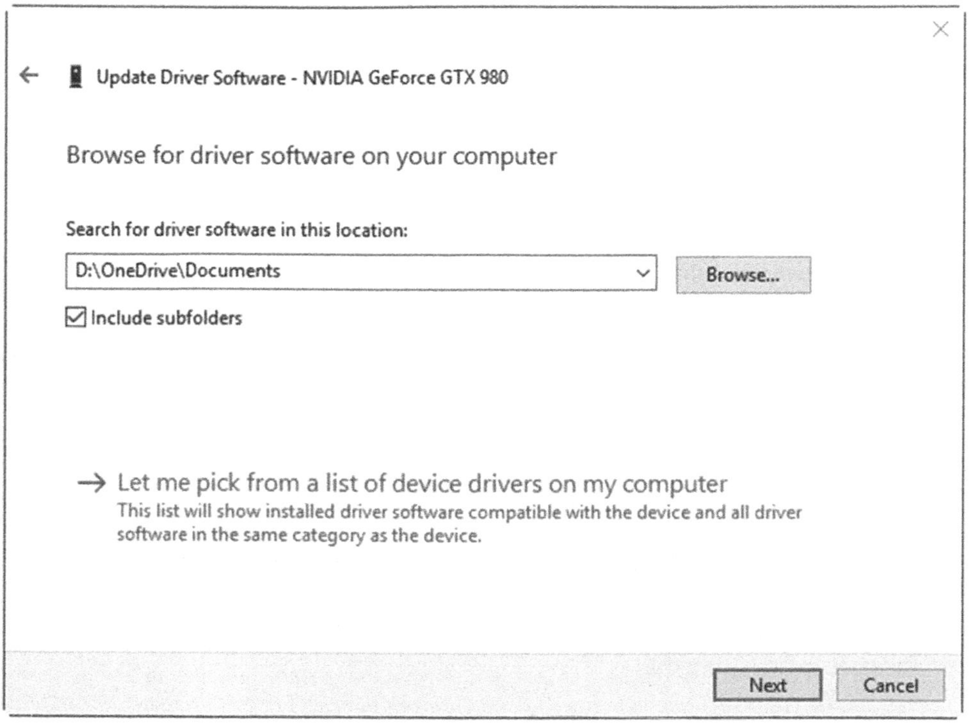

Figure 15-6. You can choose Let me pick... to choose a driver from the Driver Store

4. You will be shown a list of the drivers that Windows 10 identifies as being compatible with your hardware, see Figure 15-7. Occasionally though, and especially with an older device, you may wish to specifically search the Driver Store.

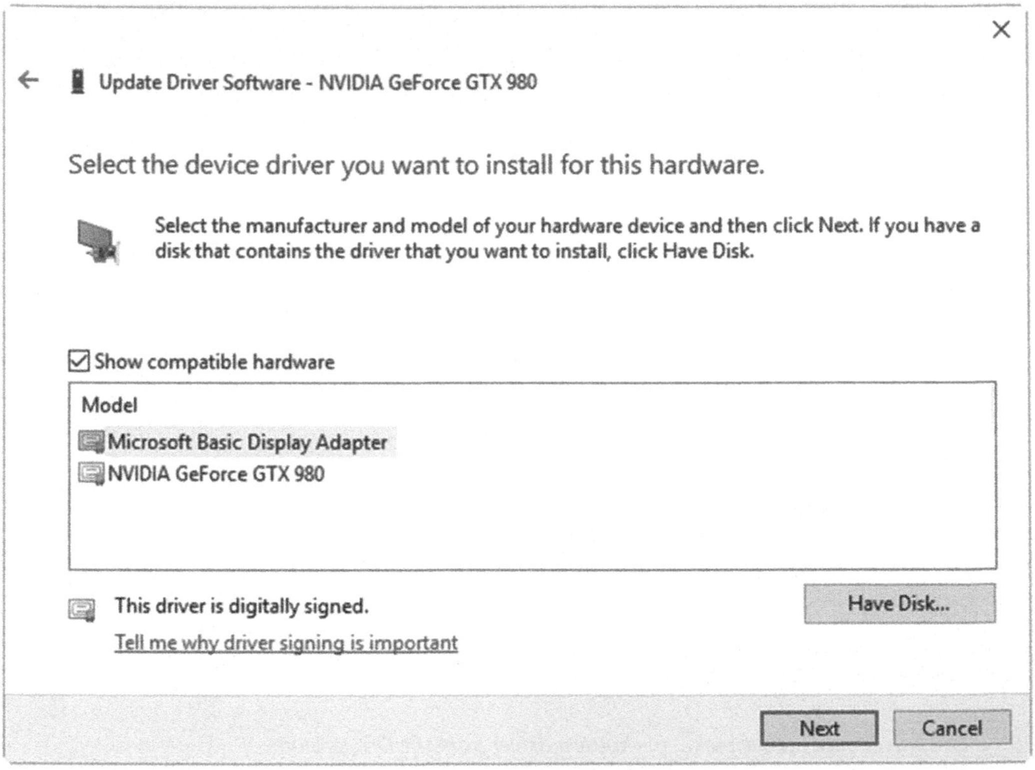

Figure 15-7. Only drivers Windows feels are compatible will be shown

5. Uncheck the Show compatible hardware option, and the contents of the Windows 10 Driver Store will become available to you, see Figure 15-8.

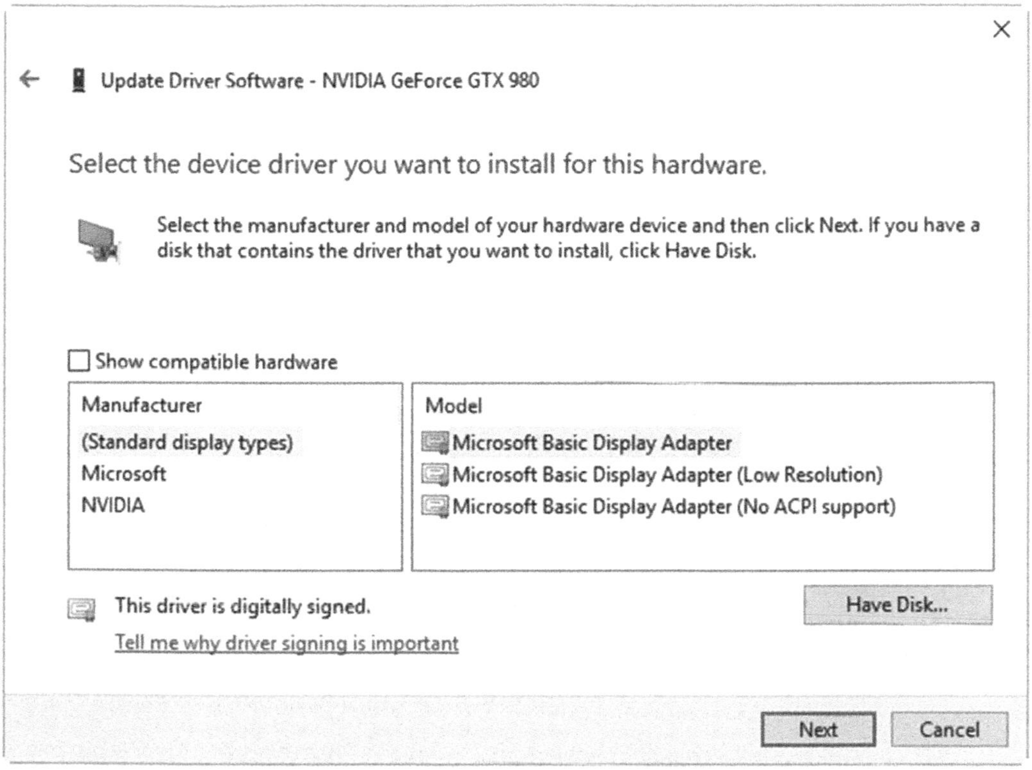

Figure 15-8. You can display all drivers for that device type

If the device type is unknown by Windows, a list of all available device categories in the Driver Store will be displayed, see Figure 15-9. Choose the correct category for the device, and compatible drivers for that category, as seen in steps 4 and 5, will be displayed.

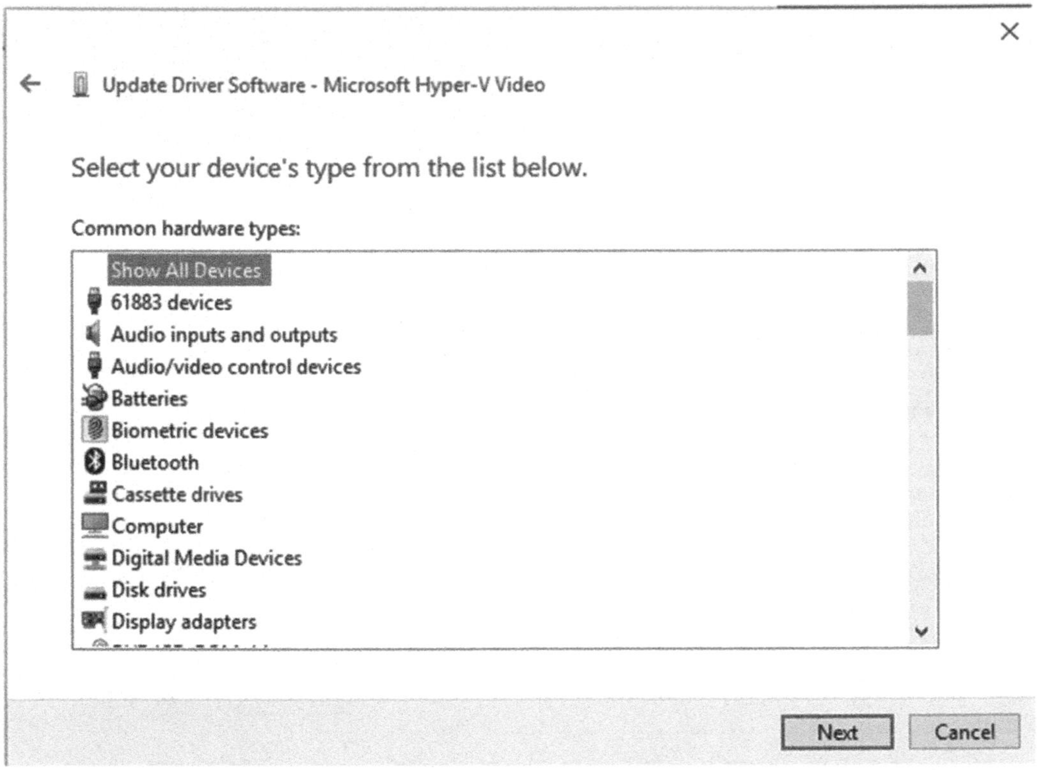

Figure 15-9. *Unknown devices will display all device types in the Driver Store*

Installing Legacy Hardware

Sometimes you will need to install non–Plug and Play devices such as older Serial or Parallel devices. These can still be regularly used in specialist scenarios such as medicine and engineering. To install a legacy driver, select *Add legacy hardware* from the Action menu in the Device Manager. You will be asked if you want Windows 10 to automatically search for and install the hardware or if you want to manually select it from a list, see Figure 15-10.

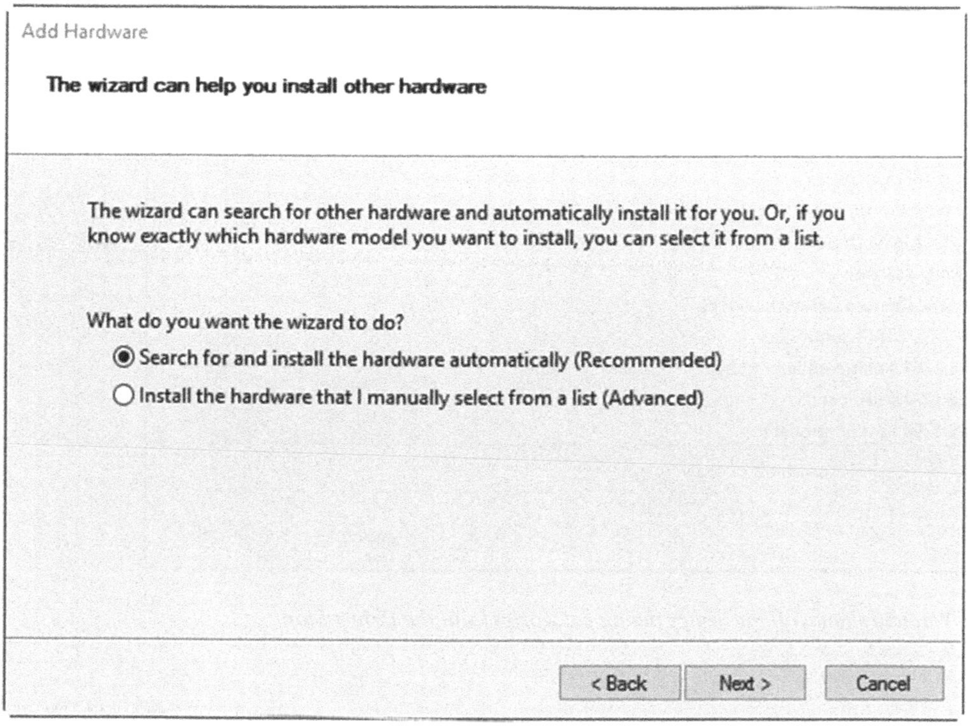

Figure 15-10. *Legacy hardware can sometimes be installed automatically*

If you choose to manually select your hardware from a list, you will be presented with a full list of all the main device types that are available in the Driver Store, see Figure 15-11.

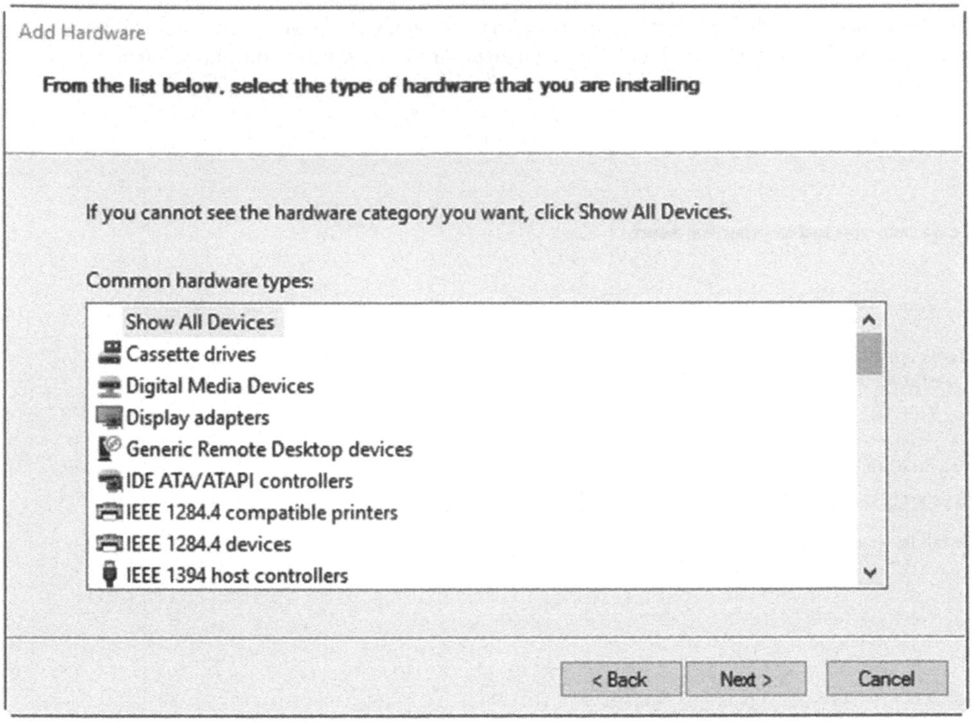

Figure 15-11. *You will shown all the legacy device categories from the Driver Store*

What happens from here will vary depending on what device category you choose. If you are, for example, installing a modem, you will be first asked if you want the modem automatically detected, or you will be taken to a list of all the legacy and smartphone modem types that are known to Windows.

If on the other hand you're installing a printer, you will be asked which port on the computer it is connected to, or if Windows needs to create a virtual port for the connection, see Figure 15-12.

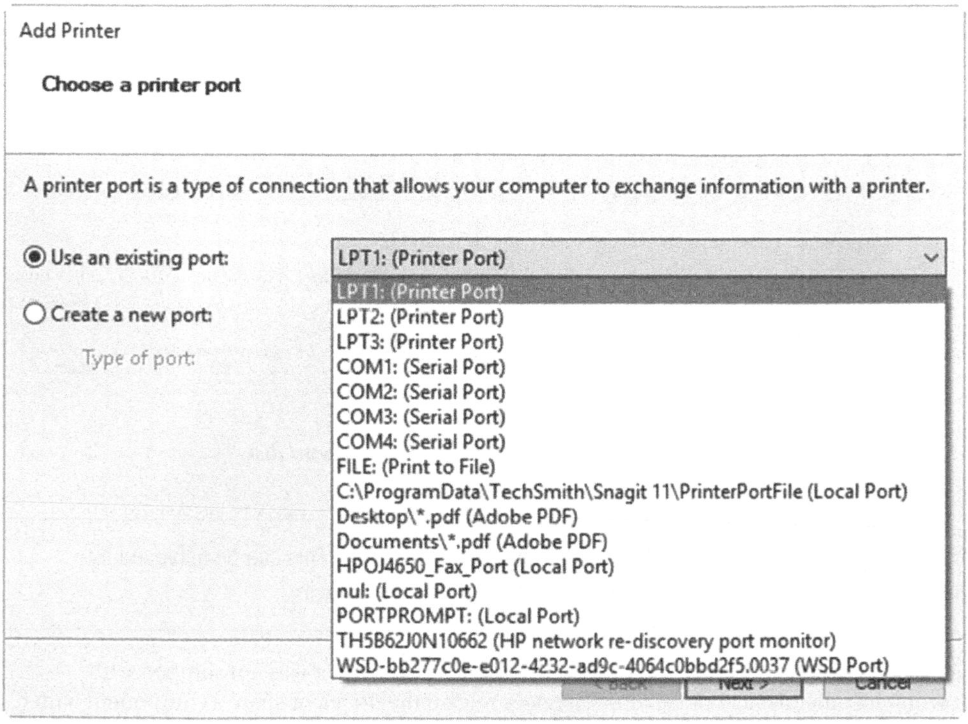

> Add Printer
>
> **Choose a printer port**
>
> A printer port is a type of connection that allows your computer to exchange information with a printer.
>
> ● Use an existing port: LPT1: (Printer Port) ˅
>
> ○ Create a new port:
>   Type of port:
>
> LPT1: (Printer Port)
> LPT2: (Printer Port)
> LPT3: (Printer Port)
> COM1: (Serial Port)
> COM2: (Serial Port)
> COM3: (Serial Port)
> COM4: (Serial Port)
> FILE: (Print to File)
> C:\ProgramData\TechSmith\Snagit 11\PrinterPortFile (Local Port)
> Desktop*.pdf (Adobe PDF)
> Documents*.pdf (Adobe PDF)
> HPOJ4650_Fax_Port (Local Port)
> nul: (Local Port)
> PORTPROMPT: (Local Port)
> TH5B62J0N10662 (HP network re-discovery port monitor)
> WSD-bb277c0e-e012-4232-ad9c-4064c0bbd2f5.0037 (WSD Port)
>
> < Back   Next >   Cancel

Figure 15-12. *Installing legacy printers will ask what port the printer is connected to*

But what happens if you have a specialist medical, engineering, or other device and you're not certain what category to choose for its installation? Point of Sale hardware has several categories available in the legacy device installer wizard, but what about everything else? Generally speaking, the categories are sensibly laid out with titles such as Network infrastructure devices, Imaging devices, and Sensors. If you cannot gain access to the manual that came with the device, there are no VEN_ and DEV_ codes you'll be able to check, though a search online for the device name and model number may reveal full installation instructions, and perhaps even a current driver.

■ **Note**   Parallel devices will connect to the *LPTx* ports on a PC, and Serial devices will connnect to the *COMx* ports, where the x in these examples represents the port number.

Uninstalling and Deleting Device Drivers

When it comes to troubleshooting device drivers, they can provide a wealth of information, and there are several tools and techniques you can use to assist you. The first of these is driver updating and removal. You can right-click a driver in the Device Manager and select *Uninstall* from the menu that appears, but sometimes you will also get an option to *Delete the driver software for this device*, see Figure 15-13.

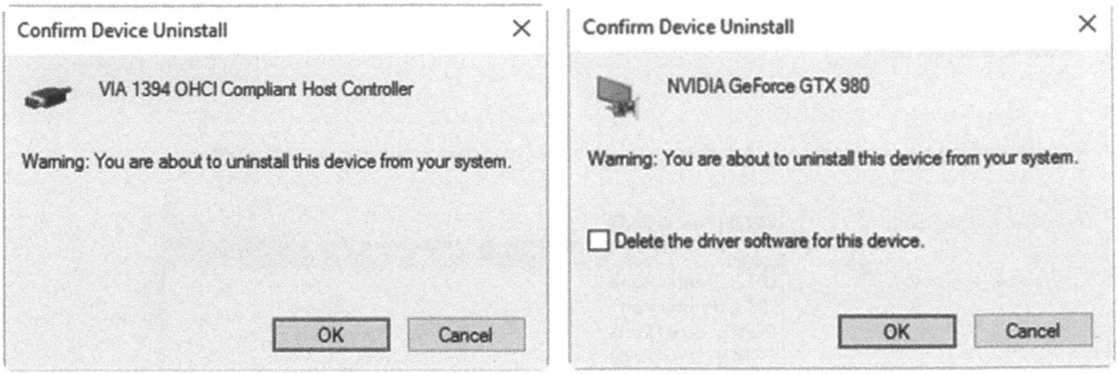

Figure 15-13. Some drivers offer the option to delete the driver files from the hard disk

---

■ **Tip** Sometimes a device isn't needed by the system and can be disabled. This can be achieved by right-clicking the device and selecting *Disable* from the contect menu that appears.

You will be offered the *Delete the driver software...* option when the driver was not shipped with Windows 10, or when no other devices or Windows services rely on the driver, or share a component with it. Checking this box will permanently delete the driver from the Driver Store. This means that when the device is reinstalled on the PC, the driver will need to be reloaded from Windows Update or reinstalled from the device installation media.

This can be very useful if a device that's causing problems is automatically being reinstalled on a restart or on a refresh of the Device Manager. If you need to install a different driver for a device, perhaps an earlier driver, and are being prevented from doing so, this may be because the faulty version of the driver is constantly being reinstalled.

■ **Tip** Sometimes you may wish to roll a driver back to the previously installed version and then block the new driver from installing. I will show you how to block driver installation shortly, but under the *Driver* tab in the Device Properties panel, you will find a *Roll Back Driver* button. If a previous driver is available for the device, this button will be available to click. Note that this system uses the Windows 10 System Restore feature and will not work if System Restore is disabled on the PC.

Blocking Device Driver and Device App Installation

Additionally, you might want to block all driver updates from Windows Update, or specific driver updates that you know are causing problems. Windows Update was changed in Windows 10 so as to deny users and administrators the option to block specific updates. I'll talk about Windows Update in full in Chapter 16, but it's still possible to block driver updates from Windows Update.

If you find that a driver is automatically downloading an app or apps from the manufacturer's web site (such as an updater app) that is either causing a problem, or that you don't want installed, you can block all of these downloads by opening *System* from the Control Panel and then clicking.

Under the Hardware tab in the System Properties window, click the *Advanced System Settings* link at the left of the window; then, in the dialog that appears, click the *Hardware* tab. This will display a *Device Installation Settings* button, which offers you the option of blocking all third-party apps that may be automatically downloaded by devices, see Figure 15-14.

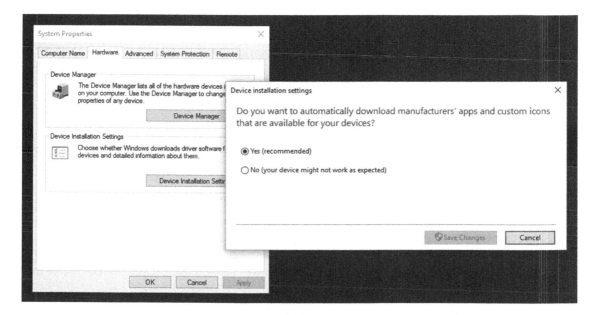

Figure 15-14. *You can block all app downloads that accompany some drivers*

Sometimes, however, you need to block a driver completely, because you know it is causing problems. To do this, you can download the Microsoft "Show or Hide Updates" Troubleshooter package from http://pcs.tv/1WXoRR3. Running this troubleshooter will enable you to block specific Windows Updates, including hardware drivers, from being downloaded and installed onto the PC, see Figure 15-15.

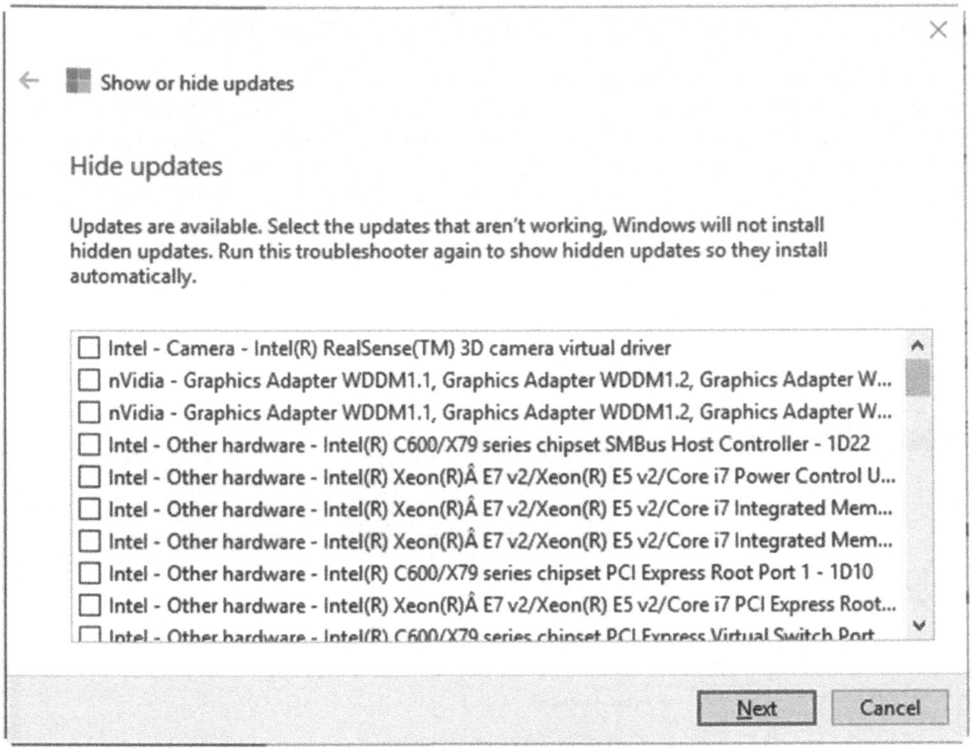

Figure 15-15. *Microsoft provides a troubleshooter that can block Windows Updates*

Finding Device Driver Details and Information

Sometimes you need to find advanced information about a driver, perhaps because you need to remove the driver files manually from a PC. A wealth of information is available for many drivers by right-clicking them in the Device Manager and selecting *Properties* from the menu that appears.

You might want to know exactly what files are installed on the PC as part of the driver installation (it's always more than one file), perhaps because you want to manually delete the files. Under the *Driver* tab in the Driver Properties dialog is a *Driver Details* button. Clicking this button will display another dialog listing all the files associated with the driver that are installed on the PC's hard disk. You can make a note of these files (sadly there's no copy button) for manual deletion, see Figure 15-16.

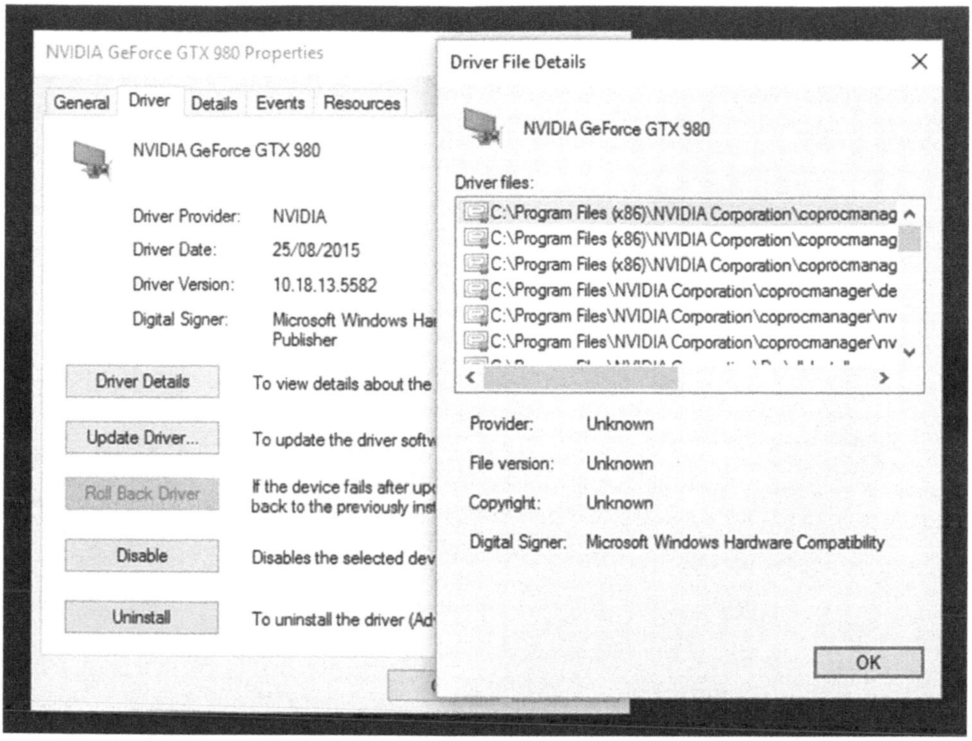

Figure 15-16. You can see the full driver file list in the Device Properties

---

■ **Note**   Some driver files may be locked by Windows due to being currently "in use." You can start the PC in Safe Mode or Diagnostic Mode to manually delete the files, and I will detail how to start the PC in these modes in Chapter 19.

Additionally, the *Details* tab of the driver properties panel diaplsys a drop-down menu with a welath of useful information, and this is where you can find the DEV_ and VEN_ codes I detailed earlier in this chapter. The information in the drop-down menu will vary from one driver and device type to another, but one very useful piece of information that's common to all devices is its version number, see Figure 15-17.

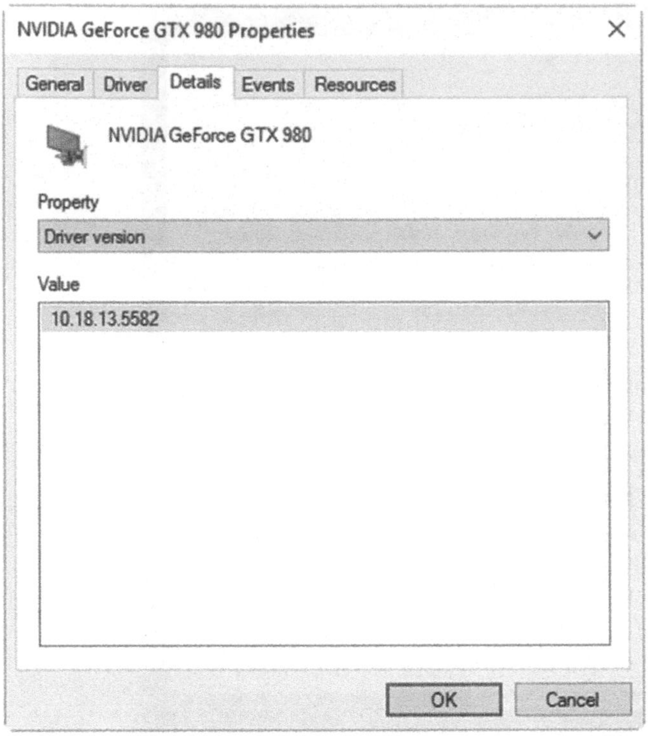

Figure 15-17. *You can get useful information about the driver such as its version number*

The version number of anything is crucial both to system administrators, who will want to exhaustively test new versions of apps and drivers before deploying them, and also when troubleshooting a problem. You can search online for the version number of a driver (or app) to see if a more recent version is available, or if the currently installed version is known to cause problems or, perhaps, was designed for an earlier version of Windows and shouldn't be installed at all.

Troubleshooting Device Drivers

At the end of the previous chapter I mentioned that the properties for some devices can be changed and reconfigured, so as to alter or improve the behavior or performance of the driver. The context I gave was network drivers where some behaviors might need to be indiviually configured to create stable connections to secure or specialist network types.

In Figure 15-18 you can see a driver, a Wi-Fi networking driver in this case, which has configurable properties under an *Advanced* tab. The options available will vary from one device and driver to another. They will, however, be configurable so that you can, in the example of this 802.11ac Wi-Fi driver, disable some of the older Wi-Fi connection protocols should it be necessary for security or, when the device may not be providing a stable connection with its default settings.

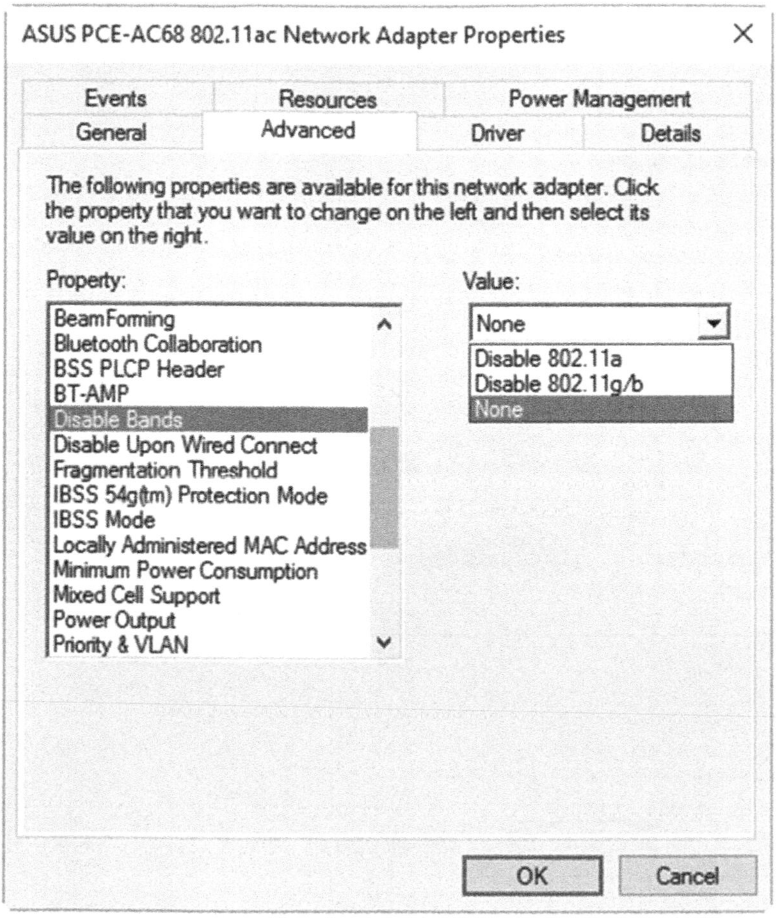

Figure 15-18. Some drivers have configurable properties

The *Resources* tab, see Figure 15-19, can provide information that's useful in determining if a device is conflicting with another device. It was common for earlier versions of Windows that IRQs or memory conflicts would take place, where the driver would be trying to address the same memory space as another device or app, or where it was trying to use the same processor interrupt channel as another device.

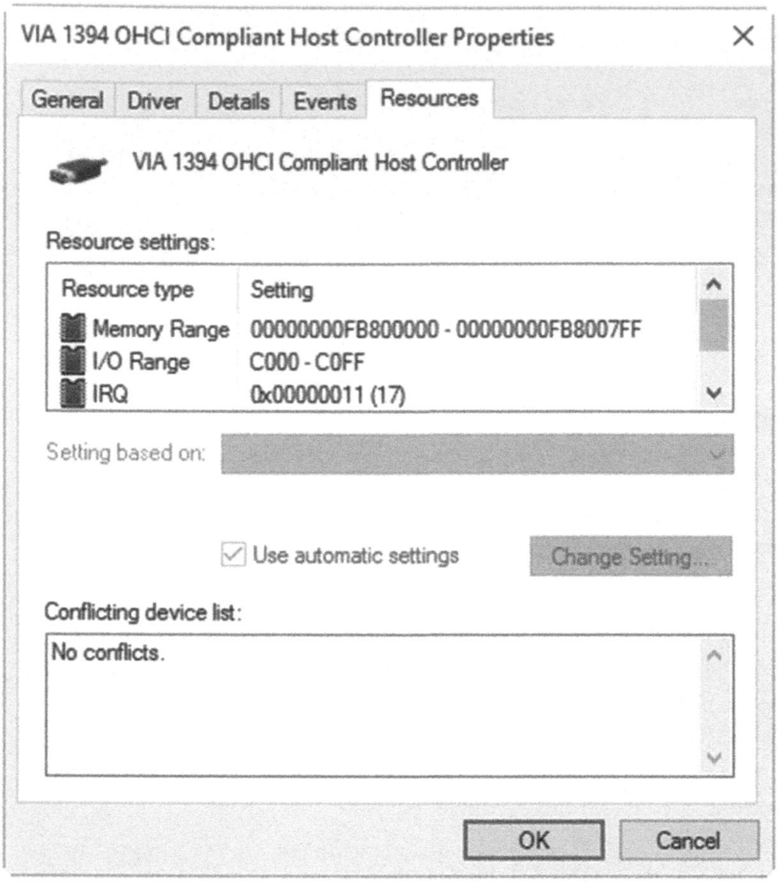

Figure 15-19. *The Resources tab can display information about memory, port, and IRQ usage*

■ **Note** Interrupts are communications channels assigned by the PC's processor to allow all apps, services, and devices to share processor time. Rather than have everything making requests of the processor all of the time, which would overload the processor's capacity, devices, apps, and services are assigned an IRQ. These IRQs are cycled by the processor, enabling everything to get an equal amount of processor time, without overloading the system.

Memory, IRQ, and I/O assignments are managed automatically by Windows 10, which uses a system called Side-by-Side. This permits multiple versions of files, drivers, and DLLs (Dynamic Linked Libraries), which are used to provide services in Windows, to operate concurrently. I will look more at Side-by-Side files, which are found in the \Windows\WinSXS folder, in Chapter 27.

Because Windows 10 manages these aspects of driver operation, you will almost always find that the *Change Setting* options under the *Resources* tab are grayed out and unavailable. In some cases, with specific hardware (such as legacy hardware) you will find that you can manually assign IRQ and other resource channels for a driver. This can be useful if you find that a device is using the same IRQ as another device with which it is conflicting.

The Events tab is extremely useful when diagnosing problems with a device. It hooks into the Event Viewer, which I detailed in Chapter 5, to list all events for the driver, see Figure 15-20. These will include configuration and error events. Clicking an event will list further details, including an 0x000... format error code if relevant. Clicking the *View All Events* button will open the full Event Viewer with all of the events for the device listed. More detailed information on the events and errors can be obtained in the Event Viewer, and tasks can be attached to errors to alert the user or a support person about the crash.

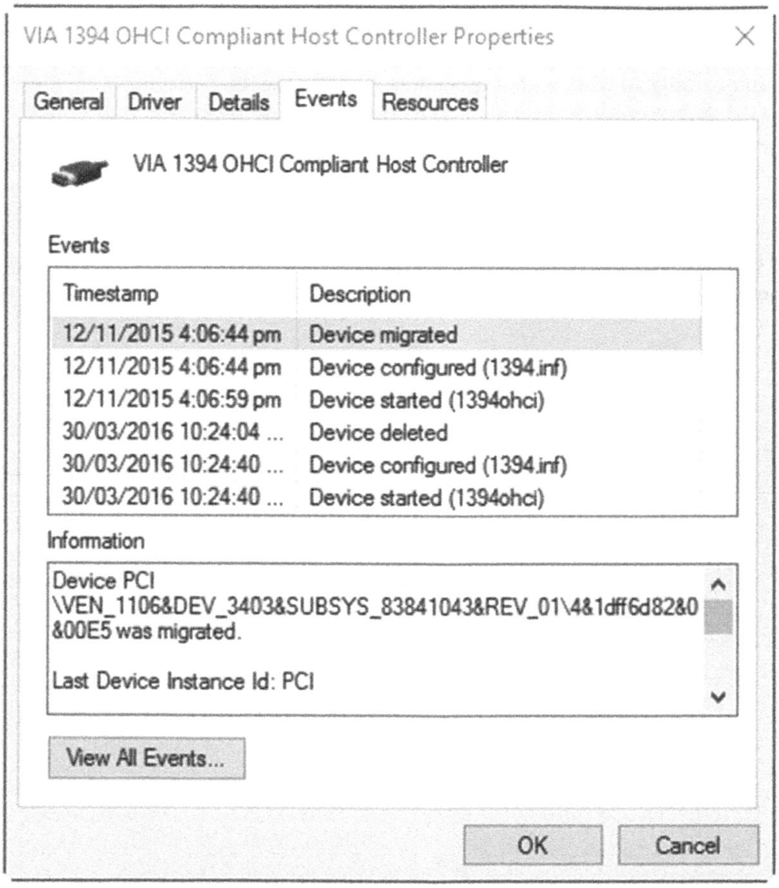

Figure 15-20. The Events tab provides details of device crashes and other events

Backing Up and Restoring the Driver Store

If you're anything like me, you'll have a partition or disk in your system in which you keep important win32 app installers and hardware drivers. When the time comes to reinstall Windows 10 from scratch, which will most likely still need doing every so often for one reason or another, these are your quick way to get the system working. This is especially so in light of the fact that Murphy's Law dictates that you won't be able to get Internet access on the PC, at the very time you need to download the network drivers.

The Windows 10 Driver Store is located in the C:\Windows\System32\DriverStore folder on your PC. You can create a backup copy of this folder, and when time comes to reinstall, either copy it back to the fresh installation or tell Device Manager to search your backup copy of the folder when reinstalling drivers.

Additionally, there is a C:\Windows\System32\Drivers folder that you may also want to back up, as it may contain device drivers required by your hardware.

If you are copying the folder back to its original location, you should only do this if the version of Windows 10 you are installing is the same as the one the backup copy of the DriverStore folder was copied from. The reason for this is that new and updated drivers for existing and new hardware types are released on a regular basis both through Windows Update and with updated releases of Windows 10.

Summary

Device drivers on a PC can be complex things to work with, especially when they're misbehaving. Some drivers, such as the graphics driver, are embedded so deeply within the operating system that troubleshooting and managing them can prove difficult. On these occasions, you'll likely need Windows 10's Safe or Diagnostic Modes, and I'll show you how to use these in Chapter 19.

In the last few chapters, we've dealt with the issues that plague PC users and system administrators the most, these being startup, networking and Internet connections, and device drivers. We've still got software and app compatibility to come in Chapter 17, but in the next chapter we'll deal with the fourth most common plague for the PC, this being Windows Updates and edition upgrade installation.

■ ■ ■

CHAPTER 16

Windows Update and System Upgrades

Windows Update received a major shake-up with Windows 10, and not everybody welcomed the changes. The short version of the story is that, whoever you are, wherever you work, it's not possible to opt out of stability and security patches for Windows 10... ever! If you are using Windows 10 Home or Pro, it's not possible for you to opt out of feature updates and upgrades either, and if you're using Windows 10 Home, you can't even delay a security or stability update that might be known to cause problems.

Why would Microsoft do such a thing? Well I want to first deal with the tricky subject of Windows 10 Home (and Pro) users who cannot or do not defer updates. Generally speaking, Windows Updates never cause problems. Of course this isn't always the case, and there are a few isolated incidents where a Windows Update has needed to be pulled by Microsoft for causing problems. Third-party hardware drivers that are released through Windows Update are another matter entirely. Nothing is ever released through Windows Update until it's been extensively tested, but problem updates do occasionally sneak through. That, frankly, is why I have a job.

So let's get back to the thorny issue of why Microsoft would do such a thing. When Windows 10 was released in July 2015, it was widely reported online that the move was made either because with Windows being free for the first 12 months, you would no longer own your own copy of the OS. Another theory held that Microsoft simply wanted to force everybody to be using Windows 10, or that the updates would at some point after the first year become chargeable. None of these reasons are true.

The truth is that when Satya Nadella took over as Microsoft CEO in 2014, he immediately took the company on a major slimming exercise. The company was bloated and inefficient. When it came to Windows, they had always had a policy of supporting each operating system for ten full years after its release, with the latter half of that being just security and stability updates. This, coupled with the ability of any Windows user to either hide specific updates, or to opt out of updates altogether, meant that Microsoft was effectively supporting a massive number of different versions of each OS. The cost for providing this support would run into tens of millions of dollars every year, but all of it was essential to keep Windows desktop PCs safe, secure, and reliable.

With Windows 10 the decision was made to cut those costs massively, and the best way to do this was to ensure that all Windows users would be in the same place, all of the time. The only way to achieve this would be to mandate Windows Updates, and remove the ability people had to opt out of receiving them.

To a large extent this makes sense. If you compare the policy to that of other technology companies, Apple only support OS X versions for 18 months after their release and the same goes with versions of their iOS operating system. Google on the other hand has a very different problem. They don't enforce or encourage OS updates in the way that Apple does, and so its OS ecosystem is extremely fragmented,

© Mike Halsey 2016
M. Halsey, *Windows 10 Troubleshooting*, DOI 10.1007/978-1-4842-0925-7_16

with many versions of Android in use simultaneously. If you examine how we use those mobile operating systems, however, we're used to having updates to apps just appear overnight. We might open an app one evening to find that it looks and operates quite differently from the way it did when we used it only that morning. This has become the norm for apps, so could or should it become the norm for operating systems as well?

A word about the feature upgrades. It's true that the Windows 10 user interface (UI) will change over time. It's also true, however, that it won't change very much. The Start Menu won't be going anywhere (much to the annoyance of this author, I can tell you), the Action Center will still operate the same way, and so on. All that will happen is that each part of the OS will gain additional functionality and be improved in usability over time.

So where does this leave you, the person having to deal with the fallout from all of this? Well, there are some workarounds and ways to configure Windows 10 to enable, and guarantee, safe and reliable service when updates do come a'callin'.

Deferring Updates in Windows 10

Let's jump right in then to deferring updates in Windows 10. As I've mentioned, if you are using Windows 10 Home you cannot defer anything but feature upgrades, but an option exists in Windows 10 Pro and Enterprise to allow updates to be deferred for a period of several months. Microsoft specify "several months" in their help documentation because *upgrades* (by which they mean new and enhanced OS features) and *updates* (stability and bug fixes) are handled differently, with the latter only being delayable by a maximum period of only 1 month.

There are three ways to defer updates in Windows 10. These are called the Current Branch (CB), the Current Branch for Business (CBB), and the Long-Term Servicing Branch (LTSB). I should point out that none of these will *ever* allow you to defer critical security updates. Microsoft is quite clear in their documentation about this fact. Full details about Microsoft's different servicing branches for Windows 10 can be found online at `http://pcs.tv/1WZqmhw`.

Current Branch

The CB is available as an option in all PC, laptop, and tablet editions of Windows 10. You can find it in the Settings app (there is no longer a Windows Update option in the Control Panel). Open *Update & Security*, then click the *Advanced Options* link in the Windows Update section.

This will reveal Windows Update's limited configuration options. One of these is a check box to *Defer upgrades*, see Figure 16-1. Checking this will activate the CB deferment option and defer feature upgrades to the operating system for a period of 4 months after their release. What it will not do is defer any security or stability updates.

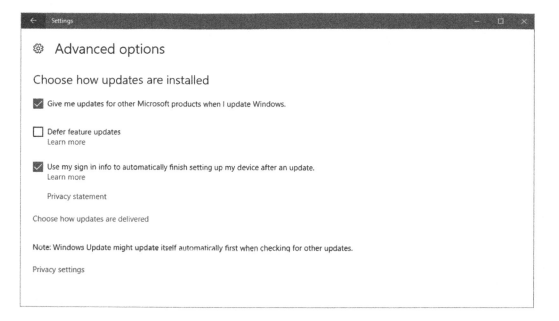

Figure 16-1. *The Defer Updates option can defer all but security updates for 3 months*

Current Branch for Business

Finer control with the CBB can be found in the Group Policy Editor. Navigate to *Computer Configuration* ➤ *Administrative Templates* ➤ *Windows Components* ➤ *Windows Update* and enable the *Defer Upgrades and Updates* policy. Here you can choose how long you want upgrades and updates to be deferred for, see Figure 16-2.

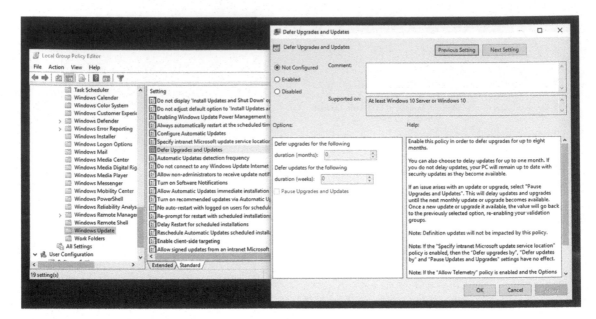

Figure 16-2. *Finer control of CBB can be found in the Group Policy Editor*

You will see here that the maximum period that upgrades can be delayed is 8 months, but for updates (by which Microsoft means stability and bug fixes) the maximum delayable period is only 4 weeks. In fairness, 4 weeks has always been more than enough time in the past for Microsoft to pull a faulty update (normally this just takes a couple of days) and to issue a replacement patch.

Additionally, for PCs enrolled on the CBB, Microsoft won't try and push feature upgrades to those PCs for a minimum period of 4 months. This is unless that is overridden in Group Policy.

Long-Term Servicing Branch

The LTSB is available only for PCs running Windows 10 Enterprise that are managed by a Windows Server Administrator. Once activated, it is similar to how the CBB works with group policy, except that the Upgrades deferment option will extend to a maximum time of 10 years.

Something of note regarding the LTSB is that it's only really intended for mission-critical systems, where operation will not change over time, and where user interaction with the desktop will be minimal. Examples of this are automatic teller machines (ATMs), medical or engineering systems, or point-of-sale terminals. These are systems where the inbuilt apps in Windows 10 would be very unlikely to be needed or used.

Because the Windows Store apps in Windows 10 are updated much more frequently, they are blocked from installation entirely on systems configured for LTSB. This includes the Microsoft Edge web browser, Cortana, and the Windows Store itself. No Windows Store apps will be available or installable on LTSB-configured Windows 10 PCs. Win32 apps will still be installable.

If a business is using its own custom Store apps, however, delivered through a custom business store (that may contain some of other third-party apps, or even Microsoft Store apps), or side-loaded onto the PC, these will still work and be updated through the store as per normal. Microsoft does advise caution when doing this, however, as changes to the app platform requiring updates to apps and future upgrades to the OS may be required for continued safe and reliable operation of the app platform. Basically here, they're covering all the bases as nobody knows exactly how Windows 10 will evolve over time.

Choosing How Updates Are Delivered

Another new feature in Windows 10 that pertains to how updates are delivered is that the OS now supports peer-to-peer update sharing. This works in three ways, see Figure 16-3.

1. Either it's off completely, in which case app updates only come direct to each PC through that PC's own Internet connection.

2. Updates provided by PCs on the local network are enabled. This means that a PC doesn't have to download part or all of an update from the Internet, which can reduce the Internet bandwidth used by multiple PCs connected to a home or work network.

3. Updates will be provided by PCs on the local network or on the Internet. This is the same as option 2, except that updates can be provided to the PC over the Internet by other Windows 10 PCs that also have all or part of the update. Each PC configured in this way will also share its Windows Updates with other Windows 10 PCs around the world.

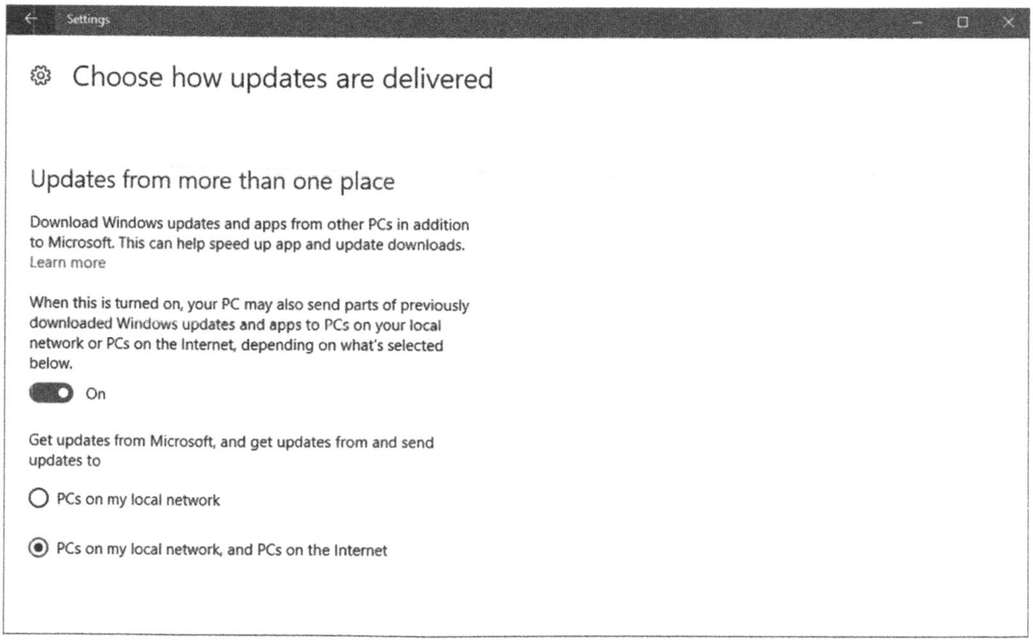

Figure 16-3. Windows Updates can be delivered via a peer-to-peer system

Uninstalling and Blocking Updates

If a Windows Update needs to be removed from a PC, perhaps because it is conflicting with an app, is a faulty driver update, or is causing the PC to become unstable, this can be done from the *Advanced Options* panel in the Windows Update Settings. Here you can click the *Uninstall updates* link, which will open a Programs and Features window where offending updates can be removed by right-clicking them, see Figure 16-4.

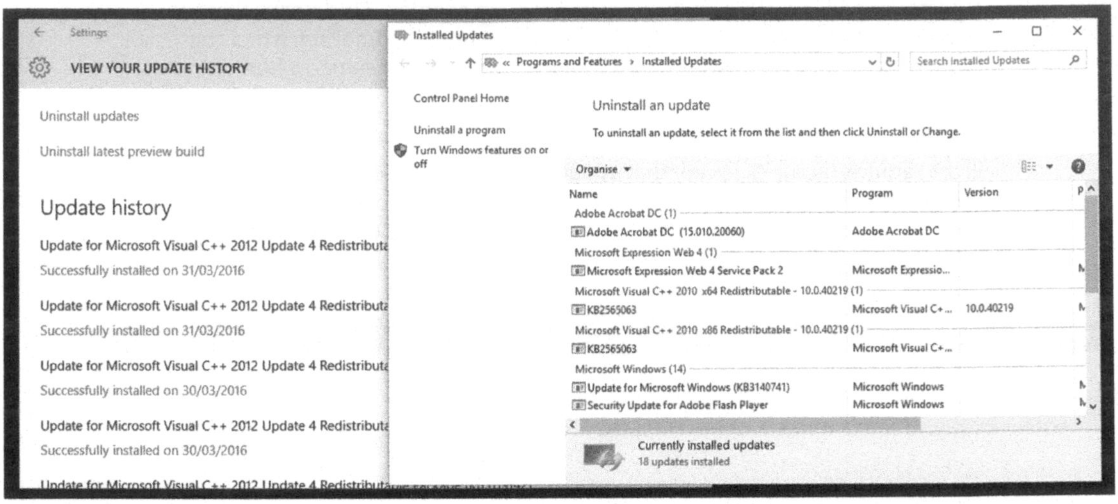

Figure 16-4. *Windows Updates can be uninstalled through the Settings app*

Shortly after the release of Windows 10, Microsoft did bow to pressure from businesses and the public and release a tool for blocking the installation of Windows Updates. You can download the *"Show or Hide Updates" Troubleshooter Package* from `http://pcs.tv/1WXoRR3`. This lists all currently available updates and provides a check box next to each that allows you to exclude an update from a PC, see Figure 16-5.

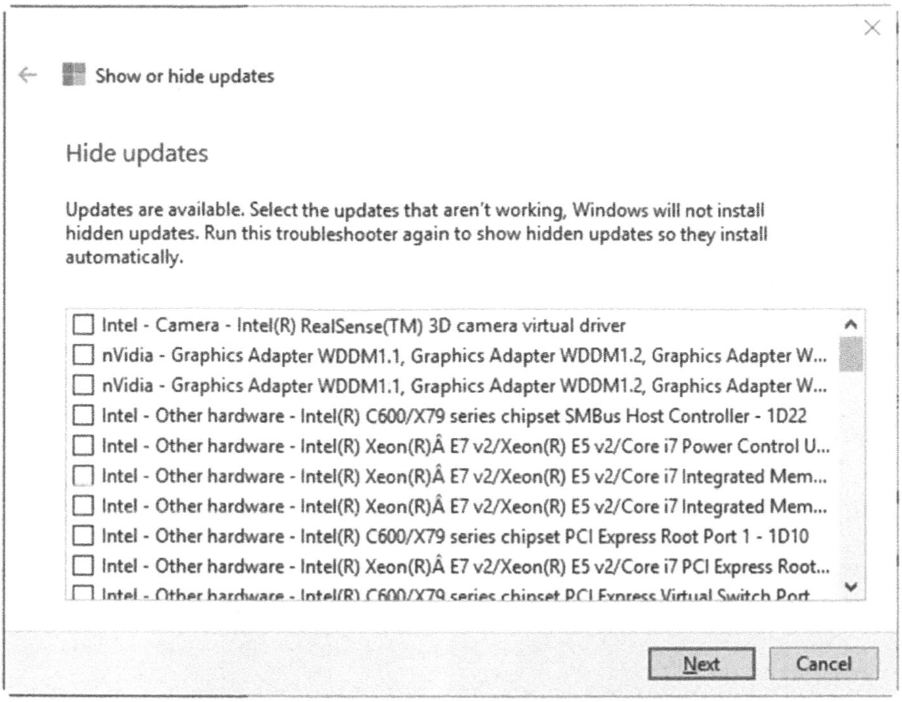

Figure 16-5. *Microsoft has released a tool that can block Windows Updates*

The Show or Hide Updates Troubleshooter works on a per-PC basis. Should you wish to block updates on PCs managed by Windows Server, you will have a tool available to you through the System Center Configuration Manager.

■ **Tip**   The *Update & security* panel in the Settings app allows PC users to enroll in the Windows Insider program. This is a beta program for new Windows 10 features and releases, and it completely overrides the current Windows Update settings. The *Insider Preview Builds* option can be disabled in Group Policy in *Computer Configuration* ➤ *Administrative Templates* ➤ *Windows Components* ➤ *Data Collection and Preview Builds*.

Troubleshooting and Repairing Windows Update

So what happens should Windows Update become corrupt and stop working? This does occasionally happen and you may find that updates will either flatly refuse to install or even refuse to download at all. In this circumstance it's straightforward to reset Windows Update, though you might need to restart your PC first if Windows Update has recently been in use.

To reset Windows Update, open File Explorer and navigate to C:\Windows\SoftwareDistribution. This folder, seen in Figure 16-6, contains all the downloads and configuration options for Windows Update. You can completely delete the entire contents of the SoftwareDistribution folder if you want, and it won't harm the PC at all. Should you do this, however, Windows Update will be completely reset, which will include any updates you may have hidden. Perhaps a preferable option is to delete the Download folder (or its contents). This will delete any updates that have partially or completely downloaded, but that will be corrupt, preventing installation.

Figure 16-6. *The SoftwareDistribution folder contains Windows Updates downloads and config files*

Windows Upgrades and the Reset Image

In Chapter 2, I showed you how you can repair and reset Windows 10 by using its inbuilt Reset feature. This is different from a System Image Backup, which is a single disk image file containing a snapshot of the disk or partiton on which Windows 10 is installed, complete with copies of the boot partitions, at the time the backup was made.

Reset doesn't have a single image file. It does work from a backup version of the main Kernel file, install.wim (the root operating system), which is hidden away in a backup partition. This file is very small though and isn't the full OS as installed on your PC. The rest of the files sit in the folders beneath the \Windows folder and are updated periodically by Windows Update.

The System Image Backup restore method is superior to the Reset feature in the following way: all of your installed Store and win32 apps, and all of your settings and configuration options, are kept intact. Where it fails is that you then have to download any and all updates to all those apps (and, crucially, to Windows 10) that have been released since the snapshot was made. This can take a considerable amount of time, especially considering you'll likely still be using the same Windows 10 installation for 10 years… or more.

Reset uses the files that come from Windows Update to make sure that, when the PC is reimaged, it's also up to date (it won't update your apps, however). This can save considerable time in downloading the half a million Windows Updates that were released since you first installed Windows 10 on the PC.

"But," you might say, "what if it's a Windows Update that buggered my PC in the first place?" The Reset feature will only use Windows Updates that have been installed on the PC for 30 days or more, the theory being that if you've been using them for the last 30 days, they'll be alright and won't cause any problems.

Occasionally, the core install.wim image backup file required to make Reset work can itself become corrupt. Microsoft has included a tool within Windows 10, however, that can check this Reset image and, if necessary, repair it. You run this from a *Command Prompt (Admin)* window from the desktop or the Recovery Environment, with the following commands.

- **DISM /Online /Cleanup-Image /CheckHealth** will verify if any corruption has been detected in the Reset Image files. It will not perform any repairs, however.

- **DISM /Online /Cleanup-Image /ScanHealth** will check for file corruption, and will take much longer than the /CheckHealth switch. It will also not perform repairs.

- **DISM /Online /Cleanup-Image /RestoreHealth** will scan the Reset image files for any corruption, and repair any damage automatically, taking the repair files it needs from your installed copy of Windows 10 and also fresh copies of appropriate files from Windows Update.

If you have a situation where you are trying to repair the Reset image, but your Windows installation is itself corrupt, you can use an existing Windows 10 installer ISO file. It's best to get a fresh one (that's up to date with all the latest upgrades) from the Windows 10 Download page. You can find this online at http://pcs.tv/1M2It5N.

Download the Media Creation tool and use it to create an ISO file (you may need to do this on another PC if your main Windows installation isn't working properly). Once the ISO file is created, you can burn it to a DVD by right-clicking it, or if it's downloaded to the PC that needs repair, double-click it to mount it.

Now use the command **DISM /Online /Cleanup-Image /RestoreHealth /Source:D:\sources\install.wim**, where D: might need to be replaced by the drive containing the install DVD or mounted disc image. The repair operation will try to use Windows Update to ensure the Reset image is repaired correctly. If you do not wish for Windows Update to be used, perhaps because you are on a metered Internet connection, you can also use the **/LimitAccess** switch to prevent the tool from accessing Windows Update.

Summary

It's very clear that Windows Update in Windows 10 is a very different beast from anything seen in earlier Windows versions. That isn't to say it's not configurable, and that it's not possible to block problematic updates. The hooks that Windows Update has into the Reset system can also be of enormous benefit.

In the next chapter, we'll look at the last of the big five problem areas, already having covered startup, network and Internet connections, device drivers, and Windows Update; I'll show to how to maintain *compatibility* with the older win32 apps, web sites, and intranets we all still need to use in our working lives.

CHAPTER 17

Maintaining App and Web Site Compatibility

Having a stable, reliable, and robust PC, with a good network and Internet connection that's fully updated and configured as you need it, isn't going to help you much if you can't use the apps or access the web sites or intranet sites that you need. Apps are everything. From the smallest utility that sits in your system tray, to a major suite such as Adobe Creative Cloud, or a custom app that was written specifically for your business, if you can't use the apps you need, you can't get anything done at all.

It doesn't stop there either. Your business may rely on web sites or an intranet site that was designed and programmed some years ago, but which needs to be maintained and kept in use. This site may rely on specific web browser plug-ins or web standards that were de rigueur at the time.

It's easy for the world to say it's moved on, and that technology and standards have moved on. If your business relies on older technologies, which would be prohibitively expensive to rewrite, at least in the short term, you have to find ways to get everything working that you need.

The good news is that Windows 10 is a very legacy-friendly operating system, both supporting win32 apps that would run happily on Windows 7, and having good compatibility solutions for those that didn't. There are also compatibility settings for web sites and intranets for both the Edge browser and Internet Explorer 11 (IE11) (which remains in the OS for all users).

Maintaining compatibility is everything. I mentioned in the previous chapter that even Windows Store apps aren't immune to compatibility problems. Should an Enterprise PC be placed on the Long-Term Servicing Update Branch (LTSB), in which only security and stability updates are delivered for 10 years, you might find that after a while your custom or even the standard Microsoft Store apps stop working. This will be because, as the app framework evolves and apps are updated, they will require new OS features that will be rolled out over the years but that won't be included in the LTSB updates.

© Mike Halsey 2016
M. Halsey, *Windows 10 Troubleshooting*, DOI 10.1007/978-1-4842-0925-7_17

Maintaining Compatibility with Win32 Apps

Let's begin with win32 apps, otherwise known as the desktop apps we've all been using since the days of Windows 95 (technically we were using them in Windows 1, but the win32 framework changed considerably with the move to Windows 95, and the onward march to the modern Windows NT kernel).

Windows 10 is quite good at detecting problems with win32 apps, and it will alert you if it detects that an app didn't start, run, or close properly. It's possible to have Windows 10 assist in making apps compatible, however, or to set compatibility manually on a per-app basis.

There are four ways to get to the app compatibility settings in Windows 10.

1. From an app that's pinned to the Taskbar, right-click it and then right-click the app name again in the jumplist that appears. From the context menu that appears, select its *Properties*, see Figure 17-1.

Figure 17-1. *You can access an app's properties panel from the Taskbar*

2. From the *All Apps* view in the Start Menu, right-click the app and from the menu that appears, click More and then click Open File Location, see Figure 17-2. In the window that appears, right-click the app (which should already be highlighted) and select *Properties* from the menu that appears.

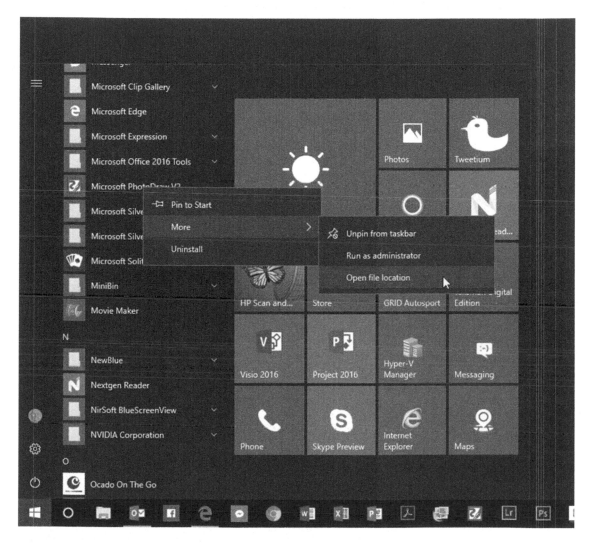

Figure 17-2. *You can access an app's properties panel from the Start Menu*

3. Open the installation folder for the app, if you know what it is. In the example I'm using here of Microsoft PhotoDraw 2000 (which I still use almost every day), it's C:\Program Files (x86)\Microsoft Office\Office. Then right-click the app launcher and select *Properties* from the menu that appears.

4. If you are having trouble installing a win32 app, right-click the installer file and select Properties from the menu that appears.

When the App properties panel appears, click the Compatibility tab, and it is here that you have several options and courses of action available to you, see Figure 17-3. At the top of this dialog will appear a button to *Run [the] compatibility troubleshooter*.

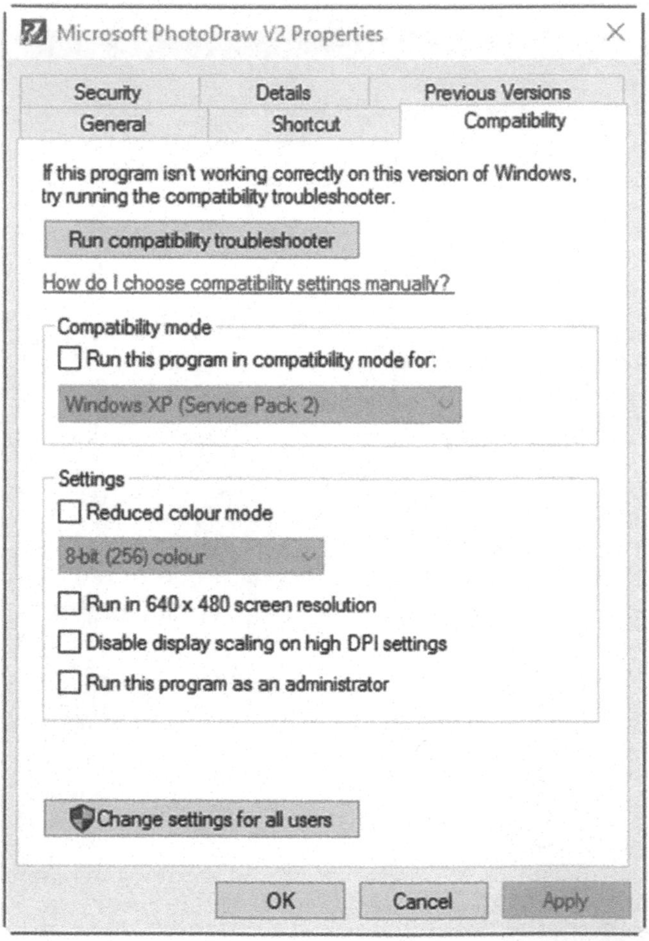

Figure 17-3. *The Compatibility tab in the App properties panel lets you manage compatibility*

Running the compatibility troubleshooter app will display a wizard that will present you with a series of options to describe the problems you experience, see Figure 17-4. These include "The program worked in an earlier version of Windows but won't install or run now." Selecting one or more of these description options will enable the troubleshooter to set app compatibility automatically. You will then be asked to run or install the app to check if the settings worked. If they don't, the troubleshooter will offer you additional options.

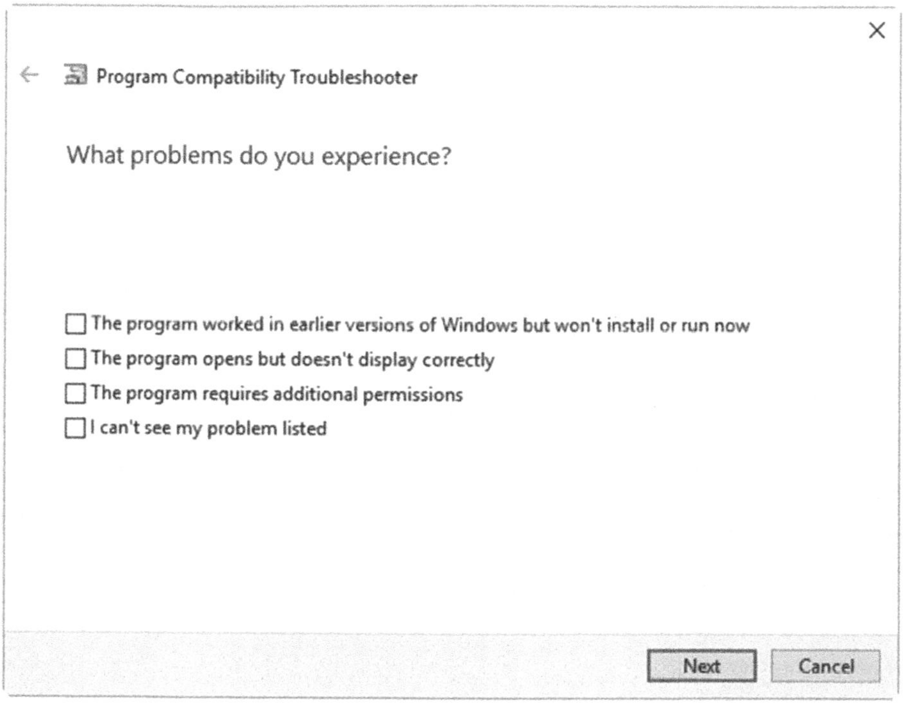

Figure 17-4. *The App compatibility troubleshooter can set compatibility automatically*

If you want or need to set app compatibility manually, there are several options available to you. The first is a drop-down menu that lists every Windows version going back to Windows 95 (20 years before Windows 10 was released), see Figure 17-5. Remember I said that the app framework before Windows 95 was very different, and I'll come to this shortly.

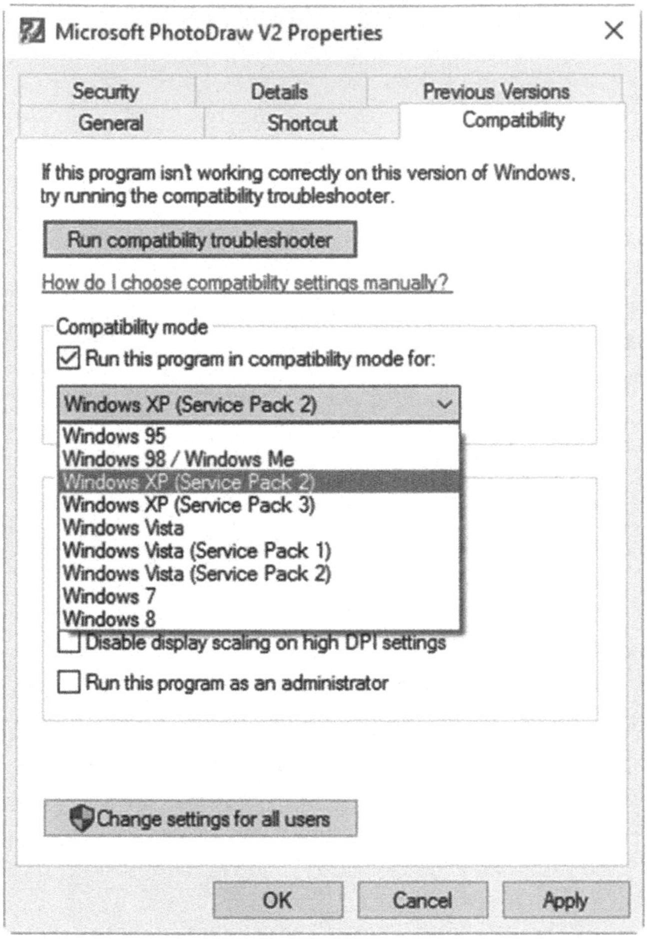

Figure 17-5. *You can choose an OS version the app ran in before*

Now, I want to stress an important caveat at this point, as simply setting *Run this program in compatibility mode for [an older OS version]* won't fix every problem. This is because, as Windows has evolved over the years, many features and services in the OS have changed or been dropped altogether.

I'm using Microsoft PhotoDraw 2000 v2 for this demonstration, which was released when Windows 98 and ME were the current desktop operating systems in use. PhotoDraw has an incompatibility today in that none of the 3D modeling features in the app will work. This is because they rely on Direct3D, which has changed so considerably since its first release in 1996 that it's completely incompatible with PhotoDraw today. This is okay for me, as I can live without the 3D features, but it's a good example of how Windows has changed and evolved with technology.

So what happens if you have a *really* old app that you still want or need to use? You might have an app that you still need to use, but that was written back in the days before high-DPI displays and User Account Control, 20 years ago or more. Below the Windows version selection drop-down menu are four additional options, see Figure 17-6.

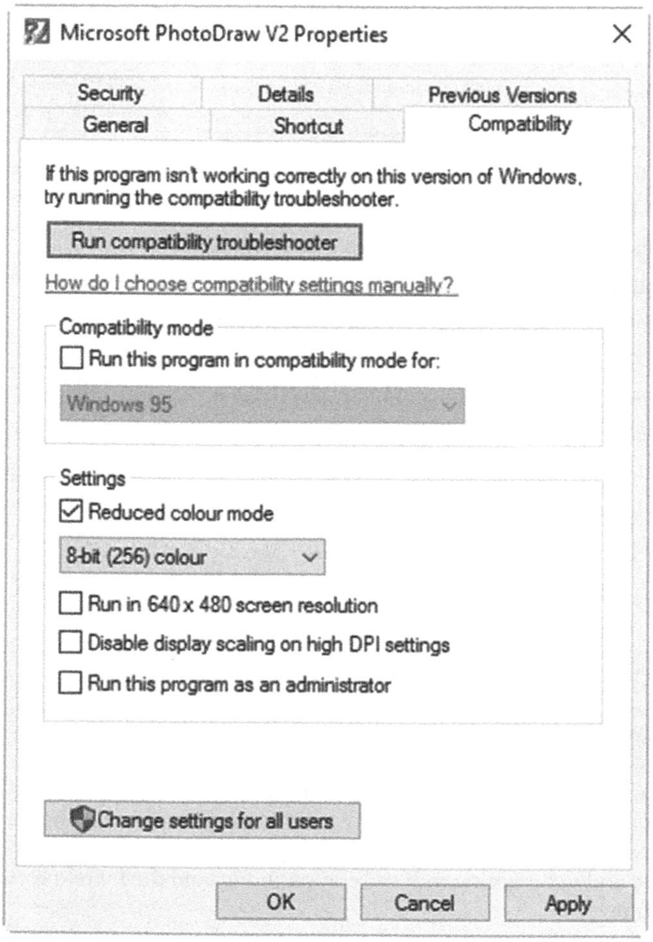

Figure 17-6. *You can set compatibility for 20-plus-year-old apps in Windows 10*

- **Reduced color mode** will force the app to run in either 8-bit, 256-color, or 16-bit, 65,535-color mode. This maintains compatibility for apps that do not render correctly, because they were designed for old VGA (Video Graphics Adapter) screens that typically used a 640- by 480-pixel resolution (I'm writing this on a 4K display that has 27 times the resolution of VGA, and can't imagine having a desktop that small any more)

- **Run in 640 × 480 screen resolution** will force the app to stay within a confines of a VGA-size window. This is used if the app doesn't display properly when resized on your screen or run in a regular Windows 10 window.

- **Disable display scaling on high-DPI screens** is used because on high-DPI screens (such as my own 4K display) it's common to tell Windows 10 to scale the desktop by 125%, 150%, or even 200%. This makes text and other items on screen larger, but it can also break the rendering of apps that were designed before this feature came about. Checking this option will force Windows to ignore desktop scaling for that app.

- **Run this program as an administrator** is a tricky one that I'd like to spend a bit more time on, so let's do just that...

■ **Caution**   Some legacy apps on Windows, and by this I mean apps that were written for Windows 95, Windows 98, Windows ME, Windows 2000, and Windows XP, were written in such as way as to exploit the fact that the default user of a PC was an Administrator who could do anything they wanted, at any time. This presented a major security risk, thus bringing about the introduction of User Account Control in Windows Vista. Because users could change any setting, delete any file, or modify any configuration option, so could malware (and it often did). It's now considered "sloppy" coding when apps relied on this functionality, and often this was a workaround meaning developers didn't have to code their apps properly. Should a legacy app require Administrative rights in order to work, this presents a security risk to your PC. Any malware that attacks the app can take advantage of its Admin rights to make any change it wants to your system, such as injecting more malware or a rootkit virus. Should an app need to be run as an Administrator, it should, ideally, be completely sandboxed in a virtual machine, and I will show you how to do this in Chapter 20.

Managing Web Site and Intranet Compatibility

Just as we use apps on our PC to accomplish tasks at home and in the workplace, web apps and intranets are also essential to our daily lives. You might use the Gmail web site to read and manage your email, or Office 365 to manage and collaborate on documents with colleagues. While these web services and web apps are regularly updated to ensure they work with the latest browsers, if you need to use an older web site or intranet site for your business, things can be trickier. The good news, though, is that both Microsoft Edge and IE come with advanced tools for managing and maintaining web site compatibility, and the better news is that these tools work the same way in both browsers.

In both Edge and IE11, you can set and manage compatibility with web sites and intranet sites using the *F12 Developer Tools*. These are accessed in the same way in both browsers, by selecting F12 Developer Tools from the browser Settings menu, see Figure 17-7, or (oddly enough) by pressing the F12 key on your keyboard (if you have an F12 key, that is).

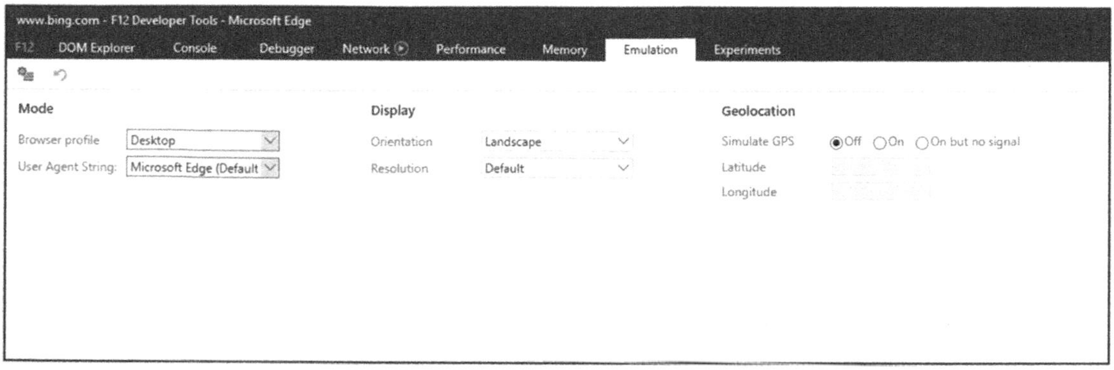

Figure 17-7. *The F12 Developer Tools are available in both Edge and IE11*

The following compatibility settings are available both Edge and IE.

- **Browser Profile** lets you choose if the web or intranet site is designed primarily for a desktop or smartphone display.

- **User Agent String** will present a long list of browsers. You can choose which one the web site or intranet site worked well with, see Figure 17-8. These include every version of IE going back to IE8 (in Edge) and IE6 (in IE11), Mozilla Firefox, Google Chrome, and Apple Safari.

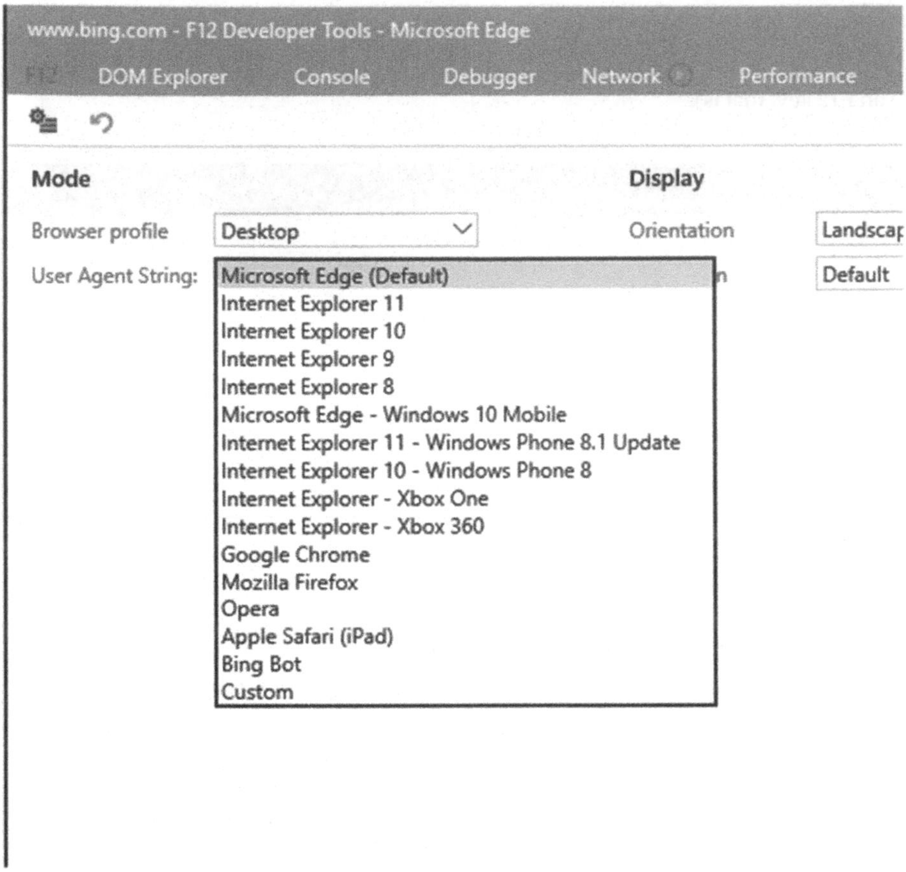

Figure 17-8. You can choose which browser the web site or intranet site worked in before

---

■ **Tip** The F12 Developer Tools in IE11 additionally support compatibility modes for IE versions 7 and 6. IE6 was around for many years, and many intranets still exist that were written for it, though the browser itself wasn't what we'd now call either "standards compliant" or "secure."

- **Orientation** allows you to set a default portrait or landscape orientation for the site. This can be used if the site does not render properly in the browser, or if the layout doesn't properly fit the browser window.

- **Resolution** is again used if the web or intranet site does not render properly in the browser window, because it was designed for a specific screen resolution on older PCs. You can set resolutions between 2560 × 1440 and 800 × 480 pixels, see Figure 17-9, or you can set Custom options if a web or intranet site requires, say, a 640 × 480 maximum resolution to function correctly.

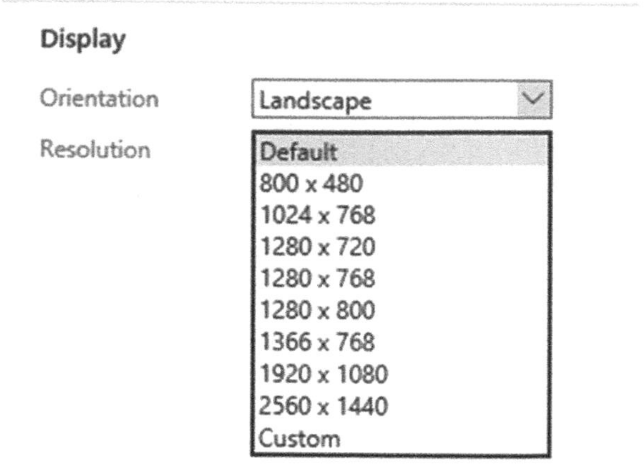

Display

Orientation   Landscape

Resolution   Default
800 x 480
1024 x 768
1280 x 720
1280 x 768
1280 x 800
1366 x 768
1920 x 1080
2560 x 1440
Custom

Figure 17-9. You can force the web site or intranet site to be constrained in a specific maximum resolution

- **Geolocation** is used only if the web site or intranet site requires the use of GPS or Windows geolocation features, but either your PC does not support them, or they have been disabled in Group Policy. You can fix a latitude and londitude that will be given to the web site by the browser.

Managing Security in IE

Earlier in this chapter, I talked about how some older apps require Administrator rights in order to function correctly. This presents a significant security risk to any PC, because if malware can successfully attack the app, then it can pretty much do whatever it likes on your computer. Web browsers aren't immune to this, as while both Google Chrome and Microsoft Edge have some formidable sandboxing technologies built into them, IE... well... doesn't. As a result, it is *the* most attacked web browser in the whole history of the Internet, helped I'm sure by the runaway popularity of IE6, which, at one point, held 99% of the browser market, putting competitor Netscape (which I always really liked) out of business completely.

IE comes bundled with all editions of Windows 10. It's initially hidden, but you can search for it in the Start Menu or Cortana, after which time it will always appear in the Start Menu's All Apps list. You manage privacy and security in the Internet Options panel, which is available from the Settings menu in IE11 itself, but is also available from the Control Panel, and controllable through Group Policy.

■ **Note**   Do you *really* need to use IE? Certainly for compatibility for legacy intranet and other sites there's a strong case for doing so, but for everything else? The recommendation of this particular author is only to use IE11 for the tasks that it absolutely *must* be used for, and that a modern, secure browser such as Edge is used for everything else.

Security in IE11 is managed through, oddly enough, the Security tab in the Internet Options (also called Internet Properties) panel, see Figure 17-10. At the top of the panel are four "zones" for which you can set security permissions.

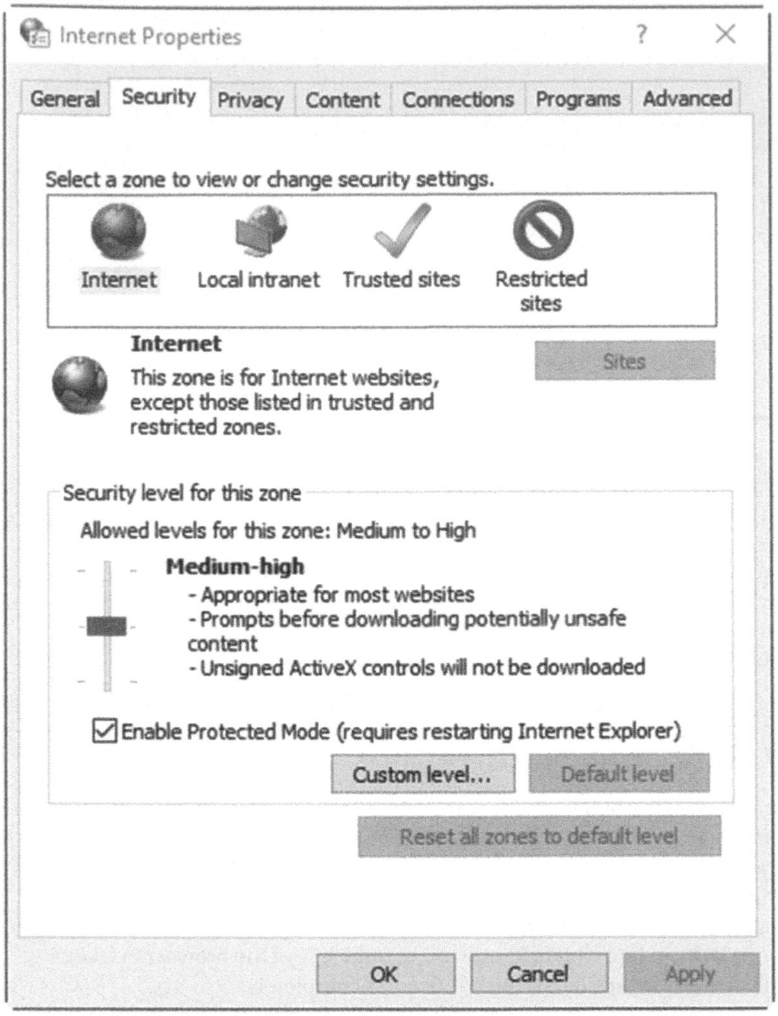

Figure 17-10. IE11 security is managed in Internet Options

- **Internet** is for, funnily enough, web sites and anything not on your local network. Clicking the *Custom level* button allows you to approve and deny access for specific web technologies, such as ActiveX, which is notoriously attacked by malware. There is also a security-level slider control you can use to automatically set Medium, Medium-High, and High levels of security for the browser. If you use IE11 only to access certain web sites, try setting the security level to high, and disabling all web technologies, re-enabling them only as necessary to ensure your web sites work correctly in the browser.

- **Local intranet** is for intranet sites run from your company network. It too has a security slider, which ranges here from Low to High, and a *Custom level* button in which you can disable specific web technologies. Additionally, there is a *Sites* button which you can click to permit only specific intranet sites. This feature can prevent malware from connecting to any web site by spoofing the site as an intranet instead.

- **Trusted sites** are web and intranet sites that you definitely trust not to harm your PC or let in malware. If you only use IE11 for your intranet and a limited number of web sites, it is good to add them to the trusted sites list.

- **Restricted sites** are web and intranet sites that you specifically do *not* want IE11 connecting to. Unfortunately, there isn't an option to "block everything except sites on the Trusted list"; instead you need to specifically add web sites you wish to block. This makes it less useful than other web filtering systems.

The *Privacy* tab is where you control (guess what) in IE11. It may sound frivolous, given that pretty much none of us have any privacy online these days, but it's very important to businesses. This is because cookies, which are small files that web sites and intranets store on our PCs and that often contain login details, can also be used to track our activities with the site online.

A web site may use its own cookies for innocuous purposes, perhaps as in the preceding example, to automatically sign you in each time you visit it. Sites can also place third-party cookies on your PC. Generally speaking, these almost always come from advertisers, through advertisements displayed on the page. Very occasionally, though, an advert can deliver malware, and then any cookies placed could be monitoring your site usage in a way you would not wish to permit.

You can click the *Sites* button to specify web sites which must always or never be allowed to use cookies, but as with the Restricted sites list, this isn't a catch-all solution. You can instead click the *Advanced* button to define specific policies on the PC for accepting or blocking both first- and third-party cookies, see Figure 17-11.

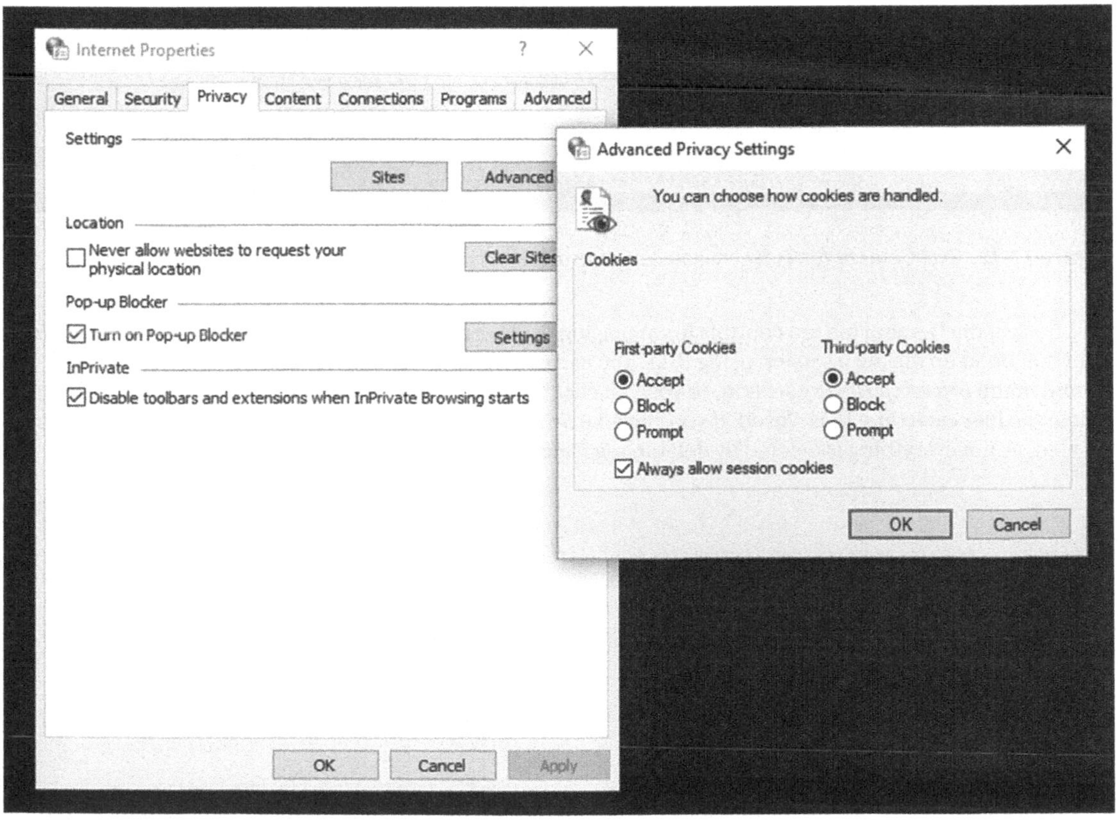

Figure 17-11. *The Privacy controls allow you to block cookies*

The *Content* tab is where you can manage IE11 features such as form, username, and password autocomplete. You can also manage security certificates through this tab, however. Secure web sites and intranet sites will have a security certificate, and here those certificates can be viewed, imported, or exported to other PCs (perhaps from a central server store) and wiped from the PC, see Figure 17-12.

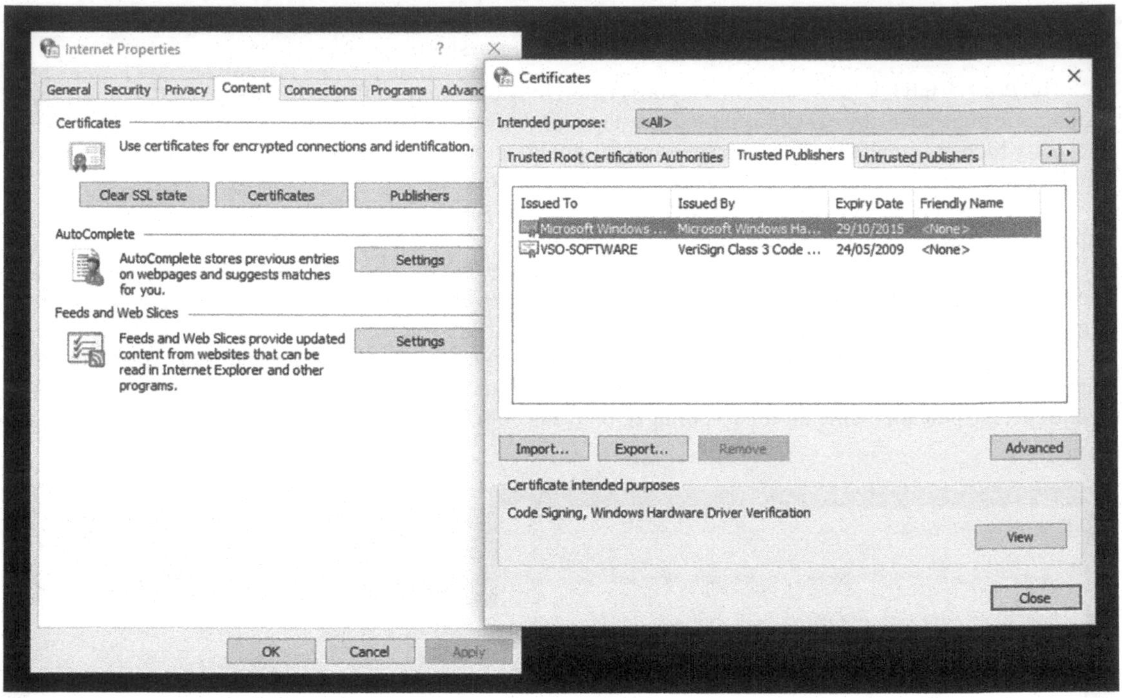

Figure 17-12. *The Content tab is where you can control security certificates for web and intranet sites*

Back at the General tab are controls for managing the files (cookies, passwords, usernames, web history, etc.) that build up during a session using IE11. You can manually delete these files by clicking the *Delete* button in the *Browsing History* section, or you can check the *Delete browsing history on exit*, to automatically delete the files each time IE is closed. If you click the *Settings* button, you can choose exactly what it is that is deleted, as not everything is deleted by default, see Figure 17-13.

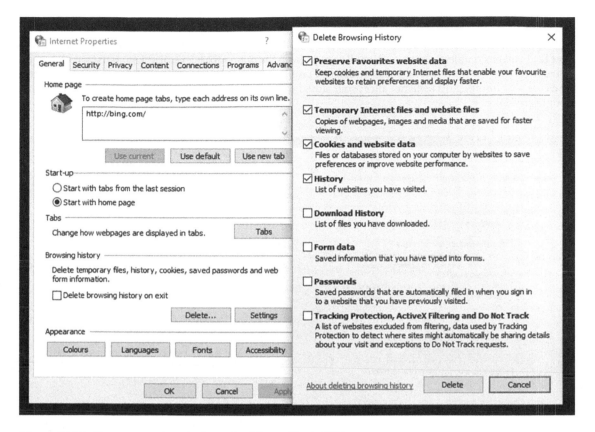

Figure 17-13. *You can manage the browsing history files in IE11*

Resetting IE

Despite all the controls available in IE11, and the Advanced tab containing yet more browsing and security options for the browser, you might find occasionally that IE11 fails to start or work reliably. Should this happen you can be faced with a problem, as you can't uninstall or reinstall the browser, nor will there ever be a newer version released you can upgrade to, as Microsoft has stated that IE11 will be the final version.

It is possible, however, to completely reset IE, which does have the same effect as completely reinstalling it (unless some core files have become corrupt, that is), in which case a reset or reimage might be required. Under the *Advanced* tab in the Internet Options is a *Reset* button. Click this and you will be told that IE11 will be completely reset, and you'll also be given the option to delete all of your personal files, as a corruption with the browser might also be causing problems with them, see Figure 17-14. I would point out, however, that resetting IE11 will not affect your stored web site Favorites, as these are stored elsewhere in your users folder.

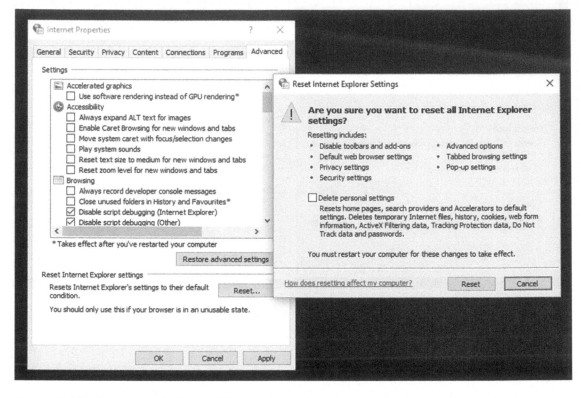

Figure 17-14. *You can completely reset IE11*

Setting Your Default Web Browser

I mentioned earlier in this chapter that it can be wise to use IE only to connect to the legacy web and intranet sites that you need it for, and to use a more secure browser, such as Edge, for everything else. There are three ways to make sure that Edge (or another browser such as Google Chrome) is your default browser.

You can open the Settings app and navigate to *System* ➤ *Default Apps*, where the default web browser can be selected, see Figure 17-15.

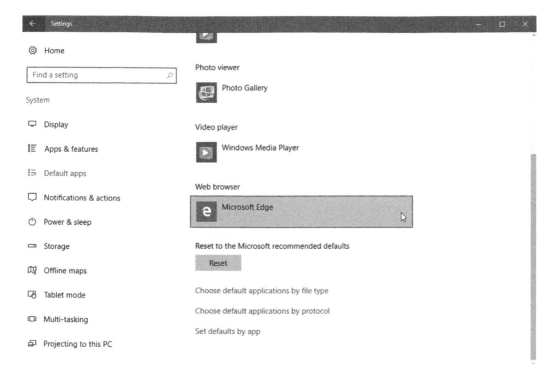

Figure 17-15. *You can set your default browser in the Settings app*

Alternatively, the Default Programs panel still exists (as you read this, anyway) in the Control Panel. We can expect its features to be fully folded into the Settings app within the first few years of Windows 10's release. Click *Set Default Programs* and a list of the apps installed on your PC will be presented. Choose the browser you want to make default and click either *Set this program as default*, or if you want finer control, *Choose defaults for this program*, see Figure 17-16.

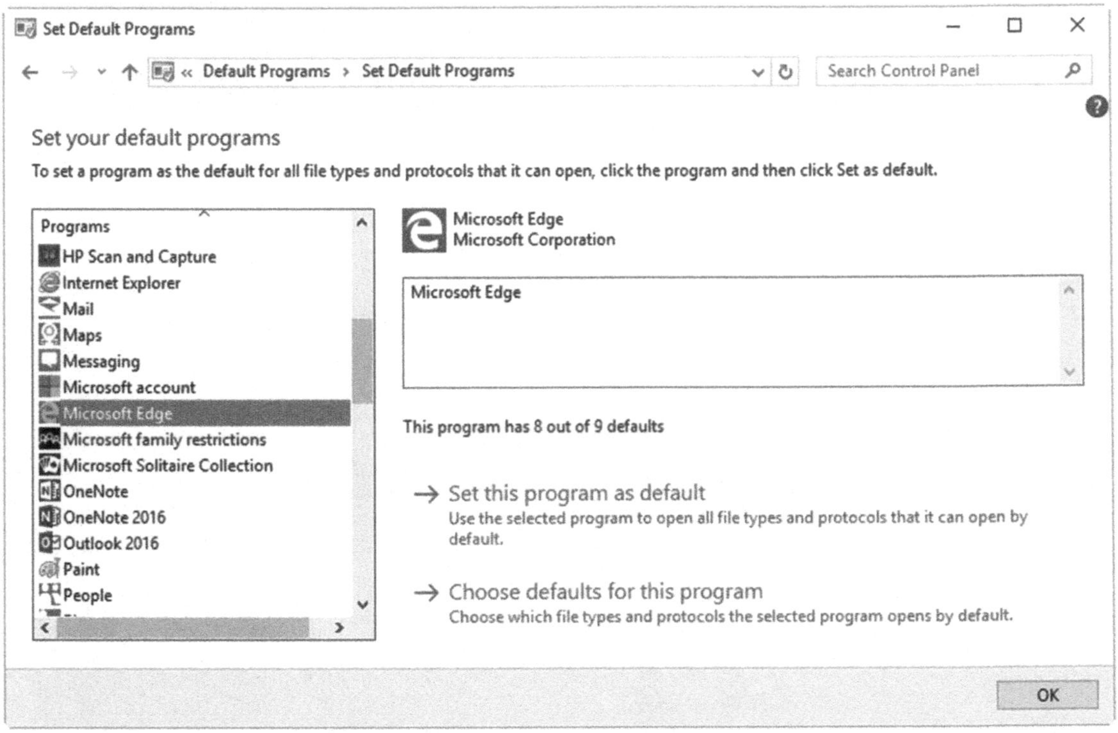

Figure 17-16. You can also set the default browser from the Control Panel

The default browser can also be set directly from within the Internet Options panel, though here you can only choose between IE and Edge, see Figure 17-17. Navigate to the *Programs* tab, and you will see an *Opening Internet Explorer* drop-down menu at the top of the dialog. Note that this menu will be grayed out if IE is not currently set as the default browser.

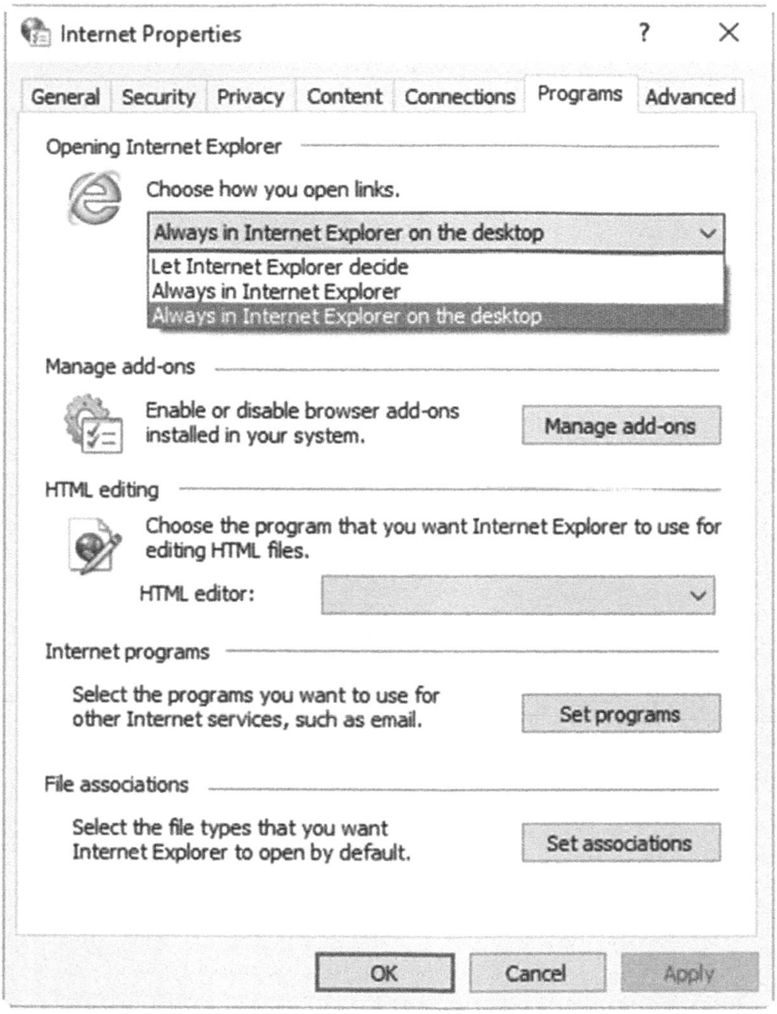

Figure 17-17. *You can also set the default browser from within the Internet Options*

Summary

Windows is, and always has been, the most compatible operating system in history. You can still run DOS programs that were written in the early 1980s in Windows 10 through the Command Prompt, and hundreds, perhaps even thousands, of apps that are over 20 years old will still install and work fine on your PC, though perhaps with a bit of compatibility tweaking.

Using any legacy app, web site, or intranet on your system, though, will always present a potential security risk, so in the next chapter I'm going to focus on that entirely and show you how to ensure that your PC, your files, and your personal information are kept safe, secure, and (as and where appropriate) encrypted and away from prying eyes.

■ ■ ■

CHAPTER 18

Managing Security and Privacy

How would you feel if your laptop or tablet were stolen, with your files and data on board, including shopping logins and passwords, financial details, and personal photos? Worse, how would you feel if you didn't have a password on your PC, or if that password were easily guessable? Now imagine how your employer would feel if it were your company laptop or tablet that were stolen, complete with confidential customer details and information on current and future projects?

It might be annoying or even humiliating to lose a personal device containing auto-logins to social networks, and some photos you'd rather the rest of the world not see. In the business space however, the use and storage of data are strictly regulated in most countries around the world. People's data is personal to them, and you have a responsibility to look after it and keep it safe.

In many countries, the fines and penalties for losing unencrypted customer, employee, and other personal data can be steep enough to shut down a small business for good. So what are the best practices for managing privacy and encryption on PCs, but also, how can you regain access to that encrypted data if you find yourself locked out?

Creating a Strong Password?

Let's begin with passwords. If you're a systems administrator or an IT Pro, you probably know already that you can open the **netplwiz** panel by searching for it in the Start Menu, and disable forcing of password entry for the PC at sign in, see Figure 18-1.

© Mike Halsey 2016

M. Halsey, *Windows 10 Troubleshooting*, DOI 10.1007/978-1-4842-0925-7_18

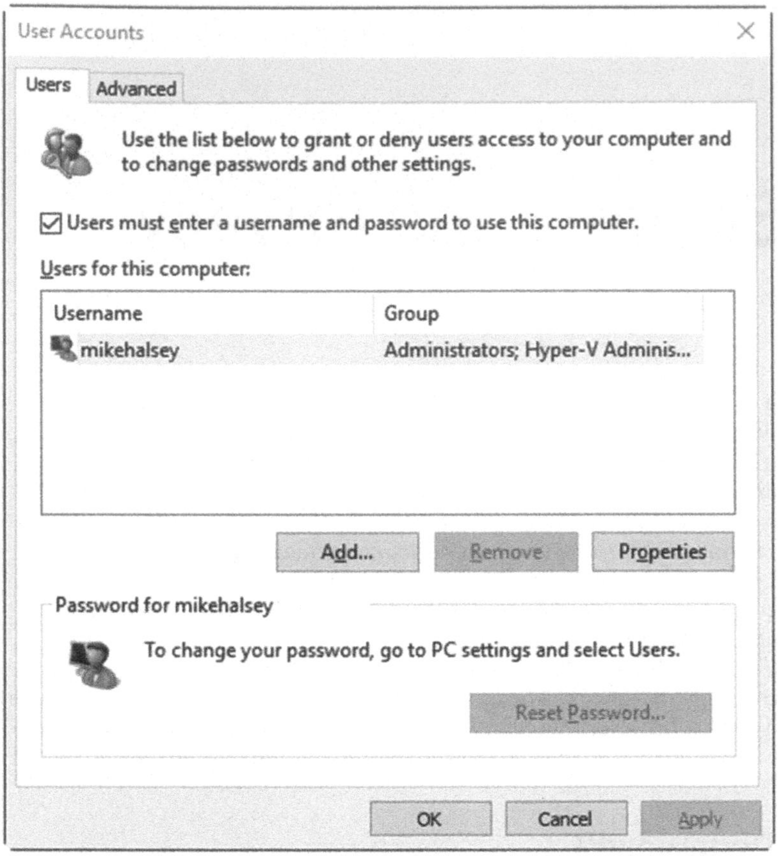

Figure 18-1. *Requiring a password at sign in can be disabled*

You may already do this on some of your PCs; I do, but only on a Surface Pro that never leaves the house, and on which I don't store any files (to be honest I only use it to watch video and TV while I'm playing Elite: Dangerous on my gaming PC). Is this secure? Well only if you use a local account on the machine to separate it from your OneDrive files, Microsoft e-mail, and the like, which I do. If the Surface Pro is stolen by a burglar, it can't be used to access any of my personal files or information.

This is a fairly expensive way to watch TV, however (in fairness the Surface Pro was a gift from Microsoft, otherwise I'd never have been able to justify it). For all of my other machines I am horrendously paranoid. I simply will not buy a PC, laptop, tablet, or desktop that doesn't come with a TPM (Trusted Platform Module) encryption chip, and while I'm a big fan of Windows Hello, because Windows Hello requires a PIN be set up, which is considerably less secure than my superstrong password, I simply won't use it on anything that leaves the house. Finally, and for good measure, on the desktops that do have a PIN and Windows Hello set up, they are securely tethered to a solid wall by use of a land anchor.

So how do you set up a good password? I have a video online that will guide nontechnical users through the process of setting one up, and you can find it online at http://pcs.tv/1B1N0ja. There are some simple rules you can follow, however, to help make your password supersecure.

- Use a phrase as the basis of your password. Perhaps a line from a song or poem.

- Choose a format for changing characters in the password, perhaps capitalizing the second, third, and last letters, or changing the first or second vowel into a number or symbol.

- Substitute numbers or symbols for letters. The following are examples of how you can do this.

  - 3, £, or # instead of E

  - $ or 5 instead of S

  - () or 0 (zero) instead of O

  - & or @ instead of A

  - 8 instead of B

  - 1, |, or [instead of L or I

  - / instead of 7

- Append to the beginning, middle, or end, of the password some unique characters to represent the service or web site for which that password is to be used. This will make the password unique to that one place.

  - eBa, or e8@ for eBay

  - Ama, @m@ for Amazon

  - D()m for the company domain

You will then have passwords that are extremely strong, fairly straightforward to remember, and utterly unique in every instance. In the following examples, you will see each password is more secure than the last, and they all follow an easy-to-remember pattern.

- imagine

- Imagine

- ImagineAllThePeople

- imAginealLthEpeOple

- 1mAg1n3&lLthEp3Opl3

- 1mAg1n3&lLthEp3Opl3g()Ogl3

You can test the strength of your own password at the web site HowSecureIsMyPassword.net, available at http://pcs.tv/howsecpwd. In the examples I've given, the first is a dictionary word and will be guessable by a hacker almost instantly. The last, which has been uniquely modified for Google sign in, would be almost completely uncrackable, and anybody who wanted to do so would need intelligence about how you create your passwords to aid them in the process.

It's not impossible to remember complex passwords either. Let's take the last exmaple, **1mAg1n3&lLth Ep3Opl3g()Ogl3**. The code here is that the vowels are changed to numbers or symbols, and always the same number or symbol, and the third letter of each word is capitalized; it's no more complicated than that.

■ **Caution**   If you are required to change your password regularly, perhaps every 90 days, please avoid incrementing the password by adding a number or letter on the end of it, 1, 2, and so on. This makes the password easy to guess if people discover the core password.

Managing Safety and Privacy for Children

Nothing is more important than the safety and security of children, or so I'm told as I haven't got any myself, which is why I have to time to write big books such as this. I do have a dog though, a rescue border collie called Jed, so for the purposes of this section, I've set him up with his own user acocunt on my PC ;)

You'll see in Figure 18-2 that I've set up Jed an account in the family section of the *Accounts* page in the *Settings* app. Adding the child (or dog in this case, but we'll call him a child as he really is just a big kid) lets you choose if the account is for a child or an adult, and then makes settings for that child available in Family Safety in your Microsoft account.

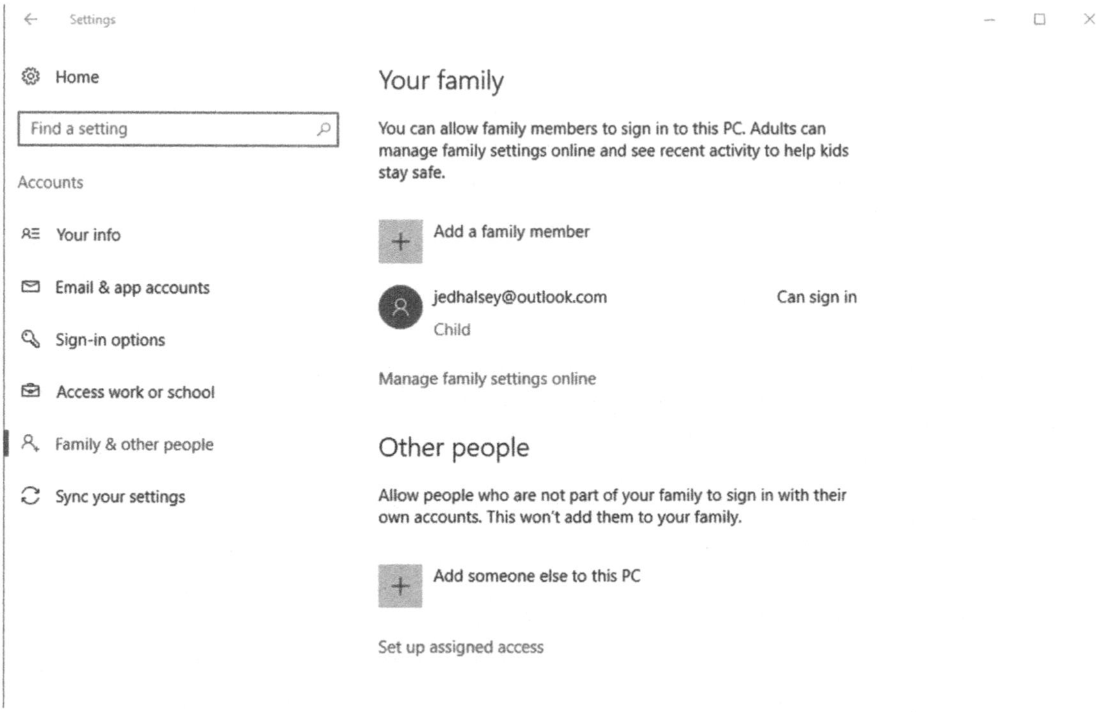

Figure 18-2. You add child accounts as family members

■ **Note**   The Family Safety feature in Windows 10 requires that the parent(s) and children all sign into the PC(s) with Microsoft accounts.

Clicking the *Manage family settings online* link in the Family Accounts panel will take you to the Family Safety page of your Microsoft account online. Here you will see a list of your children, and you can click each one to display details of their activities online (which I'm assuming for Jed was watching cat videos), and you can optionally have a weekly status report e-mailed to you for each child, see Figure 18-3.

Figure 18-3. You can get weekly activity reports from Family Safety

The Family Safety dashboard provides controls that you can activate and configure for each child. These include web filtering, time permissions, and game ratings, see Figure 18-4. Clicking one will allow you to set permissions for that child.

Block websites

You can make sure that adult websites are blocked for the kids in your family. You can also block specific sites – or choose which sites you want your kids to see.

Set good screen time habits

Together, you can talk about good habits and set limits on how much time they can spend with their screens.

A window into their digital life

Get recent activity reports on sites visited, apps used, games played and screen time. Or, check-in online at any time.

Playtime is important. Let them have fun, safely

You can allow your child to download apps and games appropriate for their age, and still make sure they don't get anything they're not ready for yet.

Figure 18-4. There are different settings available in Family Safety

When you have activated the web filtering, you will see that to make the system easy to use, Microsoft has a single-switch approach, see Figure 18-5. This activates global web filtering based on the age of the child. The filters are provided not only by Microsoft, but also child protection companies and organizations around the world, and they're very extensive.

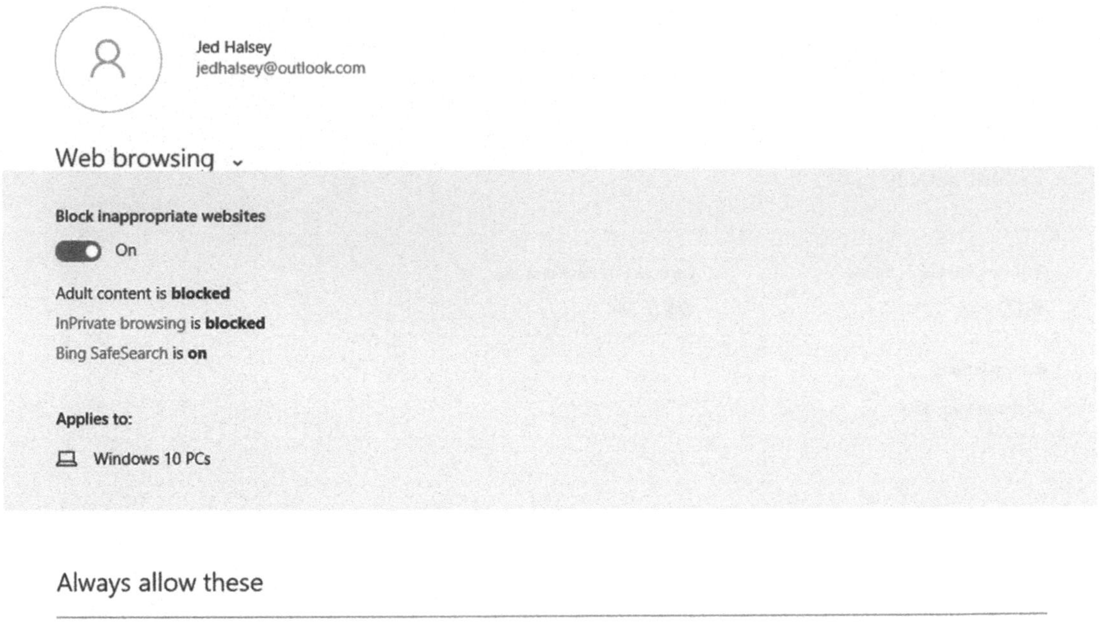

Jed Halsey
jedhalsey@outlook.com

Web browsing ⌄

Block inappropriate websites

◉ On

Adult content is **blocked**
InPrivate browsing is **blocked**
Bing SafeSearch is **on**

Applies to:

🖥 Windows 10 PCs

Always allow these

Figure 18-5. *You can use web site filtering for children*

You might find, however, that the system could still block some web sites that your child requires for school, or that some web sites are permitted when you you would rather your child not see them, perhaps on religious grounds. You can add web sites to your personal white and black lists from the Family Safety, web filtering panel, see Figure 18-6.

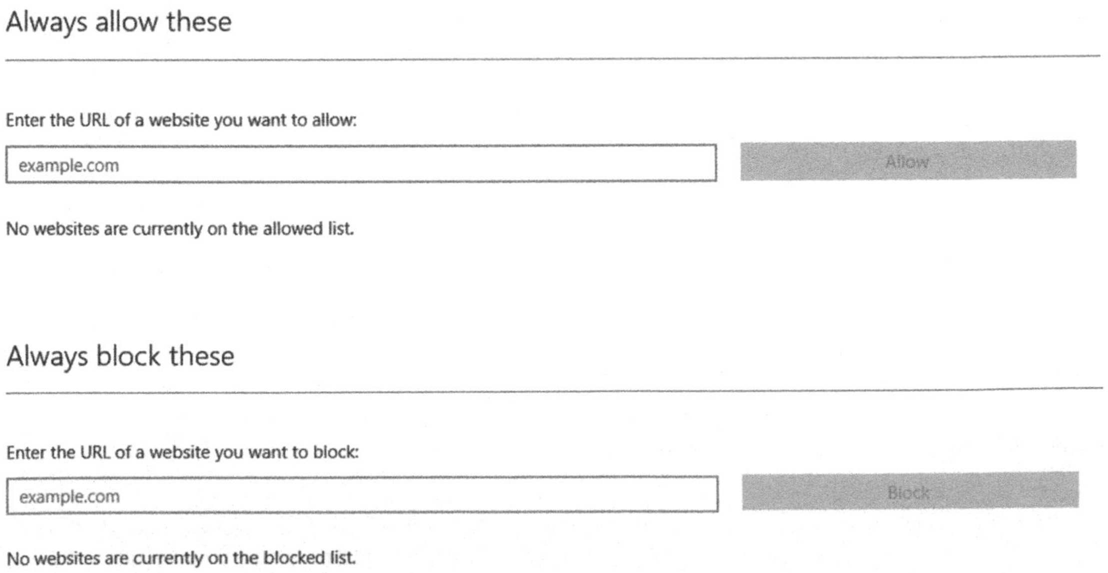

Always allow these

Enter the URL of a website you want to allow:

example.com	Allow

No websites are currently on the allowed list.

Always block these

Enter the URL of a website you want to block:

example.com	Block

No websites are currently on the blocked list.

Figure 18-6. *You can add specific sites to your white or black list*

The times controls allow you to set how often, or for how many hours a day, your child is allowed to use their PC. This might be that you don't want them using the PC after 7 p.m., but you might allow them to continue until 9 p.m. on a Friday or Saturday night. Should there be a circumstance such as a school holiday, during which you could be more flexible on the times, overrides are also available.

When it comes to games, it's important to note that this system is not a catch-all for every game. It only really works with games provided through the Windows Store. You can choose the age of the child from a drop-down menu to choose what games they should be allowed to play on their PCs, see Figure 18-7.

Figure 18-7. *Game ratings are available for children*

Using the Credential Manager

Username and password management is crucial for any computer use these days, especially given the need for supersecure passwords, as I detailed at the beginning of this chapter. You can create superstrong, perhaps even completely random, passwords, but how can you manage them or remember them if you've forgotten one?

You might use a third-party password manager but these do have problems associated with them. The first, and probably the biggest, certainly when it comes to businesses, is that they almost always only manage Internet usernames and passwords. The second, however, is that because all your password information is stored with these services in the cloud, they are a target for hackers and criminal gangs. Indeed, in recent years we've seen data breaches from these services.

I'm a big fan of not using third-party software to replace something that's already part of Windows anyway, and the good news is that the Windows 10 *Credential Manager* (search for it in the Start Menu or Cortana) is a great tool for managing local, network, and Internet security.

It's separated into two parts, your Web Credentials and your Windows Credentials, see Figure 18-8. The former will keep a list of all your Internet usernames and passwords and synchronize them between Windows 10 devices (this includes PCs and smartphones) using a Microsoft account or another account type that supports syncing, such as a Domain. You will see a list of all the web sites and web services for which details are stored, and can display a password on entering your PC account password, or by using Windows Hello.

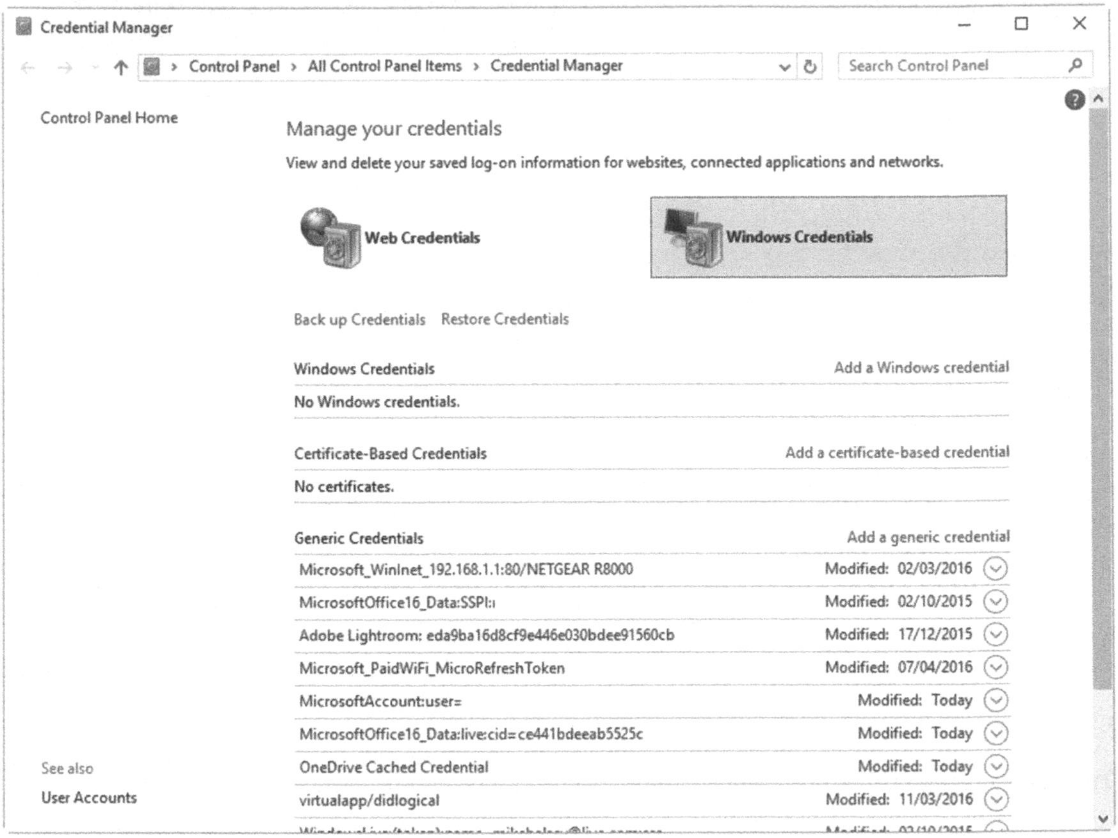

Figure 18-8. The Credential Manager allows you to store and retrieve passwords and usernames

When it comes to Windows Credentials, which include network sign-ins, these can be both backed up and restored from PCs, and credentials can be manually added by a user or administrator. It's also possible to add credentials that rely on a specific security certificate, and I'll show you how to manage security certificates later in this chapter.

Managing Encryption in Windows 10

There are three main types of encryption in Windows 10. These are the Encrypting File System (EFS), which is a file and folder-based encryption system; Bitlocker and Bitlocker To Go, which are full-volume (partition or disk) encryption systems; and the Full Disk Encryption system, which is an easier-to-manage version of Bitlocker, which is implemented on smartphones and consumer-grade tablets.

Each has its uses and I'll show you how to use and manage them shortly. Why would you want to use encryption, however? In both the personal and business space there are compelling reasons, especially given that we store much of our lives on our PCs these days. This doesn't include family, vacation, and personal photos and work or private documents, but our PCs do store, as I've just detailed, sign-in details for our shopping, banking, and other web sites.

In the business space it's even more important, as on our PCs we often carry commercially sensitive documentation, or client or customer data. Any data on anybody that you hold, be they customers, clients, or members of your own staff, will be subject to strict data protection regulations, the fines for breaches of which can be enough to put a small company out of business for good.

It's important then to choose the right type of encryption for your needs. Each one has its uses, but EFS and Bitlocker are both very different from one another.

■ **Caution**   Is any type of encryption completely secure? While EFS and Bitlocker provide extremely strong encryption for your files and data, it's true to say that no form of encryption is completely secure. As has been proven with high-profile cases involving the FBI and other security agencies, if somebody is truly determined to gain access to your data, it's likely they'll find a way to do it eventually. Also, many companies exist to recover data that has been lost, or is on damaged computers. This will include the ability to decrypt files and drives as and where necessary.

Why do I mention this? As customer and staff details are covered by data protection regulations around the world, should you operate in a high-security environment such as research, finance, or where large amounts of data on individuals are stored, it's always wise to minimize the surface for attack. This can involve laptops and tablets having on them only the data they *absolutely need* at any one time, or having all access to secure data provided only through an encrypted VPN.

Using the EFS

As I mentioned earlier in this section, the EFS is a file- and folder-based encryption system. Activating it creates a security key that can be transferred from one PC or user account to another, which means it does have an advantage over Bitlocker, where the disk or volume is encrypted, meaning that when files are copied into a nonencrypted space, such as another PC, or when attached to an e-mail, they will be decrypted.

EFS does need to be managed carefully, however, as this complete encryption can have its downsides. The first is that it is supported only on NTFS-formatted drives. This means that when transporting EFS-encrypted files you might find that their encryption becomes scrambled, and the files will become corrupt. When transporting encrypted files on an ExFAT or other Microsoft file system, you should be fine. I have encountered an issue with a third-party Network Attached Storage (NAS) drive, however, where its proprietary file system completely scrambled my backup of encrypted files, much to my own annoyance.

You can activate EFS on any file(s) or folders you have selected in File Explorer. Just right-click your selection and click *Properties* from the menu that appears. In the Properties dialog click the *Advanced* button in the Attributes section of the General tab, and a dialog will appear displaying a checkbox option to Encrypt contents to secure data, see Figure 18-9.

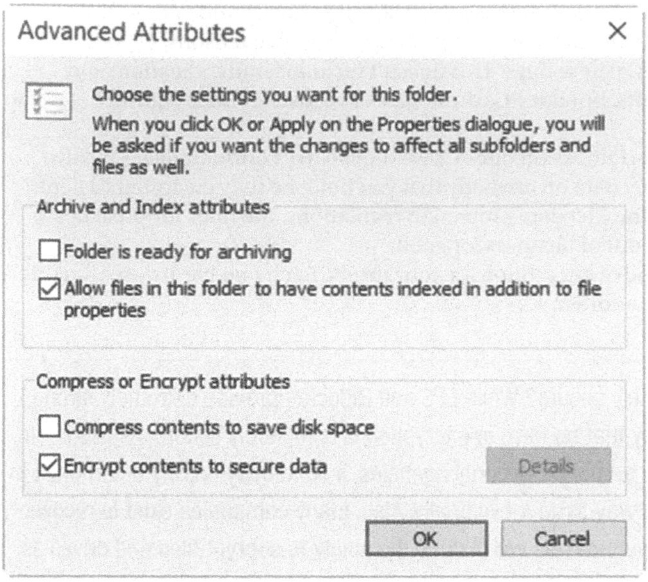

Figure 18-9. You encrypt files and folders in EFS with a checkbox option

Once the files/folders have been encrypted, a system tray alert will prompt you to back up your encryption key. Rather foolishly, it gives you the options to both do this later, or to not do it at all (why?). You really do need to back up your encryption key immediately... just in case either disaster strikes, or you get distracted by cat videos and forget.

You are asked where you want the encryption key to be stored. This should be a safe repository where it's out of reach of thieves (or is at least where they're not likely to look for it). The two places you should never store your EFS encryption key are on your Windows drive (because if disaster strikes and you need to reinstall Windows 10, you will lose it), and in a folder that's encrypted with EFS (because you could lose access to the key). In fact I'd go so far as to advise that you don't keep only one copy of the key, and don't keep it on the same physical hard disk as the encrypted files. A disk failure could mean that and backups made of those files could then be irrecoverable.

■ **Caution** Do not save your EFS Certificate to a folder that is encrypted by EFS, or you will be unable to decrypt the folder later as you will lose access to the key.

Should you at a later time need to create a backup copy of your encryption key (damn those cat videos), you can do this by searching for **encryption** in the Start Menu or Cortana, and selecting *Manage file encryption certificates* from the search results. This will display a wizard that will allow you to create backup copies of your certificate(s), see Figure 18-10.

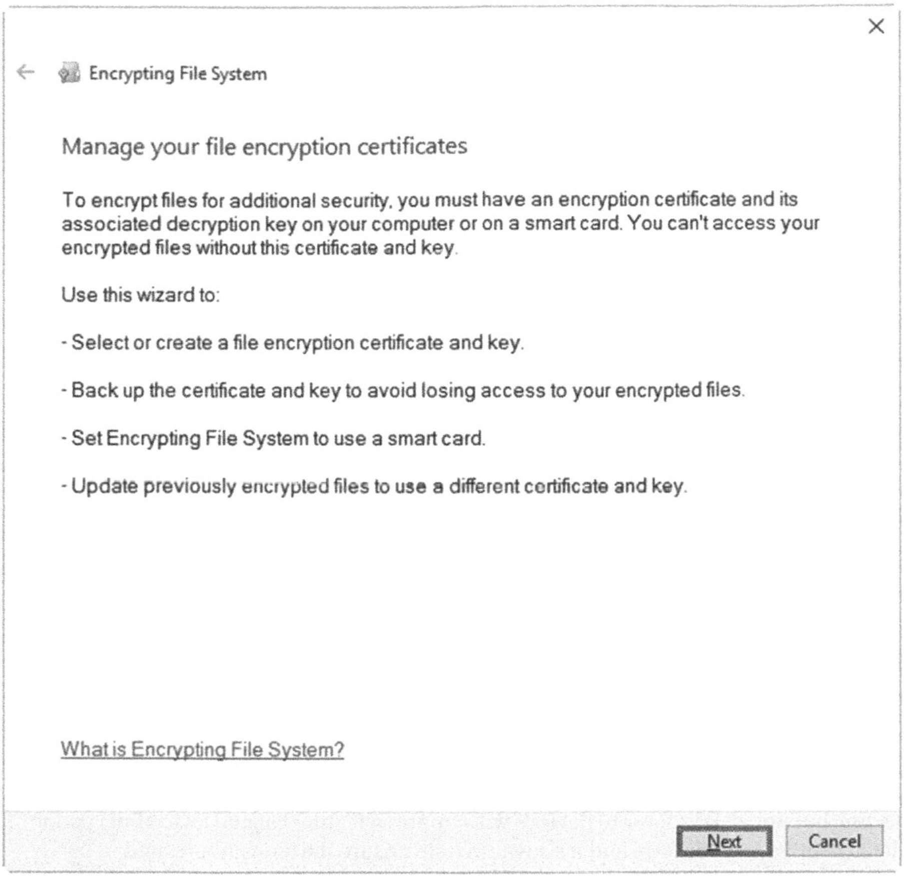

Figure 18-10. You can back up and restore EFS certificates

If you need to import your EFS certificate, perhaps because you've reinstalled Windows, or transferred encrypted files to a different user on the PC, or a different PC, you can double-click the certificate file to import it to the currently signed-in user account on the PC.

▓ **Note**   EFS certificates are locked to individual user acocunts. Should another user, with her own separate account on the PC, or on a different PC, need to access the files, she can import the certificate to her own account by double-clicking the key file.

Managing EFS Encryption with Cipher.exe

Windows 10 includes a command-line tool called *Cipher.exe*, which can be used to manage EFS encryption on PCs. It needs to be run from a *Command Prompt (Admin)* window and can be used with the following switches and syntax.

- /e encrypts files and folders in the format Cipher /e D:\Secret
- /d decrypts files and folders using the same syntax as /e

- /s tells EFS to encrypt or decrypt all subfolders as well, used in the format /s:D:\Secret

- /a performs the operation on ALL files and folders

- /f forces the operation on all files (use with care as it will also re-encrypt encrypted files)

- /q Quiet mode, does not report activity

- /h displays files with hidden or system variables, as these are not encrypted by default

- /k creates a new file encryption key

- /u updates the user's current encryption key

- /n prevents the user's current encryption key from being updated (again, use with care)

- /r:PathnameNoExtension creates a new recovery certificate and private key

- /w:Pathname deletes data from unused portions of a volume (can be used to wipe free space on a disk)

- /x[:PathName] PathNameNoExtension creates a backup of certificates and private keys for the currently signed-in user

Managing Device Encryption

Only the Pro and Enterprise versions of Windows 10 support the Bitlocker drive and volume encryption technology, which I'll detail in full, shortly. Microsoft mandated with Windows 8.1, however, that all devices with screens larger than 8 inches should be equipped with a TPM security chip.

This means that some but not all Windows 10 devices will support a feature called Device Encryption. This is effectively Bitlocker with a friendly face, and it's a way to help ensure that consumers, and nontechnical PC owners can carry tablets and laptops around with them, while keeping their personal and sensitive files and data protected.

■ **Caution**   Device Encryption will encrypt only the drive on which Windows 10 is installed. If you have partitioned your device, any additional volumes you create will not be encrypted by Device Encryption.

When I say that not all devices will come with Device Encryption, not every Windows 10 PC supports it. Typically, any device with a screen of between 8 and 11 inches that comes with both a TPM and supports Connected Standby will support Device Encryption. For devices with screens larger than this, Device Encryption will be unavailable.

■ **Caution**   It's worth noting that devices with screens of 11 inches or more, and that have Windows 10 Home installed, will not have Device Encryption available as an option in the Settings app. You will also not be able to encrypt these PCs with Bitlocker, as Bitlocker is supported only in the Pro and Enterprise editions of Windows 10. If you are purchasing a laptop or tablet with a screen of 11 inches or larger (10 inches to be on the safe side) and want to guarantee you can encrypt your drive, it's best to factor the upgrade to Windows 10 Pro into the cost of the device.

To activate Device Encryption, open the Settings app and navigate to *System*, and then to *About*. This will display, if your device supports it, a Device Encryption option, see Figure 18-11.

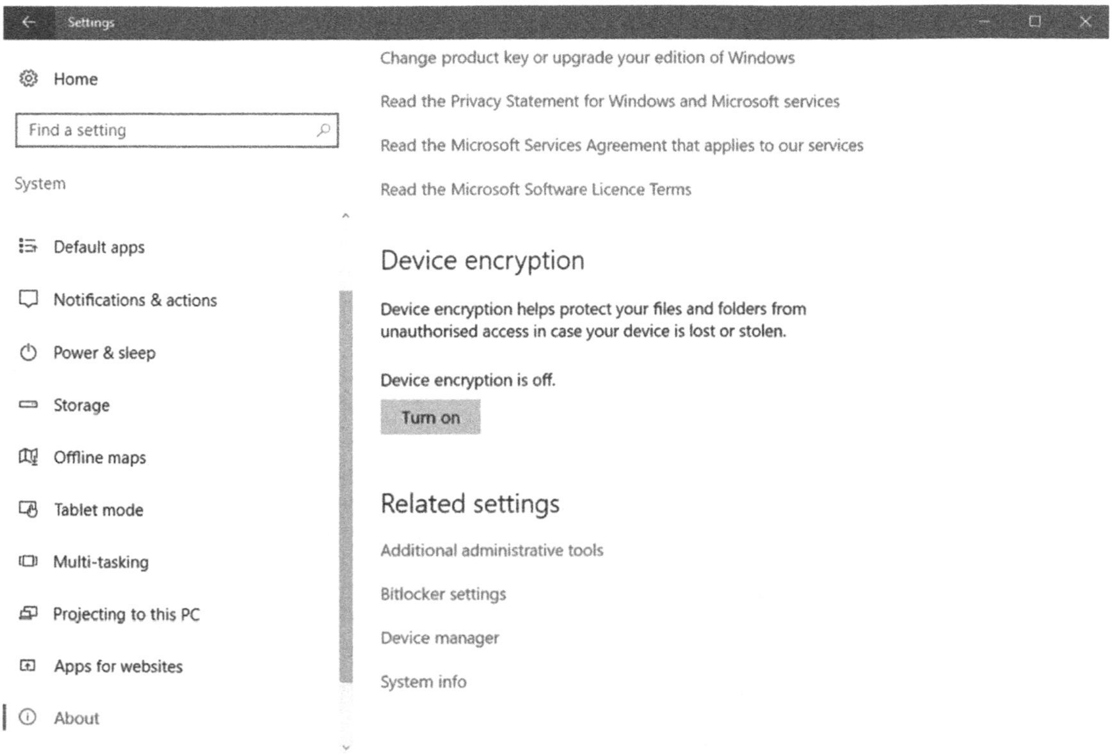

Figure 18-11. *You can manage Device Encryption in the Settings app*

So what happens with your decryption key, as it's all well and good encrypting your device, but if something goes wrong, such as the PC not starting properly, and all of a sudden you find yourself locked out and asked to enter your decryption key: where do you find it?

If you have signed into the device using a Microsoft account, you will find your Device Encryption key online at `https://onedrive.live.com/recoverykey`. I find it useful to keep a link to this in the browser on my smartphone, just in case. If you use Bitlocker with a company Domain, the recovery key is stored in Active Directory.

You can manually back up your encryption key, however, should you want a copy on a USB Flash Drive, or if you have signed into the PC using a local account. In the Start Menu or Cortana, search for **device encryption** and choose the option to *Back up your recovery key* when it appears. This will display a wizard that allows you to create a backup of the key.

■ **Caution**   Do not store the backup copy of your recovery key on a drive encrypted by Device Encryption or Bitlocker (or EFS for that matter), as you will be unable to recover the key later should you become locked out of the drive.

Encrypting Your PC with Bitlocker

On PCs running Windows 10 Pro or Enterprise, you will have an option to use the Bitlocker drive and volume encryption system to encrypt the contents of your PC. Bitlocker can be found in the Control Panel, and while it doesn't require that a TPM chip be installed on the PC, there are very compelling reasons to have one.

Bitlocker encrypts full disks and partitions on your PC. You can individually select which drives are encrypted, though you must have the partition on which Windows 10 installed encrypted if you want to encrypt any other drives, or have those drives auto-unlock when the PC starts. Before you start encrypting drives, however, you need to activate the TPM, as this is the chip on which Windows 10 stores its encryption keys. The TPM ensures that if a drive that's encrypted is removed from the PC, it cannot be decrypted. This is because the TPM is part of the motherboard on the PC and cannot be removed.[1]

Managing a TPM on Your PC and in Windows 10

The TPM chip on a PC must be activated in the BIOS or UEFI firmware. Should you want to use Bitlocker on your TPM-equipped PC, but you're receiving the message that a TPM chip isn't installed, it's because you need to go into the firmware on your PC and activate it.

You manage your TPM by opening the *Bitlocker* options in the Control Panel, or by searching for Bitlocker in the Start Menu or Cortana (it is also available by searching for **tpm.msc**). When the Bitlocker panel is open on your screen, click the TPM Administration link in the bottom left of the window.

The TPM Management screen is standard Microsoft Management Console fare with three vertical panels, see Figure 18-12. Here there are options in the right panel to prepare the TPM (basically to turn it on), turn it off, and more. If you prepare the TPM and begin using it to encrypt drives, an owner password is created automatically and stored in the chip itself. Should a problem arise and you find yourself locked out of a drive, you can use the *Reset TPM lockout* option to automatically reset your Bitlocker access permissions. You might want to set the password manually however (though there's no need to do so), and you can do this by selecting the *Change Owner Password* option.

---

[1]Some desktop PCs come with the TPM as a removable module, usually purchased separately from the motherboard itself. In these circumstances, the TPM can be moved to a different PC containing a compatible module slot (usually with a motherboard from the same manufacturer), and should unlock any encrypted drives that are moved with it once it has been enabled in the BIOS or UEFI firmware.

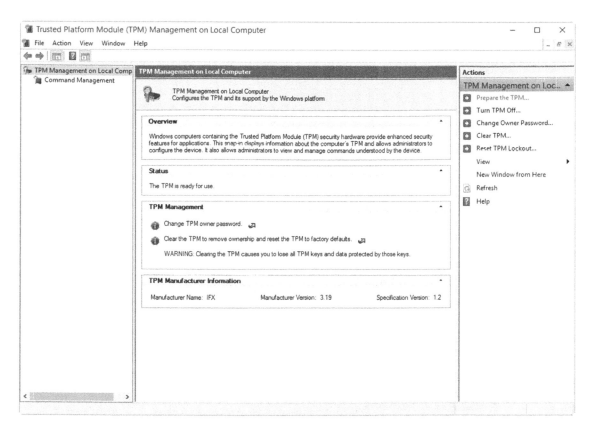

Figure 18-12. *You administer your TPM from within Windows 10*

The *Clear TPM* option can be useful if you are performing a full, clean reinstallation of Windows 10 and are not keeping any drives or partitions that have been encrypted with Bitlocker. This will delete any and all encryption keys from the TPM chip. These can build up over time as you encrypt, decrypt, and re-encrypt drives, and there's only a finite amount of storage available in the chip.

Using Bitlocker Without a TPM

It's possible to use Bitlocker on your PC without having a TPM chip installed, though I don't recommend it. Instead, you will need to have a USB Flash Drive that contains the Bitlocker key plugged into the PC every time the computer starts. While this might seem like a great way to ensure nobody can use the PC or access your data when you're away from it, a USB Flash Drive is not the same thing as a security smartcard.

The problem arises because a USB Flash Drive has a normal file system, like any drive on your PC, and this file system can become corrupt. With USB Flash Drives, an operation as simple as unplugging the drive from the PC while it's being read can cause a corruption, and as such, you really can't rely on a Flash Drive to remain stable for such a critical role as providing TPM access to a PC.

That said, should you *really* want to use Bitlocker on your PC without a TPM you can activate the option in the Group Policy editor (search for **gpedit** in the Start Menu or Cortana) and navigate to *Computer Configuration* ➤ *Administrative Templates* ➤ *Windows Components* ➤ *Bitlocker Drive Encryption* ➤ *Operating System Drives*, see Figure 18-13.

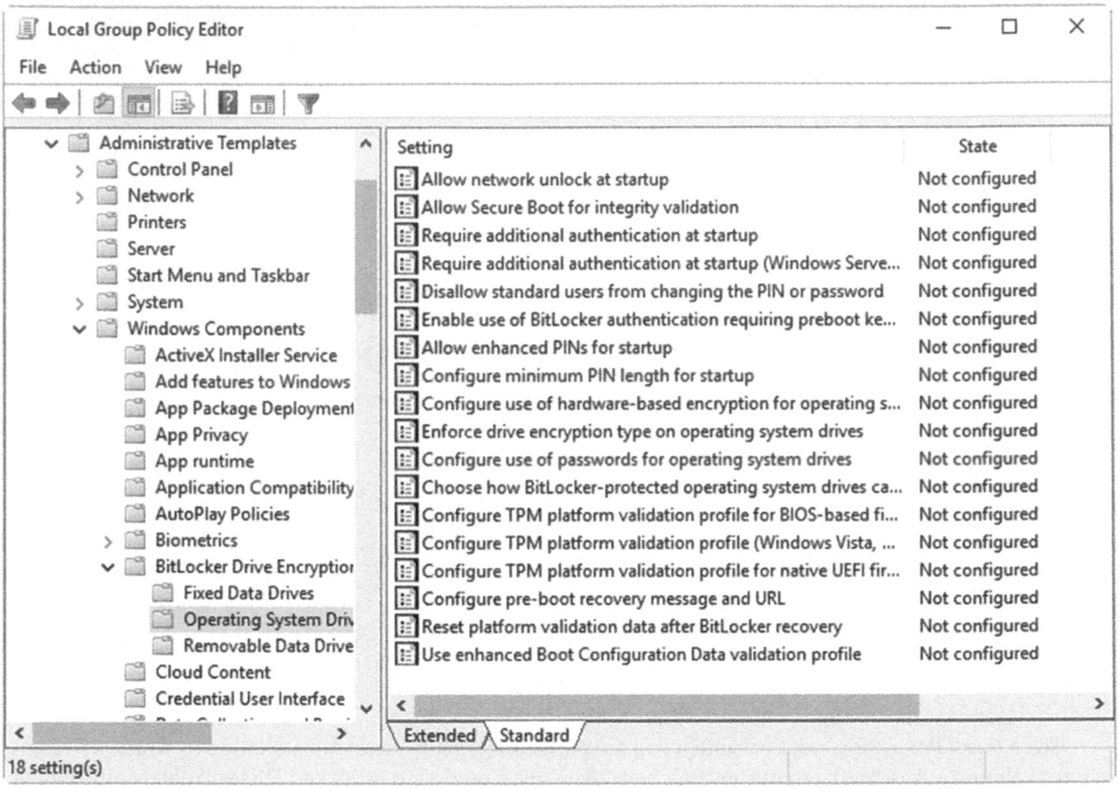

Figure 18-13. *You can configure the PC to use Bitlocker without a TPM in Group Policy*

Double-click the *Require additional authentication at Startup* option and enable the policy. You will be given a verbose description of what enabling the policy will do, and presented with a check box, which will already be checked, to require a startup key on a USB Flash Drive, see Figure 18-14. Once the policy is enabled, restart the PC to allow Bitlocker to be used without a TPM.

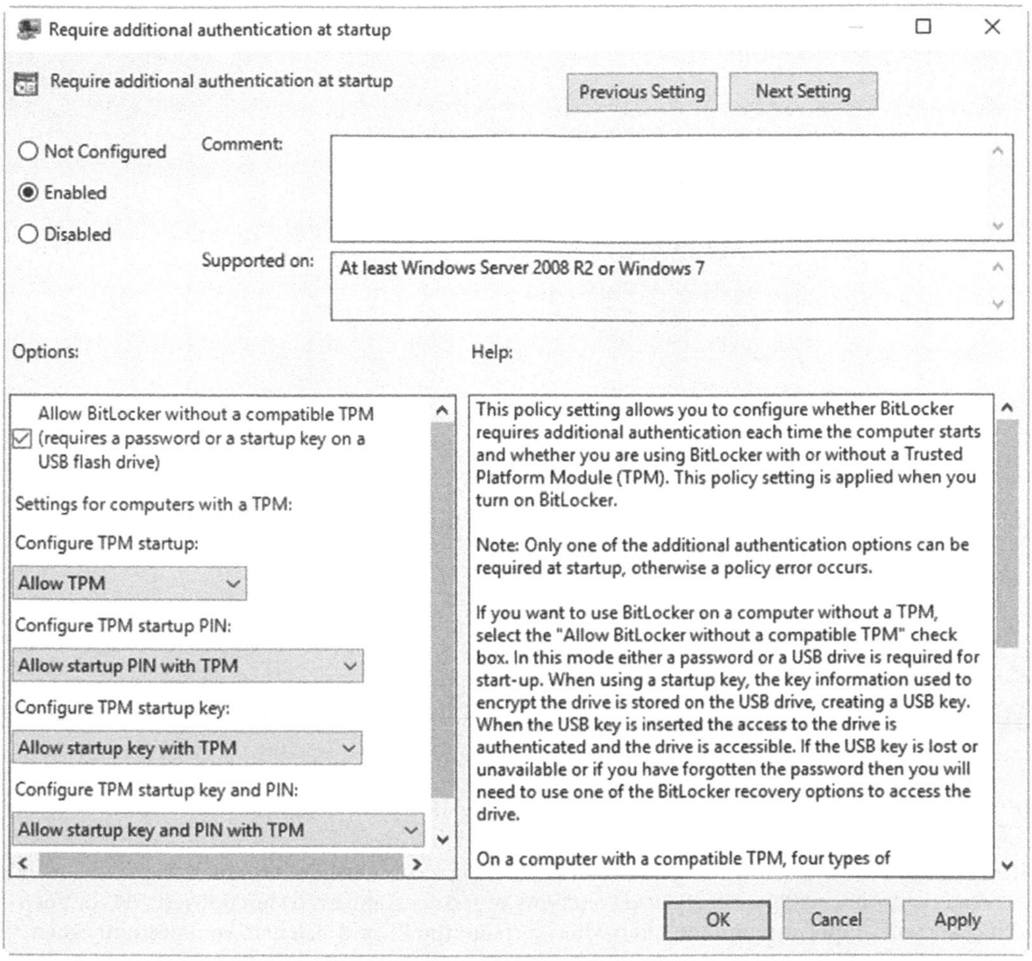

Figure 18-14. *The Group Policy editor will inform you what the policy change will do*

Managing Bitlocker Encryption on Your PC

You manage Bitlocker encryption from the main Bitlocker panel, accessible in the Control Panel, but also by searching for **Bitlocker** in the Start Menu or Cortana. You will see collapsible panels for each of your installed hard disks (and partitioned volumes), see Figure 18-15.

Expanding a drive's panel will present various options for managing Bitlocker on that particular drive. These include options for encrypting and re-encrypting the drive (fairly obviously), as well as creating a backup copy of your recovery key, adding a password or smartcard to unlock the drive, or activating or deactivating auto-unlock of the drive. You can also temporarily suspend protection, which can be useful if you are trying to undertake intentive file management tasks, while the system is encrypting your drive for the first time.

■ **Caution**   If you are updating the BIOS or UEFI firmware on your PC from the desktop, you should suspend Bitlocker protection. This is because on some firmware, Bitlocker will see what it thinks is "new" hardware and require input of your recovery key on the next restart.

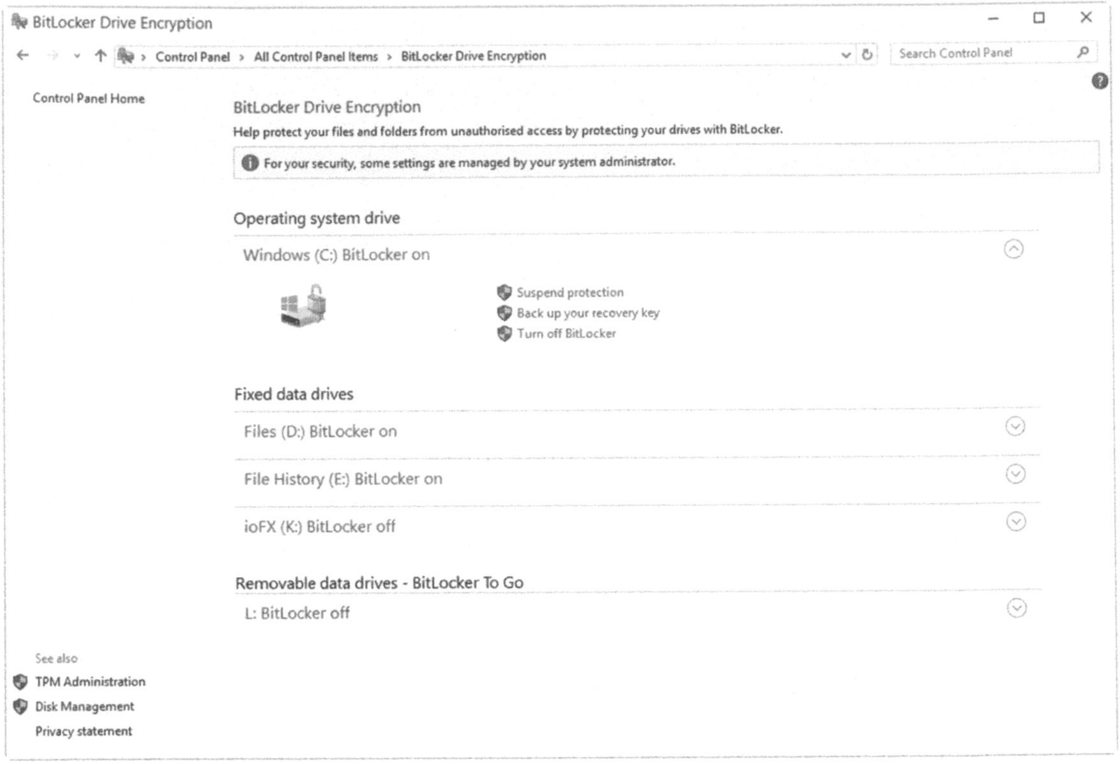

Figure 18-15. *The Bitlocker panel displays collapsible panels for all your disks and partitions*

That really is all there is to configuring Bitlocker, as it's designed as what I like to call a "fart-and-forget" system. You can carry on working while Bitlocker encrypts your drives, and even shut down the PC or put it to sleep. Bitlocker will simply resume encryption when you start the PC and sign in to your account again.

Managing Your Bitlocker Recovery Key

When you encrypt a drive using Bitlocker, you will be prompted to create a backup copy of your encryption key and, unlike EFS, the process simply won't progress until you've done so, see Figure 18-16. If you have signed into your PC using a Microsoft account, you will be prompted to save a copy of the recovery key directly to the cloud. This can be very useful should you find yourself locked out of the machine; simply point a browser on any device at `https://onedrive.live.com/recoverykey` and sign in to view the 48-character unlock code.

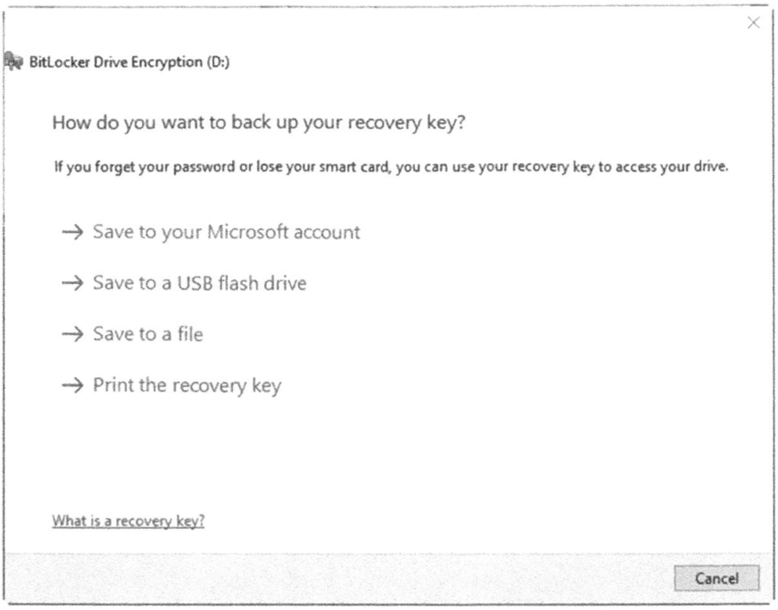

Figure 18-16. *You can back up your recovery key in various ways*

Additionally, there are options to save the recovery key to a USB Flash Drive (you'll need to plug one in at this point obviously), save it to a file, or print it. It should be noted that for your Windows 10 drive, the option to save the key to a USB Flash Drive doesn't appear. This is a little odd, but you can choose the *Save to a file* option instead, and merely point to an attached USB Flash Drive on the PC instead.

■ **Caution**   Do not store the backup copy of your Bitlocker recovery key on a drive encrypted by Device Encryption or Bitlocker (or a folder encrypted with EFS), as you will be unable to recover the key later should you become locked out of the drive. Also, if you choose to carry a USB Flash Drive with the recovery key with you when you travel, do not keep it in the same bag as your laptop or tablet, which will prevent them from being stolen together should a thief strike.

Using Bitlocker To Go

Bitlocker To Go is a tool that allows you to encrypt removable drives such as USB Flash Drives and external hard disks (and no, please don't encrypt the drive that contains your Bitlocker and EFS recovery keys, as that's just asking for trouble).

You can encrypt removable drives through the main Bitlocker panel, where they will appear listed below the hard disks and partitoins in your PC. One crucial difference is that the unlock key for a removable drive is never stored in the TPM (which also means you can use Bitlocker To Go on PCs that don't have a TPM). The reason for this is that the drives are, by their very definition, mobile, and can be used on any PC. Thus, the only options available when you encrypt a removable drive are either to set a password or to use a smartcard, see Figure 18-17. Additionally, you cannot set a drive encrypted with Bitlocker To Go to automatically unlock, as that would rather defeat the point of it being encrypted in the first place.

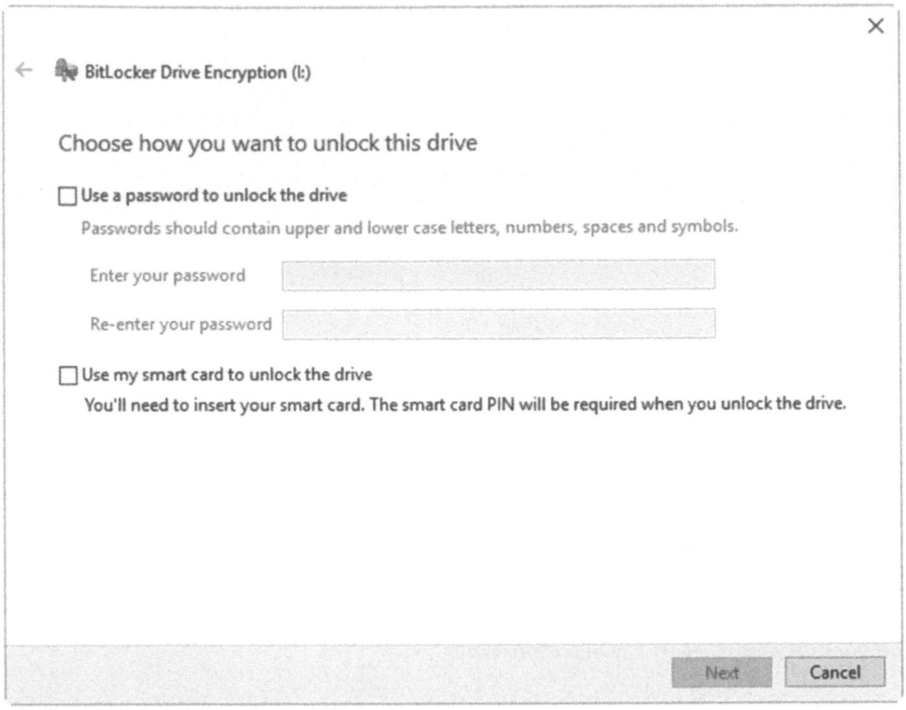

Figure 18-17. *Bitlocker To Go will not store the unlock code in your TPM*

■ **Tip** While we're on the subject of removable drives, there are two Group Policy options you can set in Windows 10 Pro or Enterprise that can significantly enhance the security of your systems. The first of these can be found in *Computer Configuration* ➤ *Administrative Templates* ➤ *Windows Components* ➤ *AutoPlay Policies*, where you can block USB and other removable media from automatically starting and opening files and apps when inserted into the PC. This is a common way for malware to spread, and so disabling AutoPlay can be a great boost to security.

You can also help guard against data theft. In *Computer Configuration* ➤ *Administrative Templates* ➤ *System* ➤ *Removable Storage Access*, you can block all manner of removable storage completey on the PC, including USB Flash Drives, CDs, DVDs and Blu-Ray disks, floppy drives, and more besides.

Summary

The encryption facilities in Windows 10 are both extensive and easy to use. They should, however, always be used with care, and some basic rules should be followed. The primary rule is always to make sure you have a backup copy of your recovery or encryption key. You should always make sure that you never store this key in a folder or on a drive that is, itself, encrypted, as you may not be able to recover it when you need to.

Encryption is a great way to prevent thieves and unwanted eyes from getting access to your files and data. This is in the same way that we use antivirus software to prevent the spread of malware to our PCs, a subject we'll be looking at in depth in the very next chapter, including how we can troubleshoot and remove malware after a PC has become infected.

■ ■ ■

CHAPTER 19

Malware and Viruses

Probably the worst fate to befall a PC is for it to become infected with malware. Long gone are the days when viruses were fairly innocuous things; the first one I got on a PC played "Yankee Doodle Dandy" to me every day at five o'clock. Nowadays viruses and malware exist to make money, real money, for the criminal gangs that create them. Why is this? Simply put, a few years ago, many criminals around the world discovered that, rather than rob banks and steal jewelry, they could make much more money sitting at home by infecting our computers.

Windows 10 includes some excellent security systems, such as SmartScreen, which can identify malicious files when downloaded from the Internet, and User Account Control (UAC), which can help defend against software that wants to be installed, or run as an administrator.

The weak point with our PCs, however, is the soft, squidgy thing that sits at the keyboard, and it's always the user who will be exploited. How will this happen? Malware will attempt to exploit both our natural tendency not to read things properly in our screens, and just click "Okay" anyway, but also the lack of technical knowledge that most PC users have.

How to Defend Against Malware

This does seem like an important place to begin, as it's always the user who is the point of entry for malware on a PC (unless the security on a PC is pretty nonexistent, it's extremely difficult for a PC to become infected any other way). If you are a systems administrator, it's very likely that you'll have your systems locked down. This will mean you will have up-to-date antivirus software installed, the apps installed on the PC, and your copy of Windows will always be kept patched and up to date, you won't have anything installed that could pose a security risk, and your users won't be administrators, so they won't be able to install malware themselves.

This, of course, is a rose-tinted view of the world, and while it might be the case in large corporations, it certainly isn't the case for many small businesses and almost every home user, where the PCs in use are much more likely to be individual, stand-alone units. It's crucial then, to educate PC users in how to identify possible malware attacks, so that they can be defended against.

Malware on PCs spreads in the following ways.

- App downloads from the Internet: these can appear as legitimate versions of the app you're really looking for, a cool new game, or perhaps a codec that's required to play video on a web site you've visited.

- Infected web sites that will encourage you to install a codec or plug-in that contains a malware payload. This is usually a web site that purports to offer something compelling or cool, such as a cartoonize yourself app, or the latest video of a naked celebrity.

© Mike Halsey 2016
M. Halsey, *Windows 10 Troubleshooting*, DOI 10.1007/978-1-4842-0925-7_19

- Some malware is injected into legitimate files, but that are hosted on web sites other than the original download source, such as a hardware driver hosted on a generic driver web site.

- Malware that's injected into legitimate web sites using vulnerabilities in the site code to permit changes to the site, which can include links to autodownload malware, or to display full-screen warnings that your PC is already infected and you have to download the fix that's offered.

- Macros in infected office documents, such as Word, Excel, and PowerPoint.

- Infected downloadable files from file-sharing (Torrent) web sites. These are commonly modified versions of existing files, such as pirated software.

- Viruses that are transferred from one PC to another, by sending themselves as a "Look at me" file via email, or by infecting USB Flash Drives or other removable media.

It's actually very easy to defend against malware on PCs, and you should make sure that the following three rules are included with any training you provide for people.

1. NEVER install or click Okay on anything unless you specifically set out to do so beforehand.

2. NEVER download anything unless you trust the source web site implicitly, or unless it's from an official Microsoft, Google, or Apple App Store.

3. NEVER perform any action on your PC simply because a web site asks you to do so.

So What Is This Malware Stuff Anyway?

Malware comes in many different forms these days, each with its own purpose, some of which is to affect your files and your PC, and some of which is to affect other systems.

- **Viruses** will affect the local PC and are increasingly rare, as their purpose is only to make it difficult to use the PC. This might include infecting the BIOS or UEFI firmware system so as to make the PC unbootable.

- **Back doors** will use your PC as a route into your network, to try to allow a hacker to steal sensitive data such as customer or staff details, or credit card details. They are also used for industrial and state-sponsored espionage.

- **Keyloggers** will record what you type on your keyboard and the web sites you visit, in order to try to harvest usernames and passwords for shopping or other sites where your credit card information is stored, or your online banking.

- **Trojans** are malware payloads that look, to all intents and purposes, like a perfectly legitimate file or app. They could even be the app installer or file you are looking for, but embedded within the code will be a malware payload.

- **Bots** are not to be confused with the chatbots released by companies such as Microsoft and Facebook, to make it easier to interact with companies online. This malware will use your Internet bandwidth to link your PC into a network of infected PCs that will collectively perform actions such as Distributed Denial of Service (DDOS) attacks on major companies' web sites and servers.

- **Rootkits** will attempt to inject themselves into the Windows 10 kernel and boot files, so as to bypass any security on the PC and load unfettered at startup. They then have full administrative access to the PC.

- **Macros** are malware programs that are embedded inside document types that permit code to be run, such as spreadsheets and other office documents.

- **Ransomware** is a particularly nasty form of malware that will encrypt any and all files found on your PC or network stores, demanding money for a decryption key, which will itself also contain malware.

Defending PCs Against Malware

Throughout this book, I'm detailing the security tools available in Windows 10 that can defend a PC against malware. I just want to run through them here though, to reiterate what each of the tools is, and why they're all important.

- **UAC** is the security subsystem in Windows 10. UAC will alert the user whenever he attempts to make a change to a PC that could affect other users on the system. Administrators will get an elevated OK/Cancel prompt, and standard users and children will be required to enter an Administrator password.

- **Windows Defender** is the free antivirus package that's included with Windows 10. It offers basic antivirus and anti-malware protection, though is not as fully featured as many third-party antivirus packages.

- **Windows Firewall** is actually a pretty good firewall defense and doesn't need to be replaced by a third-party firewall package.

- **Windows Advanced Firewall** offers configurable rules for apps, ports, and services, and is useful for people who need more control over their firewall, such as some businesses and gamers.

- **Windows SmartScreen** checks all files and apps downloaded from the Internet against white and black lists of known files held and maintained by Microsoft and many third-party security companies. If it detects a file known to contain malware it will block it, and it will alert you if it cannot recognize a file that might contain malicious code.

- **Secure Boot** is an Intel-designed system designed to prevent rootkits from gaining access to the boot system on your PC, and from infecting the motherboard firmware. It is incompatible with desktop operating systems except Windows 8.1 and Windows 10, and needs to be disabled on dual-boot systems running older versions of Windows and Linux. Not all PCs support Secure Boot. Any PC sold with Windows 8.1 and Windows 10 will support it, but older PCs may not, motherboards you purchase online may not, and PCs with the older BIOS firmware will not.

- **Windows Defender Advanced Threat Protection (ATP)** is a system released by Microsoft for corporations, as an optional extra for PCs, to analyze their networks for malware or other unwanted activity.

It's worth noting that each and every one of these security systems can be disabled. If you have a dual-boot PC, for example, running Windows 7 or Linux alongside Windows 10, Secure Boot will have to be disabled, as it would prevent those other operating systems from starting. UAC, Windows Defender, the Windows Firewall, and SmartScreen can all be disabled in Windows 10, though if you don't have installed alternatives, Defender and the Firewall will nag you to switch them back on. In fact, it's far too easy to disable some security features. SmartScreen, for example, is disabled through a simple on/off switch in the Edge browser that doesn't, in my own opinion, explain how important the feature is at all, see Figure 19-1.

Figure 19-1. *SmartScreen is all too easy to disable in the Edge browser*

It is for this reason that only users of a PC who actually MUST be administrators should be so, and every other user should be a standard user. The weak link in a PC's security will always be the soft, squidgy thing sitting at the keyboard. Criminals are extremely good at tricking people into clicking and authorizing things they shouldn't, or to entering secure details on a web site that's fake, but even with this being the case, having lax security can let a hacker or malware into your system everywhere from a coffee shop to a secure office.

Defending Your Files Against Ransomware

Ransomware is a very different beast from malware, and in many ways it's considerably more dangerous should your PC(s) become infected. Ransomware will encrypt all of your files and documents, and then damand a ransom (the clue was in the name) for the decryption key. This key is itself likely to be loaded with more malware and so the cycle will continue.

The ransom demanded for the unlock code for your files is usually several hundred dollars, and although it's known that many people, including businesses, do pay the ransom, it's also something that many other people, and especially small businesses, simply wouldn't be able to afford.

So how do you protect your PCs from ransomware? It might seem that the obvious way is to keep your files and documents that are normally stored in your Shell User Folders (Documents, Pictures, Music, and Video) in a different location on your hard disk. This does make them slightly more awkward to access, but crucially it offers no guarantee of protection, as ransomware is highly likely to scan your whole hard disk, and all other available storage, and encrypt every known document type it finds.

The trick to defending your files against ransomware is incremental backups. We used to create these all the time, perhaps once a month onto a few CDs or DVDs, or once a week through backup software onto an external hard disk. These days, with Windows features such as File History, and cloud services like Dropbox, Google Drive, and OneDrive, we've gotten used to instantaneous sync. The problem this creates is that every time a file changes (such as being encrypted), it will be reuploaded to your cloud storage.

Some cloud systems such as LiveDrive, which I use myself as a secondary cloud backup, will allow you to set a sync schedule. LiveDrive will only allow a maximum of every 48 hours, though it's possible that in the case of a ransomware infection you'll need longer than this. For this reason, I strongly suggest using dedicated backup software with an external USB hard disk. The backup can be set to run all the time, or on a schedule of up to a week or two (meaning you'd only ever lose one or two weeks' worth of file updates). The advantage though is that you can physically unplug the hard disk from your system, meaning that no malware or ransomware can get to it. This is opposed to network-attached USB hard disks and Network Attached Storage (NAS) drives, which will be viewable through your PC all the time and thus also viewable by the ransomware.

Versioning support, which is offered by File History and other backup systems and services, can also be very useful, as it allows you to roll back to previous versions of (i.e., nonencrypted) files. Where this falls down is that the people who create ransomware know this too, so versioning does not create a guarantee of file security. Only a segregated backup strategy is any guarantee that if you are infected by ransomeware, and need to completely wipe and reimage the PC, you can recover all of your files.

Manually Removing Malware from a PC

Sometimes you will need manual, file access to a PC to remove malware. This is because the "fix" might come in the form of detailed instructions from a security web site (please only use the web sites from the big security providers such as Symantec and Kaspersky for this). In this case, how do you get that file access without having the malware run automatically? Well, there are various options available to you for this.

Using Safe Mode and Diagnostic Mode

Malware, once it gets its hooks into your PC, can be extremely difficult to remove. It buries itself in the Windows services that are automatically loaded at the PCs startup, or within the OS kernel itself. Malware will commonly run a series of codependent services on the PC. This means that when you shut one down, other malware services will recognize that it's no longer running and automatically restart it. Anti-malware software can shut down all the offending services simultaneously, but this requires the malware to be identified by your antivirus software.

Should you need to remove malware manually, it can be extremely tricky, but is still possible. Some malware is relatively straightforward to remove, and can be done from within Safe Mode or Diagnostic Mode in Windows 10. Safe Mode and Diagnostic Mode (also known as Diagnostic Startup) are similar, but also very different from one another.

Starting Your PC in Safe Mode

You may already be familiar with Safe Mode. This is a reduced functionality mode in which only essential Windows services, and no third-party services or apps are loaded. There are various ways to get to Safe Mode in Windows 10. If you restart your PC while holding down the Shift key, the system will restart into the Recovery options menu. Once here, click *Troubleshoot*, then *Advanced options*, then *Startup Settings*. This will restart the PC and present a version of the legacy Windows boot menu, see Figure 19-2.

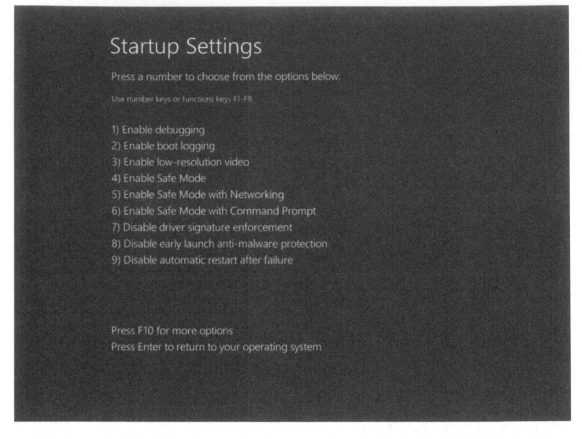

Figure 19-2. The Startup settings menu allows you to invoke Safe Mode

There are three Safe Mode options at this menu. *Safe Mode, Safe Mode with Networking*, and *Safe Mode with Command Prompt*. Safe Mode is the default option. This will load the basic, essential Windows services only with a desktop interface and basic graphics, but with all networking features disabled. Choosing this option can be useful when removing malware, as you are isolating the machine, and not allowing the malware to see other PCs or devices on your network or to gain access to the Internet.

Safe Mode with Networking will also boot the minimal Windows services, but will also load the networking drivers, giving the PC both local network and Internet access. You can use this if you do not have another PC on which to download a malware removal tool, and where the download of the tool is blocked by the malware on the regular desktop.

Safe Mode with Command Prompt starts Windows 10 in a Command Prompt–only environment, with no desktop interface. If you are proficient with command-line tools and utilities and prefer to work in this way, it is a good option for troubleshooting and malware removal.

The other way to invoke Safe Mode is through the System Configuration panel. You can best access this by searching for **msconfig** at the Start Menu or in Cortana. This displays a utility from where, in Windows 7 and earlier, you managed the startup apps on your PC (a process that's since been moved to the Task Manager). It's also from where you can invoke Safe Mode and Diagnostic Startup.

■ **Caution**   When you activate Safe Mode or Diagnostic Startup using MSConfig, the PC will then **always** start in that mode, until you open MSConfig again and select the *Normal startup* option.

Safe Mode can be invoked from the *Boot* tab, see Figure 19-3. There are various options available to you that mirror those available from the Recovery Environment menu.

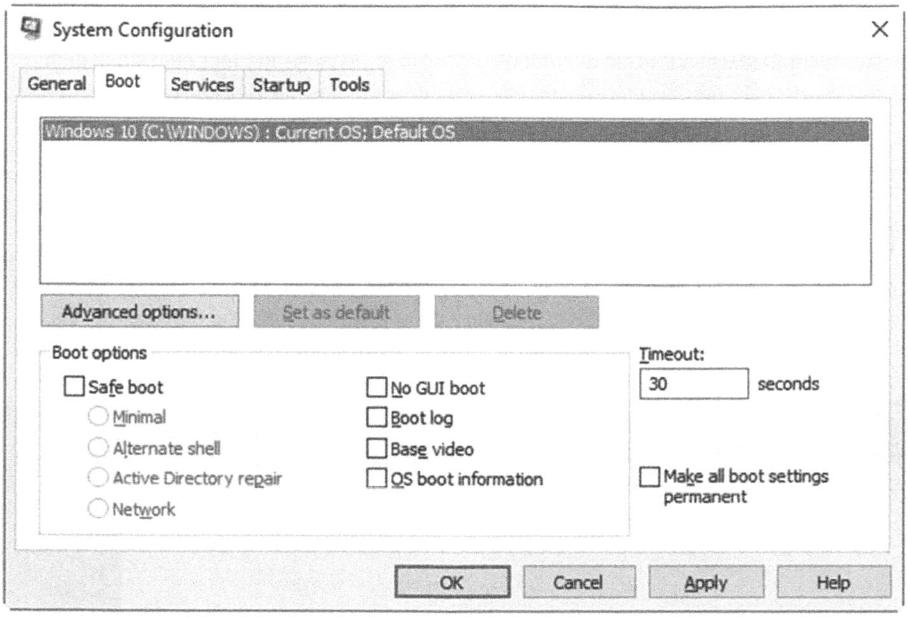

Figure 19-3. You can start Safe Mode from MSConfig

- **Safe boot - Minimal** will start the PC in the standard Safe Mode, with no networking support.

- **Safe boot - Alternate shell** will start the PC with a Command Prompt–only interface.

- **Safe boot - Active Directory repair** is an additional option that will also load the Active Directory services, in addition to networking services.

- **Safe boot - Network** loads the OS in Safe Mode with networking services also loaded.

Additionally, there are four check box options also available.

- **No GUI boot** will load the OS without displaying the the Windows loading screen. This can be used when you are troubleshooting display problems.

- **Boot log** saves a log of what starts and is loaded to the file C:\Windows\Ntblog.txt.

- **Base video** forces Safe Mode to use only the standard VGA video drivers that come with Windows. This can be useful for troubleshooting display driver issues.

- **OS boot information** can be used in conjunction with the No GUI boot option. It will display a list onscreen of services and Windows components that are loaded and run, as they are invoked. You may be familiar with Safe Mode displaying this information by default in versions up to Windows XP.

■ **Note**   You may have noticed a check box to *Make all boot settings permanent*. This isn't because you're paranoid enough to always want to start your PC in Safe Mode. It's instead because the four check box items I detailed, from No GUI boot to OS boot information, can be invoked independently of Safe Mode. Checking the Make all boot settings permanent option will write these to the boot system for your OS.

Starting Your PC in Diagnostic Mode

Diagnostic Mode is different from Safe Mode in that it's not quite as limiting. In Safe Mode, nothing except the base services and drivers are loaded when the OS starts. This leaves you with (possibly) no networking, very limited graphical functionality and, crucially, with some of the Control Panel applets disabled, see Figure 19-4.

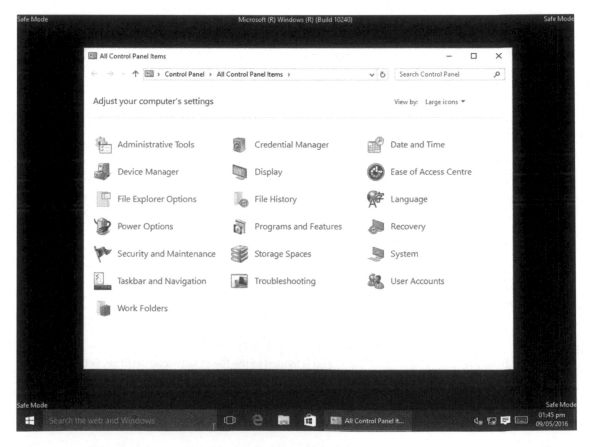

Figure 19-4. *Not all Control Panel applets are available in Safe Mode*

You may find this limiting and might, for example, need to access a feature such as the Windows Firewall when manually removing malware from the PC. For this you can use Diagnostic Startup. This is different from Safe Mode in that more is loaded when the PC starts, including the full Control Panel. The startup items include the graphics drivers, so you have a full desktop experience. It will mean, however, that some Windows or third-party services are loaded (your graphics subsystem will likely be a third-party service) that would not be loaded in Safe Mode, and these might be infected.

You can invoke Diagnostic Startup from **MSConfig**, by choosing its option under the *General* tab, see Figure 19-5. Again, remember that when you want the PC to return to normal startup, you will need to open MSConfig again, and check the *Normal startup* option.

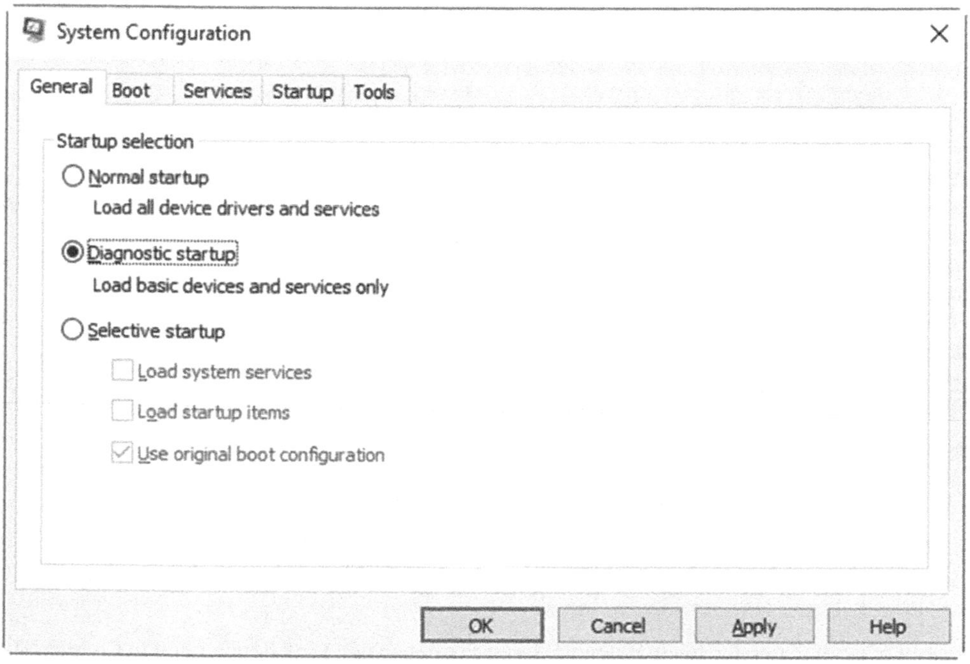

Figure 19-5. *You invoke Diagnostic Mode startup from MSConfig*

Checking Loaded Services in Safe or Diagnostic Mode

Once you have started your PC into Safe or Diagnostic Mode, you can use the MSConfig tool to check which services have been loaded, and which ones are set to load when the PC starts normally from the *Services* tab, see Figure 19-6.

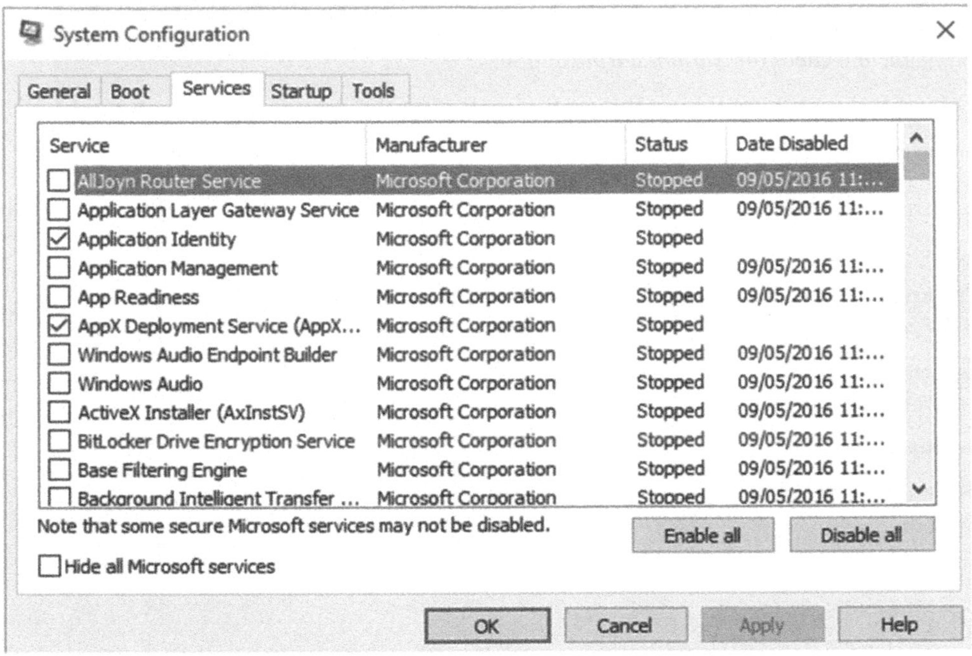

Figure 19-6. *You can manage malware services in Safe and Diagnostic Modes*

This can be much better than referring to the main Service panel, which I will detail in full in Chapter 21. In the MSConfig panel, only the services that are set to load at normal startup are included. There is also a helpful *Hide all Microsoft services* check box, which will change the view to only display third-party services. Note however it may be a Microsoft Service that has become infected.

Using the Registry Editor to Remove Malware

If you have malware on your PC, then it will certainly have embedded itself in the Windows Registry. I will show you how to use the Registry Editor in depth in Chapter 26, but it can be run by searching for **regedit** in the Start Menu or Cortana. You can also run the Registry Editor from the Command Prompt when you start the PC into the Recovery Environment, or from a Recovery Drive.

All Registry manipulation should be undertaken with great care, which is why there is an entire chapter to this book devoted to the subject. I do strongly urge you to read Chapter 26 before undertaking modifications to the Windows Registry, as making the wrong change can cause the PC to be unbootable.

Using a Portable OS to Manually Remove Malware

While Safe Mode and Diagnostic mode can be useful and effective ways of removing malware, most malware enbeds itself so deeply into the Windows OS that you'd never get rid of it completely if the core Windows kernel files are loaded at all. Under these circumstances, it used to be common for people to remove the hard disk from a PC, plug into a different PC, and remove the virus then while the hard disk was effectively dormant. This method should be used when you have to follow detailed instructions to remove malware manually from a PC.

■ **Note**   Booting your PC from a portable OS will not allow access to any disks or partitions that are encrypted with Bitlocker.

This was fine when most PCs were big towers, or laptops with removable hard disks. Nowadays, though, with ultrabooks and tablets that have nonremovable storage, this method simply isn't possible. It can be replicated, though, by booting the PC from a portable OS. This could be a downloadable disk Image (ISO) file of a Linux distro, such as Ubuntu or Mint. You can download a Linux distro on a noninfected PC and burn it to a CD or USB Flash Drive. Starting the infected PC from this will provide file access to the hard disks on the infected machine.

If you have access to a Windows To Go USB drive, you can start the PC using that and, although you would never normally have access to the host PCs hard disk(s) when using Windows To Go, you can assign drive letters in the Disk Management Console. To do this, open the Disk Management console from the *Win+X* administration menu, then right-click the drive you need to access, and select *Change Drive Letter and Paths* from the menu that appears, see Figure 19-7. Choose an available drive letter, and the drive will then appear in File Explorer.

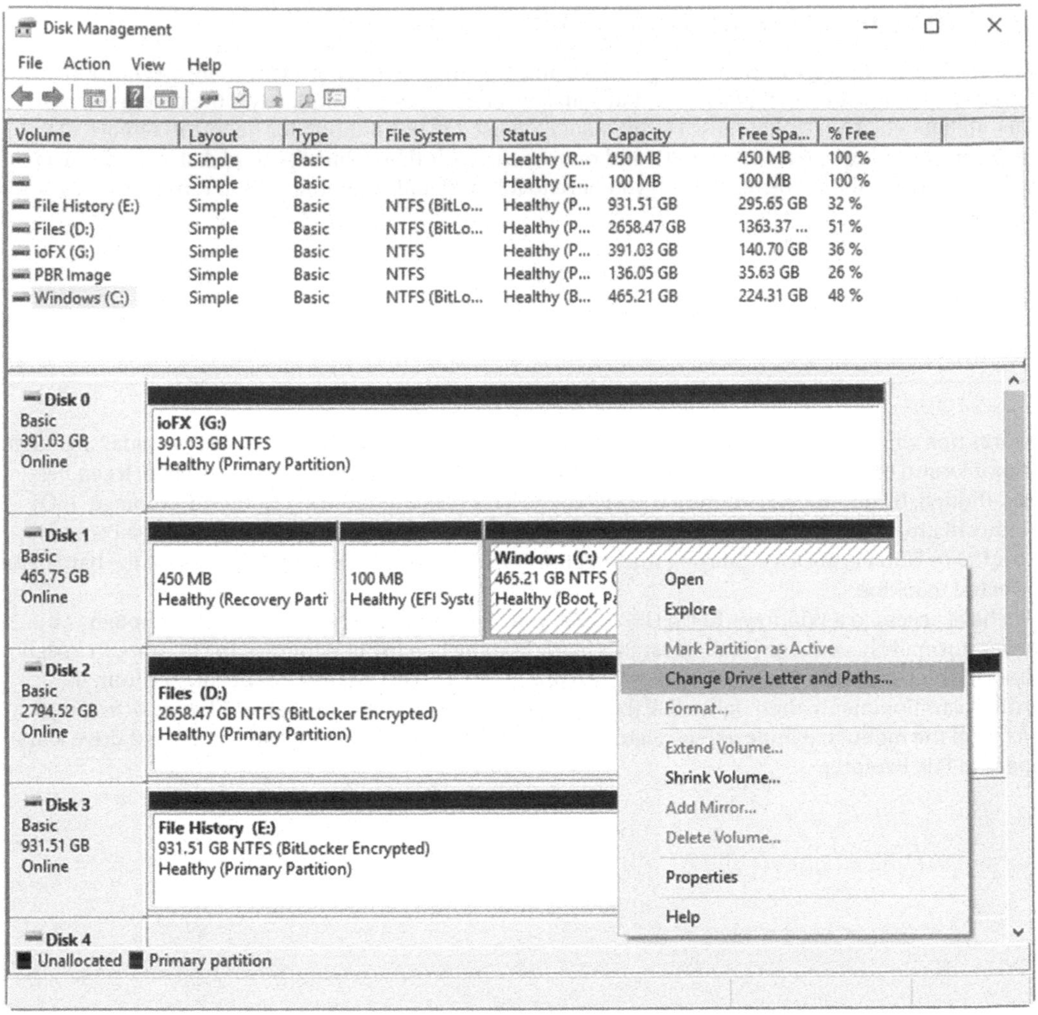

Figure 19-7. Assigning driver letters to disks in the Disk Management Console

Using Third-Party Tools to Remove Malware

By far the best and most recommended way to remove malware from a PC, when your installed antivirus software can't do the job on its own, is to use a third-party tool. There are plenty to choose from, and here I'll detail some of the very best and why you can trust them to do the job.

It's important to note that these tools need to be up to date, so you should always download (from a noninfected PC) the most current and up-to-date version of the tool before using it. This is because the malware your PC is infected with might be new, and the removal utility will only be built into the latest versions of these tools.

Microsoft DaRT

If you are in a business using the Enterprise edition of Windows 10, or if you have an MSDN account, you will have access to Microsoft's Diagnostics and Recovery Toolset (DaRT). This allows you to create recovery media for a PC that includes the following tools.

- **Computer Management console** is the same as on the host Windows 10 PC and allows you to view that PC's event logs, scheduled tasks, local users and user groups, device drivers, autorunning applications, and both Microsoft and third-party services.

- **Crash Analyzer** helps you determine the cause of crashed on the host PC, by examining the contents of the crash memory dump file(s), and having them interpreted for you.

- **Defender** is an offline version of the Windows Defender antivirus package. This can be used to scan a PC for malware, and remove it safely without the malware becoming active.

- **Disk Commander** provides tools to help you repair and recover corrupt disks and partitions.

- **Disk Wipe** can be used to delete all data from a hard disk, when you need to wipe a disk completely to eradicate a virus infection, before a reimage.

- **Explorer** is a full version of File Explorer that lets you examine and manipulate the files on the host PC. This can be used when you need to manually remove files as part of malware removal.

- **File Restore** is a file "undeletion" tool to help you recover files that were deleted accidentally, or that were too large for the PC's Recycle Bin.

- **File Search** is a general-purpose search tool for locating specific files or file types on the host PC.

- **Hotfix Uninstall** can be used to remove Windows Updates that can be causing the PC to become unstable.

- **Locksmith** lets you change and manage user account passwords for any account on the PC. This can be used if malware has locked you out of your own, or the Administrator account.

- **Registry Editor** allows you to access the Registry on the host PC and manually remove any keys placed there by malware.

- **SFC Scan**, the System File Repair Wizard, checks all the Windows OS files on the host PC to determine if any have been changed or have become corrupt. It can then be used with up-to-date installation media to replace any modified or damaged files with the proper ones.

- **Solution Wizard** is a tool that can be used if you are not sure which of the DaRT tools is best to fix your specific problem. It asks a series of questions and will suggest the best way to fix your problem.

- **TCP/IP Config** can be used to manipulate the network settings on the host PC, so that you can access local network resources or the Internet to apply fixes.

Windows Defender Offline

Windows Defender Offline is, and I know how surprised you will be to hear this, a version of Windows Defender that can be run offline. You can doanload it on a clean PC and use it to create a bootable CD, DVD, or USB Flash Drive which can scan your PC for and remove malware.

`http://windows.microsoft.com/ windows/what-is-windows-defender-offline`

■ **Note**   You can also perform an offline scan of the PC using Windows Defender by selecting *Scan Offline* in the *Update & security* ➤ *Windows Defender* section of the settings app.

ESET Online (and Offline) Scanner

Several companies, including some of those listed in this section, provide online scanners that can scan your PC for viruses through your web browser. ESET provides a scanner that can also be downloaded to use on your PC as well. This can be useful if you suspect your current antivirus software has missed a virus.

`http://www.eset.com/us/online-scanner/`

Norton Bootable Recovery Tool

Many of the following tools all fall into broadly the same category as Windows Defender Offline. Norton is the same in that it allows you to create a bootable DVD or USB Flash Drive that can be used to scan for and remove malware.

`https://security.symantec.com/nbrt/nbrt.aspx`

Sophos Bootable Antivirus

By this point, you might have guessed that the choice of which tool you download and use depends on your personal preference for antivirus vendor. It also needs to work, and not all of these tools will be up to date with the very newest viruses, however. The Sophos tool can only be used to create a bootable CD or DVD, and so it is less suitable for ultrabooks and tablets.

`https://www.sophos.com/en-us/support/knowledgebase/52011.aspx`

Kaspersky Rescue Disk

Kaspersky Rescue Disk is designed to create a bootable CD or DVD from which to remove malware, though instructions do exist on the web site for how you can create a bootable USB Flash Drive.

`https://support.kaspersky.com/viruses/rescuedisk`

Kaspersky Ransomware Decryptor

A suite of free utilities that, while they can't defend against ransomware, will help you remove ransomware from an already infected PC, and decrypt any files the ransomware has encrypted. You can download it at

`https://noransom.kaspersky.com`

AVG Bootkit Remover

The AVG Bootkit Remover is a tool that you download to an infected PC to scan for malware. If an infection is found, the tool will ask you to restart the PC so that removal and cleanup can take place.

http://www.avg.com/au-en/remove-win32-bootkit.tpl-stdfull

F-Secure Rescue CD

Can be used to create a bootable CD or DVD from which you can scan for and remove malware.

https://www.f-secure.com/en/web/labs_global/rescue-cd

Trend Micro Rescue Disk

This is another third-party tool that can be used to create a bootable CD, DVD, or USB Flash drive for scanning for and removing malware on a PC.

https://origin-www.trendsecure.com/Info/Rescue_Disk/html/download.html

McAfee Free Tools

Security firm McAfee provides a selection of free security tools, which you can find at http://www.mcafee.com/uk/downloads/free-tools and which include the following tools.

- **GetSusp** will scan for undetected malware on a PC, and can be used if you suspect you may have undetected malware on a PC.

- **Real Protect** can be used to detect suspicious activity on a PC, such as an attack or access for a hacker.

- **RootkitRemover** is a stand-alone utility for detecting and removing complex rootkit attacks.

- **Stinger** is used to remove a specific list of supported viruses and is updated regularly with the latest and most common virus definitions.

D7II

If money is no object, then subscribing to an annual licence for D7II can pay dividends. It's a complex suite to use, and should not be used unless you're proficient in maintaining and configuring PCs, but it includes a powerful anti-malware suite that includes tools from Kaspersky, Bitdefender, Sophos, McAfee, and more.

https://www.foolishit.com/d7ii/

RKill

RKill can be used to terminate the running processes that malware is using to keep itself active on a PC. This can be useful if your standard antivirus software is unable to clean the infection. Run RKill first to stop the offending processes, then use your existing antivirus software to clean the infection as per normal.

http://www.bleepingcomputer.com/download/rkill/

Junkware/Adware Removal Tools

Sometimes you can have software on your PC called junkware or adware. This isn't actually a virus, but it can be really annoying and slow down your PC. Several companies provide free software for removing junkware including

- Malwarebytes **Junkware Removal Tool**, https://www.malwarebytes.org/junkwareremovaltool
- Adlice **RogueKiller**, http://www.adlice.com/software/roguekiller/
- Xplode **AdwCleaner**, available by searching online

Microsoft SysInternals Suite

Several packages in Microsoft's excellent SysInternals Suite can be used to detect and remove malware from a PC, including AutoRuns, Process Explorer, and Rootkit Revealer. I will detail these and other SysInternal tools in full in Chapter 22.

Researching Virus Removal Online

Earlier in this chapter I wrote about how you can use Windows utilities such as the Safe and Diagnostic modes, or a portable OS, to manually remove viruses and other malware from a PC. This will be necessary if the tools I've detailed in the preceding section can't remove malware from your system. You need to be very careful when removing viruses manually, as you will need to access both the Windows Registry and the Services panel, and disabling or changing the wrong thing can cause your PC to become unstable or unresponsive.

How do you go about finding the information you need to rmeove a virus manually in the first place, though? This can be tricky as the Internet is a vast resource full of people who think they're experts in everything, but who most certainly are not. When researching a virus, it'll be because one of two things has happened. Either your antivirus software has identified a virus, and given you its name, but can't remove it. Alternatively, it could be because you know someone else who has recently had a virus called "X" which now also appears to be on your PC as well. Suffice to say, it'll always be because you already know what the malware is called.

Generally speaking, stick to the list of vendors I've listed here, companies such as Microsoft, Symantec, Sophos, McAfee, Bitdefender, and the like. They will often post manual removal instructions for malware should it be necessary, perhaps because they've not been able to update their own tools yet. DO NOT trust any other source unless you can be absolutely certain of its credibility.

When it comes to your local PC repair shop (be they a sole trader or a national company), in all the years I've worked in IT, I have almost NEVER heard of any of these types of vendor removing malware correctly. The normal response is to wipe the PC, probably losing some of your files in the process, and maybe even charging you for a new Windows licence for the reinstall. Find a techie friend or colleague if you're not certain, and use the tools I've listed in this chapter.

Summary

Virus and malware infection is a problem, a big one. Knowing what tools are available to help you remove malware is the most important step, however, and how you can manually remove any remaining files associated with the malware is a very useful skill to aquire. Armed with the information in this chapter (some of which will inevitably change over time, as some packages are changed), you can be a great IT support person.

One useful way to reduce the risks involved with malware infection is to always run your PC in a virtualized environment. In the next chapter, we'll look at exactly this: How you can use the Virtualization client that comes in the Pro and Enterprise editions of Windows 10 to run virtual machines that you can both access from your desktop and start your PC from.

CHAPTER 20

■ ■ ■

Using Virtualization to Protect PCs

Much of the work involved in troubleshooting and repairing PCs comes in the form of either finding quick solutions to problems, or to finding ways to mitigate problems entirely. Virtualization, which is the process of running an operating system and apps inside a software container, actually provides ways to achieve both of these aims, and in Windows 10, it also offers some compelling ways for IT departments to be able to quickly adapt to changing workflows.

Microsoft's Virtualization client is called Hyper-V, and it comes preinstalled in the Pro and Enterprise editions of Windows 10. You might find that it's hidden from view and unobtainable from the Start Menu, however, in which case you'll need to enable it. To do this, open the *Win + X* administration menu, and click *Programs and Features*. Next, in the window that appears, click the *Turn Windows features on or off* link.

This will display an options dialog in which you may see that the check box next to Hyper-V is unchecked, see Figure 20-1. Check the box to enable the Hyper-V Virtualization client.

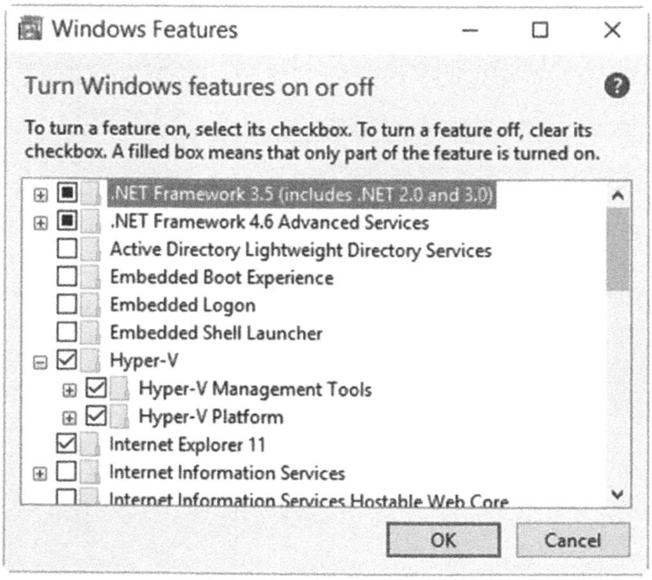

Figure 20-1. *You might need to enable Hyper-V in Windows 10*

© Mike Halsey 2016

M. Halsey, *Windows 10 Troubleshooting*, DOI 10.1007/978-1-4842-0925-7_20

So what is it that Hyper-V can do for me, I hear you ask. Virtualization has many different uses. App developers, for example, might have several Virtual Machines (VMs) open on their desktop, each running a different version of the Windows OS, so they can test their app in all the different OS versions, without needing multiple PCs. System administrators might use a VM of the standard company Windows installtion, in which they can test new updates, patches, and apps for stability and security.

When it comes to troubleshooting, however, there are several uses for VMs. These include being able to create a quick restore system, in which a PC can boot into a VM, or having a system where, using VMs, a PC can quickly be repurposed for different tasks. Perhaps most useful, however, is that Virtualization can be used to completely sandbox older operating system versions, such as Windows XP, that are completely out of support, but that might still be required for mission-critical tasks in the workplace.

Creating and Managing VMs in Hyper-V

VMs in Windows 10 are created, added, and managed in the Hyper-V Manager; search for this in the Start Menu or Cortana. This is standard Microsoft Management Console fare, with a panel on the left where the master systems (in this case, your PC) are listed, a panel on the right containing context-sensitive menu options, and a central panel with information about any VMs that have been created or imported, see Figure 20-2.

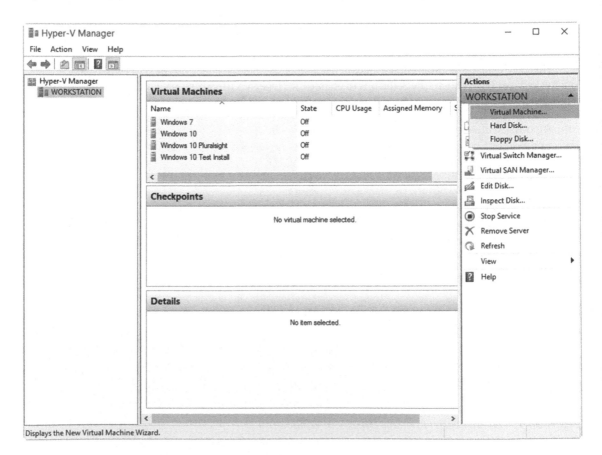

Figure 20-2. *The Hyper-V Manager in Windows 10*

You can create or import a VM (you may have one that's been created for you) by clicking the *New...
Virtual Machine* or *Import Virtual Machine* links in the top of the right panel. This will run through a wizard
that will ask how you want to set up your VM, with questions such as its storage location and more.

I want to deal with some of the more important questions that arise in this wizard interface. The first
of these is which *generation* of VM you wish to create, see Figure 20-3. If you need to create a VM running
Windows XP, for example, you won't be able to use the newer Generation 2–type VM. This is because the
Generation 2 type, which offers additional functionality such as UEFI support, Secure Boot, Boot from a SCSI
Virtual Hard Disk (VHD), and faster boot and operation times, also requires a 64-bit OS. The 64-bit version
of Windows XP was short-lived and poorly supported.

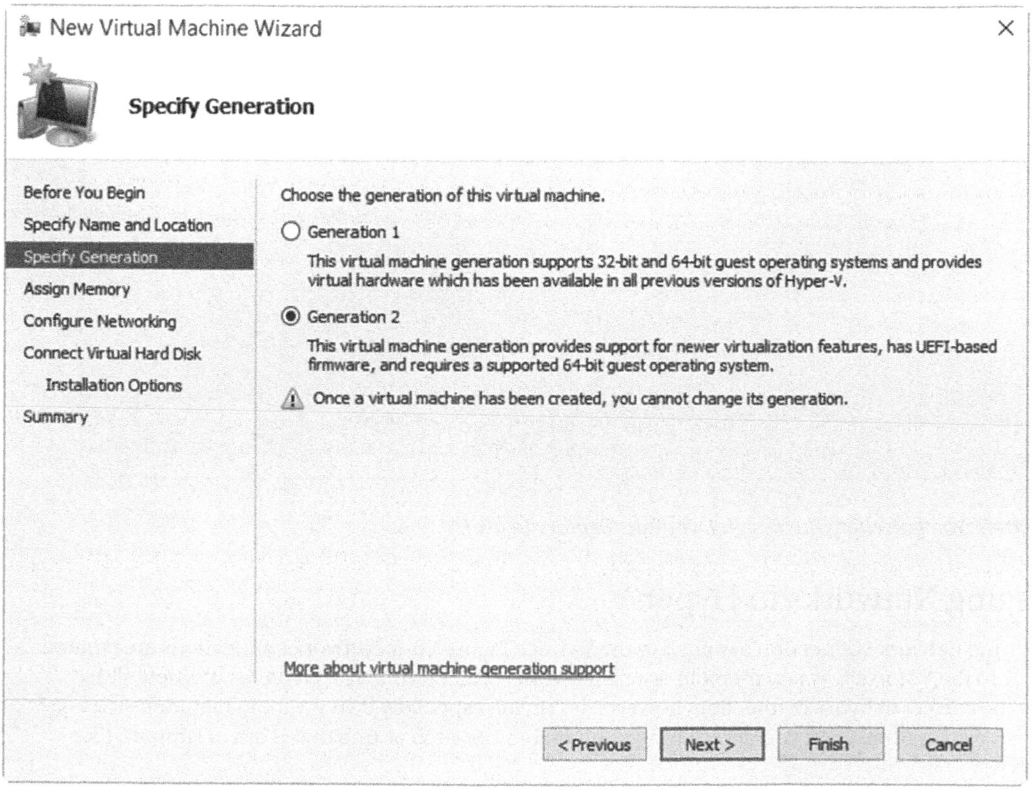

Figure 20-3. You can choose from different generations of VM type

The next option is how much memory to assign to the VM, and whether to use Dynamic Memory, see
Figure 20-4. When a VM starts, it will consume all of the memory you give it. This is memory shared with the
host OS on the PC, and you might only have so much you want to spare. Hyper-V's Dynamic Memory feature
allows the host OS to reclaim unused memory when the VM isn't using it. This can help improve the overall
performance of the host PC, especially if it is running multiple VMs.

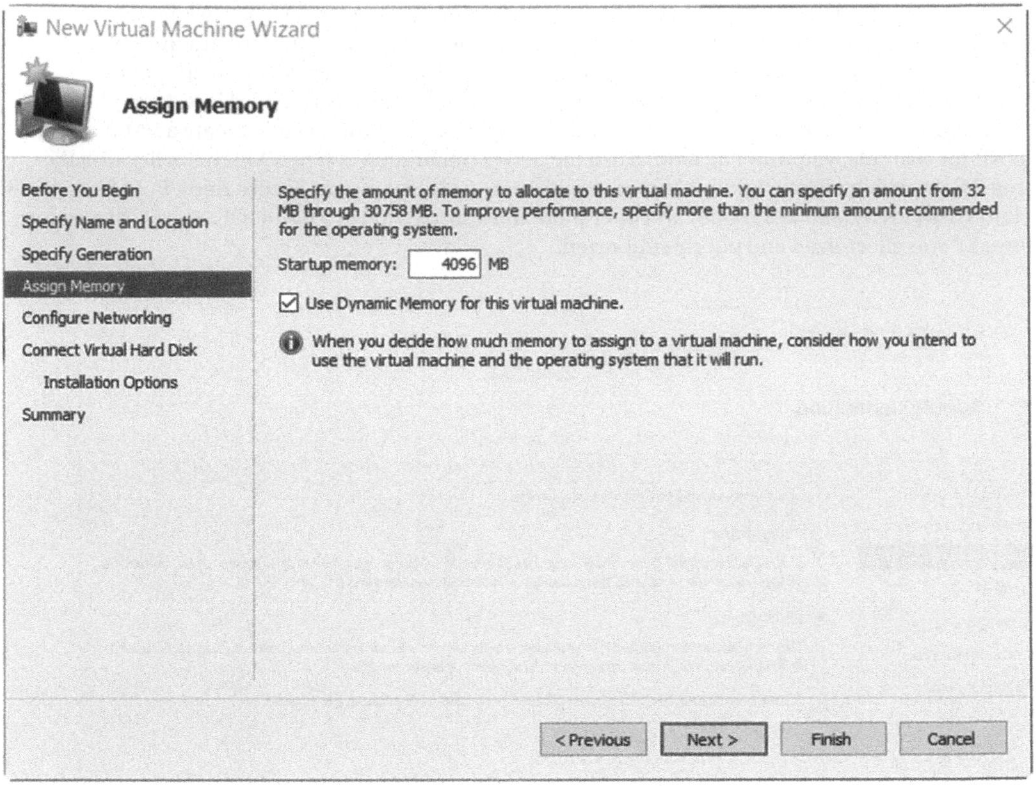

Figure 20-4. *You can choose to assign Dynamic Memory to a VM*

Managing Networks in Hyper-V

Next up is the network connection assigned to the VM, see Figure 20-5. Network connections are created separately to the VM itself, as you might have one network connection that's shared by multiple VMs. Creating the correct network connection, however, is crucial, especially if you want to maintain strict security on your systems, or if you are running a vulnerable OS, such as one that is out of support, like Windows XP.

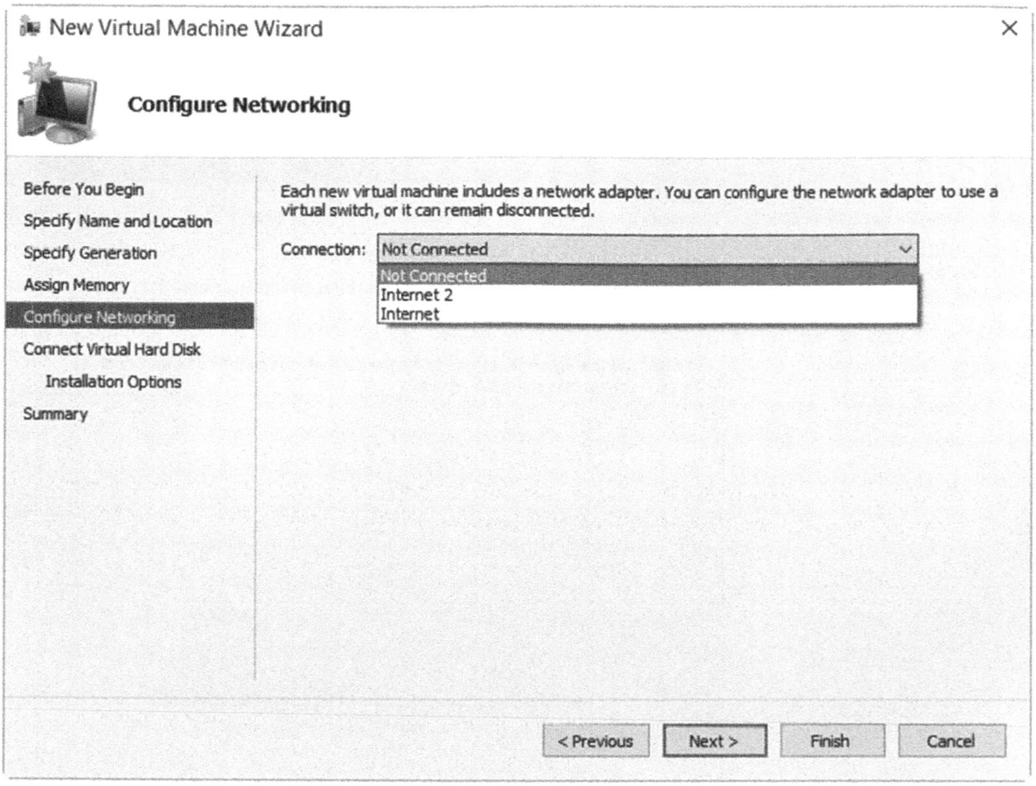

Figure 20-5. *You can assign different network types to VMs*

There are three different network connection types that you can create within Hyper-V, see Figure 20-6, and it's extremely important to maintaining good security that you choose the correct one.

- **External** networks can see everything that your physical network adapter can. This includes other machines and devices on the network, but also it means they can get full access to the Internet, if your PC also has Internet access.

- **Internal** networks are ones that are constrained to the host PC and the VMs that run on it. This means that the VM will be able to see all other locally running VMs, and also the storage resources on the local PC.

- **Private** networks are to be used if you really do need to sandbox a VM, as they provide the best security. A VM connected to a private network will only be able to see other VMs runing on the PC, and nothing else.

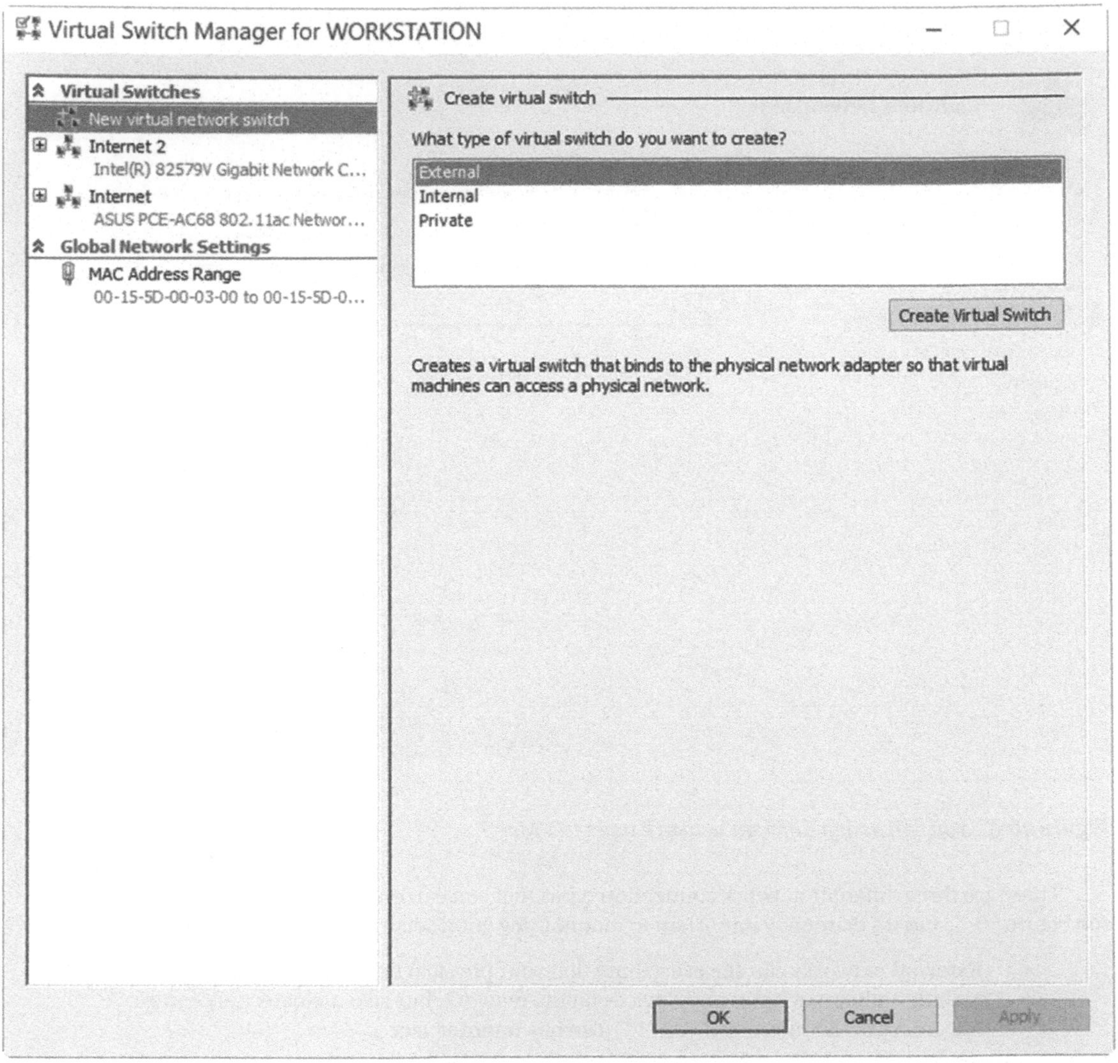

Figure 20-6. *There are three different types of network connection you can create*

■ **Tip** If you have more than one physical network adapter in your PC, perhaps two gigabit Ethernet, or Ethernet and WiFi, you can connect the Virtual Switch to the adapter you're not using for your own Internet access. This will give the VM access to PCs and VMs connected to that second network, which you can isolate for its own purposes, for instance, to create a secure network of PCs internally in your company.

That said, there's nothing to say that a VM has to be connected to a network at all. By far the best way to sandbox a VM is to not have it connected to a Virtual Network at all. You may find that the legacy app(s) you need to run on the VM don't require Internet access. It may be a payroll system where all the data is stored locally, for example, and where there is no need for any type of network connection. You can disable the network connection at any time however, which enables you to fully update and secure the VM before isolating it from the Internet and/or your network.

Creating Backups of VMs in Hyper-V

One very useful feature of Hyper-V is the ability to create checkpoints for VMs. These work like System Restore on your PC, in that they are a snapshot of the state of that VM, at the time to checkpoint was created. They can be used to test different scenarios in the VM because you can safely roll back the changes using the checkpoint afterward, if the change has resulted in an unexpected or unwanted result.

You can create and manage checkpoints in the central panel in the Hyper-V manager by selecting the appropriate VM, whereby checkpoint options will appear in the bottom right of the window, see Figure 20-7.

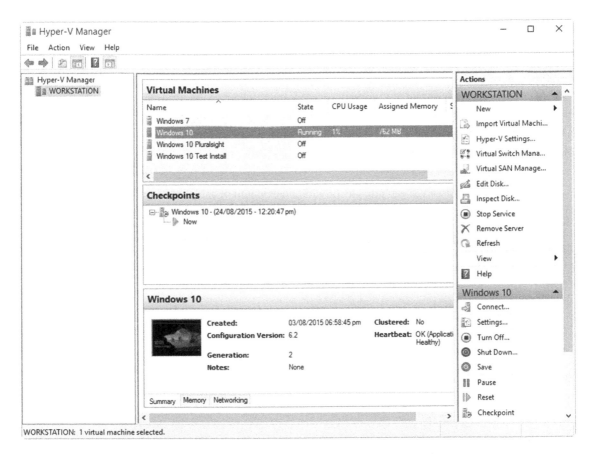

Figure 20-7. *You can create checkpoints so you can test changes to VMs*

■ **Tip** Selecting a VM in the Hyper-V Management window will present an Export option in the bottom right of the window. You can use this to create a backup copy of the VM, so that it can also be used on other PCs, or so that it can be easily copied back to the PC should there be a problem with the VM later.

Booting and Repurposing Your PC from a VM

At the beginning of this chapter, I said that you can make PCs more robust through the use of VMs. One of the methods for doing this is to boot your PC from a VM. When you do this using a VM created in Hyper-V you won't even know you're not using the host operating system, as the VM will have full access to the PCs hardware, and will run quickly and effectively.

There are several advantages to booting a PC into a VM. The first is that, from a system administrator's point of view, you will always have a working, safe, secure underlying OS that you can start the PC into if something goes wrong with the VM. Repairing the VM for the user can then become a simple task of copying a fresh copy of the VM from across your company network (you may even store VM images on the PC itself). This can be significantly faster than reimaging a PC, and has the only drawback that you may need more than one product licence for the copy of Windows on the PC.

■ **Note**   Each operating system and software package you install into a VM needs to have its own license, and if necessary for that product, its own product key. Some versions of Windows are not licensed for use inside a VM. You can find out more about licensing for your particular copies of Windows and other Microsoft software at www.microsoft.com/About/Legal/IntellectualProperty/UseTerms.

Booting your PC from a VM can provide the additional benefit of being able to quickly repurpose the machine. Let's say, for example, you are a business with a limited amount of laptops, and you need take one that's been used by a sales representative and repurpose it, so that a designer can use it instead.

Rather than having to place a base Windows image onto the laptop, and then sideload all of the apps that a designer in your company needs, you can create a VM in advance that has this preconfigured. This is pretty much the same as creating multiple installation images of Windows 10 for your company, but VMs can be easier to manage and configure.

Creating a VHD

To boot your PC from a VM you will need a VHD, and while you can create this when you install Windows, you can also create it in advance. You do this from the *Disk Management Console* (available from the *Win+X* menu). From the *Action* menu, click the *Create VHD* option, see Figure 20-8.

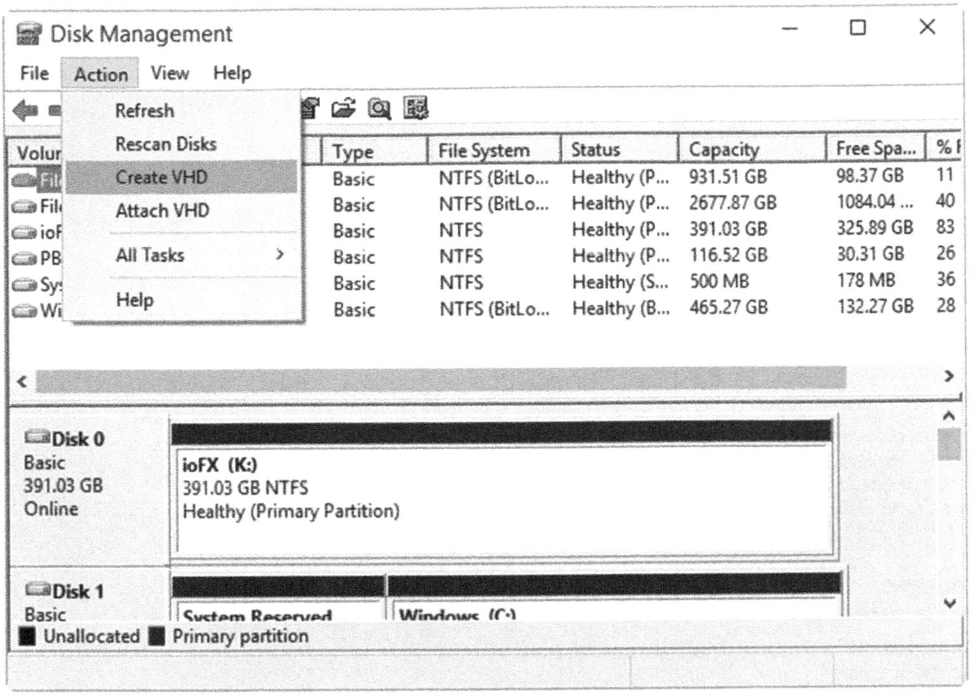

Figure 20-8. You can create VHD from the Disk Management Console

In the dialog that appears you need to choose a storage location for the VHD, the type of VHD container you want to use (both types are described well), and if the VHD is to be a fixed size or if it should expand dymnamically, see Figure 20-9. The latter option should be kept as fixed, because once you boot the PC from the VHD, it won't be able to expand dynamically anyway, as it won't be managed by the host OS.

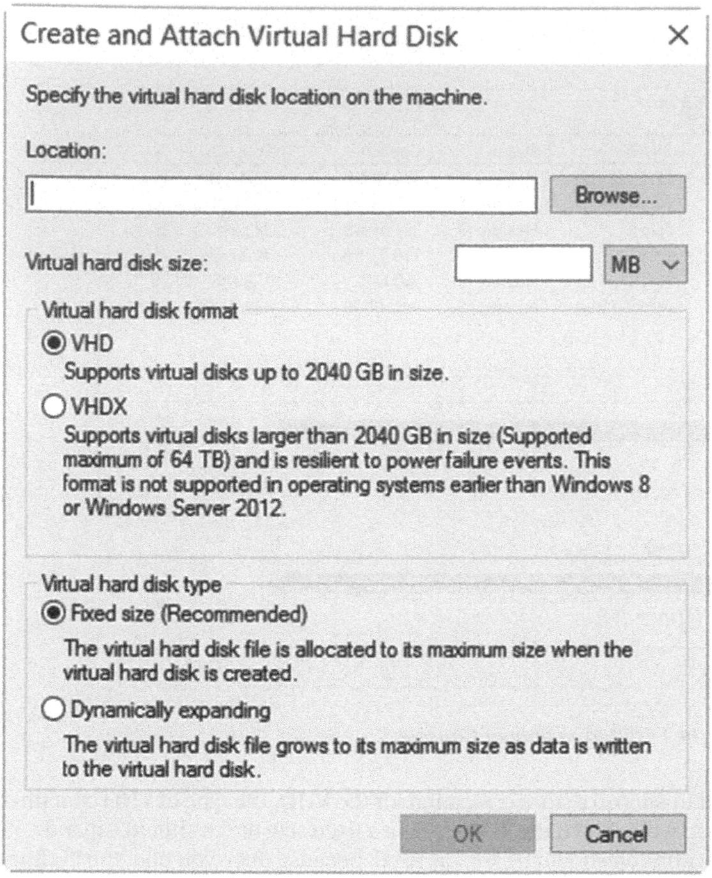

Figure 20-9. You need to choose parameters for the VHD

■ **Tip** You can also create VHDs in Hyper-V by using the *New* ➤ *VHD* option in the top right of the window.

Adding a VHD to the Boot Menu

To boot the PC from the VM, so that you can install an operating system into it, start your PC using your Windows installation media (DVD or USB Flash Drive).

1. Press **Shift+F10** at the installation screen to open a Command window.

2. Type **diskpart** and press Enter.

3. To use an existing VHD, type **Select vdisk file=C:\Path1\Path2\disk.vhd**, substituting the path and disk names for the location on the disk of the VHD and its name.

4. If you don't have an existing VHD and need to create one, type **Create vdisk file=C:\Path1\Path2\disk.vhd maximum=20000 type=fixed**, again substituting the path and disk names with where you want the VHD to be created and what you want it to be called (the path folders must already exist). Also, substitute the number of megabytes and create either a fixed or a dynamic disk.

5. If you have just created a new VHD, type **Select vdisk file=C:\Path1\Path2\disk.vhd** and press Enter to attach the VHD if you have just created one, as per step 2.

6. Type **attach vdisk** and press Enter.

7. Type **exit** and press Enter.

8. Type **exit** again and press Enter.

9. Click **Install Custom: Install Windows Only (Advanced)**.

10. Locate the newly attached VHD in the hard disk pane in which you want to install Windows. This is Disk 1 if you have only one hard disk in your computer. You can identify it by its size. Click **Next** when you are ready to install Windows onto the VHD.

The next step is to add the VHD to the PC's boot menu.

1. Press **Win+X** to open the Administration menu.

2. Click **Command Prompt** (Admin).

3. Type **bcdedit /v** in the Command window.

4. Press Enter.

5. Locate the VHD you installed and make a note of its globally unique identifier (GUID) code. It is a long string of numbers and letters in the Identifier section for the OS (see Figure 20-10).

```
■ Administrator: Command Prompt                                              —    □    ×

Microsoft Windows [Version 10.0.10240]
(c) 2015 Microsoft Corporation. All rights reserved.

C:\Windows\system32>bcdedit /v

Windows Boot Manager
--------------------
identifier              {9dea862c-5cdd-4e70-acc1-f32b344d4795}
device                  partition=\Device\HarddiskVolume3
description             Windows Boot Manager
locale                  en-GB
inherit                 {7ea2e1ac-2e61-4728-aaa3-896d9d0a9f0e}
fverecoveryurl          http://windows.microsoft.com/recoverykey
default                 {c3b6c6d7-3772-11e5-9319-9639c7488931}
resumeobject            {c3b6c6d6-3772-11e5-9319-9639c7488931}
displayorder            {c3b6c6d7-3772-11e5-9319-9639c7488931}
toolsdisplayorder       {b2721d73-1db4-4c62-bf78-c548a880142d}
timeout                 30

Windows Boot Loader
-------------------
identifier              {c3b6c6d7-3772-11e5-9319-9639c7488931}
device                  partition=C:
path                    \Windows\system32\winload.exe
description             Windows 10
locale                  en-GB
inherit                 {6efb52bf-1766-41db-a6b3-0ee5eff72bd7}
recoverysequence        {c3b6c6d8-3772-11e5-9319-9639c7488931}
recoveryenabled         Yes
allowedinmemorysettings 0x15000075
osdevice                partition=C:
systemroot              \Windows
resumeobject            {c3b6c6d6-3772-11e5-9319-9639c7488931}
nx                      OptIn
bootmenupolicy          Standard
hypervisorlaunchtype    Auto
useplatformclock        Yes

C:\Windows\system32>
```

Figure 20-10. *You will need the GUID (Identifier) of the VM*

1. Type **bcdedit /set {GUID} description "OS Name,"** substituting the actual GUID for the OS for the letters GUID and assigning the OS its proper name. Press **Enter**.

2. Optionally, you might want this VHD to be the OS that loads by default. Set this by typing **bcdedit / default {GUID}**. Press **Enter**.

The VM has now been added to the boot menu on the PC and will start as though it were a regular OS, installed on the main hard disk. This is better because as long as you keep the file name of the VHD and its storage path the same, you can swap it out with another VM and quickly repurpose or repair the PC.

Summary

VMs can be a very useful way to protect the host OS on a PC, and to ensure that repair can be implemented quickly and without fuss. It's also useful when it comes to setting up PCs, as you won't need additional tools such as the Assessment and Deployment Toolkit and System Center Configuration Manager, which are sometimes available only to Enterprise customers and can also be complicated to understand and use.

The ultimate aim of any PC administrator though is to try, as much as is humanly possible, to make the PC completely bomb-proof, so that no matter what disaster might befall it, you can be up and running again quickly. This is precisely the subject we'll be tackling in the next chapter.

PART 3

■ ■ ■

Mastering Windows 10 Troubleshooting

CHAPTER 21

■ ■ ■

Bomb-Proofing Your PC

It's fair to say that nothing ever goes wrong with a PC unless there's a human involved in some way. Machines are simply not capable of going wrong on their own, as it's going to be performing an operation, making a change, applying an update, or just not understanding correct use that can lead to anything from a minor issue to full-scale failure.

As an IT Pro, however, it's not just your job to keep systems operational and functional all of the time; it's going to be your passion as well. Sure, you probably love delving into the OS and fixing problems every bit as much as I do, but it's still a pain in the arse when you have to do it.

The ultimate aim, therefore, isn't just to make a PC system as resilient, robust, and reliable as possible, but to actually make it completely bomb-proof. I do genuinely mean bomb-proof too, as you want to be certain that if the very worst eventually did indeed occur, you could pick up quickly and carry on working with as little fuss and as minimal downtime as possible.

Creating a Robust Backup Strategy

The most important part of making any PC system bomb-proof is to create a robust and reliable backup strategy. Take major tech corporations such as Microsoft and Google, for example. These companies store and keep much if not all of our data safe for us. Almost all of my own files are synced with OneDrive, and you may have a similar system in place for your personal or company files with Microsoft, Google, Amazon, Dropbox, or any one of the multitude of cloud service providers.

Each and every one of these companies, if they're clever and the big players certainly are, will store at least two copies of your data in separate geographic locations. This means that if there's a disaster at one data center, the other will remain intact, and you will still have access to all your files while the first data center is repaired, or even rebuilt.

For people who have a robust backup strategy in place, a similar approach will be adopted. This may just involve cloud storage but it could also include offline storage as well. Remember that cloud restore can be slow, and if you want to be back up and running quickly, having hundreds of gigabytes, or even terabytes of data in the cloud, will take some considerable time to restore, even on the fastest broadband connection.

You may store an offline backup of your data at your premises, and perhaps (and I do recommend this) a mirrored copy of that backup at a separate, and again secure, location. This can be achieved in several ways. You may have backup software on your PCs that will create backups both to your local storage and to the remote storage via the Internet. You may alternatively have a Network Attached storage (NAS) drive which can automatically mirror the data it holds to the remote location. Should a catastrophe occur, you can then take one of these local backups and use them to restore all of your data quickly.

When it comes to the PCs themselves, you can store your installation image files, and all files necessary to quickly set up new PCs, as a part of your backup process. You may even have virtual machines configured that can be quickly deployed to new PCs as bootable operating environments (see Chapter 20 on how to create these) or that can be run on a remote server and accessed via Remote Desktop Services.

© Mike Halsey 2016

M. Halsey, *Windows 10 Troubleshooting*, DOI 10.1007/978-1-4842-0925-7_21

You might have noticed that I'm placing emphasis here on having more than one backup, and you'd be correct. No matter who you are, your files and data will be the most important things to you, from photos of your dog to documents about your business. I use a multitier backup strategy, of a local backup in the PC using File History, two cloud backups to OneDrive and LiveDrive, and backup to a NAS drive locally as well.

With these strategies in place you will find that, should the building in which your offices are based suddenly fall over and land in a pile of dust, your employees will be able to keep working, from home if necessary and on their own machines, with file access you can provide to them, and with full access to all the apps and services they need to get the job done.

Lock Down Your PCs with Group Policy

Not all security is about making sure your business can get up and running again quickly after a disaster. Internal security is every bit as important, especially in these days of data theft and whistleblowers (though I should say if you're doing something wrong and somebody might whistleblow on you, a change in behavior might be a better option).

It's all too easy these days for an employee to slip a tiny USB Flash Drive into a PC and copy huge amounts of data. This data might even include the personal details of employees, customers, or suppliers, all of which will be governed by strict data protection laws. So how do you prevent data loss in this manner?

If you are using the Pro or Enterprise editions of Windows 10, you will have access to the Group Policy Editor (search for **gpedit** in the Start Menu or Cortana). Group Policy allows you to lock down many aspects of the OS and your PC, but the first I want to detail is how to block removable storage.

In the *Computer Configuration* ➤ *Administrative Templates* ➤ *System* ➤ *Removable Storage Access* section are options to completely block all types of removable storage, from CDs and DVDs, to floppy drives, tape drives, and USB Flash Drives (listed as Removable Disks), see Figure 21-1.

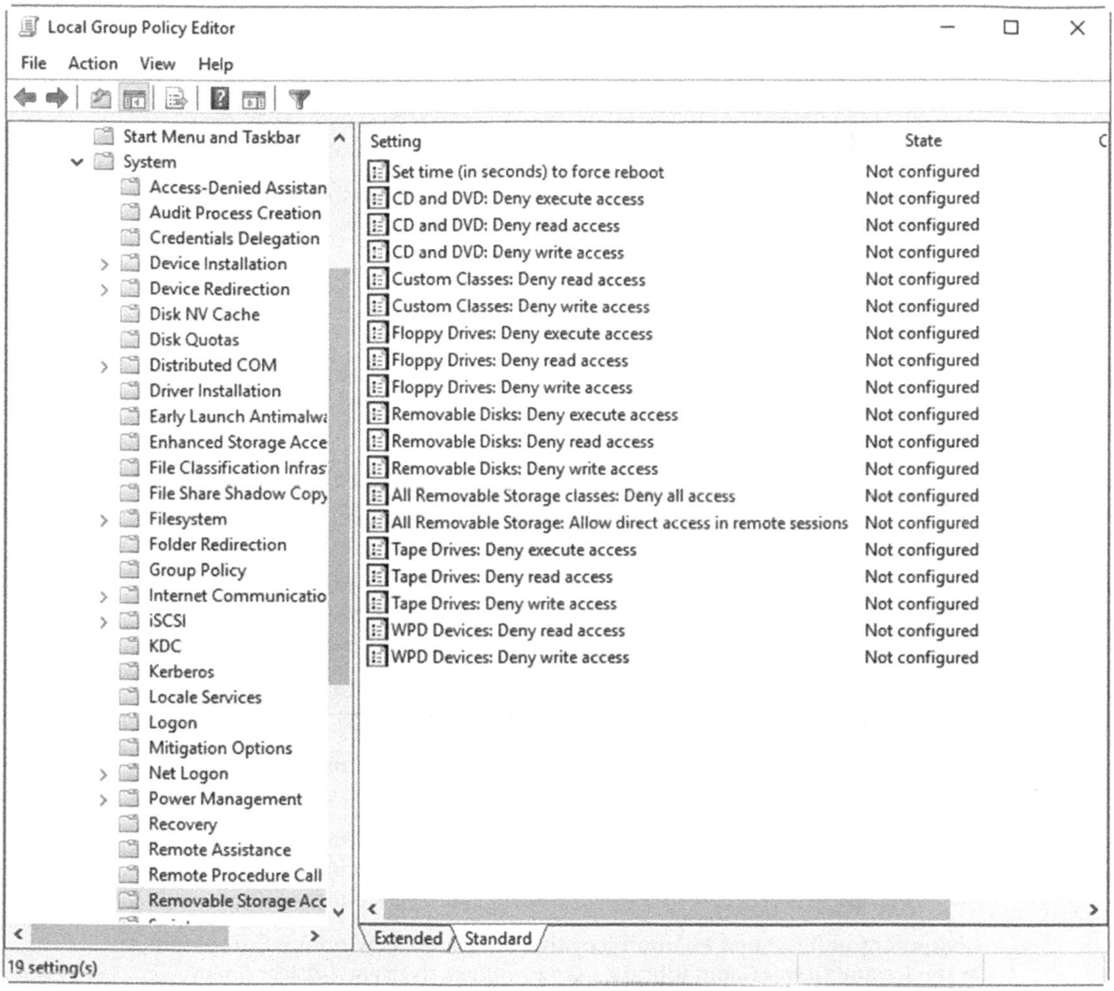

Figure 21-1. *You can manage removable storage in Group Policy*

You can even control access in such as way as to allow people to read files from removable media, but not to write data to the media or to be able to execute (run) apps from the media, which is a good way for malware to spread.

Other ways you can secure your PCs in Group Policy include being able to restrict hardware device installation and updating (as these can sometimes be updated to use nonsigned or unstable drivers). This can be found in *Computer Configuration* ➤ *Administrative Templates* ➤ *System* ➤ *Device Installation*, and can prevent unauthorized hardware being installed on your PCs.

There are other settings available in Group Policy that can be used to secure your PCs. Including the two I've already mentioned in this list, these are...

- **Computer Configuration** ➤ **Windows Settings** ➤ **Security Settings** ➤ **Account Policies**, where you can enforce password policies for the PC.

- **Computer Configuration** ➤ **Windows Settings** ➤ **Security Settings** ➤ **User Rights Management**, where you can control additional sign-in and user permissions.

- **[Computer Configuration / User Configuration] ➤ Windows Settings ➤ Security Settings ➤ Security Options**, which contains security settings that don't fall into the previous two categories.

- **Computer Configuration ➤ Administrative Templates ➤ System ➤ Device Installation**, to prevent the installation of unauthorized hardware.

- **[Computer Configuration / User Configuration] ➤ Administrative Templates ➤ System ➤ Logon**, for setting security and password rules for users.

- **Computer Configuration ➤ Administrative Templates ➤ System ➤ Remote Assistance**, where you can specify if Remote Assistance can be used, and also restrict connections to newer, more secure versions of Windows.

- **[Computer Configuration / User Configuration] ➤ Administrative Templates ➤ System ➤ Removable Storage Access**, for denying read, write, and execute rights for removable and USB Flash media.

- **[Computer Configuration / User Configuration] ➤ Administrative Templates ➤ System ➤ User Profiles**, where you can specify security rules for caching and deleting user profiles.

- **[Computer Configuration / User Configuration] ➤ Administrative Templates ➤ Windows Components ➤ AutoPlay Policies**, if you allow removable media on your PCs, you can disable autoplay, which can restrict the ability of malware to infect the PC.

- **Computer Configuration ➤ Administrative Templates ➤ Windows Components ➤ Biometrics**, to control the use of biometric sign-in on the PC.

- **Computer Configuration ➤ Administrative Templates ➤ Windows Components ➤ Bitlocker Drive Encryption**, to enforce encryption policies on the PC.

- **Computer Configuration ➤ Administrative Templates ➤ Windows Components ➤ Data Collection and Preview Builds**, used to manage what usage data is sent to Microsoft, and to prevent the user from installing prerelease builds of Windows 10.

- **Computer Configuration ➤ Administrative Templates ➤ Windows Components ➤ Device and Driver Compatibility**, used to enforce the signed-driver policy.

- **[Computer Configuration / User Configuration] ➤ Administrative Templates ➤ Windows Components ➤ Remote Desktop Services**, where you can control all aspects of Remote Desktop and its security.

- **Computer Configuration ➤ Administrative Templates ➤ Windows Components ➤ Security Center**, where you can activate the Windows (legacy) Security Center for domain-attached PCs.

- **Computer Configuration ➤ Administrative Templates ➤ Windows Components ➤ Smart Card**, where you can control smartcard sign-in and security policies.

Managing Windows Services

Services are Microsoft and third-party applets that run in the background and either perform essential tasks to keep the OS running, such as managing user sign in, or provide features that will be shared by other apps or devices on the PC, like Plug and Play or the Print Spooler.

You access the Services panel in Windows 10 by searching for **services** in the Start menu or Cortana, and it will display a list of all the services currently installed on the PC, with sortable (clickable) column headings, so that you can, for example, arrange the list by the services that are currently running, see Figure 21-2.

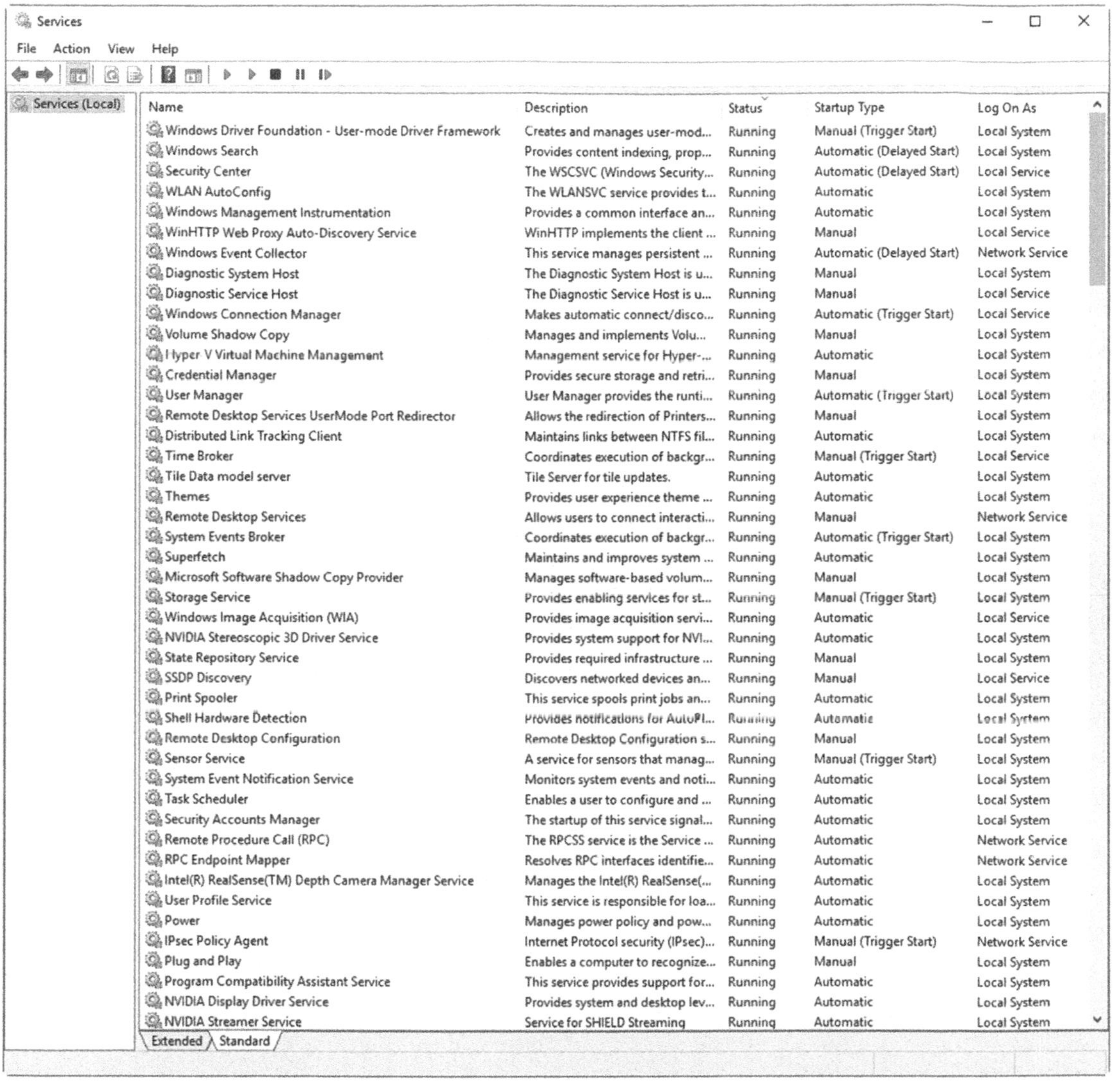

Name	Description	Status	Startup Type	Log On As
Windows Driver Foundation - User-mode Driver Framework	Creates and manages user-mod...	Running	Manual (Trigger Start)	Local System
Windows Search	Provides content indexing, prop...	Running	Automatic (Delayed Start)	Local System
Security Center	The WSCSVC (Windows Security...	Running	Automatic (Delayed Start)	Local Service
WLAN AutoConfig	The WLANSVC service provides t...	Running	Automatic	Local System
Windows Management Instrumentation	Provides a common interface an...	Running	Automatic	Local System
WinHTTP Web Proxy Auto-Discovery Service	WinHTTP implements the client ...	Running	Manual	Local Service
Windows Event Collector	This service manages persistent ...	Running	Automatic (Delayed Start)	Network Service
Diagnostic System Host	The Diagnostic System Host is u...	Running	Manual	Local System
Diagnostic Service Host	The Diagnostic Service Host is u...	Running	Manual	Local Service
Windows Connection Manager	Makes automatic connect/disco...	Running	Automatic (Trigger Start)	Local Service
Volume Shadow Copy	Manages and implements Volu...	Running	Manual	Local System
Hyper-V Virtual Machine Management	Management service for Hyper-...	Running	Automatic	Local System
Credential Manager	Provides secure storage and retri...	Running	Manual	Local System
User Manager	User Manager provides the runti...	Running	Automatic (Trigger Start)	Local System
Remote Desktop Services UserMode Port Redirector	Allows the redirection of Printers...	Running	Manual	Local System
Distributed Link Tracking Client	Maintains links between NTFS fil...	Running	Automatic	Local System
Time Broker	Coordinates execution of backgr...	Running	Manual (Trigger Start)	Local Service
Tile Data model server	Tile Server for tile updates.	Running	Automatic	Local System
Themes	Provides user experience theme ...	Running	Automatic	Local System
Remote Desktop Services	Allows users to connect interacti...	Running	Manual	Network Service
System Events Broker	Coordinates execution of backgr...	Running	Automatic (Trigger Start)	Local System
Superfetch	Maintains and improves system ...	Running	Automatic	Local System
Microsoft Software Shadow Copy Provider	Manages software-based volum...	Running	Manual	Local System
Storage Service	Provides enabling services for st...	Running	Manual (Trigger Start)	Local System
Windows Image Acquisition (WIA)	Provides image acquisition servi...	Running	Automatic	Local Service
NVIDIA Stereoscopic 3D Driver Service	Provides system support for NVI...	Running	Automatic	Local System
State Repository Service	Provides required infrastructure ...	Running	Manual	Local System
SSDP Discovery	Discovers networked devices an...	Running	Manual	Local Service
Print Spooler	This service spools print jobs an...	Running	Automatic	Local System
Shell Hardware Detection	Provides notifications for AutoPl...	Running	Automatic	Local System
Remote Desktop Configuration	Remote Desktop Configuration s...	Running	Manual	Local System
Sensor Service	A service for sensors that manag...	Running	Manual (Trigger Start)	Local System
System Event Notification Service	Monitors system events and noti...	Running	Automatic	Local System
Task Scheduler	Enables a user to configure and ...	Running	Automatic	Local System
Security Accounts Manager	The startup of this service signal...	Running	Automatic	Local System
Remote Procedure Call (RPC)	The RPCSS service is the Service ...	Running	Automatic	Network Service
RPC Endpoint Mapper	Resolves RPC interfaces identifie...	Running	Automatic	Network Service
Intel(R) RealSense(TM) Depth Camera Manager Service	Manages the Intel(R) RealSense(...	Running	Automatic	Local System
User Profile Service	This service is responsible for loa...	Running	Automatic	Local System
Power	Manages power policy and pow...	Running	Automatic	Local System
IPsec Policy Agent	Internet Protocol security (IPsec)...	Running	Manual (Trigger Start)	Network Service
Plug and Play	Enables a computer to recognize...	Running	Manual	Local System
Program Compatibility Assistant Service	This service provides support for...	Running	Automatic	Local System
NVIDIA Display Driver Service	Provides system and desktop lev...	Running	Automatic	Local System
NVIDIA Streamer Service	Service for SHIELD Streaming	Running	Automatic	Local System

Figure 21-2. *You can view and control all the Microsoft and third-party Windows services*

You will see that each service has a full description, and this can be very useful in determining exactly what a service is for, and what apps or Windows features might need to use it. After all, you don't want to disable a service that might be required, or that could even prove essential in the smooth operation of the PC.

Each service will have one of four startup types assigned to it: *Disabled*, *Manual* (where the service is run only when invoked by an app or process), or *Automatic* (where it will run on startup) and *Delayed Start* (where it loads only after everything else associated with startup has finished loading). You can display the properties inspector for a service by double-clicking it. This will display a dialog in which you can get information about and change settings for the service, such as its startup type, see Figure 21-3.

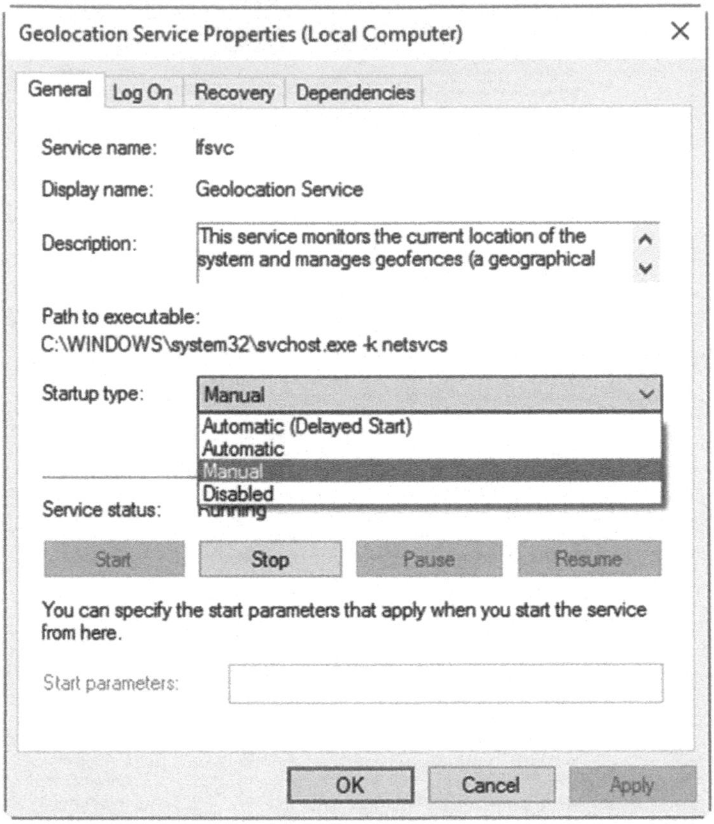

Figure 21-3. *You can control individual services by double-clicking them*

There is useful information available in each services properties panel. For example, under the *Dependencies* tab you can see if this service relies on any other services to operate. This is useful if you are considering disabling services, as you might find that something you need to run depends on the service you wish to disable being active, see Figure 21-4.

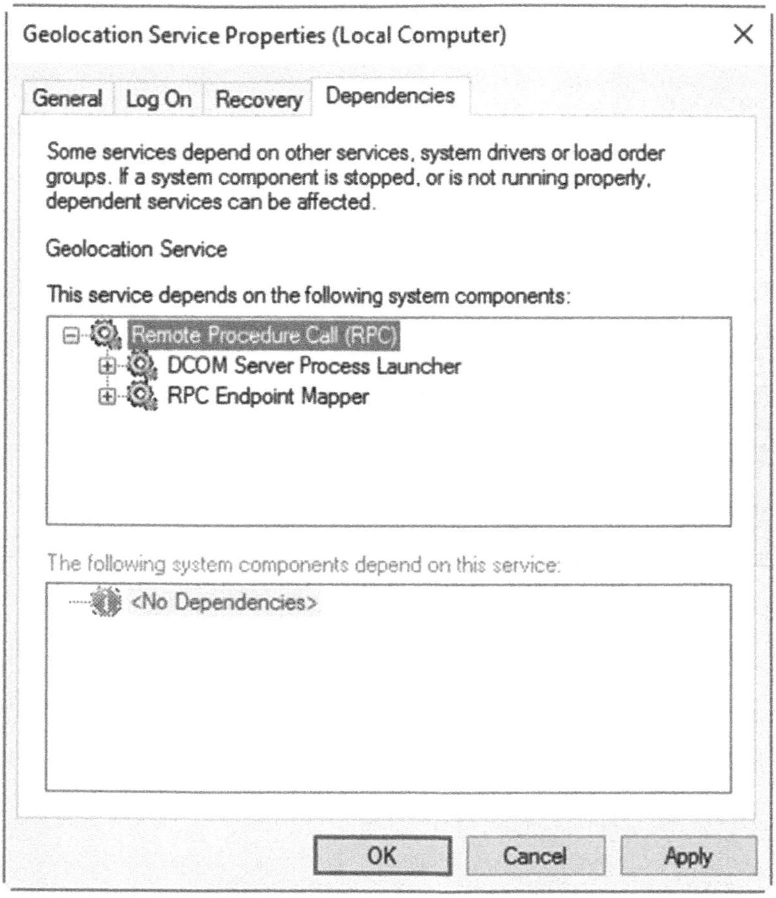

Figure 21-4. You can check if a service has any dependent services before you disable it

Additionally, the *Recovery* tab contains options for what Windows should do if a service fails or crashes, see Figure 21-5. This includes restarting the service, running a speciaic program (perhaps a dedicated troubleshooter), or restarting the PC. You can choose different actions for the first, second, and each subsequent service failure.

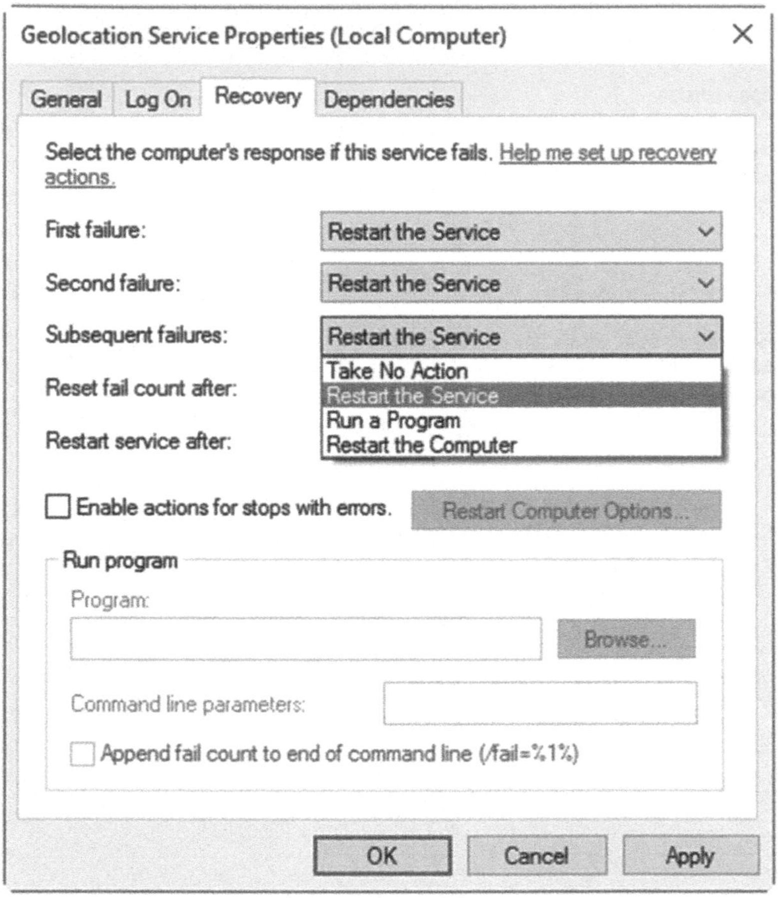

Figure 21-5. *You can set troubleshooting options for services*

Over the last few versions of Windows, Microsoft has become extremely good at enabling only the services your PC actually *needs*, in order to be able to start and operate quickly and effectively. There are services, however, that might be enabled that you won't need, and can stop. Why would you want to disable services though? Well, done properly, a PC with less running will be faster and more robust and reliable overall.

- **Third-party management and update services from companies such as AMD, Apple, Adobe, Dropbox, Google, Nvidia, and Skype.** You might want to leave the update services enabled from third-party companies, as they can install critical security updates for apps installed on your PC. There might be additional services, however, that are not necessary.

- **Auto Time Zone Updater** will not be necessary for static desktop PCs.

- **Bitlocker Drive Encryption Service** will not be necessary for PCs on which you choose not to use Bitlocker, or Bitlocker To Go.

- **Bluetooth Handsfree Service / Bluetooth Support Service** will not be necessary on PCs where you do not intend to use Bluetooth devices.

- **Downloaded Maps Manager** is not necessary on PCs where you will not be using the maps app.

- **Ecrypting File System (EFS)** is not necessary on PCs where you do not intend to use EFS.

- **Fax** is not necessary if you will not be sending or receiving faxes from the PC.

- **File History Service** is necessary only if you will be using the File Histroy backup feature.

- **Geolocation Service** is not needed if you do not wish to use the geolocation features of Windows 10 on the PC.

- **HomeGroup Listener / HomeGroup Provider** can be disabled if you do not wish to use the HomeGroup feature in Windows 10.

- **Hyper-V Services:** many can be disabled if you do not wish to use virtualization on the PC.

- **Phone Service / Telephony** is useful only for telephony features on the PC.

- **Print Spooler** can be disabled if the PC is to be used only for tasks that will not involve printing.

- **Remote Access / Remote Desktop Services** can be disabled to boost security if you do not want to permit Remote Desktop and Remote Assistance on the PC.

- **Smart Card Services** can be disabled if you will not be using smart card authentication with the PC.

- **Touch Keyboard and Handwriting Panel Service** can be disabled on nontouch PCs.

- **Windows Image Acquisition (WIA)** only provides services for the importing of photos and video from attached cameras.

- **Windows Media Player Network Sharing Service** supports media playback features such as Play-To.

- **Windows Mobile Hotspot Service** can be disabled on static desktop PCs.

- **Windows Search** is extremely useful as it manages and maintains the full search capabilities of the OS. However, if you disable it you can sometimes boost the battery life of a laptop or tablet by up to 30%

- **Windows Store Service (WSService)** can be disabled if you do not intend to use the Windows Store.

- **Work Folders** can be disabled if you will not be using the Work Folders BYOD feature.

- **Xbox Services** can be disabled if you do not want to use the gaming or Xbox streaming features of Windows 10.

Manage Your Local Security Policy

You can manage security policies for the PC, such as user permissions and sign-in controls, through the Local Security Policy panel; search for **secpol** in the Start Menu or Cortana. This contains policies that are also found in Group Policy, but it keeps all the security policies together and in one place, so they are easy to navigate, see Figure 21-6.

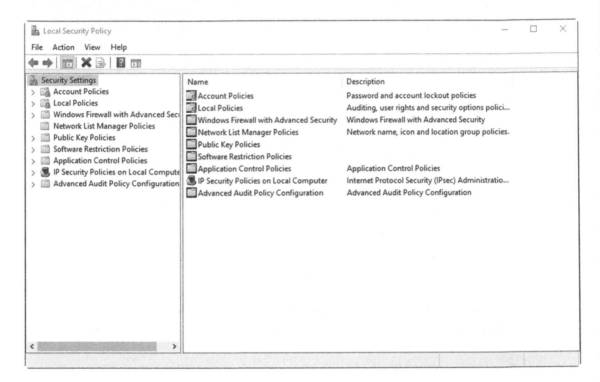

Figure 21-6. *You can manage a multitude of security policies in Windows 10*

It can be well worth spending some time examining the different options available to you. The Password Policy section, for example, can enforce minimum standards of complexity for the PC that must be met when users create or change their password. These policies can also specify that passwords must be changed on a regular basis.

If you are unsure about what any security policy does or means, double-clicking it will open its properties dialog, in which you will find an *Explain* tab. This will provide a full, plain text description of the policy and what it does, see Figure 21-7.

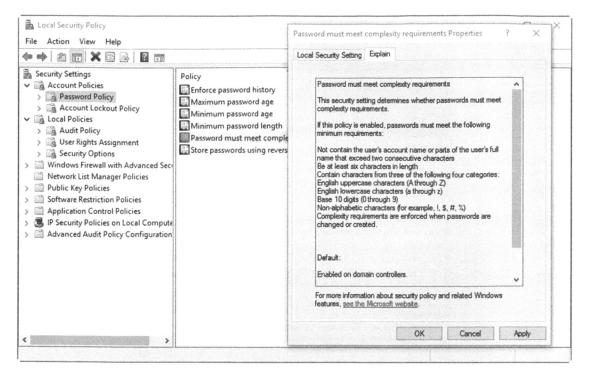

Figure 21-7. *Each policy has an Explain tab with a detailed description*

Managing Advanced Firewall Policy

When it comes to maintaining good security on our PCs, nothing is more important than a firewall. The Windows Firewall is extremely good, and there's almost never any need to replace it with a third-party option. It's boosted further by the inclusion of a *Windows Firewall with Advanced Security* panel, which you can open by searching for **firewall** in the Start Menu or Cortana.

The Advanced Firewall is standard Microsoft Management Console fare, with the usual three-column layout, see Figure 21-8. In the top left of the window you will see options to create Inbound, Outbound, and Connection Security rules. The right column contains context-sensitive options that will change depending on what is highlighted and what you are doing.

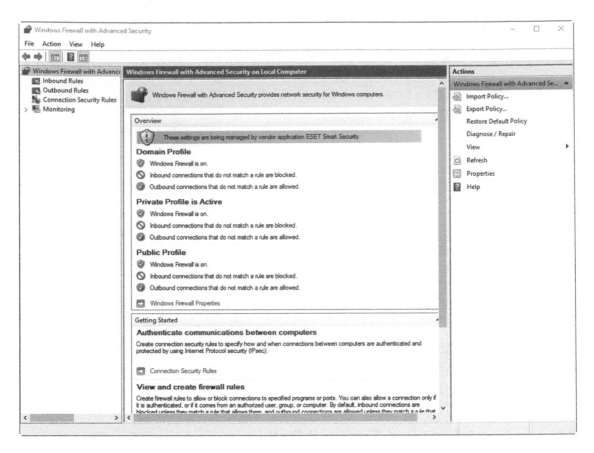

Figure 21-8. *The Advanced Firewall panel in Windows 10*

Clicking the Inbound or Outbound rules section will display a list of all the rules that are currently created, with details of whether the rules are enabled or not. You will also see a *New Rule* link appear in the top right of the window. You can click this to create new Firewall rules for the PC. There are four different types of rules you can create, see Figure 21-9.

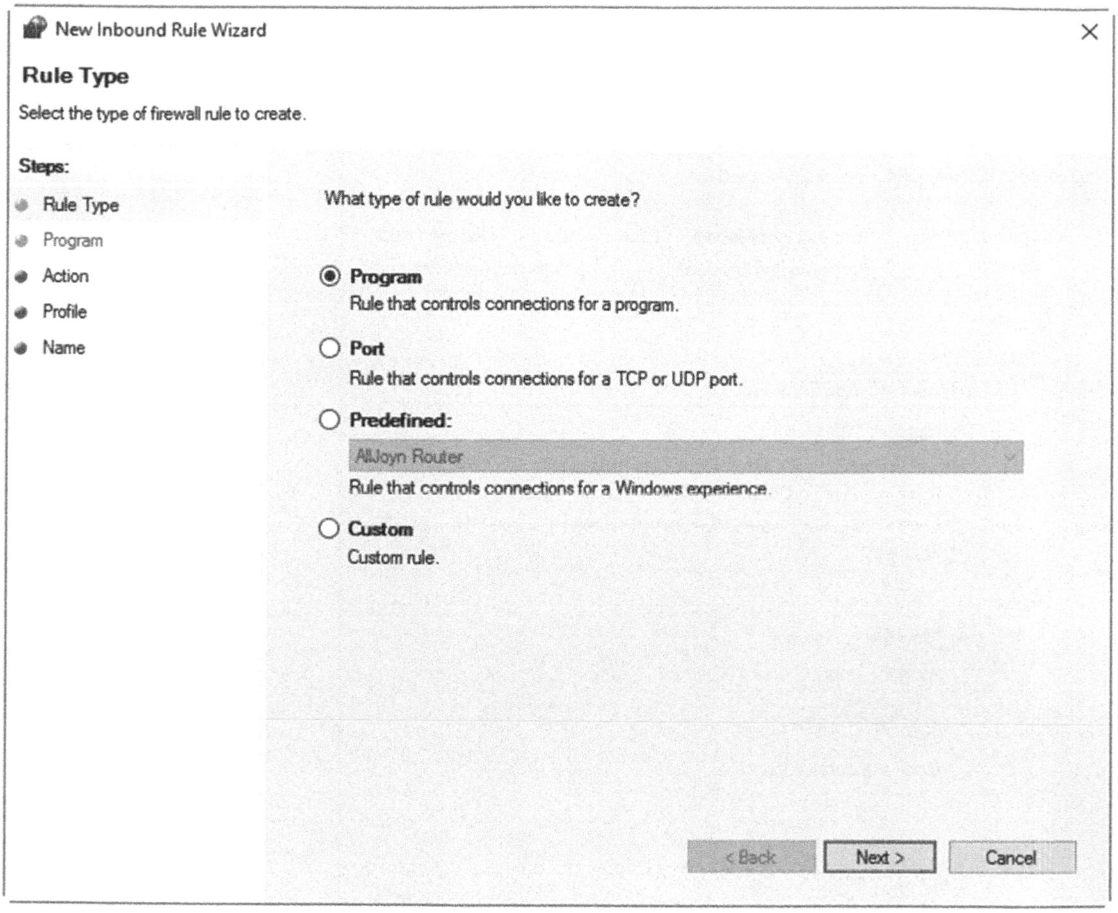

Figure 21-9. *You can create new rules in the Firewall*

- **Program** rules are those associated with a specific win32 app on your PC; Store apps are not managed here. You may find that you have a specific app on your PC which is being blocked by the firewall or that you wish to block. You can allow or deny access to the app here.

- **Port** is for allowing or denying access to specific communictaion ports on the PC. You may, for example, have a Virtual Private Network (VPN) solution that requires specific ports to be open and accessible on the PC, or you may specifically want to block ports used by file-sharing torrent apps.

- **Predefined** rules are ones that have already been configured by Microsoft to cover a wide range of business scenarios. These include rules that cover the BranchCache and Hyper-V features of the OS, along with Remote Access and Media Playback.

- **Custom** rules are defined in a very similar way to Program rules, but they also allow you to define rules that include specific Microsoft or third-party services.

You can examine and change the properties for any Firewall rule by double-clicking it to display its properties panel, see Figure 21-10. There is a wealth of information and a great many configuration options here for the firewall, including a plain text description of what the rule is, and what it is used for.

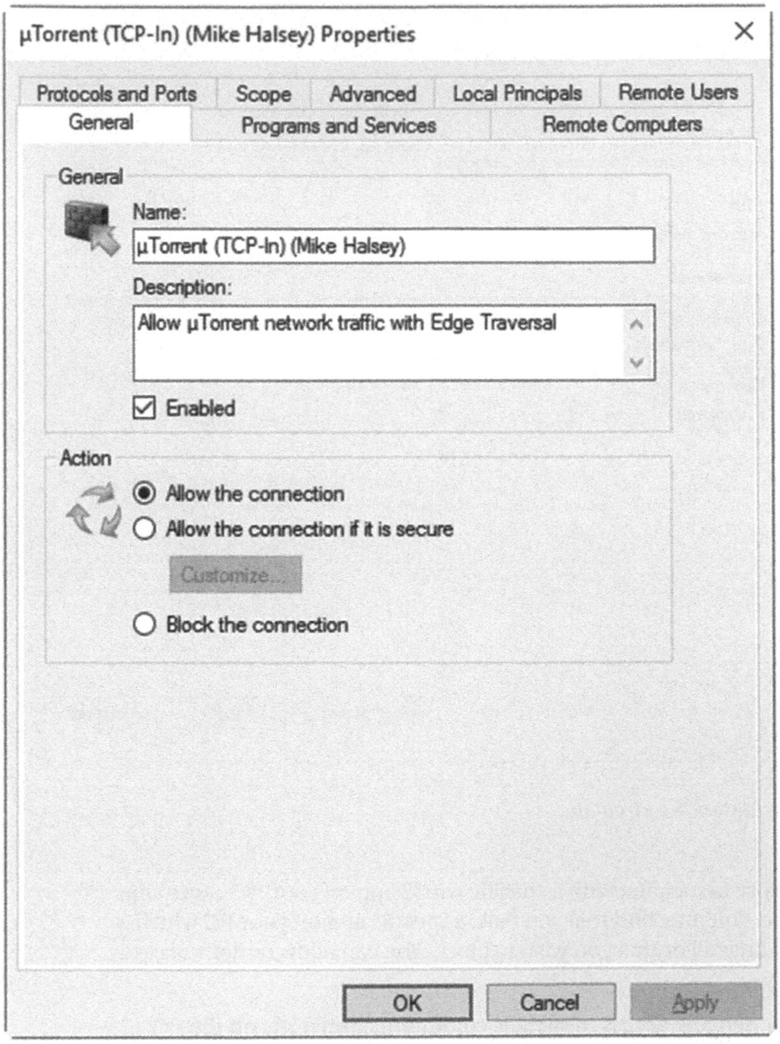

Figure 21-10. You can change the properties for any rule

In the rule properties panel, you can view and manage the following aspects of the rule.

- **Action** is used to allow or block the connection, or to only allow it if you have a secure network connection, such as a VPN.

- **Programs and Services** lets you define which apps, Application Packages (which include Store apps), and Services the rule applies to.

- **Remote Computers** allows you to define rules that will allow remote connections only from specific PCs, or that will not apply if a specific PC is connected. These can be useful for managing strong security during Remote Desktop sessions.

- **Protocols and Ports** is where you can set the communications protocol type (such as TCP, IPv6, etc.) and communications ports to which the rule applies.

- **Scope** allows you to limit access through the rule to specific IP addresses or an IP address range.

- **Advanced** is where you can specify if the rule applies to each of domain, private, and public network connection types, and where other options that don't fall into other categories reside.

- **Local Principals / Remote Users** are similar to the Remote Computers options, except that it allows you to restrict access to specific local and remote users.

The Connection Security rules are to determine security policies when using network and Internet connections that need to be tightly controlled, see Figure 21-11. These include Tunnel (VPN) connections, direct server-to-server communications, and where authentication between the different computers can be overridden.

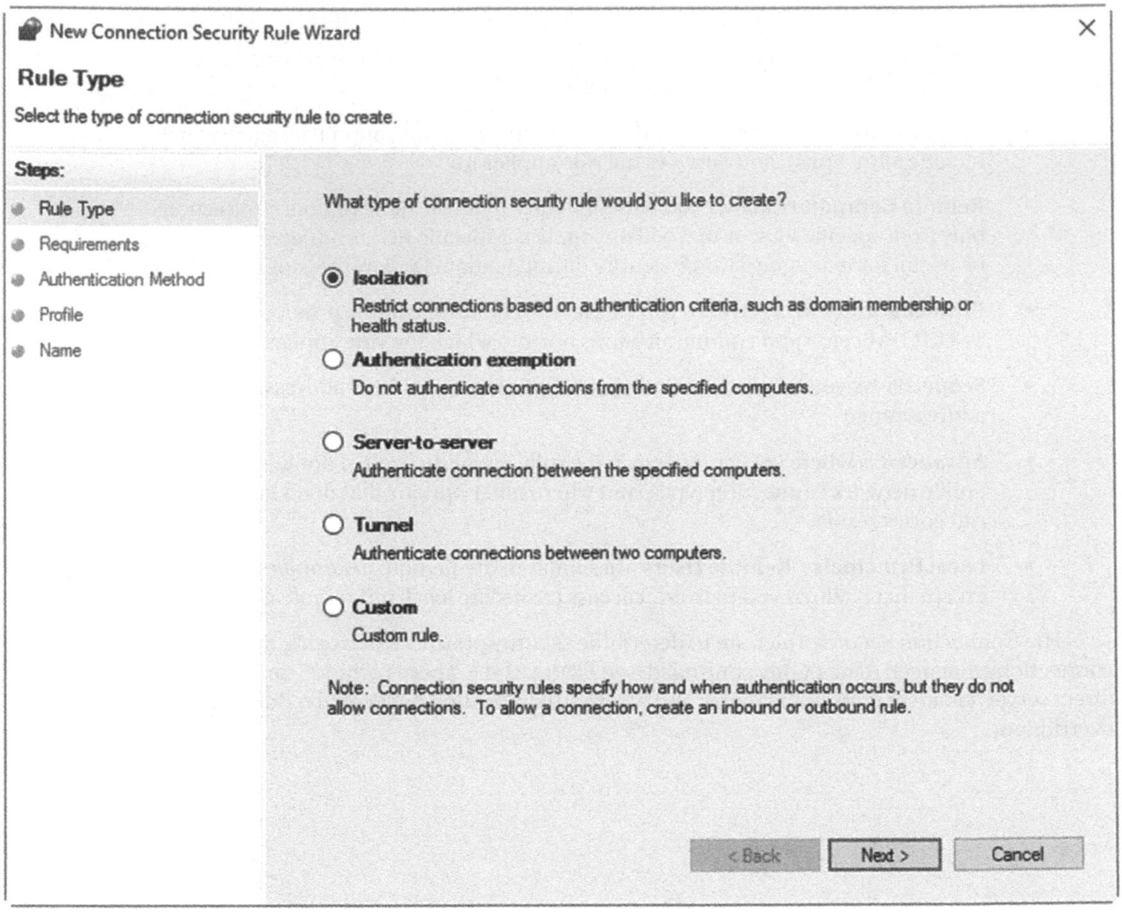

Figure 21-11. You can set Connection Security rules

Summary

Creating a bomb-proof PC system isn't limited to what I have described in this chapter, as you will also need to ensure you have a full system image backup of your PC that can be restored if required, and that you keep copies of your Windows image (ISO) installation file and all hardware drivers for your PCs safe and in multiple locations to cover you in the case of data loss.

Following this advice and setting appropriate levels of security, however, can really help you to prevent problems that can compromise your PCs and your network from occurring in the first instance. Remember that everything is connected to everything else, and thus, if your PC can see other PCs and storage systems on the network, it is a potential weak point of entry to those other systems.

Sometimes, however, we need much more detailed information when we're diagnosing and repairing PC problems. In the next chapter we'll look in depth at the excellent Microsoft SysInternals suite, and the programs it includes that can aid with troubleshooting a Windows 10 PC.

■ ■ ■

CHAPTER 22

Microsoft Sysinternals

Nothing says you're an IT Pro better than a good knowledge of Microsoft's Sysinternals suite. First developed by Bryce Cogswell and Mark Russinovich in 1996, it was bought ten years later by Microsoft, for whom Russinovich now works as a senior technical fellow, and sits as part of Microsoft's TechNet web site. You can find Sysinternals on the Microsoft web site at `https://technet.microsoft.com/Sysinternals`.

It consists of suite of stand-alone apps that perform various configuration, diagnostic, and repair tasks within the Windows OS, some of which have almost become legend. Rather than let the tools sit and stagnate, Sysinternals is an active Microsoft project, being updated on a regular basis with upgrades and new tools.

There are currently, as I write this, a massive 69 tools and utilities available as part of Sysinternals. I won't write about how to use them all here, as that would be a book on its own (which does rather give me an idea), but instead I'll focus on the tools available that can be specifically used to diagnose, troubleshoot, and repair problems with PCs.

Some of the tools I will highlight in detail. This is because these will be tools that can directly benefit troubleshooting. Others I will just reference as they are primarily configuration tools, yet can be useful when troubleshooting problems. This may mean I don't include all the commands available for a tool, but all of this information is available on the Sysinternals web site.

File and Disk Utilities

The file and disk utilities within Sysinternals will provide a wide range of functions, from helping configure PCs systems to helping you view and check the configuration options you have already made.

AccessChks

The first tool to detail falls into the "useful for checking if everything is configured correctly" category. AccessChk is run from the command line and can be used to check what access specific users or user groups have to files, directories, Registry keys, Services, and more. Full details of its command-line syntax can be found on the Sysinternals web site.

AccessEnum

AccessEnum is a graphical utility that will allow you to view a tree view of files, directories, and Registry keys, detailing what users have read and write permissions, and what users might be denied access. It is a tool that is simple to use: you simply point it at the location you wish to view permissions for and click the Scan button, see Figure 22-1.

© Mike Halsey 2016
M. Halsey, *Windows 10 Troubleshooting*, DOI 10.1007/978-1-4842-0925-7_22

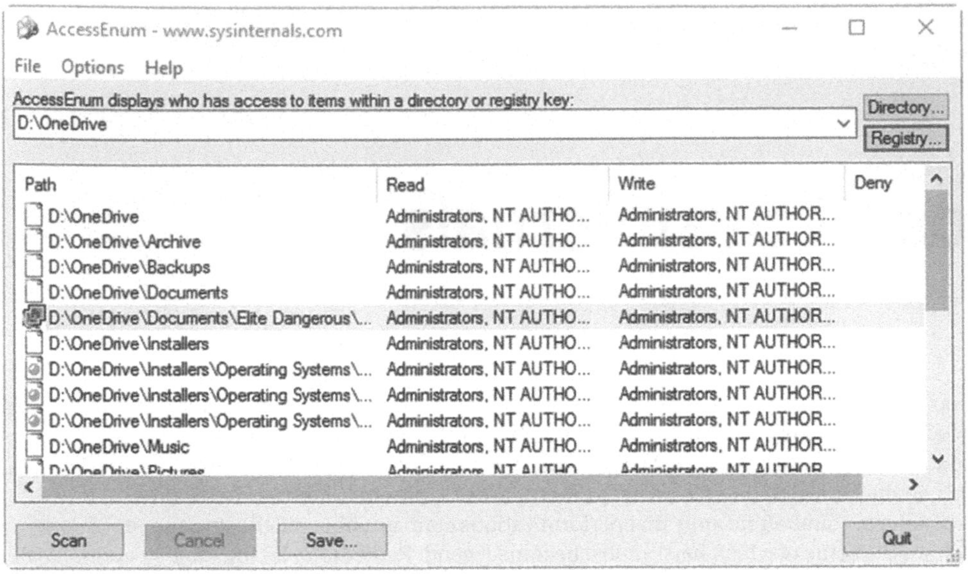

Figure 22-1. *The AccessEnum utility*

Contig

This is another command-line tool, and the switches are available on the Sysinternals web site. While Windows 10 includes a full disk defragmentation tool, the Contig tool picks up where the defragmentation tool stops by providing file-level defragmentation. This is important because defragmenting a drive won't always defragment every file on that drive, and you may occasionally find a file being reported as corrupt where this tool may be able to help.

Disk2Vhd

Sometimes you might have a hard disk in a PC that needs deep diagnosis, or perhaps a very careful recovery of files and data. Disk2Vhd can create a virtual hard disk snapshot of any hard disk or partition on the PC, even a live system. This then resides as a file that can be examined or worked on later on another PC; moreover, the file will work with Hyper-V, see Figure 22-2.

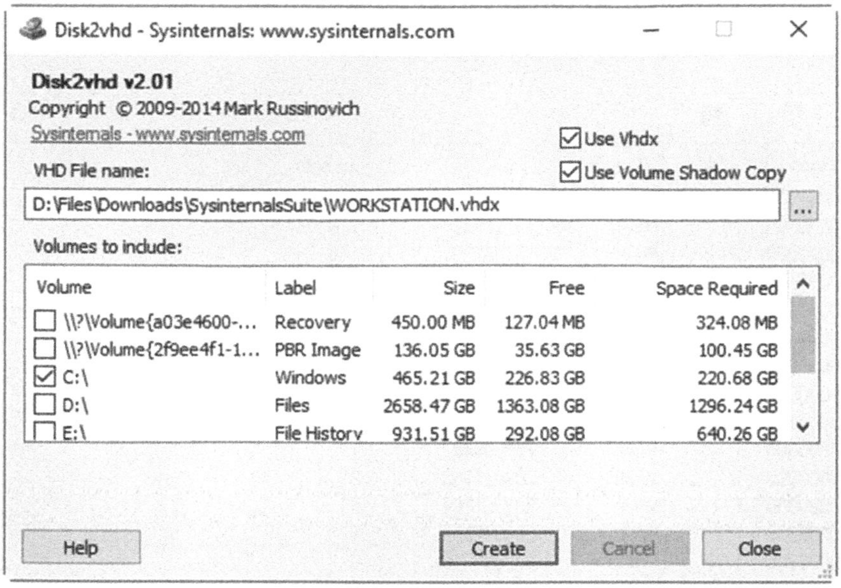

Figure 22-2. Disk2Vhd can create VHDs from disks and partitions

DiskExt

Another command-line utility, this one will list the physical disks that partitions in the PC are located on, and where on those disks the partitions are located. This can be useful when diagnosing partition issues, and for checking if a partition, such as the Windows boot partition, is located on the correct disk.

Diskmon

The first of the majorly useful troubleshooting and diagnostic tools. Diskmon provides a live report of every read and write activity that takes place on your hard disk, see Figure 22-3. This can be useful in many circumstances. For example, you may be concerned that something on the PC is accessing disk space that it should not, such as malware. Alternatively you may be trying to determine if a fault when accessing or saving a file resides in a bad sector on the hard disk, or is a problem with the file or data itself. If there are failures to read and write files and data, these will be displayed as either multiple repeated attempts by Windows, or an extended read or write duration.

#	Time	Duration (s)	Disk	Request	Sector	Length
346	19.600316	0.00000000	1	Read	5329639	1
347	19.600592	0.00000000	1	Read	13723992	128
348	19.600913	0.00000000	1	Read	13724120	128
349	19.601245	0.00000000	1	Read	13724248	128
350	19.601442	0.00000000	1	Read	13724376	128
351	19.601727	0.00000000	1	Read	13723992	8
352	19.681533	0.00000000	1	Write	187091008	8
353	19.681610	0.00000000	1	Write	187091056	16
354	19.682182	0.00000000	1	Write	118725088	32
355	19.682322	0.00000000	1	Write	15960848	10
356	19.682419	0.00000000	1	Write	202891168	8
357	19.682481	0.00000000	1	Write	202891264	8
358	19.682548	0.00000000	1	Write	202891304	8
359	19.682610	0.00000000	1	Write	202890016	8
360	19.682682	0.00000000	1	Write	64173800	8
361	19.682749	0.00000000	1	Write	5505760	8
362	19.682804	0.00000000	1	Write	5505736	8
363	19.682861	0.00000000	1	Write	5505752	8
364	21.057866	0.00000000	1	Write	7160776	24

Figure 22-3. Diskmon reports on all hard disk activity

DiskView

Perhaps slightly less useful for troubleshooting, but interesting all the same, DiskView can tell you where on your disk a file is physically located. This can be useful if you are diagnosing a corrupt or damaged disk or solid-state drive.

EFSDump

The Encrypting File System (EFS), which I detailed in Chapter 18, isn't like Bitlocker in that when you sign into the PC you have access to your files. File access needs to be granted on a per-user basis through implementation of an unlock key. The EFSDump utility can display which users have access to EFS-encrypted files on a PC.

MoveFile and PendMoves

These two utilities are very similar to one another, and can be used to move files, or to see which files are scheduled to be moved or deleted, when the next reboot takes place. They are command-line utilities for which the full syntax is available on the Sysinternals web site.

NTFSInfo

NTFSInfo is another command-line utility that can display details about an NTFS-formatted disk or partition. This includes technical information such as the allocation unit size, the location and details of key NTFS files, and information about the Master File Table.

PsFile

This is another command-line utility, and another utility that can provide information about files that are locked by the operating system. PsFile can inform you about what files have been opened by other computers on your network.

SDelete

SDelete is included here only because it's a useful tool to know about. It's a command-line utility that can be used to securely delete files on a PC. It was created to assist with deleting EFS-encrypted files, where space is not quickly overwritten afterward by new data.

ShareEnum

ShareEnum can be used to identify all file shares available on a network. This tool can be useful for helping diagnose problems with network file shares on a PC, to determine if the PC can actually see the share, or if it is a misconfigured app or firewall setting that is blocking access.

Sigcheck

The sigcheck utility will report on the file version number, timestamp, digital signature, and certificate details of any file on the PC. It is a command-line utility that can be useful if you believe that a specific system or other file has become corrupt or has been tampered with.

Networking Utilities

When it comes to troubleshooting problems on a PC, networking is right up at the top of the list of problem areas. This is because if we can't get access to our network files and resources, access to the Internet or, heaven forbid... social media, the world comes to an abrupt and shuddering halt. For anybody not interested at that point in something called the "front door," the Sysinternals suite includes some useful network troubleshooting tools.

PSPing

PSPing does exactly what you might expect it to: it displays detailed ping information to test network connections. It is a command-line utility that is much more configurable than Windows 10's standard Ping command. PSPing is used with one of four main switches and then a series of subswitches to test for ICMP (the main protocol used by routers for reporting errors), TCP, latency, and bandwidth. Full details of the switches are available on the Sysinternals web site.

PsTools

Rather than being a utility, PsTools is actually an extra suite of utilities for administering PC systems remotely. It includes utilities that can remotely execute apps, display information about files and users, kill processes detailed information about processes, and shutdown and restart the PC. Full details of the tools available can be found on the Sysinternals web site.

TCPView

The TCPView utility provides information about the endpoint network connections from your PC, including the remote or IP address of the destination and the port used by the PC to make the connection, see Figure 22-4. Using this utility, you can see every running process and service that has an active network connection, and the destination they are connected to.

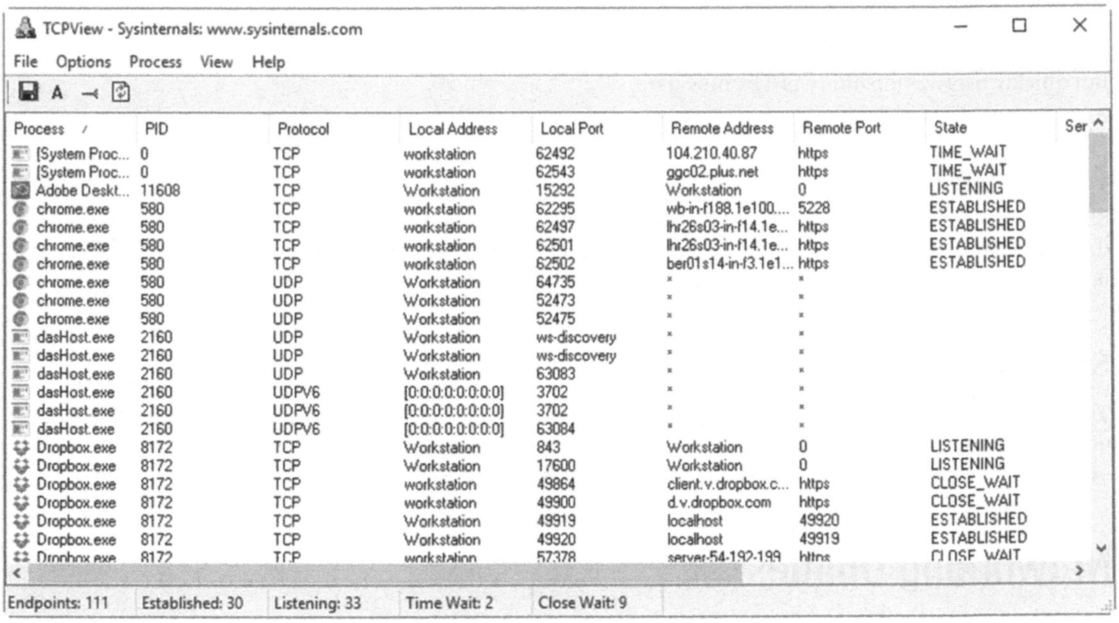

Figure 22-4. *TCPView provides useful endpoint information*

You can marry this information with the data you have on IP address ranges within your company, or company VPN, to check for misconfigured network connections, or to see where malware or rogue apps might be making connections. There is also a command-line version of this tool available in Sysinternals, called TCPVcon.

WhoIs

WhoIs is useful for providing information on who owns and maintains domain names or IP addresses to which your PC is connecting. For example, in running TCPView, I spotted that Google Chrome on my PC was connecting to the IP address 216.58.198.206, and wanted to see what company was at the end of this address. A quick search using WhoIs reveals that the connection was being made by the browser to the company MarkMonitor, which is known to be trustworthy, see Figure 22-5.

```
Administrator: Command Prompt                                    —   □   ×

D:\Files\Downloads\SysinternalsSuite>whois 216.58.198.206

Whois v1.12 - Domain information lookup utility
Sysinternals - www.sysinternals.com
Copyright (C) 2005-2014 Mark Russinovich

Connecting to NET.whois-servers.net...
Connecting to whois.markmonitor.com...

Domain ID: 1570253561_DOMAIN_NET-VRSN
Registrar WHOIS Server: whois.markmonitor.com
Registrar URL: http://www.markmonitor.com
Updated Date: 2014-10-28T12:38:28-0700
Creation Date: 2009-09-24T22:40:03-0700
Registrar Registration Expiration Date: 2019-09-24T22:40:03-0700
Registrar: MarkMonitor, Inc.
Registrar IANA ID: 292
Registrar Abuse Contact Email: abusecomplaints@markmonitor.com
Registrar Abuse Contact Phone: +1.2083895740
Domain Status: clientUpdateProhibited (https://www.icann.org/epp#clientUpdateProhibi
ted)
Domain Status: clientTransferProhibited (https://www.icann.org/epp#clientTransferPro
hibited)
Domain Status: clientDeleteProhibited (https://www.icann.org/epp#clientDeleteProhibi
ted)
Domain Status: serverUpdateProhibited (https://www.icann.org/epp#serverUpdateProhibi
ted)
Domain Status: serverTransferProhibited (https://www.icann.org/epp#serverTransferPro
```

Figure 22-5. WhoIs can provide information on IP addresses you connect to

Process Utilities

Knowing what's going on inside your PC at any one time is essential to effective troubleshooting. Perhaps you have a hung process you need to root out, or malware that restarts every time you shut it down, because there's a dependent process running in the background that has yet to be identified. The process utilities in the Sysinternals suite are powerful, flexible, and almost always completely indispensable.

AutoRuns

There are a few utilities in Sysinternals that can be considered "the daddy," and AutoRuns is most definitely one of them. Seen in Figure 22-6, it goes far beyond the startup apps list that Windows 10 includes in the Task Manager, to show absolutely everything that starts when you switch on your PC.

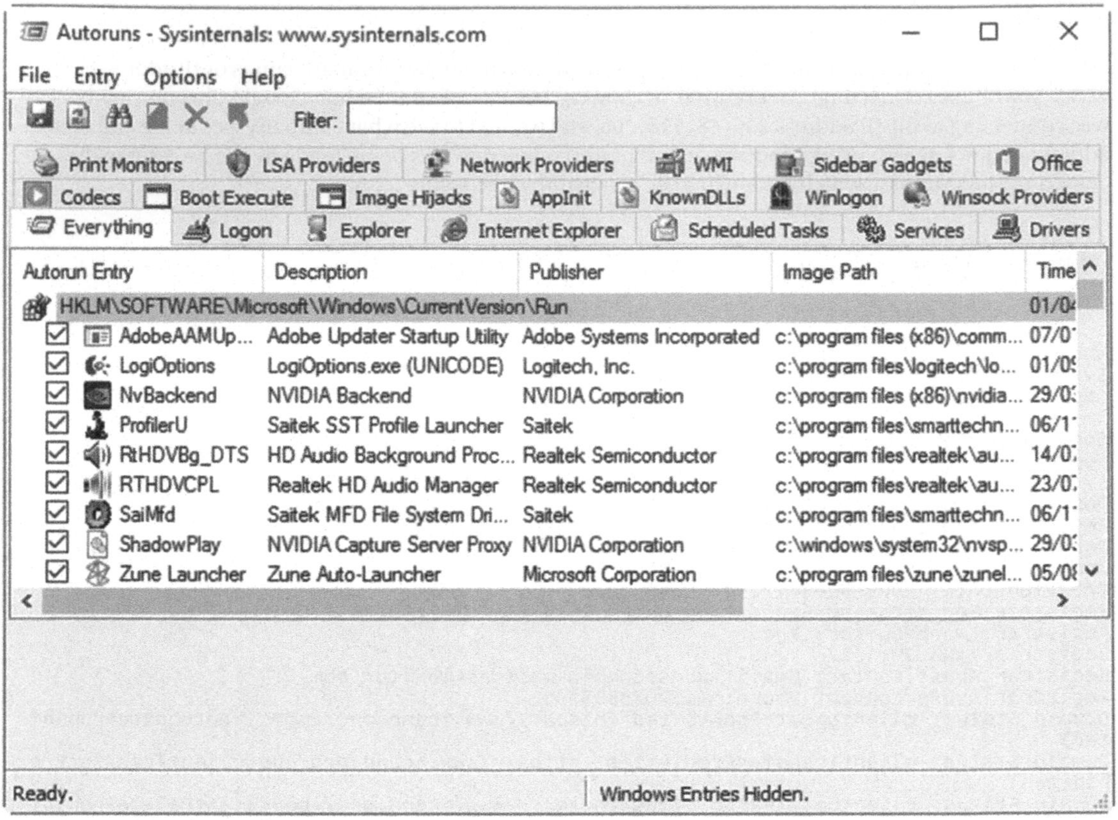

Figure 22-6. *The AutoRuns utility; the daddy of startup managers*

The information available in AutoRuns is at the far end of detailed, and every single item comes with a handy checkbox, enabling you to quickly disable anything that's causing a problem, or that you don't want running on the system.

The list of things that you might want to disable using AutoRuns is extensive and includes (but is by no means limited to) malware, unwanted or problematic audio and video codecs, software has hasn't uninstalled properly or for which the startup entries remain on the system, crapware (the term used to define all the useless apps and utilities that come bundled with new PCs), Registry keys that are associated with startup items, apps that hijack Windows functions such as ISO disk image handling or screen capture, dynamic link libraries (DLLs) that the system can no longer find, web browser plug-ins, tasks that have been set to run automatically at startup, third-party and other Windows Services, faulty drivers, or drivers that cannot be found or that were incorrectly uninstalled... the list just goes on. AutoRuns is just an amazing little utility.

Handle

Earlier in this chapter I showed you some Sysinternals utilities for dealing with locked files. Handle is a command-line utility that can provide details of which app has opened and locked a particular file or director on your PC. Full details of its switches can be found on the Sysinternals web site.

ListDLLs

DLLs are files that are bundled with Windows 10, or provided by third-party software companies, which enable apps to share functions on the PC. Back in the days of DOS, every running program had to provide its own way of managing everything, and I remember the excellent WordPerfect 5.1 word processor coming with a battery of disks that contained its own printer drivers.

DLLs took all this pain away but knowing what's running can be impossible without the use of a utility such as ListDLLs. This is a command-line utility (with switches available on the Sysinternals web site) that can list all the DLLs that have been loaded by an app or process, or to list all the processes that are accessing a particular DLL. Should you find, for example, that an app, process, or DLL is crashing, you can use this tool to see if the DLLs in use have any other dependencies which may be causing the problem.

Portmon

If you are using a PC system to which Serial or Parallel devices are attached, and they're still more common than you might think, then the Portmon utility can display all the activitiy for those ports. This includes successful and failed communications and the process using each port. This information can be useful in tracking down communication problems between the PC and attached devices.

ProcDump

ProcDump is a command-line utility with two uses. The first of these is for monitoring an app for CPU processor spikes and reporting when a spike occurs. If you have an app that is periodically, or even regularly, using huge amounts of processor time, then ProcDump can provide valuable information about what it's doing at the time.

The second use for ProcDump is to monitor apps when they are hung. Sometimes you may encounter an app for which the window appears to temporarily crash. This is because the app is doing, or trying to do something in the background and cannot proceed until that task is complete. In this circumstance, ProcDump can provide information on what is occurring with that app at the time. Full details of the switches available to use with ProcDump are available on the Sysinternals web site.

Process Explorer

I mentioned earlier that Sysinternals had more than one "daddy" in its arsenal, and Process Explorer is another. It's great if you really want to know what's going on in your PC, what app has opened a particular file or folder, what DLLs are being used by an app, how much CPU time an app is taking, how much memory it's using, what network bandwidth it's using, whether it's being run in a secure, virtualized environment or not, what permissions each user or user group has over the app, and more besides. All of this can be gained from a simple and easy-to-understand interface, see Figure 22-7.

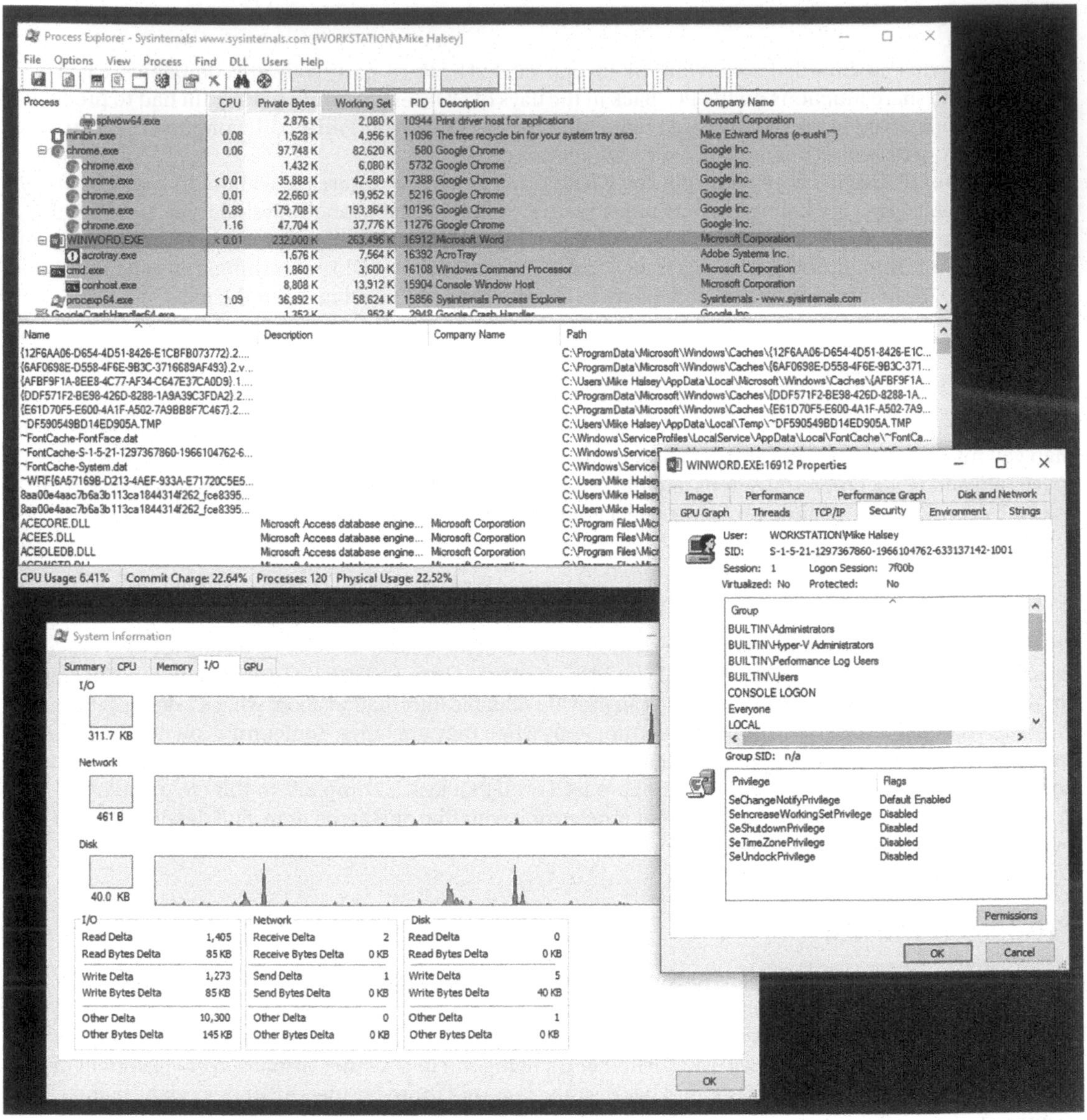

Figure 22-7. *Process Explorer provides more information on running apps than you can believe*

From Process Explorer you can kill processes, or entire process trees, which include all the dependencies for a process. You can suspend processes, restart them, find information about installed DLLs, submit suspect app samples for virus testing, disconnect and send messages to other users who are using resources on the PC, and more besides.

■ **Tip** Sometimes Process Explorer can fail to run, reporting an *"Unable to extract 64-bit image. Run Process Explorer from a writeable directory"* error. Should you encounter this, navigate to your AppData\Local\Temp folder by typing **%tmp%** into the Start menu, Cortana, or the breadcrumb bar in File Explorer, right-click the `procexp64` app, and run it as an Administrator from there.

Process Monitor

If there are any other utilities in the Sysinternals suite that stand head and shoulders above the rest, and that are constantly used and referenced by system administrators and IT Pros, then Process Monitor will definitely be one, see Figure 22-8.

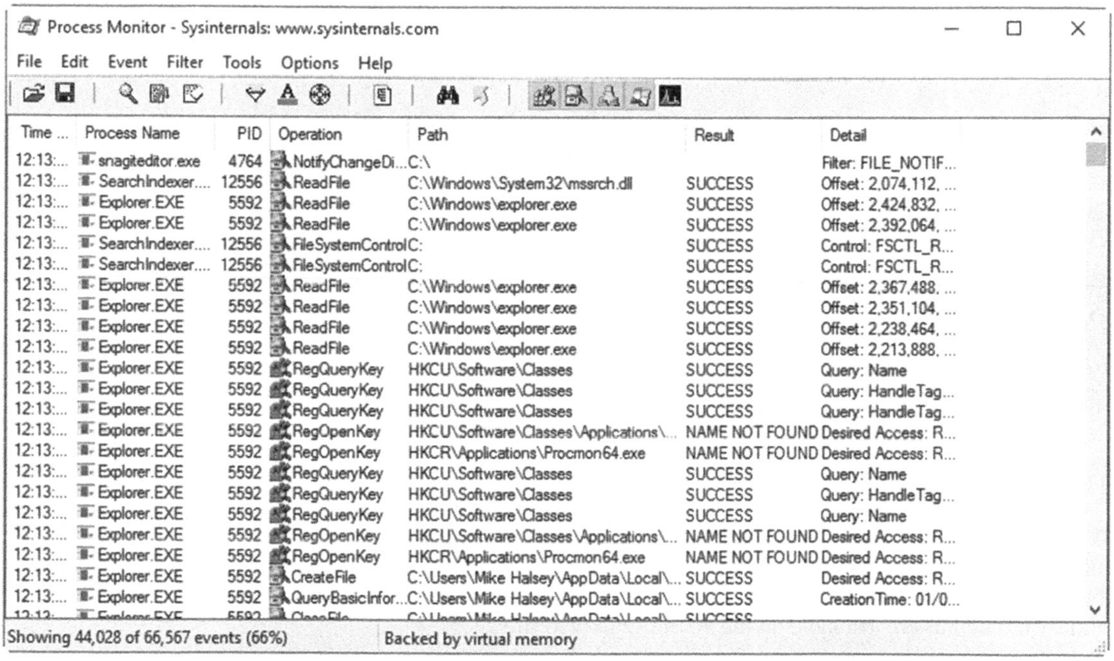

Figure 22-8. Process Monitor details everything running on the PC

This wonderful little utility is so incredibly useful when diagnosing and troubleshooting many types of problems on a PC, including hung apps and app dependencies, malware infections, misconfigured software, deleted files and Registry keys, and more besides.

Process Monitor details, in real time, every running process and service on the PC, with information about every operation they are performing, every Registry key they have open or have access to, and whether the actions they are taking are successful or are reporting an error.

Perhaps you are looking for the dependencies for malware that has infected a PC. You can use Process Monitor to identify all of the Services, DLLs, and Registry keys associated with the core malware app. You can also use Process Monitor to check the dependencies for any running app on the PC, to see what files and keys are associated with it. All of this information can come in handy when diagnosing problems with apps and Windows features, because you can see at a glance what's happening, if the tasks performed have been successful or not, or if essential Registry keys, DLLs, or Services are missing or reporting an error.

Additionally, you can filter the view to narrow the information displayed to a subset of the full available information. Lastly, if a file is locked on the PC and unable to be deleted, moved, copied, or even opened, you can also see what process is currently using and has locked the file, so that the process can be closed or terminated.

PSExec

PSExec is a command-line utility that allows you to execute programs over a remote connection to the PC. It is intended as a lightweight replacement for remote desktop or third-party remote access packages, and for installing apps onto remote PCs. Its full syntax can be found on the Sysinternals web site.

PsKill

PsKill is a command-line utility for terminating running processes on PCs. It has benefits over alternatives such as Process Explorer in that it can kill processes not only for different users on a PC, but also on different PCs across a network. The full syntax is available on the Sysinternals web site.

PsList

PsList is another command-line utility, and it will display detailed technical information about a specified process. You can find the syntax and switches for this utility on the Sysinternals web site.

PsService

PsService is another command-line utility, and it's similar in some respects to PsList. However this utility allows you to get information about and control Services on the PC, or across a network on a remote system. This includes being able to stop, restart, and pause both Microsoft and third-party Services. The full syntax and switch details are available on the Sysinternals web site.

PsSuspend

PsSuspend allows you to suspend processes on a local or remote PC. This can be preferable to killing a service completely; suspending it allows you to continue using the service later on. It is a command-line utility, and its syntax and switches are detailed on the Sysinternals web site.

ShellRunas

ShellRunas is another command-line utility, but one that allows you to launch an app or process under the sign-in credentials of a user other than the one who is already signed into the PC. You can find details of its switches on the Sysinternals web site.

VMMap

PCs don't just hold running apps and processes in memory; they also save some memory to disk in the form of virtual memory, also known as the Paging File in Windows. VMMap allows you to view the physical and virtual memory usage of a specific process, see Figure 22-9. If an app or process is hogging memory, this utility can provide detailed information on how much memory and what memory types are being used.

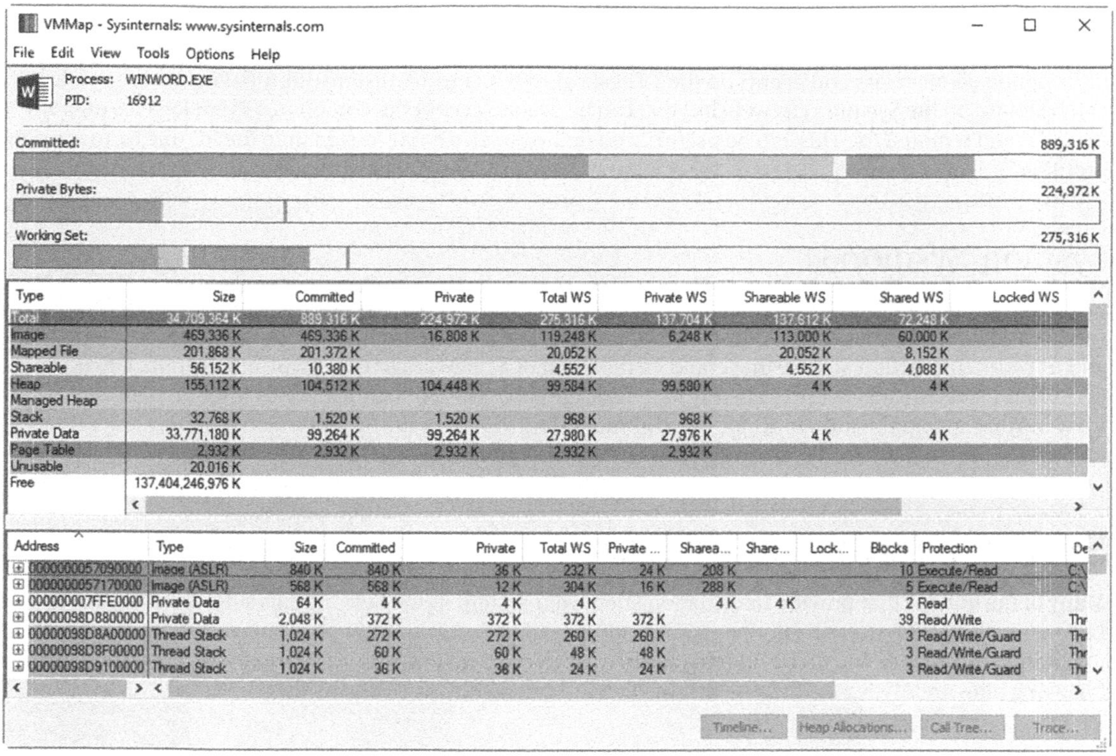

Figure 22-9. *VMMap allows you to view the memory usage for a particular process*

Security Utilities

Security is crucial to maintaining stable and reliable PCs, and to avoid data loss and malware infection. Some of the security tools available in Sysinternals, such as AccessChk and AccessEnum, have already been detailed in this chapter, but others can prove useful.

LogonSessions

LogonSessions is a command-line utility that will detail all of the current user sessions running on the PC. It can be used with the -c switch to automatically output the data as a CSV file, or it can be used with the -p switch to also list all the processes runing in a logon session. Full details and syntax can be found on the Sysinternals web site.

PsLoggedOn

This is another command-line utility for displaying details of which users are currently signed into a PC. This tool can also be used to monitor remote computers, and its full syntax and switches are available on the Sysinternals web site.

PsLogList

Back in Chapter 5, I detailed the Event Viewer in Windows 10, and how it can be used to provide detailed information about errors and events on the PC. PsLogList is a command-line utility (switches and syntax can be found on the Sysinternals website) that can be used to access the contents of Event log files on both the local and remote PCs. This can be useful if you find yourself unable to sign in to the PC due to an error or problem.

Sysmon/Sysmon64

If you suspect that a PC has been infected with malware, the Sysmon can probably help. This tool runs as a service and driver very early in the Windows boot cycle, and checks for process creation, process change, and network connection activity that could be the result of a malware or other type of infection. Once Sysmon is loaded on a PC, it runs silently in the background and reports its findings through the Event Viewer. You can find the full syntax for this command-line utility on the Sysinternals web site, and you can view a Microsoft video on how the utility works at **http://pcs.tv/1TL18TX**.

System Information Utilities

Many of the utilities that provide information about your system in the Sysinternals suite, such as LogonSessions and Process Explorer, have already been detailed in this chapter. There are a few, however, that don't also fall into one of the other categories. Not all of them are applicable to troubleshooting, but the following ones are.

Handle

Handle is a command-line utility that can report which program has a specific file or directory open. It provides all the data about a specific profess or app, and its full syntax and switches can be seen on the Sysinternals web site.

LiveKd

LiveKd is a command-line debugging tool for the Windows kernel files. It can be used on the main PC or on a Hyper-V virtual machine running on the PC, and needs to be used with the Debuggin Tools for Windows. These tools, and full details on how to use LiveKd, can be found on the Sysinternals web site.

LoadOrder

The LoadOrder utility can be used to view the order in which device drivers are loaded when a PC starts, see Figure 22-10. If a driver is failing at startup, you can see if it is loading early enough in the boot process so any dependencies load afterward. LoadOrder can also be used to detect unwanted drivers or malware infections.

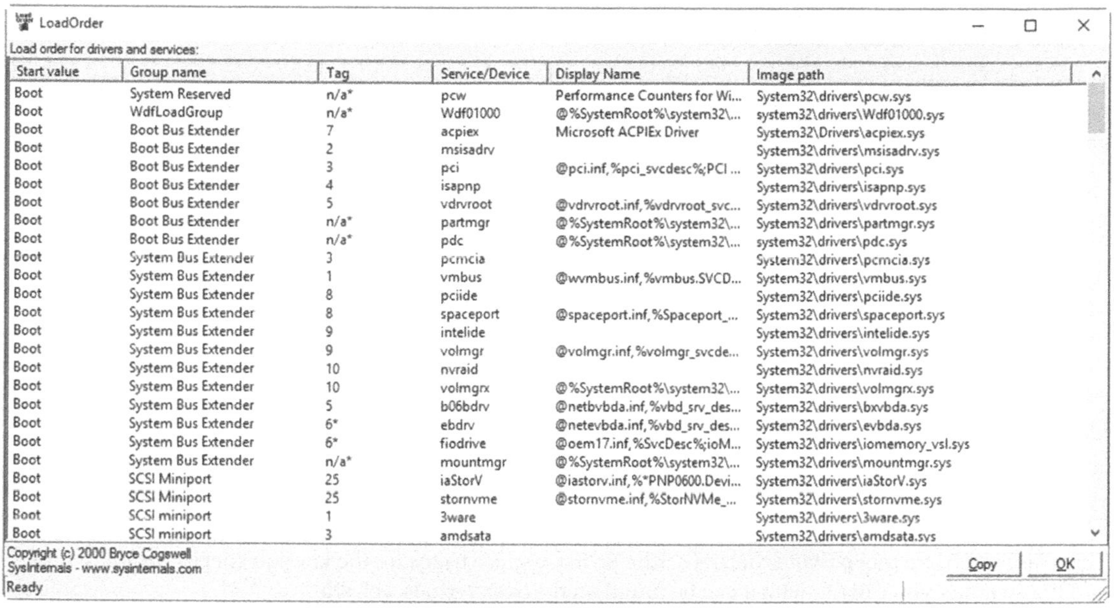

Start value	Group name	Tag	Service/Device	Display Name	Image path
Boot	System Reserved	n/a*	pcw	Performance Counters for Wi...	System32\drivers\pcw.sys
Boot	WdfLoadGroup	n/a*	Wdf01000	@%SystemRoot%\system32\...	system32\drivers\Wdf01000.sys
Boot	Boot Bus Extender	7	acpiex	Microsoft ACPIEx Driver	System32\Drivers\acpiex.sys
Boot	Boot Bus Extender	2	msisadrv		System32\drivers\msisadrv.sys
Boot	Boot Bus Extender	3	pci	@pci.inf, %pci_svcdesc%;PCI ...	System32\drivers\pci.sys
Boot	Boot Bus Extender	4	isapnp		System32\drivers\isapnp.sys
Boot	Boot Bus Extender	5	vdrvroot	@vdrvroot.inf, %vdrvroot_svc...	System32\drivers\vdrvroot.sys
Boot	Boot Bus Extender	n/a*	partmgr	@%SystemRoot%\system32\...	System32\drivers\partmgr.sys
Boot	Boot Bus Extender	n/a*	pdc	@%SystemRoot%\system32\...	System32\drivers\pdc.sys
Boot	System Bus Extender	3	pcmcia		System32\drivers\pcmcia.sys
Boot	System Bus Extender	1	vmbus	@wvmbus.inf, %vmbus.SVCD...	System32\drivers\vmbus.sys
Boot	System Bus Extender	8	pciide		System32\drivers\pciide.sys
Boot	System Bus Extender	8	spaceport	@spaceport.inf, %Spaceport_...	System32\drivers\spaceport.sys
Boot	System Bus Extender	9	intelide		System32\drivers\intelide.sys
Boot	System Bus Extender	9	volmgr	@volmgr.inf, %volmgr_svcde...	System32\drivers\volmgr.sys
Boot	System Bus Extender	10	nvraid		System32\drivers\nvraid.sys
Boot	System Bus Extender	10	volmgrx	@%SystemRoot%\system32\...	System32\drivers\volmgrx.sys
Boot	System Bus Extender	5	b06bdrv	@netbvbda.inf, %vbd_srv_des...	System32\drivers\bxvbda.sys
Boot	System Bus Extender	6*	ebdrv	@netevbda.inf, %vbd_srv_des...	System32\drivers\evbda.sys
Boot	System Bus Extender	6*	fiodrive	@oem17.inf, %SvcDesc%;ioM...	System32\drivers\iomemory_vsl.sys
Boot	System Bus Extender	n/a*	mountmgr	@%SystemRoot%\system32\...	System32\drivers\mountmgr.sys
Boot	SCSI Miniport	25	iaStorV	@iastorv.inf, %*PNP0600.Devi...	System32\drivers\iaStorV.sys
Boot	SCSI Miniport	25	stornvme	@stornvme.inf, %StorNVMe_...	System32\drivers\stornvme.sys
Boot	SCSI miniport	1	3ware		System32\drivers\3ware.sys
Boot	SCSI miniport	3	amdsata		System32\drivers\amdsata.sys

Copyright (c) 2000 Bryce Cogswell
Sysinternals - www.sysinternals.com

Figure 22-10. *LoadOrder displays the order in which drivers are loaded at startup*

RAMMap

This utility provides detailed graphical and technical data on memory usage on the PC, see Figure 22-11. This includes details of all apps and process memory usage, but also details of file memory usage. You can use RAMMap to see how memory is being allocated in Windows 10, so that you can analyze memory usage on the PC.

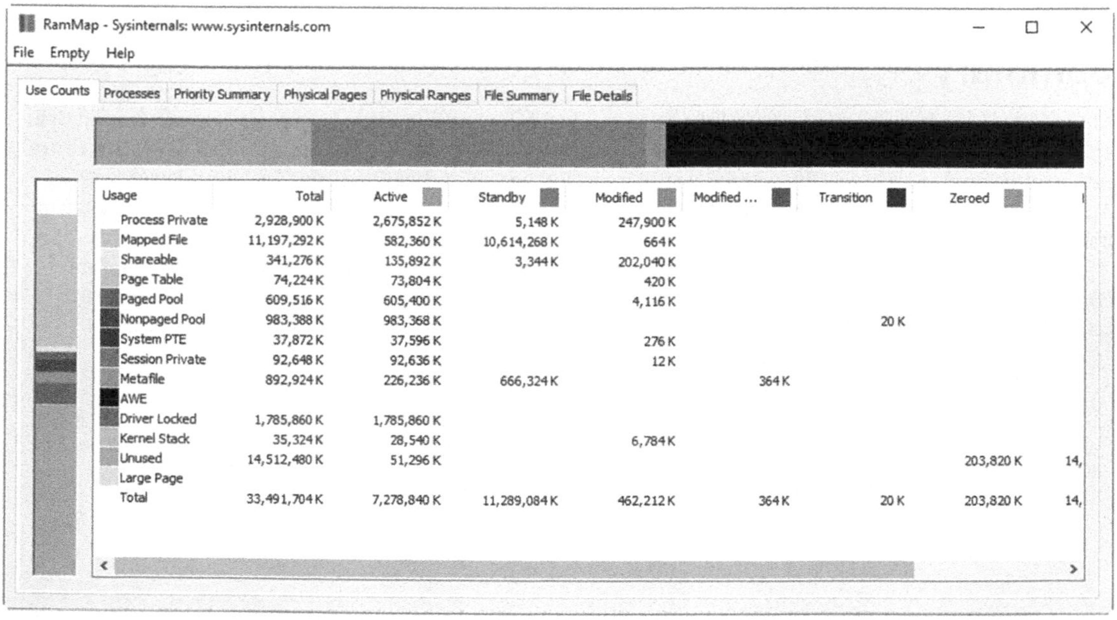

Usage	Total	Active	Standby	Modified	Modified ...	Transition	Zeroed	
Process Private	2,928,900 K	2,675,852 K	5,148 K	247,900 K				
Mapped File	11,197,292 K	582,360 K	10,614,268 K	664 K				
Shareable	341,276 K	135,892 K	3,344 K	202,040 K				
Page Table	74,224 K	73,804 K		420 K				
Paged Pool	609,516 K	605,400 K		4,116 K				
Nonpaged Pool	983,388 K	983,368 K				20 K		
System PTE	37,872 K	37,596 K		276 K				
Session Private	92,648 K	92,636 K		12 K				
Metafile	892,924 K	226,236 K	666,324 K		364 K			
AWE								
Driver Locked	1,785,860 K	1,785,860 K						
Kernel Stack	35,324 K	28,540 K		6,784 K				
Unused	14,512,480 K	51,296 K					203,820 K	14,
Large Page								
Total	33,491,704 K	7,278,840 K	11,289,084 K	462,212 K	364 K	20 K	203,820 K	14,

Figure 22-11. *RAMMap provides technical data on memory usage*

Miscellaneous Utilities

There are a few other Sysinternals utilities that don't fall into any of the main categories, but that are useful nonetheless. Not all of the miscellaneous Sysinternals tools are relevant to troubleshooting, but those that are follow.

RegDelNull

If you find yourself unable to delete a Registry key that you need to get rid of, perhaps to clean up an app that's not uninstalled properly, or to remove malware, and you're unable to delete the key, RegDelNull might be able to help. This command-line tool is used in the format `regdelnull <RegistryKeyPath> [-s]` to delete keys that have embedded-null characaters, and that are otherwise undeletable, perhaps due to a Registry corruption. The `-s` switch forces the command to include all subkeys ion the deletion. More information is available on the Sysinternals web site.

Registry Usage

This command-line tool provides details on the Registry space usage for the key you specify. Its full syntax and the switches you can use with it can be found on the Sysinternals web site.

RegJump

RegJump is a very handy little command-line utility to use, and is made even more useful in Windows 10, now that the Command Prompt fully suports cut and paste. It will force the Registry Editor to open at the key you specify, saving time having to scroll through the Registry Editor, opening paths as you go. It can be used in the format `regjump <RegistryPathName>`, or in the format `regjump -c`, which will automatically copy the Registry Address from the Windows clipboard.

Summary

Microsoft's Sysinternals suite is so useful, and so packed full of utilities, that I could never have hoped to fit all the information on how to use it for troubleshooting into anything smaller than its own book. There are many additional tools and utilities that I've not included here, but that are useful for administrating PCs. Again, you can download the Sysinternals tools and get full documentation from the Microsoft web site at `https://technet.microsoft.com/Sysinternals`.

Now seems like a good time though to bring the fopcus back to the best way to protect PCs so that complex tools like Sysinternals don't need to be used, or where their use can be minimized. In the next chapter then, we'll look at best practices for setting up, maintaining, and using PCs in the workplace.

CHAPTER 23

■ ■ ■

Best Practice in the Workplace

Much of the preventative work you can do, to help make sure problems with PCs don't occur, or at least occur infrequently, comes down to best practice methodology. In the business space this is doubly important as, whether you have six or six thousand PCs to support, troubleshooting and repair are complex and time-consuming processes. Either you've got to invest time in diagnosing the cause of a problem so that you can implement a fix, or you reimage a machine and the user then has to wait some time for all the most recent updates and patches to be installed.

But what is best practice when it comes to making sure your PCs work in a worry- and trouble-free way? Simply put, it's a common-sense approach to your work that not only helps you get things done more quickly and effectively when deploying and maintaining PCs, but that can also help the user. Indeed, some of the ideas and suggestions I'll put forward in this chapter (and you'll also have your own ideas) can save battery power, keep users working longer, and help them to be more productive in the mix.

Managing Power and Batteries

The battery seems like a great place to begin, as effective power management can help boost not just battery life on laptops and tablets, but the security on all PCs. Why do I say this? Well, it's because some of Windows 10's security features are tied in with the power management settings.

The Advanced Power Management settings can be found by opening the Power Options from the *Win+X* menu. Click the *Require a password on wake-up* option in the top left corner of the window, and then, if necessary, click the *Change settings that are currently unavailable* link. This will present options to *Require a password (recommended)* and *Don't require a password*.

Additionally though, if you click the *Choose when to turn off the display* or the *Change when the computer sleeps* option from the main Power Options screen, and then click the *Change advanced power settings* link, you will see separate options on a laptop or tablet for requiring a password on both grid power and battery, see Figure 23-1.

© Mike Halsey 2016
M. Halsey, *Windows 10 Troubleshooting*, DOI 10.1007/978-1-4842-0925-7_23

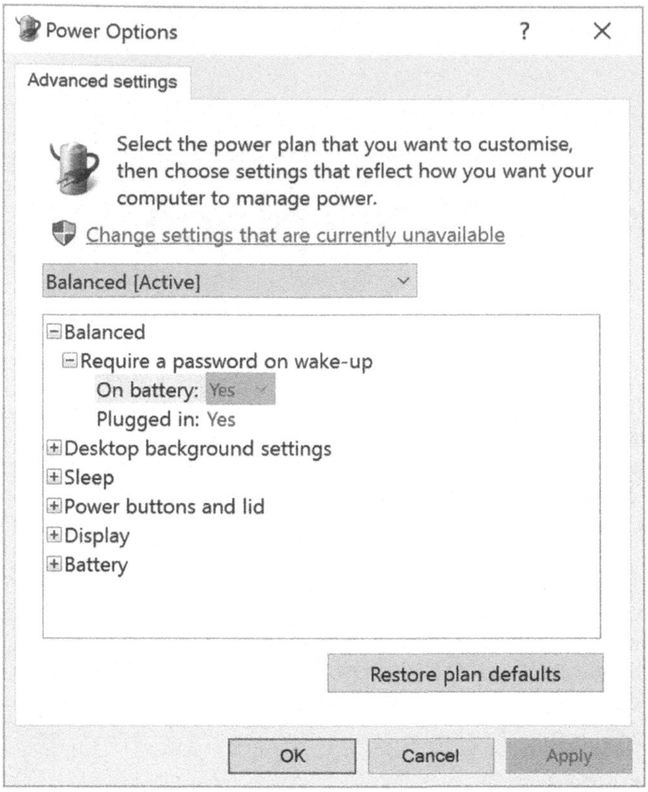

Figure 23-1. *You can disable password entry on wake-up if necessary*

Why is this significant when it's recommended that you have a password on the machine all the time anyway? Ideally yes, for reasons of good security it's preferable to have password entry every time you come back to a PC. However, if you also enforce a strong password policy, this can prove to be a chore for users who will end up having to resent it. Given that the user will have to enter their password when they start the PC in the morning anyway, you can then, as an example, enforce passwords on wake-up only if it's running on battery power. This gives the user less stress when working in the office or at home on their laptop, while also enforcing better security if they're using the laptop in a coffee shop, on a train, or elsewhere away from your premises.

■ **Tip**   If the user of a laptop or tablet doesn't need to use the file search feature of Windows 10, disabling the *Windows Search* service can sometimes boost battery life by up to 30%.

Changing the behavior of the power button on the PC can reap benefits as well. In the Power Options, clicking the *Choose what the power buttons do* link, and then the *Change settings that are currently unavailable* link if necessary, will allow you to change the shutdown and sleep behaviors of the PC, see Figure 23-2. Why might you want to do this? There are both technical and practical reasons for doing so.

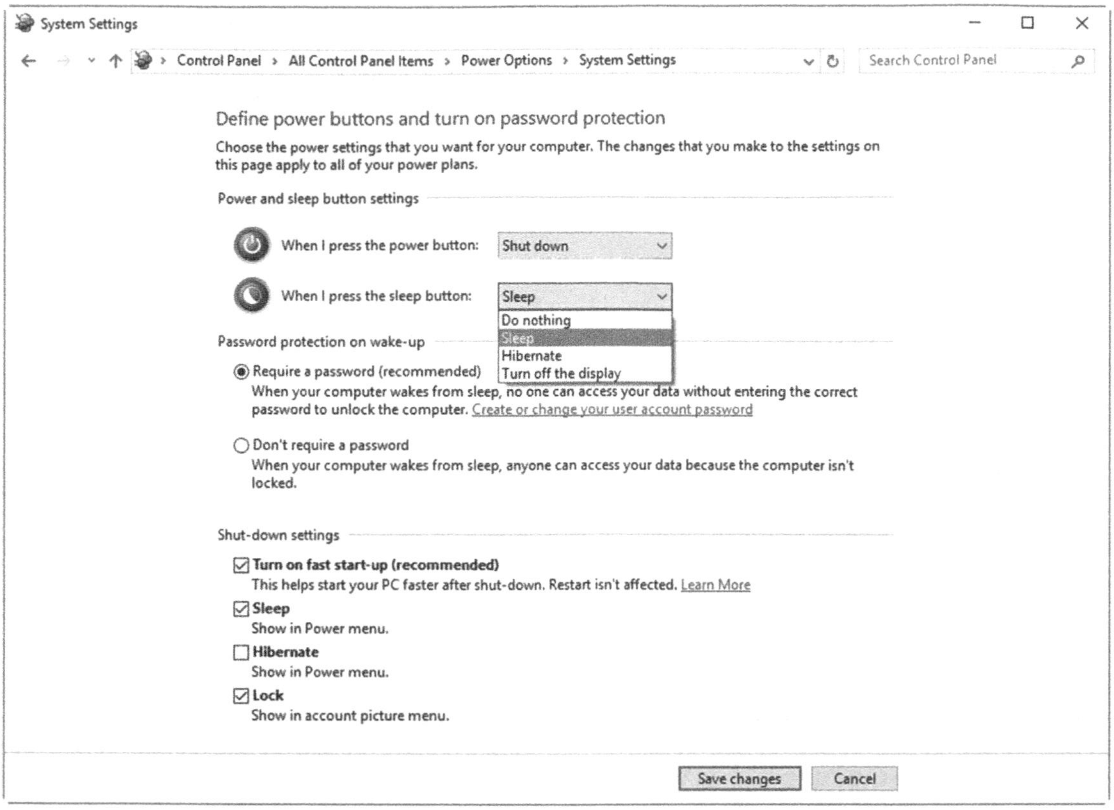

Figure 23-2. *You can change the behavior of the power buttons*

The practical reasons include the fact that modern PCs consume almost no electricity in sleep mode, and after a couple of hours in sleep, the PC will hibernate automatically, in which it will use no power at all. In these states, startup is considerably quicker than starting the PC from cold, and the effect on your power or battery usage is minimal because both Windows 10 and modern PCs are incredibly power-efficient.

It can also be annoying for a user waiting to start their PC. I'm guilty of this as I've been using laptops since they first appeared (indeed I remember the original CGA LCD screens on early laptops giving me blinding headaches after a short while), and because of the very poor battery life of laptops at the time, I long ago became used to switching them off properly. It can be a hard habit to break, so reassigning the power button action can sometimes help.

On a technical level, there are some PCs that simply don't like various sleep and hibernate states in Windows 10. You'll know this from trial and error, but symptoms can include a signal not being returned to a connected monitor, so you don't get a picture, the PC effectively hanging when you try to wake it, or a PC not really going to sleep at all.

■ **Tip**   Having one app, be it a store app or a win32 app, open full screen uses less power than having multiple apps open in separate windows on the desktop. This is because the PC's graphics processor has less to draw, and less work to do. Encouraging people to use their apps full-screen, perhaps by switching the device into Tablet Mode, and switching between them as necessary, can extend the battery life of a laptop or tablet.

Newer PCs, that is to say, ones that have been released in the Windows 8.1/Windows 10 timeframe, will usually support a feature called Hybrid Sleep, which is designed primarily for desktop PCs, and is a combination of the sleep and hibernate states. It saves the current working state of the PC to both memory and the hard disk, enabling you to carry on working quickly from sleep, or from a hibernate state, should there be a power failure.

This is different to the sleep and hibernate states that are designed for laptops and tablets, which save the current state of the PC to memory and the hard disk, respectively. As I mentioned earlier, a laptop or tablet placed in sleep will automatically hibernate after a couple of hours, though you can change this setting in the Power Options.

Fast Start-Up is slightly different, and not all PCs will support it. Indeed, you may find that some PCs which should actually support it might complain about it. Fast Start-Up saves the working state of the Windows kernel (the core OS files) that is residing in memory to the hard disk when you shut down the PC. The next time you start the PC from cold, what is effectively a hibernation file, but without your previously loaded open documents and apps, is loaded back into memory more quickly than Windows 10 can read the files individually from the hard disk.

■ **Tip** Windows Store apps consume less power than traditional win32 desktop apps. This is because they are suspended when not in focus (i.e., not in the foregound and selected on the desktop). In this suspended state they use no processor time at all. If you have people in your business who use, for example, Microsoft Office, encouraging them to switch to the Store versions of Word, Excel, PowerPoint, and OneNote can save power on their laptop or tablet, extending its battery life, while also providing most, if not all, of the functionality they need.

Managing Users and BYOD PCs

Nothing will break something on a PC faster than letting someone actually use the thing. Unfortunately, much as we would like people to stop using and therefore breaking our PCs, it's not very practical and they wouldn't get much work done. Managing users in an effective way, then, is essential to best practice and minimizing problems from occurring.

This is complicated slightly in the workplace because of the rise and rise of BYOD, known as Bring Your Own Device (and sometimes Bring Your Own Disaster). People love using using own laptops and tablets in the workplace, perhaps because the ones provided by the company are so crummy, or perhaps because it aloows them to work more freely at home.

The problems associated with BYOD however are many and bountiful. They include not being able to control the antivirus software, or Windows Updates on the PC, not being able to control the basic security of the PC, and not being able to control who else gets access to it and gets to use it. All of these are a nightmare for systems administrators.

MDM

Windows 8 was the first Microsoft operating system to feature BYOD support. These come in the form of Azure Active Directory sign in, and Work folders (a more modern and manageable version of ActiveSync for files). Mobile Device Management (MDM) is by far the most useful, however. Managed from a Windows Server system, MDM allows system administrators to specify minimum standards for Windows Updates, security settings, and malware protection. Additionally, should an employee with an enrolled PC leave the company, the administrators can remotely wipe any company files and data stored on the PC.

MDM is configured from the Settings app, in the Accounts section, see Figure 23-3, and it's a simple process that can be done by the users themselves. It doesn't affect the basic operation of their PCs, but it can prevent them from accessing the company network or files, if they do not meet, and keep up with the minimum security requirements.

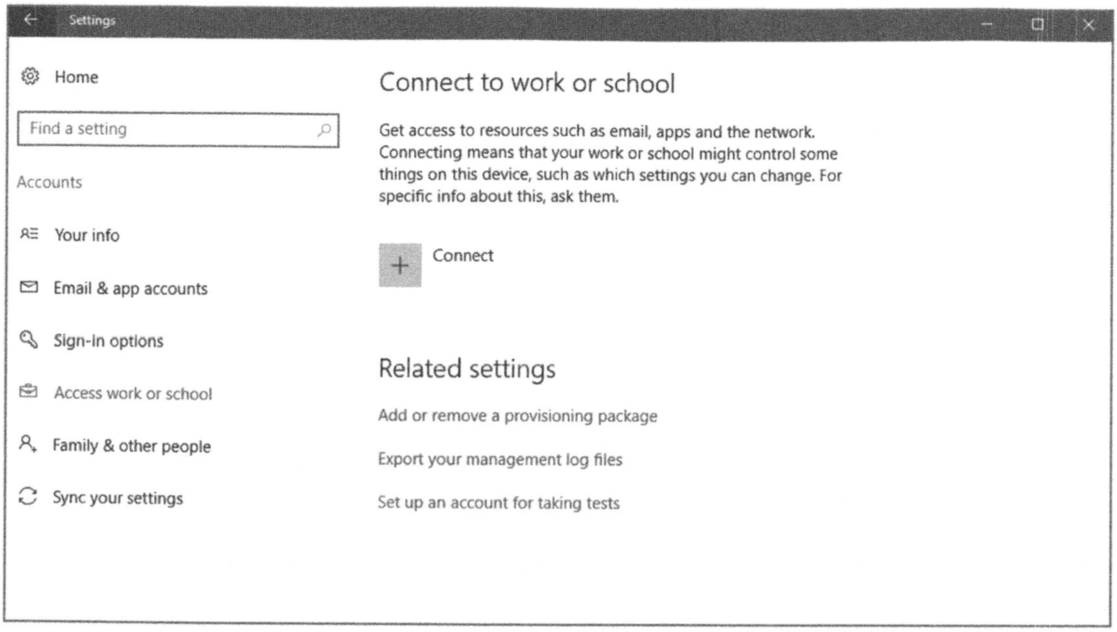

Figure 23-3. *MDM allows administrators control over BYOD PCs*

Group Policy

There are other ways to manage users as well. In Chapter 21 I showed you how you can bomb-proof your PCs using Group Policy. There's much that can be done with Group Policy to prevent users from putting PCs into a state where problems will occur. These can include blocking the installation of anything other than approved apps, and even specific versions of apps.

You can also prevent users from making any configuration changes to the PC, such as changing its power, desktop, or network settings, and you can stop users from installing Windows Updates, if you have a policy of carefully checking for compatibility and other issues before rolling these out.

Backups Best Practice

The way we back up our files and data has changed dramatically in the last few years. Do you remember the days when you'd buy a big stack of blank CDs or DVDs, and then spend several hours every month burning copies of all your files to them, only to find that when you needed to copy a file back, the disc had become corrupt and wouldn't work? I certainly do!

These days we're far more likely to rely on Network Attached Storage (NAS) or cloud backups, as they are seamless, constant, and nonintrusive in our lives. I love that the files on my PCs both are backed up and synchronized with Microsoft's OneDrive service; after all, what's not to like?

Sadly, though, maintaining your backups only in this way is also a recipe for disaster, as the world and its threats have moved on. Now, especially with the threat of ransomware, we need to be smarter about how we schedule, and where we put, our backups.

Now, what I'm going to write here is my own recommendation. You might use some or all of it, or you might have your own ideas. I'm not going to say that my way is best practice, though it's certainly good practice. It's based upon the three core principles of being prepared, staying ready to restore quickly, and maintaining a consistently high level of paranoia. My own backup strategy works as follows...

- **Backup #1**, full file backup to Microsoft's OneDrive cloud service. This creates a reliable offsite backup in case of an event such as fire or theft, while also allowing me to synchronize my files between my PC, laptop, tablet, and other devices.

- **Backup #2**, full file backup to the LiveDrive cloud service, just in case Backup #1 fails or deletes files. This has actually happened with OneDrive before, and to some of my own files as well. This backup only takes place every couple of days, which reduces bandwidth consumption, while also helping with the security reason I have for Backup #4.

- **Backup #3**, local backup using File History to a separate hard disk in my main PC. This enables version control should I need to go back to an earlier version of a file, or recover a deleted file, while also making the whole files library quick to restore if necessary. This is on a hard disk more than double the size of my total file collection, to allow for maximum version control.

- **Backup #4**, local backup performed to a NAS drive, but only on a weekly or fortnightly schedule, and not constantly like the other backups. This is my protection against ransomware, which encrypts files and damands payment to unlock them. With a backup performed on a schedule, you can only lose the most recent work should you need to reformat the hard disk and recover your files. Sadly, because of the instant or near-instant nature of Backups #1, #2 and #3, encrypted files can be transferred to those backups, wiping out previous versions before you become aware an infection has taken place.

Like I said... I'm pretty paranoid! Our files are our lives, however, and often our livelihoods as well. It's one thing for Granny Clark to dig an old photo album out of the drawer to show you photos of you when you were a baby, but quite another thing for all your precious photos to be wiped out by an accident, malware attack, or user error.

■ **Caution**   I want to deal for a moment with the issue of offsite backups. These are crucial for any individual or business as they keep you covered in the event of a fire, theft, flood, alien attack, war, asteroid strike, supervolcano eruption, or the cat peeing on the computer. There are data protection issues tied to offsite backups for business, however. Data protection regulations will differ around the world, but generally they will require any data you store on employees, customers, suppliers, and members of the public to be secure and safe at all times. It might be tempting for a small business, for example, to mirror their workplace backup to a NAS drive in somebody's home. The simple act of doing this, however, could put the business in breach of data protection law should the NAS drive later be stolen. You should always check local data protection legislation before deciding where to store your offsite backups.

Deployment and Recovery Best Practice

If you're deploying Windows 10 across a medium- to large-size organization using volume licensing, then you'll already be using the Windows Assessment and Deployment Toolkit (ADK). This affords you full control over deployment images, drivers, installed apps, and more besides. For small businesses, however, perhaps with just a few PCs, each machine must be installed individually.

Generally speaking, each PC will have come with Windows 10 preinstalled, or will have been upgraded from Windows 7 or Windows 8.1. Windows 10 is a very stable and robust OS that should operate for years on the same hardware with few problems. There are still things you should do however to make sure that if you need to reimage or redeploy the OS, you can do this quickly, easily, and without any barriers. These, then, are my top tips to aid deployment and recovery in a non-volume-licensing business environment, or in the home.

1. Keep a copy of all the drivers for your hardware in at least one safe place. I keep a copy of all drivers in cloud storage so they can be synced to devices for installation, or easily copied to a USB Flash Drive.

2. Optionally, you can also keep a copy of the `C:\Windows\System32\DriverStore` folder after installation, as this will contain drivers that can be searched for by the Device Manager. However, do not immediately merge this folder with the DriverStore folder after reinstallation, as some drivers may rely on system updates that may not be installed.

3. Install Windows 10 from fresh media (DVD or USB) created using the official Media Creation Tool, `www.microsoft.com/software-download/windows10`. This ensures you are installing the most recent build of the OS, and therefore reduces the time needed after installation to install updates and patches. This can also be downloaded to create a DVD you can use with the System File Checker, see Chapter 4.

4. **Create a USB Recovery Drive**. Yes, you just knew I was going to come back to this, but it really is the single most important thing you can do with any Windows 10 PC. Label the drive, and keep it in a safe place where you can easily find it. I detailed how to create a Recovery Drive in Chapter 2.

5. Make a backup image of your Windows 10 installation to a separate internal hard disk or partition. I create special backup partitions on all my PCs for this purpose, containing a clean installation that has all apps and drivers installed. You can find out how to create a System Image Backup in Chapter 2.

6. Always leave a spare, general-purpose machine available on standby when you're going on vacation. You can guarantee that somebody important in the business will have a major PC crisis the moment you go away. Keeping a spare, patched, and up-to-date machine on standby will enable this individual to carry on working, so as not to ruin your once-in-a-lifetime trip to the Bahamas.

Managing External and Network Hardware

The best way for any external or network hardware to cause problems is for it to become damaged, and the best way for it to become damaged is for somebody to bash into it, trip over it, or snag it. This is especially true of cabling, which can be severely damaged if pulled, not to mention what can happen to the hardware on the other end of the cable, which is also pulled.

This type of damage can result in broken plugs and sockets, ripped cables, cracked cases when hardware hits the floor... you get the idea. It's extremely easy to avoid too, because the cable tie is the system administrator's best friend. These small pieces of plastic can secure any bunch of cables together, on their own or to anything else. If your desks have cable management built in, do use it; it'll save you a lot of headaches, and please, please, keep anything that people don't actively need access to away from them. They'll definitely find a way to break it if you leave it out or lying around.

Summary

Best practice really is just common sense, and is very easy to both practice and instill into others. The end users of PCs won't exercise common sense, however, because they just want to get stuff done quickly and enjoy themselves with the minimum amount of effort, so you can't rely on them to help and will have to do things youself.

I mentioned BYOD earlier in this chapter and how you can use best practice to manage BYOD devices. In the next chapter, we'll look at this in more detail, and I'll show you how BYOD devices can be managed and configured in workplace environments.

CHAPTER 24

■ ■ ■

Managing BYOD Hardware

BYOD, or Bring Your Own Device, sprang up on the popularity of the iPad. Corporate executives would get a shiny-new tablet for Christmas or for their birthday and then proclaim to the IT department that it was wonderful and that everybody should be allowed to use them.

It's fine in theory that all computers should be able to work well together; after all, they just communicate in 1's and 0's (zeros). As you'll know, however, not only do all devices *not* communicate with each other nicely sometimes, but the risks involved in letting people use their own computers at work are enough to cause many sleepless nights for an IT Pro.

Fortunately, Microsoft stepped into the fray with Mobile Device Management (MDM); you can read all about this at www.microsoft.com/server-cloud/enterprise-mobility but the short version is that MDM is a suite of tools that allows you to manage BYOD devices running the Windows, iOS, and Android operating systems. This includes smartphones and tablets.

Why is a tool such as MDM important? Simply put, as an IT Pro you will have no control over the security and patching of devices not directly owned and maintained by your company. For all you know, the person wanting to use their Android smartphone or tablet is running an extremely old, and no longer supported, version of the OS; the person wanting to use their own Windows laptop might have let the 30-day trial of antivirus software lapse after they purchased it, thinking that they're still protected; or the person with the lovely new iPad might let their children, and all of their children's friends, play with it in the evenings. In short, BYOD is at the very least a headache and at most a nightmare.

There's a whole book in how you use MDM to manage iOS, Android, and Windows devices, and sadly I've not enough pages in this chapter to show you how to manage everything here, but I'll show you what BYOD functions exist within Windows 10 and how you and the owners of BYOD PCs can use them to help them use their own device at work, and to also give you the peace of mind and reassurance that you all need.

Managing VPNs and Secure Connections

Before we jump into all the BYOD stuff, though, I want to begin by looking at how you can get secure connections from mobile devices to your company using a Virtual Private Network (VPN). VPNs are secure, encrypted data connections that give you peace of mind when an employee is connecting to your company network from a remote location over an Internet connection.

VPNs are managed the same in Windows 10 and Windows 10 Mobile, from the *Network & Internet* section of the Settings app, see Figure 24-1.

© Mike Halsey 2016

M. Halsey, *Windows 10 Troubleshooting*, DOI 10.1007/978-1-4842-0925-7_24

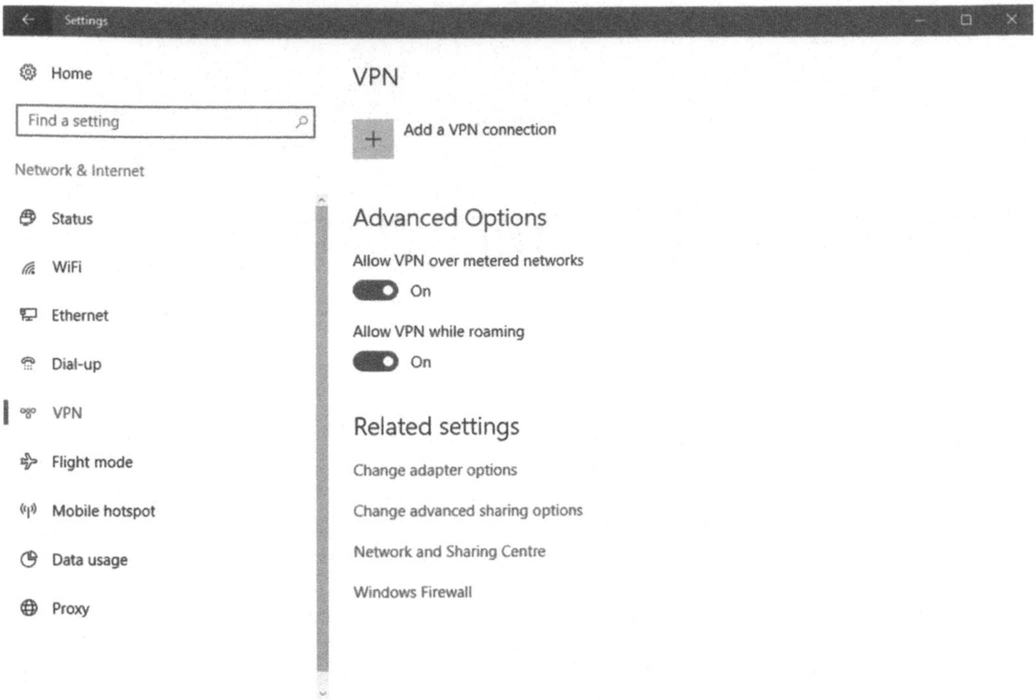

Figure 24-1. *VPNs are managed in the Settings app*

Microsoft has configured the Settings app in such a way as to make it easy and straightforward for anybody, of any technical ability, to configure the settings there. You can see in Figure 24-2 the information that you will need to provide to an employee so that she can configure her own PC to connect to your VPN.

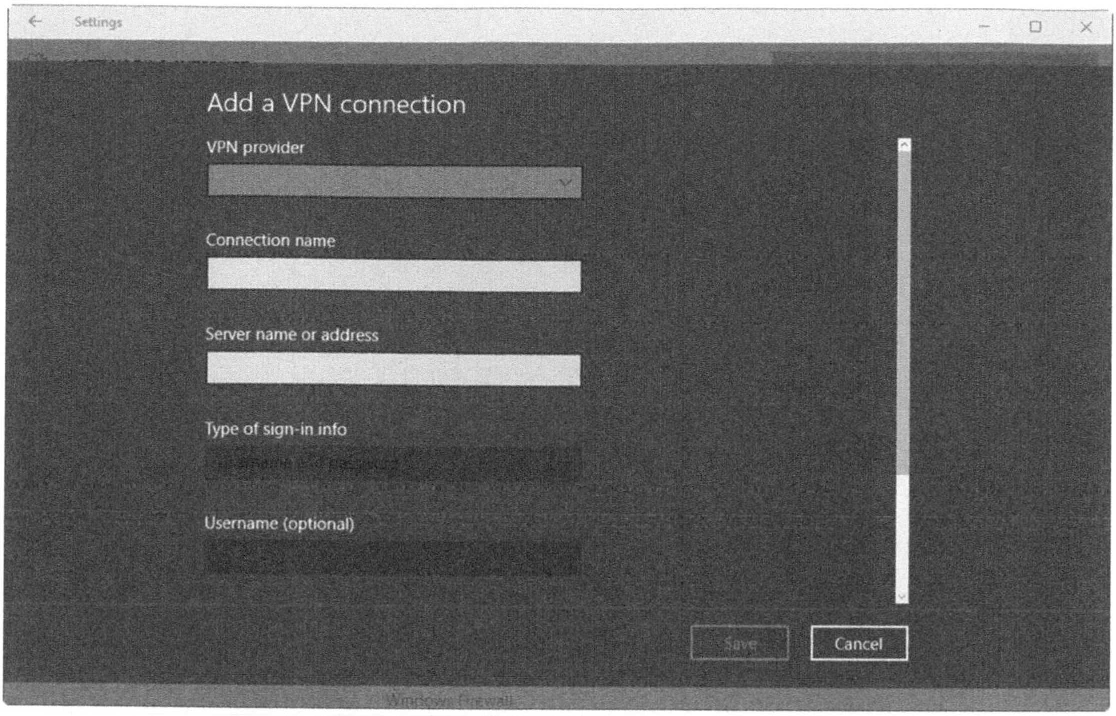

Figure 24-2. *It is easy to set up new VPN connections*

The *VPN Provider* option will use the *Windows (built-in)* default option unless you use a third-party VPN provider, for which there will no doubt be software the user will need to install on their PC first. You will then need to provide the connection name, server name or address, the VPN connection type, and details of how the user connects to the VPN, be this a username and password or a smart card.

Once the VPN is configured, the user can then connect to it from the Network & Internet panel, where *Connect, Advanced Options* (effectively editing the settings) and *Remove* options will be available to them.

Workplace Join

Whether the user is connecting their own PC to your company network remotely over a VPN, or directly in your workplace over your own Wi-Fi or wired network, there are additional options available for managing these BYOD devices.

■ **Tip**   A good security measure in the workplace is to maintain a separate Wi-Fi network for BYOD devices. This will still enable them to access workplace resources that you have connected via a switch, but can limit the surface area for attack should a device's security become compromised.

Workplace Join ties in directly with MDM, and Workplace Join can be configured to not permit connections unless the user also enrolls their device into MDM. They can do this in the Settings app, so again it's easy for them to do and understand, in the *Accounts* ➤ *Access work or school* section, see Figure 24-3.

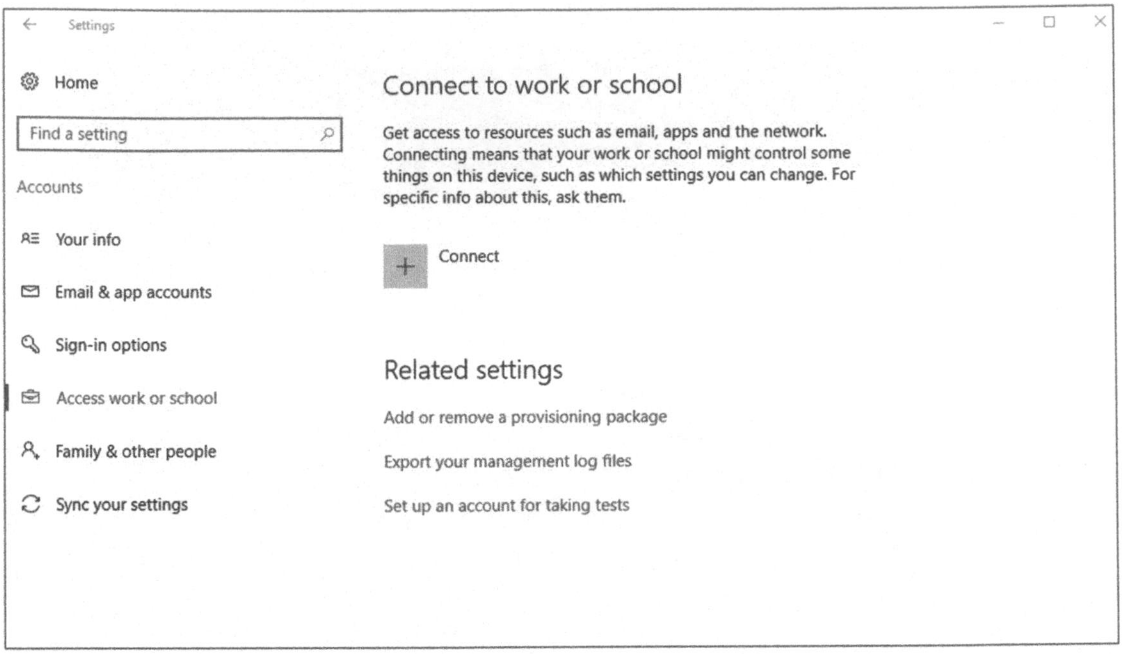

Figure 24-3. *MDM and Workplace Join are managed from the Accounts settings*

Let's spend a minute looking at what MDM allows you to do with a PC. The benefits include being able to specify minimum levels of threat protection for the device. For example, you can specify that devices for which updates and malware security are not up to date, will not be permitted to connect to the network. All of this is manageable yourself, however through Microsoft's InTune service, where you can see the current status of all BYOD (and other) PCs and push updates and apps to them as appropriate.

MDM also gives you permissions on apps. You can't stop the owner of the device from installing whatever apps they want—it is their device after all—but you can specify which ones they can use when connected to your network, and which versions of those apps can be used as well. This means that, for example, they could be prevented from using a browser where Flash is installed, or from using an older and insecure version of Adobe Acrobat Reader or Microsoft Office.

Lastly, MDM gives you authority to wipe all apps and documents related to the business from the device remotely and at any time. This means you can completely revoke a person's access should they leave the company, or for another reason, such as the PC being lost or stolen, without having to have the user or the device onsite. You specify what needs to be wiped, and the next time that device is online the instruction will be passed. You will then be able to monitor the status of the management using InTune.

Connecting to an Exchange or ActiveSync Account

The device owner can connect to your Workplace simply by clicking the *Access work or school account* link. This will drop them into the main Accounts options where they need to click the *(+) Add an account* button. This will present various options to add Microsoft Google or other e-mail account types. You can also add business accounts by clicking *Email & app accounts*, then clicking *Add an account*, which will allow them to set up Exchange or ActiveSync account types, see Figure 24-4.

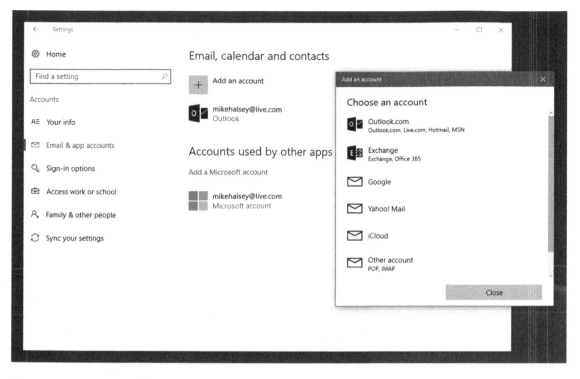

Figure 24-4. *You can add business accounts in the main Accounts settings*

Connecting to Office 365 or Microsoft Azure

If you use Office 365 or Microsoft Azure, you will need to point the user at the *Accounts* ➤ *About Access work or school* panel in the Settings app. Here they can click the *Connect* button, and then one of the two links at the bottom of the dialog that appears, to enroll their device in the company's services, see Figure 24-5. This will automatically enroll the device in MDM and allow you to manage it remotely.

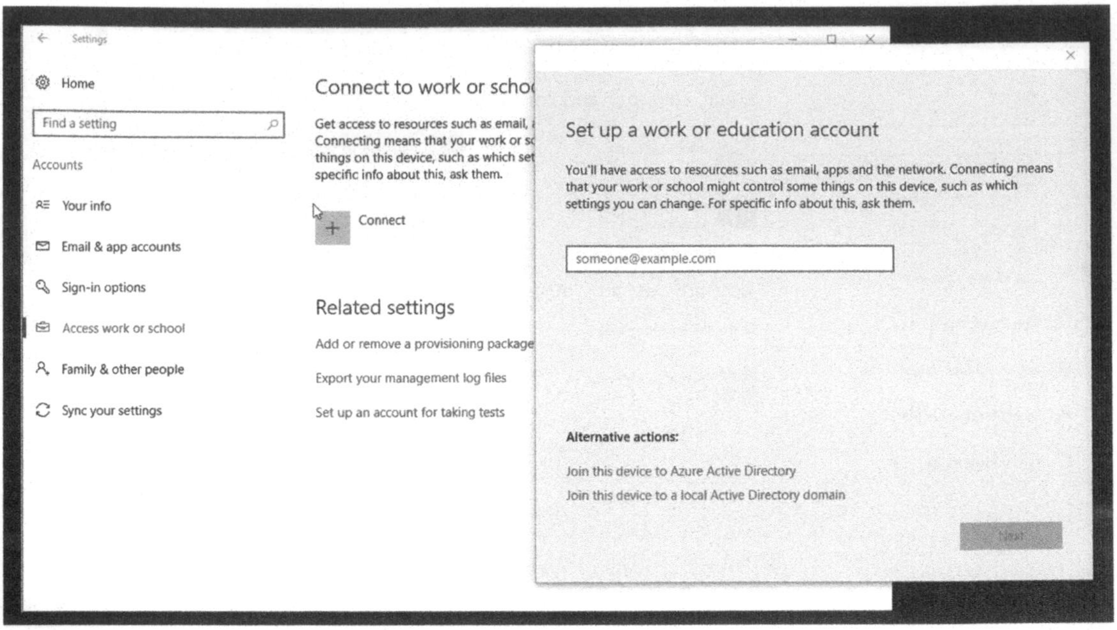

Figure 24-5. *You can easily enroll a PC in Office 365 or Azure*

Work Folders

You might be familiar with Microsoft's ActiveSync technology. This has been around since the heady days of Windows 95, and it allowed PC users to store files from the workplace directly on their device, be that a laptop or a phone running Windows Mobile or Windows CE (officially the abbreviation for Consumer Electronics by Microsoft, but always known by myself as Crap Edition). ActiveSync worked effectively for many years, but it was designed for a bygone time before we had fast Internet, or even the Internet, come to that.

In Windows 10 there is no ActiveSync, but there is a feature called Work Folders which performs the same task, but in a more modern way. Work Folders can be managed from the Control Panel, and you can most easily find it by searching for it in the Start Menu or Cortana. It's a simple affair, as you can see in Figure 24-6; there's only one item to click in its Control Panel settings.

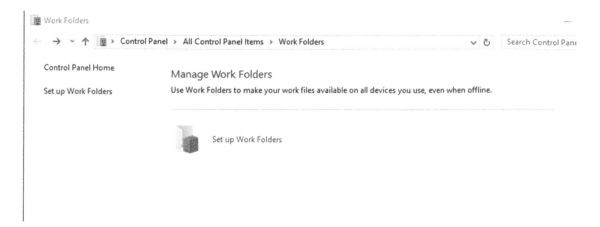

Figure 24-6. *Work Folders are easy to configure in Windows 10*

To configure Work Folders, enter the username or URL of the Work Folder access, which needs to be configured in Windows Server. A folder is configured at C:\Users\[Username]\Work Folders, where any synched files will be stored. These are automatically encrypted by Windows 10, and the user is not allowed to change the location of this store folder. The user also cannot decrypt the files.

Work Folders are designed to automatically sync on the PC and stay up to date. Should a user feel, however, that a sync has not taken place and that they do not have the latest version of their files, they can click the *Sync Now* option that will appear in the Work Folders settings in the Control Panel. That really is all there is to Work Folders. They are an alternative to ActiveSync and, just as with all other BYOD features in Windows 10, they also work with the iOS and Android operating systems.

Summary

As I mentioned at the beginning of this chapter, all MDM features in Windows 10 are managed by Windows InTune, which can also manage devices running Apple's iOS and Google's Android operating systems. InTune allows you to make sure that the security, patching, and apps on the device are both up to date and approved by yourself and your company; you can read more about it at www.microsoft.com/server-cloud/enterprise-mobility.

We're heading into the home stretch now with this troubleshooting book, and that's all now for best practice. In the next chapter, we'll begin to look at how we can really dig deep within Windows 10 and get advanced and detailed technical information about the OS, your PC, your installed apps and updates, and what different types of diagnostic and system information are available to you.

CHAPTER 25

■ ■ ■

Getting Advanced Information

In Chapter 22 I detailed the Microsoft Sysinternals suite, and it's clear from using utilities such as AutoRuns just how much there is going on inside a PC at any one time. It's not just the drivers for the hardware you can see on your desk that are installed, but the many dozens more for all the hardware on your motherboard that you can't. This is coupled with audio and video codecs, support utilities, Windows and third-party services... the list is pretty endless.

When you're troubleshooting a problem with your PC then, how do you go about getting the detailed diagnostic and support information that you need? Back in Chapter 5 I detailed the Event Viewer, and showed how powerful and useful it is to get information about errors and events. Believe me, though, the Event Viewer is just one place from which you can get useful and detailed information. There are others. Many others!

The Task Manager

If you still think of the Task Manager in Windows just as the place where you can close running and hung apps, then think again. Sure, in its simplest form, the default when Windows 10 is installed, it's just that, a list of running apps with an End Task button, see Figure 25-1. Click that More details icon however, and a whole new world opens its doors to you.

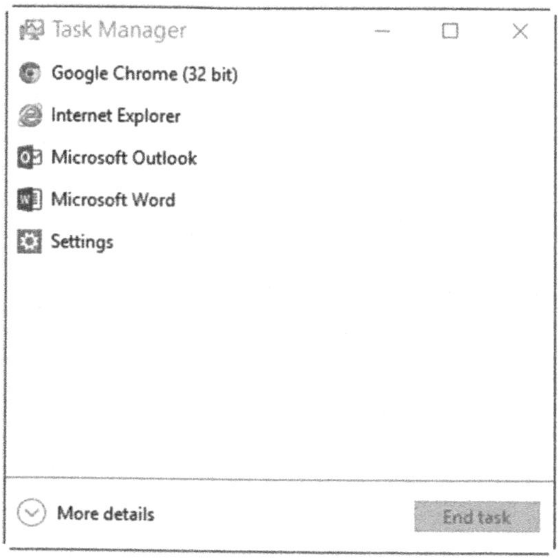

Figure 25-1. The "default" Task Manager is a simple affair

© Mike Halsey 2016

M. Halsey, *Windows 10 Troubleshooting*, DOI 10.1007/978-1-4842-0925-7_25

With the full Task Manager view open, a wealth of useful information is displayed across several tabbed panels, see Figure 25-2. The default view, the *Processes* tab, provides live information about the processor, memory, disk, and network usage of running apps and services.

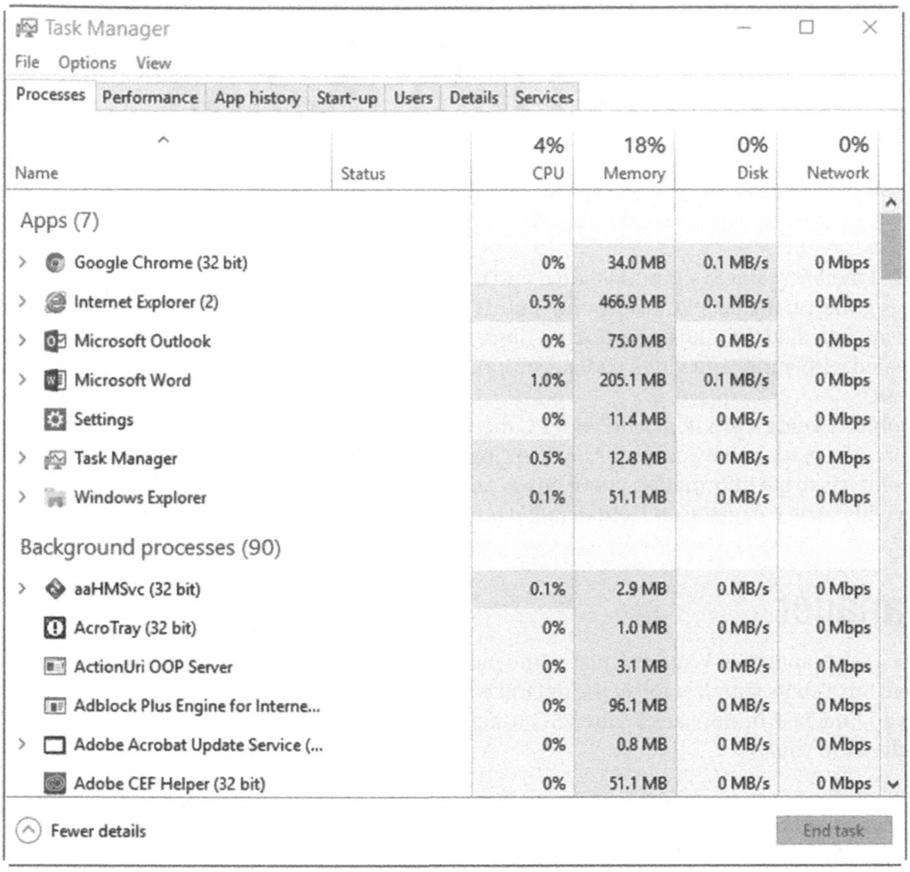

Figure 25-2. *The full Task Manager is packed with useful information*

The information the Processes tab provides is heat-mapped, enabling you to see at a glance if an app is hogging too much processor time or memory, as an exmaple. Hung apps will also be detailed, and another useful feature when it comes to managing hung apps is that if any app has a dependency, for example, it has multiple processes (sometimes called threads) running, an arrow will appear to its left. Click this and you will be able to see if you will also terminate any other processes by forcing the closure of the hung app.

The *App history* tab is useful if you use a lot of Store apps. As well as reporting on processor and network usage, it can very helpfully report on whether apps are using metered data (which can be expensive when you're on a roaming data connection), and how much data they have used to update their live tiles, see Figure 25-3.

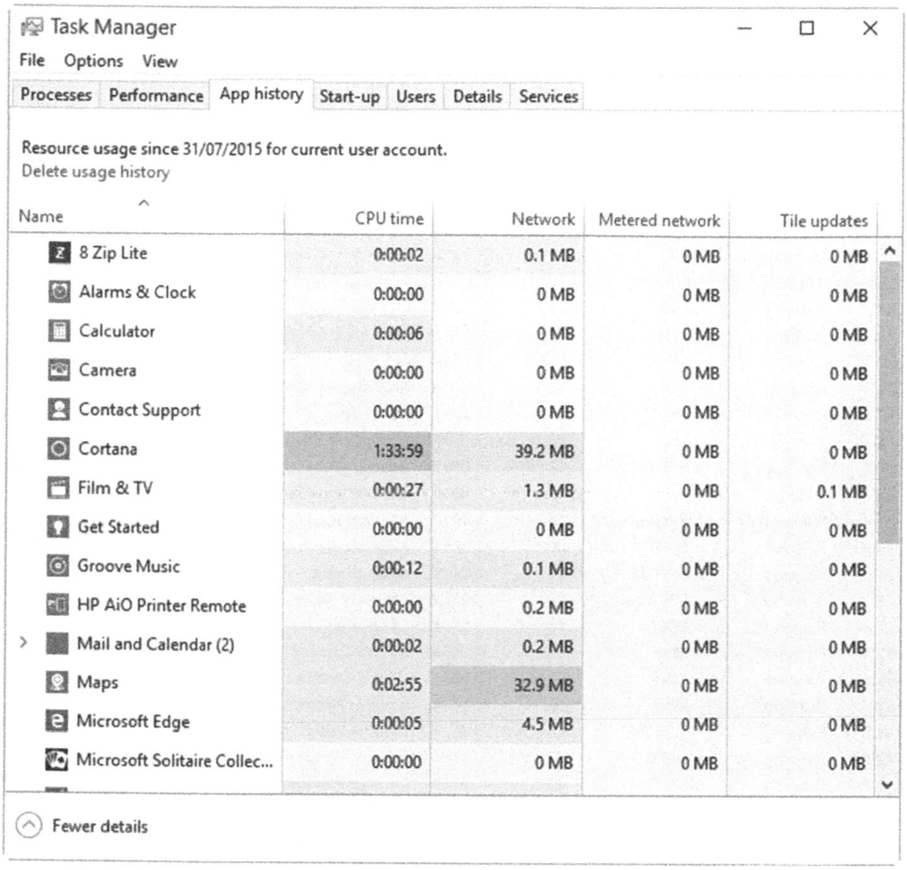

Figure 25-3. *The App History tab provides information about Store apps*

It's entirely possible, however, that you might be a Task Manager purist, and not fancy this "trimmed-down" traffic-light approach. If you were a fan of the Task Manager as it appeared in Windows XP and Windows 7 then the *Details* tab is for you. This lists all running apps and processes, complete with detailed descriptions of what each is, their CPU and memory usage, and more besides, see Figure 25-4. In many ways, this provides more information than the Processes tab, as it lists background processes which my hang or fail on the PC. The *Services* tab also lists all Microsoft and third-party services that are running on the PC.

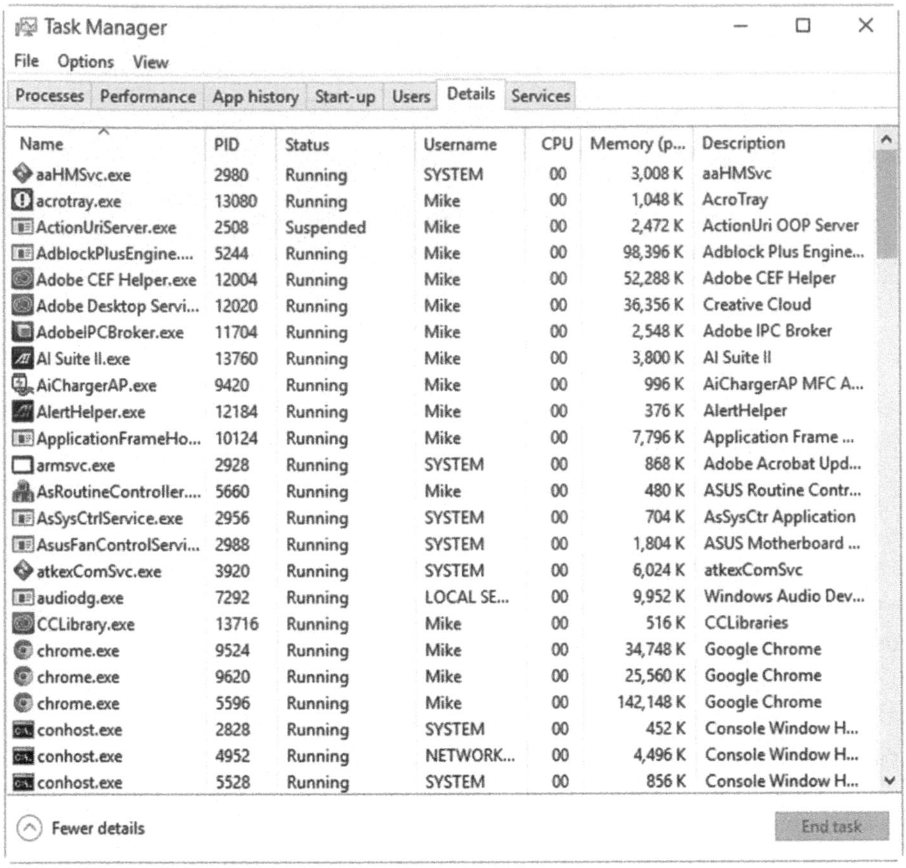

Figure 25-4. *The Details tab is a wealth of "What's going on" info*

The Task Manager's party-trick, however, is what it can do in providing live status and information panels, which you can sit on your screen, see Figure 25-5. If you right-click a graph under the *Performance* tab, you can view live data about the PC's processor, memory, hard disk (separated by disk), and network (separated by connection) usage. These can be presented as graphs or numeric metrics, and processor information can also be viewed on a core-by-core basis.

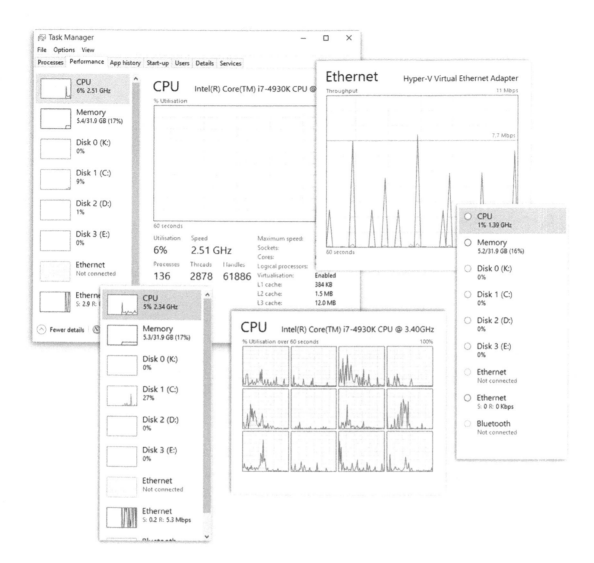

Figure 25-5. *Meet the Task Manager's party-trick, live system status panels*

If you need to monitor live information about your PC, such as the processor, memory, or network usage, then the Task Manager is by far the simplest and least intrusive way to do it. Then, last but by no means least, the *Start-up* tab is where you can manage the apps that run at startup on the PC, see Figure 25-6.

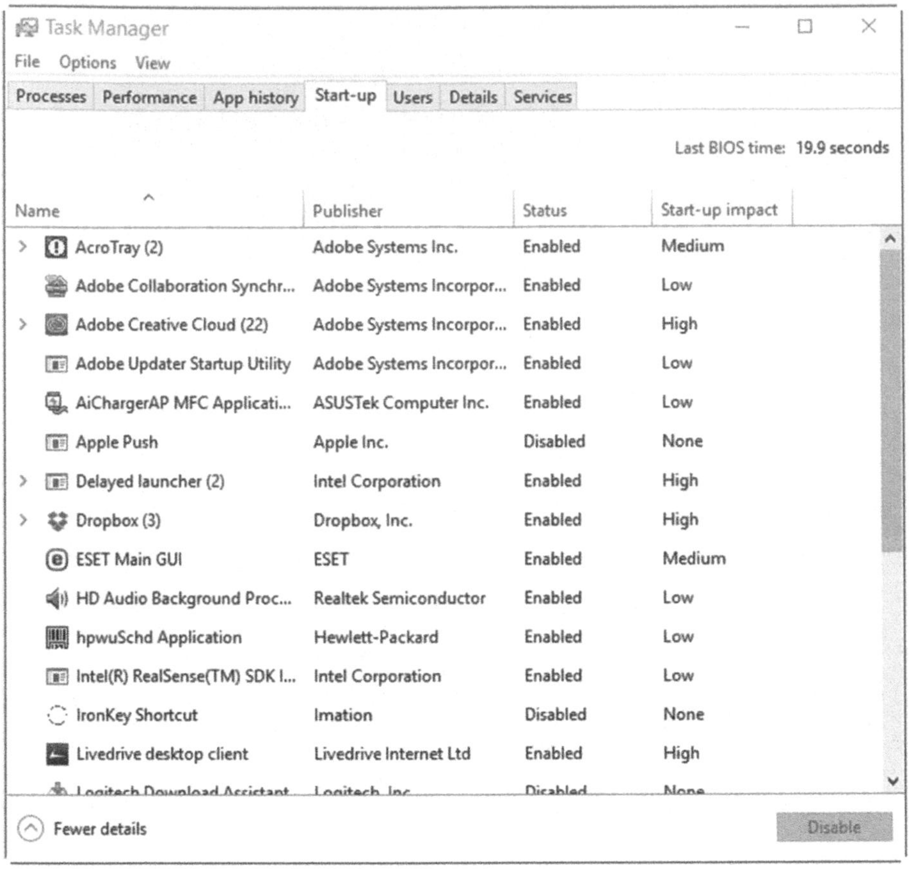

Figure 25-6. *You can manage your startup apps from the Task Manager*

The Performance Monitor

If you need to monitor more live metrics on your PC than the Task Manager can display, then the Performance Monitor is where you want to head. Everything that it's possible to monitor in Windows or on your PC can be displayed by live metrics in the Performance Monitor, from Bitlocker throughput to telephony connections.

The Performance Monitor displays a constantly updating graph above a series of check box options. By default, the processor time is displayed, but you can add any other metric to the graph by clicking the green *(+) Plus* icon on the toolbar. This will present a list of all the available metrics on your PC, see Figure 25-7. Select the metrics you want to add to the graph and click the *Add* button. Once metrics are added, they can be removed by pressing the *(X) Remove* icon, or by unchecking them below the graph.

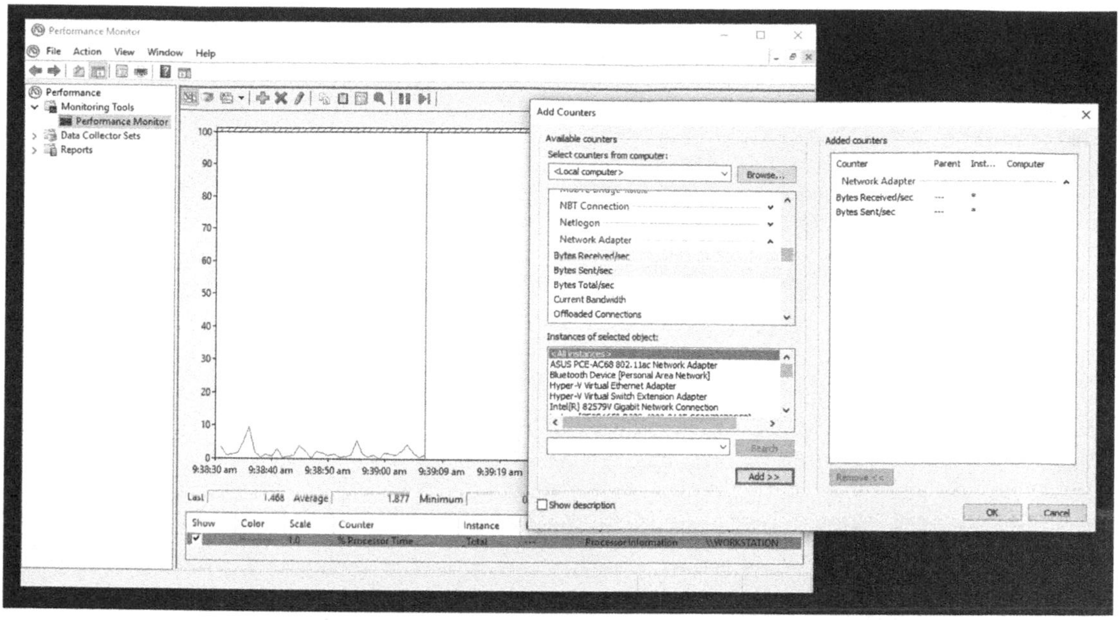

Figure 25-7. *The Performance Monitor can display hundreds of live metrics*

■ **Tip** If you have several metrics displayed in your graph but want to highlight one, select it in the panel below the graph and then click the *Highlight* icon in the toolbar.

Data Collector Sets

Sometimes you need to collect data on the operation of the PC to read later, as you will be unable to read the data live and when it happens. You can achieve this through the creation of Data Collector Sets. You can set these to monitor any available metric, which includes events for Windows features, Registry key changes, and general performance. These collector sets can be viewed later in the Performance Monitor.

You create a new Data Collector Set by clicking the *Data Collector Sets* ➤ *User Defined* link in the left panel of the Performance Monitor, and then right-clicking in a blank space in the main panel and selecting *New* from the context menu that appears.

You will be asked if you want to create a Data Collector Set from a predefined template or manually. If you choose menual, you will be given full control over the data collected from everything available to you, see Figure 25-8.

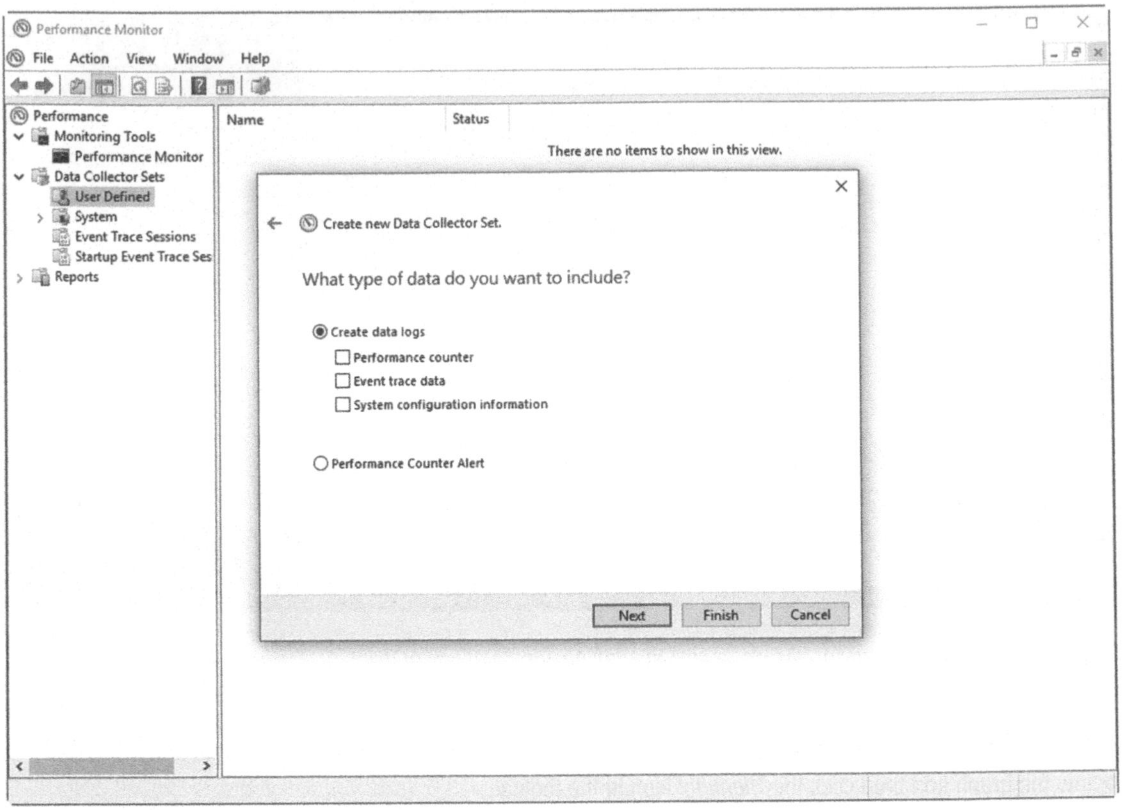

Figure 25-8. *You can create custom Data Collector Sets*

To view the data collected, you can at any time right-click the Data Collector Set to display its report. This will display in a new Reports section, which will display in the bottom left side of the window.

The Resource Monitor

Another way to view live information, and more detailed information than can often be provided by the Performance Monitor, is to use the Windows 10 Resource Monitor. This consists of a series of collapsible panels and tabs, and allows you to look at detailed breakdowns of what is happening at any one time with the PC's CPU, memory, disk, and network usage, see Figure 25-9.

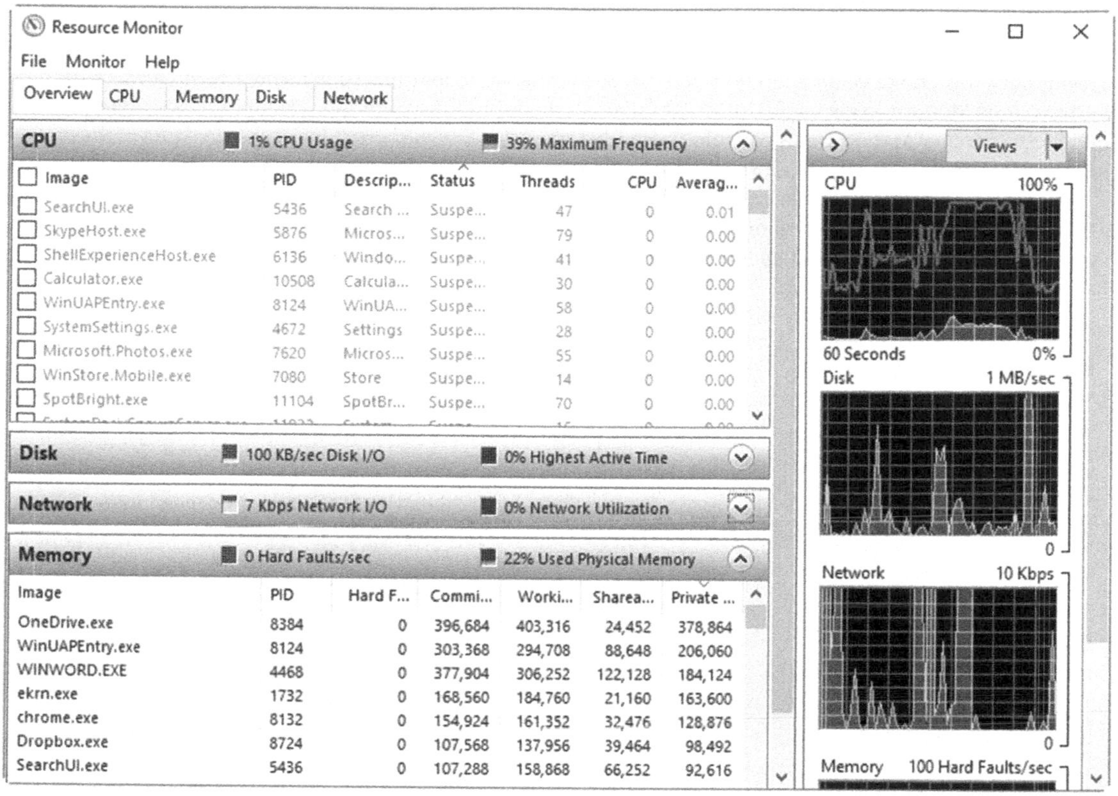

Figure 25-9. *The Resource Monitor displays very detailed metrics*

The Overview tab will give you details of all running processes: their memory, disk, and network usage. You can break this information down further, however, with the tabs along the top of the window. The CPU tab, for example, lists all running processes and services, along with their CPU usage.

Perhaps the two most useful tabs, however, are disk and network usage. The disk usage tab will show you every live disk activity, along with the read and write operations, and how much data is being read and written, by each specific app that is using the disk. You can use this if you suspect that a particular app is being a disk hog on your PC.

The Network tab is a fantastic tool for monitoring network issues and snarl-ups. Let's say, for example, that you suspect that the OneDrive sync engine isn't doing anything when it should. You can see in the Network tab exactly how much network bandwidth it is using. Alternatively, you suspect that a app is communicating with a system it shouldn't, perhaps because of a macro or other type of malware infection. The network tab can provide the IP address of the remote server. It can also provide details of the communication port(s) that an app is using, or trying to use. If you have an app, or perhaps a game, that's not communicating with the Internet properly, you can see which port it is using, and then check in the Advanced Firewall if that port is blocked for the app.

The Computer Management Console

Throughout this book I've detailed how you can use Windows 10 features such as the Event Viewer and Performance Monitor to get useful information about the Windows operating system and the status of your PC. The Computer Management console, available from *Win+X menu*, provides access to some of these tools, as well as access to the Disk Management console and the Device Manager.

Perhaps more useful, however, is the instant information it can give you on the status of folder shares and user and user group permissions. It allows you to view at a glance all of the folder and drive shares currently configured on the PC, useful if you suspect that a share is misconfigured or if another PC is unable to connect to it, see Figure 25-10.

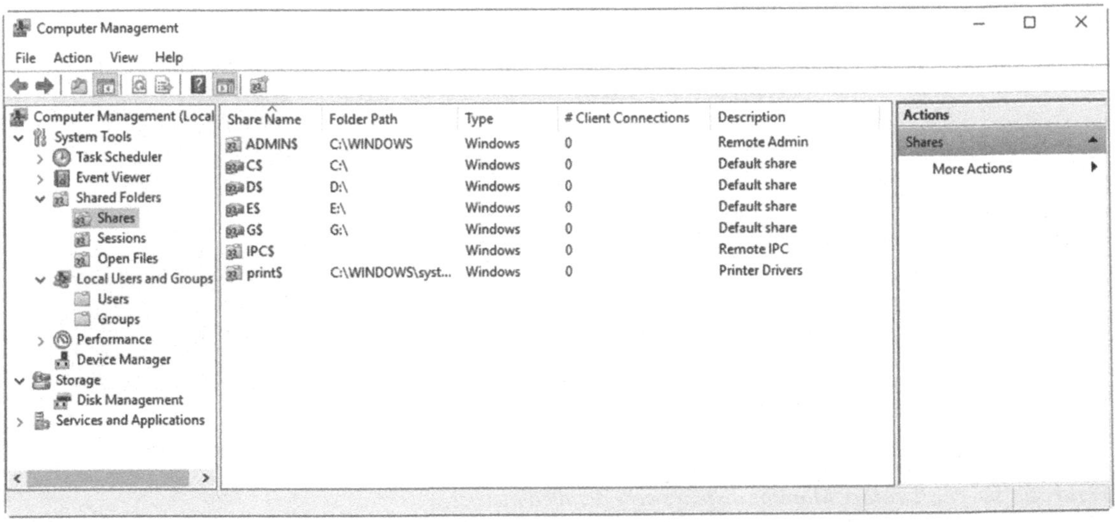

Figure 25-10. *The Computer Management console provides quick access to useful tools and information*

Additionally, the Computer Management console will display the details of any currently open folder or drive shares, with details of the PC and user connected to the share. You can also see what files are being shared, so you can get a huge amount of information about the current status of those shares. This can be useful if a user is trying to perform an action with a file or folder but permission is denied because the file is locked. Rather than just restarting the PC to unlock the file, you can first check here to see if the file or folder you need to work with is being accessed or used by another user, on another PC.

The User Groups section will detail all of the different groups of users that are configured on the PC, such as Administrator and Standard user, and you can see at a glance who is assigned to each group. You can also change the groups that a specific user is a member of. You can't change individual permissions from here, such as read, write, and modify permissions for users, but other features such as disabling an acocunt temporarily or permanently are available.

System Information

Have you ever wanted to know absolutely **everything** about a PC? I don't mean what type of processor is installed, and how much memory, but what drivers are installed for the graphics card, what the MAC (physical) address of the PC's network adapter is or what hardware devices are sharing interrupt requests (IRQ), ports, or memory addresses. I thought you might.

The System Information panel, available through the Administrative Tools window, is your one-stop shop for everything you could ever want to know about a PC, see Figure 25-11. This includes what hardware is installed, with the version numbers of the drivers, what apps are installed, again with version numbers, what print jobs are stuck in the queue, and the port addresses of the printers they're sent to. It can also tell you the full root of all the apps that begin at the PC's startup and what network protocols are configured on the PC.

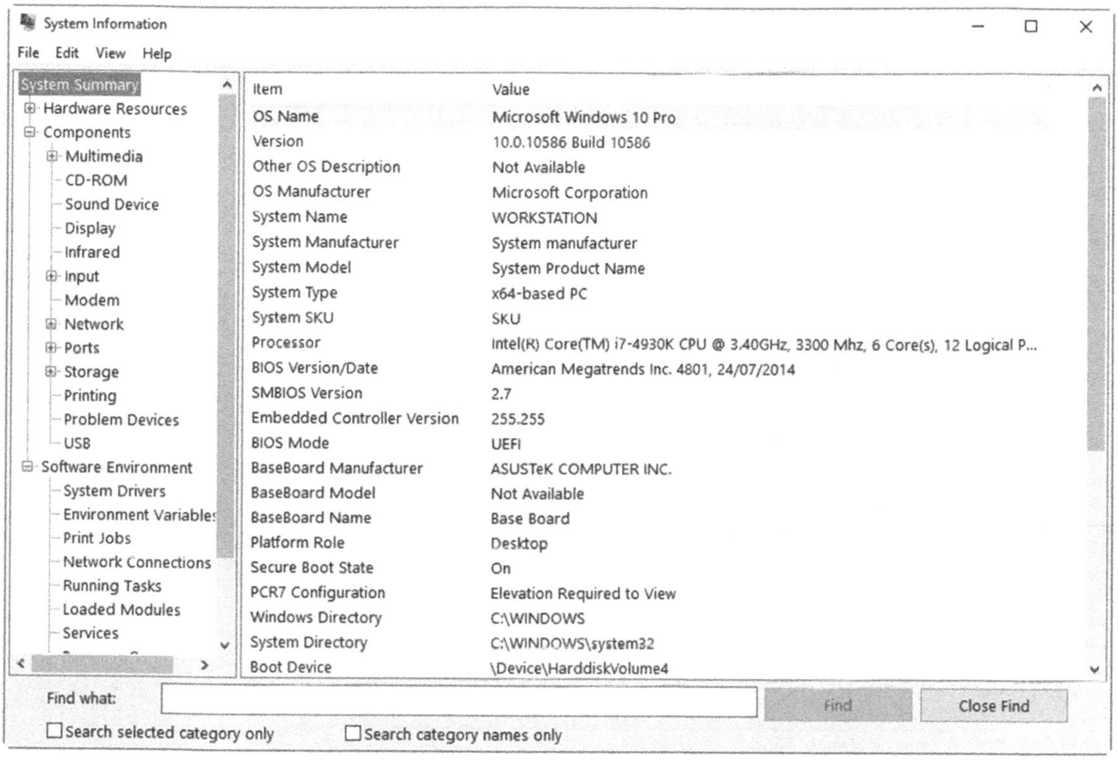

Figure 25-11. *The System Information panel is your one-stop shop for PC info*

What's even better about the System Information panel is that all of this information can be exported and e-mailed to a support person, or read on another PC. From the *File* menu, click *Save* or *Export* and you will be able to create a text file containing everything you need to know about the PC. Save will create a file that can be opened in the System Information panel on a different PC, using the *Open* option, while Export will create a plain text (.TXT) file containing the information.

You can also use the System Information panel to obtain information about other computers on your network that you have administrator access into. From the *View* menu, click the *Remote Computer* option, where you will then be able to type the name or address of the remote PC.

DXDiag

Sometimes you may suspect you have a problem with your audio or video on a PC, but how do you go about diagnosing the issue? Microsoft has for years now included the DirectX Diagnostic tool (DXDiag) in Windows, and with Windows 10 it's still present and can be found by searching for **dxdiag** in the Start Menu or Cortana. You can use this tool to get detailed information about the status of your audio and video equipment, and to export that information in a text file format for other people to read.

The Display tab, for example, will provide information on whether features such as 3D and graphics accelleration are enabled on the device, see Figure 25-12.

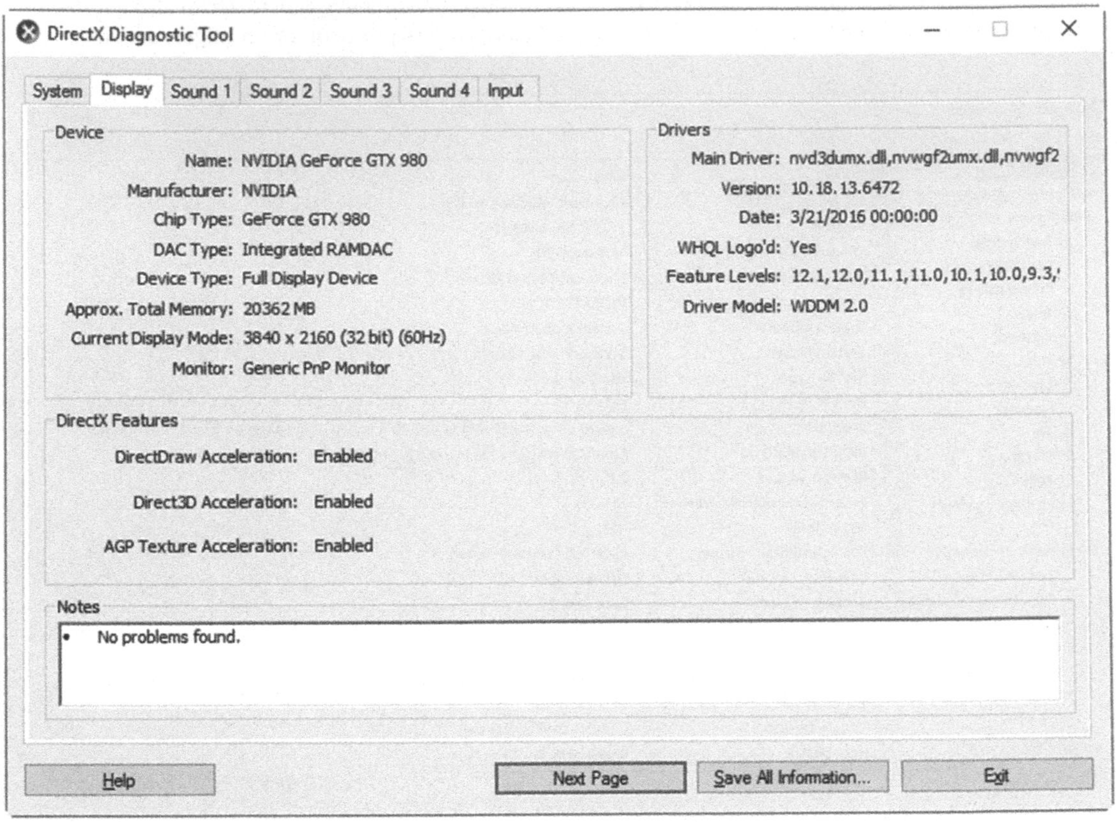

Figure 25-12. *DXDiag provides information on your audio and video equipment*

DXDiag will automatically check for problems with your audio and video hardware and report on any that it finds. You also get useful information such as the version numbers of any installed hardware. This means you can check the driver information from your PC against the manufacturer's web site, and their forums, to see if there are any known problems.

Summary

There is a massive amount of information you can get from Windows 10 about the current and past status of your PC, and the tools detailed in this chapter should not be underestimated. Indeed, being able to create Data Collector Sets in the Performance Monitor, and have them monitor from any one of hundreds of different metrics and collate that information into a report you can read at a later time, is incredibly powerful.

Another part of the Windows OS that's incredibly powerful but also unbelievably complex is the Registry. In the next chapter, I'll give you a full tour of the Windows Registry, show you what each of its different parts is for, how you can work with it safely, and how to create backups and restore those backups at a later point in time.

CHAPTER 26

■ ■ ■

The Registry in Depth

The Registry is at the heart of everything that happens on your PC. Indeed, absolutely nothing *can* happen, including drivers and services being loaded at startup, to configuration changes and app usage, without the Registry being referenced, or without a Registry change being made. It is, quite simply, the brain of the PC.

Back in the days of Windows 3.1, you might remember, each program you installed had its own .ini file. This was a plain text document in which you would set configuration options for the program, such as the folder the program was installed in. Windows 95 did away with all of this manual nonsense and introduced the Registry, where all of the configuration links, settings, and options were handled automatically by both Windows and the program.

The Registry files are no longer plain text. They are binary format files that are not readable in a text editor. This is different from the .reg files, which are exportable and importable into the Registry and are in plain text format, see Figure 26-1.

```
MinWidth Taskbar Hack - Notepad                                          —   □   ×
File  Edit  Format  View  Help
Windows Registry Editor Version 5.00

[HKEY_CURRENT_USER\Control Panel\Desktop\WindowMetrics]
"SmCaptionWidth"="-330"
"BorderWidth"="-15"
"SmCaptionHeight"="-330"
"CaptionWidth"="-330"
"IconTitleWrap"="1"
"ScrollHeight"="-255"
"CaptionHeight"="-330"
"CaptionFont"=hex:f1,ff,ff,ff,00,00,00,00,00,00,00,00,00,00,00,00,90,01,00,00,\
  00,00,00,01,00,00,05,00,53,00,65,00,67,00,6f,00,65,00,20,00,55,00,49,00,00,\
  00,00,00,00,00,00,00,00,00,00,00,00,00,00,00,00,00,00,00,00,00,00,00,00,00,\
  00,00,00,00,00,00,00,00,00,00,00,00,00,00,00,00,00,00,00,00,00,00,00,00
"ScrollWidth"="-255"
"MenuWidth"="-285"
"SmCaptionFont"=hex:f1,ff,ff,ff,00,00,00,00,00,00,00,00,00,00,00,00,90,01,00,\
  00,00,00,00,01,00,00,05,00,53,00,65,00,67,00,6f,00,65,00,20,00,55,00,49,00,\
  00,00,00,00,00,00,00,00,00,00,00,00,00,00,00,00,00,00,00,00,00,00,00,00,00,\
  00,00,00,00,00,00,00,00,00,00,00,00,00,00,00,00,00,00,00,00,00,00,00,00
"MenuFont"=hex:f4,ff,ff,ff,00,00,00,00,00,00,00,00,00,00,00,00,90,01,00,00,\
  00,00,01,00,00,05,00,53,00,65,00,67,00,6f,00,65,00,20,00,55,00,49,00,00,00,\
  00,00,00,00,00,00,00,00,00,00,00,00,00,00,00,00,00,00,00,00,00,00,00,00,00,\
  00,00,00,00,00,00,00,00,00,00,00,00,00,00,00,00,00,00,00,00,00,00
```

Figure 26-1. A .REG file opened in Notepad

© Mike Halsey 2016

M. Halsey, *Windows 10 Troubleshooting*, DOI 10.1007/978-1-4842-0925-7_26

As you can imagine then, the Registry is a huge, complex, and confusing database. If something goes wrong with it, such as a configuration change being made that causes something to become unstable, then just finding what you're looking for can be a monumental challenge in itself. Indeed, the Registry is so complex that I wrote, with fellow MVP Andrew Bettany, a whole book on it, which you can buy from Apress in the same Windows Troubleshooting range as the book you're reading now. It's *Windows Registry Troubleshooting* (Apress, 2015). For now, though, I'll give you all the information you need to get up to speed on what the Registry is, and how it works.

Registry Files

The Windows Registry isn't one big database that's stored in a hidden location on your PC. In fact, it's a collection of files scattered across various locations on your hard disk. The core Registry files on the PC are to be found in the %systemroot%\System 32\Config\ folder, see Figure 26-2. They consist of the following files.

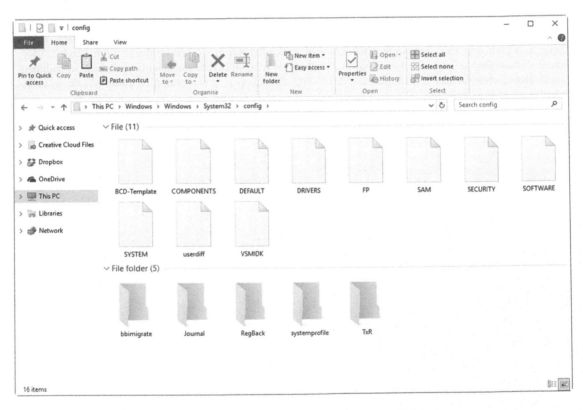

Figure 26-2. *The Core Registry Files on the PC are hidden in the System 32 folder*

- SAM (Security Accounts Manager)
- SECURITY
- SOFTWARE
- SYSTEM

- DEFAULT

- userdiff (Usedly on when the OS is being upgraded)

In addition to these, each individual user account on the PC has its own Registry files, which contain their person configuration and app options.

- %userprofile%\ntuser.dat

- %userprofile%\AppData\Local\Microsoft\Windows\UsrClass.dat

The ntuser.dat file is the one that contains the user's customization, app installation, and configuration options. The UsrClass.dat file contains additional settings for the user, such as user-specific file associations.

Registry Keys and Values

When you open the Windows Registry Editor, which is the only way to work with the Registry in the OS, you'll see that the Registry is arranged into a folder structure, see Figure 26-3. I'll show you how to use the Registry Editor later in this chapter, though you open it by searching for *regedit* at the Start Menu or Cortana. For now, I want to talk you through the different Registry sections and key types.

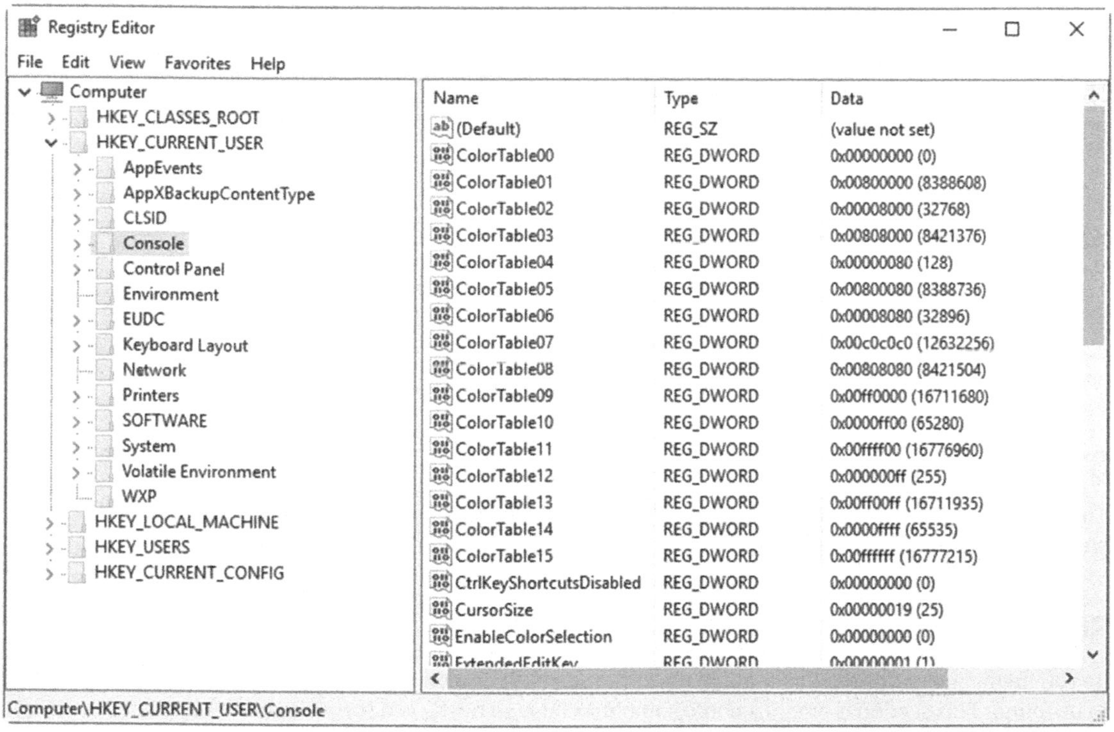

Figure 26-3. *The Windows Registry Editor*

HKEY_CLASSES_ROOT (HKCR)

This section of the Registry is where registered app information is stored. This includes file associations. Should a key be added or updated in HKCR that is also duplicated in the HKEY_CURRENT_USER\Software\ Classes section of the Registry, the HKCU key will be used as the master, as it is specific to the individual user's preferences.

HKEY_CURRENT_USER (HKCU)

This Registry section is where the configuration options for the currently signed-in user are located. This includes the disk locations for user folders, control panel settings, and app installation and configuration settings. This section is loaded from the %userprofile% folder Registry files.

HKEY_LOCAL_MACHINE (HKLM)

If you're going to be making a change to the Registry, then it's most likely going to be in HKLM. This is where all the settings for Windows, drivers, and app installations are to be found, that is, all the settings and options that are generic for all users of the PC. It is split into several subsections that relate to some of the Registry files I detailed earlier.

SAM

The Security Accounts Manager will commonly appear to be empty unless the viewing user has appropriate security permissions. This Registry section contains the security information for any domains that the PC connects to.

SECURITY

The Security section also appears empty for most users, again unless the viewing user has appropriate permissions. It is used when connecting to a domain and is linked to the security database stored in the Server Registry Hive. This contains all the security policies specified on the server that are applicable to the currently signed-in user and installed apps on the PC.

SYSTEM

The System section contains the keys that are relevant to the Windows installation, configuration, devices, and any drives attached to the PC.

SOFTWARE

As you might guess, this section is where the keys and configuration settings for all installed win32 apps are to be found. This section is organized into subfolders labeled by the vendor name for the app.

Other Sections

There are other subsections in HKLM, including DRIVERS and HARDWARE. These are created when the user signs into the PC and discarded on sign-out.

HKEY_USERS (HKU)

The HKU section contains settings and options for the currently signed-in user. It cannot be used to access settings for any other user on the PC unless you sign out and sign in as that other user.

HKEY_CURRENT_CONFIG (HKCC)

The last section, HKCC, contains information that is gathered at the PC's startup and that is relevant only to the current working session for the PC. It is created automatically and discarded when the PC is shut down.

HKEY_PERFORMANCE_DATA

Okay, so there really is another Registry section, but it's hidden from the user and nonviewable in the Registry Editor. This contains performance data provided by the Windows kernel, drivers, apps, and services. It relates only to the current operating session of the PC and is discarded when the PC is switched off.

Registry Value Types

Within these five main Registry cetagories, there are a series of different types of values...

- REG_BINARY keys store raw binary data.

- REG_DWORD are variable-length 32-bit integers.

- DWORDS are commonly used to define parameters for strings, settings, drivers, and configuration options.

- REG_SZ are field-length string values.

- REG_EXPAND are expandable length string values, also used to contain environment variables.

- REG_MULTI_SZ are multiple string arrays that can conatins a list of values, normally separated by a comma or space.

- REG_RESOURCE_LIST is a list of resources in a nested array; these are used by device drivers.

- REG_RESOURCE_REQUIREMENTS_LIST is an array list of hardware resources that is used by device drivers.

- REG_FULL_RESOURCE_DESCRIPTOR are nested arrays used to store resource lists for physical hardware.

- REG_LINK are symbolic links to other Registry keys. They specify both the root and target key.

- REG_NONE is data that does not have a specific type.

- REG_QWORD are variable-length 64-bit integers. These are not found in 32-bit editions of Windows 10.

The Registry Editor

You can view, manage, and edit the Registry using the Windows 10 Registry Editor, opened by searching in the Start Menu or Cortana for *regedit*. This is an editor that loads all of the separate Registry files into a single place, where all the keys and subkeys are sorted and arranged in plain English (well, as plain as you can be when you're a technical repository, anyway).

In the left panel of the Registry Editor is a collapsible panel of all the Registry files, showing their full folder (hierarchical) structure. The right panel will display all the keys at the currently selected hierarchy point. Additionally, there are traditional pull-down menus that allow you to perform various actions, such as adding, deleting, and renaming keys and folders, see Figure 26-4.

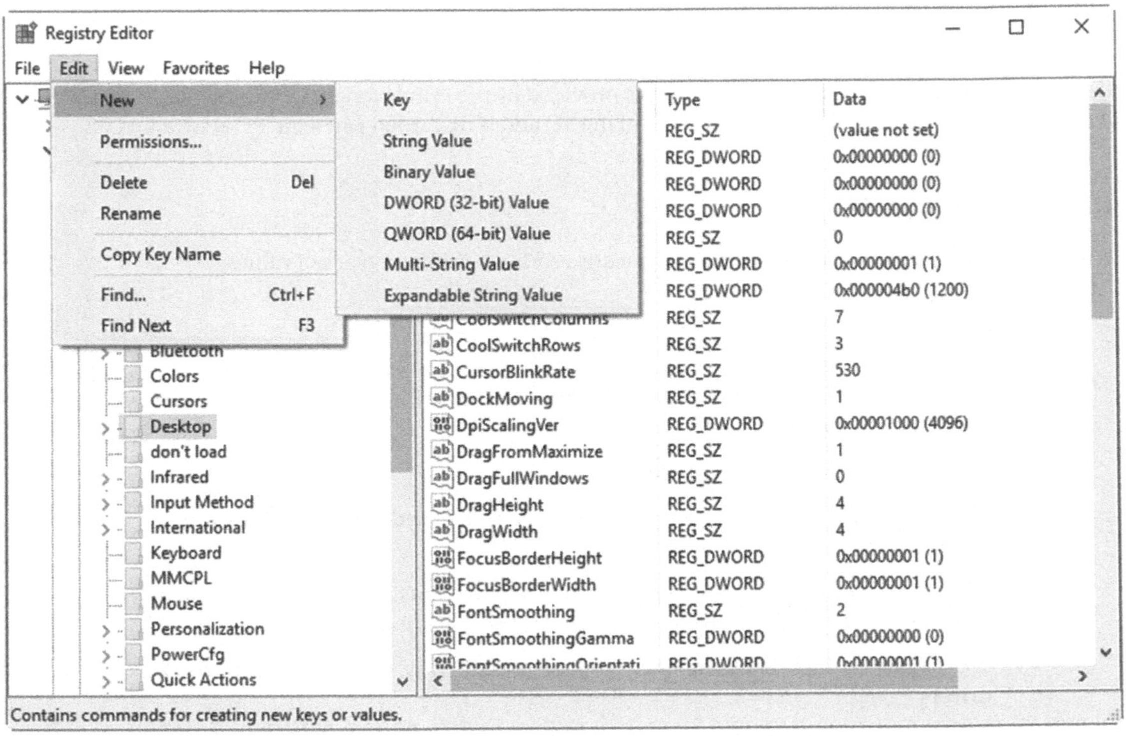

Figure 26-4. *You work with the Registry in the Registry Editor*

Backing Up and Restoring the Registry

Before you begin modifying, creating, or deleting Registry keys, you should always make a backup copy of the Registry, you know, in case something goes horrifically wrong. You can back up and reimport the Registry from the *File* menu, see Figure 26-5. This saves a copy of the Entire Registry in a plain text .reg file to any folder or drive you specify on your PC.

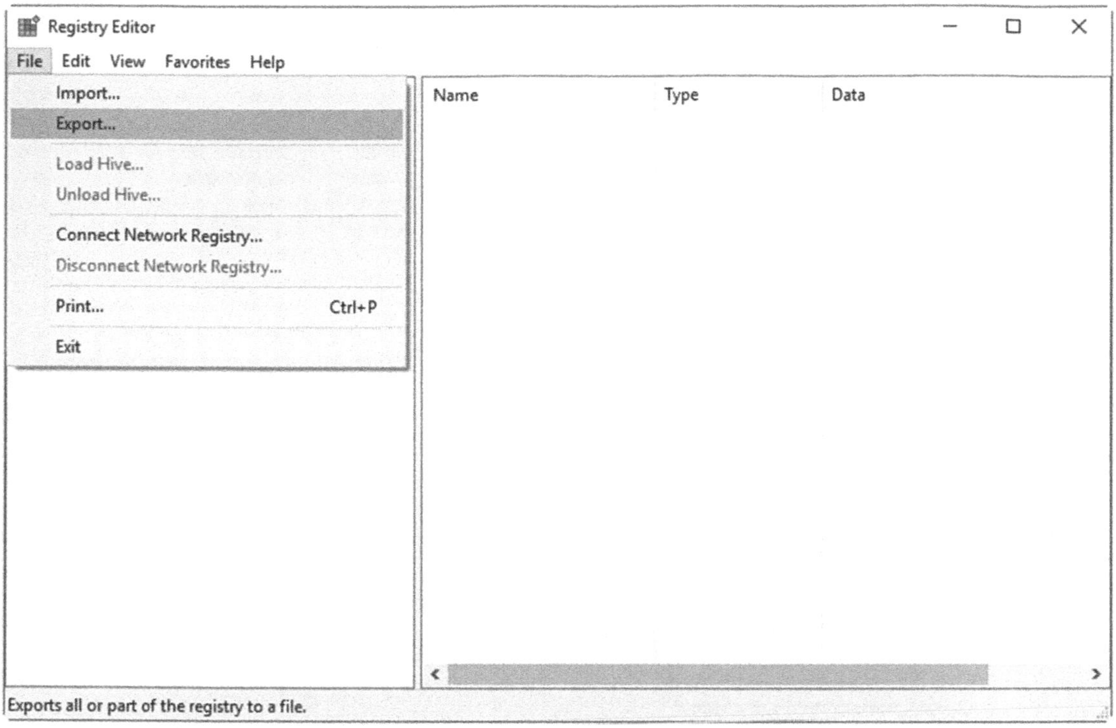

Figure 26-5. *You should always create a Registry backup when working on keys*

■ **Tip**   You can also make backup copies of any particular key by right-clicking it, in the left panel of the Registry, and selecting *Export* from the options that appear.

Creating and Modifying Registry Keys

You can create new Registry keys and values by right-clicking in the appropriate part of the Registry, see Figure 26-6. This allows you to create any type of key or value you require including both master and subkey types.

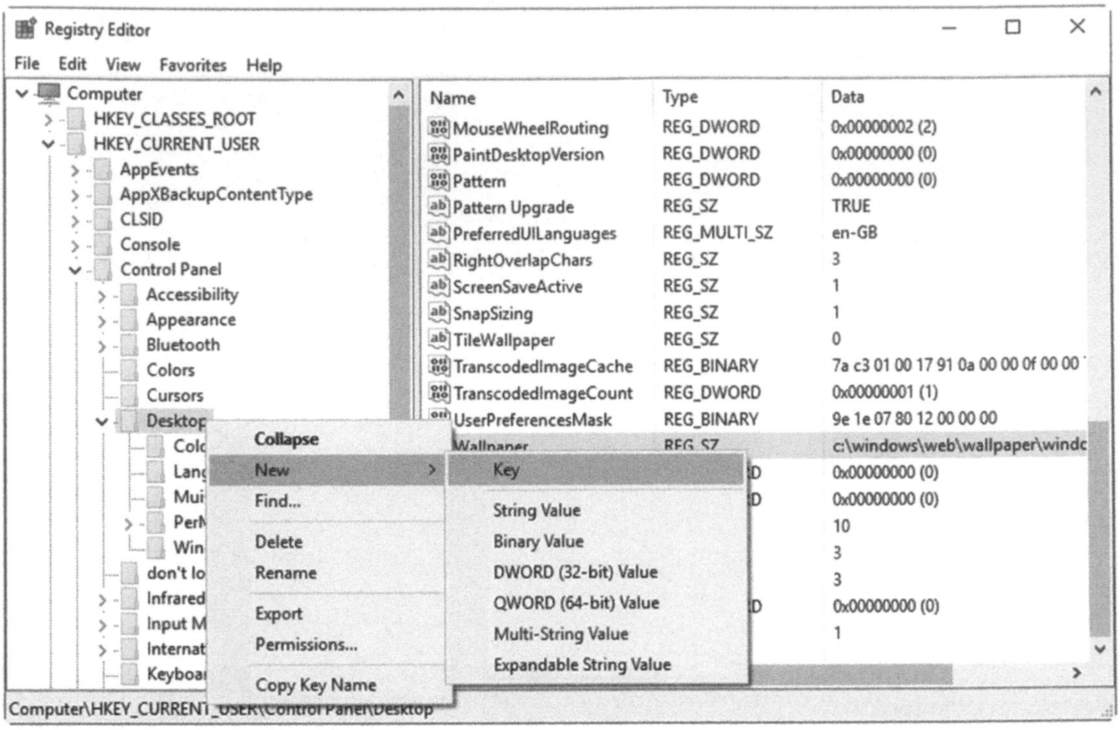

Figure 26-6. *You can create new keys in the Registry*

To edit a Registry key, right-click the key or value you want to edit and several options will become available to you, see Figure 26-7. It's the main, *Modify* option you'll need most of the time.

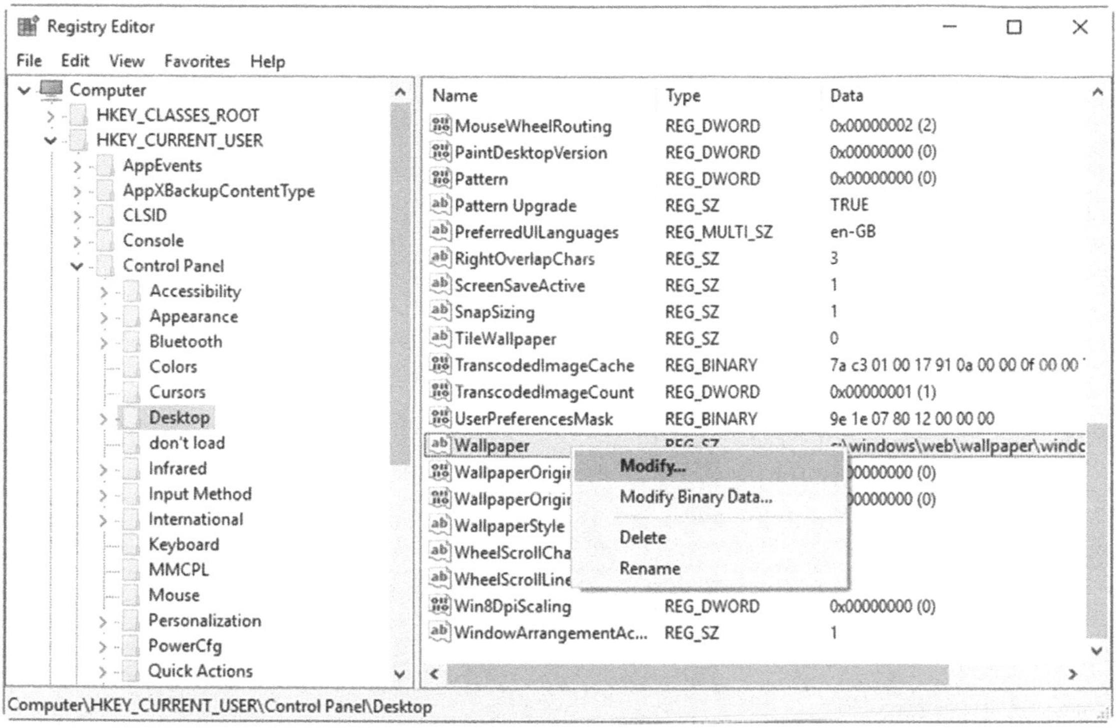

Figure 26-7. You modify Registry values on a right-click

Using REG.EXE

If you're a command-line purist, you can use the reg.exe command to edit the Windows Registry. You should always be very careful as you can't actually "see" the Registry when you're working on it in this way. There are many subcommands and switches when using reg.exe, and the full switch details can be found both in my *Windows Registry Troubleshooting book* (Apress, 2015) and on the Microsoft web site at technet.microsoft.com/library/cc732643(v=ws.11).aspx.

Editing Other Users' Registry Databases

I mentioned earlier that it's only possible to view and modify the Registry of the currently signed-in user. In the normal Regedit view, this is true; however, it is also possible to view the HKU and HKLM registries of other users on a PC, and indeed across a network. To open the Registry files of another user on the PC, follow these instructions.

1. Sign into the PC as an Administrator

2. Search for *regedit* at the Start menu or in Cortana to run the Registry Editor

3. Select the HKEY_USERS branch in the Registry Editor

4. From the *File* menu, select *Load Hive*, see Figure 26-8

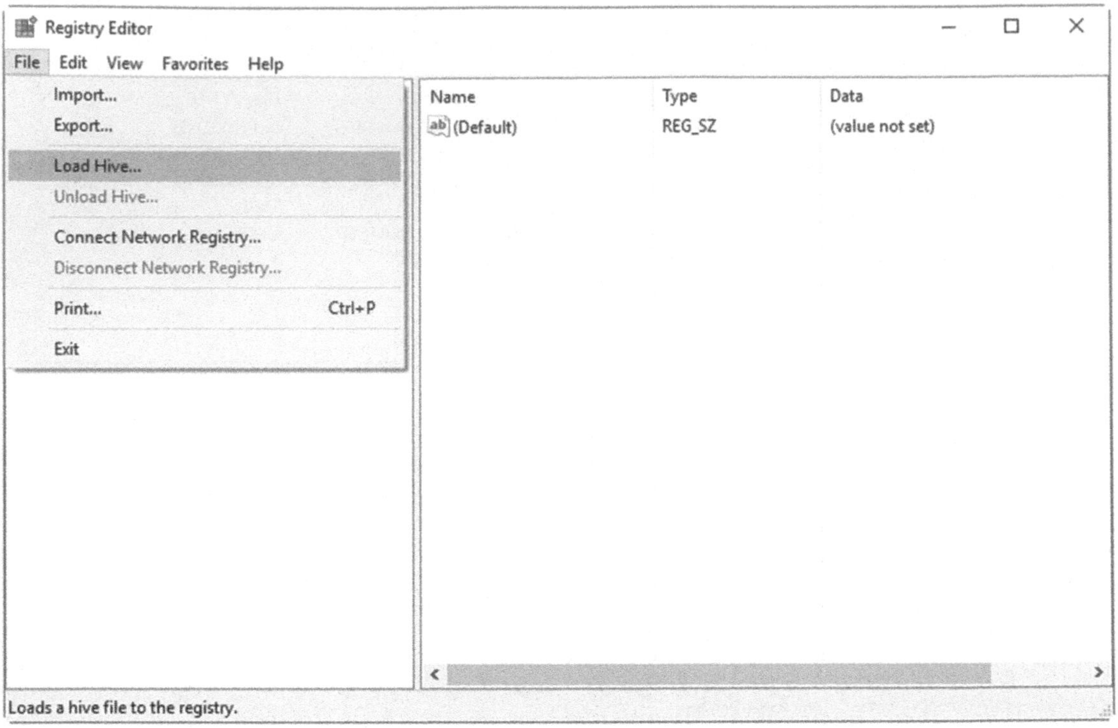

Figure 26-8. *You can connect to other users' Registries on the PC*

5. Browse to the user's profile directory on the hard disk and select the NTuser.dat file

6. When prompted for a key name, enter the user's username as a reference label

You will now be able to view and edit the Registry files for that specific user in the Registry Editor. Note that you will need to set File Explorer to show both *Hidden* and *System* files to display the NTuser.dat file. You should also make sure that when you are finished with the remote Registry file, you should highlight it in the Registry Editor, and from the *file* menu, select *Unload Hive*.

There are several steps to go through. These are detailed in full in my *Windows Registry Troubleshooting* (Apress, 2015) book, though I will summarize them here.

1. In the Group Policy Editor, you need to allow *inbound remote administration exception* connections policy. You do this in Computer Configuration ➤ Administrative Templates ➤ Network ➤ Network Connections ➤ Firewall, and then in either the Standard Profile or Domain Profile sections.

2. Also in the Advanced Firewall, open TCP ports 135 and 445.

3. Activate the *Remote Registry* service in the *services* panel on the PC you wish to access remotely.

4. Open the Registry Editor, and from the *File* menu, select *Connect Network Registry*.

5. Enter the name of the PC and user you wish to connect to.

You will now see the PC listed in the Registry Editor, and two new branches will appear, HKLU and HKU. Once you have made the changes you need to make, be sure to disconnect the Registry Editor from the remote PC using the option in the *File* menu.

▪ **Tip**   If the PC won't boot, you can run the Registry Editor from a USB Recovery Drive. You do this by entering the Command Prompt option and typing regedit, from which the Registry Editor will appear. You will then be able to connect to different user's Registry files on the PC using the method I detailed earlier.

Third-Party Registry Utilities

I mentioned at the beginning of this chapter that the Windows Registry Editor is the only way to view and manage the Registry in Windows, and strictly just within Windows 10, it is. However, some useful third-party utilities exist that can also help, especially if the PC is unbootable. These all work in various ways, but the best tools available are

- **PCRegEdit**—found by searching online

- **Hiren's Boot CD**—www.hiren.info/pages/bootcd

- **Lazesoft Recovery Suite Home**, Recovery CD—www.lazesoft.com/lazesoft-recovery-suite-free.html

- **UBCD4Win**—ubcd4win.org

- **Microsoft Desktop Optimization Pack** (DaRT)—available through Software Assurance

Summary

The Windows Registry is a very complex and utterly crucial part of the operating system. You should really only be editing it if you are following specific instructions from a hardware or software vendor, or from Microsoft itself, and you should absolutely know what it is you are doing. Making the wrong change in your Registry can not just result in hardware or apps misbehaving, but it can also render the entire Windows installation unusable.

The Registry files themselves, of which I detailed there are several, are just that, files on the PC. In fact, the file and folder structure that makes up Windows 10 is also horrifically complex, and changing or deleting the wrong thing can also render your Windows installation useless. In the next chapter, then, I'll take you right through this file and folder structure, and detail what is what, and where is where.

■ ■ ■

CHAPTER 27

Windows 10 File Structure in Depth

I just counted how many files are currently sitting on my C: drive, where Windows 10 is installed on my PC. This doesn't count my documents, pictures, music, and video, which I store elsewhere to ensure file security, but there are still almost half a million files in more than seventy thousand folders sitting on the drive.

Now, I have some big app suites installed, such as the full Adobe Creative Suite, Microsoft Office, and the Vegas Pro suite of video editing apps. These will install huge volumes of files on the PC, and then there's temporary files, configuration files, preferences files... the list goes on.

So how do we go about making sense of this file system from a troubleshooting point of view? What is the SysWOW64 folder, and what's so special about the WinSXS folder that it has to be more than 6GB in size? In this chapter I'll guide you through this file system nightmare and look at what every major part of the operating system is for, and where it can be found.

The Windows 10 File and Folder Structure

You probably don't need me to tell you that the Windows 10 OS is stored in the C:\Windows folder on your hard disk, and that user files are stored in the C:\Users folder. Things are never quite that simple though, and if you're troubleshooting the boot files for the OS, Windows Update, or System Restore, where would you look?

Many of these folders and their files are hidden from view, under two levels of protection called hidden and system files. You can unhide either or both of these file types in File Explorer by clicking the *View* tab, and then the *Options* button. In the dialog that appears, click the *View* tab, and then you can change the options for *Show hidden files, folders and drives* and *Hide protected operating system files (recommended)*, see Figure 27-1.

© Mike Halsey 2016
M. Halsey, *Windows 10 Troubleshooting*, DOI 10.1007/978-1-4842-0925-7_27

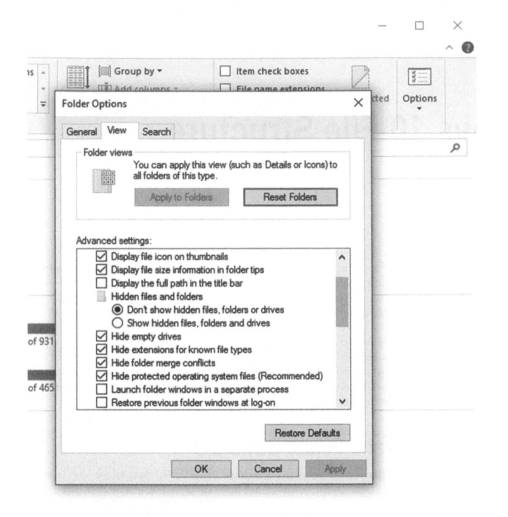

Figure 27-1. You can display both hidden and system files in File Explorer

But when you're then looking at the contents of the hard disk on which Windows is installed, and indeed every other disk, you might not recognize what some of the files and folders you see are for.

Root Windows Folders

- **MSOCache**—will be seen only on systems with Microsoft Office 2007 or a later version installed. It contains installation files for the Office suite that are used if the installed apps need to be repaired.

- **ProgramData**—contains win32 app data that applies to all users on the PC. This includes configuration and other files necessary for the apps to run. It can be a very large folder but should never be deleted.

- **System Volume Information**—seen on all of your hard disks and is used by the System Restore and File History features. It contains archived and encrypted versions of critical system files, such as the Registry and files that change on app installations. It does this with versioning control, so that System Restore can roll back to previous versions if needed. It is also used in a limited way by the File History feature for version control of your documents.

Win32 and Store App Folders

- **Program Files** and **Program Files (x86)** are the folders in which win32 desktop apps are installed. The Program Files (x86) folder is seen only on 64-bit Windows 10 installations, and it is where 32-bit software is installed.

- **Program Files\WindowsApps** is the install location for all Store apps. This folder is heavily protected by the OS, to the point where even the local Administrator account cannot gain access to it.

Windows Operating System Folders

- **Windows\AppPatch**—contains application compatibility files.

- **Windows\Boot**—contains files necessary for starting the OS; I detailed these in Chapter 13.

- **Windows\CSC**—contains offline files and documents, used for caching.

- **Windows\Cursors**—contains cursor and icon files for the OS.

- **Windows\Debug**—contains Windows error logs. I'll talk more about the log files shortly.

- **Windows\Fonts**—where all the installed typefaces on your PC are installed.

- **Windows\Globalization**—where language packs, dictionary files, and other files relating to location are stored.

- **Windows\IME**—contains Language files used by the OS and apps, also IME (x86) on 32-bit systems.

- **Windows\ImmersiveControlPanel**—contains the files that constitute the Settings app.

- **Windows\INF**—contains device driver installation files.

- **Windows\Media**—contains audio and video files that are used by the OS, such as sound packs.

- **Windows\Prefetch**—the system Windows uses to load commonly used files before you open them. The OS tries to anticipate what you want to use and open. Sometimes, this cache can become corrupt, and if so, it is safe to delete the contents of this folder.

- **Windows\Resources**—contains ease-of-access themes, accessibility themes, and other themes for Windows.

- **Windows\Security**—contains security files and logs used by Management Console snap-ins.

- **Windows\SoftwareDistribution**—the folder used by Windows Update. Should you find that Windows Update is unable to download or install any updates, you can completely delete the contents of this folder. If you do this and discovered that some files are locked by the OS, reboot the PC and try again. Note, however, that if you have hidden any Windows Updates using Microsoft's Windows Update troubleshooter tool, they will become viewable and installable again if you delete the contents of this folder.

- **Windows\System**—exists to maintain compatibility with legacy apps that do not look for the System32 folder.

- **Windows\System32**—the main repository of all files that constitute the Windows operating system.

- **Windows\System32\Config**—contains the main Registry files used by the OS. Additional Registry files can be found in the %userprofile% and %userprofile%\AppData\Local\Microsoft\Windows folders.

- **Windows\System32\Drivers**—contains installed driver files.

- **Windows\System32\Divers\etc**—contains configuration text files such as the Hosts file, which can be used to modify the mapping of host names to IP addresses.

- **Windows\System32\GroupPolicy**—contains Group Policy script and template files.

- **Windows\System32\icsxml**—contains files used by the Universal Plug-and-Play feature for hardware.

- **Windows\System32\Microsoft**—contains cryptography files.

- **Windows\System32\oobe**—contains files that are used by the Windows Out-of-Box-Experience when setting up new users on the PC.

- **Windows\System32\ras**—contains Remote Access encryption files for Windows server connections.

- **Windows\System32\Recovery**—contains files used by the Windows Reset feature.

- **Windows\System32\restore**—contains files used by the System Restore feature.

- **Windows\System32\spool**—contains files associated with your installed printers and the print spool queue.

- **Windows\SysWOW64**—used to store files necessray to maintain app and driver compatibility between 32- and 64-bit code.

- **Windows\Tasks**—contains scheduled task files.

- **Windows\WinSxS**—called the Windows Side-by-Side folder. It contains multiple copies of Dynamic Link Libraries (DLLs) and other files that are crucial to your app and OS operation, but where different versions of the same file may be required to be loaded by different apps simultaneously. This folder can grow to an enormous size but is crucial to the operation of Windows 10.

- **Windows\Web**—contains images used by the lock screen and for Windows wallpapers.

User Account Folders

- **Users\[UserName]\AppData\Local**—known also by the shortcut %localappdata%, this folder contains the data and settings that are necessary for installed apps, and for your user profile to operate correctly. Internet temporary files are also stored in this folder.

- **Users\[UserName]\AppData\LocalLow**—contains data that cannot be moved, and has lower-level access on your PC, such as when a web browser is used in privacy mode.

- **Users\[UserName]\AppData\Roaming**—can be accessed by the shortcut %appdata%. It contains data and settings that can move with your user account, such as when you are connected to a Domain.

Windows Log Folders

- **PerfLogs**—where custom Data Collector Sets that are created in the Performance Monitor are stored. See Chapter 25 for details on how to create these, and what they are.

- **Windows\Debug**—where log files that are created when an app or service crashes, or when certain audit processes are performed, such as installing Windows Updates. These logs are stored in plain text format, and can be read in Notepad.

- **Windows\Logs**—the main log folder for the Windows OS. It contains many log files such as WindowsUpdate.log. These files are sometimes stored as Extensible Markup Language (XML) files , that can be opened in a web browser. Many files, however, are stored as Event Trace Log (ETL) files. You can read these files in the *Event Viewer* by clicking the *Action* menu and then the *Open saved log* option.

- **Windows\Minidump**—contains crash reports that are created by applications and Blue Screens of Death (BSOD). They have the file extension `.dmp`. You cannot read these files in Notepad, and will need the Windows Driver Kit (WDK) or Windows Software Development Kit (SDK), both of which are available as part of Microsoft Visual Studio.

- **Users\[UserName]\AppData\Local\CrashDumps**—contains crash dump files that are pertinent to the specific user account. They can also be accessed through the address `%LOCALAPPDATA%\CrashDumps`.

Windows Temporary File Folders

- **Users\[UserName]\AppData\Local\Temp**—the main temporary file storage, stored on a per-user basis. It is used for multiple purposes, including downloaded files and web pages that are viewed in your browser. You can most easily access it by navigating to `%temp%`.

- **Users\[UserName]\AppData\Local\Microsoft\Windows\INetCache**—used for storing temporary Internet files.

- **Users\[UserName]\AppData\Local\Microsoft\Windows\Temporary Internet Files\Low**—another Internet files temporary folder.

- **Windows\Temp**—a protected temporary file store used by the OS and apps.

Windows File Types

- **Bootmgr**—a critical file required at PC startup.

- **Desktop.ini**—a file found in every folder on your PC. It contains configuration data about how that folder and its contents should be viewed in File Explorer.

- **DLL** files—contain code shared by many different apps and services. These apps and services can call upon DLLs to perform tasks that may be required by different apps, such as managing the print queue and displaying window furniture.

- **EXE** files—win32 apps that can be run on a double-click of the mouse.

- **Hiberfil.sys**—the Hibernation file that stores the PC's memory state.

- **INF** files—device driver installation files.

- **INI** files—configuration and option files for apps and Windows features.

- **Thumbs.db**—contains thumbnail images of files and documents within a folder. You may also have some ehThumbs.db files, which were used by Windows Media Center.

- **Pagefile.sys** and **Swapfile.sys**—used by the virtual memory feature in Windows 10.

- **SYS** files—contain system settings used by the OS and both software and hardware drivers on the PC.

Managing the Shell User Folders

You might find that you want to change the locations of some of the Shell User Folders on your PC. For example, I mentioned earlier in this chapter that I store my files and documents on a separate partition to my Windows installation. This ensures the files are not affected if I suffer a major problem with the OS and have to reinstall it.

There are different ways to manage the Shell User Folders, but we'll start with the temporary files folder, as this seems like a natural jumping-off point. If you open **system** [Settings] from the Start Menu or Cortana, and click the *Advanced System Settings* link, you will be presented with the system properties panel. Then clicking the *Environment variables* button in the bottom right corner of the dialog will display a dialog in which you can change the location, should you wish, of the Windows Temprary folder, see Figure 27-2.

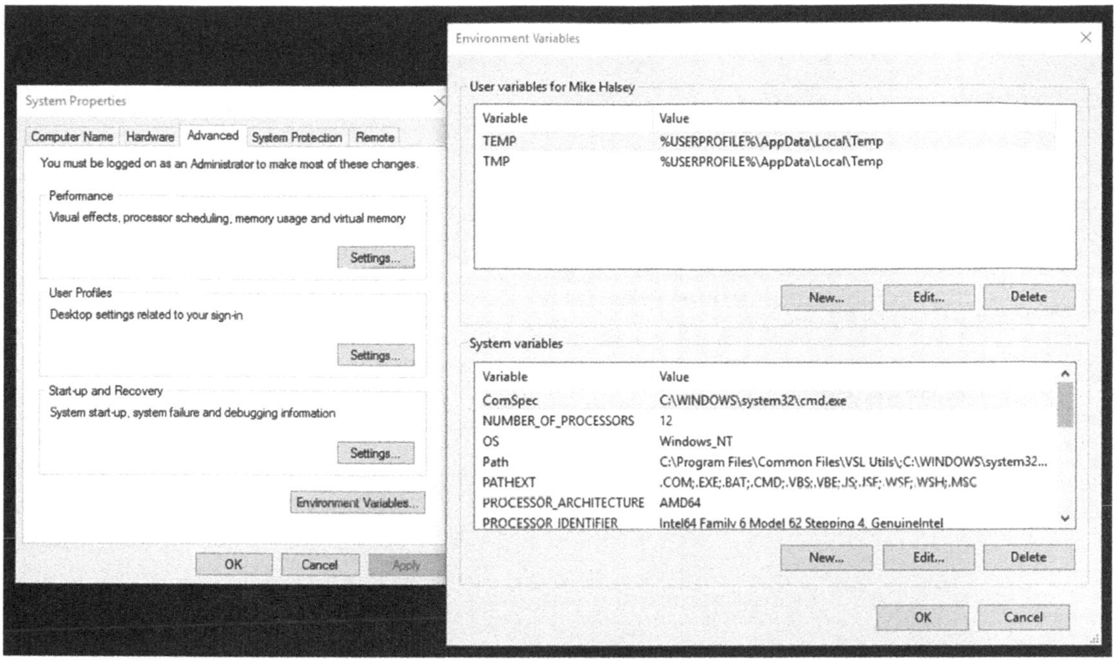

Figure 27-2. You can change the location of the Temporary folder

There are several ways to move the Shell User Folders, documents, pictures, music, video, and so on.

1. The easiest is to cut and paste the folders from their current location, to the new location where you want them to be. Windows 10 will then automatically update all the pointers for you.

2. You can also right-click a folder (this must be done individually) and select its *Properties*. Then, click the *Location* tab in the dialog that appears where you can either click *Move*, to move the folder and its contents to a new location, or *Restore Default* if something has gone wrong with it, and it needs to be reset, see Figure 27-3.

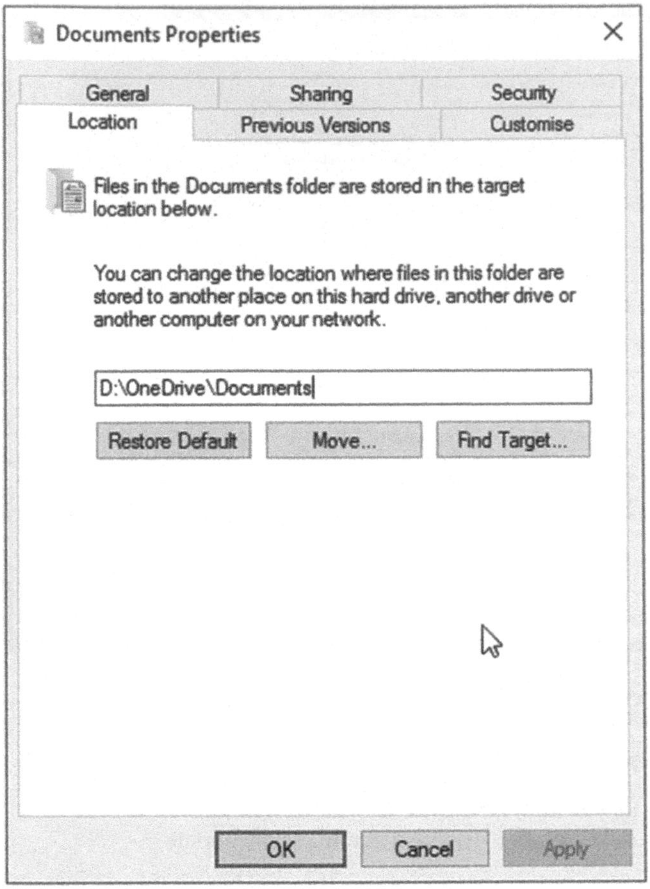

Figure 27-3. *You can move your user document folders in File Explorer*

If you want full and complete control over all the Shell User Folders, however, perhaps because the locations of one or more have become corrupt, you can find them in the Registry, see Figure 27-4. There are two Registry locations to visit.

- HKCU\Software\Microsoft\Windows\CurrentVersion\Explorer\User Shell Folders

- HKCU\Software\Microsoft\Windows\CurrentVersion\Explorer\Shell Folders

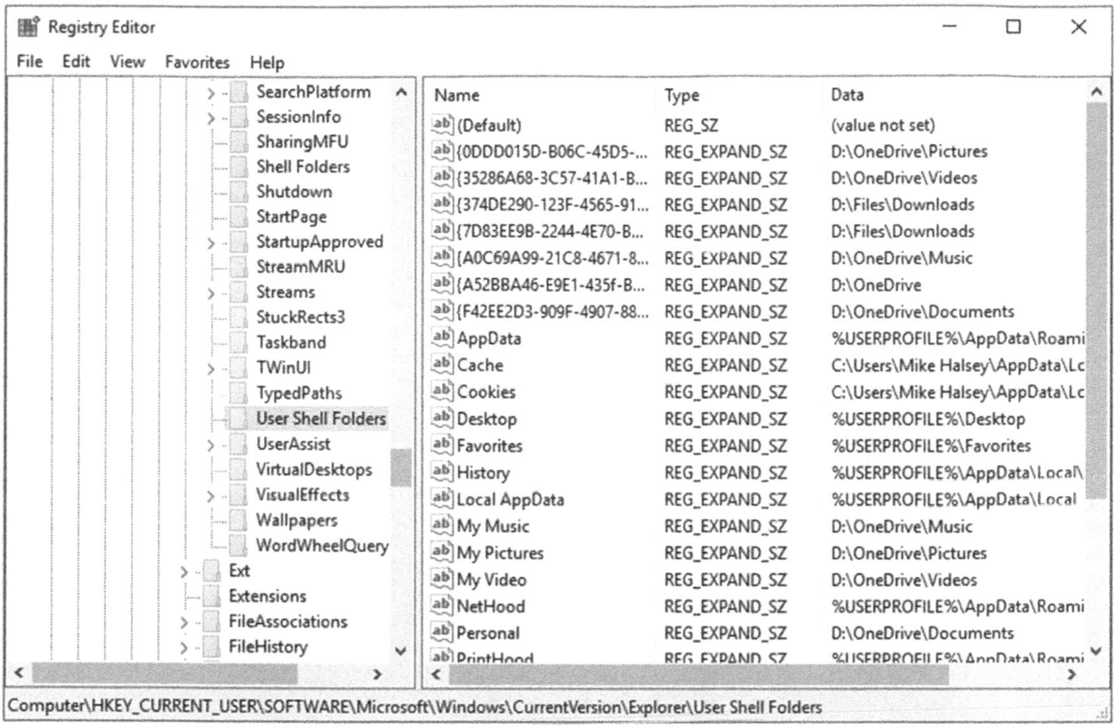

Figure 27-4. *You have full control over the Shell User Folders in the Registry*

Summary

So there you have it, an in depth breakdown of what's what and why it's there in the Windows file system. The Windows OS is indeed a horrifically complicated beast when it comes to its file structure. Knowing what the look for, where to find it, or even what the hell something is can be a very frustrating and difficult process.

While we're on the subject of difficult problems, this gives me a good segue into the next chapter, where I'll be showing you how you can use the Internet to research the more difficult troubleshooting problems you might encounter. This includes where you can look online, what to look out for, how to avoid getting the wrong advice, and what tools are available that can help you in your work.

CHAPTER 28

■ ■ ■

Researching Difficult Problems

Throughout this book I've detailed the tools and utilities available to you, both within Windows 10 and externally from Microsoft and third parties, to help provide information and diagnose and repair problems. This is all fine for straightforward issues where it's clear what the cause of the problem is, and how you can repair it. What happens, though, when the cause of a problem is less clear, when there's some obscure error message that could have one of several causes, or when finding the actual solution to the problem is like searching for the proverbial needle in a haystack?

Troubleshooting is a very similar task to detective work, I've always said. The most famous detective quote comes from Sherlock Holmes: "Once you have eliminated the impossible, whatever remains, however improbable, must be the truth." This process of elimination is crucial in determining the cause and discovering the correct solution for a problem. First, though, you need to be armed with the correct information.

Reading the Windows Log Files

Having accurate information is essential in troubleshooting any type of problem. Way back in Chapter 5, I detailed the Event Viewer, and how you can get extremely detailed information about events, errors, and crashes. Sometimes however, you also need direct access to crash logs. I detailed the locations of these in Chapter 27, but let's look at how you read them, and how you make sense of them.

Log Text Files

The Windows\Debug log files contain audit (installation, deletion, update, etc.) operation details and app crash details in plain text file formats, see Figure 28-1. The files you will find in this folder will vary, and are entirely dependent on what's been happening on the specific machine. In the following image, we can see that there are logs for the wiaservc.dll file. A search online, and I'll show you how to do this efficiently later in this chapter, reveals that this is the Windows driver associated with "still image devices." It makes sense that there would be event logs for this service, as I have been unplugging my printer (with its integrated scanner) fairly often recently, so I can plug a desk fan into its power outlet instead.

© Mike Halsey 2016

M. Halsey, *Windows 10 Troubleshooting*, DOI 10.1007/978-1-4842-0925-7_28

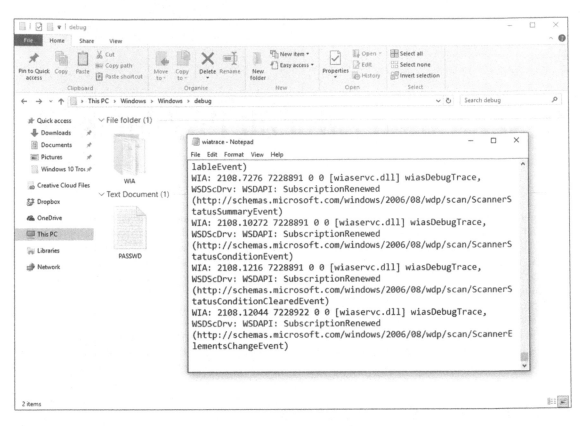

Figure 28-1. *The Windows\debug log files are stored in plain text format*

Reading .xml and .etl Files

The Windows\Logs folder is where the main Windows 10 logs are stored. They are separated into subfolders, most of which are sensibly named, such as RecoveryDrive and SystemRestore, see Figure 28-2. The log files are stored either as plain text (.txt) files, which can be opened in Notepad; as Extensible Markup Language (.xml) files, which can be opened and read in a web browser, such as Edge or Internet Explorer; or as Event Trace Log (.etl) files.

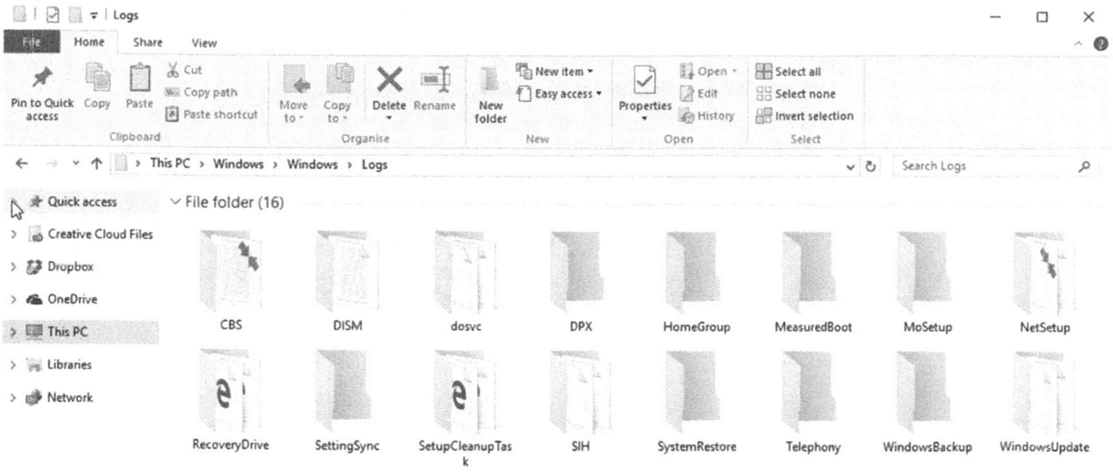

Figure 28-2. *The Windows\Logs folder contains the main Windows Logs*

Event Trace Log files are opened in the Event Viewer. They should all be available in the Event Viewer anyway, if I'm honest, though you may wish to open a file from another PC, perhaps one that's been e-mailed to you. To open an .etl file, in the Event Viewer, click the *Action* menu, and then click the *Open saved log* option, see Figure 28-3.

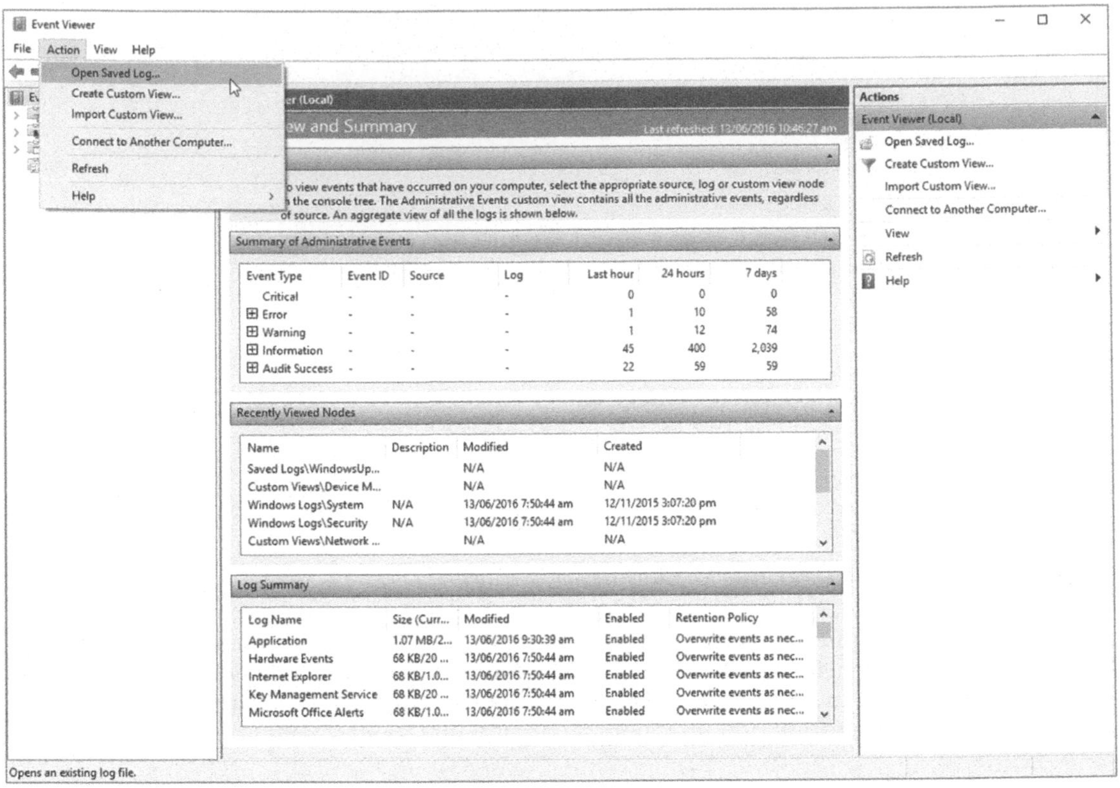

Figure 28-3. *You can open .etl files in the Event Viewer*

Once the `.etl` file has been opened in the Event Viewer, you will see it appear in the left panel in a new Saved Logs section, see Figure 28-4. You can now view it as you would any other event log.

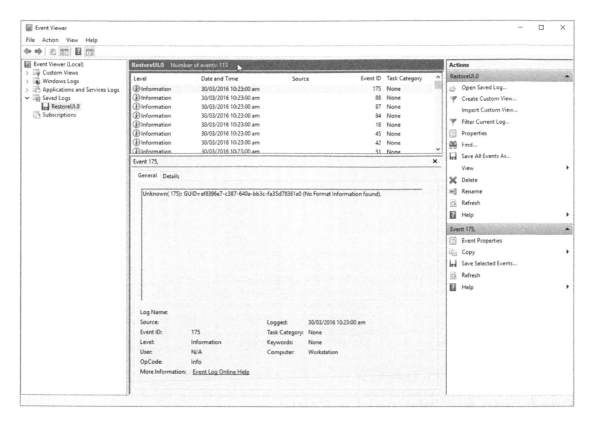

Figure 28-4. *The opened .etl file will appear in the Saved Logs section*

Reading .dmp files

The Windows\MiniDump folder is where you will find critical error log files, such as those associated with a Blue Screen of Death (BSOD). These files are stored in the slightly less friendly .dmp format and cannot be opened natively in Windows 10. There are several ways to open them, however. If you have access to Microsoft Visual Studio, you can download the Windows Driver Kit (WDK) or Windows Software Development kit (SDK). Both of these will allow you to open, and read, the contents of the .dmp file.

Perhaps a preferable option for many people will be the third-party utility *BlueScreenView*. You can download this from www.nirsoft.net/utils/blue_screen_view.html and it will automatically display the contents of all the .dmp files located in your Windows\MiniDump folder, see Figure 28-5.

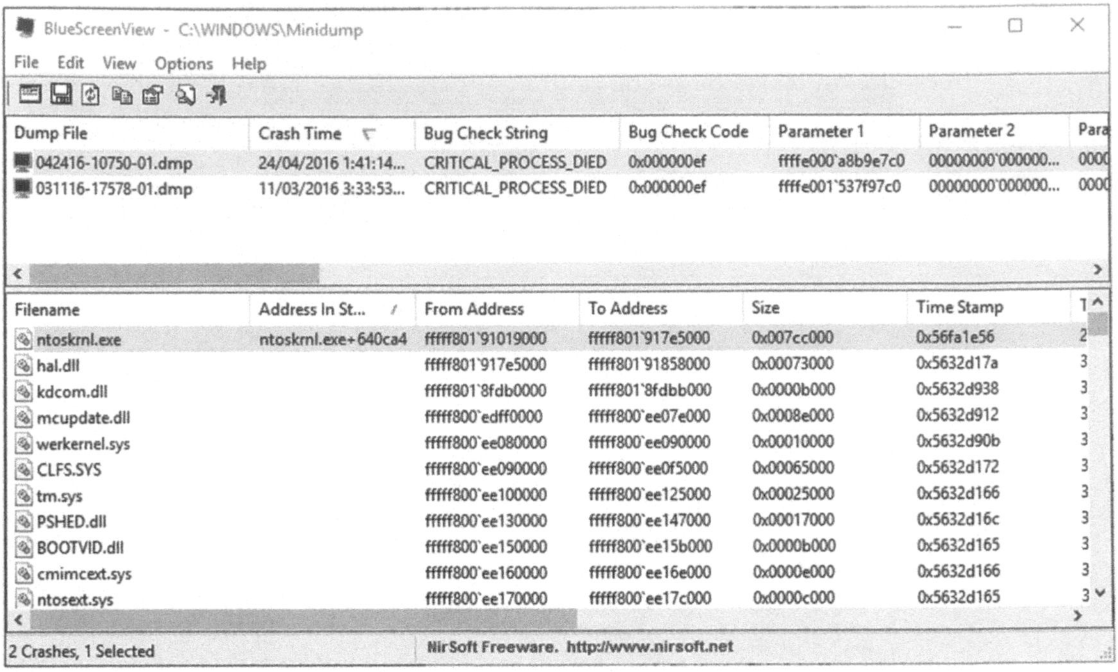

Figure 28-5. *BlueScreenView is a handy freeware utility for reading .dmp files*

Searching the Internet for Solutions

The Internet is brilliant, the Internet is amazing, the Internet is all-powerful (okay, maybe not that last one), but certainly the Internet is a fantastic tool for researching the causes of and the solutions to problems on our PCs. Sadly, the Internet is also full of bad advice, misinformation, incomplete answers, sites that are simply after your money, and... let's face it, malware.

Knowing how to use the Internet to effectively search for and find solutions to problems can be a challenge in itself. Anybody can type a search query into Google or Bing, and click the first link that appears in the search results. Is this going to provide the best result, the correct solution, or something less helpful, such as a web site that's just trying to sell you something?

An example of this is that there are usually several, or even many, different problems that can result in the same error code. You may have to spend some time digging, or try a few different things before you get the fix you need.

■ **Tip** You can make your Internet searches more effective by using search operators such as + (plus) before a word to force the inclusion of that in all the results, − (minus) before a word to specifically exclude that word from searches, and "..." (double quotes) around a search phrase to prevent the search returning results that contain each word you type individually. You can find Google search operators listed at support.google.com/websearch/answer/2466433, and Bing search operators at onlinehelp.microsoft.com/bing/ff808438.aspx.

I want to start with a warning. Well, I don't want to, but it's very important. When you're searching for solutions to problems, and especially when you're searching for hardware drivers (using either the hardware device name, or the VEN_ and DEV_ codes), there are a great many webites that will present you with their own installer, such as that seen in Figure 28-6, that I found when I searched for an Asus network card driver.

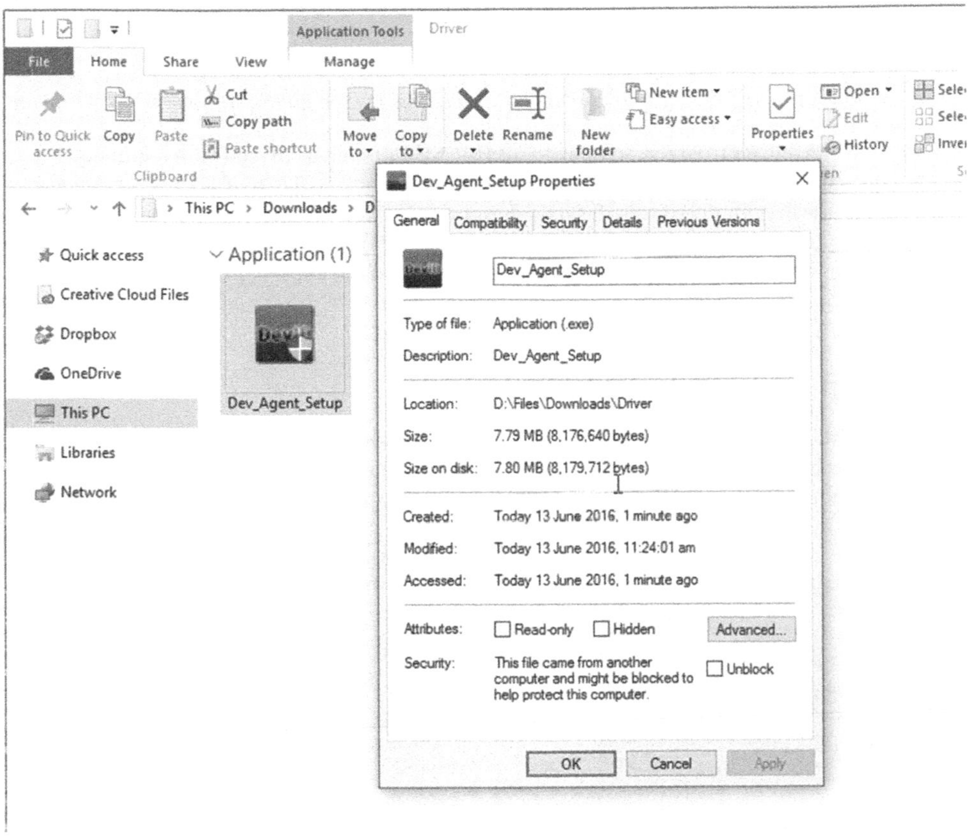

Figure 28-6. *Many "driver download" sites want you to install an unknown payload*

There is absolutely no way to know what is in these files until you click them and give them Administrator permission to install. **DO NOT EVER DO THIS** as once the installer has administrative rights, it can install whatever the hell it wants on your PC, from browser toolbars and unwanted apps to malware. I would also stress that you **MUST NEVER USE** paid-for driver download services. Drivers are always freely available online; you will not ever need to pay for them.

So what web sites can you trust to provide quality information? Here's my rundown of the best, and those I would recommend.

Answers.Microsoft.com

The Microsoft Answers site is always a great resource, not the least of which is that Microsoft has its own support staff to answer questions and provide support. This is a great example, however, of how you should not always trust the quality of the advice you are receiving. Figure 28-7 shows three "badges" that are automatically assigned to different types of forum participants.

Of these, only two can be trusted absolutely for their professionalism; can you tell which one can't? Obviously, the one labeled "*Microsoft Support Engineer*" will be a dedicated support person, employed directly by Microsoft.

Figure 28-7. The Microsoft Answers web site tells you how qualified the person giving support is

Of the other two, you can always trust the advice of an *MVP*. MVPs (such as myself) are technical experts who have been awarded with the MVP (Most Valuable Professional) badge to mark the significant contributions they have made in helping Microsoft's user communities worldwide.

An *Insider*, however, is anybody who has signed up to be a member of the Windows Insider (beta) program. Anybody can join the Windows Insider program, as it's open to the general public. As such, some answers given by insiders can be inaccurate.

Support.Microsoft.com

This is another dedicated Microsoft support site, with help across all of the company's products. There are also community forums here, in which you can search for your problem to see if anybody else has encountered it as well. Windows 10 also comes with a *Contact Support* app, see Figure 28-8, which you can find in the Start Menu.

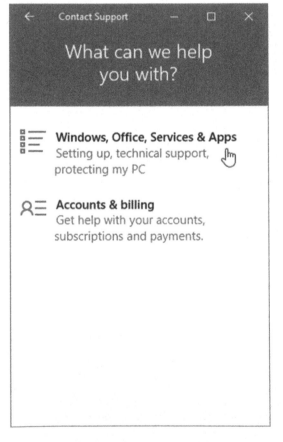

Figure 28-8. Windows 10 comes with a Support app

Technet.Microsoft.com and MSDN.Microsoft.com

Technet and MSDN (Microsoft Developer Network) are Microsoft's business-focused information and resource sites. You will find a huge amount of in-depth and technical information here. If you are researching a difficult problem, then the answers could well be found on MSDN or Technet.

Other Microsoft and Third-Party Support Sites

There are a great many excellent-quality support web sites provided by third parties. The best of these are...

- **Annoyances.org**—www.annoyances.org
- **Computing.net**—www.computing.net
- **How To Geek**—www.howtogeek.com
- **Microsoft Download Center**—www.microsoft.com/download
- **Ten Forums**—www.tenforums.com
- **Tom's Hardware**—www.tomshardware.co.uk

■ **Tip** Twitter is a great resource if you are having trouble with a PC. Occasionally a problem will hit with a driver or Windows update that will affect a great many people. You can get instant reaction, and sometimes instant help, by monitoring Twitter for search terms or hash tags.

Hardware Driver and Support Sites

I always recommend that you download hardware drivers directly from the manufacturer's web site. These web sites will also have forums in which you can post questions and get answers directly from technical staff at the company.

- **Acer**—www.acer.com/support
- **Asus**—www.asus.com/support
- **AMD**—support.amd.com
- **Dell**—www.dell.com/support
- **HP**—support.hp.com
- **Intel**—downloadcenter.intel.com
- **Lenovo**—support.lenovo.com
- **Microsoft Surface Support**—www.microsoft.com/surface/support
- **Nvidia**—www.nvidia.com/page/support.html
- **Samsung**—www.samsung.com/support

Third-Party Support Tools

Additionally, there are many excellent third-party help, information, and support tools that are favored by IT Pros; these are in addition to the Microsoft SysInternals suite that I detailed in Chapter 22.

- **Aida64**—www.aida64.com

- **CCleaner**—www.piriform.com/ccleaner

- **Disk Digger**—www.diskdigger.org

- **GRC**—www.grc.com

- **Hiren's Boot CD**—www.hiren.info/pages/bootcd

- **Sandra Utilities**—www.sisoftware.eu

- **TeamViewer**—www.teamviewer.com

- **Ultimate Boot CD**—www.ultimatebootcd.com

- **WhoCrashed**—www.resplendence.com/whocrashed

Summary

It's certainly true that because the Internet is the ultimate democratic outlet, it's also full of errors and misinformation, as well as unwanted and malicious drive-by downloads. You should always be careful from where you source information and what you trust. Certainly you should never download a driver that comes in its own container from the web site that hosts it, as you have absolutely no idea what else might be in that package.

Researching difficult problems, however, is only half of the story, and in the next chapter I'll show you how you can go about fixing them. This can include working safely with hardware, fixing the seemingly unfixable, and connecting the dots to see if the cause of your problem lies outside of the PC itself.

CHAPTER 29

■ ■ ■

Troubleshooting Difficult Problems

Troubleshooting is a process of elimination, detective work to join up the dots, making connections between different aspects of the OS, hardware, apps, and other factors, and coming to conclusions based on technical knowledge and expertise. This book can give you the technical knowledge you need to diagnose and repair problems. What do you do, though, in terms of the actual detective work?

Well, you might be surprised that this can be taught as well. (You can tell I'm a teacher by trade, can't you?) Troubleshooting requires that you look at your PC holistically. It might appear, on the face of things, that a problem is being caused by a graphics driver, or that a nonbootable PC might have a faulty power supply. What do you do with the more complex problems, however, perhaps those that only occur occasionally or under certain circumstances?

"Mike Halsey's Holistic Troubleshooting Agency"

Back in 1987, acclaimed science fiction author Douglas Adams—he of the famous *Hitchhiker's Guide to the Galaxy* (Pan, 1979), some Monty Python contributions, and fondly remembered episodes of Doctor Who—released a novel called *Dirk Gently's Holistic Detective Agency*. The protagonist, the aforementioned Dirk Gently, believed in the "fundamental interconnectedness of all things," and used this principle to solve all manner of difficult and dangerous cases, from messy divorces to missing cats.

Silly an idea as this might be for a novel, it's a sound principle to begin with when troubleshooting PC problems. To give an example of this, let's look at a typical PC system (it can be any type of PC), and how interconnected and interdependent it is on other services and devices. Our typical PC is connected to, at some point or another, each of the following...

- Keyboard
- Mouse
- External monitor
- External hard disk/NAS drive
- Power cable(s)
- Monitor cable(s)
- Network cable
- Wireless dongle / aerial
- USB hub (and cables)
- Router / switch

© Mike Halsey 2016
M. Halsey, *Windows 10 Troubleshooting*, DOI 10.1007/978-1-4842-0925-7_29

- Telephone socket / cable socket

- Telephony / cable network

- Telephone exchange

- Datacenter (with all the PCs, cabling, routers, etc., that entails)

- Company server (with all the routers, switches, storage, and cabling that entails)

...to be honest I could continue this list ad infinitum, but you probably get the point that when troubleshooting a problem on a PC, you might not see that problem contained within the apps, drivers, and OS structure that we're typically used to.

Gauging Both Internal and External Factors

I'll give you a couple of hypothetical scenarios. In the first, a PC user has called tech support to report a problem. "It's only intermittent," he says, only happening very occasionally. "Right!" you might proclaim, knowing that it's probably something he's doing, or something that's going on at that specific time. It could be a problem that only occurs when he runs the payroll software on the PC (so a software error or database connection failure), when he uses the printer (a driver, configuration, cable, or hardware fault), or about once a month on a Tuesday (could it be linked to Microsoft's Patch Tuesday update cycle for Windows?).

In Scenario Two, a worker in a busy office has a problem on their PC that's caused her to have to stop work. She details the issue she's having on her PC, but completely fails to mention that three other people in her office are also having trouble with their PCs this morning. Those are different problems though, so she didn't think it worth mentioning. When you look at these problems separately, though (Office 365 not connecting, VPN connection dropping, NAS storage problem, and a PC that is hanging on a black screen at startup), it's reasonable to assume that none of the problems are local to the PCs themselves, but that all of them exist elsewhere on the company network (a PC hanging on a black screen at startup can sometimes be fixed by temporarily unplugging its Ethernet cable).

There are also all manner of external factors which can cause problems with PCs...

- Dust / pet hair collecting in vents and fans, or when a laptop/tablet is somewhere such as a construction site or the beach.

- Extreme heat/cold (though modern hardware is extremely resilient to these).

- Thick brick or stone walls (these can block Wi-Fi and other radio signals).

- Using the PC at a different location (another office or outside of the company).

- Poor cable routing (can lead to snagged and damaged plugs and cables).

- Insufficient amounts of available power, or an unreliable electricity supply, can cause PCs to fail to start, restart periodically, or to shut down occasionally.

- Human beings (who really are capable of being complete idiots).

Indeed, one of my all-time favorite phrases from the aforementioned Douglas Adams is that "the problem people face in trying to make something completely foolproof, is that they frequently underestimate the ingenuity of complete fools."

■ **Tip** Some problems can be caused by the use of poor-quality cabling. Unshielded Twisted Pair (UTP) cables are commonly used for networking, as they're cheap. Good-quality shielded cables, however, can prevent many of the problems associated with UTP cables, such as picking up interference from television, radio and cellular signals, microwave ovens, and powerful motors.

It's the same when looking for problems internally on the PC as well. I had a problem on my own workstation PC last year where the machine was completely and very suddenly failing to start. There was nothing happening when I turned the PC on, short of the power light coming on and a faint whirr of some fans. On the face of it you might think, as I initially did, that the power supply had failed, or that it just wasn't producing enough power any more to get the PC going. As it turned out, however, the graphics card had failed and was causing the entire system to hang in the BIOS. Because I had no picture though, I couldn't see the error it was producing.

Another example, this one from this book's tech reviewer Dustin Harper, is that he was troubleshooting a PC that kept switching itself off after a few seconds. It transpired that the PC had been dropped, and the power button was pushing inward, remaining depressed. Releasing the power button rectified the problem.

Using Troubleshooting Tools Together

There are a lot of Windows, Microsoft, and third-party troubleshooting and diagnostic tools available for Windows 10 and that I've detailed throughout this book. Sometimes, though, you might find that just looking in the Event Viewer, or checking what's going on in the Resource Monitor, isn't enough. You might need to use more than one of these tools, perhaps even three or four, together at one time.

Using tools in concert with one another such as this can help you get a clearer picture of what's going on. Let's say you have a network problem. It might be caused by a driver, configuration, cable, or other issue, but the PC is pinging the network and the connection keeps dropping. With the Task Manager open, you can see the overall network usage; with the Resource Monitor, you can see exactly what apps are trying to use the network connection; and with the Event Viewer, you can set up a Data Collector Set to record warnings, events, and errors on everything those specific and running services apps are doing.

None of the diagnostic and troubleshooting tools I've detailed should always be used in isolation. You might see a rogue process in the Resource Monitor and not know what it is. The Task Manager's *Details* and *Services* tabs allow you to right-click a process name and search online for details of what it might be, see Figure 29-1. In the *Details* tab, you can also open its file location on the hard disk. You can then perhaps use Process Monitor to check the startup and other status of the app or process.

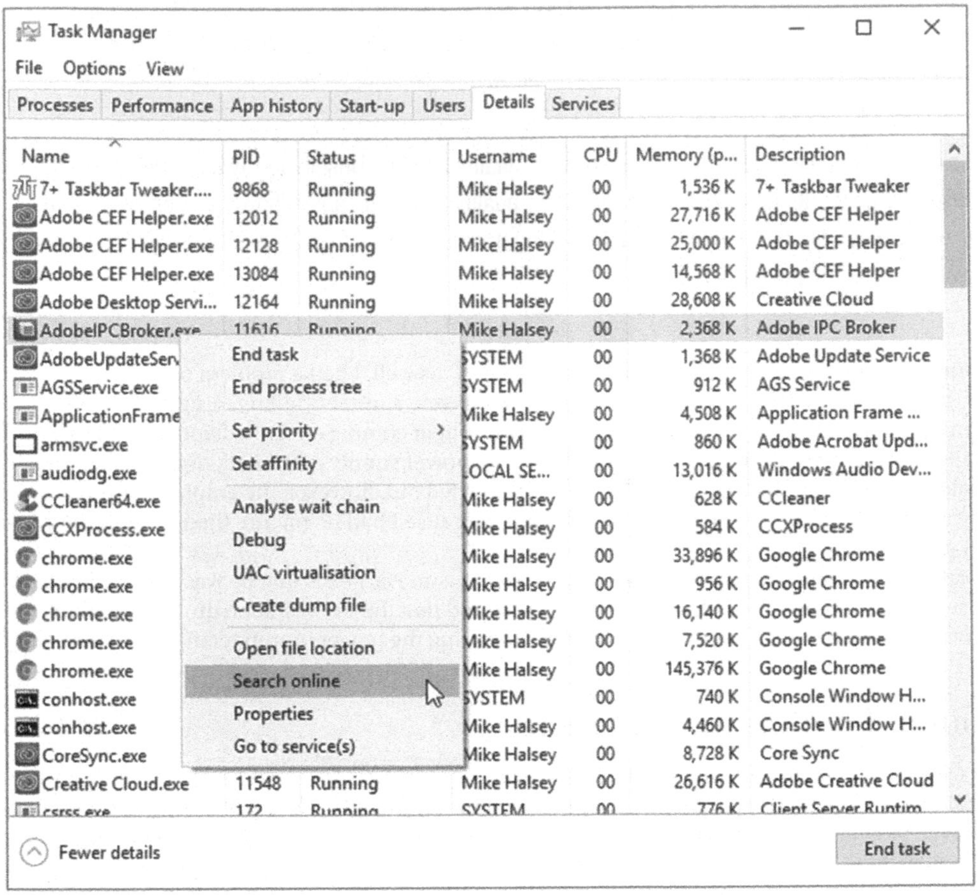

Figure 29-1. *You can search online for details about an app or process*

Troubleshooting and Repairing Hardware

When it comes to troubleshooting and repairing hardware there are several important considerations. The first of these is safe working, not for you (though you don't want a PC landing on your foot because the table leg is wonky). If you are working on any electrionics or electrical equipment, you should also follow these simple rules.

1. Disconnect the equipment from wall power.

2. Remove any trailing or dangling cables.

3. Use an antistatic wristband, see Figure 29-2.

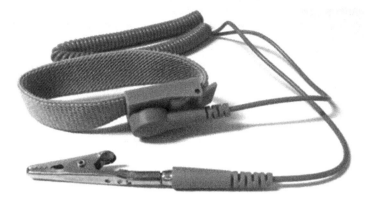

Figure 29-2. *An antistatic wristband can protect delicate electronics*

The latter is very important, as modern electronics can have components that run on microvolts. Any static electricity you have on your person, which can be picked up from nylon carpets, clothing, or metal surfaces, can have a profoundly damaging effect on hardware.

There are also the obvious rules to follow for putting the hardware on a safe and stable surface, keeping any unnecessary tools and equipment out of the way, and keeping the equipment away from water or any other liquids.

■ **Note** Many laptops and tablets these days are seemingly unrepairable, being sealed thin units with no obvious way into the case. iFixIt, found at www.ifixit.com, has repair guides for many of these devices, and they also sell dedicated repair toolkits that can include custom tools required for some devices from companies such as Apple. You should note, however, that opening these devices will void any manufacturer's warranty.

Minimal Boot Configuration and Jumpstarting PCs

I mentioned earlier in this chapter that I had a problem on my own workstation PC about a year before writing this book, where the PC wouldn't start at all. The lights would come on and the fans would spin up, but nothing else happened.

Initially, I thought it might be the power supply that was at fault. Power supplies fail more than any other piece of hardware due to the heat they build up, their fan(s), and how much work they have to do. It turned out, however, that it was the graphics card, actually one of two in an SLI configuration, that had blown up and was causing the system to hang on the BIOS.

I didn't have a picture on my monitor (fairly obviously) so I couldn't see that the BIOS was hanging, but was able to figure out the problem's cause by using a minimal boot configuration. So what is this, and how does it work?

Minimal boot configuration means stripping a PC's hardware down to the absolute basics and seeing what works and what doesn't. Disconnecting all the optical and hard disk drives, except the one on which Windows 10 is installed, removing all but one memory card, and removing the graphics card (if your motherboard has onboard graphics) and any PCI expansion cards can result in a PC that requires considerably less power to operate. This can be a good way to test both the power supply, which can produce less power as it gets older, just like a motor engine, but also individual components.

You can then try each memory card in turn (remembering to power down the PC when you switch components, obviously), different graphics cards, and expansion cards, and maybe even swap out the power supply for another.

■ **Note**   Jumpstarting a PC is the process of using the power supply from one PC to temporarily replace the PSU in another. You will probably need to physically unscrew the power supply from the "loan" PC, but then might only need to plug in its motherboard plugs to the PC you wish to test.

It was using this minibal boot configuration that I was able to quickly diagnose the problem with my workstation and trace it to one specific graphics card, which had spectacularly failed.

Summary

Using joined-up thinking and looking at problems holistically can really help when troubleshooting PC problems. If you've been doing PC troubleshooting and repair for many years, as I have, it's all too easy to think of the PC as a stand-alone device. That really isn't the case anymore, however, as the ecosystem into which our PCs plug themselves is both extensive and complex.

We're going to finish this book, though, by going back to the stand-alone principle and looking at installation of the OS. This will include how to troubleshoot problems in upgrading a PC to Windows 10 from Windows 7 or Windows 8.1, and how to nondestructively reinstall the OS, so that in the event of a disaster, you can save all of the files and documents of the user on the system.

CHAPTER 30

■ ■ ■

Installation and Restore

When Windows 10 first launched into its "free for a year" offer, there were plenty of horror stories of people getting unstable systems after upgrading from Windows 7 and Windows 8.1, or from people who couldn't get the new OS installed at all.

The upgrade process to Windows 10 is actually the slickest and most reliable of any Windows upgrade process in the past, though it might sometimes be difficult to believe such a thing. Of the upgrade problems that people had, the fault lies, I'm sorry to say, were with the end users and the hardware and software makers. If you have a completely clean installation of Windows 7 or Windows 8.1 and upgrade it to Windows 10, you'll get a completely clean and fully working installation.

Sadly, hardware driver writers are almost always very slow to update their drivers when changes made to the underlying OS require such updates. The same is true too of many software houses. Then you get the end user who wants to use really old versions of software. In many cases this is perfectly understandable and justifiable. I still use Microsoft PhotoDraw 2000 v2, as I've never found anything as powerful yet easy to use, and many people still like to use Microsoft Money. Then there are all third-party apps that are out of support.

Many apps are still in support, however, and I know of people who are still using version 2.x of CCleaner (we're on version 5.x as I write this) as they just don't like having to update software all the time. Again, this is understandable to a certain extent, and it's great that the Windows Store updates apps silently and automatically in the background.

So in short, I'm not defending Microsoft's practices during this first free upgrade year, as many of the tactics employed to get people to upgrade bordered on underhand trickery. Upgrade failures with Windows 10 are very rarely the fault, or completely the fault though of Microsoft.

This doesn't mean that problems don't occur, and I want to spend some time in this last chapter looking at how these problems can be fixed, and to show you how to nondestructively refresh or reinstall Windows 10 if there isn't an image backup already available on the PC.

Troubleshooting the Windows 10 Upgrade

It's common when upgrading a PC to Windows 10, to do this by downloading the Windows 10 Upgrade Tool, which is available to download from www.microsoft.com/software-download/windows10. This will allow you to purchase an upgrade licence, if necessary, and upgrade in place from Windows 7 or Windows 8.1 to Windows 10.

What happens occasionally is that the upgrade process hangs completely, reporting a "can't install Windows 10" or similar error. By this time, it's already downloaded 3GB of Windows 10 files, and if you try to run the tool again, you're still presented with the same error, as it might not be able to download the files again afresh. There is a simple fix for this, however. This tool creates a $WINDOWS.~BT folder, and can also create a $Windows.~WS folder in the root of your C: drive, see Figure 30-1, and it is to this folder that the downloaded files are placed. You may also or instead see a Windows10 Upgrade folder. If you are having trouble with the Upgrade Tools, you can delete these folders and begin your download of Windows 10 again.

© Mike Halsey 2016

M. Halsey, *Windows 10 Troubleshooting*, DOI 10.1007/978-1-4842-0925-7_30

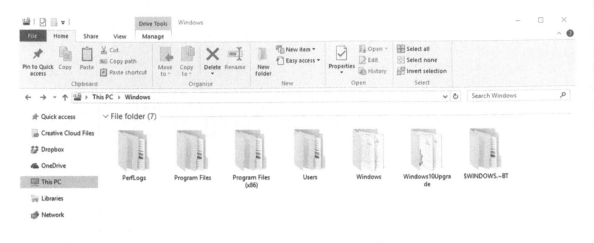

Figure 30-1. *The Windows 10 Upgrade Tool creates a $WINDOWS.~BT folder*

■ **Tip** If you are upgrading a PC with only a very small amount of storage, and the Disk Cleanup Wizard is not freeing up enough space for the Windows 10 download, you can use the Upgrade Tool with an external USB Flash Drive, though you may also need an On The Go (OTG) cable to connect this to the PC. The installation files will be downloaded to this USB drive, but bear in mind that your backup copy of Windows 7 or Windows 8.1 will also be placed on the USB drive. This means that you should not delete the contents of the Flash Drive until you are absolutely certain that there are no problems with Windows 10 on that device, and that you will not need to roll back to your previous OS.

Installing Windows 10

Not everybody wants to upgrade their PC systems to Windows 10, however. Many people, including myself, see the benefits in performing a clean instalaltion of the OS. There's also the plain fact that you might have been using Windows 10 for a while now (the chances of that given that you're reading this book are fairly high), and will need to reinstall it at some point. This might be because you've encountered a massive problem with the OS that can be solved only by a complete reinstall.

Obtaining Up-to-Date Installation Media

One of the problems with every version of Windows is that you would install the OS from your original installation DVD, and then you'd have months, perhaps even years of updates and patches to install. This could take days, and if you only had a Windows 8 disc, you'd then also had to perform the major upgrade to Windows 8.1. All of this was a real pain.

With Windows 10 being the last major version of the OS, Microsoft sought to address this, and at the same time address the fact that so many people never kept, or would lose their installation DVD. There's also the fact that if you upgraded in place from Windows 7 or Windows 8.1 during the first year in which Windows 10 was free, you wouldn't get physical installation media anyway.

The Windows 10 Media Creation Tool, available to download from www.microsoft.com/software-download/windows10, will let you create a USB Flash Drive or an ISO file that can then be burned to a DVD, from which you can install Windows 10, see Figure 30-2. The best part is that because this tool downloads Windows 10 from Microsoft's servers, it will *always* download the latest build. This means you'll never have more than a few months of Windows updates to install afterward, if at all.

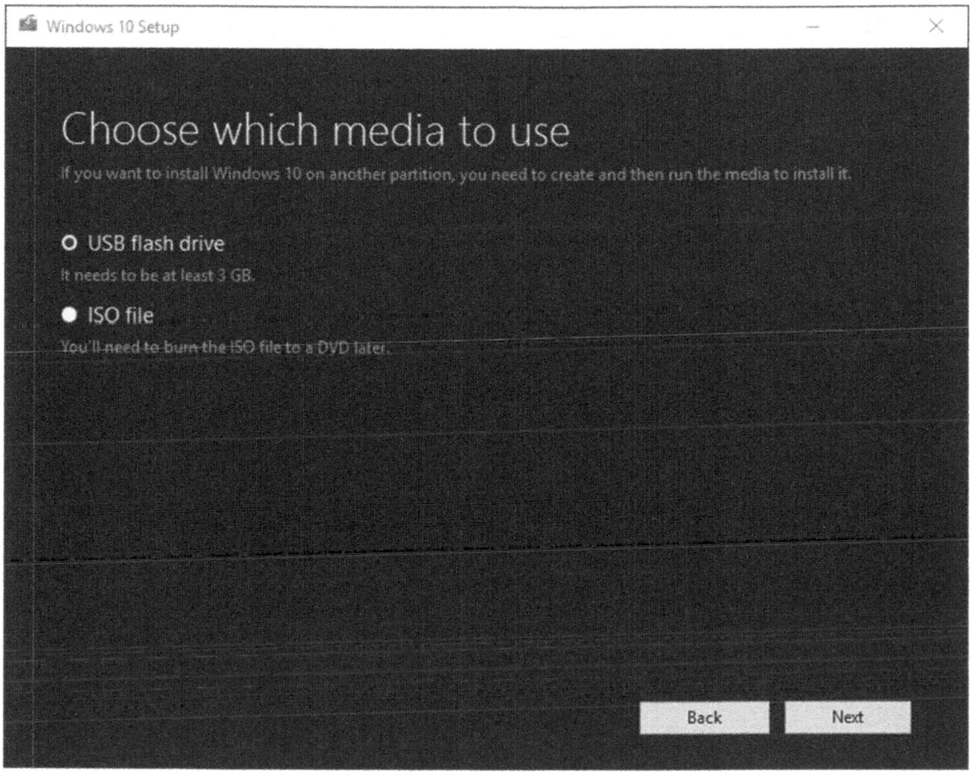

Figure 30-2. You can create installation media of the latest Windows 10 build at any time

■ **Note**   Where does the Windows 10 Media Creation Tool stand with Original Equipment Manufacturer (OEM) versions of Windows 10? With all previous versions of Windows, the product key you had on your PC could be locked to an edition of Windows you bought from a company such as HP, Dell, Lenovo, and so on, and you couldn't install a "regular" copy of Windows with that product key if something went disastrously wrong.

With Windows 10, you will be able to use the Media Creation Tool with **all** Windows 10 installations. This is because Windows 10 installations are product key agnostic. Provided a copy of Windows 10 has been previously activated on that PC, you will always be able to reinstall Windows 10 on the same hardware.

Creating Customized Installation Media

What if you're in a business environment, however, and need a customized version of the Windows 10 installation media? There are many reasons why you might want to do this. At its most basic you might have bought a job-lot of PCs for the business, all with the same hardware, and you want to embed the appropriate hardware drivers, and perhaps a series of core apps, into the Windows installation media, to reduce the overall installation time and Internet bandwidth usage.

You might additionally be on one of the business branches for Windows Update, either the Current Branch for Business, in which you get feature updates months after they're rolled out to all other Windows PCs, or the Long-Term Servicing Branch, where you'll get only security and stability updates for up to 10 years.

Neither of these scenarios can be used with the Windows 10 Media Creation Tool, which will always include all the latest feature packs rolled into the installer. So what can you do to create custom media?

With Windows 10, Microsoft has actually made it very difficult to create custom installation media, in which you have injected drivers and apps. These are called "slipstreamed" installers. You will either need the Windows 10 Installation and Deployment Toolkit, or will need to follow incredibly complex and difficult instructions using the DISM (Deployment Image Servicing and Management) tool that's built into the OS.

Fortunately, third parties have stepped in with various solutions that allow you to create custom installation media. Here I want to talk about just one, a very powerful tool called NTLite (www.ntlite.com). This utility, see Figure 30-3, of which there is a free version, can be used to perform a wide variety of tasks.

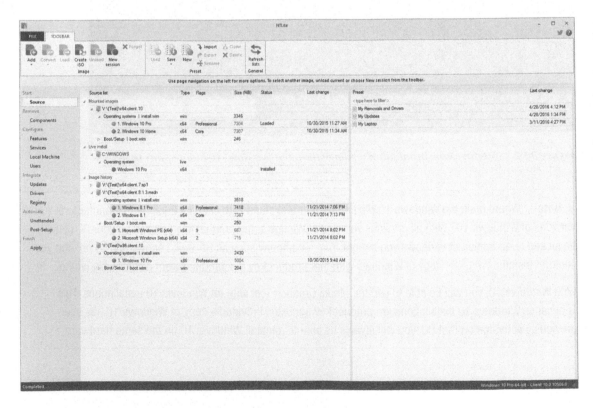

Figure 30-3. *NTLite allows you to easily create slipstreamed media*

NTLite will let you add drivers, Windows updates, language packs, and apps to your installation media. Additionally, however, you can use it to remove specific Windows components, tweak the OS, configure disk partitions in advance of installtion (useful if you want to separate files and documents, or have a separate image backup partition), automate the installation process, and more besides.

Nondestructively Reinstalling Windows 10

Let's say then that you've encountered a problem that is so bad you have no choice but to completely reinstall Windows 10 on the PC. The user(s) on the PC, however, will likely have files and documents on the same partition as the corrupt OS installation (if those haven't already been moved to or been stored on a separate partition or hard disk) that will need to be kept. So how do you perform a nondestructive reinstallation of the OS?

It might seem obvious that you can use your installation media to *Upgrade* Windows 10 on the PC. You can do this by starting the Windows 10 installer from the desktop. If you can't get to the desktop, though, you can seem a bit stuck.

Never fear, however, as there is an easy solution. Start your PC from your Windows 10 installation media, be this a USB Flash Drive or DVD, and click *Install* as per normal. When asked if you want to upgrade or perform a custom installation, you won't be allowed to click the *Upgrade* option (this can be selected only by starting the installer from the desktop). Instead, click *Custom: install Windows only (advanced)* option, see Figure 30-4, and when asked on what disk or partition you want to install Windows 10, choose the partition on which it's already installed.

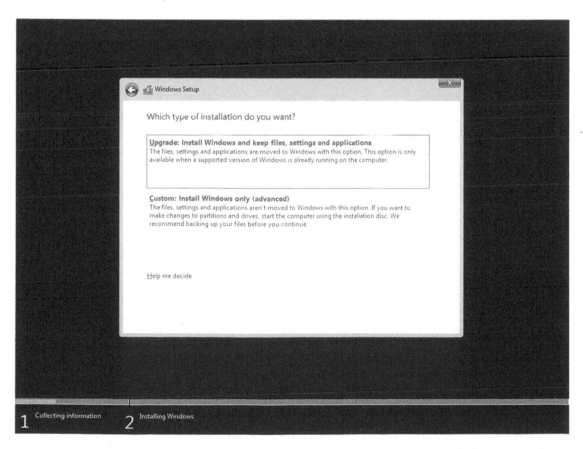

Figure 30-4. Do not upgrade Windows if you need a nondestructive installation

The difference now is that, if we were performing a clean installation of the OS, we'd open the disk tools options in the installer and format the partition, or perhaps even delete the partition and create a fresh one. To nondestructively reinstall the OS, though, **do not** format or delete the partition. When you click *Next,* you will then be told that the installer has found a previous copy of Windows, which it will move to a Windows.old folder, see Figure 30-5.

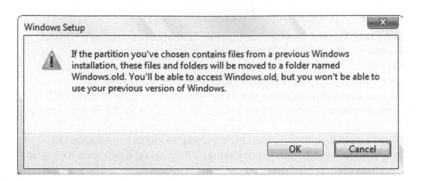

Figure 30-5. *You will be informed that a Windows.old folder will be created*

Once the Windows 10 reinstallation is complete, you will have a fresh install into which you will need to reinstall drivers, apps, updates, and so on, but you will also have this Windows.old folder, in which there will be a Users folder containing all the files and documents stored on the PC previously, as well as anything else you might have kept there, such as downloaded files, installers, driver backups, and more besides.

■ **Note**   In addition to the Windows 10 Media Creation Tool, Microsoft has also released a *Windows 10 Refresh Tool*, which can be downloaded from http://pcs.tv/23dD1AM. This tool works similiarly to the Media Creation Tool, but is intended to help you reinstall Windows 10 nondestructively on PCs where the currently installed version is unrecoverable.

Windows 10 SysPrep

It's worth spending a short time looking at the SysPrep tool in Windows 10, what it is, and how you can use it. When you install Windows 10 on a PC, you will be presented with the Out-of-Box Experience (OOBE). This will ask you for your Microsoft account details, present you with privacy and other options, and install the core Store apps.

SysPrep can be invoked either at the very beginning of the OOBE experience, by pressing *Ctrl+Shift+F3,* or after the OOBE expeience from the C:\Windows\System32\sysprep folder. Once activated SysPrep will present itself on the desktop, see Figure 30-6. You will now be able to install drivers, make configuration changes, and install apps that will apply to **all** users on the PC. Note that you cannot use SysPrep to make changes on a per-user basis, nor will it allow you to create user accounts.

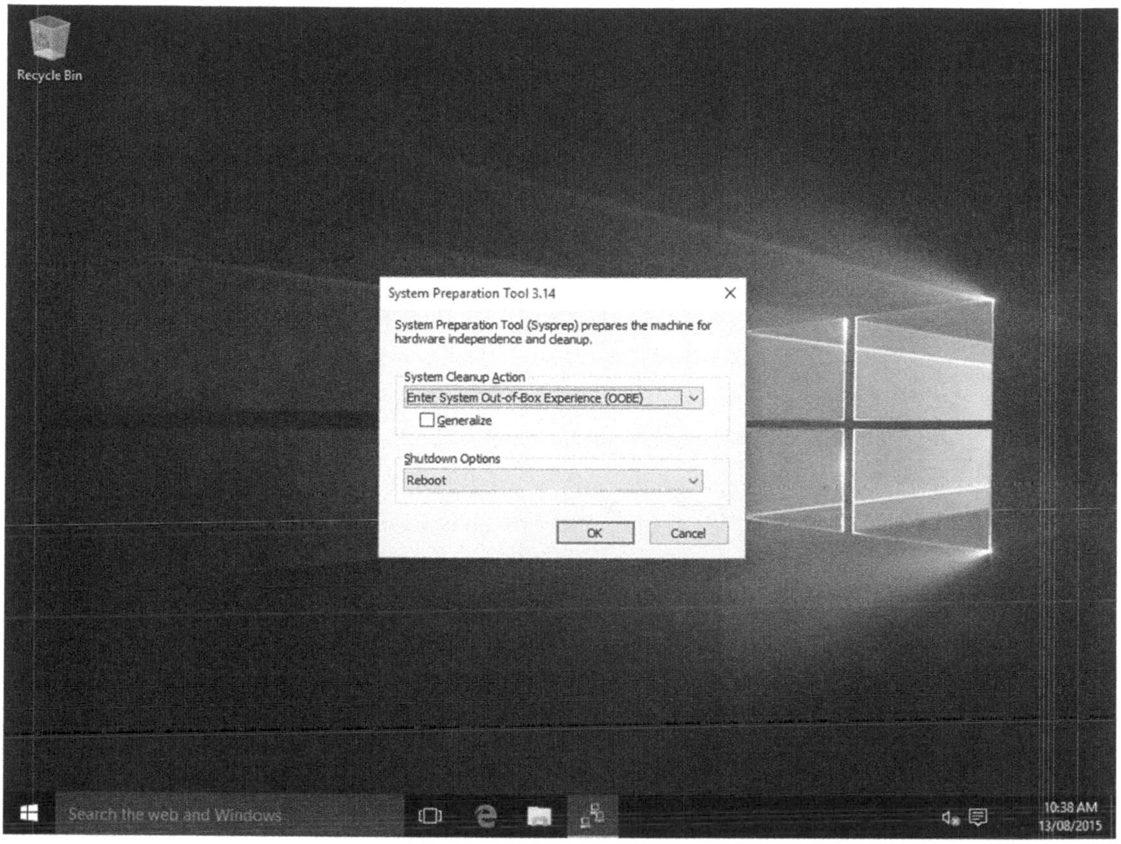

Figure 30-6. *SysPrep allows you to make changes to an OS without changing the OOBE*

It's important to leave the SysPrep window open on the PC when you are configuring Windows 10. Should you have to restart the PC at any time, you will need to invoke SysPrep again if you have not restarted the PC through the SysPrep tool itself. When you're finished you can use the SysPrep window to shut down the PC. The next time it starts, the user who is receiving the PC will get the full OOBE experience. SysPrep can be a great tool to use then if you are preparing PCs that are purchased by, or are to be given as a gift to other people. It can also be used with third-party imaging software, such as Symantec Ghost, for making image backups that can then be rolled out across other machines in a small to medium-sized business. Note that the Windows Image Backup system won't operate in SysPrep.

Summary

I always like to end on a happy note, and the thought of giving a PC to somebody as a present is a very happy one indeed. You'll probably be asked to support that PC, however, but throughout this book I have shown you everything you need to know about diagnosing and repairing problems on PCs. More importantly, I've shown you how to mitigate and prevent problems from occurring in the first instance. I sincerely hope you've found this book helpful, educational, informative, and authoritative.

More help is available through other books in this *Windows and Windows Server Troubleshooting Series*, which you can purchase online at `http://pcs.tv/1UADAyk`. These include specialist books dedicated to the Windows Registry, File System, Installation and Updating, Software and Hardware Compatibility, Malware, and Viruses, Networking, and Group Policy, through to advanced server topics including Troubleshooting Windows Using Powershell, and Troubleshooting BYOD and Mobile Device Management.

For now, I'd like to thank you for reading. This book has really been a labor of love. I hope you've got as much from it as I have put into it, and now that you know how to troubleshoot and repair any type of problem on a PC, I sincerely hope you never need to ;)

Index

Get the eBook for only $5!

Why limit yourself?

Now you can take the weightless companion with you wherever you go and access your content on your PC, phone, tablet, or reader.

Since you've purchased this print book, we're happy to offer you the eBook in all 3 formats for just $5.

Convenient and fully searchable, the PDF version enables you to easily find and copy code—or perform examples by quickly toggling between instructions and applications. The MOBI format is ideal for your Kindle, while the ePUB can be utilized on a variety of mobile devices.

To learn more, go to www.apress.com/companion or contact support@apress.com.

Lightning Source UK Ltd.
Milton Keynes UK
UKOW04f1456220916

283564UK00008B/211/P